WILLIAM K. KERSHNER

THE
SIXTH EDIT

ADVANCED PILOT'S FLIGHT MANUAL

Including FFA Written Test Questions (Airplanes) plus

Answers and Explanations and Practical (Flight) Test

IOWA STATE UNIVERSITY PRESS / AMES

TO MAC AND SARAH LISENBEE

WILLIAM K. KERSHNER began flying in 1945 at the age of fifteen, washing and propping airplanes to earn flying time. By this method he obtained the private, then the commercial and flight instructor certificates, becoming a flight instructor at nineteen. He spent four years as a naval aviator, most of the time as a pilot in a night fighter squadron, both shore and carrier based. He flew nearly three years as a corporation pilot and for four years worked for Piper Aircraft Corporation, demonstrating airplanes to the military, doing experimental flight testing, and acting as special assistant to William T. Piper, Sr., president of the company. Kershner holds a degree in technical journalism from Iowa State University. While at the university he took courses in aerodynamics, performance, and stability and control. He holds airline transport pilot, commercial, and flight and ground instructor certificates and has flown airplanes ranging from 40-HP Cubs to jet fighters. He also is the author of THE STUDENT PILOT'S FLIGHT MANUAL, THE INSTRUMENT FLIGHT MANUAL, THE FLIGHT INSTRUCTOR'S MANUAL, and THE BASIC AEROBATIC MANUAL. Kershner operates a one-airplane, one-instructor aerobatic school using a Cessna 152 *Aerobat*. He received the General Aviation Flight Instructor of the Year Award, 1992, at the state, regional, and national levels. The Ninety-Nines awarded him the 1994 Award of Merit.

ILLUSTRATED BY THE AUTHOR

© 1994 William K. Kershner. Previous editions and printings © 1985, 1976, 1970 Iowa State University Press, Ames, Iowa 50014
All rights reserved

Authorization to photocopy items for internal or personal use, or the internal or personal use of specific clients, is granted by Iowa State University Press, provided that the base fee of $.10 per copy is paid directly to the Copyright Clearance Center, 27 Congress Street, Salem, MA 01970. For those organizations that have been granted a photocopy license by CCC, a separate system of payments has been arranged. The fee code for users of the Transactional Reporting Service is 0-8138-1303-4/94 $.10.

♾ Printed on acid-free paper in the United States of America

Fourth edition, 1976
Fifth edition, 1985 *(through nine printings)*
Sixth edition, 1994
Second printing, 1995

© 1962, 1965 as *The Private Pilot's Flight Manual*

Library of Congress Cataloging-in-Publication Data

Kershner, William K.
　　The advanced pilot's flight manual: including FAA written test questions (airplanes) plus answers and explanations and practical (flight) test/William K. Kershner. — 6th ed.
　　　　p.　　　　　cm.
　　Includes bibliographical references (p.　　) and index.
　　ISBN 0-8138-1303-4 (alk. paper)
　　　1. Airplanes — Piloting. I. Title.
TL710.K42　　　1994
629.132′52 — dc20　　　　　　　　　　　　　　　94-29137

CONTENTS

INTRODUCTION
TO THE FIRST EDITION

IT HAS LONG BEEN the writer's opinion that the average pilot could learn the basics of airplane performance very easily if the involved mathematics were bypassed. One of the purposes of *The Advanced Pilot's Flight Manual* is to bridge the gap between theory and practical application. If pilots know the principles of performance they can readily understand the effects of altitude, temperature, and other variables of airplane operation.

GAMA (General Aviation Manufacturer's Association) and the FAA together have established a *Pilot's Operating Handbook,* which will include information now scattered among several different sources. It has a standardized format so that the pilot can quickly find information (for instance, emergency procedures), whether flying a Piper, Cessna, or other makes. The older planes will still have several sources for finding operating information. *Pilot's Operating Handbook* will be used as a general term to cover all sources of information available to the pilot.

When it is said here for instance, "You can find the center of gravity limits in the *Pilot's Operating Handbook,*" the term is meant to cover all sources of information currently available to the operator. You may be able to open the *Owner's Handbook* and get this information *or* you may have to go out to the airplane and look at something called "Operations Limitations" or "Airplane Flight Manual."

So, rather than repeat each time, "You can find this information in either the *Owner's Handbook* (or *Owner's Manual*) or *Pilot's Handbook,* or *Flight Handbook,* or *Airplane Flight Manual,* or "Operations Limitations," or in the form of placards or markings," the writer has used one term: *Pilot's Operating Handbook (POH).*

Thumb rules are used throughout as a means of presenting a clearer picture of the recommended speeds for various performance requirements such as maximum range, maximum endurance, or maximum angle of climb. Such rules of thumb are not intended in any way to replace the figures as given by the *POH* or comparable information sources, if available. However, the knowledge of even the approximate speed ranges for various maximum performance requirements will enable pilots to obtain better performance than if they had no idea at all of the required airspeeds. Naturally, this practice must be tempered with judgment. If a pilot flies a rich mixture and high power settings until only a couple of gallons of fuel are left, setting up either the rule of thumb or the manufacturer's recommended airspeed for maximum range still won't allow making an airport 75 mi farther on. The same applies to maximum endurance. Waiting to the last minutes of fuel to set up the maximum endurance speed will have no perceptible effect on increasing endurance.

Many of the rules of thumb are based on the use of calibrated stall airspeeds, which are in turn based on the max certificated weight of the airplane (unless otherwise noted). Airplane weight variation effects on recommended airspeeds are to be ignored unless specifically mentioned.

The material in this book includes what the writer believes is of the most interest to the pilot who wants to go more in detail about airplane performance. For instance, the chapters on checking out in advanced models and types are intended to cover the questions most often asked by pilots checking out in those airplanes.

It is hoped that the material whets the reader's desire for more information. If so, then the mission of this book will have been accomplished. The books listed in the Bibliography are recommended for further study.

INTRODUCTION
TO THE SIXTH EDITION

THE PURPOSE of this edition is to update material, to go more deeply into basics of flight instruments and navigation, and to include 651 questions for airplanes from the FAA *Commercial Pilot Written Test Book,* with answers and explanations. In recent years the tendency in flight training is to pass too lightly over the fundamentals, and there has been some decline in the ability of pilots to fly an airplane to the edges of its envelope. Some math is included to allow the aspiring professional pilot to better understand the basics of airplane performance and other factors that affect the operation of a particular airplane.

ACKNOWLEDGMENTS

The writer has been fortunate in having knowledgeable people available to comment on the manuscripts for each edition and would like to thank the following people for their help (these acknowledgments are not meant to imply endorsement of *The Advanced Pilot's Flight Manual* by any of the organizations mentioned and should not be construed as such).

American Aviation Publications for permission to take parts of articles I wrote for *Skyways* magazine.

Harold Andrews of the Stability and Control Section of the Bureau of Naval Weapons, Washington, D.C., for his pertinent comments on the chapter on Stability and Control and other parts.

Merritt Bailey, my editor at Iowa State University Press, who was instrumental in assuring that this book, like the *Student Pilot's Flight Manual,* was published in a manner more readable than that evidenced by my sometimes rambling discussions in the manuscript.

Michael Beaumont of Houston, Tex., who sent information on gyro instruments.

Don Bigbee, of Castleberry Instruments and Avionics, who sent photos and data on gyro instruments and gave permission for them to be used in Chap. 4.

Lynne Bishop, editor at Iowa State University Press, for her work on the sixth edition.

Business/Commercial Aviation magazine for permission to use material from some of my articles on airplane performance.

Capt. M. R. Byington, Jr., of the Aeronautical Science Department at Embry-Riddle Aeronautical University, who made suggestions for improvement of later printings of the fifth edition and who gave me permission to include references to his report, *Optimized Engine Out Procedures for Multi Engine Airplanes* (May 1988).

Bill Carlon, of Sigma-Tek, Inc., who furnished brochures and data and gave permission to use photos of gyro instruments that were a great aid in Chap. 4.

Bernard Carson, instructor in the Aeronautical Engineering Department at Pennsylvania State University, who reviewed parts of the manuscript and made helpful comments on flight limitations.

Cessna Aircraft Company, for furnishing actual curves of Drag and Thrust horsepower required and available and other information on Cessna airplanes and for allowing me to insert copyrighted material (performance charts, schematics of systems, and placards).

Leighton Collins, Editor of *Air Facts,* who reviewed parts of the manuscript and whose suggestions on methods of presenting some of the more technical parts were of particular value.

Joe Diblin of Avco Lycoming, who furnished very valuable information on Lycoming engines and let me use material from the Avco Lycoming *Flyer*. His easy-to-understand writing style makes learning about engines a pleasure.

Employees at Aero Design, Beech, Mooney, and other companies, who helped me in quests for sometimes obscure reports and information.

Dudley C. Fort, Jr., M.D., of Sewanee, who gave me added information on carbon monoxide for Chap. 18.

Hartzell Propeller Inc., of Piqua, Ohio, and McCauley Industrial Corp., of Dayton, Ohio, for furnishing much-needed data on propellers.

Allen W. Hayes, veteran flight instructor of Ithaca, N.Y., whose cogent arguments on the subject of flight mechanics were the greatest factor in researching and inserting a chapter on that subject.

John Paul Jones, Chief of the Engineering and Manufacturing Branch of the FAA Training Center, and H. E. Smith, Jr., engineering pilot of the Center, who reviewed the complete manuscript and made valuable comments and suggestions.

Ralph Kimberlin of the University of Tennessee Space Institute, who provided general data on stability and control for Chap. 10.

Arthur L. Klaastad, of Kent, Wash., whose letters on analysis of flight mechanics were most useful in revising Chap. 3.

T. M. Koenig, of Bolivar Aviation (Tenn.), who provided a very good analysis, with drawings, of the forces and moments acting on a light twin with an engine out.

Ken Landis, Chief Controller at the Williamsport, Pa., airport, who kindly reviewed that part of the manuscript dealing with communications procedures.

Dr. Robert Langel, Goddard Space Flight Center, NASA, who furnished charts of magnetic variation and changes in variation for Chap. 4.

Jack LeBarron, of the Navy's *Approach* magazine, who always managed to find and furnish performance information when it was most needed.

Capt. Arthur Lippa, Jr., General Manager, Aircraft Division of U.S. Steel, who gave permission to use material from the booklet "Medical Factors in Flight."

Audrey J. Little, flight instructor of Nashville, whose reviews and many suggestions were useful.

Stanley R. Mohler, M.D., Chief, Aeromedical Applications, FAA, who furnished information on the use of oxygen.

Piper Aircraft employees who reviewed parts of the manuscript that covered their special areas and who made valuable suggestions and comments, including Clyde R. Smith, Flight Test Supervisor; Calvin Wilson, Aerodynamicist; Elliot Nichols, Design Engineer, Power Plants Installation; and Richard Wible.

Hampton Pitts, of Nashville, Tenn., who sent an excellent analysis of gyro precession and who also recommended books and papers for further reading on the subject.

Robert M. Potter for suggestions and information on hydroplaning.

Delbert W. Robertson, W. R. Wright, and Hugh Pritchard of the Chattanooga Weather Bureau Airport Station and Jack Merryman of the Nashville WBAS, who answered questions and furnished actual sequence reports and other weather data for publication.

William Schmedel, Director of Training, National Aviation Academy, St. Petersburg, Fla., who pointed out errors in earlier printings.

Robert Scripture, Jennie A. Smith, and G. M. Yerkes, of Safetech, Inc., who allowed me to make photos of E-6B models FDF-47 and FDF-57-B for the navigation problems in Chap. 17.

Hugh R. Skinner, Jr., of Barfield Instrument Corporation, who sent material on the pressure instruments, including a print of his informative paper, "The Altimeter Credibility Gap."

Fred C. Stashak, Chief Stress Engineer of Piper Aircraft Corporation, who furnished information on Piper airplanes.

Dr. Mervin Strickler, of the FAA Public Affairs Office, who aided in getting the manuscript to the right people in the FAA.

F. C. Taylor, of Mooney Aircraft Corporation, who furnished detailed power-required and -available curves on the Mooney 231.

W. D. (Bill) Thompson, of Precise Flight, Inc., who furnished information on descent rate control, mentioned in Chap. 8, information concerning the use of thumb rules for performance, in addition to furnishing answers to specific questions concerning Cessna aircraft.

Eleanor Ulton, who typed the smooth copy of the manuscript and smoothed, as well, some of the rougher edges of my writing.

Harry Weisberger, of Sperry, who sent material on gyroscopes that was of great help in writing Chap. 4.

Calvin Wilson, Aerodynamicist, of Piper Aircraft Corporation, who furnished data on Piper airplanes. Also, Cal furnished speed-power information and gave permission to use information from the Aztec E *Pilot's Operating Handbook*.

Special thanks to my wife, whose encouragement has never faltered and who has furnished practical help in the form of typing or keyboarding the manuscripts. Without her help, these editions could not have been completed. And special thanks also to my son, Bill, who flies for a major airline, for help with the answers and explanations to the questions on the Commercial Written Test, all of which are included in this book.

Bill Kershner

Sewanee, Tennessee

PART 1

AIRPLANE PERFORMANCE AND STABILITY FOR PILOTS

1 Introduction to Airplane Performance

A REVIEW OF MATHEMATICS FOR PILOTS

A pilot doesn't have to know calculus to fly an airplane well, and there have been a lot of outstanding pilots who could add, subtract, multiply, and divide—and that's about it. *But* since you are going to be an "advanced pilot," this book goes a little more deeply into the whys and hows of airplane performance, including a little math review.

Trigonometry. Trigonometry can turn into a complex subject if you let it, but the trigonometry discussed here is the simple kind you've been using all along in your flying and maybe never thinking of it as such.

Take a crosswind takeoff or landing: you've been using Tennessee windage in calculating how much correction will be needed for a wind of a certain strength at a certain angle from the runway centerline. You correct for the crosswind component and know that the headwind component will help (and a tailwind component will hurt).

You have been successfully using a practical approach to solving trigonometric functions. (If an instructor had mentioned this factor earlier, some of us might have considered quitting flying.)

What it boils down to is this; whenever you fly you're unconsciously (or maybe consciously) dealing with problems that involve working with the two sides and hypotenuse of a right triangle. Flight factors involved include (1) takeoffs and landings in a crosswind, (2) max angle climbs, (3) making good that ground track on a VFR *or* IFR cross-country, (4) working a max range curve (if you are an engineer, too), and (5) calculating max distance glides. The following chapters will cover all these areas of performance in more detail.

Looking at a takeoff in a crosswind, you're dealing with the sines and cosines of a *right triangle,* a triangle with a 90° angle in it (Fig. 1-1).

SINE. The sine (normally written as "sin," which perks it up a little) for an angle (α here) is the ratio of the nonadjacent side A to the hypotenuse (side C) (Fig. 1-1). The Greek letters α (alpha) and β (beta) are used for the angles here because, well, it gives the book more class, and the Greek letters *are* used in aerodynamics equations. More Greek letters will be along shortly. The sides of a triangle are normally denoted by our alphabet (A, B, C).

Look at a 30°-60°-90° triangle (Fig. 1-2). The internal angles always add up to 180°; thus the other two angles of the right triangle (which has a 90° angle) always add up to 90° (10° and 80°, 45° and 45°, etc.) Another interesting point about right triangles is that the sum of the squares of the two sides is equal to the square of the hypotenuse, or $A^2 + B^2 = C^2$ (Fig. 1-3). (This is what the Scarecrow recited after the Wizard of Oz gave him a diploma—and a brain.)

COSINE. For a 30° angle (β in Fig. 1-2) the relationship of sides A and C (the hypotenuse), side A is *always* 0.866 the length of side C (the cosine of 30° is 0.866; A/C = 0.866). Engineers add a zero before the decimal point for a value less than 1 so that it is clear that there isn't a missing number.

Looking at the angle α in Fig. 1-2, note that the relationship of length of the adjacent side B at the 60° angle to the hypotenuse (side C) is the *cosine* of *that* angle, *always* 0.50 (B/C = 0.50).

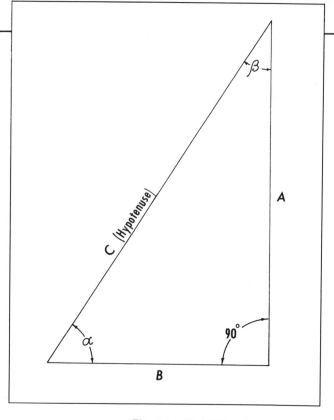

Fig. 1-1. Right triangle components.

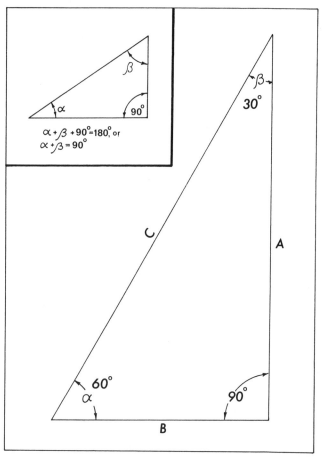

Fig. 1-2. A right triangle with 30° and 60° acute (less than 90°) angles.

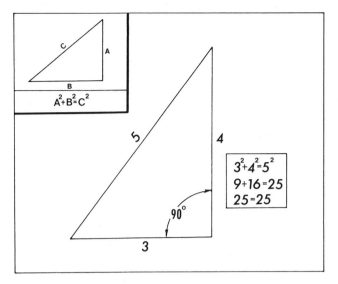

Fig. 1-3. Classic example of the relationship of the hypotenuse of a right triangle. (Another is a triangle with 7 and 24 sides and a 25 hypotenuse: $7^2 + 24^2 = 49 + 576 = 625$; $25^2 = 625$).

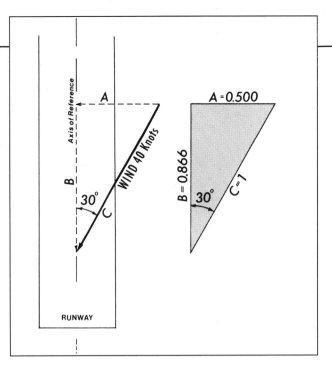

Fig. 1-4. Finding the headwind and crosswind components.

Looking from the same angle of 60° (α) it is a fact that the *sine* (the nonadjacent side A divided by the hypotenuse, or A/C), is 0.866; that is, the length or value of side A is 0.866 the length of the hypotenuse. The sine of the 60° angle is the same as the cosine of a 30° angle—and why not? That's the same side (A). For side B, 0.500 is the cosine of the 60° angle and the sine of the 30° angle. (Got that?)

$$\text{(Fig. 1-2)}-\cos \alpha = B/C = 0.500$$
$$\sin \beta = B/C = 0.500$$

Take a practical situation: You are taking off in a jet fighter from a runway with a 40-K wind at a 30° angle to the centerline. What are the crosswind and headwind components? You're working with a right triangle with 30° and 60° acute angles (Fig. 1-4). Solving for the crosswind component for the wind at a 30° angle you find that the ratio of A to C is 0.50 to 1, or one-half. The component of wind working across the runway is 0.50 of that of the total wind speed of 40 K, or a 20-K crosswind component, which means the same side force as if the wind were at 20 K at a 90° angle to the runway.

To make takeoff calculations in the *Pilot's Operating Handbook* (*POH*) you'd need to know the headwind component (B/C), or the cosine of the 30° angle, which is *always* 0.866. So...0.866 × 40 K is 34.64 K. (Heck, call it 35 K.) If, however, the wind was *60°* to the runway at 40 K, the situation would be reversed and the *crosswind* component would be 0.866 × 40 = 34.64 (35) K (and the *headwind* component would be 0.50 × 40 = 20 K), as can be seen by checking the graph (Fig. 1-5). What we've started here is a wind component chart like that found in a *POH*; here the engineers work out the sines and cosines for various angles the wind may make with the runway and all you have to do is read the values off the graph. Note that the triangle in Fig. 1-4 and the shaded area of Fig. 1-5 are the same. The wind speed in the graph is always the hypotenuse (side C) of the triangle.

TANGENTS. The tangent is the relationship between the *far side* (the nonadjacent side) and the *near side* (the side adjacent to the angle in question). Look back at Fig. 1-2. The relationship A/B is the tangent of the angle α (60° shown there), and

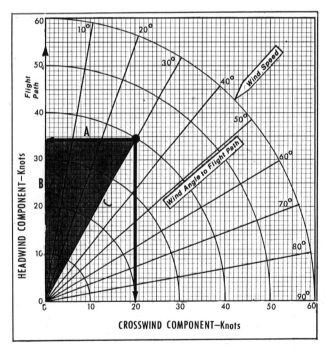

Fig. 1-5. The wind component chart is a prepared set of right triangles, with sines and cosines precalculated and drawn. Horace Endsdorfer, private pilot, assumes that Fig. 1-5 can only be used for crosswinds from the right, since that's the way it's drawn, but Horace has other problems as well (see Chap. 7—Endurance).

looking ahead at Fig. 1-8 you can see that the tangent of 60° is 1.732. In a 60° angle, side A is 1.732 times as long as side B. The tangent is useful in such factors as finding the angle of climb, where the relationship of feet upward versus feet forward is essential.

To digress a little, Fig. 1-6 shows the procedure probably first used in measuring the height of an object too high to be scaled easily. Although the example is better as a problem in geometry, it shows that for a given angle (the sun's rays form-

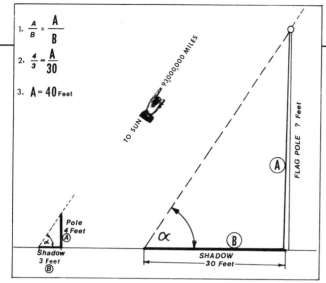

1. $\dfrac{A}{B} = \dfrac{A}{B}$

2. $\dfrac{4}{3} = \dfrac{A}{30}$

3. $A = 40$ Feet

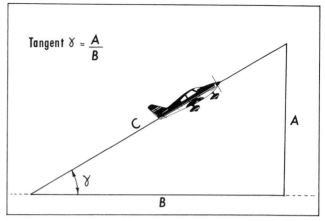

Tangent $\gamma = \dfrac{A}{B}$

Fig. 1-6. Using the relationship between similar triangles to find the height of a flagpole by measuring sides A and B of the small triangle and side B of the large triangle to find side A (the height of the flagpole). It is assumed that the flagpole is greased so that it cannot be climbed and measured with a tape. (There's the old story of two physics students who were each given a very expensive barometer and told to find the height of a certain tall building. One dropped the barometer off the top and measured its fall with a stopwatch. The other went to the janitor and said, "If you tell me exactly how high this building is, I'll give you this fine barometer." Scientific research methods vary, it seems.)

Fig. 1-7. Max angle of climb (γ) is a tangent function and depends on the highest ratio of A (vertical height) to B (horizontal distance). Gamma (γ) is normally used to depict climb or descent angles.

Fig. 1-8. (below) A. Sine, cosine, and tangent values. Notice how the tangent value increases rapidly as the angle approaches 90°; for instance, from 85° to 89.5° (4.5°) the value increases over 10 times and goes to infinity at 90°. B. A graphical representation of the sine, cosine, and tangent values. Note that the tangent goes off the scale at a value of 1.0 at 45°. The examples are for the sine, cosine, and tangent of 30°.

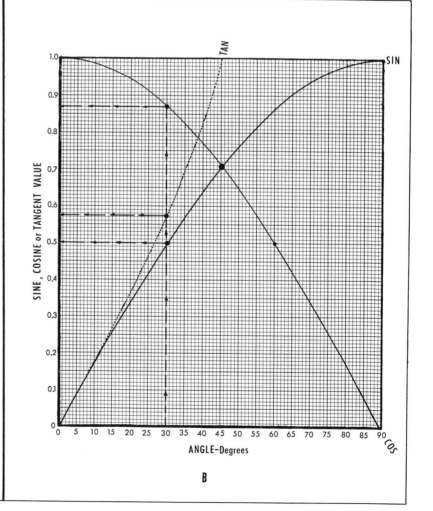

ANGLE-Degrees	SINE	COSINE	TANGENT
0	0	1.00	0
2	0.0349	0.999	0.0349
5	0.0872	0.996	0.0875
6.6	0.115	0.993	0.116
10	0.174	0.985	0.176
15	0.259	0.966	0.268
20	0.342	0.940	0.364
25	0.423	0.906	0.466
30	0.500	0.866	0.577
35	0.574	0.819	0.700
40	0.643	0.766	0.839
45	0.707	0.707	1.00
50	0.766	0.643	1.192
55	0.819	0.574	1.428
60	0.866	0.500	1.732
65	0.906	0.423	2.14
70	0.940	0.342	2.75
75	0.966	0.259	3.73
80	0.985	0.174	5.67
85	0.996	0.087	11.43
89	0.9998	0.017	57.29
89.5	0.99996	0.00873	114.59
90	1.00	0	Infinite

A

B

ing the shadow), the sides of a right triangle have the same ratio.

If you were assigned the job of finding the height of the flagpole on a sunny day you could set up a vertical pole 4 ft tall and measure the shadow (3 ft here). You would then quickly measure the flagpole shadow to establish the ratio of the two poles (Fig. 1-6). Your numbers would not likely work out as evenly as these, however, and there would be a problem on a cloudy day or at night.

If you had a device set on the ground for measuring the angle α (53° here) and knew the distance of that device from the flagpole (B) you would come up with tan α = A/30; A = 30 tan α; α = 53°, tan α = 1.33, A = 30 × 1.33 = 40 ft.

Okay, to review:

The sine of an angle is the ratio between, or relative value of, the "far" (nonadjacent) side of the right triangle and its hypotenuse and, like the cosine and tangent, is always the same for any given angle.

The cosine is the ratio between, or relative value of, the "near" (adjacent) side of the right triangle and its hypotenuse.

The tangent is the ratio of the "far" side to the "near" side of an angle of the right triangle.

The tangent shows the relationship in a climb between vertical and horizontal distances covered.

The sine (0.500) of a 30° angle is the same as the cosine of a 60° angle. The sine of 55° equals the cosine of 35°, sine 20° equals cosine 70°, etc. (The "etc." is to cover the fact that the first time you encounter it this can be as confusing as an FAA directive.)

Fig. 1-8 is a table of sine, cosine, and tangent functions for angles from 0° to 90° in 5° increments, plus three other selected angles that will be discussed later. Using a trig table (or the right pocket calculator) you could, for instance, find the sine of an angle of 6°36′ (6 degrees 36 minutes) or 6.6°, which turns out to be 0.1149372. (That's *all* you need — to be fumbling around with a trig table or calculator while you're

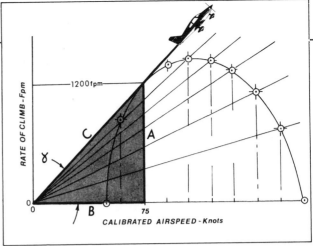

Fig. 1-9. Rate of climb versus airspeed, finding the angle of climb at sea level (no wind).

flying.) But again, what it says is that the ratio of the value of the *far side* of the triangle to its hypotenuse is 0.115 (rounded off in Fig. 1-8); it's about 11.5% as long as the hypotenuse.

Max Angle Climb. A good example of finding the max angle of climb of an airplane at a particular density-altitude is shown in Fig. 1-9, which is a variation of Fig. 6-7. (You might take a look at Fig. 6-7 now.)

As noted in Chap. 6, the max angle climb speed is found by running a line from the origin of the graph (zero climb and zero knots) tangent to or touching (and passing) the curve.

The angle of climb (γ, or gamma) is the tangent, or the ratio of A to B (A/B); tan γ = rate of climb/velocity — or is it?

The rate of climb is 1200 ft per minute (fpm) and the velocity is 75 K, so tan γ = 1200/75 = 16, which would give a climb angle (after referring to your trig table or using a calculator) of 86.4°. *Now that's a climbing airplane!* (Fig. 1-10)

Fig. 1-10. Using the dimensions cited in the example gives the airplane extraordinary climb performance.

Of course, 86.4° is *not* the answer because we're dealing in apples and oranges, knots and feet per minute. One of the values must be converted to the other; for simplicity, convert the 75 K to feet per minute. The conversion for knots to feet per second is 1.69; multiply that by 60 to get the distance covered in a minute: 1.69 × 75 × 60 = 7605 (call it 7600).

So the tangent of the angle is 1200/7600 = 0.158, or, looking at Fig. 1-8, the angle of climb is 8.98° (call it 9°). Wait a minute. It's easy to fall into a trap using the graph shown in Fig. 1-9, although at shallow angles of climb the error is not too great. At first glance, it seems a simple matter of solving the tangent: you just plot climb distance versus airspeed and look up the tangent. The kicker is that the airplane is traveling up along its *climb path flight angle* at the airspeed given for max climb.

Look at the problem again after setting up equal values: $\sin \gamma = 1200/7600 = 0.158$; $\gamma = 9.09°$ (call it 9.1°). The point is that at *shallow* angles (usually considered as less than 15°) the sine and tangent are quite close together and in this case would create an error of 0.11°, or a little over 0.1° ($9.09° - 8.98° = 0.11°$).

A problem might be set up as follows: Through earlier flight testing it was found that the max angle of climb for our new Rocket Six is 10.0° at sea level density. Find the horizontal distance required from *lift-off* to clear a 50-ft obstacle under the condition given. Assume that the airplane has the max angle climb speed at lift-off.

The *tangent* of the angle of climb is important here because you're finding the distance to clear a 50-ft obstacle as part of the takeoff and climb distance for insertion in the *POH*. The vertical part of the triangle is known (A = 50 ft), as is the angle of climb (10.0°), so you would need to find B, or the horizontal distance required (Fig. 1-11). Tan γ = tangent of 10.0° (checking Fig. 1-8, you'll find the answer is 0.176). Note again in Fig. 1-8 that the tangent of the angle is very close to the sine value. So A (the height of 50 ft) is 0.176, or about 17.6% of B, the ground distance. You can see that the distance required after lift-off to clear the obstacle is 50/0.176 = 284 ft. Solving algebraically and doing some reshuffling, tan γ = A/B; B tan γ = A; B = A/tan γ, or 50/0.176, or 284 ft. (That's why it's called the "Rocket.")

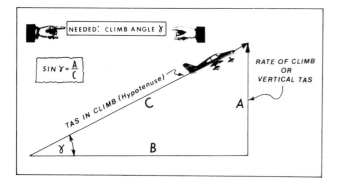

Fig. 1-11. Finding the climb angle of an airplane at a particular climb speed (TAS) and rate of climb.

The ground run would be added to this to get total distance to clear a 50-ft obstacle at sea level density-altitude. The same idea would be used for different pressure altitudes and temperatures (and different Weights) until the takeoff distance chart or graph is complete.

Look at a canned problem of finding the climb angle at the maximum *rate* of climb for an airplane at a particular altitude and temperature. You are the test pilot and set up a climb at 5000 ft density-altitude. You (and the airplane) will be flying the hypotenuse (side C); the rate of climb will be side A. (See Fig. 1-11 again.) So...

1. If two sides of a right triangle are known, or

2. If *one* side and *one* of the acute angles of a right triangle are known, all other factors may be found.

Two items are known:

1. The IAS is read off the airspeed indicator, converted to CAS (or EAS, as needed) and then to TAS (knots).

2. The rate of climb is either timed or read off the extra-accurate vertical speed indicator especially built for this problem.

The TAS up the climb path is in knots and the rate of climb is in feet per minute (fpm). Again it's apples and oranges, so you convert one of the values to the other. For this problem, the TAS along the climb path is to be 89 K and the rate of climb is found to be 900 fpm. One solution is to convert both to *feet per second* (although you could convert the TAS to feet per minute to match the rate of climb usage). To convert 89 K to feet per second, use the conversion multiplier 1.69. The airplane is traveling at 150 feet per second (fps) along the hypotenuse.

The rate of climb is 900 fpm, or 60 sec × 15 (fps).

The sine of the angle of climb, then, is side A/hypotenuse or rate of climb (fps)/TAS (fps) = 15/150 = 0.10. See Fig. 1-8B to get the angle.

$$\text{Sin } \gamma = 0.10$$
$$\gamma = 5.8° = 5°48'$$

You could use "fathoms per fortnight" for both TAS and rate of climb, just as long as both factors are given in the same terms.

FIXED ANGLE OF ATTACK PERFORMANCE FACTORS

There are several factors in calculating airplane performance based on a fixed angle of attack; in order to fly at that angle of attack (without an angle of attack indicator) the airspeed must be varied as the square root of the Weight change. The following performance parameters for reciprocating engine airplanes depend aerodynamically on a constant coefficient of Lift (or constant angle of attack).

Stall Speed. The stall occurs at the maximum coefficient of Lift (C_{Lmax}) for the configuration chosen (clean or a chosen flap setting). The C_{Lmax} with flaps extended will be higher than unflapped, naturally, which means that the stall speed (V_{stall}) will be *lower*.

Look at the equation for Lift (see Chap. 2 for a more thorough discussion): Lift = $C_L S(\varrho/2)V^2$, where ϱ = air density (slugs per ft³), C_{Lmax} = maximum coefficient of Lift, S = wing area (ft²), and V^2 = true velocity (fps²). Assuming that Lift = Weight (W), and solving for V_{stall}, you'd find $V_{stall} = \sqrt{2W/S\varrho C_{Lmax}}$.

Following are the steps used in finding the stall speed:

$$L = W = C_{Lmax}S(\varrho/2)V^2$$
$$V_{stall}^2 = \frac{W}{C_{Lmax}S(\varrho/2)} = \frac{2W}{C_{Lmax}S\varrho}$$

(The "2" is moved to the top of the equation to simplify things a little.)

To solve for V_{stall}, square roots are taken of each side of the equation:

$$V_{stall} = \sqrt{2W/C_{Lmax}S\varrho}$$

You can see that the greater the C_{Lmax}, the lower the stall speed. (V_{stall} is TAS here.)

Double the Weight and the stall speed is increased by a factor of the square root of 2 ($\sqrt{2}$), or 1.414. Two numbers to remember if you plan to follow up on this are $\sqrt{2} = 1.414$ and $\sqrt{3} = 1.732$. Spend your time memorizing them instead of watching TV news; it's less depressing.

Max Range Airspeed. Max range distance depends on maintaining the maximum ratio of C_L to C_D (C_L/C_D), or maintaining a constant *angle of attack* throughout the trip. As fuel is burned off, the Weight decreases and the dynamic pressure must be reduced to reduce Lift so as to maintain straight and level flight at this constant angle of attack. If you don't reduce power as Weight decreases, the airplane will climb. (This is one technique of long-range cruise control, that is, letting the airplane gain altitude as Weight decreases; but the usual procedure for max range is to maintain a constant altitude and reduce airspeed as fuel is burned.)

Looking at the Lift equation again, assuming straight and level flight:

$$L = W = C_{LR}S(\varrho/2)V^2 = C_{LR} \times S \times \varrho/2 \times V^2$$

where C_{LR} = coefficient of Lift at the max *range* angle of attack and $(\varrho/2)V^2$ = dynamic pressure (pounds per square foot, or psf).

Taking a fictitious airplane weighing 3600 lb at the start of a max range exercise at a constant 5000-ft density-altitude and a wing area of 180 ft², find the speeds for max range at Weights of 3600 lb and of 2700 lb near the end of the trip. The C_L for max range (C_{LR}, or max C_L/C_D) is 0.500 for this airplane. The density at 5000 ft is 0.002049 slugs per ft³ (see Fig. 4-4). Of course, you aren't going to carry a standard atmosphere chart around in the airplane, but do the problem anyway.

The true airspeed (V_T) to be carried at 5000 ft at a Weight of 3600 lb is

$$V_T^2 = \frac{2W}{C_{LR}S\varrho} = \frac{2 \times 3600}{0.002049 \times 180 \times 0.500} = \frac{7200}{0.1844}$$
$$= 39{,}096$$

$$V_T = \sqrt{\frac{2W}{C_{LR}S\varrho}} = \sqrt{39{,}096} = 198 \text{ fps}$$

To convert from feet per second to knots, the factor is 1.69; 198/1.69 = *117 K* (rounded off). The true airspeed to be carried for max range at 5000 ft density-altitude at 3600 lb is 117 K. Using an E-6B computer or electric calculator, the *calibrated* airspeed is found to be *109 K* at 5000 ft.

At a Weight of 2700 lb near the end of the trip, the *only* variable is Weight. Going through the process again to find TAS:

$$V_T^2 = \frac{2W}{C_{LR}S\varrho}$$
$$V_T = \sqrt{\frac{2W}{C_{LR}S\varrho}} = \sqrt{\frac{5400}{0.18441}} = \sqrt{29{,}283}$$
$$= 171 \text{ fps, or } 101 K$$

You would again use a calculator to find the CAS at 5000 ft (94 K).

The question comes up as to the variation of max range indicated (or calibrated) airspeed with respect to different *density-altitudes*. Take still another look at the Lift equation (Lift = Weight): $L = W = C_{LR}S(\varrho/2)V^2$.

Assume that the Weight is the same at the different density-altitudes so that L (or W) is constant but ϱ varies. Since $(\varrho/2)V^2$ is dynamic pressure (CAS), if the other factors (L,

C_{LR}, and S) are constant, then dynamic pressure must remain so.

The *combination* of one-half the density times the velocity, or TAS, squared of the air molecules moving past the airplane gives the dynamic pressure required to support it.

Suppose that an airplane at a certain Weight and C_L requires a minimum calibrated airspeed of 100 K, or a dynamic pressure of 33.9 psf, to maintain level flight. The 33.9 psf may be obtained by flying at sea level at a calibrated and true airspeed of *100 K* (169 fps), or at 10,000 ft with a true airspeed of *116 K*. In both cases the calibrated airspeed is 100 K. The point is this: Once the C_{LR} is found you would fly the airplane at the same calibrated (or indicated) airspeed at any of the lower operating altitudes to get max range.

Max Endurance. *Maximum endurance* for propeller airplanes is also a function of a constant coefficient of Lift (C_{LE}, or max endurance coefficient of Lift) as far as aerodynamics is concerned. It is found at a higher angle of attack than max range and, in aerodynamic theory at least, is the lowest point on the power-required curve.

As in the cases of maximum range and the stall speed, the airspeed required to maintain the C_{LE} is decreased with the *decrease of the square root of the Weight* (and for the same reasons). More about this in Chap. 7.

Max Distance and Minimum Sink Glides. These are fixed angle of attack performance factors also varying with the square root of the Weight change. More about this in Chap. 8.

Maneuvering Speed. The maneuvering speed (V_A) also depends on a constant C_L (C_{Lmax}, or the stall angle of attack); therefore V_A must be reduced with the decrease of the square root of the Weight: $V_{A2} = V_{A1}\sqrt{W_2/W_1}$; $V_A = \sqrt{n} \times V_s$, where n = limit load factor (discussed in Chap. 11).

A thumb rule for finding the effects of Weight change on airspeed for *any parameter requiring a constant C_L is to reduce the airspeed* (V_A here) *by one-half of the percentage of the Weight reduction.*

Suppose at 3000 lb an airplane has a maneuvering speed of 100 K (chosen for simplifying the arithmetic). At 2400 lb, or at *20%* Weight reduction, this rule says reduce the 3000-lb maneuvering speed by *10%* to 90 K. At 1800 lb, a Weight reduction of 40%, the original 3000-lb (100-K) maneuvering speed should drop by 20%, to 80 K.

To check it out, actually solve for the square roots (the technical way of doing it) and compare. Instead of the thumb rule of 90 K at the lower Weight of 2400 lb, the computer gives an answer of 89.44 K. At the Weight drop of 40%, the "real" answer is 77.45 K, as compared with the estimate of 80 K.

Fig. 1-12 is a graph used to see the relationship between Weight change and required airspeeds for the performance parameters that result from, or require, a fixed angle of attack, or more accurately, a constant C_L. The graph is a quick and easy way to get the numbers; you can still work it out yourself if you like.

Following are operating speeds (CAS):

Stalls = V_{S0}, V_{S1} (landing configuration and clean respectively)

Maneuvering speed = V_A

Maximum range speed = V_{MR}

Maximum endurance speed = V_{ME}

Each of these operating speeds decreases as a function of the square root of the decrease in Weight. V_{S1}, as noted in Chap. 4, is the stall speed for a particular configuration; in this book it will be the clean stall speed at a particular Weight.

To use Fig. 1-12, assume a fictitious airplane with a maximum certificated Weight of 3600 lb. The airspeeds (CAS or EAS) at that Weight for this problem are $V_{S1} = 62$ K, $V_A = 120$ K, $V_{MR} = 106$ K, $V_{ME} = 80$ K. To find the required airspeeds at a Weight of 2990 lb, divide: 2990/3600 = 0.83. The new Weight is 0.83 of the max certificated Weight (rounded off).

Selecting 0.83 on the ratio of weights scale, move across to intercept the reference line and then down to find the CAS (or EAS) multiplier of 0.91 for this problem. Solving for the *new* airspeeds (rounded off) at the lower Weight of 2990 lb: $V_{S1} = 0.91 \times 62 = 56$ K; $V_A = 0.91 \times 120 = 109$ K; $V_{MR} = 0.91 \times 106 = 96$ K; $V_{ME} = 0.91 \times 80 = 73$ K. Fig. 1-12 works for any Weight ratio you may use; 3600 and 2990 lb were just examples.

Fig. 1-12. CAS or EAS multipliers to correct for Weight change with the fixed angle of attack performance factors (stall speeds, maneuvering, max range, and max endurance speeds). It's assumed for the graph that the lowest Weight will not be less than 50% (0.50) of that of the maximum Weight. You could use the graph to find Weights much lower than the 2990 lb used as an example by having it as the "new" max Weight. For instance, to find the maneuvering speed at 1555 lb for that same (originally 3600-lb) airplane you could set up the ratio 1555/2990 = 0.52. Looking at 0.52 on the ratio of Weights scale in this figure and moving over to the line and down—as was done earlier—you'd get an answer of about 0.72. The V_A at 1555 lb is 0.72 that of 2990 lb. V_A at 2990 pounds was 109 K, as was found earlier. V_A at 1555 lb would be $0.72 \times 109 = 78$ K (rounded off).

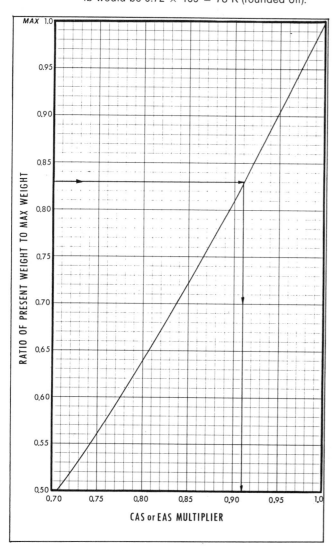

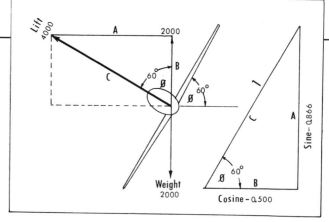

Fig. 1-13. The cosine of 60° is 0.500; the Weight is 2000 lb. Cosine ϕ (phi or phee, the Greek letter used to denote bank) = cosine 60° = 0.500. The Lift required $= \dfrac{1}{\cos \phi} = \dfrac{1}{0.500} = 2$. Lift required = $2 \times 2000 = 4000$ lb.

TURNS

Looking at a 2000-lb airplane in a steady state, coordinated, constant-altitude turn in a bank of 60° (Fig. 1-13): The "up" and "down" forces must be in balance if the airplane is to maintain a constant altitude. The items known are the airplane's Weight, which is acting directly downward, and the 60° angle of bank. It is also known that Lift acts perpendicular to the wingspan (the hypotenuse, or side C), and for now it can be given a value of 1.

Side B (the vertical component of Lift) must be 2000 lb in order to balance the Weight of 2000 lb, and here it is 0.500 of the value of the total Lift (the hypotenuse, or side C) required to maintain a constant altitude. The Lift (C) acting perpendicular (as always) to the wingspan must be 4000 lb. Lift required $= 1/\cos \phi = 1/0.500 = 2$, or C = 2B's (B = 2000 lb).

The g's being pulled here are Lift/Weight = 4000/2000 = 2 g's. In any constant-altitude balanced turn, the load factor being exerted is the Lift-to-Weight ratio, or load factor (LF) = $1/\cos \phi$.

Look back at Fig. 1-8, or use your calculator, and find the load factor for a 25° banked turn; cos ϕ = B/C, or cos ϕ = 0.906, or LF = 1/0.906 = 1.104 g's. You could make up your own curve as shown in various textbooks or *POH*s by picking bank angles from 0 to 90°, plotting the points, and joining them. You can use Fig. 1-8 to find the cosine of a particular bank and divide "1" by that.

This brings up the point about the *stall speed increase* with increased bank angle in the balanced, constant-altitude turn; the stall is affected by the load factor, which is an indication of how much the airplane "weighs." The stall speed increases as the *square root* of the load factor increases (or Weight increases, as was discussed earlier and is shown in Fig. 1-12).

Suppose that the airplane is in a bank of 35° ($\phi = 35°$). What is the load factor and increase in stall speed? Referring to Fig. 1-8 you'd see that the cosine of 35° is 0.819 (call it 0.82). The load factor in the 35°-banked constant-altitude turn is $1/\cos \phi = 1/0.82 = 1.22$. The pilot (and airplane) is feeling 1.22 g's flying the 35°-banked turn. The stall speed increase is the *square root* of the load factor (or apparent Weight increase), or $\sqrt{1.22}$, or 1.10. The stall speed has increased by 10% in the turn (more about this in Chap. 2).

Radius of Turn. Many times you'd like to have a good idea of what radius of turn would be expected at a given angle of bank and airspeed (TAS, knots).

$$\text{radius (ft)} = \frac{V^2}{11.26 \tan \phi}$$

For example, what is the turn radius of an airplane at a 30°
bank at 150 K?

$$\text{bank angle } (\phi) = 30°$$
$$V^2 = (150)^2 = 22,500$$
$$\tan 30° = 0.577 \text{ (look back at Fig. 1-8)}$$
$$\text{radius} = \frac{22,500}{(11.26)(0.577)} = \frac{22,500}{6.497} = 3463 \text{ ft}$$

The radius at 300 K (which is twice as fast as the 150 K
just used) will be 4 times as large because the radius is a
function of the square of the velocity.

$$V^2 = (300)^2 = 90,000$$
$$\tan 30° = 0.577$$
$$\text{radius} = \frac{90,000}{(11.26)(0.577)} = \frac{90,000}{6.497} = 13,852 \text{ ft}$$

Since you know that the radius goes up as V^2 you could multiply the radius found at 150 K by 4, rather than go through all
the arithmetic again.

The "new" radius, if you know the "old" one, is proportional to $(V_2/V_1)^2$ times the "old" radius. For example, the
radius at 150 K was 3463 ft. What would be the "new" radius
of turn at 190 K?

$$(190/150)^2 = (1.267)^2 = 1.604, \text{ or } 1.604 \times 3463 = 5554 \text{ ft}$$

Turn Rate. For those interested in instrument flying the *rate*
of turn is an important factor; the rule of thumb of dividing
the TAS (K) by 10 and adding one-half of that answer works
very well for the standard rate of turn of 3° per second. As an
example, the rule of thumb indicates that at an airspeed of
130 K a standard rate of turn would require a bank of 19.5°
(call it 20°).

$$\text{turn rate (degrees per second)} = \frac{1091 \tan \phi}{V}$$

where ϕ is the bank angle and V is TAS in knots (130 K here).
The turn rate is 3° per second, so turning the equation around
a little:

$$3 = 1091 \tan \phi/V$$
$$3V = 1091 \tan \phi; \quad 3V/1091 = \tan \phi$$
$$\tan \phi = (3 \times 130)/1091 = 390/1091 = 0.3575.$$

Using a calculator or trig table (or Figure 1-8) you'd find that
the angle of bank (ϕ) is 19.67°, a value "easily" flown on the
attitude indicator (sure it is). You could look at Fig. 1-8 and
see that the tangent of 20° is 0.3640 and that the tangent of
the angle sought here would be slightly less than that. Or you
could interpolate between 0.3640 (for 20°) and 0.2680 (for
15°).

There is a certain amount of error involved in interpolating between tangent values because as the angle increases the
tangent value increases at a *much* higher rate. For instance,
the tangent of 60° is *not* 3 times the value of the tangent of
20°. Looking back at Fig. 1-8 you'd note that the tangent of
60° is 1.732; the tangent of 20° is 0.364, for a ratio of 4.76 to
1 (1.732 divided by 0.364), not 3 to 1. It gets even more out of
hand as the angle approaches 90°.

SUMMARY

This chapter is an introduction or review of trigonometry, as well as briefly covering certain aspects of airplane performance. The following chapters will cover climbs, turns,
glides, and cruise performance in much greater detail. After
you've read each chapter on performance you might want to
check back to this one for a quick review of the basic factors
involved.

2 The Four Forces

BACKGROUND

Lift, Drag, Thrust, and Weight are the Four Forces acting on an airplane in flight (Fig. 2-1). The actions of the
airplane are affected by the balance (or imbalance) of these
forces, and while each will be discussed separately in this
chapter, don't get the idea that each works completely separately.

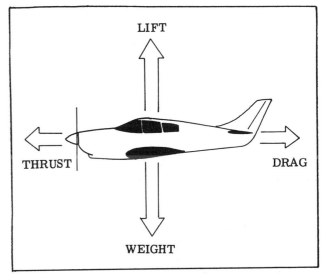

Fig. 2-1. The Four Forces.

Sure, you can fly an airplane without knowing how Lift
or the other of the Four Forces work, *but* a good idea of the
factors affecting each of them can lead to analyzing and predicting the performance of your airplane under different conditions of Weight, altitude, etc. This chapter takes a look at
how each Force is developed, and Chap. 3 shows how it *acts*
in flight.

LIFT

Lift is the force exerted primarily by the wings (although
the fuselage contributes, and even the tail helps under certain
special conditions) and is created by the action of the air moving past the airfoil (cross-section of the wing). *Lift is considered to act perpendicularly to the relative wind and to the
wingspan* (Fig. 2-2).

The airfoil produces Lift by its shape, which is such that
the pressure, velocity, and downwash distribution results in
effective Lift, meaning that the Lift required for the airplane's
various performance actions does not result in excessive drag
and high power requirements. In other words, the airfoil gives
a high Lift-to-Drag ratio (more about that later). You might
use a flat plate of sufficient size to "lift" a 2000-lb (or 200,000
lb) airplane, but the power required to fly it would be prohibi-
tive.

As the airfoil moves through the air, either in powered or
gliding flight—or as the air moves past it as in a wind tun-
nel—pressure distributions around it result in a downwash
action (Fig. 2-3). This action creates the reaction of the airplane being supported in flight. (Fig. 3–5 shows some pres-

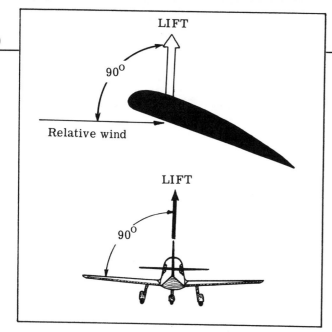

Fig. 2-2. Lift acts perpendicular to the relative wind and to the wingspan.

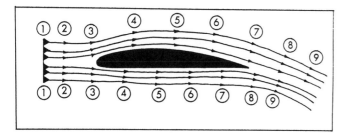

Fig. 2-3. Relative velocities and downwash around a nonsymmetrical airfoil.

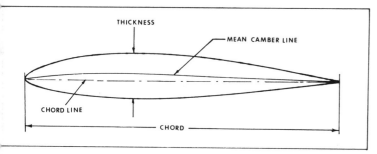

Fig. 2-4. Airfoil nomenclature. The chord line is the shortest distance between the leading edge to the trailing edge of the airfoil.

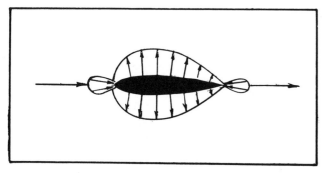

Fig. 2-5. Pressure patterns around a symmetrical airfoil moving at a zero angle of attack.

sure distribution patterns around an airfoil at two different low angles of attack.) The air, moving past the airfoil, has different velocities at different positions.

Fig. 2-4 gives some airfoil nomenclature. Note that the mean camber (average curve) line is equidistant from each surface. Fig. 2-5 shows a symmetrical airfoil (no camber) at zero angle of attack. The pressure distributions on each side of the airfoil are lower but equal, there is no downwash, and Lift doesn't exist. In Fig. 2-6 downwash is present and the pressure distribution is such that Lift is being produced.

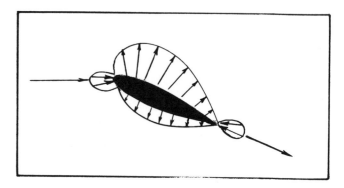

Fig. 2-6. Pressure patterns around a symmetrical airfoil at a positive angle of attack. By comparing Fig. 2-5 and 2-6 you can see that Lift isn't produced by a symmetrical airfoil until an angle of attack occurs. Most aerobatic airplanes have symmetrical or near-symmetrical airfoils for better inverted flight characteristics. (The airfoil in Fig. 2-3 would be inefficient in inverted flight.)

If you are interested in the mathematics of Lift, take another look at the following equation, which was introduced in Chap. 1.

$$L = C_L S(\varrho/2)V^2, \text{ or } \text{Lift} = C_L \times S \times \frac{\varrho}{2} \times V^2$$

where L = Lift, in pounds
  C_L = coefficient of Lift (It varies with the type of airfoil used and angle of attack.)
  S = wing area, in square feet (Fig. 2-7 shows how it is usually measured.)

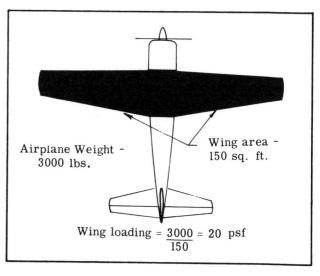

Airplane Weight - 3000 lbs.

Wing area - 150 sq. ft.

Wing loading = $\frac{3000}{150}$ = 20 psf

Fig. 2-7.

$\varrho/2$ = air density (ϱ) divided by 2. (Rho, or ϱ, is air density, which for standard sea level conditions is 0.002378 slugs per cubic foot. If you want to know the mass of an object in slugs divide the Weight, in pounds, by the acceleration of gravity, or 32.16. The acceleration caused by gravity is 32.16 ft per second, per second at the earth's surface.)

V^2 = true velocity (true airspeed) of the air particles in feet per second (fps) squared.

Coefficient of Lift is a relative measure of an airfoil's lifting capabilities. Comparatively high-lift airfoils, such as the Clark Y type with its curved or cambered upper surface and flat lower surface, may have a maximum C_L of 1.8. A thin airfoil, such as might be used on a jet, may have a maximum C_L of only 0.9. The airplane having the higher maximum coefficient of Lift, or C_{Lmax}, will use less runway on landing (assuming two airplanes of equal wing loading operating in the same air density). Having available the C_L versus angle of attack curves of various airfoils, the engineer can decide which airfoil would be better to use for a particular airplane. Your contact with the term is only through control of the angle of attack while flying.

A plot of C_L versus angle of attack for a typical general aviation airplane type of airfoil shows that the C_L increases in a straight line with an increase in angle of attack until the stalling angle is reached, at which point the C_L drops off rapidly (Fig. 2-8).

Fig. 2-9 shows the C_L versus angle of attack for a high-speed symmetrical airfoil such as may be used on jets. Its maximum C_L is only 0.9, which means that the airplane would have a high landing speed.

These airfoil designations describe the airfoil properties and shape. The 23012 is an unsymmetrical airfoil. The "12" indicates that the airfoil maximum thickness is 12% of its chord. The 0006 airfoil is a symmetrical airfoil (the first two zeros tell this) with a thickness ratio of 0.06 or 6%.

Take the 3000-lb plane with the 150-ft² wing area in the earlier example. Assume that there are two airplanes exactly alike with this Weight and wing area; one has a 23012 airfoil, and the other a 0006. The plane with the 0006 high-speed airfoil will cruise faster because of less Drag but will also land faster. In fact, it may land so fast as to be useless for many smaller airports.

It has been found that a "birdlike" airfoil (Fig. 2-10) has a comparatively high C_{Lmax}. Earlier planes used this type and had low landing speeds—but also had low cruise speeds because of the higher Drag at all angles of attack. A good setup would be to have a 0006 airfoil for cruising and a birdlike airfoil for landing. Flaps accomplish just that; when you lower the flaps you raise the C_{Lmax} and have a lower landing speed.

Fig. 2-11 shows plots of the C_L versus angle of attack for two airfoils. Notice the similarity of the curves of the 0006 with flaps and the 23012. It can be readily seen that although the flaps installation adds Weight, flaps make it possible for fast airplanes to land at low speeds. The two airplanes of the same Weight and configuration in the example would probably use the same amount of runway for landing, assuming the plane with the 0006 airfoil used 60° of flaps and the one with the 23012 airfoil did not have flaps and, of course, the air density (density-altitude) was the same for both airplanes.

By using the Lift equation ($L = C_L S(\varrho/2) V^2$, and solving for velocity, an actual comparison of the two airplane landing speeds can be found. For convenience, we'll assume that the two airplanes are landing at sea level, that Lift just equals Weight at the touchdown, and that the C_L in the equation is

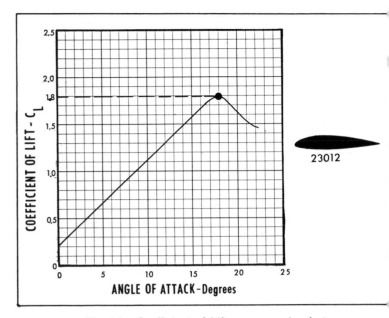

Fig. 2-8. Coefficient of Lift versus angle of attack, NACA (now NASA) 23012 airfoil.

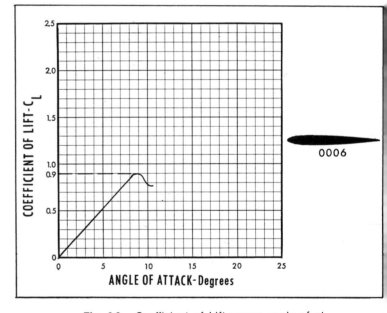

Fig. 2-9. Coefficient of Lift versus angle of attack, NACA 0006 airfoil.

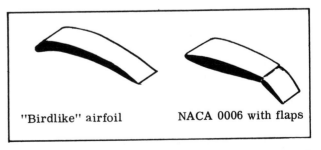

"Birdlike" airfoil   NACA 0006 with flaps

Fig. 2-10.

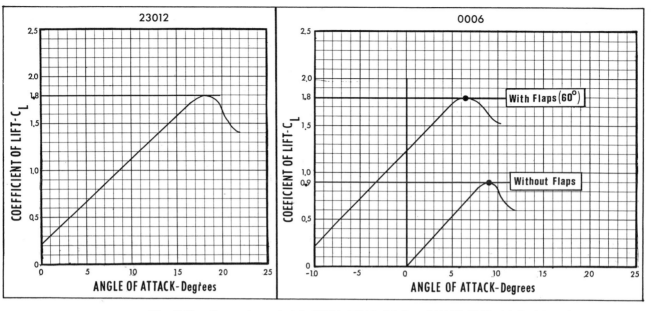

Fig. 2-11. Comparison of plain NACA 23012 airfoil and NACA 0006 airfoil with and without flaps.

C_{Lmax} (both will touch down at the maximum angle of attack or minimum speed).

First solve for the landing speed of the airplane with the 23012 airfoil and do a little algebraic shuffling of the Lift equation:

$$V = \sqrt{2L/C_{Lmax}S\varrho}.$$

Everything inside the square root enclosure is known: L (Weight) = 3000 lb, C_{Lmax} (for this airfoil) = 1.8, S = 150 square feet, and ϱ = 0.002378 slugs per cubic foot.

$$V = \sqrt{\frac{6000}{1.8 \times 150 \times 0.002378}} = \sqrt{\frac{6000}{0.64}} = \sqrt{9380}$$
$$= 97 \text{ fps}$$

Thinking in terms of miles per hour, V = *66 mph* or 57 K (true airspeed, or TAS).

Do the same thing for the airplane with the 0006 airfoil (no flaps); C_{Lmax} is 0.9 instead of 1.8 (everything else is the same):

$$V = \sqrt{\frac{6000}{0.9 \times 150 \times 0.002378}} = \sqrt{\frac{6000}{0.32}} = \sqrt{18,750}$$
$$= 137 \text{ fps or } 93.5 \text{ mph or } 81 \text{ K (TAS)}$$

(At sea level the indicated and true airspeeds will be the same, assuming no airspeed instrument or position error.) A pretty "hot" airplane but it could be cooled down by adding the flaps mentioned earlier.

Getting back to Lift in general, the funny thing about it is that you really don't worry about how much Lift you have in normal flying—you fly by the airplane and Lift takes care of itself. Sure, you can be flying along at cruise and increase Lift by pulling back on the wheel but you can *feel* that Lift is greater than it should be by the way you are being pressed down in the seat. As Drag is increased by the increase of Lift, you'll find that the airplane slows—and Lift will tend to regain its old value again.

One time when you *are* interested in watching Lift increase is on takeoff. If your 3000-lb airplane with the 23012

airfoil (or any airfoil) is taking off at a high elevation (where the density is low) it must have a higher V^2 (TAS, squared) in order to make up for the lower density to get the required Lift for lift-off. This is *one* of the reasons why a longer takeoff run is required at airports at higher elevations. (The big reason is that the engine is producing less power in the less dense air, but this will be covered in later chapters.)

High-Lift Devices. The effects of flaps, as noted, can increase the maximum C_L compared with the wing without flaps. While the term *high-lift device* is commonly used, actually *the purpose of flaps, slots, or slats is to provide the same Lift as before (say 3000 lb) at a lower airspeed, not to increase the Lift over that required.* If you are flying at a high speed and suddenly put the flaps down it is true that Lift will be increased suddenly and the airplane will *accelerate* upward—and you will again be pressed down sharply in the seat. You could find that "increasing the Lift" in such a fashion could cause certain problems (such as leaving a trail of flaps and other parts of the airplane fluttering behind). *So the high-lift devices are used at low speeds.* More about this in Chap. 11.

FLAPS. Flaps are the most widely used high-lift device. Many types are in use, a few of which will be covered here.

1. *Plain flap*—A simple means of changing the camber of the airfoil for use at low speeds (Fig. 2-12).

2. *Split flap*—You can see in Fig. 2-13 that there is a low-pressure region between the flap and the wing so that for equal flap areas and settings, the split flap tends to cause greater Drag than the plain flap, particularly at lesser angles of deflection.

3. *Fowler flap*—This flap combines a camber change with an increase in wing area—a good combination to lower the stall speed for landing but the system may be too complex and heavy for lighter planes (Fig. 2-14).

4. *Zap flap*—This split-type flap increases wing area in the same way as the Fowler type (Fig. 2-15).

5. *Double-slotted flap*—By putting slots in the flaps, a combination of camber change and smoother flow is obtained (Fig. 2-16).

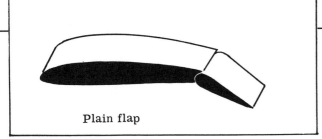

Plain flap

Fig. 2-12.

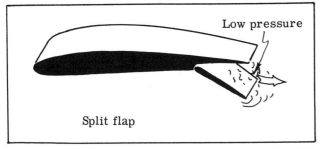

Low pressure

Split flap

Fig. 2-13.

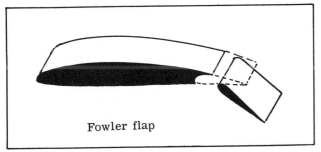

Fowler flap

Fig. 2-14.

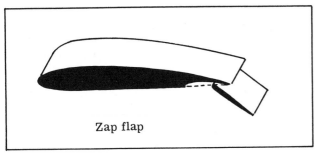

Zap flap

Fig. 2-15.

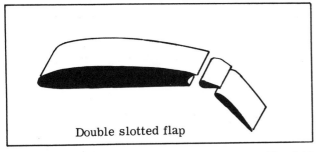

Double slotted flap

Fig. 2-16.

SLOTS. The leading-edge slot is a means of keeping a smooth flow at higher angles of attack than would be possible with an unslotted wing. Slots usually are placed near the wing tip to aid in lateral (aileron) control at the stall and to insure that the tips don't stall first, or they may be used along the entire span.

You are familiar by now with the idea of a wing dropping during the stall and, like most pilots, probably prefer an airplane that has a good, straight-ahead stall break (Fig. 2-17).

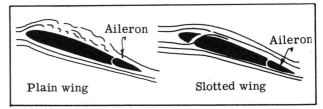

Aileron

Aileron

Plain wing   Slotted wing

Fig. 2-17. Comparison of plain and slotted wing at higher angles of attack.

SLATS. Slats are movable leading-edge vanes that form slots. The slot causes Drag at higher speeds and, as the slat can be retracted more or less flush with the leading edge, it is a boon to higher-speed airplanes. Some jets use a "droop snoot" in combination with flaps to obtain a birdlike airfoil for lower landing speeds (Fig. 2-18).

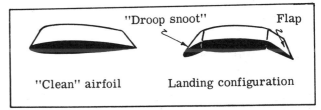

"Droop snoot"   Flap

"Clean" airfoil   Landing configuration

Fig. 2-18.

The high-lift devices complement each other—that is, by adding flaps to a plain airfoil, the maximum C_L is raised; adding slots or slats to this flap-equipped wing results in a further increase in C_{Lmax}.

Boundary Layer. You've probably heard this term many times. A good illustration of boundary layer can be seen on a dusty wing; you fly the airplane at speeds up to 200 K, but the dust isn't affected. The boundary layer effect is one factor that helps to keep the dust on. The boundary layer is that thin layer of air adjacent to the surface of a moving body. The velocity of the boundary layer air varies in speed from zero at the surface to the free stream velocity (TAS) at a certain distance from the surface. The thickness of a boundary layer varies for different conditions of velocity, surface roughness, etc., but normally may be considered in terms of very small fractions of an inch.

There are two types of boundary layers: (1) laminar or layered smooth flow and (2) turbulent. The laminar type creates much less skin friction Drag than the turbulent type; aeronautical engineers are particularly interested in maintaining a laminar boundary layer over as much of the wing and other components as possible at high speeds. Fig. 2-19, a typical airfoil for a light trainer, shows that both types are present.

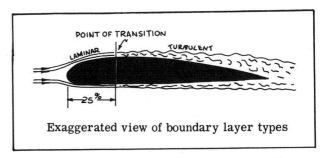

POINT OF TRANSITION

LAMINAR   TURBULENT

25%

Exaggerated view of boundary layer types

Fig. 2-19.

From a Drag standpoint then, it is advisable to have this transition from laminar to turbulent flow as far aft as possible, or have a large amount of the wing surface within the *laminar* portion of the boundary layer. As the transition usually occurs at approximately the thickest part of the airfoil (where the pressure is lowest) some airfoils are designed with the thickest parts at a position of 40 to 50% of the chord instead of the usual 25 to 30% (Fig. 2-20).

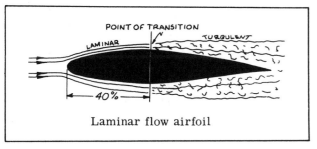

Fig. 2-20.

These laminar types of airfoils are now being used on various high-performance general aviation planes.

While maintaining a laminar flow as long as possible is a decided advantage from a Drag standpoint, it doesn't always work quite so well for stall characteristics. One of the first steps in a stall is the separation of the boundary layer, and the longer it remains intact the more delayed the stall (higher angle of attack and a greater C_{Lmax} at stall). The laminar layer tends to break down more suddenly than the turbulent layer so that the laminar flow airfoil usually does not have quite as good stall characteristics as found in older airfoil types (all other things being equal). The designer must compromise between low Drag and good stall characteristics on the airplane using the laminar flow airfoil.

Some general aviation trainers use NACA 64 and 65 series airfoils, which are considered to be in the laminar flow family. The Piper Cherokee 140 has a 65_2-415 airfoil, which has the maximum thickness of 40% aft of the leading edge (the "4" in its designation) and a thickness-to-chord ratio of 0.15, or 15%.

One problem encountered in actual operations is that mud or other protrusions on the wing surface may cause the laminar flow to become turbulent at a point well forward of the desired or designed point. Fig. 2-20 shows the "perfect" situation. But insects smashed against the leading edge may cause the flow behind the point to become turbulent, with a resulting loss of cruise efficiency. It would seem that any kind of roughness (scratches *or* protrusions) could cause problems, but aerodynamicists note that a scratch or depression has little effect on transition, compared with a protuberance of the same dimension.

BOUNDARY LAYER CONTROL. For many years engineers have worked to find means of delaying boundary layer separation at higher angles of attack. Two methods are generally used: (1) suction, which removes the boundary layer at various points of the airfoil, drawing it inward, and (2) blowing, which adds energy to the boundary layer and in essence works as if the entire airfoil has a turbulent layer (with its resulting better stall characteristics because of later separation). Boundary layer control requires a great deal of energy, which only can be furnished by adding Weight in the forms of pumps, piping, etc. Jets use bleed-air from the compressor sections.

Angle of Attack Indicators. The U.S. Navy has for some years used angle of attack (α) indicators both for operational carrier airplanes and for those in the Training Command preparing pilots for their flying with the fleet.

The airplane will always stall, clean, at a certain α and, with a given amount of flap deflection, at another constant α—Weight, airspeed, or g force has no effect on it. The max range and max endurance will each have a requirement for a certain fixed C_L as will the max distance or minimum sink glide. By knowing the different angles of attack (sometimes given in degrees, but more often in *units*) required for the various performance phases just cited, the pilot may hold them constant during the period of that particular phase. The same value of angle of attack would be maintained on the A/A indicator throughout, say, a 5-hr max range flight where, because of fuel burn, the Weight may decrease by 30 to 40%. To maintain the max range conditions without an A/A indicator, the airspeed must be reduced as the square root of the Weight change, as was noted in Chap. 1. (See Fig. 1-12 for a graph to correct the airspeed for constant phases, depending on a constant C_L value.)

Since angle of attack is the criterion for performance in these earlier mentioned areas, variable Weight or density (atmospheric pressure and temperature) has no effect on the A/A readings for the various maneuvers. If, for example, the airplane stalls at an indicated 15 units with full flaps in bitterly cold Antarctica at a very light Weight, it will also stall at 15 units with full flaps at max Weight in Central Africa on a hot summer day. The calibrated airspeeds at stall will be different but in this case only because of the Weight. The approach units would be the same value in both cases; the approach *airspeeds* would be different, however.

The A/A indicator uses a probe (well calibrated and usually on the fuselage) to check the airflow. Taken into account are the angle of incidence and other factors that would result in different angles between fuselage and wing flow.

DESIGN OF THE WING

Every airplane is made up of compromises, and this is particularly noticeable in wing design. For speed, a tapered wing is better than a rectangular wing. But the tapered wing with no twist has poor stall characteristics, as the tips tend to stall first. Common sense tells you that the tapered wing has less Drag because of less area near the tip—which results in less induced (vortex) Drag than on a rectangular wing of equal area (assuming the two planes have the same span loading). The elliptical wing (like that of the WW II *Spitfire*) is more efficient but does not have as good stall characteristics as the rectangular wing (other factors being equal).

Wing Design and the Stall. There are several solutions to this problem of the stall. In every case the tips should stall *last*. You want lateral (aileron) control throughout the stall. An airplane with bad rolling tendencies at the stall break is viewed with a jaundiced eye by pilots. The best stall pattern is to have the wing stall at the root area first, with the stall progressing outward toward the tips. This may be accomplished by several means: washout or twist, slots, stall strips, and spanwise airfoil variation.

WASHOUT OR TWIST. The wing may have a built-in twist so that the tip, having a *lower* angle of incidence (resulting in a lower angle of attack during the approach to a stall), will be flying after the root section has stalled. Generally this difference in incidence is no more than 2° to 3° from root to tip. The tips are said to have *washout* in this case (Fig. 2-21). *Washed-in* tips would have a *higher* angle of incidence—hardly conducive to pilot ease during the stall as the tips naturally tend to stall first.

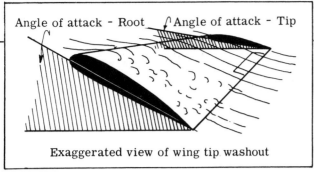

Exaggerated view of wing tip washout

Fig. 2-21. Wing tip washout as a means of maintaining lateral control during the stall.

SLOTS. Slots are not only a high-lift device but also a lateral control aid. Planes with slots usually have them only in the section near the wing tip so that lateral control can be maintained throughout the stall, or at least so that a wing won't drop suddenly with little warning, as may sometimes happen in a landing or practice stall (unmodified tapered wings have this tendency). Slots give the tapered-wing airplane the benefit of added lateral control in the stall and tend to dampen any rolling tendency. If the tips stalled first (remember, some airplanes have a different twist in each wing to counteract torque), a sizable rolling moment could be produced.

Some STOL (short takeoff and landing) airplanes have full-length slots or slats, which make for good slow-speed characteristics (Fig. 2-22).

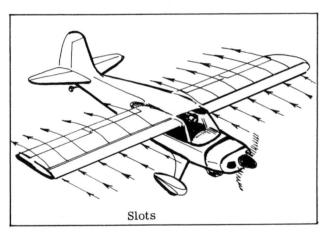

Slots

Fig. 2-22.

STALL STRIPS. Stall strips, or spin strips as they are sometimes called, are strips attached to the leading edge of the wing near the root. As the angle of attack increases, these strips break up the flow, which gives the desired effect of the root area stalling first (Fig. 2-23).

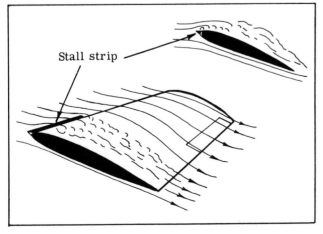

Stall strip

Fig. 2-23. The stall or spin strip.

SPANWISE AIRFOIL VARIATION. This high-sounding title simply means that some wings may have a high-speed-type airfoil at the root and a low-speed-type at the tip. An extreme example would be a laminar flow airfoil at the root and a birdlike airfoil at the tip. The birdlike tip will be flying after the high-speed section at the wing root has stalled (Fig. 2-24). In some cases several of these wing design techniques may be combined. The fact that the root section stalls first tends to cause a flow disturbance that usually results in tail buffeting and warning of the impending stall.

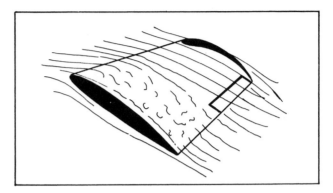

Fig. 2-24. Different airfoils at root and tip.

Wing Tip Tanks or End Plates. Many jets and several of the new high-performance light planes use tip tanks. The aerodynamic effect of tip tanks or end plates is an increase in effective aspect ratio (ratio of span to average chord), and you'll see in the next section that a larger aspect ratio results in lower induced Drag. In most cases the tip tanks more than offset any additional penalty such as increased frontal area or skin friction area.

DRAG

Anytime a body is moved through a fluid such as air, Drag is produced. Airplane aerodynamic Drag is composed of two parts: induced Drag (the Drag caused by Lift being created) and parasite Drag (form Drag, skin friction, and interference Drag). Drag acts rearward and parallel to the flight path.

Parasite Drag. The following factors affecting parasite Drag are similar to those affecting Lift (assume as each factor is discussed that the others remain constant).

Coefficient of parasite Drag—A relative measure of the parasite Drag of an object. The more *streamlined* an object the *lower* its coefficient of parasite Drag (Fig. 2-25).

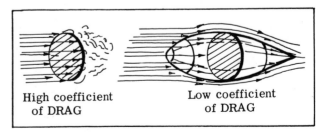

High coefficient of DRAG   Low coefficient of DRAG

Fig. 2-25. A comparison of the Drag of a flat plate and a streamlined shape with the same cross-section area at the same air density and velocity.

Air density—The greater the density of the fluid moving past an object, the greater the parasite Drag, assuming the velocities are the same. Note the difference in effort required to move your hand through water and air at the same speeds.

Velocity—Double the airspeed and parasite Drag is quadrupled.

Area—Parasite Drag increases directly with the size of the object in the airstream. The engineers normally base the total Drag of an airplane on its wing area, so as to establish some basis for comparison between airplanes.

The total coefficient of Drag is the sum of C_{Di} (coefficient of induced Drag) and the C_{Dp} (coefficient of parasite Drag), or $C_{Dtotal} = C_{Di} + C_{Dp}$ (more about C_{Di} later). Total Drag = $(C_{Di} + C_{Dp})S(\varrho/2)V^2$.

FORM DRAG. This is the Drag caused by the frontal area of the airplane components. When you were a kid you no doubt stuck your hand out the car window when you went riding (until your parents noticed). When your hand was held palm forward, the Drag you felt was nearly all form Drag. When your hand was held palm down the Drag was caused mostly by skin friction. This can probably be best described by looking at a very thin flat plate (Fig. 2-26).

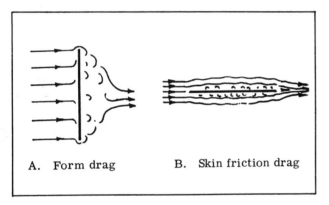

Fig. 2-26. Form Drag and skin friction Drag.

Note that in Fig. 2-26A the Drag existing is principally caused by the form of the plate whereas in Fig. 2-26B the largest part of the Drag is skin friction. This form Drag is the reason why streamlining is necessary in order to reach higher cruise speeds (Fig. 2-27).

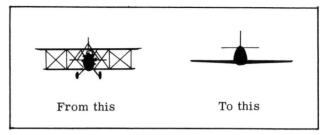

Fig. 2-27.

SKIN FRICTION DRAG. This is the Drag caused by the air passing over the airplane's surfaces. Flush riveting and smooth paint are good ways of decreasing skin friction Drag. A clean, polished airplane may be several miles per hour faster than another of the same model that is dirty and unpolished. Waxing and buffing will help an aerodynamically clean airplane because a large proportion of its parasite Drag is due to skin friction. Waxing the Wright Brothers' Flyer would have been a waste of elbow grease as far as getting a noticeable added amount of airspeed because the largest percentage of its Drag was form Drag.

INTERFERENCE DRAG. Interference Drag is caused by the interference of the airflow between parts of the airplane such as are found at the intersection of the wings or empennage with the fuselage. This Drag is lessened by filleting these areas so that the mixing of the airflow is more gradual (Fig. 2-28).

Interference Drag *increases* as the angle between the fuselage and wing or tail decreases from 90°. A midwing configuration (round fuselage) would have less interference Drag than a wing placed low on the same fuselage (assuming no fairing). Without fairings, Drag increases radically for the low wing at higher angles of attack.

A good example of increased interference Drag is during gear retraction or extension. The acute angles between the landing gear and wing or fuselage can raise the Drag considerably, and this can be a problem during a lift-off in close-to-stall conditions.

Induced Drag. Induced Drag is a byproduct of Lift. As discussed in the section on Lift, there is a difference in the pressure on the top and bottom of the wing, and as nature abhors a vacuum (or at least tries to equalize pressures in a system such as unconfined air), the higher-pressure air moves

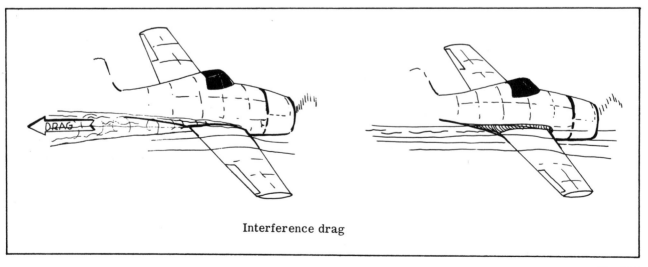

Interference drag

Fig. 2-28.

over the wing tip toward the lower pressure on top. Wing tip vortices result because as a particular mass of air gets over the tip the wing has moved on out from under it (Fig. 2-29).

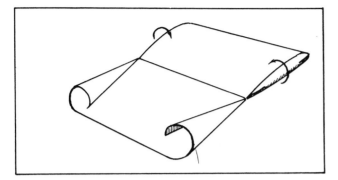

Fig. 2-29. Wing tip vortices.

Because of action of these vortices the relative wind passing the wing is deflected downward in producing Lift. The downward deflection of the air means that the wing is actually operating at a lower angle of attack than would be seen by checking the airplane's flight path, because it's flying in an "average" relative wind partly of its own making (Fig. 2-30).

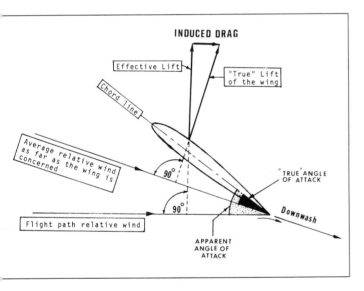

Fig. 2-30. Induced Drag.

Fig. 2-30 shows that the "true" Lift of the wing is operating perpendicularly to its *own* relative wind rather than perpendicularly to the air moving relative to the whole airplane (or the relative wind you, as a pilot, think about). Of course you know that the angle of attack is the angle between the chord line of the wing and its relative wind.

As the C_L (angle of attack) increases, the strengths of the wing tip vortices get greater with a resulting increase in downwash (and differences in angles of attack). This makes the difference between effective Lift and the wing's "true" Lift even greater, which would make the retarding force, induced Drag, increase (Fig. 2-30).

Keep in mind that wing tip vortices can be very powerful for large airplanes (which are producing many pounds of Lift) and are particularly vicious when they are flying clean at low speeds (high C_L). Following closely behind an airliner on approach or takeoff can be an extremely exciting activity for a lightplane.

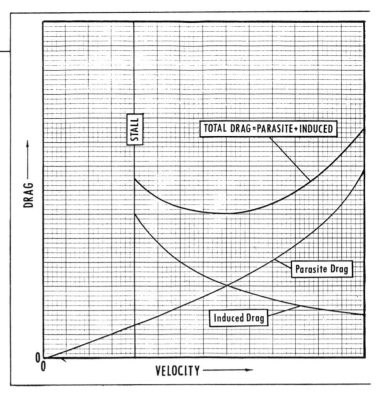

Fig. 2-31. Total Drag is a combination of parasite and induced Drag.

Fig. 2-31 plots parasite and induced Drag versus airspeed for a fictitious airplane at a specific Weight in the clean condition. As you can see, the total Drag at various speeds is made up of the sum of the two types. Induced Drag rises sharply as the airplane slows and approaches the stall speed (or more correctly as it approaches the maximum C_L) and at a point just above the stall speed, it may be 80 to 85% of the total drag. It gets lower as the speed increases (as the angle of attack, or C_L, decreases). It will never disappear because as long as any Lift is being produced it's a resulting evil.

Induced Drag is inversely proportional to the aspect ratio of the wing; that is, longer thinner wings mean less induced Drag if indicated airspeed, airplane Weight, and wing area are equal. (Aspect ratio is the wingspan-to-average-chord ratio or, more correctly, the ratio of the span squared, divided by the wing area.) If the wing had an infinite span the wing tip vortices would naturally not exist and induced Drag would be zero. The power of the wing tip vortices is tied in directly with "span loading" (the amount of Lift produced per foot of wingspan), which is another way of talking about aspect ratio. Aircraft that require good aerodynamic efficiency rather than high speed and that operate the majority of the time at comparatively high coefficients of Lift need high-aspect-ratio wings (sailplanes and the U-2). For airplanes such as jet fighters that operate at high speeds where induced Drag is small compared with parasite Drag, the aspect ratio must be low, both from an aerodynamic and a structural standpoint.

GROUND EFFECT. When the airplane wing operates close to the ground the downwash characteristics are altered, with a resulting decrease in induced Drag. This happens because the strength of the vortices is decreased and the downwash angle is also decreased for a particular amount of Lift being produced. This means that the wing's true Lift and effective Lift are working closer to each other (the angle between the two forces is less) and the retarding force (induced Drag) is less. (Check Fig. 2-30 again.)

When the airplane approaches the ground as for a landing, ground effect really enters the picture at about a wingspan distance above the surface. Its effects are then increased radically as the plane nears the ground until at about touchdown induced Drag *can* possibly drop by about 48%. All other things equal, the low-wing airplane is more affected than the mid- or high-wing because the wing is closer to the ground. Fig. 2-32 shows the decrease in percent of induced Drag in terms of span height for airplanes of general configuration. (Remember the effects vary with aspect ratio.)

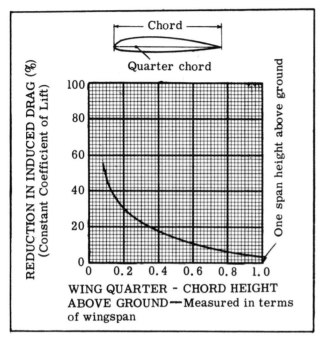

Fig. 2-32. Reduction of induced Drag with decrease in height above the ground.

Basically, ground effect means that you are getting the same Lift for less induced Drag. As induced Drag can make up 80 to 85% of the total Drag at lift-off or touchdown, a 48% decrease in induced Drag could mean a *decrease in total Drag of around 40%* for a specific angle of attack. This amount of Drag decrease could fool a pilot into thinking on takeoff that the airplane is ready to fly and climb out like a tiger, only to discover after getting a few feet above the ground that it's more like an anemic house cat. The power required to fly the airplane rises sharply as the induced Drag increases, and a deficit in power would result in a sink rate. The pilot meanwhile is holding the same nose attitude, trying to get some climb out of the suddenly inherited "lead sled." As the airplane starts settling, the angle of attack is increased because of the downward movement; since the angle was at the raw edge to begin with, the airplane stalls and abruptly contacts the ground again (sounds of bending metal in the background).

Ground effect also has a bearing on the longitudinal (pitch) stability of the airplane. An airplane is more stable in ground effect; that is, the nose is "heavier" for any trim setting. In fact, ground effect is a major factor in deciding the forward center of gravity (CG) limits of the airplane. More up-elevator is needed near the ground because the wing downwash angle is decreased. The down force exerted on the stabilizer-elevator is a mixture of free stream velocity, slipstream (which is weak in the power-off condition), and downwash from the wing. It may take anywhere from 4° to 15° more up-elevator to obtain the max angle of attack at landing as compared with that in free flight at altitude, depending on the make and model of the airplane.

As the airplane is more nose heavy in ground effect, an airplane loaded at (or past) the rearward CG limits might appear to be acceptably stable immediately following the takeoff, but as it gained a few feet could tend to nose up, catching the pilot sleeping. The influence of ground effect on stability will be covered more thoroughly in Chap. 10.

You can see by looking at Fig. 2-32 that the wing quarter chord would have to be about 3½ to 4 ft above the surface (this is about one-tenth the span of most current lightplanes) in order to get a 48% decrease in induced Drag.

The pilot's misunderstanding of ground effect has caused more than one landing accident when the airplane has "floated" the length of the runway while the pilot sat there with paralysis of the throttle hand thinking "it would settle on any day now."

You can use ground effect to aid you in acceleration to climb speed after takeoff. Induced Drag is greater than parasite Drag at this point, so leave the gear down until you're sure the airplane is going to stay airborne (landing gear represents parasite Drag). Don't let yourself be fooled into lifting off before the plane is ready.

It was noted earlier that interference Drag may increase during gear retractions as the gear and doors go through their process. If the airplane's takeoff performance is depending on ground effect, the retraction of the landing gear while moving up and out of ground effect could be the factor that puts the airplane back on the ground—with the gear partially retracted. Chap. 5 will cover this idea again.

Another reason for not getting the gear up too soon is that an engine failure could result in a gear-up landing with plenty of landing area ahead. Under normal conditions leave the gear down until you can no longer land on the runway ahead.

Ground effect has also enabled pilots to get out of ticklish situations on takeoff and landing and has been used by pilots of multiengine airplanes on overwater flights when an engine (or engines) failed. Taking advantage of this phenomenon allowed them to keep flying under conditions that would have otherwise resulted in a ditching. Glassy water, which is best for ground effect can be hazardous as far as judging heights are concerned. You can see in Fig. 2-32 that a few feet can make a lot of difference as far as ground effect is concerned.

The wing's lifting function is more efficient in ground effect (it's as if the wing has a higher aspect ratio) and needs a *lower angle of attack* to get the required Lift. The C_L versus angle of attack curve (straight line portion) is steeper. Looking back at Fig. 2-8, you can see that at an angle of attack of 10°, a C_L of about 1.10 is obtained; in ground effect the slope of the line might be steeper so that at 10° the C_L could be 1.3 or so. Of course, as an airplane climbs *out* of the ground effect it loses this advantage; the C_L versus angle of attack curve reverts to the situation shown in Fig. 2-8, and a *higher angle of attack* is needed to get the required Lift. This could cause problems in increased Drag and result in a stall if the pilot pulls the nose up sharply to keep from settling back in.

Lift-to-Drag Ratio. One measure of an airplane's aerodynamic efficiency is its maximum Lift-to-Drag ratio. The usual engineering procedure is to use the term C_L/C_D since the other factors of Lift and Drag (density, wing area, and velocity) are equally affected. (The C_D is the coefficient of *total* Drag.) This means that at a certain angle of attack the airplane is giving more for your money. The angle of attack and ratio of this special point varies with airplanes as well as with a particular airplane's configuration (clean or dirty). Pilots hear the term C_L/C_D maximum and automatically assume that this point is found at C_{Lmax}, or close to the stall. This is not true because, while the C_L is large at large angles of attack, the total C_D is *much* larger in proportion because of induced Drag. Following are figures showing how the Lift-to-Drag (or

C_L/C_D) ratio varies for a sample airplane in the clean condition.

C_L	C_D	C_L/C_D Ratio
0.935	0.080	11.7 (low speed)
0.898	0.075	12.0
0.860	0.070	12.1
0.820	0.065	12.6
0.772	0.060	12.9
0.725	0.055	13.2
0.671	0.050	13.4
0.620	0.045	13.7
0.562	0.040	14.1
0.500	*0.035*	*14.3*
0.418	0.030	13.9
0.332	0.025	13.3
0.200	0.020	10.0 (high speed)

The italicized figures show the values for C_L/C_D maximum.

The maximum Lift-to-Drag ratio is the condition at which maximum range and maximum glide distance will be found (this will be covered in more detail later). It is found at the point of minimum Drag for the airplane.

THRUST

Thrust, the force exerted by a propeller, jet, or rocket, is used to overcome aerodynamic Drag and other forces acting to retard the airplane's motion in the air and on the ground. It can be explained by one of Newton's laws of motion: For every action there is an equal and opposite reaction.

The propeller is a rotating airfoil that accelerates a comparatively large mass of air rearward, resulting in an equal and opposite reaction—the airplane moves forward. The Thrust exerted is proportional to the mass and the velocity of the accelerated air.

The jet engine accelerates a smaller mass of air and fuel at a faster velocity than does the propeller. The rocket takes an even smaller mass (of its fuel and oxidizer) and accelerates it to a very high speed.

Thrust Available and Drag. The greatest Thrust for the *propeller-driven* airplane is found in the static condition; that is, when you are sitting on the end of the runway with the engine running at full power the propeller is producing the greatest Thrust. As the plane moves the Thrust force available decreases with speed increase.

For straight and level flight the Thrust available (pounds) and Drag (pounds) are considered equal if a constant airspeed is maintained. For speeds in the area of cruise where the airplane's Thrust line is acting along the flight path (the nose is not "cocked up" as is the case for slower speeds) this assumption is a valid one (Fig. 2-33). The variations of the Four Forces in different maneuvers will be shown in Chap. 3, and this particular point will be covered.

Propeller. The propeller, a rotating airfoil, is subject to stalls, induced Drag, and other troubles that affect airfoils. As you have noticed, the blade angle of the propeller changes from hub to tip with the greatest angle of incidence (highest pitch) at the hub and the smallest at the tip (Fig. 2-34).

This twist is necessary because of the difference in the actual speed through the air of the various portions of the blade. If the blade had the same geometric pitch all along its length (say 20°), at cruise the inner portion near the hub would have a negative angle of attack and the extreme outer portion would be stalled. This is hardly conducive to get up and go—so the twist is necessary.

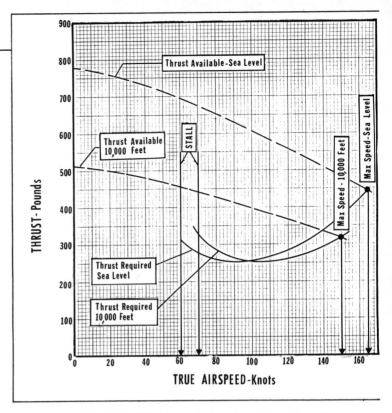

Fig. 2-33. Thrust required and maximum thrust available versus true airspeed at sea level and 10,000 ft for a fictitious high-performance four-place airplane (gross Weight).

Fixed-pitch propellers come in two main categories, climbing and cruising. Regardless of which prop is on the plane, you always wish you had the other one. The climbing prop with its lower pitch results in higher rpm and more HP developed, which gives efficient takeoff and climb performance—but poor cruise characteristics. The cruise propeller with its higher pitch results in lower rpm and less HP developed, which is efficient for cruise but gives comparatively poor performance in takeoff and climb. Two terms are used in describing the angles of incidence and propeller effectiveness: (1) *geometric pitch,* or the built-in angle of incidence, the path a chosen portion of the blade would take in a nearly solid medium such as gelatin and (2) *effective pitch,* or the actual path the propeller is taking in air at any particular time. Okay, looking at geometric pitch you might see a number on the fixed-pitch prop of an airplane such as M58 D74 or D7458. The "74" tells you the diameter of the propeller (74 in.), and the "58" tells the advance of a particular station of the blade,

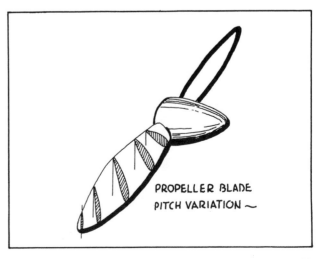

PROPELLER BLADE PITCH VARIATION ~

Fig. 2-34.

per revolution (58 in.). A "D7452" propeller would be more of a "climb" prop (the selected station only advances 52 in. per revolution, hence a lower pitch); the engine would be revving up more, and it would be more efficient at lower airspeeds. Different prop manufacturers may have different codes but you might ask some of the local mechanics about the code for a particular prop if you aren't sure.

The difference between the geometric pitch and the effective pitch is the angle of attack (Fig. 2-35). The climbing propeller has a lower *average* geometric pitch than the cruising prop and revs up more, developing more HP (Fig. 2-36).

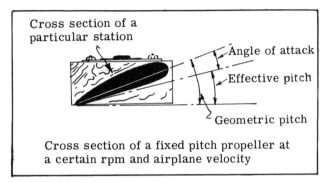

Fig. 2-35.

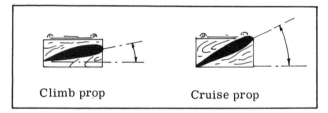

Fig. 2-36. Climbing and cruising propellers — a comparison of geometric pitch at the same station (same distance from hub).

Take an airplane sitting at the end of a runway with a cruise-type propeller revolving at 2400 rpm. Fig. 2-37 shows that as the plane is not moving, the geometric pitch and angle of attack are the same, and a large portion of the blade is stalled. A vector diagram would show the difference in the efficiency of a propeller at 0 mph and 100 mph (at 2400 rpm).

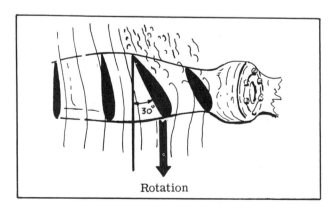

Fig. 2-37. Airplane stationary — a portion of the blade stalled.

The velocity of a *particular station* of the blade can be readily found. Let's pick a station at a point slightly more than 1½ ft from the hub center so that the point chosen travels 10 feet each revolution. At 2400 rpm the velocity at this point is 400 fps. Assuming a geometric pitch of 30° at this point, the prop stalls at an angle of attack of 20°, so this portion of the blade is stalled.

Therefore the only part of the blade developing Thrust under this condition would be the portion having a geometric pitch of less than 20° — or the outboard portion of the blades. The Thrust pattern would look like that shown in Fig. 2-38.

Fig. 2-38. Thrust pattern of the propeller of a stationary airplane.

For the same airplane moving at 89 K, or 150 fps (again chosen for convenience), the result can be seen by vectors (Fig. 2-39). You will notice that the blade is operating at a more efficient angle of attack. As the propeller is an airfoil, it is most efficient at the angle of attack giving the greatest Lift-to-Drag ratio. A climb prop would be more efficient at low airspeeds because a greater portion of the blade is operating in this range. At high airspeeds it is operating at a lower angle of attack and is not producing efficient Thrust.

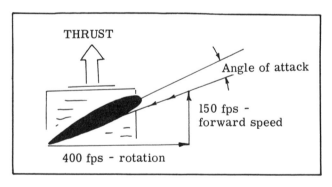

Fig. 2-39. Angle of attack of the same portion of the blade at a forward speed of 150 fps (89 K).

At a higher pitch the Drag of the blades is higher and the engine is unable to get as high an rpm and develop as much HP as would be obtained with a lower-pitch propeller. *The fixed-pitch propeller is efficient only at one particular speed range.*

The solution to this is the variable-pitch propeller, which can be set to suit the pilot;

1. For takeoff and climb — LOW PITCH, which results in HIGH RPM and high power. (The British call this "fine pitch.")

2. For cruise — HIGH PITCH, which results in LOW

RPM and efficient cruise. (The British call this "coarse pitch.")

With a variable-pitch prop the rpm still varies with airspeed, as with the fixed-pitch prop. In other words, if you set a cruise rpm of 2400, a climb or dive will cause it to vary. The constant-speed prop, which is an "automatic" variable-pitch propeller, will maintain a constant rpm after being set. Once the desired setting is made changes in airspeed do not affect it.

THE CONSTANT-SPEED PROPELLER (OIL-COUNTERWEIGHT TYPE). The constant-speed propeller setting is the result of a balance between oil pressure (using engine oil) and the centrifugal force exerted by the propeller counterweights. This balance is maintained by the governor, which is driven by the crankshaft through a series of gears. The governor has two main parts, the flyweight assembly and the oil pump. The governor is set by the prop control(s) in the cockpit. Assume you have set the rpm at 2400 for cruise. The oil pressure and counterweight forces are equal because the flyweights in the governor are turning at constant speed and the oil valve to the prop pistons is closed, with oil pressure locked in the propeller hub. Now assume that you pull the nose up. The airspeed drops, causing the prop rpm and engine rpm to drop. The centrifugal force on the governor flyweights decreases because of the drop in rpm. The contraction of the flyweight causes a two-way valve to be opened so that increased pressure to the pistons moves the propeller to a lower pitch, allowing it to maintain 2400 rpm.

If the plane were dived, the prop would tend to overspeed; the resulting increase in centrifugal force of the governor flyweight would cause the oil valve to open so that the oil pressure in the propeller hub dome would decrease. Centrifugal force on the propeller counterweights would then cause the prop to be pulled into a higher pitch; the increased blade angle of attack would result in more Drag and the propeller would not overspeed. To summarize:

Lower pitch (higher rpm) is caused by added oil pressure.

Higher pitch (lower rpm) is caused by centrifugal force on prop counterweights.

The operation of most noncounterweight propellers is the reverse of that of the oil-counterweight types. The blade in creating Thrust creates a moment that tends to decrease its pitch (the same thing happens to a wing, as will be covered in Chap. 3). A spring may be added to help this natural force. This is opposed by governor oil pressure, which tends to increase its pitch.

Newer makes of propellers use compressed air or nitrogen in the dome to increase pitch and feather. This force opposes the pitch-lowering tendency caused by the blade moment and the governor oil pressure. Because counterweights are not necessary a great deal of Weight is saved. In effect, the compressed air does the job of the counterweights.

To get an idea of how a variable-pitch or constant-speed propeller can increase the efficiency of a propeller let's set up a hypothetical situation. To simplify matters, assume that a certain engine can only be run at a certain rpm for cruise—no other can be used; 2400 is a good round figure so that's the number for this problem. (The propeller is direct-drive and turns at this same rpm.) Fig. 2-40 shows the efficiencies of a particular propeller at different pitch settings of the propeller blade (at a station three-quarters, or 75%, of the radius from the hub) at various airspeeds.

The constant-speed propeller will change its angle to maintain a constant rpm so as the airspeed increases, the pitch setting will also increase automatically. The dashed line (envelope) shows that as the airspeed increases, the efficiency remains fairly constant over the entire range. The propeller pitch changes as needed to keep a constant angle of attack.

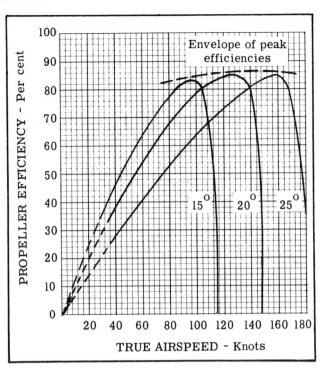

Fig. 2-40. Efficiency of a particular propeller at various blade settings and airspeeds (constant 2400 rpm).

Notice that the solid line curves for different pitch settings have a comparatively narrow range of airspeed for peak efficiency. For this airplane a pitch (at the station at 75% of the radius of the prop) of 15° is 80% (or higher) efficient only between the speeds of 85 and 104 K, or has its peak efficiency at about 95 K. At a pitch setting of 20° the range of 80% or higher efficiencies is from about 104 to 140 K, with the peak at about 128 K, etc. Shown are the ranges of efficiencies for fixed-pitch versions of that propeller at 15°, 20°, and 25° pitch respectively. Notice in Fig. 2-40 that the efficiencies for these pitches drop rapidly at the upper ends of their speed ranges. The constant-speed prop has practically an infinite number of pitch settings available within the airplane's operating speed ranges; this is shown by the envelope of peak efficiencies.

Use of the variable-pitch and constant-speed propeller also will be covered in later chapters.

TORQUE. You have long been familiar with *torque*, the pilot's term for that force or moment that tends to yaw or turn the plane to the left when power is applied at low speeds. It is also the price paid for using a propeller. Knowing that the propeller is a rotating airfoil, you realize that it exerts some Drag as well as Lift. This Drag creates a moment that tends to rotate the airplane around its longitudinal (fuselage) axis opposite to prop rotation.

Although normally torque is thought of as one force, it is, in fact, several combined forces.

1. *Slipstream effects*—As the propeller turns clockwise, a rotating flow of air is moved rearward, striking the left side of the fin and rudder, which results in a left yawing moment. The fin may be offset to counteract this reaction, with the fin setting built in for maximum effectiveness at the rated cruising speed of the airplane, since the plane will be flying at this speed most of the time (Figs. 2-41 and 2-42).

If it were not for the offset fin, right rudder would have to be held at all speeds. As it is, the balance of forces results in no yawing force at all and the plane flies straight at cruise with no right rudder being held (Fig. 2-41).

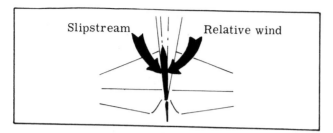

Fig. 2-41. The offset fin is designed so that the angle of attack of the fin is zero (the forces balance) at cruise.

Sometimes the fin may not be offset correctly, due to manufacturing tolerances, and a slight left yaw is present at cruise, making it necessary to use right rudder to keep the airplane straight. To take care of this, a small metal tab is attached to the trailing edge of the rudder and bent to the left. The pressure of the relative air against the tab forces the rudder to the right (Fig. 2-42).

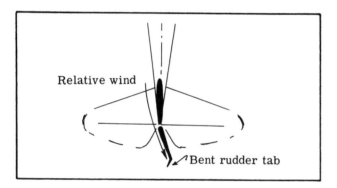

Fig. 2-42. The rudder trim tab.

On lighter planes this adjustment can be done only on the ground, and it may require several flights before a satisfactory setting is found. For heavier planes a controllable rudder tab is used, allowing the pilot to correct for torque at all speed ranges. If the tab has been bent correctly (or has been set in the cockpit) for cruise, the torque and impact forces are balanced.

Some manufacturers use an offset thrust line, or "cant" the engine to counteract torque at cruise; the airplane's reactions are the same as for the offset fin.

In a climb, right rudder must be held to keep the plane straight. In a dive, left rudder is necessary to keep it straight. In larger planes the rudder tab may be set during flight for these variations from cruise.

In a glide there is no yawing effect. Although the engine is at idle and torque is less, the impact pressure on the fin is also less. *The slipstream effect is the most important torque force working on the single-engine airplane.*

2. *Equal and opposite reactions*—Newton's Law of equal and opposite reactions is only a minor factor in torque effects. The airplane tends to rotate in a direction opposite that of the propeller's rotation. In some cases the left wing or wing tip area may have *washin* to compensate for this. Washin means that the angle of incidence is increased and the wing is bent up into the airstream for more Lift. *Washout* can be thought of as the wing turning down out of the relative wind for less Lift, as noted earlier in the chapter. Washin may also contribute very slightly to a left-turning effect.

3. *Asymmetric loading* or propeller disk asymmetric loading (also called P-factor)—This condition, caused by the air not striking the prop disk at exactly a 90° angle, is usually encountered in a constant positive angle of attack such as in a climb or in slow flight. The down-moving propeller blade, which is on the right side as seen from the cockpit, has a higher angle of attack and consequently a greater Thrust, which results in a left-turning effect. This can be visualized by checking Fig. 2-43.

To find the exact difference in the Thrust of the two sides of the propeller disk, a vector diagram must be drawn that includes the propeller blade angles, rotational velocity, and the airplane's forward speed and angle of attack. If the airplane is yawed, the P-factor effect is encountered. A left yaw would mean a slight nose-down tendency and a right yaw a slight nose-up tendency (you can reason this out). As climbs and slow flights are more usual maneuvers than are yaws, these will be the most likely spots to encounter P-factor effects.

P-factor has been given a great deal of credit for contributing to left-turning tendencies in situations where it has little, if any, effect on the airplane's yawing tendencies. For instance, the attitude of the tricycle gear on the takeoff roll pretty well assures that the prop disk is perpendicular to the line of "flight"—yet the airplane still turns radically to the left. Let's see, there's no problem with torque (sure, the left wheel may be pressing on the runway a few pounds harder

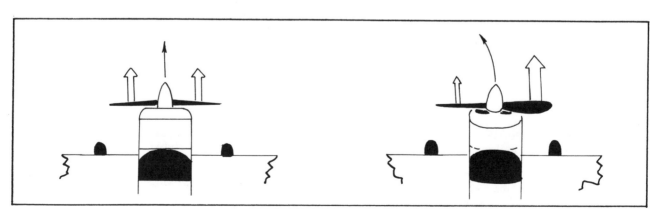

Fig. 2-43. Asymmetric disk loading effects.

because of "equal and opposite reaction," but the turning effect is negligible). There is little or no difference in the angle at which the prop encounters the relative wind, so the rotating slipstream is the culprit here.

Prop manufacturers are advised to take the P-factor effect into account when running a vibration evaluation of their propellers (FAA AC 20-66).

Some older twins used to have engines toed-in or -out and this gave a "permanent" P-factor effect. You can get an idea of P-factor roughness in an airplane parked in a strong crosswind with the engine idling.

4. *Precession* – You encounter precession when, in a tailwheel-type airplane, you try to force the tail up quickly on a takeoff run. The airplane wants to get away from you as it suddenly yaws to the left. Precession affects the airplane only *during* attitude changes.

Precession is a gyroscopic property (the gyro will be covered more thoroughly in Chap. 4). If a force is exerted against the side of the gyro, it reacts as if the force had actually been exerted in the same direction at a point 90° around the wheel (Fig. 2-44).

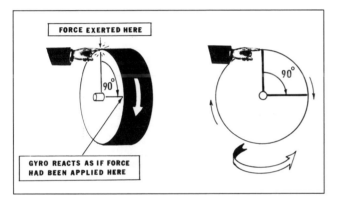

Fig. 2-44. Precession.

The propeller disk makes a good gyro wheel, as it has mass and a good rotational velocity. Another property of a gyro is "rigidity in space." This property is used in ships' gyros and aircraft attitude indicators and heading indicators. The rotating gyro wheel tends to stay in the same plane of rotation in space and resists any change in that plane (Fig. 2-45). If a

Fig. 2-45. The gyro wheel has the property of "rigidity in space."

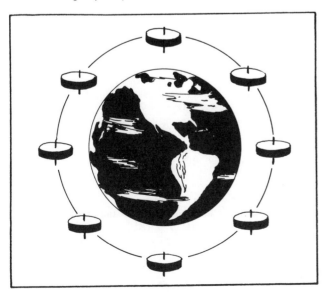

force is insistent enough in trying to change this plane of rotation, precession results.

When you're rolling down the runway in the three-point position (in a tailwheel-type plane), the propeller is in a certain rotational plane. You are using full power and are fighting the other torque effects (rotating slipstream, asymmetric loading, etc). When you shove the wheel or stick forward and the tail rises, the plane reacts as if the force were exerted on the right side of the propeller disk from the rear. The result is a brisk swing to the left. You can further reason out the reactions of the propeller plane to yawing, pull-ups, or push-overs. You're most likely, however, to notice precession effects on getting the tail up for takeoff because the rudder is comparatively ineffective at this low speed and the sudden yaw is harder to control.

SUMMARY OF TORQUE. These forces or combinations of them make up what pilots call "torque," the force that tends to yaw the plane to the left at low speeds and high power settings. This discussion is presented so that you may get to understand your airplane better; the objective is to compensate for torque and to fly the airplane in the proper manner. There are a lot of good pilots flying around who wouldn't know what "asymmetric disk loading" was if they were hit in the face with it. The nose yaws to the left and they correct for it – and so should you.

The Power Curve

FORCE, WORK, AND POWER. In order to understand power and horsepower it is necessary to discuss *force* and *work*.

A *force* may be considered a pressure, tension, or weight. Thrust, Lift, Weight, and Drag are forces; our present system uses the term *pounds* to express the value or strength of a force.

You can exert a *force* against a heavy object and nothing moves; that still doesn't alter the fact that force has been exerted. If the object doesn't move no *work* has been done as far as the engineering term is concerned (tell this to your aching back). So *work*, from an engineering standpoint, is a measure of a *force* times *distance* (in the direction in which the force is being exerted). If a constant force of 100 lb is exerted to move an object 10 ft, the deed has accomplished 1000 ft-lb of *work*.

For instance, your Zephyr Six airplane weighs 2200 lb and you must push (or pull) it by hand 100 ft to the gas pit. It does *not* require 220,000 ft-lb of work to accomplish this as you could see by attaching a scale to the tow bar and checking the force required to move the airplane at a steady rate; for our purposes we'll say that it requires a constant force of 55 lb to keep the airplane rolling across the ramp. This job would require 5500 ft-lb of work on your part (55 lb times 100 ft).

If you lifted the airplane to a *height* of 100 ft at a constant rate, the work done *would* be 2200 lb × 100 ft or 220,000 ft-lb. The force you would need to exert would be the Weight of the airplane, once you got it moving at a steady rate upward. And, obviously you would do less work pulling the airplane 100 ft than lifting it the same distance because less force is required to pull it than to lift it.

The amount of work done has nothing to do with time; you can take a second or all week to do the 5500 ft-lb of work in pulling the airplane. This brings up another term – *power*. *Power* is defined as a time rate of work. If you pulled the airplane the 100 ft over to the gas pit in 1 sec you would have been exerting a power of 5500 ft-lb per second. (And if you are strong enough to accomplish such a feat you don't need an airplane; just flap your arms when you want to fly.) Suppose that it takes 10 sec to do the job. The power used would be work/time = 5500 ft-lb/10 sec = 550 ft-lb per second or 375 mi-lb per hour. You would have to exert 1 HP for 10 sec to do the job. The most common measurement for power is the term *horsepower*, which happens to be a power of 550-ft-lb per second.

Thrust horsepower (THP) is the HP developed by a force (Thrust) exerted to move an object (the airplane) at a certain rate. Remembering that a *force* times the distance it moves an object is *work*, and when divided by time, *power* is found, the equation is THP = TV/550, where T = propeller Thrust (pounds) and V = the airplane's velocity (fps). As velocity can be considered to be distance divided by time, TV (or T × V) is *power* in foot-pounds per second. The power (TV) is divided by 550 to obtain the HP being developed. If you wanted to think in terms of *miles per hour* for V, the equation would be THP = TV/375 (375 is the constant number used for miles per hour). For V in knots, THP = TV/325.

As far as the airplane is concerned there are several types of horsepower of interest.

Indicated horsepower is the actual power developed in the cylinders and might be considered to be a calculated HP based on pressure, cubic-inch displacement, and rpm.

Brake horsepower (BHP) is so named because in earlier times it was measured for smaller engines by the use of a braking system or absorption dynamometer such as the "prony brake." The HP thus exerted by the crankshaft was known as *brake horsepower* or *shaft horsepower*. The fact that there is internal friction existing in all engines means that all the HP in the cylinders doesn't get to the crankshaft, so a

loss of HP from indicated horsepower, called *friction horsepower loss*, results. The reciprocating engine is always rated in BHP. If your airplane has an unsupercharged (or normally aspirating) engine, for example, the specification will note that the engine is rated as a certain HP at full throttle at a certain rpm at sea level (meaning standard sea level conditions of air density). For supercharged engines the specification cites a specific manifold pressure and rpm at sea level and also at the critical altitude (above which even full throttle can't hold the required manifold pressure to get the rated HP). This idea will be covered in more detail in later chapters.

The term *75% power* means *75% of the normal rated power, or max continuous available at sea level on a standard day* (59°F and a pressure of 29.92 in. of mercury). For instance, a particular engine may have a takeoff power rating of 340 HP and a *normal rating* of 320 HP. The takeoff rating label means that the engine can be run at this power only for a *limited time* as given in the engine specifications. If you use the engine power chart and set up manifold pressure and rpm to get 75% power for that engine, your HP will be 75% of 320 (the normal rated power), or 240 HP.

For other engines, the takeoff rating and normal rating are the same. That is, they develop a certain maximum amount of HP and can be run continuously at this power if necessary. In effect, there is no takeoff rating, or no special higher than normal, limited-time power setting.

BHP also increases slightly with intake ram effect but is normally considered to remain constant, hence it's use as a standard for setting power by the power chart.

Thrust horsepower, as discussed earlier, is considered to be a percentage of BHP if propeller efficiency is taken into account: THP = η BHP. The term η (eta) is the propeller efficiency which runs *at best* up to 0.85 (85%) for most engine-propeller combinations and varies with airspeed. (This was covered back in the section on the propeller.)

As an example of the various steps of getting from the ignition of the fuel-air mixture to the THP being developed, take a look at the following:

Indicated HP (work done in cylinders)	325 HP
Drive loss (friction and accessories)	− 25 HP
Resulting *Shaft* or *Brake HP*	300 HP
Loss from propeller (80% efficient at a particular speed)	− 60 HP
Horsepower available as *THP*	240 HP

Fig. 2-46 shows the *maximum* HP available for the two types of power at various speeds. The point at which the maximum HP available equals the HP required establishes the maximum level flight speed of the airplane, whether in terms of HP or THP (points 1 and 2):

Notice how the available THP varies with airspeed. As THP = TV (K)/325, you can see that although at zero velocity the Thrust might be high, no HP is being developed because V = 0, and a number times zero is still zero. As the airplane picks up speed THP starts being developed, increasing fairly rapidly at first. This is because Thrust is high at the lower speeds (check back to Fig. 2-33). THP increases at a lower rate as the speed picks up (and Thrust decreases.)

You will also note that more BHP than THP is required by the airplane at any speed; this is because, as was mentioned, the propeller is not 100% efficient and there's some loss. In other words, the engine has to produce more than enough effort to get the required amount of HP actually working to fly the airplane.

For the same airplane of Fig. 2-46 the amount of BHP necessary to get the THP required rises sharply at lower speeds because the propeller efficiency drops rapidly in that

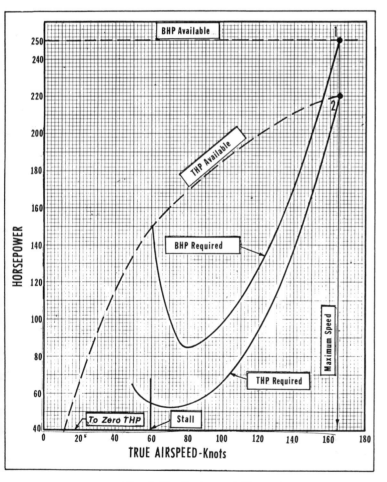

Fig. 2-46. Brake and Thrust horsepower available and required versus true airspeed for a four-place airplane with the engine rated 250 BHP at sea level (gross Weight). (In order to save space the HP was started at 40 rather than 0.)

area. The THP required does not rise as sharply in this area as either the Drag or BHP-required curves because, while the Drag is rising rapidly, the required THP is also a function of velocity—THP = TV/325 or DV/325 and the decrease in speed *tends* to offset the effects of the increase in Drag (the velocity used here is in knots).

To give an idea of the comparison between BHP and THP, suppose that instead of the prop an iron bar of equal Weight and Drag is attached on the hub. The engine would still be putting out a certain amount of BHP as measured by a dynamometer, but the iron bar would be producing no Thrust and therefore no THP could ever be developed by the engine in that configuration—the efficiency (η) would be zero.

In thinking in terms of setting power, a curve for BHP is more effective; for performance items such as climbs or glides, THP gives a clearer picture.

Fig. 2-47 shows some pertinent points on a power-available and power-required versus velocity curve as expressed in BHP for a fictitious airplane at the maximum certificated Weight of 3000 lb at sea level in the clean condition.

The shaded area shows the areas of normal cruise power settings and airspeeds for this particular airplane. As you know, power settings most commonly used are from 60 to 75% of the normal rated power. The majority reciprocating engine airplanes avoid cruise (or continuous) power settings above 75% because of increased fuel consumption and engine wear.

By now you've also noticed that the power-required curve (for both THP and BHP) has a characteristic U shape similar to the Drag curve. This is because the power required to fly the airplane at a constant altitude varies with the Drag exist-

ing at different airspeeds—the values, of course, are different as one is expressed in pounds and the other in HP. If you had a Drag versus airspeed curve for your airplane you could draw your own THP-required curve by selecting particular airspeeds and using the Drags in the equation for THP.

Because of the varying power needed to maintain a constant altitude, the airplane can fly at two speeds for the lower power settings (Fig. 2-47). It is unlikely that in actuality it could fly at a slow enough speed to require close to 100% power (250 BHP for this airplane) to maintain a constant altitude because the stall characteristics of the airplane wouldn't allow it—the break would occur at an airspeed higher than that. If the stall could be delayed appreciably through use of, say, boundary layer control, it might well work out that it could fly at a slow speed where 100% power is required to maintain a constant altitude.

The power required varies with Weight, altitude, and airplane configuration. Fig. 2-48 shows the effects of various Weights on the power required for the airplane in Fig. 2-47. The solid line represents the curve of Fig. 2-47.

Added or subtracted Weight affects the existing induced Drag and power required at various airspeeds. (The engineers speak of this as induced power required.) You can also see that the stall speed is lower with less Weight and vice versa. *Notice that a variation in Weight has comparatively little effect on the max speed. The effects of Weight are felt mostly where induced Drag is predominant.*

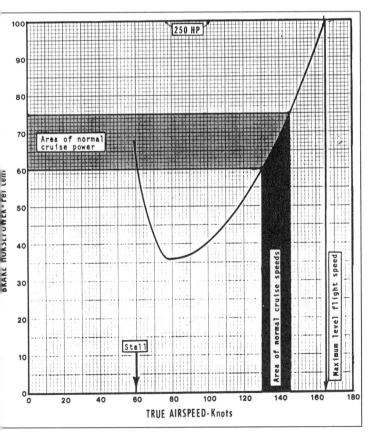

Fig. 2-47. Brake horsepower required and available versus airspeed for a particular airplane at sea level (gear and flaps retracted). Assume TAS = CAS.

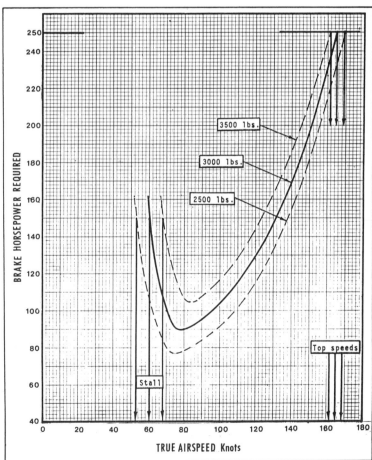

Fig. 2-48. The effects of Weight on the airplane in Fig. 2-47 (TAS = CAS). The stall speed effects are slightly exaggerated here for clarity. For calculating the exact stall speeds for Weight change use Fig. 1-12.

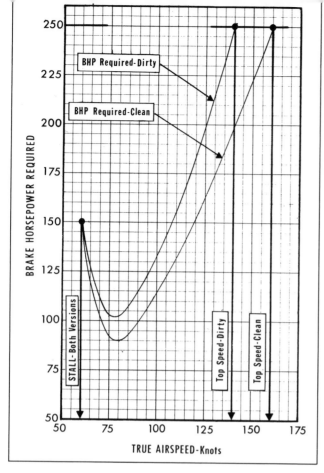

Fig. 2-49. The effects of parasite Drag (extended gear) on the airplane in Fig. 2-47.

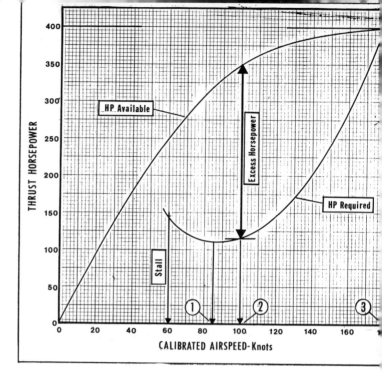

Fig. 2-50. Thrust horsepower available and required versus airspeed for a light twin at gross Weight at sea level. (Assume CAS = TAS at sea level.)

Fig. 2-49 shows the effects of parasite Drag on the power-required curve in Fig. 2-47. The new curve represents the power required (at the original Weight of 3000 lb) with the gear extended. In this case, the maximum speed would be greatly affected because parasite Drag (or parasite power required) is the largest factor in that area. The cruise speed *would* be affected because it is also in an area of high parasite Drag. In this example, *the stall speed would not vary and comparatively small effects would be felt at the lower flight speeds where parasite Drag is low.*

The *total* power required equals induced power required *plus* parasite power required.

Fig. 2-50 shows THP required and available versus airspeed for a light twin at gross Weight at sea level. This curve is important in that the rate of climb of the airplane depends on the excess THP available. The maximum rate of climb, then, is found at the airspeed where the maximum excess THP is available because that is the HP working to raise the airplane. Notice that as you slow down past the point of minimum power required (point 1) the THP required starts increasing again. The excess HP available depends on the characteristics of *both* the THP-available and THP-required curves. The airspeed at which the maximum excess horsepower exists (Point 2) is therefore the speed for a max rate of climb for this airplane at the particular Weight and altitude. Point 3 shows the maximum level flight speed at sea level.

Chaps. 3 and 6 will go into more detail on climb requirements and how excess THP works in making the airplane climb.

JETS AND PROPS. The jet engine exerts a constant Thrust at all airspeeds, compared with that shown for the propeller in Fig. 2-33. Therefore, the THP developed by the jet increases in a straight line with velocity: THP = TV (mph)/375 or TV(K)/325.

Fig. 2-51 is a power-required and power-available versus velocity curve for the light twin of Fig. 2-50 when it is equipped with either jets or reciprocating engines. To simplify, assume that the airplane could be equipped with either jet engines or reciprocating engines with no difference in parasite Drag or gross Weight. This means that the power-*required* curve in Fig. 2-51 would be exactly the same for either version.

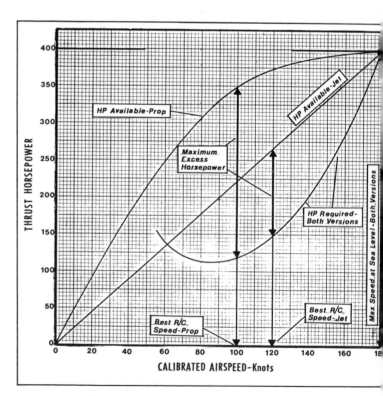

Fig. 2-51. A comparison of prop and jet versions of the light twin in Fig. 2-50.

Suppose that the top speed of the reciprocating version of our fictitious airplane is 180 K at sea level and it requires 400 (Thrust) horsepower to fly at this speed. (The top level flight speed is that point at which the power required equals the total power available, you remember.) We'll also say that the jet version is equipped with two engines developing maximum Thrust at sea level of 361 lb each, for a total of 722 lb of Thrust. If the airplanes are at the same Weight and have the same parasite Drag, it can be shown (Fig. 2-51) that the top speed of the jet version is also 180 K because, as noted above, it required 400 THP to fly level at this speed and that just happens to be what our jet engines are producing at that speed:

$$THP = TV/325$$
$$\frac{722 \text{ (lb Thrust)} \times 180 \text{ (K)}}{325} = 400 \text{ THP or}$$
$$\frac{722 \times 208 \text{ (mph)}}{375} = 400 \text{ THP}$$

THP-available curves are given both for props and jet engines. Note that the THP produced by the jet version is a straight line—it is directly proportional to velocity.

As was mentioned before, the rate of climb for any airplane is proportional to the excess HP available. It can be noted in Fig. 2-51 that the maximum rate of climb is found for the airplane at a speed of 100 K when it uses reciprocating engines, and at the higher speed of 120 K when the jet engines are installed.

The higher speed used for climb in a jet airplane is one of the hardest things for the ex–prop pilot to get used to. Notice in Fig. 2-51 that the performance of the jet-equipped version would be poor in the climb and low-speed regime because of the smaller amount of excess HP available, compared with one with props. In fact, at speeds close to the stall a power deficit could exist in that airplane. If you tried to hurry the airplane off the ground at takeoff you might get it too cocked up and find that you can't get, or stay, airborne. (This sometimes happens even in airplanes with a reasonable amount of power or Thrust available.)

Obviously this jet version is underpowered—even though it has the same top speed as the propeller version of the airplane. The low-Thrust engines in this example certainly would not be used for this particular airplane; the jet engines would actually be more streamlined and the manufacturer would put higher-Thrust engines in, so that the jet version would be much faster. But the big point here is that jet engines just aren't very practical in an airplane designed for a top speed of 180 K.

Because of its relatively poor acceleration at low speeds, and because of the time required for the engine to develop full Thrust when the throttle is opened all the way from idle (it may take several seconds), a comparatively high amount of power is usually carried by the jet airplane on approach until the landing is assured.

The power curve will be covered in more detail as it applies to flight requirements throughout the book.

WEIGHT

The Weight of the airplane, as the Weight of any other object, always acts downward toward the center of the earth. Weight and Drag, the detrimental forces, are the main problems facing aeronautical engineers.

Weight acts toward the center of the earth so you can see by Fig. 2-52 that the Australians and other people in that area fly upside down as far as we're concerned. However, they seem quite happy about it, have been doing it for years, and it's too late to mention it to them.

There are several Weight terms with which you should be familiar:

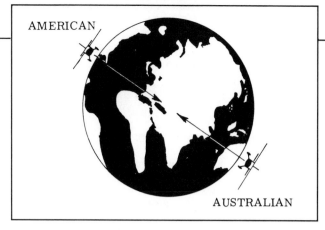

Fig. 2-52. As far as Americans are concerned, the Australians fly inverted all the time (and vice versa).

1. *Empty Weight as weighed* is the actual Weight as obtained from the scale readings (after the Weight of extra items such as braces or chocks is subtracted). It may be empty of oil, any fuel, or hydraulic fluid, but these are considered later in Weight and balance problems worked for the airplane.

2. *Licensed Empty Weight* is the empty weight of the airplane including *undrainable oil, unusable fuel,* and *hydraulic fluid.* This term applies to airplanes *manufactured before 1976* and indicates that the airplane is painted and ready to go except for oil and usable fuel (and pilot).

3. *Standard Empty Weight* is the term used for general aviation airplanes in models produced *in 1976 and after* and includes *full oil, unusable fuel, and hydraulic fluid.* In other words, oil is considered in this empty Weight. It's the empty Weight of a "standard" airplane of that model. The airplane may be actually weighed without oil or be bare of paint; these are added mathematically to get the *standard empty Weight and moment.*

4. *Basic Empty Weight* is the standard empty Weight plus the Weight of optional equipment. (A particular airplane has its own basic empty Weight.)

5. *Gross Weight* is the maximum allowable Weight for the airplane. The manufacturer's performance figures are usually given for the gross Weight of the airplane, although in some cases graphs or figures in the *POH* also show performance at Weights below gross Weight. *The term as used in this book refers only to the maximum FAA-certificated Weight.* This is the most commonly accepted use of the term. Airplane loading will be covered in Chap. 10.

AND IN CONCLUSION

Maybe some of the material in this chapter needs a little thinking about, and much of it will be repeated as it applies in following chapters. It's possible after reading this that you may subscribe to Dr. Horatio Zilch's belief that airplanes, etc., are really held up by a very strong and very fine wire, which simplifies the subject considerably.

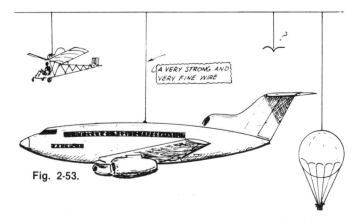

A VERY STRONG AND VERY FINE WIRE

Fig. 2-53.

3 Flight Mechanics

THIS CHAPTER has nothing to do with the people who work on aircraft; *flight mechanics* are the forces and moments acting on the airplane in flight. While the Four Forces are fresh in your mind from the last chapter it would be well to see how they act on the airplane.

The term *force* was covered in the last chapter, and you've used moments in computing Weight and Balance problems. A moment normally results from a force (or weight) acting at the end of an arm (at a 90° angle to it) and is usually expressed as pound-inches or pound-feet (Fig. 3-1).

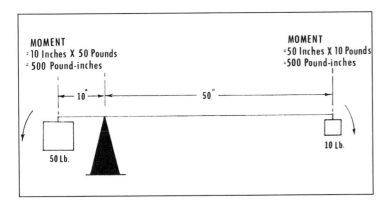

Fig. 3-1. A system of moments in equilibrium.

The airplane in steady-state flight—that is, in a steady climb, a glide, or in level unaccelerated flight (this includes steady level turns)—must be in *equilibrium,* that is, the forces acting in opposite directions on the airplane must cancel each other out. (The same thing goes for the moments.)

A *vector* is an arrow used to represent the direction and strength of a force. You've had experience with vectors in working out wind triangles in navigation and also unconsciously discuss vector systems when you talk about headwind

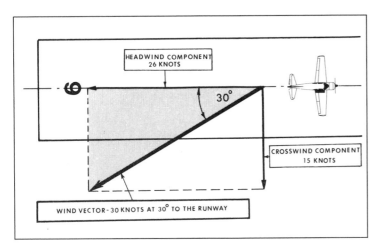

Fig. 3-2. A vector system as faced by the pilot during a takeoff or landing in a crosswind that is 30° to the runway at 30 K (Chap. 1).

and crosswind components for takeoffs and landings (Fig. 3-2). As a pilot you use the runway centerline as a reference and consciously (or unconsciously) divide the wind into components acting along and perpendicular to this reference axis.

You are interested in the component of wind acting across the runway (for example, 15 K) and, if you were interested in computing the takeoff run, you would use the headwind component, or the component of the wind acting down the runway (say, 26 K). You usually don't go so far as to figure out the exact crosswind component but note the wind velocity and its angle to the runway and make a subconscious estimate of how much trouble it might give you on takeoff or landing. You set up your own axis and work with what would seem a most complicated system if people started talking about axes, vectors, and components. What you do is break down the wind's vector into the two components of most interest to you, as was done in Chap. 1. The same general idea will be used here for the forces acting on the airplane.

The reference axis for operating the airplane is the flight path or line of flight, and the forces are measured as operating parallel and perpendicular to it (Fig. 3-3). For an airplane in a *steady-state condition* of flight such as straight and level unaccelerated flight, a constant-airspeed climb or glide, or a constant-altitude balanced turn of a constant rate, the forces acting parallel to the flight path must be balanced. The same thing applies for those forces acting perpendicular, or at 90° ("up" or "down"), to the flight path—they must cancel each other. Each of the vectors shown in Fig. 3-3 may represent the total of several forces acting in the direction shown.

The following must be realized in order to see the mechanics of flight:

1. *Lift* always acts perpendicular to the relative wind (and, hence, perpendicular to the flight path). This is the *effective* Lift discussed in the last chapter, or the Lift acting perpendicular to the actual path of the airplane.

2. *Drag* always acts parallel to the relative wind (and flight path) and in a "rearward" direction.

3. *Weight* always acts in a vertical (down) direction toward the center of the earth.

4. *Thrust,* for these problems, always acts parallel to the centerline of the fuselage. (In other words, at this point we'll assume no "offset" thrust line and that Thrust is acting parallel to the axis of the fuselage.)

This chapter will take a look at the Four Fundamentals of flight—*straight and level, climbs, descents, and turns*—and analyze the factors in each.

THE FORCES AND MOMENTS IN STRAIGHT AND LEVEL FLIGHT

Take an airplane in straight and level *cruising* flight: The average airplane in this condition has a tail-down force because it is designed that way (the need for this will be covered in Chap. 10). Let's examine the forces and moments acting on a typical four-place airplane in straight and level flight at a constant speed at *cruise.*

For simplicity, rather than establishing the vertical acting forces with respect to the center of gravity (CG), which is the usual case, these forces will be measured fore and aft from the center of Lift. Assume at this point that Lift is a string holding the airplane up; its value will be found later (this is legal). The airplane in Fig. 3-4 weighs 3000 lb, is flying at 154 K CAS, and at this particular loading the CG is 5 in. ahead of the "Lift line."

Summing up the major moments acting on the airplane (check Fig. 3-4 for each):

1. *Lift-Weight moment*—The Weight (3000 lb) is acting 5 in. ahead of the center of Lift, which results in a 15,000-lb-in. *nose-down* moment (5 in. × 3000 lb = 15,000 lb-in.).

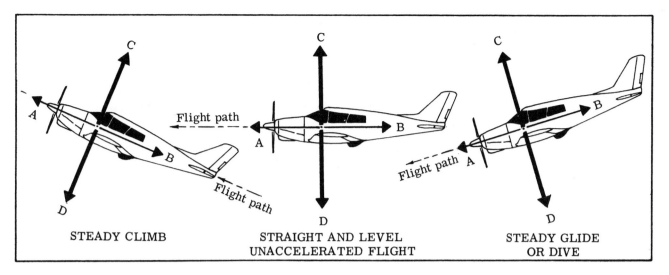

Fig. 3-3. In steady-state flight the sum of the forces acting parallel to the flight path (A–B) must equal zero; the same applies to those acting perpendicular. Minus signs may be given to forces acting in a "downward" or "rearward" direction.

2. *Thrust moment*—Thrust is acting 15 in. above the CG and has a value of 400 lb. The *nose-down* moment resulting is 15 × 400 = *6000 lb-in.* (The moment created by Thrust will be measured with respect to the CG.) For simplicity it will be assumed that the Drag is operating back through the CG. Although this is not usually the case, it saves working with another moment.

3. *Wing moment*—The wing, in producing Lift, creates a nose-down moment, which is the result of the forces working on the wing itself. Fig. 3-5 shows force patterns acting on a wing at two airspeeds (angles of attack). These moments are acting with respect to the aerodynamic center, a point considered to be located about 25% of the distance from the leading to the trailing edge for all airfoils.

Notice that as the speed increases (the angle of attack decreases) the moment becomes greater as the force pattern varies. If the airfoil is not a symmetrical type the nose-down moment created by the wing increases as the *square* of the airspeed. (There is no wing moment if the airfoil is symmetri-

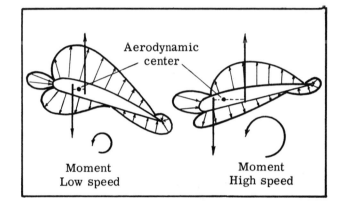

Fig. 3-5. The moments created by the unsymmetrical airfoil at two different airspeeds. The angles of attack and pressure patterns around the airfoil have been exaggerated.

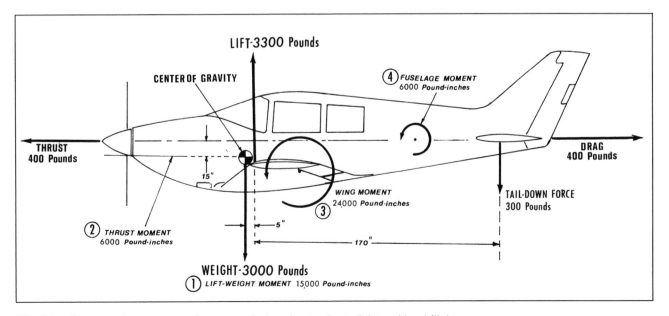

Fig. 3-4. Forces and moments acting on an airplane in steady straight and level flight.

cal because all of the forces are acting through the aero-dynamic center of the airfoil.)

For an airplane of the type, airspeed, and Weight used here, a nose-down moment created by the wing of 24,000 lb-in. would be a good round figure. Remember that this would vary with indicated airspeed. *Nose-down moment created by wing = 24,000 lb-in.*

4. *Fuselage moment*—The fuselage may also be expected to have a moment about its CG because it, too, has a flow pattern, which, for the airplane type and airspeed in this example, would be about *6000 lb-in. nose-down*. (This is not always the case.)

Summing up the nose-down moments:

Lift-Weight moment	= 15,000 lb-in.
Thrust moment	= 6,000 lb-in.
Wing moment (at 154 K)	= 24,000 lb-in.
Fuselage moment (at 154 K)	= 6,000 lb-in.
Total nose-down moment	= 51,000 lb-in.

For equilibrium to exist there must be a *tail-down* moment of 51,000 lb-in., and this is furnished by the tail-down force. Fig. 3-4 shows that the *arm* (the distance from the Lift line to the center of the tail-down force) is 170 in. So, the moment (51,000 lb-in.) and the arm (170 in.) are known; the force acting at the end of that arm (the tail-down force) can be found: 51,000 lb-in./170 inches = 300 lb. The airplane nose does not tend to pitch either way.

The *forces* must also be balanced for equilibrium to exist. Summing up the forces acting perpendicular to the flight path (in this case because the flight path is level, it can be said also that the *vertical* forces must be equal—in a climb or glide the forces acting perpendicular to the flight path will not be vertical) (Fig. 3-3). The "down" forces are the Weight (3000 lb) and the tail-down force (300 lb). The "up" force (Lift) must equal the down forces for equilibrium to exist so that its value must be 3300 lb. Now the moments *and* forces acting perpendicular to the flight path are in equilibrium. As can be seen, Lift is not normally the same as Weight in straight and level unaccelerated flight. Of course, the CG can be moved back to a point where no nose-down moment exists and no tail-down force is required. This, however, could cause stability problems, which will be covered in Chap. 10.

In the situation just discussed it was stated that the airplane was at a *constant cruise* speed so that the force (lb) acting rearward (Drag) and the force (lb) acting forward (Thrust) are equal. (It is assumed that at higher speeds the Thrust line is acting parallel to the flight path so it can be considered to be equal to Drag.)

Thus it can be said without too much loss of accuracy that in the cruise regime Thrust equals Drag and normally Lift is slightly greater than Weight when the forces are balanced.

But what about a situation where the airplane is flying straight and level at a constant airspeed in *slow flight*? Again the forces must be summed as shown in in Fig. 3-6. Now the Thrust line is *not* acting parallel to the flight path (and opposite to Drag); for purposes of this problem it will be assumed that it is inclined upward from the horizontal by 15°.

As a pilot, for straight and level slow flight you set up the desired airspeed and use whatever power is necessary to maintain a constant altitude; you don't know the value of Drag, Thrust, or Lift (and may have only a vague idea as to what the Weight is at that time, but for this problem it's 3000 lb, as before). The tail-down force will be assumed to be 200 lb. (At this high angle of attack it likely will be less than for cruise.) In the problem of straight and level *cruising* flight it was just assumed that Thrust equaled Drag and we weren't particularly interested in the values. Look at Fig. 3-7 for a typical Drag versus airspeed curve for the type of airplane being discussed.

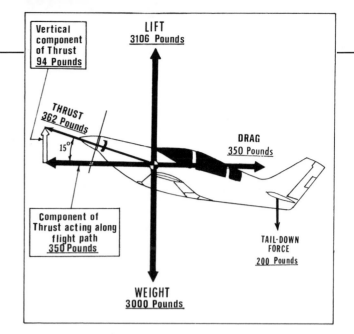

Fig. 3-6. The forces at work on the airplane in straight and level slow flight just above the stall. The vertical component of Thrust has been moved out ahead of the airplane for clarity. Because of the placement of the various forces it would appear that the moments are not in equilibrium. They will be assumed to be so for this problem.

In summing the forces parallel to the flight path in slow flight with this airplane, Drag is 350 lb; the component of Thrust acting opposite Drag must be 350 lb also. No doubt you are already ahead of this in your thinking and realize that because it is inclined at an angle, the actual Thrust must be greater than Drag if its "forward" component along the flight path is equal to Drag. You could look in a trigonometry table and find that at a 15° angle, the *actual* Thrust must be about 3½% higher, or about 362 lb compared with 350 lb of Drag.

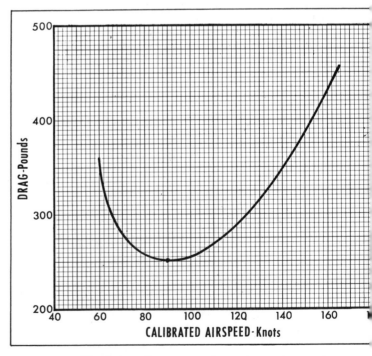

Fig. 3-7. A Drag versus airspeed curve for a fictitious, four-place, high-performance, single-engine airplane at gross Weight. The values are in the area currently expected of that type of airplane.

Thrust also has a component acting at a 90° angle to the flight path parallel to Lift. A check of a trigonometric table would show that this force is 26% of the actual Thrust and has a value of about 94 lb (which is a fair amount).

Now, summing the forces perpendicular to the flight path (the "up" forces must equal the "down" forces):

Forces "down" = Weight + tail-down force = 3000 + 200 = *3200 lb*

Forces "up" = Lift + vertical component of Thrust = Lift + 94 lb = *3200 lb*

Lift, of course, is found as 3200 − 94 = 3106 lb, using our arbitrary values. So Lift is less at low-speed level flight (3106 lb) than at cruise (3300 lb), if you are talking strictly about each of the Four Forces. You don't worry about this in practical application but fly the airplane and set the power and airspeed to get the desired result.

As the vertical component of Thrust helps support the airplane, the wings only have to support 3106 lb rather than the full 3200 lb (Weight plus tail-down force) in slow flight and therefore the wing loading is less than would be expected. The airplane always stalls at a lower airspeed with power on (for the same flap setting and Weight) than in the power-off condition. The effect of the slipstream across the wing helps lower the stall speed, too.

The greater that Thrust is in proportion to Weight, the greater this effect. For instance, if the airplane had an engine-propeller combination capable of producing 3000 lb of Thrust the airplane would be capable of "hanging on its prop" and in theory the power-on stall speed would be zero.

So, in summary, in straight and level flight in the *slow flight regime* it may be expected that (1) the actual Thrust exerted by the propeller (lb) is greater than the Drag of the airplane and (2) Lift is less than at higher speeds. The location of the CG, the angle the Thrust line makes with the flight path, and other factors can have an effect on these figures, of course.

FORCES IN THE CLIMB

To keep from complicating matters, the tail-down force will be ignored for the first part of each section of flight mechanics. It exists, of course, and varies with CG and angle of attack (airspeed) but is comparatively small in most cases so Lift will be considered equal to Weight, at least at the beginning. We'll also assume that all moments are balanced and won't have to consider them further, and the Four Forces will be drawn as acting through a single point (the CG) of the airplane to avoid complicating the drawings.

One of the biggest fallacies in pilots' thinking is believing that the airplane climbs because of "excess Lift." For purposes of this problem the Drag (lb) of the example airplane will be 250 lb at the recommended climb speed of 90 K (Fig. 3-7). The figures for the values for Drag have been rounded off.

Again, remembering that all forces (and moments) must be in balance for such equilibrium to exist, the following is noted. Because the flight path is no longer level, Weight, for the first time, is no longer operating in a direction 90° to the flight path. As the forces must be in equilibrium both parallel and perpendicular to the flight path, Weight must be broken down into the components acting in these directions (as you do with the wind when it is neither right down the runway nor straight across it) (Fig. 3-8).

Fig. 3-9 shows the forces acting on the airplane in a steady-state climb of 90 K (CAS). The airplane has an angle of climb of 8° to the horizontal and requires an angle of attack of 6° to fly at the climb airspeed of 90 K. We are assuming that the angle of incidence is zero (the wing chord

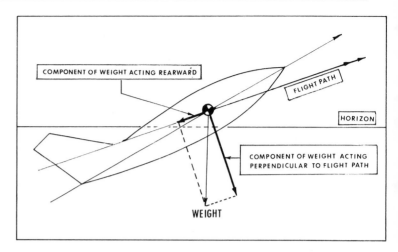

Fig. 3-8. As Weight is no longer acting perpendicular to the flight path it must be broken down into components as shown.

line is exactly parallel to the fuselage centerline) and that the Thrust line is offset "upward" from the flight path by 6° in this climb. In the following drawings the angles will be exaggerated and a simplified airplane silhouette used for clarity.

To sum up the forces *parallel* to the flight path:

The forces acting rearward along the flight path are aerodynamic Drag (250 lb) (see Fig. 3-7 again) *plus* the rearward component of Weight, which by checking a trigonometric table for the 8° angle of climb (in round numbers) is found to be 417 lb. The *total* rearward acting force is aerodynamic Drag (250 lb) plus the rearward acting component of Weight (417 lb), or *667 lb*.

For the required equilibrium (steady-state climb condition) to exist, there must be a balancing force acting forward along the flight path; this is furnished by Thrust. The fact that the Thrust line is offset upward from the flight path by 6° further complicates the problem. Because of its inclination the actual Thrust produced by the propeller must be greater than 667 lb in order to have that force acting along the flight path. The actual Thrust, you will note, is the hypotenuse of a right triangle, and you remember from your geometry (and Chap. 1) that the hypotenuse of a right triangle is always longer than either one of its sides; the longer of the two other sides is the

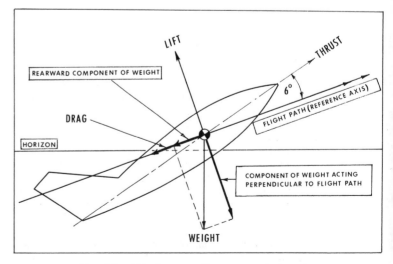

Fig. 3-9. The forces acting on an airplane in a steady climb.

component of Thrust acting along the flight path, which must be equal to the rearward acting force(s). The sum of the forces equals zero.

Again, a check of a trigonometric table shows that to have 667 lb along the flight path the *actual* Thrust must be about 0.55% greater (a little more than one-half of 1%) so that its value is 3 lb greater, or about 670 lb (a nit-picking addition, to be sure) so the forces acting *parallel* to the flight path at the climb speed of 90 K and Weight of 3000 lb are balanced (Fig. 3-10).

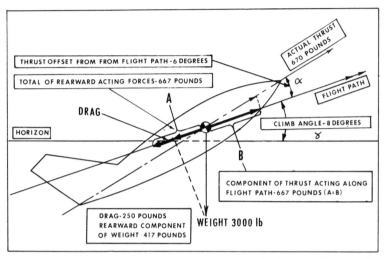

Fig. 3-10. A summary of the forces acting *parallel* to the flight path in the steady-state climb.

To sum the forces acting *perpendicular* to the flight path:

The component of Weight acting perpendicular (more or less "downward") to the flight path at the climb angle of 8° turns out to be 2971 lb according to the trigonometric table (the cosine of 8° is 0.9902). As this is considered to be the only force acting in that direction (now that the tail-down force is being neglected) it must be balanced by an equal force (or forces) in the opposite direction. The two forces acting in that direction are (1) Lift and (2) the component of Thrust acting at 90°, or perpendicular, to the flight path (Fig. 3-11).

As Thrust is now a known quantity, we can solve for that component acting in the same direction as Lift. For a 6° angle of inclination the component for 670 lb of Thrust is 70 lb (rounded off). This means that Lift must have a value of 2901 lb in this case (2971 − 70 = 2901 lb), or Lift (2901 lb) + Thrust component (70 lb) = Weight component (2971 lb). The forces acting perpendicular to the flight path are balanced.

Lift (2901 lb) is found here to be *less* than the airplane's Weight (3000 lb) in the steady-state climb. Thrust (670 lb) is *greater* than aerodynamic Drag (250 lb).

What happened to the idea that an airplane makes a steady climb because of "excess" Lift? Even considering the tail-down force, which for this airplane's airspeed, Weight, and CG location could be expected to be about 250 lb, Lift is hardly greater than Weight. In any event, there is no "excess Lift" available—it's all being used to balance the tail-down force and the component of Weight acting perpendicular to the flight path. (Lift would have to be 2901 lb plus 250 lb, or 3151 lb.)

You remember from the last chapter that the Thrust horsepower equation is THP = TV/325 (the 325 is for the airspeed in knots) so that the THP power being developed along the flight path is (667 × 90)/325 = 185 THP. The "V"

in the equation is *true* airspeed; it will be assumed that the airplane is operating at sea level at this point so that the calibrated climb airspeed of 90 K equals a TAS of the same value.

The rate of climb of an airplane depends on the amount of *excess* THP available at a particular airspeed. This excess THP means the horsepower that is working to move the airplane vertically. The recommended best rate of climb speed is that one at which the greatest amount of excess THP is available. The following equation may be used to determine the rate of climb in feet per minute:

$$\frac{\text{excess THP} \times 33,000}{\text{airplane Weight}}$$

Power is *force* times *distance per unit of time* and 1 HP is equal to 550 ft-lb per second or 33,000 ft-lb per minute. That's where the 33,000 in the equation comes in; it's set up for a rate of climb (RC), or vertical displacement, in feet per minute. Going back to the original idea for horsepower (in this case THP), the equation for the THP (excess THP) used to climb would be as follows:

$$\frac{\text{airplane Weight} \times \text{RC (fpm)}}{33,000}$$

The THP required to climb is that raising a certain Weight (the airplane) a certain vertical distance in a certain period of time.

But to find the rate of climb for the example airplane it would be well first to find out how much THP is required to fly the airplane *straight and level* at a constant altitude at sea level at 90 K. As Weight in *level flight* will not have a component acting rearward to the flight path, the only retarding force is aerodynamic Drag, which was found to be 250 lb. The

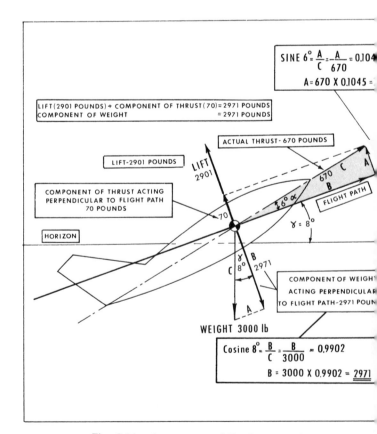

Fig. 3-11. A summary of the forces acting *perpendicular* to the flight path in the climb.

Thrust component acting along the flight path must be equal to this, or 250 lb. Assuming that the angle of attack and the angle Thrust makes with the flight path is 6°, to get this value the actual Thrust would be about 251 lb (rounded off to the 250) (Fig. 3-12).

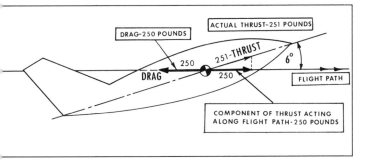

Fig. 3-12. The forces acting parallel to the flight path for the airplane flying *straight and level* at the recommended climb speed of 90 K.

In the earlier look at the climb at 90 K, 667 lb of Thrust was being exerted along the flight path. This is 417 lb more than required for level flight and is, in effect, the "excess Thrust" needed for a climb angle of 8° at 90 K. (The rearward component of Weight was 417 lb.)

Solving for excess Thrust horsepower (ETHP):

$$ETHP = \frac{\text{excess Thrust} \times \text{velocity (K)}}{325}$$

$$ETHP = \frac{417 \times 90}{325} = 115 \text{ THP}$$

Solving for rate of climb:

$$RC = \frac{ETHP \times 33,000}{\text{Weight}}$$

$$RC = \frac{115 \times 33,000}{3000} = 1265 \text{ fpm}$$

The brake horsepower (BHP) required to get such performance for a 3000-lb airplane with the described characteristics could be estimated. It can be assumed here that at the climb speed the propeller is 74% efficient (efficiency varies with airspeed, you remember from Chap. 2) and that the THP being developed is 74% of the BHP being developed at the crankshaft. The *total* THP being used in the climb is THP = (T × V)/325 = (670 × 90)/325 = 185 THP (rounded off). The Thrust acting along the flight path was 667 lb, but the *total* Thrust exerted was 670 lb; this is what must be used to work back to the BHP requirement.

This, then, is approximately 74% of the horsepower developed at the crankshaft, so the BHP required to get this performance for the fictitious airplane would be 185/0.74, or approximately 250 BHP (0.74 × 250 = 185).

The rate of climb found is in the ball park for current four-place retractable-gear airplanes ("our" airplane may be cleaner or dirtier aerodynamically than others). All of this resulted from our arbitrarily selecting an aerodynamic Drag (250 lb), an angle of attack in the climb (6°), and a climb angle of 8° at a climb speed of 90 K. The figures were picked to give a reasonable idea of how such airplane types get their climb performance. The 74% used for propeller efficiency is also arbitrary, although the figure is close to that expected for the airplane type and speed discussed.

The more practical aspects of the climb will be covered in Chap. 6.

FORCES IN THE GLIDE

As you have probably already reasoned, anytime the flight path of the airplane is not horizontal, Weight has to be broken down into two components. The glide or descent at an angle of 8° to the horizontal would have the same percentages of Weight acting perpendicular and parallel to the flight path as for the 8° angle of climb just mentioned—except that in the glide the component of Weight parallel to the glide path is not a retarding force but is acting in the direction of flight.

For this situation it is assumed that the power is at idle and *no Thrust exists*. The tail-down force will be neglected at first. The forces acting parallel to the flight path are (1) the component of Weight, which must be balanced by (2) aerodynamic Drag in order to keep the airspeed constant in the descent. For an 8° angle of descent the component of Weight acting along the flight path would be 417 lb, as for the climb—except that it's now working in the direction of motion. The aerodynamic Drag must equal the component of Weight acting along the flight path for a steady-state condition to exist. Looking back to Fig. 3-7, you see that for an 8° angle of descent this value of Drag (417 lb) exists at about 157 K.

The more usual situation would be to use the power-off glide speed recommended by the manufacturer. For this example 90 K will be used as the recommended (clean) glide speed. We'll also ignore the effects of power decrease or windmilling prop on the Drag curve and say that aerodynamic Drag at 90 K is 250 lb as it was for the power-on climb. The speed of 90 K may or may not be the best one for maximum glide efficiency (it depends on the airplane), but the niceties of that will be covered further on.

Illustrating the same reasoning as in the other steady-state flight conditions, Fig. 3-13 shows the forces acting parallel to the flight path in a power-off glide. (Again, the tail-down force is neglected for simplicity.)

Realizing that the component of Weight acting along the flight path must have a value equal to the 250 lb of aerodynamic Drag, the glide path will be of a certain angle for this

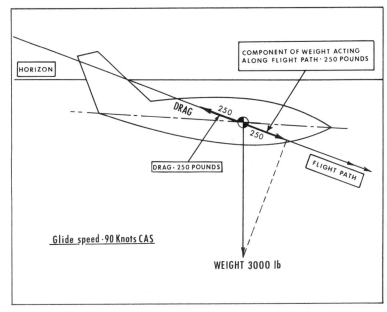

Fig. 3-13. The forces acting parallel to the flight path in the power-off glide at 90 K.

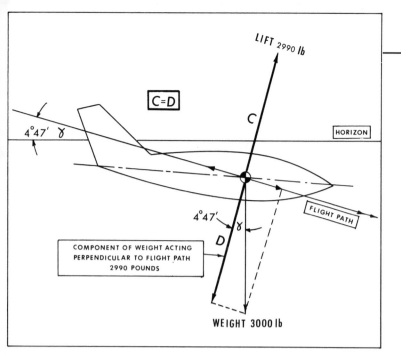

Fig. 3-14. The forces acting perpendicular to the flight path in the glide.

mined from Fig. 3-7 this would be the minimum glide angle (or *maximum distance* glide) for the example airplane. Anytime Drag is increased, the efficiency of the glide is *decreased*. With a faster or slower glide speed than the 90 K chosen, a check of Fig. 3-7 shows that Drag will increase—and the glide ratio will suffer.

One method of increasing Drag would be to glide with the landing gear extended (an increase in parasite Drag, which would result in an increase in total Drag). With the gear down a typical figure for Drag for an airplane of this type at 90 K would be 300 lb. The glide angle would be greater and the glide ratio would suffer.

Assume that the pilot starts gliding "clean" and the glide ratio is 12 to 1. The nose is at a certain attitude to get the 90 K (and the 4°47′ angle of descent); for most airplanes of that type the nose will be approximately level.

The gear is extended and suddenly the forces acting parallel to the flight path are no longer in balance; Drag is greater than the component of Weight and the airplane would start slowing if the nose were kept at the same position. Deciding to glide at 90 K as before, the pilot must drop the nose and change the flight path so that the component of Weight acting along the flight path would equal the 300 lb of aerodynamic Drag. The new glide ratio at 90 K with the gear down would be Lift (3000 lb)/Drag (300 lb), or about 10 to 1; the glide angle would be about 6° relative to the horizon.

The method of finding the rate of sink of the airplane can be compared to that of solving for the rate of climb. The rate of sink, however, is a function of the *deficit THP* existing at the chosen airspeed:

$$\frac{\text{deficit THP} \times 33{,}000}{\text{airplane Weight}}$$

The aerodynamic Drag for the airplane is a force of 250 lb acting rearward along the flight path at the airspeed of 90 K (the airplane is clean and weighs 3000 lb). The equivalent THP required to be acting in the direction of flight to equal the effects of Drag at 90 K would be THP = DV/325 = (250 × 90)/325 = 69. The combination of Thrust and velocity would have to equal 69 THP for level flight at 90 K, or TV/325 = 69 THP. However, in this case Thrust is zero and, as you know, zero times any number (90 K in this case) is still zero. So, there's no THP being developed by the engine; the airplane is 69 THP in the hole, or there is a deficit of 69 THP. The rate of sink can be calculated: (69 × 33,000)/3000 = 760 fpm (rounded off).

This could be checked by looking at the situation in Fig. 3-13 again. The airplane is descending down a path inclined at an angle of 4°47′ at 90 K forward speed. Converting the 90 K to feet per minute it can be said that the airplane is moving down the path at a rate of 9130 fpm. It was already found that the glide ratio was 12 to 1 so that the feet down per minute would be one-twelfth that traveled along the glide path, or about 760 fpm.

FORCES IN THE TURN

Analysis of the turn can be quite complicated but we'll take a simple look at it.

For normal flying (the Four Fundamentals) the turn is the only maneuver in which Lift is deliberately and maliciously made greater than Weight and is the only one of the Four Fundamentals in which g forces exist in a steady-state condition.

For a balanced turn at a constant altitude the up forces must equal the down forces as in straight and level flight. For ease of discussion we'll ignore the tail-down force in this section on the turn.

condition to occur; a check of a trig table shows this to be 4°47′ (4 degrees and 47 minutes), or nearly a 5° angle downward in relation to the horizon. Knowing the glide angle, the forces acting 90° to the flight path (Lift and the component of Weight acting perpendicular to the flight path) can be found (Fig. 3-14).

That Weight component, which can be found by reference to a trig table, is 2990 lb, so Lift must also equal this value for a steady-state (or constant) glide under the conditions of ignoring the tail-down force.

For shallow angles of glide the variation of Lift from Weight is usually ignored. In this case, Lift is 2990 lb to a Weight of 3000 lb, a variation of about one-third of 1%.

In the climb a final figure for Lift required at 90 K (considering the tail-down force) was 3151 lb. For the glide the tail-down force for this airplane would be in the vicinity of 225 lb because of the lack of a moment created by Thrust. The component of Weight acting perpendicular to the flight path at the 90-K glide was 2990 lb and Lift required to take care of this would be 2990 + 225 or *3215 lb. There are 64 more pounds of Lift in the glide than in the climb, or Lift would be greater in the glide than in the climb under the conditions established!*

The angle that Weight varies from being perpendicular to the flight path is also the angle of glide or descent. If *aerodynamic Drag is cut to a minimum, the components of Weight acting parallel to the flight path can also be a minimum for a steady-state glide.* In other words, if the aerodynamic Drag could somehow be halved for this airplane the angle of glide would be halved; the airplane would descend at an angle of about 2.5° to the horizontal *and would glide twice as far for the same altitude.*

As the airplane's Weight is considered to be constant for a particular instant of time the solution is that the farthest distance may be covered with the airplane flying at the angle of attack (or airspeed) with the minimum aerodynamic Drag. For instance, assuming that at small angles of descent Lift equals Weight (3000 lb), the angle of glide of the example airplane is 3000 lb (Lift or Weight)/250 lb (aerodynamic Drag) = 12. The glide ratio for our example airplane at 90 K is 12 to 1, or 12 ft forward for every 1 ft down. And as the point of minimum aerodynamic Drag (250 lb at 90 K CAS) was deter-

As noted in Chap. 2, Lift acts perpendicular to the relative wind and *to the wingspan*. The latter consideration is of particular importance in discussing the turn.

As you know from turning a car, your body is forced toward the "outside of the circle," and that force increases as an inverse function of the turning radius. (The smaller the radius or tighter the turn for a given speed, the greater the apparent "side force" working on you.) If you drive faster and try to turn in the same radius as that at a slower speed, the force is greater. So, your discomfort is a function of either the radius or the velocity during the turn, or both. If in a turn the car should suddenly hit a spot of oil or ice, it would move toward the outside of the circle (or more correctly, its path would be tangent to the circle). The tendency for the car to travel in a straight line is normally offset by the *centripetal* force, or the holding (friction) force of the tires against the road surface. When the oil spot or ice is encountered, the friction providing the centripetal force decreases suddenly and the car departs the beaten path for new adventures through somebody's hedge.

You'll hear, and probably use, the term "centrifugal force," which is not a true force (and not even a proper term in physics) but is the result of a body (the airplane, for example) tending to continue in a straight line.

To repeat: the acceleration, or g forces in a balanced turn, depends on the bank; a Cessna 152 and an F-15 in a 30° bank at cruise will have the same force acting on each of the pilots. The turn radius of the F-15 will be much greater as will be reviewed later.

You can set up a balanced turn and can play airspeed versus bank angle to vary the effects of rate and radius of turn. You also know that in doing steep turns you could control altitude by changing bank angle and back pressure (angle of attack). Generally you don't increase airspeed in a constant-altitude turn (you don't have all that much capacity in the average general aviation airplane), but if you did you'd have to relax back pressure (*decrease* the angle of attack) *or increase* the bank angle if a constant altitude is to be held.

In balanced, constant-altitude and constant-radius turns, the tendency of the airplane to continue in a straight line is overcome by the component of Lift (centripetal force) acting toward the center of the turn (after the turn is established).

Centripetal force (C.F.) = WV^2/gR = horizontal component of Lift (L).

where
- W = Weight of the airplane (lb)
- V^2 = tangential velocity (fps), squared. (You can call it TAS in feet per second, squared.)
- g = acceleration of gravity (32.16 fps, per second)
- R = radius of turn (ft)

$$WV^2/gR = L \sin \phi \quad (\phi = \text{bank angle})$$

If the velocity is *doubled* at the same bank, the g forces will remain the same but the turn radius will be *quadrupled*. (More about this later.)

Figure 3-15 shows that the airplane would like to go straight (A), but you are in command and want to turn (left in this particular case) (B).

Figure 3-16 shows the forces acting to keep the airplane in a constant-altitude balanced turn. The vertical component of Lift (A) is balancing the Weight of the airplane, while the horizontal component (B) of Lift is acting to turn it.

For instance, take two airplanes of the same Weight; one has a great deal more power and can maintain a level turn at twice the cruising speed of the other. Both will be banked at 30° in a balanced level turn (Fig. 3-17). Both airplanes are

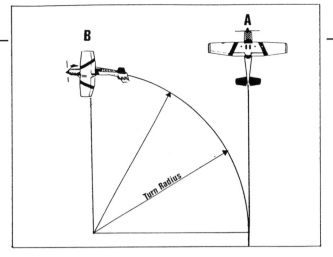

Fig. 3-15. The airplane wants to proceed straight ahead (A), but by your skillful control of the Lift force direction and value, you are able to follow path (B).

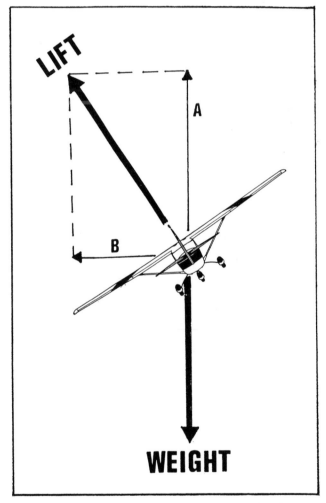

Fig. 3-16. In a balanced constant-altitude turn, Lift may be considered to be broken down into a vertical component (A) and a horizontal component (B).

pulling the same load factor or number of g's, but there is quite a difference in their turn radii. (The load factor is a function of the Lift-to-Weight ratio if the tail-down force is ignored; Lift in each case is 3460 lb; the airplanes are pulling 3460/3000, or 1.15 g's.) In the balanced turn, as was mentioned earlier, centripetal force is furnished by the horizontal component of Lift, which for the bank of 30° is found to be 1730 lb (Fig. 3-17).

Everything is known except the radius of turn (R) for each airplane under the conditions given (W = 3000 lb, g = 32.16 fps, per second, CF (horizontal component of Lift) = 1730 lb, V = 150 and 300 fps). Solving for R of Airplane A requires a little algebraic shuffling and rounding off:

$$R = \frac{WV^2}{g(CF)} = \frac{3000 \times (150)^2}{32.16 \times 1730} = 1210 \text{ ft}$$

The turning radius of airplane A in a 30°-banked turn at 150 fps, or about 90 K, is about 1210 ft, or slightly less than ¼ mi. If it made a 360° turn, the diameter of the turn would be a little less than ½ mi.

For airplane B, turning at a velocity of 300 fps, the radius of turn would be (rounded off):

$$\frac{3000 \times (300)^2}{32.16 \times 1730} = 4850 \text{ ft, or } r = \frac{V^2(K)}{11.26 \tan \phi}$$

The radius of its turn would be 4850 ft, or *four times* that of the airplane of the same Weight and angle of bank traveling at one-half the speed. (The numbers in this exercise have all been rounded off to the nearest 10 feet.)

Suppose the pilot of airplane B wanted to make the *same radius of turn* as A but still at the higher speed of 300 fps (about 178 K). You've no doubt already figured out that the airplane must be banked more steeply; this can be found by reshuffling of the equation and working back to the bank required to get a radius of turn of 1210 ft, like Airplane A.

This time the centripetal force required at the speed of 300 fps for a radius of turn of 1210 ft is (rounded off):

$$CF = \frac{WV^2}{g(R)} = \frac{3000 \times (300)^2}{32.16 \times 1210} = 6940 \text{ lb}$$

So, the horizontal component of Lift must equal this value of 6940 lb. It's also a fact that the vertical component of Lift *must* be 3000 lb (to equal Weight) so the Lift value and angle could be readily found by checking a trig table (Fig. 3-18). It's found that the angle of bank must be about 66.6°. The Lift value must be 7560 lb, or the airplane's Lift-to-Weight ratio is 7560/3000 = 2.52 g's. The pilot's face is sagging downward trying to stay in the turning circle of the slower airplane (the pilot of which probably feels quite comfortable at a 1.15-g loading in the 30° bank). Fig. 3-19 shows the two airplanes in the turn.

In instrument flying the *time* to make a turn (rate of turn) is important, and you'll find that the faster the airplane the steeper the bank must be in order to make a balanced standard-rate turn of 3° per second (Chap. 1). Chap. 4 will also go into this requirement in more detail.

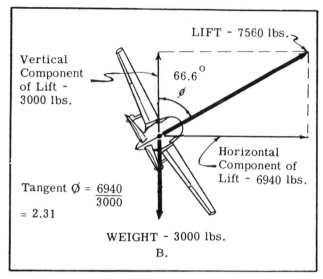

Fig. 3-18. Forces existing and bank required for Airplane B to make a turn with a radius of 1210 ft at its speed of 300 fps.

The radius of turn does not depend on the Weight of the airplane. If airplane B turned at the same velocity as A (150 fps) but weighed 6000 instead of 3000 lb, its radius of turn would be the same because the centripetal force required would also be doubled (in a balanced turn) and the ratio of Weight to CF would be the same. The equations with Weight included show actual vector values. The Japanese Zero in World War II had a maximum Weight of 6500 lb and the F4U-4 *Corsair* had nearly twice the maximum Weight (12,500 lb). Because of the Zero's lower Weight (lower wing loading) as compared with the F4U-4, it could fly (and turn) at a *much slower speed*. U.S. pilots knew better than to try to outturn the Zero. (This writer had the honor of flying the F4U-5N *Corsair* during an 8-month carrier deployment in the Far East in 1954. Needless to say, no Zeros were encountered at that late date.)

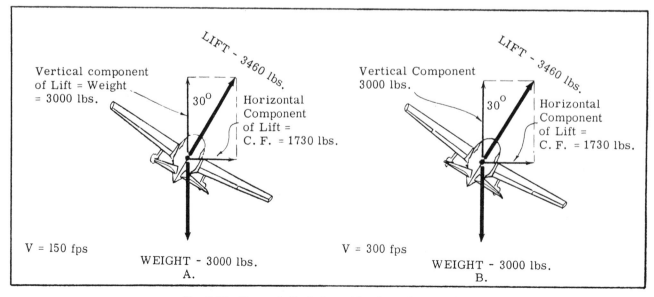

Fig. 3-17. Forces in the balanced level turn for two airplanes flying at *different speeds* at a 30° bank. Note that the forces are the same.

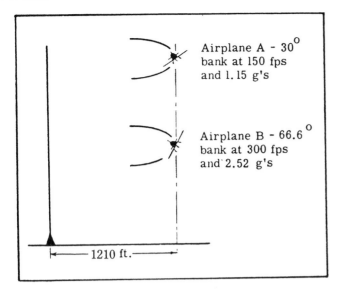

Fig. 3-19. A comparison of the two airplanes making the same radius of turn.

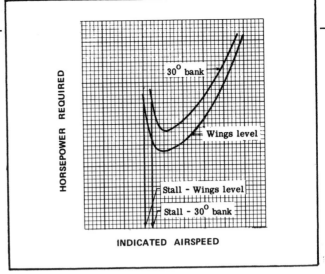

Fig. 3-20. A comparison of the horsepower required to maintain a constant altitude (and stall speeds), wings level and in a 30° bank.

A couple of things were neglected in this discussion of the turn. The tail-down force was considered to be zero, which it certainly would not be in a turn (you could expect it to increase appreciably in steeper turns). And because of the increased angle of attack in the turn, Thrust has components acting inward (helping centripetal force) and upward. However, putting all this into an illustration might result in a pretty confusing situation.

Figure 3-20 shows the power-required curves for an airplane in straight and level flight and in a 30°-banked constant-altitude turn. Note that it is quite similar to Figs. 2-48, 7-3, and 7-5, since the airplane does "weigh" more in the turn.

As was mentioned, the turns in this chapter have been balanced; Fig. 3-21 takes a look at the forces acting on the slip indicator in skidding and slipping turns.

Another Look at the Turn. Interestingly enough, the usual idea is to think of the balanced, constant-rate, level turn as a "static" condition even though the nose is moving around the horizon and g's are being pulled. In a wings-level turn (assuming a bank of, say, 0.001° and also that the longitudinal axis is level with the horizon), a steeper bank would require pulling the nose up and spoiling this initial concept.

During a banked, level turn the airplane is actually rotating about the vertical (Z) axis *and* the lateral (Y) axis. Take two exaggerated examples. In a "flat" (no-bank), constant-altitude turn the airplane is rotating only around the vertical axis (yaw). In a 90°-banked, *nose*-level turn the airplane

would be rotating (pitching) only about the lateral (Y) axis (Fig. 3-22).

In the foregoing discussion the notation was made that those were nose-level turns. (Nothing was mentioned about maintaining altitude—which would be a chore in the 90° banked turn.)

Take a look at a chandelle: it's a maximum performance climbing turn with 180° change in direction. The maneuver requires that the last 90° of turn has a constant (fairly high) nose position and the maneuver ends with the airplane just above stall. One fallacy in describing a chandelle is that it is "a loop on an inclined plane." Not so—the nose does not rise perpendicularly to the wingspan as would be the case of a loop. (A loop, straight up or inclined, is movement *only* around the lateral axis, or pitch only; the nose movement and path of the airplane are as shown in Fig. 3-23.)

Assume that a bank of 30° is set at the beginning of the chandelle and the stick or control wheel is brought straight back; the bank will increase to about 45°—as 90° of turn is reached because the airplane's pitch is not changing as much as the turn change (Fig. 3-23C).

You can take a model airplane and see how under some circumstances and attitudes movement around one axis can affect the attitude of the airplane about one or both of the others.

SUMMARY

There is a lot of misunderstanding concerning the actions of the Four Forces in various maneuvers and the most common one is that "excess Lift" is what makes the airplane

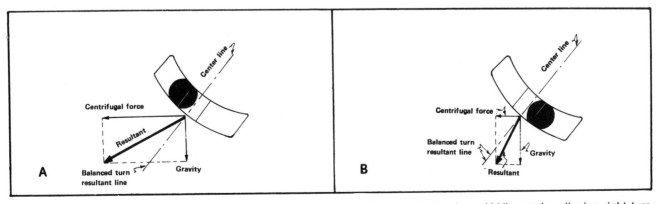

Fig. 3-21. The forces acting on the slip indicator in a skidding and a slipping right turn. Remember that centrifugal force is only an apparent force and is a popular, *not* a physics, term.

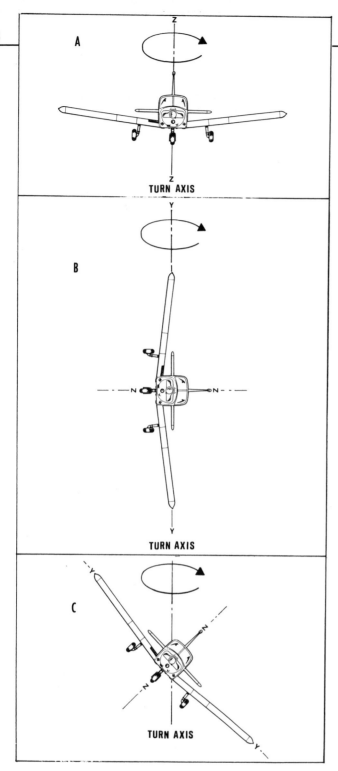

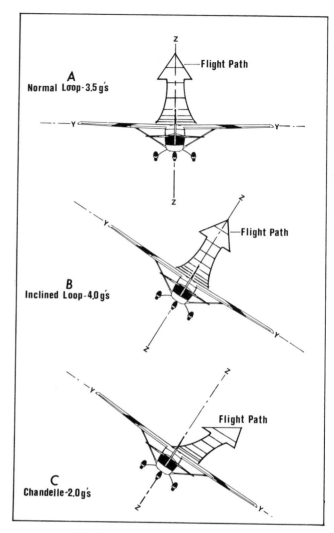

Fig. 3-23. A. The "normal" loop. B. The inclined loop. C. The chandelle. You can see that the chandelle does not follow the inclined loop idea. In the loops the airplane is rotating only about the Y axis. Note the pull-up forces in each maneuver.

Fig. 3-22. An exaggerated look at constant-altitude turns. A. The skidding, wings-level turn; the airplane is rotating only about the vertical (Z) axis. B. The 90°-banked, nose-level turn; the airplane is rotating only about the lateral (Y) axis. C. A 45°-banked, nose-level turn; the airplane is rotating equally about the Y and Z axes, but neither of the two is the turn axis. The ratio of rotation about the Y and Z axes depends on the bank angle. (Don't bank 90° in a normal category airplane.)

didn't overdo it and the wings are still with you, the airplane will *accelerate* upward (and then assume a normal steady-state climb if that's what you wanted). When you exerted back pressure the up force (Lift) was greater than the down forces (Weight, etc.) at that time—you increased the angle of attack almost instantly and the airplane was still at the cruise speed so the dynamic pressure q, which is $(\varrho/2)V^2$, was still of the same high value.

The measurement of positive g's is the Lift-to-Weight ratio, and at the instant of rotation Lift may be increased radically. Of course, as you know, an increase in angle of attack (coefficient of Lift) means an increase in Drag (induced), and Lift will tend to reassume its old value, depending on the new flight path. If you had wanted to climb at a certain airspeed (with a certain angle and rate of climb resulting) Lift would soon settle down to the required value. In flying the airplane you, as a pilot, decide what the airplane must do and keep this requirement by use of power, the airspeed, and/or altimeter. When you have established a steady-state condition such as a steady climb or glide or straight and level flight, the forces settle down of their own accord. *You* balance the forces auto-

climb. This is not to deny that it will climb when an excess Lift exists, but in that case acceleration forces, or g's, will be exerted. Suppose you are flying along at cruise and suddenly exert back pressure on the wheel or stick. Assuming that you

matically by setting up a steady-state condition.

If the up forces (working toward the ceiling of the airplane cabin) are greater than the down forces (working toward the floor) you feel positive g's and feel heavier in the seat; this is the effect in a normal level turn, the steeper the turn the greater the effect.

Probably a large number of stall-type accidents have occurred because the pilot unconsciously thought in terms of "increasing the Lift" to climb over an obstacle.

Another idea not often considered is that a tail-down force exists for the majority of airplanes throughout most of the range of flight speeds and loadings. Most laymen think that "little wing back there is always helping to hold the airplane up." In one sense perhaps it is, in that it is required for good stability, which is important to flight.

You can prove that a tail-down force exists by a very simple experiment. In Chap. 2 the drawings showed that the wing tip vortices curled over the tip toward the low pressure or "lifting" (top) side of the wing. Knowing this to be the case you can "see" this wing tip vortex action by taping a ribbon or string with a light weight on the free end to each wing tip and to the tip of each stabilizer. The rotation of the string will be as shown in Fig. 3-24).

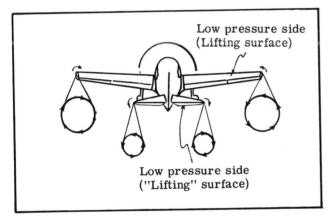

Fig. 3-24. An experiment for checking if a tail-down force exists.

Note in Fig. 3-24 that the string-weight combination is rotating in the opposite direction at the stabilizer tips than it is at the wings—the low pressure or "lifting" side is on the bottom—so a tail-down force exists.

You need only to do one wing and stabilizer tip to see the action. Check the actions of the strings at cruise and watch the wing tip as the airplane is slowed (the angle of attack or C_L is increased). You can readily see that vortex strength increases with a decrease in speed (increase in C_L).

By now you have likely figured that the airplane is actually flown by the Thrust-to-Drag relationship and that little is done in the way of controlling Lift in normal 1-g flight. By setting up a steady-state condition, Lift takes care of itself and actually varies very little in wings-level climbs and glides and straight and level flight. *Keep it in mind.*

From the turn theory in this chapter you can note some information that could be of practical value. The radius of the turn is a function of the velocity squared, $R = (f)V^2$, for a given bank angle. Should you get into marginal VFR weather with poor visibilities in strange territory, slow the airplane up so that you can make small-radius turns if necessary to avoid an obstruction such as a mountain or TV tower that suddenly looms up out of the mist. (Don't stall.) *Don't* go boring along at low altitudes in low visibilities at full cruise speed. (Better yet, preplan so that you avoid such a possibility.)

4 The Airplane Instruments

FLIGHT INSTRUMENTS AND AIRPLANE PERFORMANCE

The earlier chapters were somewhat theoretical in their approach to airplane performance and were necessary for background in preparation for this and the following chapters in Part 1.

In order to get the most from your airplane you must have a good understanding of its instruments and know what affects their operation. Whether you plan to go on to the commercial certificate or to continue to fly for personal business or pleasure, pride in your flying ability will cause you to want to learn more about your airplane.

There are certain relationships between the density, temperature, and pressure of the atmosphere. An airplane's performance depends on the density-altitude, and density-altitude has an interlocking relationship with temperature and pressure. For instance, cold air is denser than warm air—so that a *decrease* in temperature (if the pressure is not changed) means an *increase* in density. If the pressure is *increased* (assuming no change in temperature) the density is *increased* (more particles of air compressed into the same volume). This chapter on instruments is a review, but it may introduce information that you didn't run into during your study and training for the private certificate.

Equation of State. For those interested in the mathematics, the equation of state explains the exact relationships between the three variables: temperature, pressure, and density.

$$\varrho = \frac{P}{1716T_R}$$

This form of the equation of state says that the air density (ϱ), in slugs per cubic foot, equals the pressure (P), in pounds per square foot (psf), divided by 1716 times the temperature (T), in degrees Rankine. The figure 1716 is a constant number derived from the product of the constant for air (53.3) and the acceleration of gravity (32.2).

A slug is a unit of mass, as was mentioned in Chap. 2. The mass of an object in slugs may be found by dividing the Weight by the acceleration of gravity, 32.16 feet per second (fps) per second; hence a 161-lb man has a mass of 5 slugs (161/32.16 = 5).

The temperature in degrees Rankine may be found by adding 460° to the Fahrenheit reading; for a standard sea level day the temperature is 59°F or 519° Rankine.

The density at sea level on a standard day may be found as follows: ϱ (rho, air density) = 2116 (sea level pressure, psf)/(1716 × 519), or ϱ = 0.002378 slugs per cubic foot. Or, checking for pressure, pressure = density × temperature × 1716.

The equation of state and the symbols for density, pressure, and temperature will be used throughout the book.

The three factors directly affect each other. If you know your pressure altitude and the temperature, the density-altitude can be found with a graph or computer.

A REVIEW OF PRESSURE FLIGHT INSTRUMENTS

As the name implies, these instruments operate because of air pressure or air pressure changes.

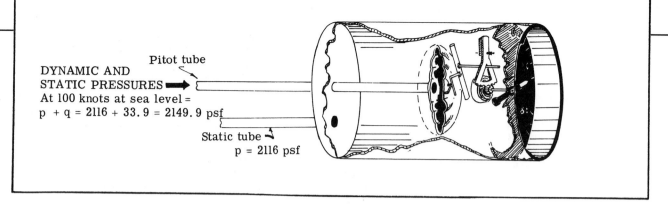

DYNAMIC AND
STATIC PRESSURES ➡
At 100 knots at sea level =
$p + q = 2116 + 33.9 = 2149.9$ psf

Pitot tube

Static tube
$p = 2116$ psf

Fig. 4-1. Airspeed indicator. The combination of the static and dynamic pressures in the pitot tube is labeled *total pressure*, or $P_T = p + q$.

Airspeed Indicator. The airspeed indicator is nothing more than a specialized air pressure gage. The airspeed system comprises the pitot and static tubes and the airspeed indicator instrument. An airplane moving through the air creates its own relative wind. This relative wind exerts a ram pressure in the pitot tube where its effects are passed on into a diaphragm linked to an indicating hand (Fig. 4-1).

This relative wind force is calibrated in miles per hour, or knots, rather than pounds per square foot of pressure. The static tube acts as a neutralizer of the static pressure around the airplane and within the instrument, so that *only* the dynamic pressure is measured. For lighter planes the pitot and static tube inlets are together. But for greater accuracy, the static tube opening is placed at some point on the airplane where the most accurate measurement of the actual outside air static pressure is found. A usual spot is on the side of the fuselage somewhere between the wing and stabilizer. No doubt you've noticed these static pressure sources, accompanied by a sign, "Keep this hole free of dirt." These points are selected as being the places where the static pressure is least

affected by the airflow about the airplane. It is difficult to find a spot on the airplane entirely free of static pressure error—and so the term *position error*. The proper placing of the static tube opening to minimize this error is responsible for no few ulcers in aircraft manufacturing. In addition to the position error in the system there is usually some error in the airspeed indicator instrument itself. This *instrument error* is another factor to contend with in airspeed calibration (Fig. 4-2).

The pitot tube position is also important. It must be placed at a point where the actual relative wind is measured, free from any interfering aerodynamic effects. A particularly bad place would be just above the wing where the air velocity is greater than the free stream velocity.

Error is introduced into the airspeed indicator at high angles of attack or in a skid. You've seen this when practicing stalls. The airplane had a stall speed of 50 K according to the *POH*, yet there you were, still flying (though nearly stalled) with the airspeed indicator showing 40 K (or even zero). It wasn't because of your skill that you were able to fly the

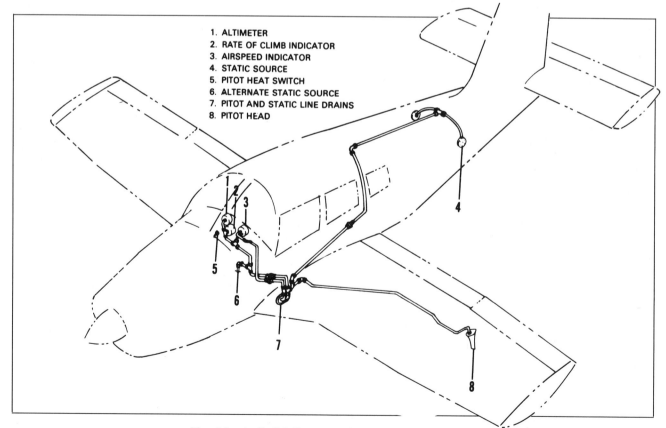

1. ALTIMETER
2. RATE OF CLIMB INDICATOR
3. AIRSPEED INDICATOR
4. STATIC SOURCE
5. PITOT HEAT SWITCH
6. ALTERNATE STATIC SOURCE
7. PITOT AND STATIC LINE DRAINS
8. PITOT HEAD

Fig. 4-2. A pitot/static system for a four-place airplane. Others may have the static sources in the forward part of the fuselage just aft of the engine compartment.

airplane at this lower speed—the angle of the airplane to the airstream introduced an error. While at first the pitot tube, being at a fairly high angle of attack, seems to be the culprit, this is not the case. For the airplane that stalls at the usual 15° to 20° angle of attack this effect is small, although for STOL-type airplanes it could be a real factor in airspeed error. Flight test airplanes use an elaborate extended boom with a swivel pitot head, which results in much greater accuracy at high angles of attack. This is obviously not practical in cost or weight for normal lightplane installation. The *major* source of error, however, is the static system; the pitot tube contributes a minor amount.

So, static pressure error can also be introduced at angles of attack or angles of yaw, the amount of error depending on the location of the static opening; this will be covered again a little later.

The dynamic pressure measured by the airspeed indicator is called "q" and has the designation $(\varrho/2)V^2$, as indicated earlier. You will notice that dynamic pressure is a part of the Lift and Drag equations. This *dynamic pressure,* which is one half the *air density* (slugs per cubic foot) *times* the *true air velocity* (feet per second squared), is pressure in *pounds per square foot.*

At sea level on a standard day, at a speed of 100K(169 fps), q would be $\dfrac{0.002378 \times 169^2}{2} = 33.9$ psf. The lightplane airplane airspeed indicator is calibrated for standard sea level conditions with a temperature of 15°C or 59°F and a pressure of 29.92 in. of mercury, or 2116 psf.

The perfect airspeed indicator would work as follows:

Pitot tube measures dynamic and static pressure.

Static tube equalizes static pressure or "subtracts" it from the pitot tube reading.

Airspeed indicator indicates dynamic pressure only.

So the airspeed indicator only measures the dynamic pressure, which is a combination of density and airstream velocity (squared). As altitude increases, the air density decreases so that an airplane indicating 100 K (or 33.9 psf dynamic pressure) at 10,000 ft actually has a higher TAS than the airplane at sea level *indicating* the same dynamic pressure (airspeed).

This airspeed correction for density change can be worked on your computer, but a good rule of thumb is to add 2% per 1000 ft to the indicated airspeed. A plane with a calibrated airspeed of 100 K at 10,000 ft density-altitude will have a TAS close to 120 K. (By computer it's found to be 116 K.)

Fig. 4-3. CAS versus EAS. At sea level and less than 250 K EAS and CAS are equal. At higher speeds and altitudes EAS is less. The differences at 5000 and 10,000 feet are noted by X and Y respectively.

There are airspeed indicators on the market today that correct for TAS; the TAS can be read directly off the dial. One type has a setup where the pilot adjusts the dial to compensate for altitude and the temperature effects (density-altitude) and the needle indicates the TAS in the cruising range. Another more expensive instrument does this automatically for certain speeds well above stall or approach speeds. The reason for not having corrections at lower speeds is that the pilot might fly by *true airspeed* and get into trouble landing at airports of high elevation and/or high temperatures. Perhaps an explanation is in order.

An airplane will stall at the same indicated (or calibrated) airspeed regardless of its altitude or the temperature (all other things such as Weight, angle of bank, etc., being equal). An airplane that stalls at an indicated 50 K at sea level will stall at an indicated 50 K at a density-altitude of 10,000 ft because the airspeed indicator measures q and it still takes the same amount of q to support the airplane. However, the *true airspeed* at 10,000 ft would be approximately *60 K*. If you were flying by a TAS instrument, you might get a shock when the plane dropped out from under you at an airspeed 10 K higher than you expected (it always stalls at 50 K down at sea level—what gives?). Of course, the airspeed indicator isn't likely to be accurate at the speeds close to the stall anyway, but you might not give yourself enough leeway in the approach in this case. (These are unaccelerated stalls.)

Several terms are used in talking about airspeed:

Indicated airspeed (IAS)—the airspeed as read off the standard airspeed indicator.

Calibrated airspeed (CAS)—indicated airspeed corrected for instrument and position error.

Equivalent airspeed (EAS)—calibrated airspeed corrected for compressibility effects.

True airspeed (TAS)—equivalent airspeed corrected for density effects.

Some Airspeed Theory

NOTES ON EQUIVALENT AIRSPEED. Equivalent airspeed (EAS) is the "correct" calibrated airspeed, and you couldn't go wrong by using the term in all of your hangar flying discussions for *corrected* indicated airspeed. Calibrated is fine for lower airspeeds and lower altitudes.

EAS, the actual dynamic pressure acting on the airframe, is used to get a correct picture of stresses on the airplane or to work out TAS problems if compressibility error is a factor. Fig. 4-3 is an exaggerated example of CAS versus EAS for sea level, 5000 and 10,000-ft pressure altitudes.

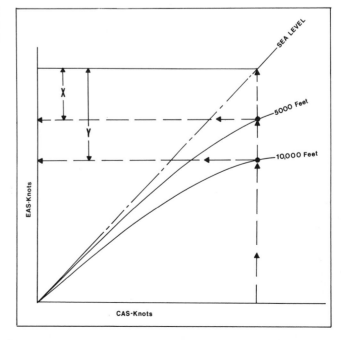

The point is that CAS is equal to, *or greater than,* EAS; the difference becomes greater with an increase in altitude and airspeed. The speed of sound decreases with altitude (and the temperature decrease), and as the airplane's airspeed increases, the compressibility "edge" is reached. One way it has been explained is that as the airplane gets into compressibility effects the *static pressure in the pitot tube* (and within the diaphragm as shown in Fig. 4-1) increases, causing the indicated—and calibrated—airspeeds to read erroneously high. A detailed correction table for a number of altitudes and airspeeds is available to pilots of higher-performance airplanes. (One table works for *all* airplanes for various airspeed and pressure altitudes.)

EAS, then, is the indicated airspeed corrected for instrument and position error (which gives CAS), and CAS is then corrected for compressibility effects.

One point about compressibility effects—it's assumed by a lot of people that the airplane itself has to be flying right at the speed of sound for the phenomenon to occur. However, curved parts of the airplane (canopy, wing, etc.) have the relative wind moving past them at near sonic velocities because of Bernoulli's theorem, even though the airplane's TAS is significantly lower than the transonic range. Some WW II fighters began to nibble at the edges of compressibility because of this factor, but stories of propeller fighters diving to supersonic speeds were exaggerated. Some late and post–WW II prop fighters (the Grumman F8F *Bearcat,* for example) had speed brakes to use if compressibility problems were encountered.

TRUE AIRSPEED. To find TAS or to establish a performance relationship between altitudes, engineers use the density ratio σ (sigma), which is the ratio between the air density at some altitude (ϱ_a) and at sea level (ϱ_0): $\sigma = \dfrac{\varrho_a}{\varrho_0}$.

The *true airspeed* (V) portion of the dynamic pressure, or $(\varrho/2)V^2$, is a function of the *square root* of the ratio of densities, or $V = f\sqrt{\varrho_a/\varrho_0}$, or $V = f\sqrt{\sigma}$; the relationship of dynamic pressure for a given CAS is

$$\frac{\varrho_a}{2}V_a^2 = \frac{\varrho_0}{2}V_0^2$$

To repeat, a CAS of 100 K at sea level is the same dynamic pressure as a CAS of 100 K at 10,000 ft; the airspeed indicator can't determine which factors (density or velocity) are making the diaphragm expand to register the same CAS (V_{cal}) in both instances. To solve for TAS (V_a) at, say, 10,000 ft you could use the square root of the density ratio. (The 2's can be eliminated since there's one on each side of the equation.)

$$V_a^2 = \frac{V_0^2}{\left(\frac{\varrho_a}{\varrho_0}\right)} = \frac{V_0^2}{\sigma}, \ V_a = \frac{V_0}{\sqrt{\sigma}}$$

$$\text{TAS} = \frac{\text{CAS (or EAS)}}{\sqrt{\text{density ratio}}} = \frac{\text{CAS}}{\sqrt{\sigma}}$$

$$V_{T10} = \frac{V_{cal}}{\sqrt{\sigma}}$$

See Fig. 4-4 for a standard atmosphere chart. At 10,000 ft ϱ is 0.001756; at sea level it's 0.002378, so using your calculator, or working it out in longhand and giving V_{cal} a universal value of 1:

$$V_{T10} = \frac{V_{cal}}{\sqrt{\dfrac{0.001756}{0.002378}}} = \frac{V_{cal}}{0.85933} = \frac{1}{0.85933} = 1.16369$$

STANDARD ATMOSPHERE CHART

Altitude (ft)	Pressure (in. Hg)	Pressure (psf)	Temp (°C)	Temp. (°F)	Density-slugs per cubic foot
0	29.92	2116.22	15.0	59.0	.002378
1,000	28.86	2040.85	13.0	55.4	.002309
2,000	27.82	1967.68	11.0	51.9	.002242
3,000	26.82	1896.64	9.1	48.3	.002176
4,000	25.84	1827.69	7.1	44.7	.002112
5,000	24.89	1760.79	5.1	41.2	.002049
6,000	23.98	1695.89	3.1	37.6	.001988
7,000	23.09	1632.93	1.1	34.0	.001928
8,000	22.22	1571.88	-0.9	30.5	.001869
9,000	21.38	1512.70	-2.8	26.9	.001812
10,000	20.57	1455.33	-4.8	23.3	.001756
11,000	19.79	1399.73	-6.8	19.8	.001701
12,000	19.02	1345.87	-8.8	16.2	.001648
13,000	18.29	1293.70	-10.8	12.6	.001596
14,000	17.57	1243.18	-12.7	9.1	.001545
15,000	16.88	1194.27	-14.7	5.5	.001496
16,000	16.21	1146.92	-16.7	1.9	.001448
17,000	15.56	1101.11	-18.7	-1.6	.001401
18,000	14.94	1056.80	-20.7	-5.2	.001355
19,000	14.33	1013.93	-22.6	-8.8	.001310
20,000	13.74	972.49	-24.6	-12.3	.001267

Fig. 4-4. Standard atmosphere chart.

The TAS at 10,000 ft is about 16% more than, or 1.164 times, that at sea level for the same calibrated (or better yet, equivalent) airspeed. A CAS of 100 K would give a TAS of about 116 K, as noted earlier.

For another problem, find the TAS for an airplane with a calibrated (equivalent) airspeed of *186 K* at a standard altitude of 17,000 ft. The value of ϱ at sea level is (still) 0.002378, and at 17,000 ft it's 0.001401 (Fig. 4-4). So the CAS (EAS) is divided by the square root of the ratio of the two densities. Under normal circumstances you'll have no problem figuring out that the square root of the ratio would be *less* than 1 because the TAS will *normally* be higher than the CAS or EAS (more about the word *normally* a little later). So $V_T = V_{cal}/\sqrt{\sigma}$; the divisor of the CAS is $\sqrt{\dfrac{0.001401}{0.002378}}$, or $\sqrt{\dfrac{1401}{2378}} = \sqrt{0.589} = 0.7675$ (rounded off). The TAS is $\dfrac{186}{0.7675} = 242$ K. Your computer does this for you.

The earlier comment about TAS *normally* being greater than CAS or EAS is correct, but in an unusual situation where the airplane is flying in an air density greater than sea level the TAS may be less than CAS or EAS. Suppose you are flying just off the surface of the Dead Sea in standard conditions. Since the Dead Sea is below mean sea level the airspeed indicator could have a density error "the wrong way." In extremely cold conditions at lower altitudes (but still above sea level) the density could be well above standard, so that things would be the reverse of normal. The airspeed indicators used for lower speeds and altitudes (say, below 250 K and below 10,000 ft) are set up on the base of using sea level density, and variations of the density *either way* from sea level must be corrected for. In usual (above sea level) flying, the density at the altitude being flown is always less than the density at sea level so the usual correction is made (TAS greater than CAS or EAS).

MACH AND MACH NUMBER. Ernst Mach (1838–1916), an Austrian physicist, published works on ballistics and fast-moving bodies in gases in the late 1870s and the 1880s. His major work preceded even the advent of aviation, much less transonic and supersonic flight, but it could be that he was getting ready for the airplane. (Many people also believe that the Federal Aviation Administration was established in 1803, a hundred years early, "just in case somebody should ever invent a flying machine." It's not true about the FAA, but Mach's studies were ready when higher-speed flight was attained).

The term *Mach number* is the ratio of the velocity of a

body in a gas to the speed of sound in that gas. As a pilot, you are interested in the speed of sound in *air*; it would be different in other gases and other mediums.

The speed of sound in air, 661 K at standard sea level, decreases with altitude (temperature), becoming 584 K at 36,000 ft where the temperature stabilizes for another 30,000 ft—at roughly −69°F.

An equation for finding the speed of sound (fps) is 49.1 $\sqrt{T_R}$ (49.1 times the square root of the temperature in degrees Rankine, which was discussed at the beginning of this chapter). You'd add 460° to the temperature (Fahrenheit) and take the square root of the sum. For instance, standard temperature at sea level is 59°F; 460 + 59 = 519°F. The speed of sound at sea level is $49.1\sqrt{519}$ = 1118 fps, or 661 K.

MACH METER. The Mach meter is designed to give the pilot the ratio of the airplane's airspeed to that of the speed of sound for both subsonic and supersonic flight (with corrections for the usual airspeed indicator problems of position and instrument errors). It has bellows to correct for static pressure and total and static pressure differences and reads this ratio at all altitudes and speeds.

MORE ABOUT AIRSPEED ERRORS. Starting out with IAS, which, as you've heard since you started flying, is what the instrument indicates, you may manipulate the system to get some far-off readings. One less than scrupulous used-airplane seller some years ago had a plastic ring set up around the pitot/static head of an airplane so that it would indicate higher airspeeds than could be explained by natural law. The light-plane, which at cruise normally would indicate about 90 mph, was suddenly converted into a 120-mph bombshell. The new owner was proud to have the hottest Buzzwind Two in the area, since it cruised 30 mph faster than the others and required much more pilot skill because it also landed at about 75 mph, compared with 45 mph for run-of-the-mill models. The seller got the money and the new owner the prestige (temporarily at least).

A *particular* airspeed indicator may indicate wrong because somebody dropped it on the way to installing it in the airplane, but this is an unusual situation.

FAR 23 (*Airworthiness Standards: Normal, Utility and Acrobatic Category Airplanes*) sets up the following maximum allowable system error for the manufacturer:

23.1323 Airspeed indicating system.
(a) Each airspeed indicating instrument must be calibrated to indicate true airspeed (at sea level with a standard atmosphere) with a minimum practicable instrument calibration error when the corresponding pitot and static pressures are applied.
(b) Each airspeed system must be calibrated in flight to determine the system error. The system error, including position error, but excluding the airspeed indicator instrument calibration error, may not exceed three percent of the calibrated airspeed or five knots, whichever is greater, throughout the following speed ranges:
(1) 1.3 V_{S1} to V_{MO}/M_{MO} or V_{NE}, whichever is appropriate with flaps retracted.
(2) 1.3 V_{S1} to V_{FE} with flaps extended.

(V_{MO}/M_{MO}, the maximum operating limit or Mach speed, is associated with higher speed aircraft.)

The airspeed correction tables in the *POH* (Fig. 4-5) assume that all the instruments in the various airplanes have the same problems and that no individual needles were bent, etc. Fig. 4-5 is for the normal static system and doesn't include the changes associated with use of alternate air sources (to be

AIRSPEED INDICATOR MARKINGS

MARKING	KIAS VALUE OR RANGE	SIGNIFICANCE
White Arc	42 - 85	Full Flap Operating Range. Lower limit is maximum weight V_{S0} in landing configuration. Upper limit is maximum speed permissible with flaps extended.
Green Arc	47 - 107	Normal Operating Range. Lower limit is maximum weight V_S at most forward C.G. with flaps retracted. Upper limit is maximum structural cruising speed.
Yellow Arc	107 - 141	Operations must be conducted with caution and only in smooth air.
Red Line	141	Maximum speed for all operations.

AIRSPEED CORRECTION TABLE
(Flaps Up)

IAS	40	50	60	70	80	90	100	110	120	130	140
CAS	51	57	65	73	82	91	100	109	118	127	136

(Flaps Down)

IAS	40	50	60	70	80	90	100				
CAS	49	55	63	72	81	89	98				

Fig. 4-5. Airspeed indicator markings and correction table (normal source).

covered later). (Airplanes manufactured as *1975 models or earlier* have the airspeed indicator markings as *calibrated* airspeed and usually in *mph*.)

To get CAS, corrections must be made for instrument and position error; if, for instance, you aren't sure of the accuracy of your airspeed indicator, you can fly the airplane between two points a known distance apart and work out your own correction table for instrument and system error. For example, to calibrate the airplane's airspeed system it would be nice to have a convenient railroad track with white-painted ties at each end of the run (Fig. 4-6).

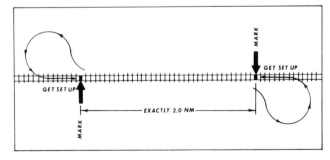

Fig. 4-6. Using a conveniently located railroad track or other straight reference, get set up and then start and stop the timing at the marks.

In books the distances are always easy to make even. "Your" track, however, could be 1.79 (or 2.87, etc.) mi long so you have to set up a correction factor. Picking a calm, early morning period and taking along an observer with a stopwatch, you would fly the route both ways at a low altitude at each airspeed desired. You might end up with a table like that in Fig. 4-7.

		FLAPS UP			
PA _1500'_	OAT _10°C_			CAS = TAS × $\sqrt{\sigma}$	
RUN	IAS-Knots	TIME-Sec	GS=TAS	AVER.TAS	CAS
1 EAST	60	110	65	—	—
WEST	60	108	67	66	65
2 E	70	96	75	—	—
W	70	98	74	74	73
3 E	80	87	83	—	—
W	80	88	82	82	81
4 E	90	79	91	—	—
W	90	79	91	91	90
5 E	100	72	100	—	—
W	100	73	99	99	97 RERUN
6 E	110	66	110	—	—
W	110	66	110	110	108
7 E	120	60	120	—	—
W	120	60	120	120	118
8 E	130	55	130	—	—
W	130	55	130	130	128
9 E	140	52	137	—	—
W	140	52	137	137	135
10 E	150	49	147	—	—
W	150	49	147	147	145

Fig. 4-7. A table made up from the runs in Fig. 4-6 (flaps up).

The point is that in calm conditions, groundspeed (GS) equals TAS, and since you have set your airplane's well-calibrated altimeter to 29.92, you're flying a known pressure altitude. With this, combined with the outside air temperature at that altitude read from the well-calibrated outside air temperature (OAT) gage on board, you can find density-altitude and work back from TAS (GS) to CAS. So for each IAS picked, you come up with a number of indicated and calibrated airspeeds to set up a table like that found in a *POH* (Fig. 4-8).

FLAPS UP										
KIAS	60	70	80	90	100	110	120	130	140	150
KCAS	65	73	81	90	97	108	118	128	135	145

Fig. 4-8. A correction card made for the airplane in Figs. 4-6 and 4-7.

In flying the airspeed calibration, if there is a crosswind you don't correct for drift but maintain a heading parallel to the railroad track (Fig. 4-9). The time start would be made when the reference point(s) is directly off the wing tip. The error is negligible for the distance flown because the airplane is flying within the air mass and doesn't "know" it's drifting.

There is some argument as to whether headwind and tailwind components cause error to creep in. By picking the calmest conditions possible, any error introduced is minimized, but look at an exaggerated example. If flying the 2-mi route in *no-wind* conditions requires 60 sec for each leg, the GS and TAS would be 120 K; the average for the two legs would be (120 + 120)/2 = 120 K.

Suppose there is a 30-K steady direct headwind on one leg and a 30-K direct tailwind on the other. The time required to fly the 2-mi leg in the headwind condition would be at 90 K,

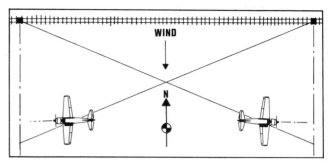

Fig. 4-9. Flight path in a crosswind.

or 80 sec. With a 30-K tailwind the stopwatch time for that distance would be at 150 K and would take 48 sec. Comparing:

Total time to go 4 mi (no wind) = 120 sec, or GS = *120 K*

Total time to go 4 mi (30-K wind) = 128 sec; 128/4 = 32 sec per NM, or *112.5 K*.

Airspeed calibration shouldn't be done in such conditions and any error would be much smaller as conditions approach calm, but the principle should be considered.

As noted earlier, flight test airplanes use an extended boom to get more accurate pitot (total pressure) and static pressure. This is fine for accuracy but would be too expensive for use on all airplanes.

Another one of the several methods for calibrating airspeeds is the *pacer method*, in which the airplane to be tested is "paced" at various indicated airspeeds by an airplane with a corrected airspeed system.

Sometimes pilots ask if each airplane manufactured is flown to the design dive speed (V_D—see Chap. 11), or has the airspeed indicator calibrated as just discussed, or has stability and control testing done. The answer is *no*. The prototype and test bed airplanes come up with the numbers and manufacturing tolerances that apply to all the airplanes that are manufactured later. Fig. 4-10 is actual airspeed calibration for a normal static source given in a *POH*.

Ground effect, or rather an airplane's proximity to the ground, can affect an airspeed system so that some *POH*s may

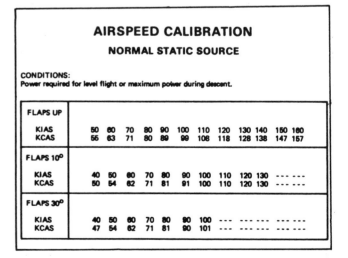

AIRSPEED CALIBRATION

NORMAL STATIC SOURCE

CONDITIONS:
Power required for level flight or maximum power during descent.

FLAPS UP											
KIAS	50	60	70	80	90	100	110	120	130	140	150 160
KCAS	56	63	71	80	89	99	108	118	128	138	147 157
FLAPS 10°											
KIAS	40	50	60	70	80	90	100	110	120	130	- - - - - -
KCAS	50	54	62	71	81	91	100	110	120	130	- - - - - -
FLAPS 30°											
KIAS	40	50	60	70	80	90	100	- - -	- - - - - -		
KCAS	47	54	62	71	81	90	101	- - -	- - - - - -		

Fig. 4-10. Airspeed calibration, normal static source, for a four-place retractable-gear airplane.

AIRSPEED CALIBRATION

ALTERNATE STATIC SOURCE

HEATER AND DEFROSTER FULL ON AND WINDOWS CLOSED

FLAPS UP										
NORMAL KIAS	50	60	70	80	90	100	110	120	140	160
ALTERNATE KIAS	46	58	69	79	88	98	108	117	136	155
FLAPS 10°										
NORMAL KIAS	50	60	70	80	90	100	110	120	130	...
ALTERNATE KIAS	45	58	69	80	90	100	109	119	128	...
FLAPS 30°										
NORMAL KIAS	50	60	70	80	90	100	...	...	...	...
ALTERNATE KIAS	46	58	68	78	87	96	...	...	...	...

Fig. 4-11. Airspeed calibration (alternate static source) for the airplane in Fig. 4-10.

have an additional correction graph or table for the takeoff run ("rotation at 90 K IAS = 94 K CAS"). The airplane in Fig. 4-10 has an alternate air source that supplies static pressure from inside the cabin if it's suspected that the normal static source (a port on each side of the forward fuselage in this airplane) is being affected by ice or water. Fig. 4-11 is an airspeed calibration for the alternate static source.

Note that the calibration is with the heater and defroster full ON and the windows closed, a likely setup when flying in icing or cold rain conditions (where problems with the normal system are most apt to occur).

Fig. 4-11 brings up an interesting point. It's usually considered that the pressure in the cabin (unpressurized airplane) will be slightly less than the ambient (outside) static pressure because of the effects of the relative wind moving past the airframe. Apparently, however, under the conditions cited the cabin pressure must be slightly higher to give the shown effect on the IAS.

Notice, too, in Fig. 4-11 that the alternate system IAS is nearly always lower than that for the normal system. There are some equal readings at 80, 90, and 100 K at 10° flaps, but basically the airspeed indicator reads less than normal.

Look at Fig. 4-11 and assume for purposes here that the KIAS with the *normal* source is "correct," that is, KIAS = KCAS. Also assume that the airplane is flying at sea level (pressure = 2116 psf, density = 0.002378 slugs per cubic

foot) at a normal KIAS (KCAS) of 120 K, flaps up. There is a 3-K difference caused by the higher cabin pressure here. You can find the difference between cabin pressure and outside pressure by the following equation: KIAS (KCAS also, for this example) = $(\varrho_0/2)V^2$. (It's assumed for now that the static pressure in the diaphragm and in the case are equal at 2116 psf. In other words, it's easier at first to assume that the imbalance is caused by a *low* dynamic pressure, find the value, and then correctly give that value to a higher cabin, or instrument case, pressure).

Check the dynamic pressures (rounded off), as if the airplane were *actually* going through the air at 120 and 117 K respectively and converting to feet per second (1.69 factor):

At 120 K, $\dfrac{\varrho_0 V^2}{2}$ = 0.002378/2 × (120 × 1.69)² or

$$\frac{\varrho_0 V^2}{2} = 0.002378/2 \times (202.8)^2 = 48.9 \text{ psf}$$

At 117 K, $\dfrac{\varrho_0 V^2}{2}$ = 0.002378/2 × (117 × 1.69)² or

$$\frac{\varrho_0 V^2}{2} = 0.002378/2 \times (197.7)^2 = 46.5 \text{ psf}$$

The 3-K drop was actually caused by a 2.4-psf *increase in cabin pressure* rather than a change (drop) in dynamic pressure (a change of pressure of 2.4/2116 = 0.001134, or a little over 0.11%).

The *total* pressure P, which equals the static and dynamic pressures p + q, at an indicated 120 K is 2116 + 48.9 = 2164.9. The actual total pressure (in the pitot tube and in the diaphragm) at an indicated 117 K should be the same (2164.9) because the airplane is actually moving at 120 K, but an error in indication has been introduced by a change in static pressure in the cabin and in the instrument case. (It has increased and is causing the diaphragm to be "compressed," resulting in a lower airspeed indication.) Fig. 4-12 gives an idea of what's happening.

The *POH* in this example does not have an altimeter correction for the alternate static source, but based on the just-learned facts, you know the altimeter would read *lower* on the alternate static source than on the normal source. (The reason, of course, is that the substitute *static* pressure being furnished to the altimeter is higher *so the altimeter "thinks" the airplane has descended*).

Checking Fig. 4-4 again and doing a little arithmetic, you will find that the altimeter, if zeroed at sea level on the normal source, would read about 32 ft lower when on the alternate

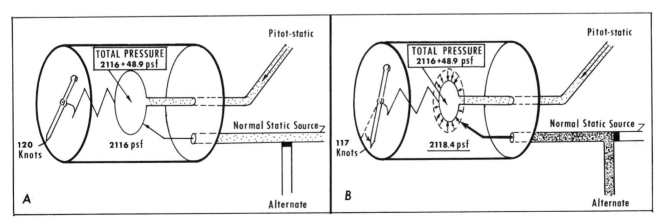

Fig. 4-12. A. The static pressure within the diaphragm and within the case are equal, so only the dynamic pressure is read, as it should be. B. Even though the total pressure (within the diaphragm) is correct, the *extra* pressure in the case induced by the alternate source allows the diaphragm to expand only about 117 K worth.

AIRSPEED CALIBRATION

ALTERNATE STATIC SOURCE

NOTES:
1. Indicated airspeed assumes zero instrument error.
2. The following calibrations are not valid in the pre-stall buffet.

VENTS AND HEATER CLOSED

FLAPS UP								
NORMAL KIAS	80	100	120	140	160	180	200	210
ALTERNATE KIAS	87	112	133	154	175	195	215	225
FLAPS 10°								
NORMAL KIAS	70	80	90	100	120	140	160	175
ALTERNATE KIAS	74	85	97	108	130	151	172	186
FLAPS 30°								
NORMAL KIAS	60	70	80	90	100	110	125	- - -
ALTERNATE KIAS	66	75	85	96	106	117	133	- - -

VENTS AND/OR HEATER OPEN

FLAPS UP								
NORMAL KIAS	80	100	120	140	160	180	200	210
ALTERNATE KIAS	85	108	130	151	171	192	211	221
FLAPS 10°								
NORMAL KIAS	70	80	90	100	120	140	160	175
ALTERNATE KIAS	73	84	95	106	127	147	167	182
FLAPS 30°								
NORMAL KIAS	60	70	80	90	100	110	125	- - -
ALTERNATE KIAS	62	72	81	93	102	113	129	- - -

ALTIMETER CORRECTION

ALTERNATE STATIC SOURCE

NOTE:
Add correction to desired altitude to obtain indicated altitude to fly.

VENTS AND HEATER CLOSED

CONDITION	CORRECTION TO BE ADDED - FEET							
	KIAS							
	80	90	100	120	140	160	180	200
FLAPS UP								
Sea Level	40	60	90	150	200	240	290	330
10,000 Ft.	50	80	120	180	250	310	370	430
20,000 Ft.	60	110	160	250	340	430	510	590
FLAPS 10°								
Sea Level	30	40	60	110	150	200	250	- - -
10,000 Ft.	40	60	90	140	200	260	330	- - -
20,000 Ft.	60	90	130	210	290	375	460	- - -
FLAPS 30°								
Sea Level	30	50	70	100	- - -	- - -	- - -	- - -
10,000 Ft.	40	60	80	130	- - -	- - -	- - -	- - -
20,000 Ft.	- - -	- - -	- - -	- - -	- - -	- - -	- - -	- - -

VENTS AND/OR HEATER OPEN

CONDITION	CORRECTION TO BE ADDED - FEET							
	KIAS							
	80	90	100	120	140	160	180	200
FLAPS UP								
Sea Level	20	30	50	90	130	190	240	300
10,000 Ft.	30	50	70	120	180	250	310	380
20,000 Ft.	50	80	110	180	260	350	440	530
FLAPS 10°								
Sea Level	10	30	40	80	110	150	190	- - -
10,000 Ft.	20	40	60	100	140	190	240	- - -
20,000 Ft.	30	60	90	150	210	270	340	- - -
FLAPS 30°								
Sea Level	10	20	30	50	- - -	- - -	- - -	- - -
10,000 Ft.	10	30	50	70	- - -	- - -	- - -	- - -
20,000 Ft.	- - -	- - -	- - -	- - -	- - -	- - -	- - -	- - -

Fig. 4-13. Alternate source corrections for the airspeed and altimeter of a particular airplane.

source. The reason is that sea level pressure is 2116 psf while at 1000 ft it's 2041 psf (rounded off), or a drop of 75 psf in that 1000 ft. The static pressure is 2.4 psf *higher* than standard for that altitude so it will change the altimeter indication *downward* by the following factor:

$$\frac{\text{static error (psf)} \times 1000}{\text{pressure change per 1000 ft (psf)}} = \frac{2.4}{75} \times 1000 = 32 \text{ ft}$$

The error would have to be 75 psf to get a 1000-foot change, but it was only 2.4 psf; $\frac{2.4}{75} \times 1000$, or about 32 ft). So the the altimeter will read about 32 ft low under the conditions cited.

Not too much error would be introduced if this was also the assumption for altitudes 1000 ft either side of sea level. Again checking Fig. 4-4 and subtracting, you'll find the pressure drop is 75 psf from sea level to 1000 ft, 73 psf from 1000 to 2000 ft, and 71 psf from 2000 to 3000 ft.

Fig. 4-13 has correction tables for a twin for airspeed and

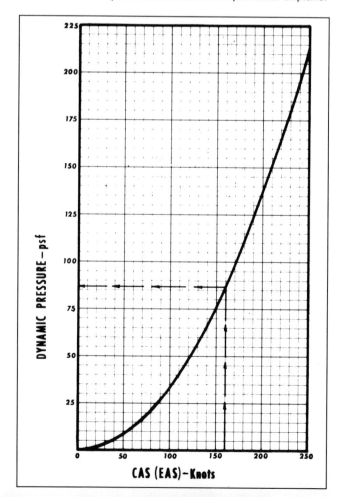

Fig. 4-14. Approximate pressure (psf) for various calibrated (or more accurately, equivalent) airspeeds. For example, at 160 K the dynamic pressure is approximately 87 psf.

altimeter when on the alternate system. The alternate system is vented within the nose section. Note that altitude is not a factor when correcting for CAS because calibrated airspeed (again) is a function of the combination of $(\varrho/2)V^2$. You can have a large ϱ and a comparatively small V, or at altitude ϱ may be small and V large. But at a particular airspeed (CAS or EAS, as applicable) q will always be the same, so a graph like Fig. 4-14 could be made.

You'll note, however, that altitude does have an effect on the altimeter correction because of the difference in rate of pressure change at various altitudes (Fig. 4-4). If the airspeed reads higher when on the alternate static source, so should the altimeter. In other words, if the static system pressure lowers when on the alternate system, it means that *the pressure in the ASI and altimeter instrument cases will be low.* And conversely if the airspeed on alternate indicates lower than the actual value, the altimeter will read lower than actual, as was worked out earlier.

The real point, of course, is to use the available *POH* corrections for airspeed and altimeter.

FAR 23 cites the following standards for a static pressure system:

23.1325 Static pressure system.

(a) Each instrument provided with static pressure case connections must be so vented that the influence of airplane speed, the opening and closing of windows, airflow variations, moisture, or other foreign matter will least affect the accuracy of the instruments except as noted in paragraph (b)(3) of this section.

(b) If a static pressure system is necessary for the functioning of instruments, systems, or devices, it must comply with the provisions of paragraphs (b)(1) through (3) of this section.

(1) The design and installation of a static pressure system must be such that—

(i) Positive drainage of moisture is provided;

(ii) Chafing of the tubing, and excessive distortion or restriction at bends in the tubing, is avoided; and

(iii) The materials used are durable, suitable for the purpose intended, and protected against corrosion.

(2) A proof test must be conducted to demonstrate the integrity of the static pressure system in the following manner:

(i) *Unpressurized airplanes.* Evacuate the static pressure system to a pressure differential of approximately 1 inch of mercury or to a reading on the altimeter 1,000 feet above the aircraft elevation at the time of the test. Without additional pumping for a period of 1 minute, the loss of indicated altitude must not exceed 100 feet on the altimeter.

(ii) *Pressurized airplanes.* Evacuate the static pressure system until a pressure differential equivalent to the maximum cabin pressure differential for which the airplane is type certificated is achieved. Without additional pumping for a period of 1 minute, the loss of indicated altitude must not exceed 2 percent of the equivalent altitude of the maximum cabin differential pressure or 100 feet, whichever is greater.

(3) If a static pressure system is provided for any instrument, device, or system required by the operating rules of this chapter, each static pressure port must be designed or located in such a manner that the correlation between air pressure in the static pressure system and true ambient atmospheric static pressure is not altered when the airplane encounters icing conditions. An anti-icing means or an alternate source of static pressure may be used in showing compliance with this requirement. If the reading of the altimeter, when on the alternate static pressure system differs from the reading of the altimeter when on the primary static system by more than 50 feet, a correction card must be provided for the alternate static system.

(c) Except as provided in paragraph (d) of this section, if the static pressure system incorporates both a primary and an alternate static pressure source, the means for selecting one or the other source must be designed so that—

(1) When either source is selected, the other is blocked off; and

(2) Both sources cannot be blocked off simultaneously.

(d) For unpressurized airplanes, paragraph (c)(1) of this section does not apply if it can be demonstrated that the static pressure system calibration, when either static pressure source is selected, is not changed by the other static pressure source being open or blocked.

(e) Each system must be designed and installed so that the error in indicated pressure altitude, at sea level, with a standard atmosphere, excluding instrument calibration error, does not result in an error of more than ±30 feet per 100 knots speed for the appropriate configuration in the speed range between 1.3 V_{s0} with flaps extended and 1.8 V_{s1} with flaps retracted. However, the error need not be less than ±30 ft.

Fig. 4-15 is a graphical presentation of an airspeed calibration chart (normal source). As an example, an IAS of 120 K results in a CAS of approximately 118 K.

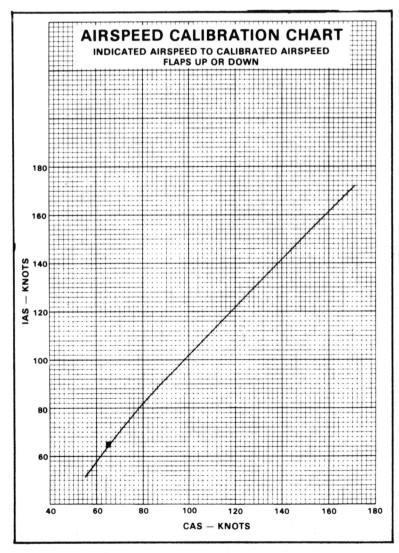

Fig. 4-15. Graphical presentation of an airspeed calibration chart.

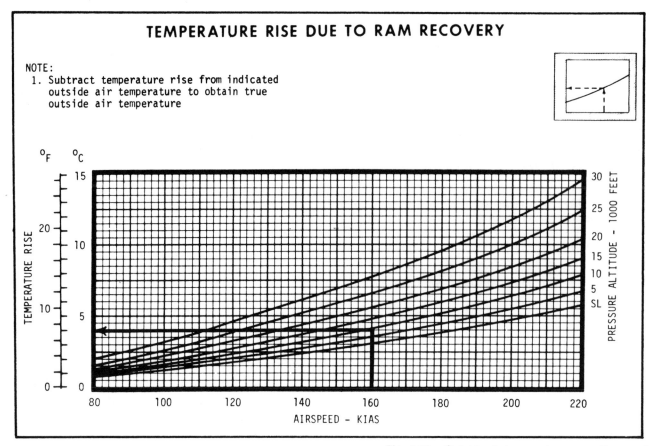

Fig. 4-16. Outside air temperature correction graph.

OTHER AIRSPEED FACTORS. Fig. 4-16 is a correction graph for the outside air temperature gage. At 160 K IAS at 10,000 ft you should *subtract* approximately 4°C (7°F) from what the OAT gage indicates.

While it might not directly apply to the previous discussion about airspeed, you should be aware that most airplanes of normal configuration, with a stabilizer or stabilator and a tail-down force, stall at a higher indicated (or calibrated or equivalent) airspeed with a forward CG because, as was noted earlier, as the CG moves forward the tail-down force must be increased to maintain equilibrium. Fig. 4-17 is an actual stall speed chart for most rearward and forward CGs for a particular weight.

The altimeter problems associated with using the alternate static system were discussed briefly earlier. However, any problems caused by use of the alternate are minor compared with having a totally plugged static system. In many nonpressurized airplanes the alternate static system gets static pressure from the cabin area; for pressurized airplanes this wouldn't work, since the cabin may be at 8000 ft and the airplane (and outside pressure) at 20,000 ft. Fig. 4-18 shows the normal pitot/static system and the alternate static system for a popular pressurized twin.

AIRSPEED INDICATOR MARKINGS. The FAA requires that the airspeed indicator be marked for various important speeds and speed ranges.

Red line—never-exceed speed (V$_{NE}$). This speed should not be exceeded at any time.

Yellow arc—caution range. Strong vertical gusts could damage the airplane in this speed range; therefore it is best to refrain from flying in this speed range when encountering turbulence of any intensity. The caution range starts at the maximum structural cruising speed and ends at the never-exceed speed (V$_{NE}$).

STALL SPEEDS

CONDITIONS:
Power Off
Gear Up or Down

NOTES:
1. Maximum altitude loss during a stall recovery may be as much as 230 feet.
2. KIAS values are approximate

MOST REARWARD CENTER OF GRAVITY

WEIGHT LBS	FLAP DEFLECTION	ANGLE OF BANK							
		0°		30°		45°		60°	
		KIAS	KCAS	KIAS	KCAS	KIAS	KCAS	KIAS	KCAS
2650	UP	46	54	49	58	55	64	65	76
	10°	42	52	45	56	50	62	59	74
	30°	39	50	42	54	47	59	56	71

MOST FORWARD CENTER OF GRAVITY

WEIGHT LBS	FLAP DEFLECTION	ANGLE OF BANK							
		0°		30°		45°		60°	
		KIAS	KCAS	KIAS	KCAS	KIAS	KCAS	KIAS	KCAS
2650	UP	51	57	55	61	61	68	72	81
	10°	46	54	49	58	55	64	65	76
	30°	42	51	45	55	50	61	59	72

Fig. 4-17. Stall speeds at center of gravity extremes.

PITOT STATIC SYSTEM

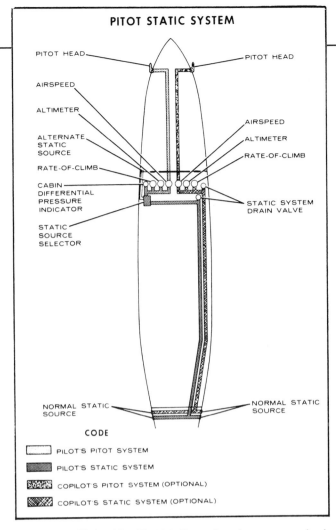

PITOT HEAD

PITOT HEAD

AIRSPEED

ALTIMETER

AIRSPEED

ALTERNATE
STATIC
SOURCE

ALTIMETER

RATE-OF-CLIMB

RATE-OF-CLIMB

CABIN
DIFFERENTIAL
PRESSURE
INDICATOR

STATIC SYSTEM
DRAIN VALVE

STATIC
SOURCE
SELECTOR

NORMAL STATIC
SOURCE

NORMAL STATIC
SOURCE

CODE

☐ PILOT'S PITOT SYSTEM

▨ PILOT'S STATIC SYSTEM

▨ COPILOT'S PITOT SYSTEM (OPTIONAL)

▨ COPILOT'S STATIC SYSTEM (OPTIONAL)

Fig. 4-18. Pitot/static system for a pressurized twin. Note that the alternate static air source is in the nose compartment.

Green arc—normal operating range. The airspeed at the lower end of this arc is the flaps-up, gear-up, power-off stall speed at gross weight (V_{S1}) (for most airplanes, the landing gear position has no effect on stall speed). The upper end of the green arc is the maximum structural cruising speed (V_{N0}), the maximum IAS where no structural damage would occur in moderate vertical gust conditions.

White arc—flap operating range. The lower limit is the stall speed at gross weight with the flaps in the *landing position,* and the upper limit is the maximum flap operating speed.

Airplanes manufactured as 1976 models or later have the airspeed indicator markings as *indicated* airspeed and knots. (Instrument markings before that were CAS and usually mph.)

FAR 1 gives the following definitions of various airspeeds (the maneuvering speed V_A and max landing gear extended speed V_{LE} are not marked on the airspeed indicator):

V_A means design maneuvering speed.

V_B means design speed for maximum gust intensity.

V_C means design cruising speed.

V_D means design diving speed.

V_{DF}/M_{DF} means demonstrated flight diving speed.

V_F means design flap speed.

V_{FC}/M_{FC} means maximum speed for stability characteristics.

V_{FE} means maximum flap extended speed.

V_H means maximum speed in level flight with maximum continuous power.

V_{LE} means maximum landing gear extended speed.

V_{LO} means maximum landing gear operating speed.

V_{LOF} means lift-off speed.

V_{MC} means minimum control speed with the critical engine inoperative.

V_{MO}/M_{MO} means maximum operating limit speed.

V_{MU} means minimum unstick speed.

V_{NE} means never-exceed speed.

V_{NO} means maximum structural cruising speed.

V_R means rotation speed.

V_S means the stalling speed or the minimum steady flight speed at which the airplane is controllable.

V_{S0} means the stalling speed or the minimum steady flight speed in the landing configuration.

V_{S1} means the stalling speed or the minimum steady flight speed obtained in a specific configuration.

V_X means speed for best angle of climb.

V_Y means speed for best rate of climb.

V_1 means takeoff decision speed (formerly denoted as critical engine failure speed).

V_2 means takeoff safety speed.

V_2 *min* means minimum takeoff safety speed.

Altimeter Review. The altimeter is an aneroid barometer calibrated in feet instead of inches of mercury. Its job is to measure the static pressure (or ambient pressure as it is sometimes called) and register this fact in terms of feet or thousands of feet.

The altimeter has an opening that allows static (outside) pressure to enter the otherwise sealed case. A series of sealed diaphragms or "aneroid wafers" within the case are mechanically linked to the three indicating hands. Since the wafers are sealed, they retain a constant internal "pressure" and expand or contract in response to the changing atmospheric pressure surrounding them in the case. As the aircraft climbs, the atmospheric pressure decreases and the sealed wafers expand; this is duly noted by the indicating hands as an increase in altitude (or vice versa).

Standard sea level pressure is 29.92 in. of mercury and the operations of the altimeter are based on this fact. Any change in local pressure must be corrected by the pilot. This is done by using the setting knob to set the proper barometric pressure (corrected to sea level) in the setting window.

True altitude is the height above sea level. *Absolute altitude* is the height above terrain. *Pressure altitude* is the altitude read when the altimeter is set to 29.92. This indication shows what your altitude would be if the altimeter setting were 29.92—that is, if it were a standard pressure day. *Indicated altitude* is the altitude read when the altimeter is set at the local barometric pressure corrected to sea level.

Density-altitude is the pressure altitude computed with temperature. The density-altitude is used in performance. If you know your density-altitude, air density can be found by tables and airplane performance calculated. You go through this step every time you use a computer to find the TAS. You use the pressure altitude and the outside air temperature and get the TAS. Usually there's not enough difference in pressure altitude and indicated altitude to make it worthwhile to set up 29.92 in the altimeter setting window, so that the usual procedure is to use the *indicated* altitude.

The fact that the computer used pressure altitude and temperature to obtain density-altitude in finding TAS didn't mean much as you were only interested in the final result. You may not even have been aware that you were working with the density-altitude during the process. Some computers also allow you to read the density-altitude directly by setting up pressure altitude and temperature. This is handy in figuring the performance of your airplane for a high-altitude and/or high-temperature takeoff or landing. The *POH* gives graphs or figures for takeoff and landing performance at the various density-altitudes. After finding your density-altitude, you can find your predicted performance in the *POH*.

The newest route is for the manufacturer to furnish performance data for various temperatures and pressure altitudes (a combination resulting in density-altitudes); you can then use the graph or table information to get answers for particular situations. Fig. 4-19 is an altitude conversion chart that might be part of a graphical presentation of, for instance, a takeoff chart.

Suppose you are at an airport at a pressure altitude of 6000 ft and the temperature is 80°F. Using the conversion chart you see that your density-altitude is 8500 ft (Fig. 4-19). Looking at the takeoff curves you can see that your expected distance to clear a 50-ft obstacle will be nearly 2300 ft at your gross Weight of 4800 lb (Fig. 4-20). This is more than double the distance at sea level and might be a handy fact to know.

You and other pilots fly indicated altitude. When you're flying cross-country you will have no idea of your exact altitude above the terrain (although over level country you can check airport elevations on the way, subtract this from your indicated altitude, and have a barnyard figure). Over mountainous terrain this won't work, as the contours change too abruptly for you to hope to keep up with them. As you fly you'll get altimeter settings from various ground stations and keep up to date on pressure changes.

The use of indicated altitude for all planes makes good sense in that all pilots are using sea level as a base point. If each pilot set the altimeter at zero before taking off, you can imagine what pandemonium would reign.

ALTIMETER ERRORS. *Instrument error*—Being a mechanical contrivance the altimeter is subject to various quirks. If you set the current barometric pressure—corrected to sea level—for your airport (if you have a tower or Flight Service Station), the altimeter should indicate the field elevation when you're on the ground.

FAR 91 specifies that airplanes operating in controlled airspace (IFR) must have had each static pressure system and each altimeter instrument tested by the manufacturer or an FAA-approved repair station within the past 24 calendar months.

Pressure changes—When you fly from a high-pressure area into a low-pressure area, the altimeter "thinks" you have climbed and will register accordingly—even if you haven't changed altitude. You'll see this and will fly the plane down to the "correct altitude," and will actually be low. When you fly from a low- to a high-pressure area the altimeter thinks you've let down to a lower altitude and registers too low. A good way to remember (although you can certainly reason it out each time) is HLH—High to Low, (altimeter reads) High; LHL—Low to High, (altimeter reads) Low.

You can see that it is worse to fly from a high- to a low-pressure area as far as terrain clearance is concerned. You might find that the clouds have rocks in them. So get frequent altimeter settings as you fly cross-country. (Don't try flying IFR unless rated.)

Temperature errors—Going back to the equation of state for air where pressure = density × temperature × 1716, you see the relationship between temperature and pressure. For our purposes we can say that pressure is *proportional* to density × temperature ($P \propto \varrho T$) and get rid of the constant number 1716. Assuming the density remains constant, for simplicity you can then say that pressure is proportional to temperature. Therefore, if you are flying at a certain altitude and the temperature is higher than normal, the pressure at your altitude is higher than normal. *The altimeter registers*

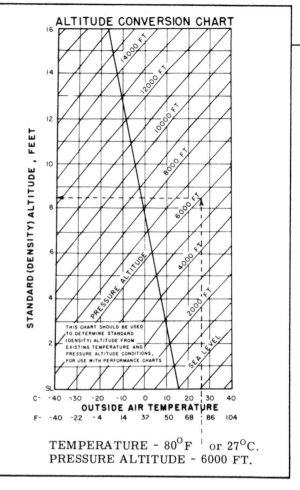

TEMPERATURE - 80°F or 27°C.
PRESSURE ALTITUDE - 6000 FT.

Fig. 4-19. Altitude conversion chart.

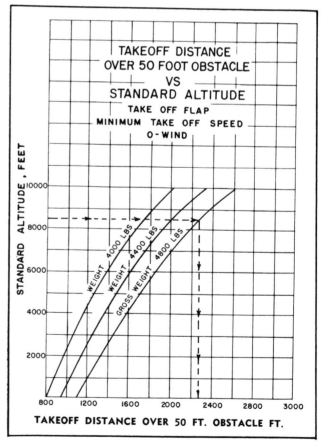

Fig. 4-20.

this as a lower altitude. If the temperature is lower, the pressure is lower and the altimeter will register accordingly — *lower temperature, altimeter reads higher.*

You might remember it this way, using the letters H and L as in pressure changes: temperature High, (altimeter reads) Low — HL; temperature Low, (altimeter reads) High — LH. Or perhaps you'd prefer to remember HALT (High Altimeter because of Low Temperature). The best thing, however, is to know that higher temperature means higher pressure (and vice versa) at altitude and reason it out from there.

The temperature error is zero at the surface point at which the setting is obtained and increases with altitude, so the error could easily be 500 to 600 ft at the 10,000-level. In other words, you can have this error at altitude even if the altimeter reads correctly at the surface point at which the setting originated. Temperature error can be found with a computer (Fig. 4-21). For indicated altitude this error is neglected, but it makes a good question for an FAA written exam or flight test — and it has been used!

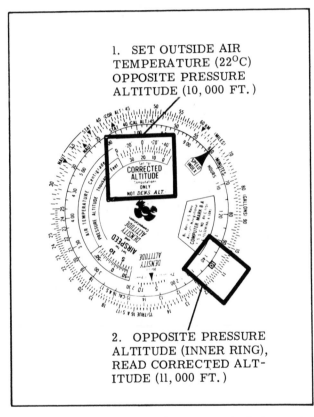

1. SET OUTSIDE AIR TEMPERATURE (22°C) OPPOSITE PRESSURE ALTITUDE (10,000 FT.)

2. OPPOSITE PRESSURE ALTITUDE (INNER RING), READ CORRECTED ALTITUDE (11,000 FT.)

Fig. 4-21. Using the computer to find corrected pressure altitude.

These errors (particularly temperature errors, which are normally ignored) affect everybody in that area (though slightly different for different altitudes) so that the altitude separation is still no problem. Temperature errors *could* cause problems as far as terrain clearance is concerned, however.

Hugh R. Skinner (see the Introduction to the Fifth Edition) has suggested some pilot considerations to observe before and during flight; here are a couple of particularly important ones:

1. Check the static ports. If the static ports are clogged or if there are large dents or protrusions *in the vicinity* of the ports a considerable static pressure error can be created, especially at high airspeeds. (For instance, mud blobs may have

been splashed up on the airframe *near* the ports and cause an erroneous static pressure.) You generally check the static ports themselves but may not notice that dried mud or new large dent near them.

2. Check for barometric correlation as often as possible, preferably before departure. Unless a large error exists don't jump on the instrument too quickly. Temperature, pressure, aircraft elevation, mechanical recovery (has it settled down?), and other problems cause short-term discrepancies in the indication of a good altimeter. Note the error and apply it to subsequent altimeter setting reports until further checks can be made. If the error persists, corrective service should be done.

ALTIMETER TIPS. You can convert your indicated altitude to pressure altitude without resetting the altimeter to 29.92 by looking at your altimeter setting. Suppose your altimeter registers 4000 ft and the current setting is 30.32 in. of mercury. Your pressure altitude is 3600 ft and is arrived at by the following: the pressure corrected to sea level is 30.32 in., but to get pressure altitude the setting should be based on 29.92 in. This shows that the actual pressure of 30.32 is *higher* than standard; therefore the pressure altitude is *less.* (Higher pressures at lower altitudes.) Using a figure of 1 in. per 1000 ft you see that the pressure difference is 0.40 inches of mercury or 400 ft. The pressure altitude is 4000 − 400 = 3600 ft. This will be as close as you can read an altitude conversion chart anyway. If the altimeter setting had been 29.52 your pressure altitude would be 400 ft higher (29.92 − 29.52 = 0.40 in. = 400 ft) or 4400 ft.

For estimation of pressure altitude without resetting: If your altimeter setting is *lower* than 29.92, *add* 100 ft to your indicated altitude for each 0.10 in. difference. If your altimeter setting is *higher* than 29.92, *subtract* 100 ft from your indicated altitude for each 0.10 in. difference to get the pressure altitude. The reason for this little mental exercise is to get you familiar with working between pressure and indicated altitude. You may prefer to note your altimeter setting (so you can return the altimeter to the indicated altitude after getting the pressure altitude), and then set the altimeter to 29.92 to get the pressure altitude. After this is done you can return to the original indicated altitude setting.

For computer work you are told to use the *pressure altitude* to find the TAS. For practical work use *indicated altitude* (current sea level setting) for TAS computations. Remember that the TAS increases about 2% per 1000 ft so the most you will be off will be 2%. That is, your sea level altimeter setting could possibly be 28.92 or 30.92, but this is extremely unlikely. So...

Assume that a total error of no more than 1% will be introduced by use of indicated altitude. For a 200-K airplane this means you could be 2 K off for TAS. But the instrument error or your error in reading the instrument could be this much.

One thing to remember concerning the altimeter that is useful for written tests and hangar flying sessions: *If you increase the numbers in the setting window* (by using the setting knob, naturally), *the altitude reading is also increased* — and vice versa. If you have the altimeter originally set at 29.82 as the sea level pressure while flying and get an altimeter setting of 30.02 from a station in your area, you'll find that in rolling in that *additional* 0.20 in. you've also given the altimeter an *additional* 200 ft of *indicated* altitude. This also follows from the earlier LHL idea; when flying from a Low (29.82) to a High (30.02) the altimeter reads Low (until you put it right by rolling in the added 0.20 in. in the setting window and adding another 200 ft to your indicated altitude).

ENCODING ALTIMETER. As you progress in aviation (you may

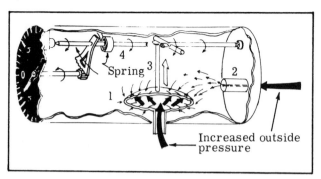

Fig. 4-23. Vertical speed indicator. As the airplane descends, the outside pressure increases. The diaphragm expands immediately (1). Because of the small size of the capillary tube (2), the pressure within the case is not increased at the same rate. The link (3) pushes upward rotating the shaft (4), which causes the needle to indicate the proper rate of descent. The spring helps return the needle to zero when pressures are equal and also acts as a dampener.

Fig. 4-22. Two types of encoders. (*King Radio Corporation*)

have your instrument rating before you read this) you'll use more sophisticated electronics equipment, including encoding altimeters (Fig. 4-22).

The encoding altimeter, which is part of the transponder system (Mode C), provides automatic altitude reporting to equipped ATC facilities. A 4096 code transponder with Mode C equipment is required for operating within Group I Terminal Control areas.

The two basic types of installations are (1) an altimeter with an internal altitude encoder and (2) a "blind" encoder for use with an existing altimeter. (Or matched sets are available as shown in Fig. 4-22.)

ALTIMETER SUMMARY. On the commercial written test (airplane) be ready to answer questions on the relationship of temperature and pressure effects on indicated and density-altitude. There are also questions on the test about the altimeter and alternate air sources and the usual assumption is that if the emergency alternate static source of an airplane is used the altimeter will always read *high*. In some airplanes, particularly with vents or windows open, the "correct" altitude may be noticeably lower than on the altimeter, and the amount will vary with airspeed. The answer is, of course, to check the *POH* for *your* airplane.

Rate of Climb or Vertical Speed Indicator. Like the altimeter, the vertical speed indicator has a diaphragm. But unlike the altimeter, it measures the *rate of change* of pressure rather than the pressure itself.

The diaphragm has a tube connecting it to the static tube of the airspeed indicator and altimeter (or the tube may just have access to the cabin air pressure in the case of cheaper or lighter installations). This means that the inside of the diaphragm has the same pressure as the air surrounding the airplane. Opening into the otherwise sealed instrument case is a capillary tube.

Fig 4-23 is a schematic diagram of a typical rate of climb indicator. As an example, suppose the airplane is flying at a constant altitude. The pressure within the diaphragm is the same as that of the air surrounding it in the instrument case. The rate of climb is indicated as zero.

When the plane is put into a glide or dive, air pressure

inside the diaphragm increases at the same rate as that of the surrounding air. However, because of the small size of the capillary tube, the pressure in the instrument case does not change at the same rate. In a glide or dive the diaphragm expands, the amount of expansion depending on the difference of pressures. As the diaphragm is mechanically linked to a hand, the appropriate rate of descent in hundreds (or thousands) of feet per minute is read on the instrument face. In a climb the pressure in the diaphragm decreases faster than that within the instrument case, so the needle will indicate an appropriate rate of climb.

Because in a climb or dive the pressure in the case is always "behind" the diaphragm pressure in the above described instrument, a lag of 6 to 9 sec results. The instrument will still indicate a vertical speed for a short time after the plane is leveled off. For this reason the rate of climb indicator is not used to maintain altitude. On days when the air is bumpy, this lag is particularly noticeable. The rate of climb indicator is used as a check of the plane's climb, dive, or glide rate. The altimeter is used to maintain a constant altitude.

There is a more expensive rate of climb indicator (Instantaneous Vertical Speed Indicator) on the market that does not have lag and is very accurate even in bumpy air. It contains a piston-cylinder arrangement whereby the airplane's vertical acceleration is immediately noted. The pistons are balanced by their own weights and springs. When a change in vertical speed is effected, the pistons are displaced and an immediate change of pressures in the cylinders is created. This pressure is transmitted to the diaphragm, producing an almost instantaneous change in indication. After the acceleration-induced pressures fade, the pistons are no longer displaced, and the diaphragm and capillary tube act as on the old type of indicator (as long as there is no acceleration). The actions of the acceleration elements and the diaphragm-capillary system overlap for smooth action.

It's possible to fly with this type of instrument as accurately as with an altimeter, but the price may be out of the range of the owner of a lighter plane.

MAGNETIC COMPASS

The Earth's Magnetic Field. As noted in hundreds of aviation books, the magnetic poles are not located at the geographic poles; this may be a large or small factor in navigation, depending on where you are.

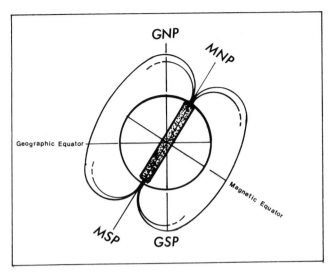

Fig. 4-24. The earth as a bar magnet.

close to the poles and there are some prodigious variation values there. (Incidentally, if you do the experiment with the magnet and iron filings keep a sheet of paper between the two systems unless you particularly enjoy picking filings off a magnet.)

Note that the western hemisphere and the United States have relatively small variation values, which is an aid to navigation in those major aviation areas; it's doubtful if nature planned it that way.

Fig. 4-26 shows the isogonic lines for the United States in 1980. The agonic line (0° variation) runs down the eastern edge of Lake Michigan, through the western edge of Franklin County, Tenn. (point A), and along the west coast of the Florida peninsula.

A brief review if you've laid off the theory for a while: The magnetic compass naturally points to the Magnetic North Pole, and this leads to the necessity of correcting for the angle between the Magnetic and Geographic North Poles. Normally a course will be measured on the chart from a meridian at a midpoint distance; this is the "true course" (the course as referred to the True or Geographic North Pole). To get the magnetic course, remember that *going from true to magnetic* (whether a course or heading):

East is least—subtract East variation as shown on the sectional or WAC chart.

West is best—add West variation as shown on the sectional or WAC chart.

The variation (15° E or 10° W) given by the isogonic lines means that the Magnetic North Pole is 15 degrees east or 10 degrees west of the True North Pole—from your position as far as the compass is concerned. Naturally, if you happen to be at a point where the two poles are magnetically in line, the variation will be zero.

The earth may be considered as a bar magnet in a sphere (Fig. 4-24), and for the record the magnetic poles are displaced about 11° from the geographic ones. It would seem by looking at Fig. 4-24 that the solution is a straightforward, straight line correction for the "angle" between the poles and that the flux lines would be symmetrical, as illustrated in a simple experiment with a magnet and iron filings. It's not so simple for the earth. As shown on navigation charts and in Fig. 4-25, the isogonic lines (lines of equal variation) seem to have a random pattern. The line system gets rather cluttered

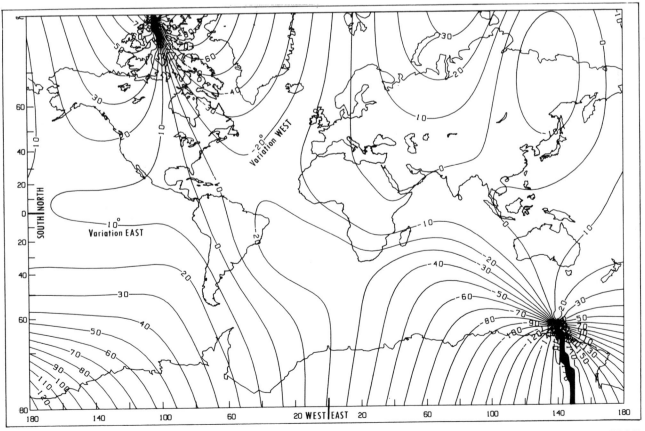

Fig. 4-25. Worldwide variation values (1980). A minus sign indicates westerly variation. (*NASA*)

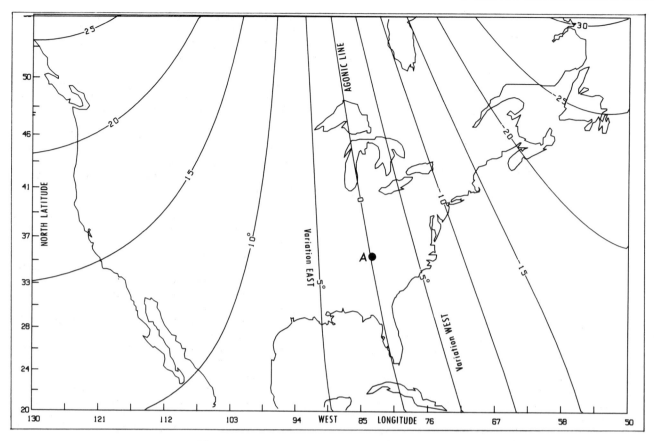

Fig. 4-26. Variation for the United States (1980). Point A will be looked at again. (*NASA*)

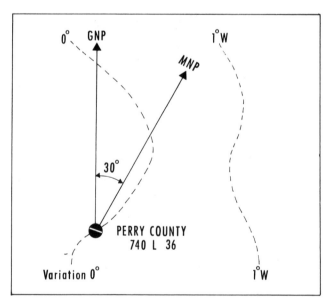

Fig. 4-27. An exaggerated look at isogonic line bending.

Fig. 4-27 shows that the variation is a magnetic angle rather than a geometric one. In this exaggerated example, at Perry County airport the geometric angle between the poles is 30° but the variation (magnetic angle) is 0° because the agonic and isogonic lines wander and set up their own "magnetic meridians."

In addition to the overall effects of the earth's magnetic field, there are also local and regional anomalies. These are considered to be the result of clockwise and counterclockwise vortices of electric currents located at the earth's core beneath these points. Large deposits of iron ore may affect the magnetic compass indications in certain locations (Fig. 4-28).

Magnetic pole reversals have been indicated over the past 6,000,000 years (don't ask who did the studies), and during that period the average lifetime of a geomagnetic field polarity, either normal or reverse, was 230,000 years but individual lifetimes varied considerably. This means that you'd better quit dragging your feet and get that commercial certificate before these data on magnetism are obsolete.

Variation of variation — Variation varies (sorry) from year to year (Fig. 4-29). You'll notice that in the southeastern United States the variation is moving "westerly" by 10 min per year (or at least that was the rate during 1980). The rate may vary from year to year. As Fig. 4-29 shows, there are pockets of fairly high variation change such as in South America and southern Africa.

Fig. 4-30 shows the change in variation for the United States and part of Canada. The area at point A (on the agonic line) has westward movement of variation at the rate of 10 min per year; in other words, variation lines are moving westward at that rate.

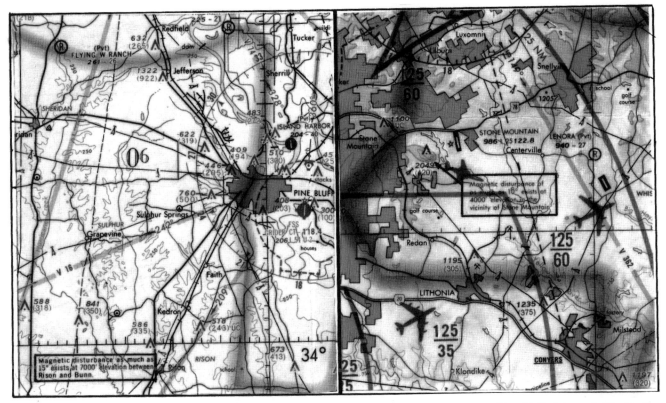

Fig. 4-28. Examples of local magnetic disturbances, near Pine Bluff, Ark., and Atlanta, Ga.

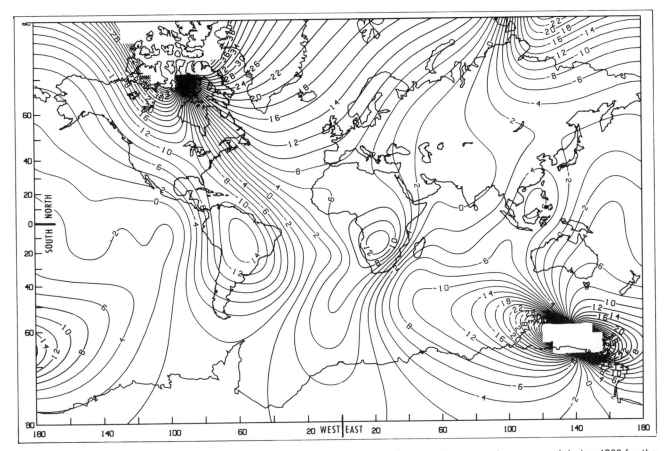

Fig. 4-29. Variation change, minutes of longitude per year (as measured during 1980 for the world). A minus sign indicates that the variation is becoming more westerly. (*NASA*)

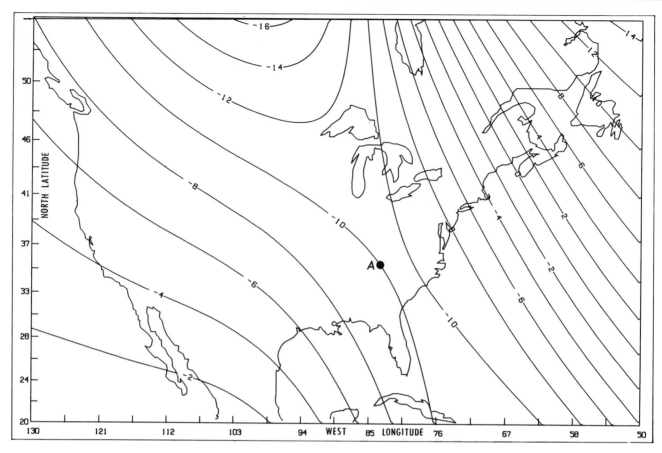

Fig. 4-30. Variation change for the United States and part of Canada (1980). Point A is Sewanee, Tenn. (*NASA*)

To better illustrate this, look at Fig. 4-31. Note that in 1960 the agonic line was at Knoxville, but in 1982 that line had moved geographically *west* to just east of Nashville, from there meandering southward to near Sewanee. Looking at a point just east of Nashville where the 1982 agonic line and the 1960 3° E isogonic line cross, you can see that variation at that geographic point has changed 3° (180 minutes) in 22 yr, an average of a little over 8 minutes per year. This was slightly below the actual change of 10 minutes given for 1980 in Fig. 4-30.

Compass Factors. Okay, so the magnetic compass is a magnet that aligns itself with the Magnetic North Pole while the airplane turns around it (Fig. 4-32). You are familiar enough with the compass so that an involved description isn't needed, but some review on using the compass may be helpful. The magnets in the compass tend to align themselves parallel to the earth's lines of magnetic force. This tendency is more noticeable as the Magnetic North Pole is approached. The compass would theoretically point straight down when directly over the pole (Figs. 4-24 and 4-33). The compass card is mounted so that a low CG location fights this dipping tendency. Dip causes certain errors to be introduced into the compass readings and should be noted as follows.

NORTHERLY TURNING ERROR. In a shallow turn the compass

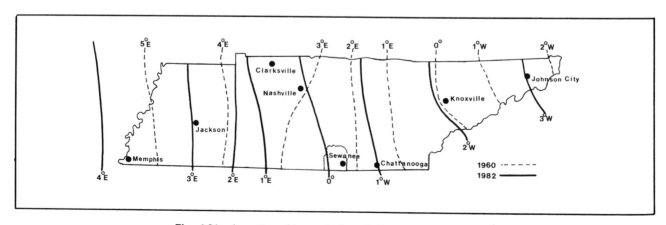

Fig. 4-31. Location of isogonic lines in Tennessee in 1960 (dashed lines) and 1982 (solid lines).

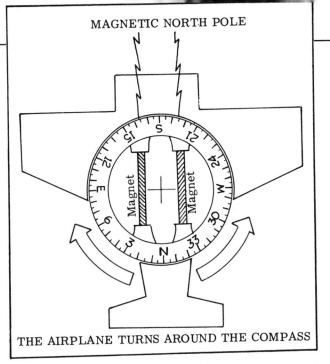

Fig. 4-32. The magnetic compass.

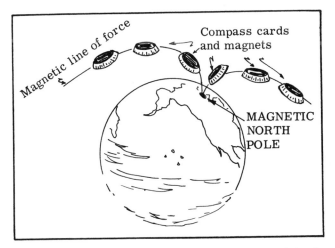

Fig. 4-33. The compass magnets tend to lie parallel with the earth's lines of magnetic force.

leads by about 30° when passing through South and lags by about 30° when passing through North (30° is a rule of thumb for U.S. use). On passing East and West headings in the turn, the compass is approximately correct.

For instance, you are headed South and decide to make a *left* turn and fly due North. As soon as the left bank is entered, the compass will indicate about 30° of left turn, when actually the nose has hardly started to move. *So, when a turn is started from a heading of South, the compass will indicate an extra fast turn in the direction of bank.* It will then hesitate and move slowly again so that as the heading of East is passed, it will be approximately correct. The compass will lag as North is approached so that you will roll out when the magnetic compass indicates 030° degrees (or "3"). (See Fig. 4-34.)

If you make a right turn from a South heading, the same effects occur: an immediate indication of turn in the direction of bank, a correct reading at a heading of West, and a compass lag of 30° when headed North.

If you start a turn from a heading of North, the compass will initially register a turn in the opposite direction but will soon race back and be approximately correct as an East or West heading is passed. It will then lead by about 30° as the airplane's nose points to Magnetic South. The initial errors in the turn are not too important. Set up your turn and know what to expect after the turn is started.

Here is a simple rule to cover the effects of bank (assuming a shallow bank of 20° or less—if the bank is too steep the rule won't work).

NORTHERLY TURNING ERRORS—NORTHERN HEMISPHERE. North heading—compass *lags* 30° at start of turn, or in the turn.

South heading—compass *leads* 30° at start of turn, or in the turn.

East or West heading—compass correct at start of turn, or in the turn.

Just remember that North *lags* 30° and South *leads* 30°, and this covers the problem. *Actually 30° is a round figure; the lead or lag depends on the latitude, but 30° degrees is close enough for the work you'll be doing with the magnetic compass and is easy to remember.*

ACCELERATION ERRORS. Because of its correction for dip, the compass will react to acceleration and deceleration of the airplane. This is most apparent on East or West headings, where

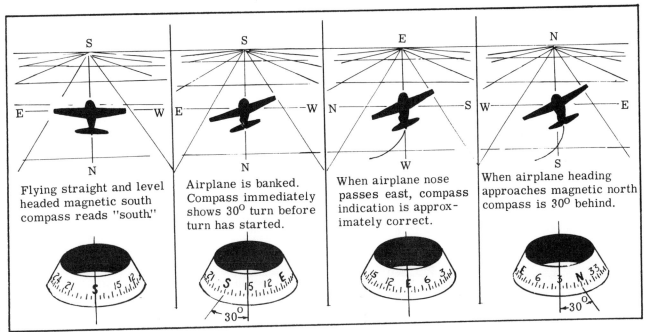

Flying straight and level headed magnetic south compass reads "south."

Airplane is banked. Compass immediately shows 30° turn before turn has started.

When airplane nose passes east, compass indication is approximately correct.

When airplane heading approaches magnetic north compass is 30° behind.

Fig. 4-34. Compass reactions to a turn.

acceleration results in a more northerly indication. Deceleration gives a more southerly indication. You might check this the next time you're out just boring holes in the sky. (Remember ANDS? *A*cceleration = *N*orth, *D*eceleration = *S*outh.)

The magnetic compass reads correctly *only* when the airplane is in straight and level unaccelerated flight (and sometimes not even then). In bumpy air the compass oscillates so that readings are difficult to take and more difficult to hold. The fluid in the case (acid-free white kerosene) is designed to keep the oscillations at a minimum, but the problem is still there.

DEVIATION. The compass also has an instrument error due to electrical equipment and metal parts of the plane. This error varies between headings and a correction card is placed near the compass, showing these errors for each 30°. The compass is "swung," or corrected, on a *compass rose*—a large calibrated circle painted on the concrete ramp or taxiway away from metal interference such as hangars. The airplane is taxied onto the rose and corrections are made in the compass with a nonmagnetic screwdriver (the engine should be running and normal radio and electrical equipment on). Attempts are made to balance out the errors—better to have all headings off a small amount than some correct and others badly in error.

In order to use the compass you must allow for corrections, and for navigation purposes the following steps apply:

1. True course (or heading) plus or minus Variation gives Magnetic course (or heading).

2. Magnetic course (or heading) plus or minus Deviation gives Compass course (or heading).

You can remember TVMDC (True Virgins Make Dull Company, or The Very Mean Department of Commerce—left over from the days when aviation was under the jurisdiction of the Department of Commerce).

Swinging the Compass.

You may never be called upon to swing a compass but as a professional pilot you should have some idea of the procedure so as to understand whether the magnetic compass in your airplane indicates within 90° of what it should. (Sure, you'll be flying airplanes with gyrosyn compasses but once in a while you may have to step back down to a float compass again.) If you work as a flight instructor as your career progresses you may be disappointed at the conditions of some of the magnetic compasses in the trainers on the line. It may have been so long since some of the compass correction cards have been corrected that they're in Gothic script, or even have Magellan's signature on them. Also you'll note that some of the cards have *no* deviation

indicated and apparently are accurate indeed. Later when you become chief instructor or chief pilot of an organization it may be your responsibility to see that the trainers' compasses are accurate enough to assure that the student pilots flying on solo cross-countries don't end up at unplanned destinations.

THE COMPASS ROSE. The compass is "swung" on the compass rose with the engine running at a speed to have the alternator working, and with radios on. For the most accuracy, the airplane should be in the level flight position. Tricycle-gear airplanes give little problem in this regard. Again, the compass rose should be painted on a ramp in an area well away from outside ferrous (iron or steel) or electrical influences. It is oriented with respect to Magnetic North and has lines painted every 30° around the circle (Fig. 4-35).

The magnetic compass has two compensating magnets: the North-South magnet has its own screw adjustment as does the East-West magnet. A nonmagnetic screwdriver (easily made by grinding a short section of ³⁄₁₆-in.-diameter copper wire if necessary) is used to make adjustments.

Aircraft Alterations (EA-AC 43.13-1A and 2A), which gives acceptable methods, techniques and practices for aircraft inspection and repair, gives some techniques for swinging aircraft magnetic indicators on the ground:

a. Move the aircraft to a location free from the influence of steel structures, underground pipes and cables, reinforced concrete or other aircraft.

b. Place the aircraft in level flight position.

c. Check the indicator for fluid level and cleanliness. If fluid is required, the compass is defective.

d. Remove the compensating magnets from the chambers or reset the fixed compensating magnets to neutral positions, whichever is applicable, before swinging.

e. Check the pivot friction of the indicator by deflecting the card with a small magnet. The card should rotate freely in a horizontal plane.

f. Align the aircraft with North magnetic heading and compensate with the compensating magnets. Repeat for the East magnetic heading. Then place on South and West magnetic headings and remove half of the indicated error by adjusting the compensators. The engine(s) should be running.

g. Turn the aircraft on successive 30° headings through 360°. Prepare a placard to show the correction to be applied at each of these headings. When significant errors are introduced by operation of electrical/electronic equipment or systems, the placard should also be marked at each 30° heading showing the correction to be applied when such equipment or systems are turned on or energized.

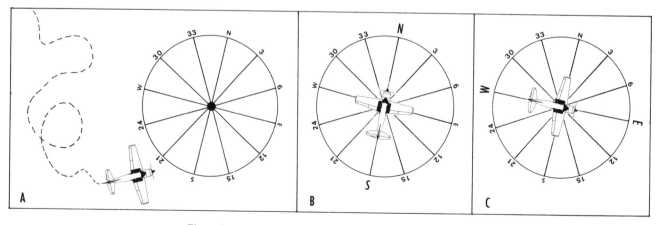

Fig. 4-35. The compass rose. A. The pilot taxis skillfully onto the rose. B. and C. North and East (then South and West) headings are corrected. The correction placard is filled in for every 30° heading.

Adjustment of remote indicating gyro compasses and other systems of this type may be accomplished by the "ground swinging" technique. Reference should be made to the manufacturer's manual for special tools, instructions and procedures.

Fig. 4-36 is a correction card for an aircraft compass that the writer "swung" on a small compass rose on his (wooden) desk (no electrical or ferrous metal inputs). Naturally, turning that compass was much easier than turning a full-sized airplane.

FOR	N	030	060	E	120	150	S	210	240	W	300	330
STEER	358	025	059	089	121	153	179	206	239	269	298	325

Fig. 4-36. A deviation card for an aircraft compass.

One point you may not have considered is that the magnetic compass may be used as a direction *and* bank indicator if you've lost all the gyro instruments. In the section called Northerly Turning Errors you'll note that when the compass turned from a heading of South it turned the correct way but exaggerated the amount of turn. You can use this fact to make a straight letdown through an overcast on South heading because bank (and turn) will be indicated more quickly and in the proper direction so that early deviations may be corrected. (Since on North the compass initially turns the opposite, no little confusion might result. On East or West, deviations are not so exaggerated.)

The magnetic compass has many quirks but once you understand them, it can be a valuable aid. One thing to remember—the mag compass "runs" on its own power and doesn't need electricity or suction to operate. This feature may be important to you some day when your other more expensive direction indicators have failed.

GYRO FLIGHT INSTRUMENTS

Vacuum-driven Instruments. For the less expensive airplanes the gyro instruments are usually vacuum driven, either by an engine drive pump or venturi system. A disadvantage of the venturi system is that its efficiency depends on airspeed, and the venturi tube itself causes slight aerodynamic Drag. Although a venturi system can be installed on nearly any airplane in a short while, the engine-driven vacuum pump is best for actual instrument operations, as it starts operating as soon as the engine(s) start. Multiengine airplanes usually have a vacuum pump on each engine so that the vacuum-driven instruments will still operate in the event of an engine failure. Each pump has the capacity to carry the system.

Errors in the instruments may arise as they get older and bearings get worn, or the air filters get clogged with dirt. Low suction means low rpm and a loss in efficiency of operation.

Some airplanes use a pneumatic (pressure) pump rather than a vacuum pump to move air through the gyro instruments. The instruments work effectively, and, in addition, the positive pressure system may be set up to operate de-icer boots or work with the turbochargers to pressurize the cabin. (More about that in Chap. 19). Now there is consideration to having a venturi installed to back up the system, should the engine-driven vacuum pump fail.

Electric-driven Instruments. The electric-driven gyro instruments got their start when high-performance aircraft such

as jets began to operate at very high altitudes. The suction-driven instruments lost much of their efficiency in the thin air and a different source of power was needed.

Below 30,000 ft either type of gyro performs equally well. It is common practice to use a combination of electric- and vacuum-driven instruments for safety's sake, should one type of power source fail. A typical gyro flight instrument group for a single-pilot plane would probably include a vacuum-driven attitude gyro and heading indicator, and an electric turn and slip or turn coordinator. Large airplanes have two complete sets of flight instruments, one set vacuum-driven and one set electric-driven.

More about Rigidity in Space. You know that once a gyro is rotating at its operating speed it resists any force trying to change its plane of rotation or its axis alignment (that is, it has rigidity in space). The resistance to change is a function of the angular velocity, weight (mass), and radius at which the weight is located. To confirm this, take two objects of the same weight and diameter and drill a hole in the center of each to insert an axis and establish equal rotation rates (Fig. 4-37). The dumbbell-shaped object (lower) has more "gyroscopic inertia" because its mass is distributed farther out from the axis and the moment of inertia depends on the *square* of the radius of the center of the mass. (Inertia is the property of a matter by which it either wants to stay put or, when moving, to continue in a straight line, according to Newton's First Law.) The moment of inertia—and you've run enough Weight and balance problems by now to know what a moment is—is the distance (radius) squared, times the mass. In other words, the farther out the center of the mass of *each half* of the shapes shown in Fig. 4-37, the much greater the inertia.

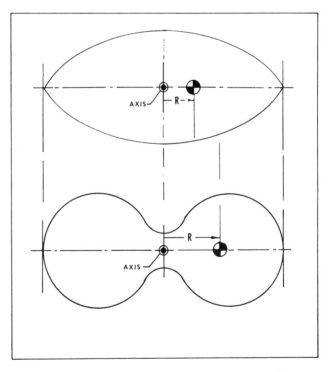

Fig. 4-37. Cross sections of two differently shaped objects of equal Weight (mass), diameters, and rpm. Note the radii of the CGs of the rotating shapes.

In order to take advantage of this property, the gyro wheel (rotor) is made so that as much of the mass (Weight) as possible is located near the rim (Fig. 4-38). From a physics

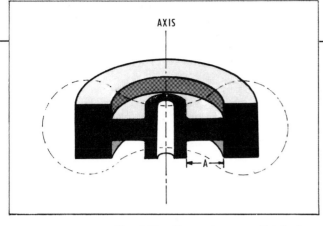

Fig. 4-38. Gyro rotor mass distribution.

standpoint it would be good to have section A in Fig. 4-38 very thin so as to move the CG of a rotor segment as far out toward the rim as possible, but structural considerations limit this, since the rotation rate may in some cases be up to 30,000 rpm and precession forces could cause destruction of the rotor-axis system. (Precession will be covered shortly.)

Or looking at it another way, Newton's Law stating that a body in motion tends to remain in motion and move in a straight line unless disturbed by an outside force doesn't, at first glance, seem to apply to rotating bodies. However, it does if you look at the gyro as a "bunch of chunks" (Fig. 4-39). As the wheel rotates at a high speed each particle tends to continue in a straight line and leave the system, but it can't because it's attached to the rest. The particle wants to continue in a line in the plane of rotation since there are no forces from the side acting on it for this example.

Looking at two of the equal-weight particles at different radii on the wheel (Fig. 4-39), you can note the following. The wheel in Fig. 4-39 has a radius of just over 2 in. and is rotating at 10,000 rpm. The circumference of a circle is $2\pi r$. Particle 1 is centered 1 in. from the center; particle 2 is 2 in. from the center and close to the edge of the wheel. The velocity for particle 1 is $2\pi r = 2 \times 3.1416$ in. $= 6.2832$ in. per revolution, or 62,832 in. per minute at 10,000 rpm. Converting to feet per second, you'd divide the inches by 12 to get feet per minute, and then divide that answer by 60: $62,832/12 = 5236$; $5236/60 = 87.3$ fps (linear velocity at any point in that radius).

Doing the same thing for particle 2 the linear velocity is found to be 174.6 fps.

Since kinetic energy (KE) is a function of one-half the mass times the velocity squared, particle 2 contributes 4 times as much to the gyro inertia; $KE = \frac{1}{2} MV^2$. Both have the

same Weight or mass so that's not a factor. The point is that the "outside" particle (2) is contributing 4 times as much as the inside particle (1), and it's a gaining proposition to move as many "particles" outboard as is structurally possible.

A 12-in.-diameter heavy gyro rotor turning at a very high speed would provide an effective gyro system. The only problem is that size and weight have to be considered for installation in an airplane's instrument panel. The older attitude indicators (or artificial horizons, or gyro horizons) and heading indicators (directional gyros) were both larger and heavier with lower rpm used (Fig. 4-40).

GYROS AND GIMBALS. It's all well and good to see the theory of how gyros work, but they have to be mounted into the instruments and here's where the gimbals (supporting rings) come in (Fig. 4-41).

When the gyro wheel is mounted (Fig. 4-41D) it has freedom around two axes. Following the logic, the gyro system is now complete. The gyro gimbals (support rings) stand (sit?) on the earth, which in turn (or at least legend has it) sits on the back of a great turtle (Fig. 4-42).

Fig. 4-42. The gyro system and earth on the back of a great turtle.

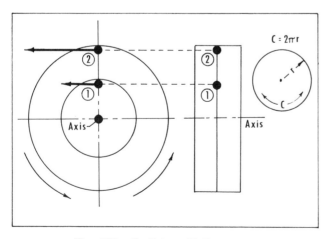

Fig. 4-39. Particles with the same mass at varying radii on a rotating wheel.

Attitude Indicator. The plane of rotation of the attitude indicator (A/I) is horizontal (the axis is vertical), and the airplane rolls, pitches, and yaws around it (Fig. 4-40 A,B). A/Is may be powered electrically or by vacuum pressure sources.

The electrically driven type may be further divided into those that use 14- and 28-volt DC (direct current) sources and those that have 115-volt AC (alternate current) sources. The latter must be equipped with an inverter to provide the required AC power. These electric A/Is are usually 360° rotation in pitch and roll and may be more expensive than the

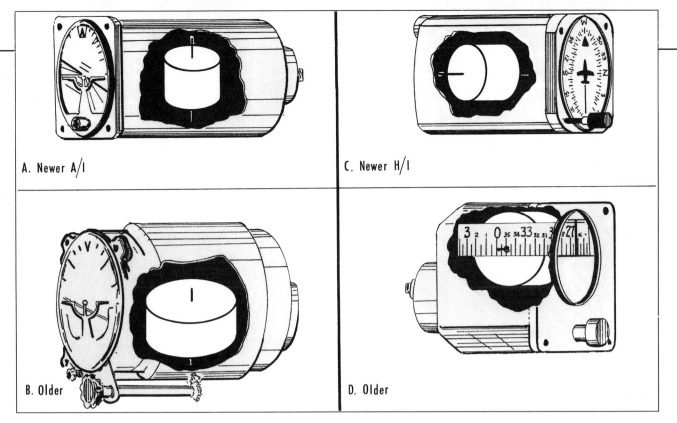

A. Newer A/I

C. Newer H/I

B. Older

D. Older

Fig. 4-40. A comparison of old and new gyro instruments. The rotor diameters were decreased so the instruments could be smaller, requiring a higher rpm to get the same gyroscopic inertia.

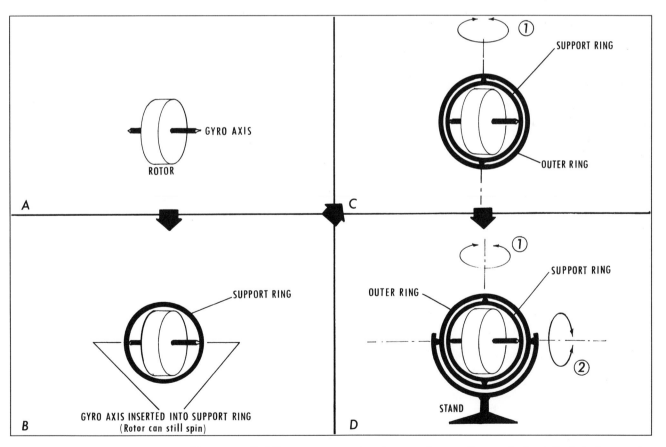

A

ROTOR

GYRO AXIS

B

SUPPORT RING

GYRO AXIS INSERTED INTO SUPPORT RING
(Rotor can still spin)

C

SUPPORT RING

OUTER RING

D

OUTER RING

SUPPORT RING

STAND

Fig. 4-41. Building up a gyro system (assume for now the gyro isn't rotating). A. A gyro rotor and axis (axle). B. Since a gyro can't just hang around without support, it's inserted into a support ring (or gimbal) that would allow it to rotate. C. An outer ring is added and attached so that the gyro rotor and support ring can turn within it (1). The rotor and supporting ring are restricted to turning in only one plane at this point. D. By adding a stand with axis attachments as shown, the *gyro system* can also turn 360° around that axis (2). By rotating the system (1 and 2) an infinite number of positions relative to the stand can be attained. If the gyro rotor is rotating and rigidity in space is maintained, the outer ring and stand may be moved around the wheel, as would be the case when an airplane does rolls or loops around the horizontal rotor in the attitude indicator.

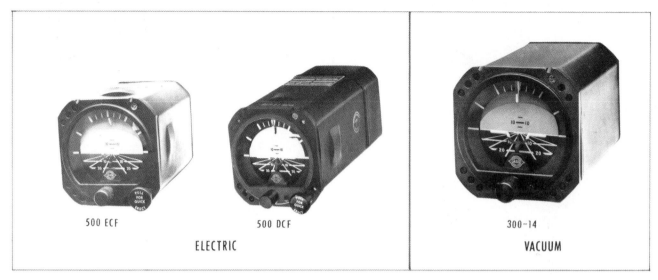

Fig. 4-43. Sample types of electric and vacuum attitude indicators. (*Aviation Instrument Manufacturing Corporation*)

vacuum/pressure-driven types (some of which also are considered nontumbling, self-erecting) (Fig. 4-43).

When you're checking out in that more complex twin your corporation is buying, you'll need to know which gyro instruments depend on electrical and which on vacuum/pressure sources. Most lighter airplanes use a vacuum/pressure-driven attitude indicator (also known as a "horizon reference indicator") and heading indicator ("directional gyro") with an electrically driven turn and slip or turn coordinator as a backup. You may find an installation with an electric-powered A/I and H/I with a vacuum/pressure-driven turn and slip, particularly on the copilot's side in heavier twins.

The electric instruments have a warning flag or indicator that pops into view when power to the instrument is lost, which should also be showing when the airplane is shut down sitting at the ramp. (A quick look and an "I see that the A/I on the pilot's side is electric" will establish your expertise at once.)

A/I power requirements — Newer - vacuum/pressure-driven A/Is normally require a suction of between 4.5 to 5.2 in. of mercury differential at a maximum flow of 2.1 ft³ of air per minute (measured at the instrument) as compared with 3.8 or 4.2 in. for earlier models (which makes sense because of the higher rpm required for the smaller sized gyro rotors). Some of the elecric types require the following power:

28-volt DC systems — 0.8 amperes

14-volt DC system — 1.5 amperes

115-volt AC system — 16 volt-amperes for starting and 13 volt-amperes while running

The newer A/I gyro rotors are 1.375 in. in diameter and 1.300 in. "long," and usually rotate at 20,000 to 25,000 rpm. The *heading indicator* (H/I) rotors have a diameter of 1.375 in. and are 1.500 in. "long."

Incidentally, older A/I instruments have an operating rotor speed of approximately 12,000 rpm and weigh about 4.5 lb as compared with 2.7 lb for a current, lighter model. Most of these also have pitch and bank limits (before tumbling) of 70° and 100° respectively.

Attitude indicator problems — If the A/I is slow to erect or shows deviation from level flight when you, with your great skills, are really flying level, the problem could be caused by worn bearings or maybe the gyro rotor isn't getting the power (electric or vacuum) that it should. After the flight and you've shut down the engine and the gyros are winding

down, listen for noise indicating bearing wear or damage. You should also check the vacuum gage or electric power indicators and power source connections for problems. Smoking in the cabin is bad for vacuum/pressure-driven instruments because the filters will eventually clog up, and air flow is cut with a resulting decrease in rotor rpm (and gyro inertia).

A/Is precess and react to *acceleration* by falsely indicating a *nose-high* attitude. This can be bad on an actual instrument takeoff when the airplane is accelerating for climb; the pilot thinks the airplane's nose is too high and may ease it over, settling back into the surface (trees, etc.). These A/Is falsely indicate a *nose-low* attitude during *deceleration*. Also, precession error is at a maximum after a 180° turn when all of the forces have been acting in the same direction. A 180° turn in the opposite direction or continuing the turn for 360° cancels the error.

Note in Fig. 4-43 that those electric A/Is have a manual quick erection system in addition to the normal adjustment knob for the small airplane.

The Heading Indicator (or Directional Gyro). The heading indicator (H/I) functions because of rigidity in space, as does the A/I; but note, looking back at Fig. 4-40, that the plane of the rotor is "vertical" (or the axis is "horizontal," if your prefer to look at it that way). The gyro is fixed relative to the card, and the airplane turns around it. Most heading indicators, both old and new types, have the gyro axis lined up with North and South indications.

The newer H/Is with vertical faces, although mechanically attached (through gears), also indicate North or South when the gyro axis is aligned with the long axis of the instrument.

The older H/Is weighed as much as 3.75 lb and operated at 10,000 rpm, compared with 2.9 lb and 24,000 rpm for some more recent models. Both types use the same gyro position (vertical plane) for their principle of operation (Fig. 4-44).

The nonslaved heading indicator must be reset to the magnetic compass when it is reading correctly; this is usually in straight and level, unaccelerated flight about every 15 min.

The older and some newer models have limitations of 55° pitch or bank, although if you are, for instance, doing a roll with the H/I indicating North or South, or a loop on an indication of East or West, this limitation does not apply since the airplane is moving *around* the rotor in these cases and is

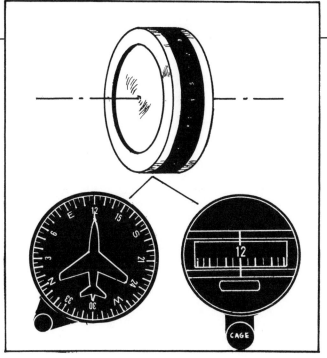

Fig. 4-44. The heading indicator. The airplane turns around the vertical gyro wheel.

not forcing the rotor against the stops. (*Don't do loops or rolls except in an aerobatic airplane.*)

A slaved gyro system continually corrects for gyro drift and compensates for magnetic dip, deviation, and oscillation. You set the H/I to the magnetic compass with the card set knob at the beginning of the flight and the system continually corrects itself while operating. The remotely mounted flux detector (the magnet portion of the system) is normally mounted in the wing tip or other area away from ferrous material.

Fig. 4-45 shows different types of vacuum/pressure-driven heading indicators. Fig. 4-46 shows some different types of electrically powered heading indicators.

PRECESSION, DRIFT, AND THE HEADING INDICATOR. Precession effects on the H/I are caused by three main factors: (1) bearing problems, (2) effect of the airplane being turned and hence trying to "turn" or move the gyro wheel from its plane of rotation, and (3) apparent precession ("drift" caused by the earth's rotation). Of these, only gyro drift can be predicted since the condition of the bearings depends on (1) the age and history of the particular instrument and (2) the number (and degree) of turns done within a given time during a flight.

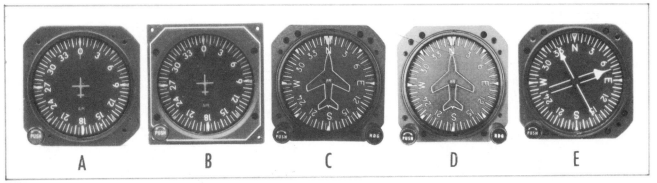

Fig. 4-45. Vacuum/pressure heading indicators (directional gyros) using 4.5–5.2 in. of mercury. A. A "standard" type of instrument used on many trainers. B. H/I with an ARINC or international standards bezel (pronounced "bezzle") or panel cutout shape. The standard bezel for an instrument is round with a diameter of 3.125 in. Notice that this instrument has a modified octagonal cutout (white outline). C. H/I with a different indicator and a "bug" and 45° references to aid the pilot to set a heading reference. D. This model provides autopilot heading select outputs. E. Slaved instrument. It has optional RMI (radio magnetic indicator) pointers for simultaneous VOR/ADF displays. Included with the installation is a slaving indicator and a magnetic flux detector (usually in the wing tip or in a part of the airplane well away from ferrous or electrical influence). (*Aviation Instrument Manufacturing Corporation*)

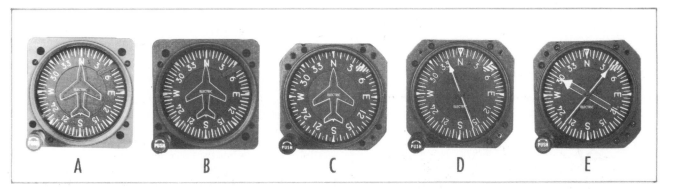

Fig. 4-46. Electric heading indicators. A. 28- or 14-volt DC free (nonslave) gyro. B. 115-volt, 400-Hz (cycles) free directional gyro. C. 115-volt, 400-Hz slaved heading indicator. D. Slaved H/I with RMI (115-volt, 400-Hz). E. Slaved H/I and RMI with dual pointers (115-volt, 400-Hz). (*Aviation Instrument Manufacturing Corporation*)

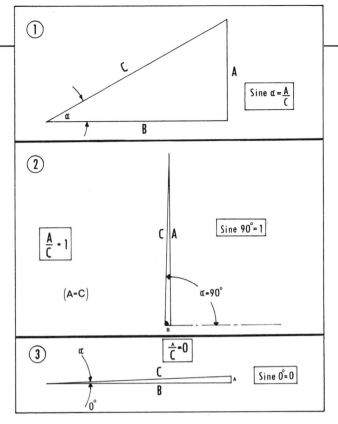

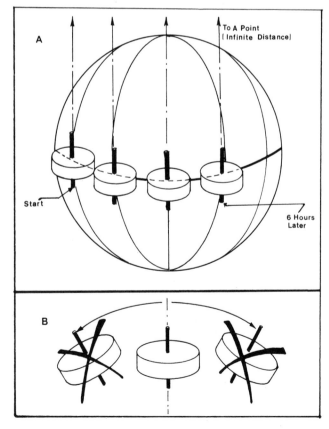

Fig. 4-47. A review of sine values for 0° and 90°.

Computing the effect of the earth's rotation (gyro drift) can be complicated but a look at the idea will give you a chance to use some of that trigonometry you did so well with in Chap. 1. The value of the error caused by the earth's rotation (apparent precession) *per hour* is: 15.04 × sin latitude. The earth turns 15.04° per hour. We've always rounded it off to 15° in basic navigation and Coordinated Universal Time

Fig. 4-48. A. A gyro rotating at the equator with the axis parallel to the surface and aligned True North and South. B. The gyro axis will remain constant as the earth rotates.

(UTC) problems. The sine of an angle, if you recall, is zero at 0° and 1 at 90° (Fig. 4-47).

Suppose the airplane is sitting tied down on the ramp at the equator (latitude = zero) facing North with the heading indicator in operation. The gyro axis is lined up with a point in space, say, an infinite distance away. The earth turns 15.04° per hour, so in 6 hr it will have turned a little over 90°. The gyro axis is still lined up with that point, with no measurable error because of the angle involved (Fig. 4-48).

The gyro principle of rigidity in space keeps the gyro axis pointed at that point an infinite distance away. You are rotating *around* that line but have not changed the angle of the gyro axis in reference to that line. The point is that the gyro hasn't turned with respect to the original setting.

Fig. 4-49 shows the top view of an operating gyro system at the equator that has the plane of the gyro pointing toward North (or the axis pointed toward the ground, rather than parallel to it as in Fig. 4-48). Note that as the earth rotates, the gyro rotor, while maintaining a constant rigidity in space, is radically changing its relationship to the earth. The "face" of the wheel is pointing at the ground at position 1. At position 7, 12 hr later (180° rotation), it has apparently turned upside down and is pointing straight up. After another 12 hr it will be back to "normal."

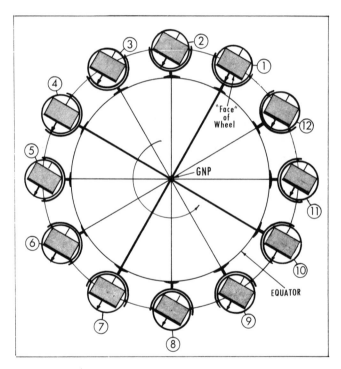

Fig. 4-49. A gyro system (rotor at speed) at the equator with the "face" of the wheel pointing at the ground. As the earth rotates for 24 hr the gyro rotor apparently turns 360° in its gimbal system.

Take an airplane sitting *tied down* with the engine running and the H/I in operation right at the Geographic (or True) North Pole. You've set the H/I on a heading of North for this example. (Actually all headings from the True North Pole are South but for this example you can set it on North for easy reference) (Fig. 4-50). The H/I that was set on North 6 hr earlier now reads West even though the H/I was not reset and the airplane is still tied down, pointing directly at the same igloo, or the original "North." The equation to determine precession error (per hour) is 15.04 × sin latitude. At the equator (latitude 0°), 15.04 × sin 0° = 15.04 × 0 = 0, or

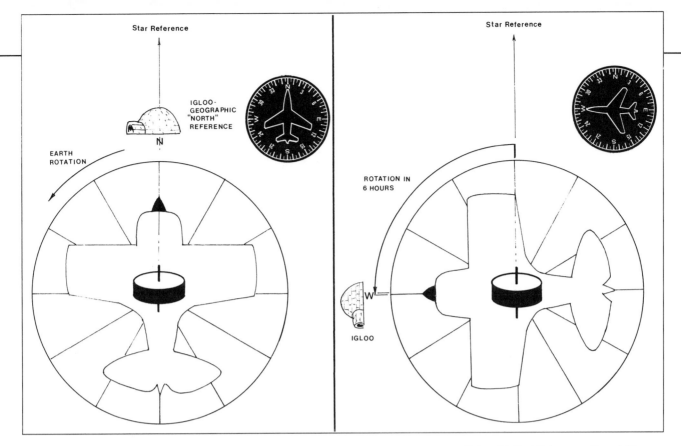

Fig. 4-50. An airplane tied down at the True North Pole with its H/I in operation. Add numbers with the setting knob to correct for the apparent drift.

no error. At the True North or South Pole (latitude = 90°), 15.04 × sin 90° = 15.04 × 1 = 15.04° precession error per hour, or the *maximum possible.*

The question now is, How does that affect the H/I, or *in which direction* is the correction to be made for the stationary H/I used in the example in Fig. 4-50? The airplane is still pointed at the igloo, our original "North" (360°), but the H/I shows *270*, or West. To use the same geographic reference and starting all over (the pilot slept for 6 hr and woke up to discover the problem), the H/I must be mechanically rotated clockwise 90° (*add* numbers) from a reading of West to a reading of North. This effect lessens as the airplane (or fixed

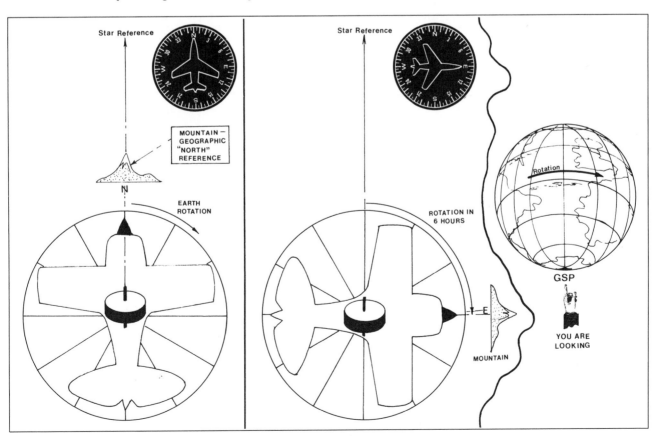

Fig. 4-51. An airplane tied down at the True South Pole with its H/I in operation. Subtract numbers with the setting knob to correct for the apparent drift.

H/I) is closer to the equator. In the northern hemisphere *add* numbers to correct the error caused by the earth's rotation.

At a latitude of 30° N you would expect an error per hour of 15:04 × sin 30° = 15.04 × 0.5 = 7.52° per hour (fixed position). You must *add* this amount to the H/I indication each hour to correct the error.

What if an airplane were tied down with the H/I at the *True South Pole*? Look at Fig. 4-51. From a point directly "below" the True South Pole, the earth's rotation appears to be in reverse, but you're looking at it from the opposite direction from that in Fig. 4-50. The earth is rotating to the "East." The airplane is tied down at the True South Pole on a heading of North, pointing at the mountain peak (geographic reference) with the H/I in operation.

After 6 hr the H/I is indicating East (090°) while the airplane is still facing *its* North reference (the peak). The reading would have to be *decreased* by 090° to correct for the gyro drift caused by the earth's rotation. Figs. 4-50 and 4-51 show the extreme of the contrasts between north and south latitudes; each hemisphere's *error would decrease* as the positions chosen *approach the equator*.

In review, *to correct for gyro drift or apparent precession:*

North latitudes—*increase* numbers on the H/I
South latitudes—*decrease* numbers on the H/I
This is the error for a stationary gyro.

You're not going to go into the problem so deeply in every flight; the old "set your H/I with the magnetic compass every 15 minutes" works fine but later you may use the Inertial Navigation Systems or other advanced equipment and should have a look at the principle involved.

Looking at some other factors: Suppose that an airplane at 30° N latitude is flying on a heading of True East (the airspeed to be decided later).

You know that on the equator every degree of longitude is 60 NM and when a stationary point there has turned 90° (earth's rotation) it will have "moved" 5400 NM. (For example purposes here, round off the earth's rotation to 15° per hour and 900 NM per hour at the equator.) You also know that the

meridians converge at the True North and South Poles and every degree of longitude on those points is 0 NM.

Fig. 4-52 shows an idea of "mileage covered" for a stationary point on the equator and one at 30° N latitude when the earth has rotated 90°. The cosine of 30° is 0.866 (Fig. 1-8); a point at 30° N would move a distance 0.866 as far as the point (moving 900 K) at the equator. That point at 30° N will move "east" 0.866 × 900 = 780 NM per hour (rounded off). The numbers show the comparative distance covered in 6 hr.

An example: You are flying a jet on a true course of 270° (True West) at 30° N latitude at 780 K ground speed and pass over a city (Fig. 4-53, point A) at 1100Z. The situation is that the airplane is staying at that *point in space* and no gyro drift is occurring. The airplane is certainly traveling hell-bent-for-election west over the earth itself but is holding its own with respect to that point in space when time zero (1100Z) occurs. The jet is canceling out the movement of that point on the earth's surface, which is moving east at 780 K with respect to the original reference an infinite distance away.

You are staying over the same point in reference to space while geographically flying 780 mi due west, cancelling out the apparent drift. An analogy would be that of a person walking down an "up" escalator at its exact speed, moving with reference to the escalator (that is, stepping on different steps) but not moving as far as the store "space" is concerned. (Astronomers: *Don't* write to mention that the earth is moving around the sun and the universe is expanding and ask for some extra velocity components to be thrown in here—we're having enough trouble as it is.)

If the airplane is traveling due *east* at 780 K at 30° N, *the apparent drift error is compounded;* the airplane is aiding and abetting the problem by adding its speed to that of the earth's rotation.

Earlier it was noted that the drift (precession) error at 30° N latitude would be 7.52° per hour and also that a point on the earth at that latitude would be traveling "eastward" at 780 K because of the rotation. If that airplane is traveling due east at 780 K its apparent drift would be another 7.52° for a total error of 15.04°, or the same error that would be present

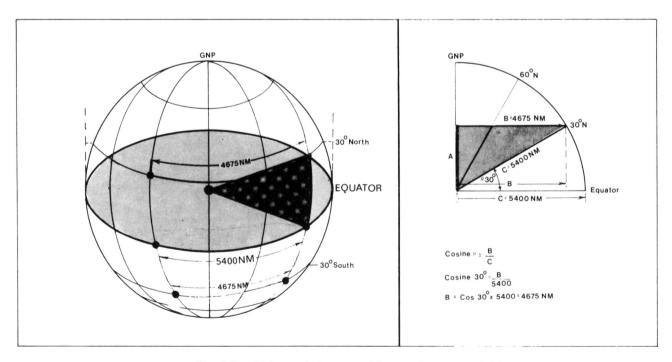

Fig. 4-52. Distances between meridians at the equator (5400 mi) and at 30° N or 30° S (4675 mi). The numbers have been rounded off for neatness and clarity of thought.

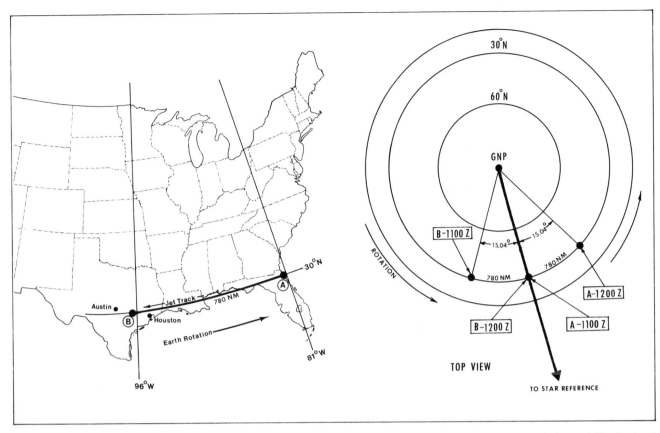

Fig. 4-53. A jet flying true west at 30° N at 780 K would cancel out the gyro drift effects. It departed point A at 1100Z and arrived at point B at the same point in space at 1200Z.

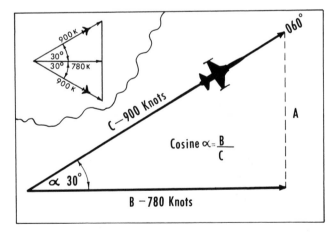

Fig. 4-54. The airplane traveling at 900 K on a true course of 060° is moving true east at 780 K.

at the geographic poles (and obviously this is a canned problem).

So, in the northern hemisphere, *if the airplane is flying westerly, the component of its flight path parallel to the equator, or parallel to the earth's rotation, decreases the drift error. Flying easterly, the error is compounded.*

The component of its flight path parallel to the equator is the one causing (or helping) the problem. Fig. 4-54 shows the idea. The airplane's component of flight parallel to the equator is 780 K and equal to the travel of a fixed point on the earth, so here, too, the error is apparently doubled. Actually the fact that the airplane is traveling in a northerly direction at

that speed causes the error to be more than doubled. As the latitude is increased (which would be the case of a course of 060°) *the drift error is increased* since the error is a function of 15.04 × sin latitude. Flying *east* or *north* (northern hemisphere), the apparent drift error is *increased* over that of the stationary gyro. Flying *west* or *south* (again northern hemisphere) would *decrease* the apparent drift error from that of a stationary gyro.

You could calculate the error caused by the increase in latitude for the airplane in Fig. 4-54 by simple trigonometry: The flight angle from True East is 30°; at the end of an hour the airplane will have traveled north by the factor $\sin \alpha = A/C$; $A = C \times \sin \alpha = 900 \times 0.5 = 450$ NM. Realizing that each 60 NM north adds another degree of latitude to the 30° N at the start, the airplane would be at 37.5° N at the end of 1 hr (450/60 = 7.5). The error would be greater at the end of the hour. If the airplane is flying a heading of 120° true, the error at the end of the hour would be that for 22.5° N, using the reasoning above.

The Precession Instruments. The turn and slip (T/S) and turn coordinator (T/C) use the principle of precession for operation, as you've been aware of since you first read about it as a student pilot. The point is that the gyro rotor tends to stay in the same plane of rotation (or keeps the axis pointed in the same direction relative to space, whichever you prefer) and any outside force acting perpendicular to the plane of rotation causes the gyro wheel to move as if the force had been applied 90° around the rim in the direction of rotation.

Precession depends on the gyro rotor rpm and the force acting to tilt the rotor. The higher the gyro inertia (which again depends on the mass, radius of the center of the mass, and rpm), the more resistant it is to precession. The greater

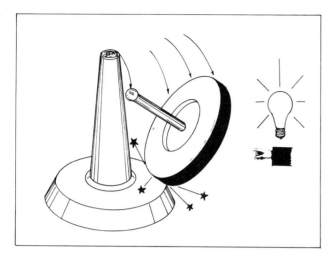

Fig. 4-55. The nonrotating gyro will fall off the stand. A degree in physics is not necessary to predict this.

the value and/or rate of application of the acting side force, the greater the precession effects if all other considerations are equal.

A toy gyroscope may be used to illustrate precession. If the end of the axis of the *non*spinning rotor is placed on the pedestal, it will obviously fall off as gravity cannot be denied (Fig. 4-55). The CG of the system is well outside the point of support. Strange things happen if the gyro rotor is rotating within a certain rpm value range. The rotor wants to fall but if the rpm is right, will instead precess or rotate around the stand, the axis remaining level. Gravity causes the rotor to want to tilt forward and down, but its rotation sets up a couple system that instead causes the gyro rotor and axis to rotate horizontally on the stand. In Fig. 4-56 the rotor itself is shown rotating counterclockwise around the axis as seen from "head-on" and you can see in the top view that the system (rotor and axis) is rotating around the stand in a counterclockwise direction.

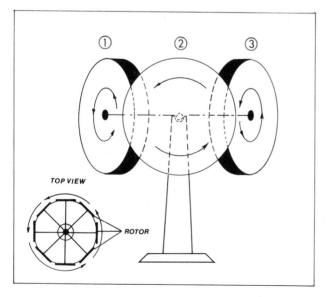

Fig. 4-56. Rotating gyro wheel reactions at a certain rpm.

In trying to fall, the weight of the rotor sets up a force-couple system that reacts with the counterclockwise rotation

so that the system turns to the left (as seen from above) rather than falling. As the rotation slows, the forces and couples will no longer be in balance and the rotor will oscillate and move downward and eventually fall.

The T/S and T/C are limited to movement of one degree of freedom. The gyro wheel "tilts" in two directions with respect to the instrument, "leftward" and "rightward" (Fig. 4-57).

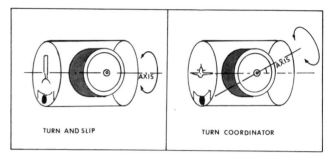

Fig. 4-57. Turn and slip and turn coordinator axis alignment.

THE TURN AND SLIP. The turn and slip (or needle and ball, or turn and bank as it used to be known) was *the* instrument for "blind flying" in earlier days. It was powered by a venturi on the side of the fuselage, usually most effective at around 85 K, which meant that the airplane was airborne and committed before the pilot knew whether the instrument was working or not. Also, structural ice could be a "minor nuisance" as it plugged the venturi.

The tilting movement of the rotor is limited by stops; the instruments have springs to dampen the movement and to lower chances of shock damage as the system reaches its stops. The needle of the T/S reacts to the yaw component only, so that a "flat" turn would give the most accurate value of the rate of nose movement around the horizon (Fig. 4-58).

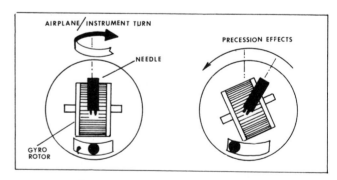

Fig. 4-58. Needle and ball reactions to a "flat turn."

Later some T/Ss used engine-driven vacuum pumps for power, and a restricter valve was necessary to lower the pressure by 1.8 to 2.2 in. of mercury rather than the 3.8 to 4.2 in. used by the "artificial horizon" and "directional gyro" of pre- and early post–WW II years. The T/Ss installed in general aviation airplanes for a number of years after WW II were surplus instruments using the lower pressure drop. There are now original manufactured vacuum T/Ss that can use either 1.8- to 2.2-in. or 4.6- to 5.2-in. pressure/vacuum values (Fig. 4-59).

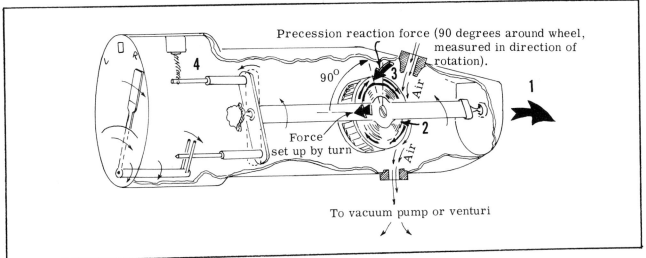

Fig. 4-59. A schematic of a vacuum/pressure-driven turn and slip reacting to a right turn.

Since it's best to have the flight instruments on different power sources so that all won't fail at once, the usual installation is to have the A/I and H/I vacuum/pressure driven and the T/S electric. Other setups have electric A/I and H/I with a vacuum/pressure T/S. Or for larger airplanes the instruments may be the two combinations just discussed, one for the pilot and the opposite arrangement for the copilot's panel.

A note with the literature for a particular T/S indicates that the instrument can be installed and used with instrument panels that are tilted as much as 8° from vertical.

There is some confusion about the markings on various models of the T/S, since some have "4 minutes" on the face, others "2 minutes," and others have no indication of any kind. The "2 minutes" indicates the time required to complete a standard rate turn of 360° at 3° per second *if the needle is deflected one needle width from center*. The 4-minute-turn instrument is used for higher-speed airplanes where 1½° per second is a standard rate to avoid too-steep banks.

In Chap. 1 it was explained that the turn rate was a function of the tangent of the angle of bank, or working further and using 3° per second as a fixed rate, it's possible to set up this equation: $\tan \phi = 3V/1091$. You would set in the airspeed (knots here) to solve for the tangent of the angle of bank and use Fig. 1-8 to find the bank.

TURN COORDINATOR. At this writing all turn coordinators are electrically driven. The axis of lateral movement of the T/C rotor is at a 30° angle to the long axis of the instrument. The T/S reacted only to yaw because of its installation and the fact (again) that precession acts 90° around the rotor.

The T/C was designed so that the pilot would get a roll input, as well as a response to yaw. The primary role of the instrument, however, was to measure the yawing of the nose (rate of turn) so the long axis would be moved up only 30°, leaving yaw as the primary mover of the indicator.

Fig. 4-60 shows a T/C (electric) and vacuum/pressure and electric T/Ss.

ENGINE INSTRUMENTS

Tachometer. For airplanes with fixed-pitch propellers the tachometer is the engine instrument to check for an indication

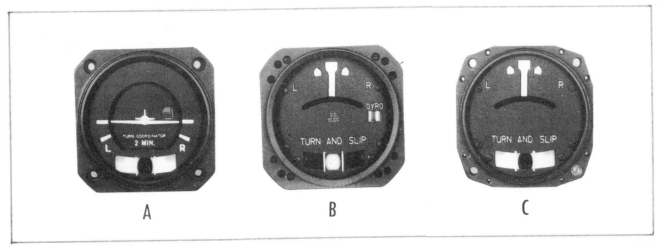

Fig. 4-60. A. Turn coordinator (electric 14 or 28 volts DC). Note the warning flag that indicates electrical power is not getting to the instrument. B. Electric turn and slip indicator (28 volts DC) with warning flag. C. A vacuum/pressure turn and slip indicator. This instrument can use differentials of 1.8 to 2.2 or 4.6 to 5.2 in. mercury as desired. Lighting is optional for these instruments. (*Aviation Instrument Manufacturing Corp.*)

of power being used. The centrifugal tachometer operates on the same principle as a car speedometer. One end of a flexible shaft is connected to the engine crankshaft and the other connected to a shaft with counterweights within the instrument. The rate of turning of the crankshaft (and cable) causes expansion of the counterweight system. The instrument hand is mechanically linked to the counterweight assembly so that the engine speed is indicated in revolutions per minute.

For direct-drive engines, the engine and propeller rpm are the same (Lycoming O-320, O-540, O-360). The geared engine (Lycoming GO-480, etc.) has different engine and propeller speeds; this is noted in the *POH* (the propeller rpm is *less* than the engine rpm). The tachometer measures engine rpm and this is the basis for your power setting. (There are a few exceptions to this "rule.")

Another type of tachometer is the magnetic, which utilizes a flexible shaft that turns a magnet within a special collar in the instrument. The balance between the magnetic force and a hairspring is indicated as rpm by hand on the instrument face. This type of tachometer does not oscillate as sometimes happens with the less expensive centrifugal type.

A third type is the electric tachometer, which depends on a generator unit driven by a tachometer drive shaft. The generator is wired to an electric motor unit of the indicator, which rotates at the same rpm and transmits this through a magnetic tachometer unit that registers the speed in rpm. This type of tachometer is also smoother than the centrifugal type.

Most airplanes have a recording tachometer from which various maintenance requirements may be made, such as 100-hr checks, oil change, or airworthiness directives. As an example, one recording tach is based on 2310 rpm, and if the engine is at lower power settings "tach time" is not built up as fast.

When trailing behind another airplane, you can "check" its rpm by looking through your prop at its prop. You would move the throttle (or propeller control with a constant-speed prop) until the other propeller "stops." Assuming that *your* tachometer is accurate, you can then read on it the other airplane's rpm. This is particularly useful when you're flying cross-country behind a friend who has the same make and model airplane but is running away from you (who swears to

carrying only 2100 rpm but you find that 2400 is indicated through your prop). Stroboscopic effect and science triumph.

Manifold Pressure Gage. For airplanes with controllable (which includes constant-speed) propellers this instrument is used in combination with the tachometer to set up desired power from the engine. The manifold pressure (mp) gage measures the air or fuel-air mixture pressure going to the cylinders and indicates it in inches of mercury.

The mp gage is an aneroid barometer like the altimeter, but instead of measuring the outside air pressure it measures the *actual* pressure of the mixture or air in the intake manifold. When the engine is not running the outside air pressure and the pressure in the intake manifold are the same, so that the mp gage will indicate the outside air pressure as would a barometer. At sea level on a standard day this would be 29.92 in. of mercury, but you can't read the mp this closely and it would appear as approximately 29 or 30 in.

You start the engine with the throttle cracked or closed. This means that the throttle valve or butterfly valve is nearly shut. The engine is a strong air pump, taking in fuel and air and discharging residual gases and air. At a closed- or cracked-throttle setting the engine is pulling air (and fuel) at such a rate past the throttle valve that a decided drop in pressure is found in the intake manifold and is duly registered by the mp gage. As the engine starts, the indication of 30 in. drops rapidly to 10 in. or less at idle. It will never reach zero as this would mean a complete vacuum in the manifold (most mp gages don't even have indications of less than 10 in.). Besides, if you tried to shut off all air (and fuel) completely the engine would quit running.

As you open the throttle you are allowing more and more fuel and air to enter the engine and the manifold pressure increases accordingly (Fig. 4-61).

As you can see in Fig. 4-61, the unsupercharged engine will never indicate the full outside pressure on the mp gage. The usual difference is 1 to 2 in. of mercury. The maximum indication on the mp gage you can expect to get is 28 to 29 in. on takeoff.

The supercharged engine has compressors that bring the fuel-air mixture to a higher pressure than the outside air be-

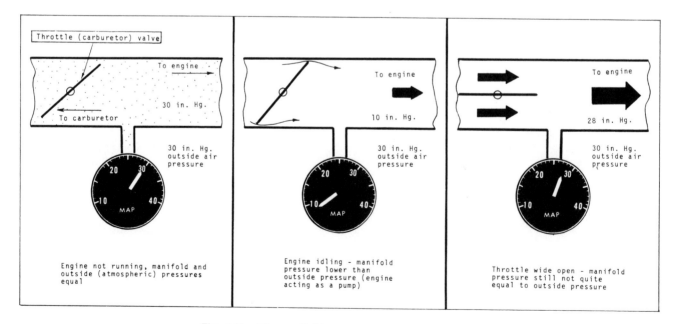

Fig. 4-61. The manifold pressure gage principle (unsupercharged engine). A value of 30 in. is used as an example, but you might see 29 in. (or lower) before start, depending on the pressure altitude at the airport.

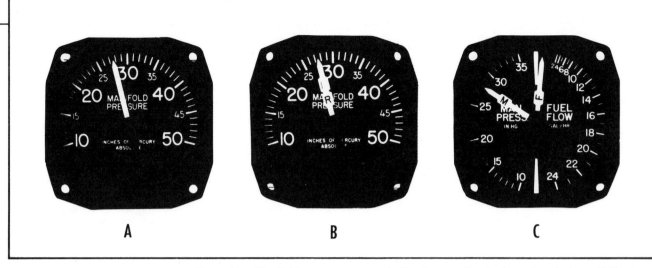

Fig. 4-62. Manifold pressure gages. A. Simple gage for single-engine airplane. B. Dual needles used for a twin. C. Combination fuel-flow and manifold pressure gage. (*Sigma Tek*)

fore it goes into the manifold. This makes it possible to register more than the outside pressure and results in more HP being developed for a given rpm, as HP is dependent on rpm and the amount of fuel and air (mp) going into the engine.

When the engine is shut down, the mp gage indication moves to the outside air pressure. The techniques in using a mp gage will be discussed later in Part 2, Checking Out in Advanced Models and Types. Fig. 4-62 shows some examples of various mp gages available.

Oil Pressure Gage. The oil pressure gage consists of a curved Bourdon tube with a mechanical linkage to the indicating hand that registers the pressure in pounds per square inch (Fig. 4-63). As is shown, oil pressure tends to straighten the tube and the appropriate oil pressure indication is registered. This is the direct-pressure-type gage.

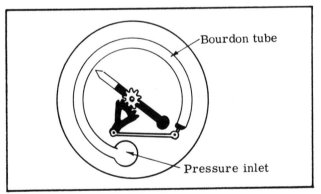

Fig. 4-63. Oil pressure gage.

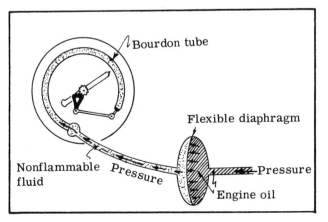

Fig. 4-64. Oil pressure gage utilizing a flexible diaphragm and nonflammable fluid.

Another type of oil pressure gage uses a unit containing a flexible diaphragm that separates the engine oil from a nonflammable fluid that fills the line from the unit into the Bourdon tube. The oil pressure is transmitted through the diaphragm and to the Bourdon tube by this liquid because liquids are incompressible (Fig. 4-64).

Oil Temperature Gage. The vapor type is the most common type of oil temperature gage in use. This instrument, like the oil pressure gage, contains a Bourdon tube connected by a fine tube to a metal bulb containing a volatile liquid. Vapor expansion due to increased temperature exerts pressure, which is indicated as temperature on the instrument face.

Other types of oil temperature gages may use a thermocouple rather than a Bourdon tube.

Cylinder Head Temperature Gage. The cylinder head temperature gage is an important instrument for engines of higher compression and/or higher power. Engine cooling is a major problem in the design of a new airplane. Much flight testing and cowl modification may be required before satisfactory cooling is found for all airspeeds and power settings. The engineers are faced with the problem of keeping the engine within efficient operating limits for all air temperatures. An engine that has good cooling for summer flying may run too cool in the winter. Cowl flaps, which are controlled by the pilot, aid in compensating for variations in airspeed and power setting. Many of the older high-performance airplanes use "augmenter cooling" instead of cowl flaps. Air is drawn over the cylinders by venturi action of a tube around the exhaust stacks (Fig. 4-65).

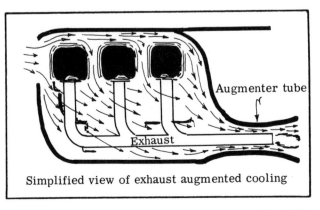

Simplified view of exhaust augmented cooling

Fig. 4-65.

The cylinder head temperature gage usually warns of any possible damage to the engine before the oil temperature gage gives any such indication.

The "hottest" cylinder, which is usually one of the rear ones in the horizontally opposed engine, is chosen during the flight testing of the airplane. A thermocouple lead replaces one of the spark plug washers on this cylinder.

The cylinder head temperature gage uses the principle of the galvanometer. Two metals of different electrical potentials are in contact at the lead. As the electric currents of these two metals vary with temperature, a means is established of indicating the temperature at the cylinder through electric cables to a galvanometer (cylinder head temperature gage), which indicates temperature rather than electrical units.

Some pilots use cylinder head temperature as an aid in proper leaning of the mixture. Generally, richer mixtures mean lower head temperatures; leaner mixtures mean higher head temperatures, all other things (airspeed, power settings, etc.) being equal. But the engine may not be developing best power at the extremes. Too rich a mixture means power loss plus excessive fuel consumption, and too lean a mixture means power loss plus the possibility of engine damage. Leaning procedures will be discussed in more detail in Part 2.

Fuel Gage. The cork float and wire fuel gages of earlier days have gone by the board. The corks sometimes got "fuel logged" and registered empty all the time. Worse, the wire sometimes got bent and the pilot had an unrealistic picture of fuel available. These indicators were followed by metal floats and indicators, and finally by the electric transmitter type now in popular use. (Check your fuel visually before the flight.)

The electric transmitter type may be broken down into the following components: (1) float and arm, (2) rheostat-type control, and (3) the indicator, a voltmeter indicating fuel either in fractions or in gallons. The float and arm are attached to the rheostat, which is connected by wires to the fuel gage. As the float level in the tank (or tanks) varies, the rheostat is rotated, changing the electrical resistance in the circuit—which changes the fuel gage indication accordingly. This is the most popular type of fuel measuring system for airplanes with electrical systems (Fig. 4-66).

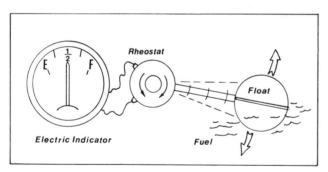

Fig. 4-66. Electric transmitter-type fuel gage.

Frequent checks of the fuel gage are a good idea; sudden dropping of the fuel level indication may be caused by a serious fuel leak and you should know about it.

Engine Instrument Marking. Following are some guidelines on engine instrument markings as given by the FAA, including some instruments not covered in detail in this chapter. You may pick up some pointers as to the limitations of what is measured by each instrument.

Carburetor air temperature (reciprocating engine aircraft)
Red radial—At the maximum permissible carburetor inlet air temperature recommended by the engine manufacturer

Green arc—Normal operating range for trouble-free operation with the upper limit at the maximum permissible carburetor inlet air temperature and the lower limit at the point where icing may be anticipated. Additional green arc may be required in the temperature range below the icing range

Yellow arc—Range indicating where icing is most likely to be encountered

Cylinder head temperature (reciprocating engine aircraft)
Red radial—At the maximum permissible cylinder head temperature

Green arc—From the maximum permissible temperature for continuous operation to the minimum recommended by the engine manufacturer for continuous operation

Yellow arc—From the maximum temperature for continuous operation to the maximum permissible temperature

Manifold pressure (reciprocating engine aircraft)
Red radial—At the maximum permissible manifold absolute pressure for dry or wet operation, whichever is greater

Green arc—From the maximum permissible pressure for continuous operation to the minimum pressure selected by the aircraft manufacturer for cruise power

Yellow arc—From the maximum pressure for continuous operation to the maximum permissible pressure

Fuel pressure (reciprocating and turbine engine aircraft)
Red radial—At the maximum and/or minimum permissible pressures established as engine operating limitations

Green arc—Normal operating range

Yellow arc—Cautionary ranges indicating any potential hazard in the fuel system such as malfunction, icing, etc.

Oil pressure (reciprocating and turbine engine aircraft)
Red radial—At the maximum and/or minimum permissible pressures established as engine operating limitations

Green arc—Normal operating range

Yellow arc—Cautionary ranges indicating any potential hazard due to overpressure during cold start, low pressure during idle, etc.

Oil temperatures (reciprocating and turbine engine aircraft)
Red radial—At the maximum and/or minimum permissible temperatures established as engine operating limitations

Green arc—Normal operating range

Yellow arc—Cautionary ranges indicating any potential hazard due to overheating, high viscosity at low temperature, etc.

Tachometer (reciprocating engine aircraft)
Red radial—At the maximum permissible rotational speed (rpm)

Green arc—From the maximum rotational speed for continuous operation to the minimum recommended for continuous operation (except in the restricted ranges, if any)

Yellow arc—From the maximum rotational speed for continuous operation to the maximum permissible rotational speed

Red arc—Range(s) in which operation is restricted, except to pass through, for all operating conditions because of excessive stresses, etc.

Electrical System. Fig. 4-67 is an electrical system diagram for a four-place airplane. This is a 28-volt DC system with a belt-driven 60-amp alternator to maintain the battery's state of charge. (Alternators have replaced generators because alternators provide more electrical power at lower engine rpm.)

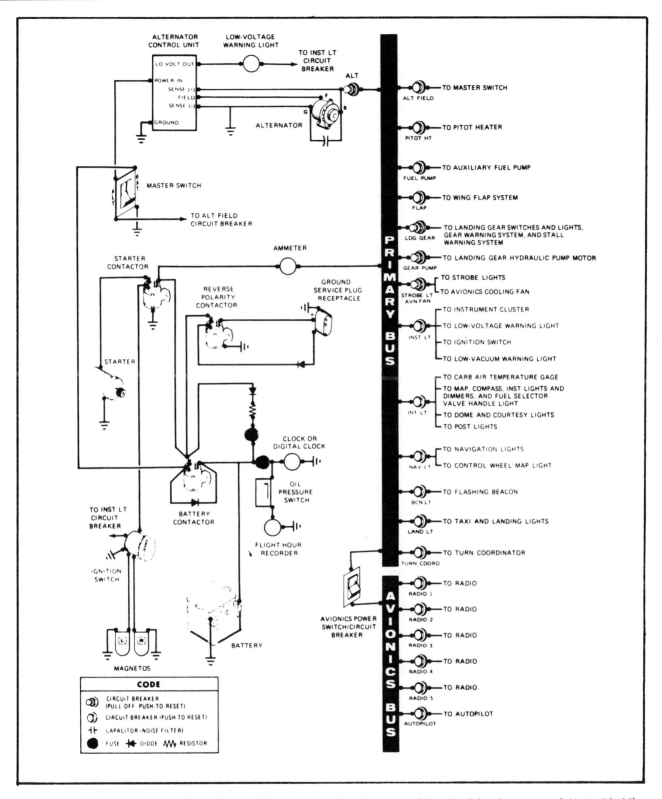

Fig. 4-67. Electrical system. Note that most of the circuit breakers are push-to-reset but the strobe lights, landing gear hydraulic pump motor, and landing gear switches and lights are protected by pull-off-type CBs. The clock and flight-hour recorder have fuses. You no doubt have long known that the magnetos have self-contained magnets and aren't part of the airplane's electrical system.

The *Ammeter* indicates the amount of current, in amperes, from the alternator to the battery or from the battery to the electrical system. When the engine is operating and the master switch is on, the ammeter indicates the charging rate applied to the battery. If the alternator isn't working, or the electrical load is too high, the ammeter shows the battery discharge rate. A low-voltage light is included in the system to warn of an alternator problem. The master switch can be turned off and then back on to reset the alternator control unit.

Learn what circuit breakers protect what units of the electrical system for *your* airplane.

Vacuum System. Fig. 4-68 is a schematic of the vacuum system for a four-place single-engine airplane. Note that the low-vacuum warning light circuit breaker is the 8th breaker from the top in Fig. 4-67.

Fig. 4-69 is the vacuum system for a twin with a vacuum pump on each engine. The system is set up so that one pump can carry the load if the other fails. Chap. 19 will discuss a pressure or pneumatic pump system for the instruments.

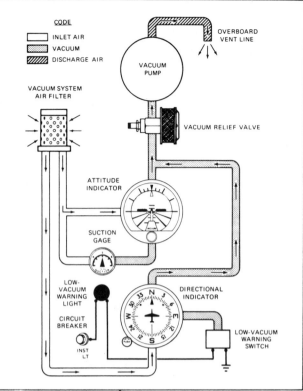

Fig. 4-68. (*above*) Vacuum system for a single-engine airplane.

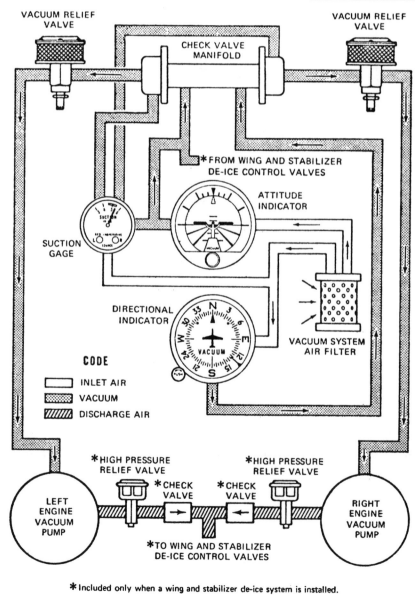

Fig. 4-69. Vacuum system for a light twin.

5 Takeoff Performance

The first measurement of a good pilot is headwork—thinking well in an airplane. Running a close second for the experienced pilot is the ability to get the most out of the plane when it is needed. If you don't know what your airplane can do you may either set such a high safety margin that performance suffers, or such a low margin as to damage your airplane and yourself. Sometimes it takes a great deal of intestinal fortitude to do what's right—for instance, during a short-field takeoff with high trees at the far end. Logic and knowledge tell you that forcing the plane off too soon will cost takeoff performance, while instinct pushes for you to get it off *now*. It requires an understanding of airplane performance and sometimes a lot of argument with yourself to do what's right in a particular situation.

The following chapters on performance will be based on your understanding of the following:

1. The air density in slugs per cubic foot is 0.002378 at sea level (standard day) and decreases with altitude.

2. The sea level standard pressure is 29.92 in. of mercury, or 2116 lb per square foot, and decreases at the rate of approximately 1 in. of mercury, or 75 lb per square foot, per 1000 ft. This is only an approximation. We will be considering only the lower part of the atmosphere (up to 10,000 ft) in this chapter.

3. The standard sea level temperature is 59°F, or 15°C, and decreases 3½°F, or 2°C, per 1000 ft (the temperature normal lapse rate is 3½°F or 2°C per 1000 ft). Performance thumb rules and data are based on normally aspirated engines (no superchargers) unless specifically stated.

TAKEOFFS IN GENERAL

The takeoff is usually the most critical part of the flight because (1) the plane is most heavily loaded at this point, and (2) if the field is somewhat soft or has high grass or snow, the takeoff suffers (but the landing roll is helped if it's not so soft as to cause a nose up). Because of these two factors in particular, it's possible for you to get into a field from which you can't fly out.

Takeoff Variables

ALTITUDE AND TEMPERATURE EFFECTS. The air density decreases with altitude and, as you remember, air density (ϱ) is a factor of Lift.

Let's say that at the point of takeoff, Lift just equals Weight (this is for a takeoff at any altitude). It would also simplify our discussion to say that the plane lifts off at the maximum angle of attack. In most cases this doesn't happen—that is, you don't "stall it off"—but it makes for easier figuring here, so we'll do it. So, the maximum angle of attack (without stalling) and wing area are the same for the takeoff at any altitude, and the density is less at higher altitudes. Assuming the Weight of the airplane is the same as you had at a sea level airport, at higher altitudes you'll have to make up for the decrease in density by an increased true airspeed before the airplane can lift off. The *indicated* airspeed will be the same for a high-altitude takeoff as it is at sea level, but it will take longer to get this indicated airspeed, the big reason being that the engine can't develop sea level HP. The result is that more runway is required with an increase in density-altitude. This increase in takeoff run can be predicted. As one pilot said after trying to take off from a short field at a high altitude and

going off the end of the runway, through two fences, a hedge, across a busy highway, and through a yard, "About this time I began to wonder if I was going to get off."

The atmospheric density does not decrease in a straight line, like temperature. At 20,000 ft the density is about half that of sea level. At 40,000 ft the density is approximately half that of 20,000 ft, and so on, with the density halving about every 18,000 to 20,000 ft. Density is a function of pressure altitude and temperature.

The FAA has produced two density-altitude computers, one for fixed-pitch-propeller airplanes and the other for variable-pitch-propeller airplanes. The computers are used to check the takeoff and climb performance of these two airplane types at higher density-altitudes.

How do you find the density-altitude without a computer? Here are the temperatures for standard altitudes (density-altitudes) from sea level to 8000 ft (rounded off to the nearest degree):

Sea level	59°F, 15°C		5000	41°F, 5°C
1000	55°F, 13°C		6000	38°F, 3°C
2000	52°F, 11°C		7000	34°F, 1°C
3000	48°F, 9°C		8000	31°F, −1°C
4000	45°F, 7°C			

Keep this in mind: For every ±15°F or ±8½°C variation from standard temperature at your pressure altitude, the density-altitude is increased or decreased 1000 ft.

For instance, you are ready to take off and set the altimeter to 29.92. The pressure altitude given is 3000 ft and the outside air temperature is +22°C. The *standard* temperature at 3000 ft is +9°C, or the temperature is 13°C *higher than normal*. This higher temperature means that the air is *less* dense and the airplane is operating at a *higher* density-altitude. This 13°C higher-than-standard temperature means adding another 1500 ft, for a *density*-altitude of 4500 ft.

You should use the *POH* figures if they are available rather than using the FAA computers or the following thumb rules.

A high temperature, even at sea level or a low altitude airport, can hurt the airplane's takeoff performance. You can check by looking at the equation of state: $\varrho = P/1716T$. If the temperature increases, the density decreases and vice versa (constant pressure). The relative humidity also affects performance. *Moist air, for the same temperature, is less dense than dry air.* Common sense would seem to tell you that water is heavier than air and the more water vapor present, the denser the air should be. *This is not the case.*

If you had high school or college chemistry you might be interested in the following analogy: As you know, the air is made up of approximately 78% nitrogen and 20% oxygen, with other gases making up the very small remainder. For this example, forget the other gases and say that air is composed of a ratio of 4 molecules of nitrogen to 1 molecule of oxygen. The atomic weights of the basic elements are hydrogen—1, oxygen—16, nitrogen—14. The molecular weights of the basic elements (2 atoms to a molecule) are H_2—2, N_2—28, O_2—32. (H_2O [water] is 18.) Assuming then that a particle of air has 4 nitrogen and 1 oxygen molecules, the total weight would be $N_2 = 4 \times 28 = 112$ and $O_2 = 1 \times 32 = 32$; $112 + 32 = 144$. So, a particle of "dry" air composed of 5 molecules "weighs" (has a relative density of) 144.

If all 5 of those molecules were replaced by water molecules, the results would be $5 \times 18 = 90$.

The moist air, based on this highly exaggerated example, would have a density of 90/144 = 0.62, or 62% of the completely dry air. Well, it's not quite that simple, for several reasons, but the fact is that moist air is "lighter" than dry air and won't allow as much Lift—and particularly HP and

Thrust—to be produced. If you calculated the effects of changing air from a very low relative humidity to 100% relative humidity at 100°F (which is a highly moist condition since every 20°F increase in temperature allows a parcel of air to double its ability to hold moisture), you'd find that a given air density would decrease approximately 2 to 3%. The effects on *Lift* would be negligible in reasonable situations but the reciprocating engine may lose up to 12% power depending on the amount of moisture existing. So, the aerodynamics of the takeoff are not so affected as is the power. Turbojet engines are not affected so much by increased moisture.

Back in Chap. 4, in discussing altimeter errors, it was mentioned that wide variations from standard temperature at your altitude can cause errors in the altimeter indications. In the case of a takeoff or landing at the airport giving the altimeter setting, any errors due to variations from standard temperature will have been compensated for in the setting. (On takeoff you will set your altimeter to field elevation, anyway.) Remember that the altimeter-temperature error is zero at the surface of the airport at which the setting is obtained (sea level is often used as an example but it's true for any airport elevation).

AIRCRAFT LOADING EFFECTS. Aircraft loading and its effect on stability and control will be covered in a later chapter, but the effects of Weight itself on takeoff runs should be noted here. Weight has a decided influence on the distance required for lift-off; the factor is (present weight/max certificated Weight)². If the airplane is 10% over the Weight given for a particular ground run value, the new distance would be 1.1^2 = 1.21, or 21% longer. (The worst situation for takeoff would be an overloaded airplane on a short, soft field at high altitude on a hot, moist day in tailwind or no-wind conditions—but more about the other factors later.)

Getting back to Weight effects alone, the same equation applies for lower Weights as well. For instance, an airplane requiring a ground run (roll) of 1000 ft at its max certificated Weight of 3000 lb would require a run of approximately 640 ft at a Weight of 2400 lb at that same density-altitude and wind and runway conditions, or $(2400/3000)^2 = (0.8)^2 = 0.64$. The airplane would require about 640 ft to lift off at the lower Weight. The *POHs* give takeoff distances at several Weights (as well as at different pressure altitudes and temperatures).

RUNWAY SURFACE EFFECTS. A soft or rough field, high grass, or deep snow can affect your takeoff distance—but common sense has been telling you this for some time. The ground drag of your airplane caused by the runway surface is called *rolling resistance*. The equation for this resistance is $R = \mu(\text{Weight} - \text{Lift})$, where μ is the coefficient of friction for that particular runway surface. The following table shows rolling resistance coefficients and thumb rules for added takeoff roll for some surfaces at *sea level*.

Takeoff Surface	μ	Required Takeoff Roll
Concrete or asphalt	0.02	*POH* figure
Firm turf	0.04	*POH* figure + 7%
Short grass	0.05	*POH* figure + 10%
Tall grass	0.10	*POH* figure + 25%
Soft field, deep snow	0.10–0.30	*POH* figure + 25%–infinity

These figures are approximate only and are based on airplanes with a power loading of 10 to 16 lb per HP, or max Weight per takeoff HP = 10 to 16 lb per HP. These figures vary with power loading. Airplanes with a lower power loading, that is, *less Weight per HP, are affected proportionately less* by increased rolling resistance than is a heavy airplane with little power. At a higher density-altitude the required takeoff distance increases for a given airplane because the engine is unable to develop full sea level HP, yet the airplane has the same max certificated Weight. Its power loading is increased and so are the rolling resistance effects. That's why it should be noted that the thumb rules for runway surface here are for *sea level*.

The percentage of additional runway required rises sharply at a μ higher than 0.15. In fact, none of the airplanes used as samples could even move at a μ of 0.30.

As an example, a certain four-place airplane has a max certificated Weight of 3000 lb and a static Thrust of 865 lb at sea level. At a μ of 0.30 (soft field, deep snow, etc.) the rolling resistance at gross Weight is $\mu(\text{Weight} - \text{Lift})$ or 0.30(3000 − 0). There is no Lift at the beginning of the roll and the result is μ times Weight = 0.30 × 3000 = 900 lb, *or 35 lb more than the Thrust available at full power*. It won't move. That's where the term infinity comes in, although in this extreme case infinity would be a better term for the *time*

Fig. 5-1. Overloading means extra-long takeoff runs.

required to get airborne, since the distance traveled would be zero ft.

One point—pilots' definitions of short or tall grass vary. One of your flying buddies may consider grass as being short if it's less than waist high while you may think that grass on a putting green is tall.

Because of this rolling resistance, for a soft-field takeoff you will want to get the Weight off the wheels as soon as possible. (Okay, so you knew that already.)

Fig. 5-2 is a general look at the two retarding forces (Drag and rolling resistance) versus calibrated airspeed from zero motion to lift-off speed on a *level concrete surface*. The total retarding force is the sum of the two, and you can note that rolling resistance is the big factor for the first part of the run, becoming zero at the lift-off (where there's no Weight on the wheels). Aerodynamic Drag is the big factor in the later part of the ground run (after the airspeed at point A).

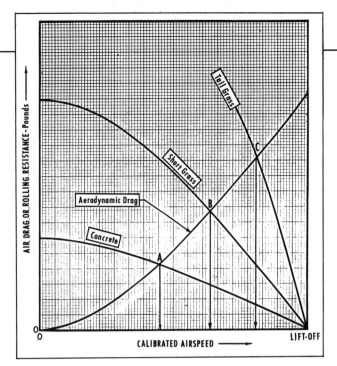

Fig. 5-3. A general comparison of the effects of concrete, short grass, and tall grass surfaces for the ground run portion of the takeoff.

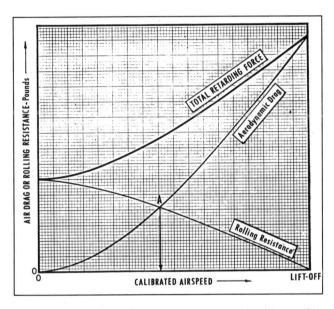

Fig. 5-2. Aerodynamic Drag and rolling resistance versus calibrated airspeed.

Fig. 5-3 shows some exaggerated effects of short and tall grass compared with the concrete surface of Fig. 5-2. All surfaces are level.

Points A, B, and C (airspeeds) indicate that (as you probably know by now) the higher the rolling resistance, the sooner the Weight should be taken off the wheels. If when taking off in tall grass you keep the nose down, maintaining a level-flight altitude, the total retarding force (mainly rolling resistance) will considerably extend the required lift-off distance.

Fig. 5-4 is a look at some approximate numbers for that 3000-lb airplane with 865 lb static Thrust that was mentioned awhile back. Some actual numbers are used, though rounding off was done and some assumptions made (for instance, that the pilot held a certain constant coefficient of Lift, or C_L, in the run until 55 K, then rotating to the lift-off altitude, or lift-off C_L, and accomplishing lift-off at 65 K). Note that the Thrust decreases from 865 lb at 0 K to 640 lb at 65 K (lift-off).

The *net accelerating force* (NAF) is the difference between the Thrust available and the total retarding force, and as you can see *in this case the NAF decreases as the airspeed increases*. Note also that total aerodynamic Drag increases at a fairly predictable rate until at 55 K when the pitch attitude is increased. The aerodynamic Drag increases rapidly there (be-

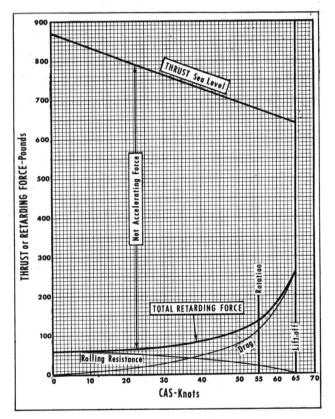

Fig. 5-4. Thrust and retarding forces for a 3000-lb, four-place airplane developing 865 lb of static Thrust at sea level on a dry concrete runway surface.

cause of the increased induced Drag) until 65 K is obtained, and then it is the total retarding force after lift-off.

Wait a minute—there seems to be a problem here. Earlier you read that in straight and level unaccelerated flight Thrust and Drag are equal, or the maximum level-flight speed of an airplane is when the maximum Thrust is equaled by the total

Drag. Looking at Fig. 5-4 and extending the Thrust and Drag curves you'll see that they would intersect at (roughly) 80 K. Based on that it would seem that this airplane is close to the mythical one you've heard about that takes off and cruises (and lands) at the same airspeed.

Fig. 5-5 shows that the physics of takeoffs (ground portion) and flight have two different requirements. The airplane in Fig. 5-4 does have different Drag characteristics in the two types of operation; "use power to go faster" doesn't always work when airborne. When you lift off you are transitioning from a ground vehicle to one of flight. If you are smooth it's not the abrupt transition implied by Fig. 5-5. (Note in Fig. 5-5 that the maximum level-flight speed is 145 K, not the approximately 80 K that might be derived from extending the curves in Fig. 5-4.)

Fig. 5-6 shows the same 3000-lb airplane taking off at sea level, again rotating at 55 K and lifting off at 65 K. This time, it's in tall grass with a μ of 0.10, so that the initial rolling resistance is $3000 \times 0.10 = 300$ lb. Comparing the NAF with that of dry concrete in Fig. 5-4 you can see that NAF is lower at the beginning of the run but is the same value at lift-off (since aerodynamic Drag is the same). The point is that it would be better to rotate earlier than 55 K to do the job. Again note that the total retarding force is the sum of the two forces (Drag and rolling resistance).

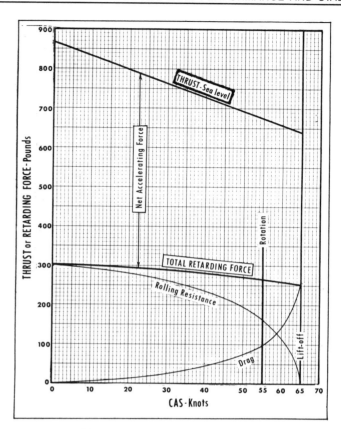

Fig. 5-6. Thrust and retarding forces, at a Weight of 3000 lb, at sea level, in tall grass (μ = 0.10).

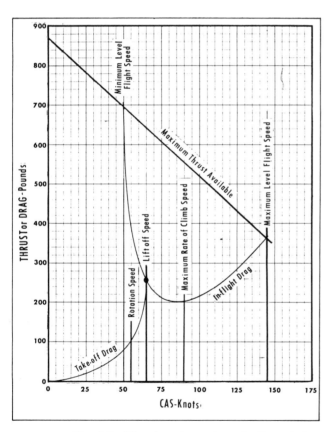

Fig. 5-5. Thrust and aerodynamic Drag during the takeoff run (dry concrete) and in flight at sea level for the airplane in Fig. 5-4.

RUNWAY SLOPE EFFECTS. This one is hard to handle. If you have figures on the slope of the particular runway you're using and are handy with mathematics (as well as having plenty of time), you can figure it out. Obviously if you are taking off uphill, more runway will be required; downhill, less. It's factors like runway slope that shoot some beautiful takeoff calcu-

lations right out the window. For safety, add 10% for an uphill run at sea level. At higher density-altitudes the slope effects will be a bigger factor since available Thrust for acceleration will be less.

There is always the question of whether to take off uphill and upwind or downhill and downwind. This depends on the wind and runway slope, of course. If you are operating from the average hard-surface airport where slopes are within certain maximum allowable values it is better to take off into the wind and uphill *if the headwind component is 10% or more of your takeoff speed.* On off-airport landings or at small airports where slopes may be comparatively steep you'll have to make your own decision according to the conditions.

FAA airport design standards (utility airports) limit the maximum slope on portions of the runway to 2%, or a little over 1.2°. Fig. 5-7 shows the effects of a *2° slope* on a 3000-lb airplane. (The angle is exaggerated a *little*.) As you can see, the rearward component of Weight has a value of 105 lb, which has a significant effect even at sea level, since the static Thrust available is only 865 lb.

Fig. 5-8 shows the effects of a 2° slope, aerodynamic Drag, the rolling resistance of tall grass, and a density-altitude of 5000 ft on the net accelerating force. (Compare Fig. 5-4 and 5-8 to see how the added factors can increase the takeoff run.)

The aerodynamic Drag is equal for Figs. 5-4, 5-5, 5-6, and 5-8, since the airplane set up the same C_L for the run up to 55 K and rotated at that point to the C_L required to lift off at 65 K. (This part of pilot technique will be covered shortly.) In looking at the curves, note the points that could give some general expectations about takeoff performance. The sample airplane used here has a fixed gear, a constant-speed propeller, weighs 3000 lb, and (again) has a *static* Thrust of 865 lb that decreases to 640 lb at 65 K at sea level.

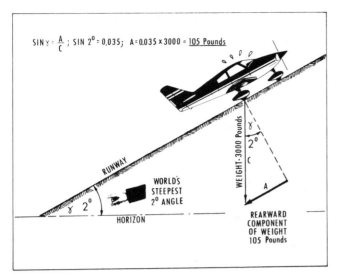

$SIN \gamma = \frac{A}{C}$; $SIN\ 2^\circ = 0.035$; $A = 0.035 \times 3000 = \underline{105\ Pounds}$

Fig. 5-7. Effects of a 2° slope on the rearward component of Weight.

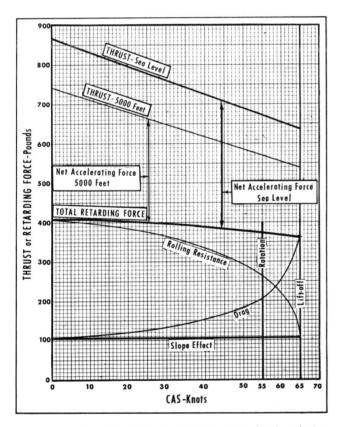

Fig. 5-8. Thrust available at sea level and at a 5000-ft density-altitude and the total retarding force in tall grass with an upslope of 2°. The total retarding force at any point in the takeoff run is the sum of rolling resistance, aerodynamic Drag, and slope effect.

The rate of acceleration will generally decrease as the takeoff run continues. The net acceleration force (NAF) will be less as the calibrated airspeed picks up, as noted earlier. The point is that if the acceleration is bad at the beginning it's not apt to *increase* as the airspeed picks up. Comparing Figs. 5-4 and 5-6 (remember that both are for sea level) you can see that the total retarding force is greatly affected by the rolling

resistance existing but the *drop* of Thrust available with increasing airspeed is the big factor in decrease in the NAF. On soft-field takeoffs your subjective feeling may be that the airplane, in the initial part of the run, is not accelerating as on dry concrete (naturally) but seems to be doing as expected for this condition. There seems to be a point about halfway to the expected lift-off spot that the airspeed stops increasing and sort of hovers around a particular (too-low) value. *This is the decision time:* (1) close the throttle and taxi back for another shot at it (this can be a useful technique in some cases, to pack the snow or press the grass down with a few dummy runs) or (2) keep at it and hope that it will pick up airspeed again, break loose, and let you clear the trees? You might prepare for the decision by stepping off the limit of the distance available to get off and safely clear obstacles. Use 2.5 ft as your measure for each "normal" step and if you are slogging through snow or tall grass better cut this down to 2 ft. If you assume a 3-ft pace, you might find the hard way that a 400-pace (what you think is 1200-ft) distance could be much closer to 800 ft. One possibility is to correctly pace off the *safe distance for lift-off* and put a marker at the halfway point. If you don't have an indicated (calibrated) airspeed of 0.7 (or 70%) of the lift-off speed at that halfway marker you will not likely have lift-off speed at the end point. (This naturally assumes a constant coefficient of rolling resistance—if the "second half" of the surface is softer the airplane may slow down and never get off.)

For example, you are taking off from a small grass airport and you've estimated that to clear the trees 1800 ft is the maximum that can be used for the takeoff run. The airplane has to break ground at the usual rotation speed to get the max angle climb speed, V_x, and get over the obstacle(s). You put a rag or marker that can be readily seen on the side of the takeoff area at the 900-ft point. With a lift-off speed (CAS) of 65 K you'll need (0.7 × 65) = 45.5 K. Call it 45 K, an easily seen value on the airspeed indicator.

Look at Figs. 5-4 and 5-8 to compare the net accelerating forces if you had been accustomed to dry, level, concrete runways at sea level and now find yourself on a runway with tall grass at gross Weight at a 5000-ft density-altitude. At 40 K (for instance) the sea level NAF (dry, level concrete) is about 640 lb; in the example at 5000 ft the NAF is about 230 lb. You won't have to worry about passengers' whiplash injuries during the run in the latter case.

WIND CONDITION EFFECTS. The wind affects the takeoff both in time and distance; of the two, distance is the most important. The headwind component is the important factor, and you need to know its value. For instance, a 30-K wind at a 30° angle to the runway would have a headwind component of 26 K—you might take a look back at Figs. 1-5, 1-8, and 3-2. (The cosine of 30° is 0.866; 0.866 × 30 = 26 K, rounded off.)

The graph in Fig. 5-9 shows that the wind effects are not as straightforward as they might at first seem. For instance, if the wind down the runway is 25% of the takeoff speed, Fig. 5-9 shows that the length required for lift-off would be only 58% of that required under no-wind conditions. Common sense would seem to tell you that 75% is the answer.

Fig. 5-10 is a quick way to find the multipliers for headwind and crosswind components. For instance, if the wind is at a 20° angle to the runway at 20 K you would see by referring to it that the headwind and crosswind components would be 18 K and 7 K respectively. You gain more by having a headwind than you might at first think.

PILOT TECHNIQUE EFFECTS. The figures for takeoff distance in the *POH* are obtained by experienced test pilots and show better performance than a 75-hr private pilot might get, but these published figures at least give some basis for compari-

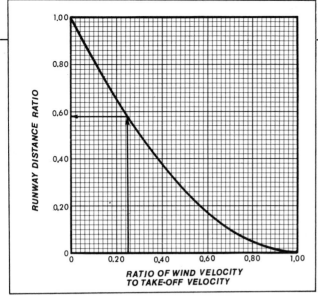

Fig. 5-9. Effects of wind on takeoff run (or roll). Use the headwind component.

son. The disheartening thing is that takeoff techniques even vary between equally experienced pilots. In fact, it's very doubtful whether anyone could make two consecutive take-offs just alike even though runway and wind conditions were exactly the same.

Assume that you carefully calculate pressure altitude and temperature effects, Weight, and wind effects before takeoff—and then use sloppy techniques. The effect is as if you measured something carefully with a micrometer, marked it exactly, and then cut it off with a blunt ax. Nevertheless, you

The Angle That the Wind Makes With the Runway	Cos α Multiplier for Headwind Component	Sin α Multiplier for Crosswind Component
0° (straight down the runway)	1.0	0
10°	1.0	0.15
15°	0.95	0.25
20°	0.90	0.35
30°	0.85	0.50
40°	0.75	0.65
45°	0.70	0.70
60°	0.50	0.85
75°	0.25	0.95
90° (Direct Crosswind)	0	1.0

Fig. 5-10. Headwind and crosswind components for the wind at various angles to the runway (rounded off).

should have some idea of the effects of variables on the take-off run to have a rough estimate of how much distance you'll need.

Assume an airplane with a constant-speed propeller that grosses at 3000 lb and according to the *POH* requires 1000 ft to break ground at sea level on a standard day (no wind). Suppose the pilot finds that the pressure altitude for the air-port on that day is 3400 ft. (The airport may actually be only 3000 ft above sea level but due to local low-pressure condi-tions the pressure altitude is higher than the actual elevation.) The temperature is 76°F and the wind is 30° to the runway at 10 K. The airplane's power-off stall speed for the takeoff con-figuration is 60 K. The takeoff speed is generally considered to be 1.2 times the power-off stall speed, so 72 K will be the

takeoff speed used for these calculations. Assume that the runway is hard surfaced and level. The plane weighs 3300 lb because, although it's illegal to be over gross, the pilot wants to take an extra passenger wedged in the back seat (plus some extra baggage).

The following steps apply:

1. *Pressure altitude and temperature effects*—Note that the pressure altitude is 3400 ft (standard temperature for this altitude is 47°F or 8°C) and the temperature is 76°F (24°C) or 29°F higher than normal. Remember that each added 15°F or 8½°C above standard equals another 1000 ft of density-alti-tude. The density-altitude is 2000 ft higher (rounded off) than the pressure altitude. *The airplane will perform at a density-altitude of 5400 ft, no matter what the altimeter says.* Add 12% per 1000 ft (5.4 × 12 = 65%). *The takeoff roll at this point will be 1650 ft.*

2. *Weight effects*—The airplane's Weight is (present Weight/gross Weight)² = (3300/3000)² = 1.1² = 1.21; 1.21 × 1650 = 1995 ft now needed to break ground (call it 2000 ft).

3. *Wind effects*—Assuming that the takeoff is into the wind (although anyone who overloads an airplane so much might decide to take off downwind just for the heck of it), the multiplier for the headwind component for a wind at an angle of 30° to the runway is 0.85 (Fig. 5-10); 0.85 × 10 = 8.5 K. If your airspeed indicator is in mph, you can convert this wind speed to mph by multiplying by 1.15; 1.15 × 8.5 = 9.8 mph (call it 10 mph).

In order to use Fig. 5-9 the ratio of wind velocity to takeoff velocity is needed; $V_{wind}/V_{takeoff}$ = 8.5 K/72 K = 0.118 or 0.12. Referring to Fig. 5-9 you find that the ratio takeoff distance (wind)/take-off distance (no wind) = 0.80. So finally: 0.80 × 2000 = *about 1600 ft runway required at a pressure altitude of 3400 ft, temperature of 76°F, weight of 3300 lb and a wind of 10 K at an angle of 30° to the runway. This doesn't take into account runway slope or bad pilot tech-nique.* Another thing to remember (again) is that tall grass, snow, or mud could possibly double this distance.

What about the climb? It's affected also. At sea level you can expect the distance (after lift-off) to clear a 50-ft obstacle to be about 80% of the takeoff roll. The sample airplane with a takeoff roll of 1000 ft would likely require another 800 ft to clear a 50-ft obstacle. The distance to clear a 50-ft obstacle increases with increase in density-altitude and Weight, but the airplane with the fixed-pitch propeller suffers more.

RULE OF THUMB TAKEOFF VARIABLES FOR UNSUPERCHARGED ENGINES

1. *Add 12% to the takeoff run, as given in the POH for sea level, for every 1000 ft of pressure altitude at the takeoff point.*

2. *Add 12% to the above figure for every 15°F or 8.5°C above standard for the field pressure altitude.*

3. *Weight effects*—The *POH* takeoff figures are for the gross Weight of the airplane unless otherwise stated. The take-off run is affected approximately by the square of the Weight change. For example, a 10% Weight change causes a 21% change in length of takeoff run.

4. *Wind effects*—The ratio of wind velocity (down the runway) to your takeoff speed (in percentage) subtracted from 90% gives the expected ratio of *runway length needed to break ground.* If wind = 20% of takeoff velocity, 90 − 20 = 70%. You'll use 70% of the runway distance as given by the *POH* for no-wind conditions. This rule of thumb can be used if you don't have Fig. 5-9 handy. Consider any headwind com-ponent less than 5 K to be calm and to have no effect on takeoff run if you use the just-mentioned rule of thumb.

Fig. 5-11. Sometimes you don't have time for computing.

THE NORMAL TAKEOFF

Tricycle-Gear. For computing takeoff distance, engineers sometimes use a speed at lift-off of 1.1 times the power-off stall speed. You know, as a pilot, that you can lift a plane off at stall speed, but this is usually reserved for special occasions such as soft-field takeoffs. The 1.1 figure is recommended to preclude your getting too deeply in the backside of the power-required curve.

If you pull the plane off in a cocked-up attitude and try to climb too steeply, you will use a great deal of your power just keeping the plane flying, much less getting on with your trip.

This too-nose-high attitude is particularly critical for jet takeoffs. Jet pilots pulling the nose too high during the takeoff run have found themselves running out of runway with the plane having no inclination to make like a bird. In fact, a 100-mi-long runway wouldn't be any better—you'd still be sitting there waiting for something to happen when there was no more runway left (Fig. 5-11).

The prop plane has more HP to spare at low speeds and will accelerate or climb out of the bad situation more quickly. But accelerating takes time and distance, and if there are obstacles off the end of the runway, you may wish you had shown a little more discretion in your method of lift-off. This problem is more evident in propeller planes of high power loadings (power loading = Weight/HP).

The "back side of the power curve" is also important on approaches. You can get your airplane so low and slow on final that by the time you accelerate or climb out of this condition, you may have gone through a fence and killed somebody's prize Hereford bull a good quarter mile short of the runway. You can get out of this region, but it may take more distance than you can spare at the moment.

If you feel that the nose is too high on the takeoff roll and the plane isn't accelerating as it should, then the nose must be lowered and the plane given a chance to accelerate—even though you don't particularly want to do this when there's not much runway left.

In an airplane that has an effective elevator and a not-so-effective rudder, it doesn't make for ease of mind if you yank the nosewheel off at the first opportunity, particularly in a strong left crosswind. On the other hand, nothing seems quite so amateurish as the pilot who runs down the runway hell-for-leather on all three wheels until the tires are screaming and then yanks it off. Just because it's a tricycle-gear doesn't mean that it should be ridden like a tricycle. The best normal take-off in a tricycle-gear plane is one in which after a proper interval of roll the nosewheel is gently raised and shortly afterward the airplane flies itself off. No book can tell you just when to raise the nosewheel for all the different airplanes. *In fact, no book can tell you how to fly, as you are well aware of by now.*

Although retractable-gear airplanes will be covered in detail later, there are a couple of points to be mentioned. Too many pilots have the idea that it makes them look "hot" to pull up the gear as soon as the plane breaks ground. Airplanes have been known to settle back on the runway after a takeoff. The plane doesn't roll too well with the gear partially retracted. Don't retract the gear too soon, even if you are *definitely* airborne. That is, don't pull up the gear until you have reached the point where in case of engine failure the airplane can no longer be landed on the runway wheels *down*. It would be very embarrassing to use 500 ft of a 10,000-ft runway and then have to belly it in when the engine quit because you didn't have time to get the gear back down (Fig. 5-12).

Delaying the gear raising has its aerodynamic and performance advantages, too. For some airplanes, the transitioning of the gear (up *or* down) can increase parasite Drag as the gear doors open and shut. An airplane that has been forced off in a marginal condition and is barely holding its own staggering along just above the runway may have enough added interference Drag and form Drag during the gear raising that

Fig. 5-12. Haste can make waste.

aerodynamic laws would require it to settle back down on partially retracted gear, no matter how good your pilot technique might be (Fig. 5-13).

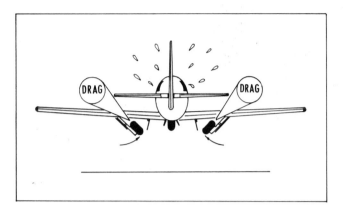

Fig. 5-13. The transition of the landing gear may cause unacceptable Drag.

Common Errors (Tricycle-Gear)

1. Holding the nosewheel on and jerking the airplane off the ground (a less violent technique similar to this is good for takeoffs in strong crosswinds but some people do it under all wind and weather conditions).

2. The other extreme, pulling the nose up too high and too early, which increases chances of poor directional control in a crosswind and extends the takeoff run. A typical case is one in which the pilot pulls the nosewheel off by brute force before it's ready, and has to apply lots of right rudder. The nose, not ready to stay up, falls back down with nosewheel cocked. This makes for a funny feeling.

Takeoffs for Tailwheel Types. Things being as they are today, it may be that you haven't checked out in a tailwheel airplane yet. For a long time there were few if any tricycle-gear trainers and everybody learned to fly in airplanes with tailwheels. Now the trend is reversed and nearly all the new planes have tricycle gear. This section is presented to give you a little background should you get a chance to check out in the tailwheel type.

The takeoff roll may be broken down into three phases.

PHASE 1. This phase usually gives the most trouble to the pilot checking out in this type. It's slightly harder to go from the tricycle-gear to the tailwheel-type than vice versa, but you'll have no trouble after the first few takeoffs and landings.

The big problem in this phase seems to be the inability to see over the nose at the beginning of the takeoff roll. You've been used to looking directly over the nose all through the tricycle-gear takeoff, and this may be a habit hard to break. You'll have to get used to looking down the side of the nose in most cases, although some tailwheel airplanes have low nose positions comparable to tricycle types.

Ease the throttle open. This is important for the tailwheel airplane because (1) the rudder-tailwheel combination has less positive control at low speeds and the sudden application of power causes torque effects that could make directional control a problem at first and (2) the high nose makes it harder to detect this torque-induced movement and may delay your corrective action.

The tailwheel will be doing most of the steering with the rudder becoming more effective as the airspeed picks up. In a high-powered, propeller airplane it may take a great deal of

rudder to do the job at the beginning of the takeoff run.

The elevators should be left at neutral or slightly ahead of neutral because you don't want to force the tail up too quickly and lose directional control.

You may for the first takeoff or two have a tendency to "walk the rudder." You've had enough experience by now to recognize this mistake and correct it yourself.

PHASE 2. As the plane picks up speed, allow (or assist slightly) the tail to come up until the airplane is in the attitude of a shallow climb. When the tail comes up, tailwheel steering is lost and the rudder itself is responsible for keeping the airplane straight. This means that added rudder deflection must make up for the loss of steering of the tailwheel. Your biggest steering problems will be at the beginning of the takeoff and at the point at which the tail comes up.

If the tail is abruptly raised, our old friend "precession" has a chance to act. The rotating propeller makes an efficient gyro, and when the tail is raised, it is as if a force were exerted at the top of the propeller arc, from the rear. The airplane reacts as if the force had been exerted at a point 90° around the propeller arc, or at the right side (Fig. 5-14). The precession force is added to the torque forces and could cause a *left* swerve if you are unprepared. The opposite occurs if the nose is abruptly raised in flight.

PHASE 3. The airplane is now in a shallow climb attitude and will fly itself off. However, you can help a little by slight back pressure. The rest of the takeoff and climb are just like the procedures you've been using with the tricycle-gear plane.

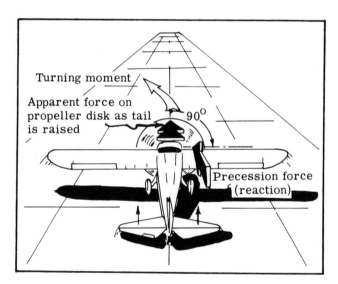

Fig. 5-14. Precession effects due to abrupt raising of the tail.

Common Errors (Tailwheel-Type)

1. Poor directional control.
2. Raising the tail abruptly and too high.
3. Trying to pull the plane off too early.

THE SHORT-FIELD TAKEOFF

The short-field takeoff is used in conjunction with the climb to clear an obstacle. Only the ground roll will be covered in this section; the maximum angle or obstacle climb will be covered in Chap. 6.

The airplane accelerates best when in the air if it is not "stalled off." The comparative amount of acceleration between the airplane at a given speed on the ground and airborne naturally depends on the surface. The airplane is ready to fly before the average pilot wants to; the pilot generally uses more runway than is necessary in becoming airborne. This is good under normal takeoff conditions as well as in gusty air, as it gives a margin of safety at lift-off. *But* in the case of the short-field takeoff, you don't have the runway to spare.

Some pilots are firm believers in the idea of holding the plane on until the last instant and then hauling back abruptly and screaming up over the obstacle. This makes the takeoff look a great deal more flashy and difficult than if the pilot had gotten the plane off sooner and set up a maximum angle climb. The rate of climb is a function of the excess HP available, as will be discussed in Chap. 6. In the maximum angle climb, you are interested in getting *more altitude per foot of ground covered,* rather than the best rate of climb. This is a compromise between a lower airspeed and lower rate of climb in order to clear an obstacle at a specific distance. True, you're not climbing at quite as great a rate, but on the other hand, because of the lower speed you're not approaching the obstacle as quickly either.

The recommended takeoff procedure is close to the soft-field technique. Get the plane airborne as soon as possible without stalling it off. In most cases the airplane will be accelerating as it climbs. Only in underpowered and/or overloaded airplanes will it be necessary to definitely level off to pick up the recommended maximum angle climb speed.

Some sources recommend that you rotate to lift-off just as the best angle of climb airspeed is attained and maintain that speed until the assumed obstructions have been cleared. This is a standardized procedure. The main drawback is that the average pilot tends to let the airspeed pick up after lift-off and get well over the best angle of climb speed, losing performance. You can talk with pilots experienced in your airplane and work out the best technique for takeoff and climb. It may very well be that rotating at V_x is best, and you can hold this exact speed after lift-off.

Use of Flaps. Manufacturers recommend a certain flap setting for the short-field takeoff because they have found that this flap setting results in a shorter takeoff run and better angle of climb. For some airplanes, the manufacturers recommend that no flaps be used on the short-field takeoff and for best performance it is wise to follow the recommendations given in the *POH*.

There are two schools of thought on the technique of using flaps for a short-field takeoff. One is to use no flaps at all for the first part of the run and then apply flaps (generally full flaps) when the time seems ripe. This technique generally disregards the fact that there is rolling resistance present. The first part of the roll usually is made with the airplane in a level-flight attitude, the pilot counting on the sudden application of flaps to obtain Lift for the takeoff. There is no doubt that aerodynamic Drag is less in the level-flight attitude than in a tail-low attitude, but rolling resistance is the greatest factor in the earlier part of the run and this is often overlooked. If the field is soft, an inefficient and perhaps dangerous (particularly in the tailwheel type) condition may be set up because Weight is not being taken from the main wheels and a nosing-up tendency is present.

The ideal point at which to lower flaps differs widely between pilots.

The effect of full flaps on the obstacle climb (unless the plane design calls specifically for the use of full flaps) results in a low Lift-to-Drag ratio—that is, an increase of proportionally more Drag for the amount of Lift required, so the climb angle suffers.

There is usually a loss in pilot technique (particularly in

the tailwheel type) during the flap lowering. The pilot has to divide attention between the takeoff and flap manipulation. This can be overcome as the pilot becomes more familiar with the airplane, but in most cases the flap handle is located in an awkward position or requires attention to operate. The flaps generally are designed to be operated at a point where the pilot can direct attention to them if necessary—that is, *before* takeoff, on the base leg or on final. The takeoff itself requires more attention than these other procedures. The pilot attempting to deflect the flaps the correct amount during the takeoff run may get two notches instead of three, or over- or undershoot the desired setting if the flaps are hydraulically or electrically actuated.

The other, and better, technique is to set the flaps at the recommended angle *before* starting the takeoff run and then forget about them until the obstacle is well cleared. Fly the airplane off and attain, *and maintain,* the recommended climb speed. *After* the obstacle is cleared, ease the nose over slightly and pick up airspeed until you have a safe margin to ease the flaps up. Some pilots clear the obstacle, breathe a sigh of relief, jerk the flaps up, and grandly sink back into the trees. On some airplanes the *POH*-recommended maximum angle of climb speed is fairly close to the power-on stall speed. Although you had a good safety margin with the flaps down, when you jerk them up at this speed at a low altitude, you could have problems in gusty air. (A common error, however, is to be overly cautious.)

Short-Field Takeoff Procedure (Tailwheel or Tricycle-Gear)

1. Before takeoff, use a careful pretakeoff check and a full power run up to make sure the engine is developing full power. Don't waste runway; start at the extreme end. Set flaps as recommended by the *POH*. (Lean the mixture as necessary.)

2. Open the throttle wide (smoothly) as you release the brakes. (Don't wait until the throttle is completely open before releasing the brakes.)

3. Keep the airplane straight and avoid "rudder walking," as this slows the takeoff.

4. Get the airplane airborne as soon as is safely possible without "stalling it off." This means that the nosewheel of the tricycle-gear type is raised as soon as practicable (not *too* high) and on the tailwheel-type the attitude is tail low, similar to that of the soft-field takeoff. In both cases, the airplane is flown off at a slightly lower-than-usual airspeed.

5. Attain and *maintain* the recommended maximum angle climb speed as given in the *POH*. Continue to use full power until the obstacle is cleared.

6. Retract the landing gear (if so equipped).

7. Assume a normal climb. (The climb will be discussed later.)

Some pilots argue for a 90° rolling takeoff, but this is hard on tires and landing gear assemblies for very little, if any, gain. It's agreed that the fixed-pitch prop is inefficient at low speeds (Chap. 2) but you might ground loop using the 90°-run technique.

It's possible that a too-sharp turn onto the runway could "unport the fuel" on one side. Suppose you're making an extra-sharp high-speed left turn onto the runway and have selected the right wing tank for takeoff. (That was the fullest and the one selected before the run-up.) As you make that turn centrifugal force moves the fuel away from the port opening of the fuel line. You could have a loss of power during the takeoff run or right after lift-off (Fig. 5-15).

Common Errors

1. Poor directional control when the brakes are released.

2. Trying to hurry the plane off the ground, resulting in high Drag and actually slowing the takeoff.

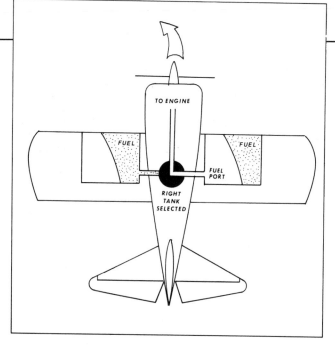

Fig. 5-15. The centrifugal force of the sharp left turn moved the fuel from the tank port and the engine is being starved at a bad time. (There is usually just enough fuel left in the line to let the airplane get too far to land on the runway.) One solution used over the years is that of baffles in the fuel tank to slow, or stop, fuel "sloshing."

3. Holding the plane down after breaking ground, letting the airspeed pick up past the maximum angle of climb speed and losing climb efficiency.

THE SOFT-FIELD TAKEOFF

(Use flaps as recommended by the *POH*.)

Maybe the only soft-field takeoff procedures you've used so far were the simulated ones practiced for the private flight test. But sooner or later you'll find yourself in a spot where the field may be too soft for a normal takeoff.

Generally speaking, mud, snow, and high grass can be considered to fall into the category where a special takeoff technique is required. This same technique is useful on a rough field where it's better to get the plane off as soon as possible to minimize chances of damaging the landing gear.

Tricycle-Gear. Keep the airplane rolling. If you stop to think things over in the middle of the takeoff area, you may find yourself watching the wheels slowly sinking in the muck. It may take full power to even move once you've stopped. The propeller will pick up mud and gravel and throw it into the stabilizer or stabilator. This doesn't help either the prop or the tail surfaces.

Rolling resistance is high, so you will want a tail-low attitude on the takeoff run to help overcome this resistance.

1. The airplane is kept rolling, full throttle is applied, and the wheel (or stick) is held back for two reasons: (1) to get the Weight off the nosewheel, which will decrease rolling resistance as well as lessen chances of the nosewheel hitting an extra-soft spot and being damaged and (2) to increase the angle of attack as soon as possible so that the Weight on the main wheels is minimized.

2. As soon as the plane is definitely airborne, lower the nose and establish a normal climb.

Common Errors (Tricycle-Gear)

1. Not keeping the airplane moving as it is lined up with the takeoff area, requiring a great deal of power to get rolling again and increasing the possibility of prop damage.

2. Not enough back pressure. Most pilots tend to underestimate the amount of back pressure required to break the nosewheel from the ground at lower airspeeds.

Of course, you may be able to get the nose too high and suffer the same results as in the normal takeoff under these conditions—that is, no takeoff at all.

Tailwheel-Type. The soft-field takeoff is a little more touchy with the tailwheel airplane because of the greater chances of nosing up if a particularly soft spot, deeper snow, or higher grass is suddenly encountered. The tailwheel airplane has some advantage in that there is no large third wheel to cause added rolling resistance. The tailwheel is small and has comparatively little Weight on it to cause rolling resistance. *But* this could cause a nose up in a situation where the tricycle-gear plane would have no particular trouble. (It could break the nosewheel, however.)

You had soft-field takeoffs on the private flight test and, if you used a tailwheel-type plane, have a pretty good idea of the technique.

As with the tricycle-gear plane, the plane should be kept rolling onto the runway (invariably someone else is coming in for a landing and you'll have to wait anyway, but if you do, try to pick a firmer spot so you won't get mired down). This means that the pretakeoff check should be run at a good spot so that after ascertaining that there is no traffic coming in, you can get on the takeoff area and get about your business (Fig. 5-16).

Review Fig. 5-3 to get a nonquantitative comparison of the effects of tall grass or soft ground. You can see by comparing Figs. 5-4 and 5-6 that the initial ($V = 0$) rolling resistance for concrete and tall grass are 60 lb and 300 lb respectively.

Procedure

1. Keep the airplane rolling onto the runway and apply full power in the same manner as for a normal takeoff. Don't ram it open!

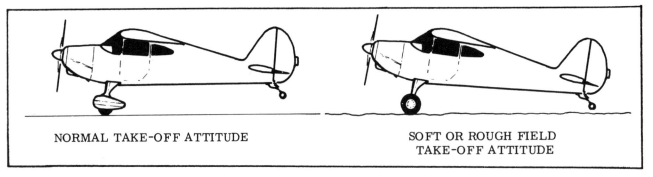

NORMAL TAKE-OFF ATTITUDE   SOFT OR ROUGH FIELD TAKE-OFF ATTITUDE

Fig. 5-16. Takeoff attitudes.

2. Keep the wheel (or stick) back to stop any early tendencies to nose over. Then—

3. Ease the tail up to a definitely tail-*low* position so that (1) the plane doesn't have a tendency to flip over and (2) the angle of attack is such as to get the plane airborne (and the Weight off the main wheels) as soon as possible.

4. As soon as the airplane is definitely airborne, lower the nose and establish a normal climb.

Common Errors (Tailwheel-Type)

1. Holding the stick back too firmly and too long, causing added tailwheel rolling resistance as well as aerodynamic Drag.

2. Getting the tail too high, with the danger of nosing up.

A REVIEW OF CROSSWIND TAKEOFFS

Tricycle-Gear. The wind's effect on both the tricycle-gear and tailwheel airplane on the ground generally is the same. That is, the airplane tends to weathercock into the wind and lean over as well (Fig. 5-17). The tricycle-gear plane does not have as strong a tendency to weathercock because the nose-wheel is large and there is more Weight on it, so there is a greater ground resistance, compared with the tailwheel-type.

In order to make a smooth crosswind takeoff you'll have to overcome these wind effects. Some lightplanes are hard to control when taken off in a strong left crosswind. The weathercocking tendency plus torque effects make it extremely difficult to have a straight takeoff run.

Procedure. Line up with the centerline of the runway, or on the downwind side if you think weathercocking will be so great as to make it impossible to keep the plane straight. If the wind is this strong, however, you might be better off to stay on the ground.

Assume, for instance, there is a fairly strong left crosswind component (10 K). It will require conscious effort on your part to apply and hold aileron into the wind. This is probably the most common fault of the relatively inexperienced pilot. It doesn't feel right to have the wheel or stick in such an awkward position. It is natural that the correction be eased off unconsciously shortly after the run begins. This may allow the wind to lift that upwind wing.

Another common error is the other extreme. The pilot uses full aileron at the beginning of the run and gets so engrossed in keeping the airplane straight that, when the plane does break ground, the full aileron may cause the airplane to

start a very steep bank into the wind. This does little for the passengers' peace of mind and is actually useful only if the pilot is interested in picking up a handkerchief with his wing tip.

Notice in Figs. 5-18 and 5-19 that the aileron into the wind actually has two effects: (1) it offsets the "leaning over" tendency (the ailerons have no effect in a 90° crosswind until the plane gets moving, though) and (2) the Drag of the down aileron helps fight the weathercocking tendency. Of course, most airplanes these days have differential aileron movement (the aileron goes further up than down) and the down aileron Drag has little effect on the tricycle-gear plane because of its takeoff attitude. Still, you'll have to fight the leaning tendency and the ailerons will be the answer.

This is a takeoff where you definitely should not rush the airplane into flying. The crosswind takeoff feels uncomfortable. It's perfectly natural to want to get the plane airborne

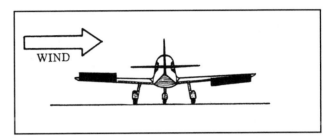

Fig. 5-18. Tricycle-gear attitude and use of ailerons to compensate for a crosswind.

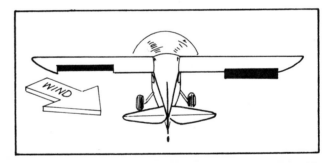

Fig. 5-19. Aileron deflection at the beginning of the crosswind takeoff (tailwheel-type).

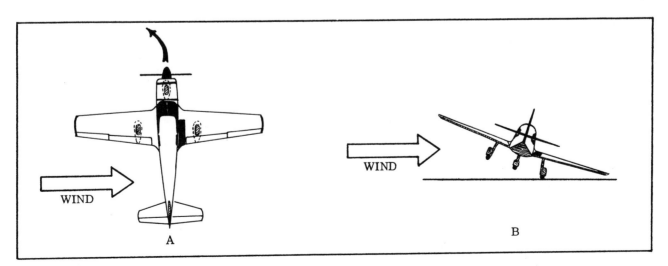

Fig. 5-17. Airplane tends to weathercock (A) as well as lean (B).

and stop all this monkey business. Keep the plane on the ground until you are certain it is ready to fly, then lift it off with definite, but not abrupt, back pressure. If the plane should skip into the air, try to keep it flying, if possible. It will start drifting as soon as you are off the ground, and it won't help the tires and landing gear assembly to hit again when you're moving sideways.

In other words, don't try to ease the nosewheel off as in a normal takeoff. The weathercocking effect in a large crosswind component may be more than you can handle with rudder alone (no nosewheel help). Again, this is particularly true in a left crosswind. In a right crosswind, torque and weathercocking tend to work against each other. The airplane should be kept on all three wheels until at the lift-off point.

The idea of keeping the plane on the ground longer applies to the tailwheel type for the same reasons as for the tricycle-gear airplane. The attitude of the plane during the run will be slightly more tail high than for the normal takeoff (which for the tailwheel type, you remember, was the attitude of a shallow climb).

A common failing of pilots in both types of airplanes is that a poor drift correction is set up on the climbout. There are the hardy but misguided souls who still believe that holding rudder into the wind or holding the upwind wing down is the best way to correct for a crosswind *on the climbout.*

You know by now that the average plane, if trimmed properly, will make its own takeoff, but this may not be the most efficient procedure, particularly under abnormal conditions. Many pilots have never flown their airplanes at gross Weight until one day they attempt it under adverse conditions—and leave an indelible impression on some object off the end of the runway.

SOME PRACTICAL CONSIDERATIONS

It's good to know the theory and factors that affect takeoff performance but you'll have to know how to use the charts for *your* airplane. The following charts are examples for review, starting with the simple and moving on to the more complex. Some people prefer a graphical presentation and others a tabular listing, but you should be prepared to use either one.

Fig. 5-20 is for a noncomplex trainer; you may have used this chart in your student and earlier private pilot days. The tabular form is self-explanatory, but you might work a couple of problems for review. Note that short-field techniques are used.

TAKEOFF DISTANCE

SHORT FIELD

CONDITIONS:
Flaps 10°
Full Throttle Prior to Brake Release
Paved, Level, Dry Runway
Zero Wind

NOTES:
1. Short field technique as specified in Section 4.
2. Prior to takeoff from fields above 3000 feet elevation, the mixture should be leaned to give maximum RPM in a full throttle, static runup.
3. Decrease distances 10% for each 9 knots headwind. For operation with tailwinds up to 10 knots, increase distances by 10% for each 2 knots.
4. For operation on a dry, grass runway, increase distances by 15% of the "ground roll" figure.

WEIGHT LBS	TAKEOFF SPEED KIAS		PRESS ALT FT	0°C		10°C		20°C		30°C		40°C	
	LIFT OFF	AT 50 FT		GRND ROLL	TOTAL TO CLEAR 50 FT OBS	GRND ROLL	TOTAL TO CLEAR 50 FT OBS	GRND ROLL	TOTAL TO CLEAR 50 FT OBS	GRND ROLL	TOTAL TO CLEAR 50 FT OBS	GRND ROLL	TOTAL TO CLEAR 50 FT OBS
1670	50	54	S.L.	640	1190	695	1290	755	1390	810	1495	875	1605
			1000	705	1310	765	1420	825	1530	890	1645	960	1770
			2000	775	1445	840	1565	910	1690	980	1820	1055	1960
			3000	855	1600	925	1730	1000	1870	1080	2020	1165	2185
			4000	940	1775	1020	1920	1100	2080	1190	2250	1285	2440
			5000	1040	1970	1125	2140	1215	2320	1315	2525	1420	2750
			6000	1145	2200	1245	2395	1345	2610	1455	2855	1570	3125
			7000	1270	2470	1375	2705	1490	2960	1615	3255	1745	3590
			8000	1405	2800	1525	3080	1655	3395	1795	3765	1940	4195

Fig. 5-20. Takeoff chart for a light trainer.

For instance, an airplane at 3000 ft pressure altitude (PA) and 10°C (at 1670 lb) requires a 925-ft ground roll and a total distance of 1730 ft to clear a 50–ft obstacle. At 1500 ft pressure altitude and 15°C you'd have to interpolate between 1000 and 2000 ft at 10°C and at 20°C. For example, 1000 ft at 10°C = *765* and *1420 ft;* 1000 ft at 20°C = *825* and *1530 ft;* 1000 ft at 15°C = 1590/2 and 2950/2 ft = *795* and *1475 ft.*

At 1000 ft PA and 15°C the airplane will require a 795-ft ground roll and 1475 ft to clear a 50-ft obstacle. Doing the interpolation for 2000 ft PA and 15°C, 2000 ft at 10°C = *840* and *1565 ft;* 2000 ft at 20°C = *910* and *1690 ft;* 2000 ft at 15°C = 1750/2 and 3255/2 = *875* and *1630 ft.* Finally, the two answers are averaged to get the performance at 1500 ft PA

and 15°C: (795 + 875)/2 and (1475 + 1630)/2 = *835* and *1555 ft* (rounded off).

Assuming no wind and taking off on a dry, grass runway at 1500 ft PA and 15°C you would add 15% of the ground roll (run?) figure to *both* distances: 0.15 × 835 = 125 ft; 835 + 125 = 960 ft ground roll; 1555 + 125 = *1680 ft total distance over a 50-ft obstacle.*

Assuming that a 9-K headwind has suddenly sprung up just as you start the roll on that dry, grass runway you would use approximately 10% *less* of the distance.

Fig. 5-21 is a takeoff distance chart for a more complex airplane with performance for two Weights given. You can interpolate altitudes, temperatures, *and* Weights with this.

TAKEOFF DISTANCE
2500 LBS AND 2300 LBS
SHORT FIELD

CONDITIONS:
Flaps Up
2700 RPM and Full Throttle Prior to Brake Release
Cowl Flaps Open
Paved, Level Dry Runway
Zero Wind

NOTES:
1. Short field technique as specified in Section 4.
2. Prior to takeoff from fields above 3000 feet elevation, the mixture should be leaned to give maximum power in a full throttle, static runup.
3. Decrease distances 10% for each 9 knots headwind. For operation with tailwinds up to 10 knots, increase distances by 10% for each 2 knots.
4. For operation on a dry, grass runway, increase distances by 15% of the "ground roll" figure.

WEIGHT LBS	TAKEOFF SPEED KIAS		PRESS ALT FT	0°C		10°C		20°C		30°C		40°C	
	LIFT OFF	AT 50 FT		GRND ROLL	TOTAL TO CLEAR 50 FT OBS	GRND ROLL	TOTAL TO CLEAR 50 FT OBS	GRND ROLL	TOTAL TO CLEAR 50 FT OBS	GRND ROLL	TOTAL TO CLEAR 50 FT OBS	GRND ROLL	TOTAL TO CLEAR 50 FT OBS
2500	56	61	S.L.	835	1400	895	1495	960	1595	1025	1705	1100	1820
			1000	910	1525	975	1635	1045	1745	1120	1865	1200	1995
			2000	995	1670	1070	1790	1145	1915	1225	2050	1315	2195
			3000	1090	1835	1170	1965	1255	2105	1345	2260	1440	2420
			4000	1195	2015	1280	2165	1375	2325	1475	2500	1580	2685
			5000	1310	2230	1410	2400	1515	2580	1625	2780	1740	2990
			6000	1440	2470	1550	2665	1665	2875	1790	3105	1920	3355
			7000	1585	2760	1710	2980	1840	3230	1975	3500	2120	3800
			8000	1755	3095	1890	3360	2035	3655	2185	3980	2350	4350
2300	54	59	S.L.	690	1160	740	1240	790	1320	845	1405	905	1500
			1000	750	1265	805	1350	860	1440	920	1535	985	1635
			2000	820	1380	880	1475	940	1575	1010	1680	1080	1795
			3000	895	1505	960	1610	1030	1725	1105	1845	1180	1970
			4000	980	1650	1050	1770	1130	1895	1210	2025	1295	2170
			5000	1075	1815	1155	1950	1240	2090	1325	2240	1420	2400
			6000	1180	2005	1265	2150	1360	2310	1460	2485	1565	2670
			7000	1295	2220	1395	2385	1500	2570	1610	2765	1725	2980
			8000	1430	2465	1540	2660	1655	2875	1775	3105	1905	3355

Fig. 5-21. Takeoff chart for a four-place airplane at two Weights.

Fig. 5-22 is the takeoff ground distance chart for a four-place airplane (0° flaps). The example is self-explanatory.

Fig. 5-23 is a chart for the *total distance* over a 50-ft

barrier for the airplane in Fig. 5-22. (Note the headwind difference for the two examples.) Fig. 5-24 is the same type of graphical presentation but for a heavier twin.

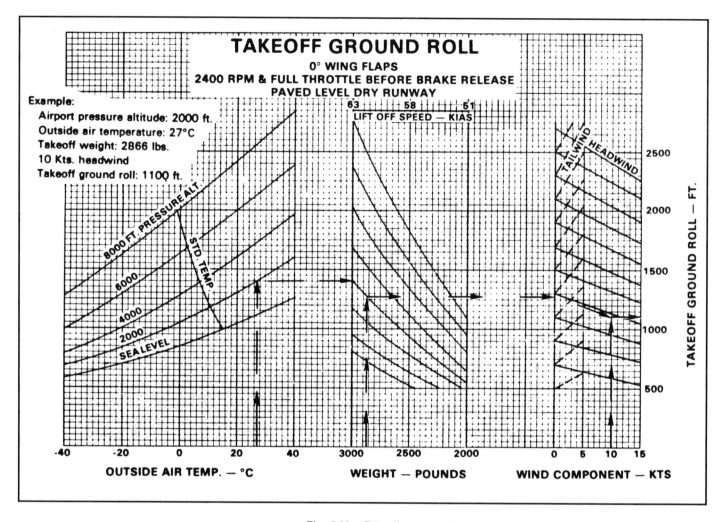

Fig. 5-22.   Takeoff ground roll—graphical presentation of a four-place airplane.

Check the notes on the charts so that you aren't computing the performance for the wrong Weight or flap configuration. These charts, like all performance or navigation charts in this book, are *not* to be used in actual situations.

Study and know the *POH*. If in doubt, read it again, and, above all, *always give yourself a safety factor, particularly in takeoffs.*

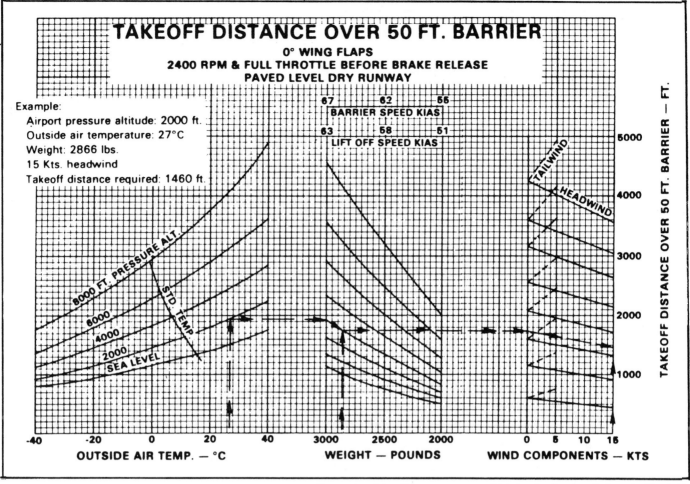

Fig. 5-23. Takeoff distance over a 50-ft barrier for the airplane in Fig. 5-22.

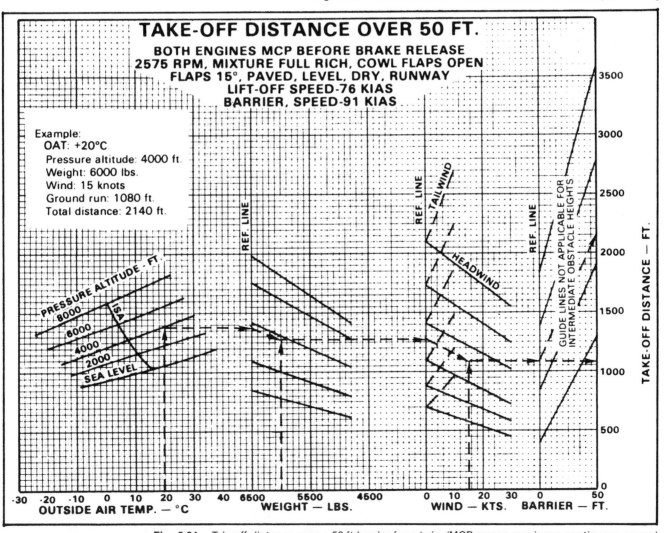

Fig. 5-24. Takeoff distance over a 50-ft barrier for a twin. (MCP means *maximum continuous power*.)

6 The Climb

An airplane's rate of climb is a function of excess HP available. This can be approximated by this equation: rate of climb (fpm) = (excess Thrust horsepower × 33,000)/airplane Weight, or R/C (fpm) = (ETHP × 33,000)/W, or

$$R/C = \frac{ETHP \times 33,000}{W}$$

Looking again at a HP-required and HP-available (THP) versus velocity curve for a particular altitude (we'll choose sea level for simplicity) you can note the following (Fig. 6-1). At a particular velocity, the difference between the THP available at recommended climb power and the HP required is the maximum. By looking at this graph for a particular airplane, you would immediately know the best rate of climb speed at sea level. With a series of these curves up to the airplane's ceiling, you can find the speed for best rate of climb for any altitude (Fig. 6-2). Looking at Fig. 6-2 you can see that at 90 K at sea level a power of about 59 THP is required to fly the airplane straight and level and 178 THP is the available power, or an

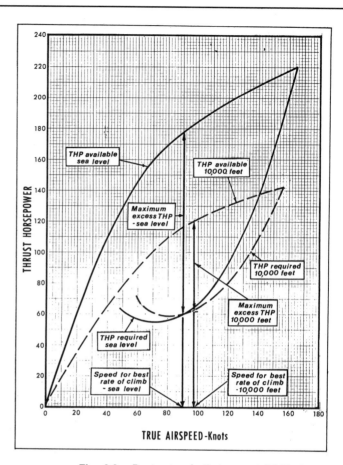

Fig. 6-2. Best rate of climb speed (TAS) at sea level and 10,000 ft (density-altitude), unsupercharged engine.

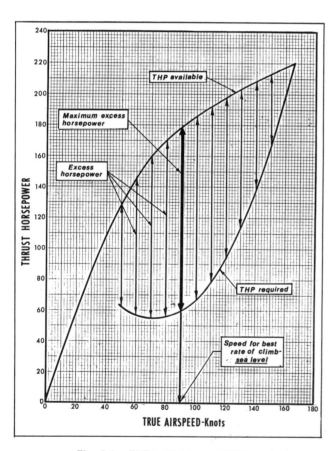

Fig. 6-1. THP-available and THP-required curve for a high-performance general aviation airplane at sea level. (Calibrated airspeed equals true airspeed at sea level.) The best rate of climb is found at the speed where there is the greatest amount of excess THP available. (Airplane Weight – 3000 lb)

excess of 119 THP exists. Using the equation for rate of climb: R/C = (ETHP × 33,000)/Weight (the Weight for this airplane is 3000 lb), R/C = (119 × 33,000)/3000 = 1309 fpm at sea level. The climb angle is found to be 8°15′ relative to the horizon. If you remember back in Chap. 3 the rate of climb for this fictitious airplane was found to be 1265 fpm (a climb angle of an *even* 8° was set up for the climb speed of 90 K and the problem was worked "backward"). The extra 55 fpm here shows that the airplane was slightly underrated by that method (and numbers were rounded off).

Checking the rate of climb at 10,000 ft at the best climb speed (given as TAS here but the pilot would use IAS or CAS, which computed for the TAS of 97 K at 10,000 ft would work out to be a CAS of about 84 K). The THP required is about 62 and the THP available is 120 (Fig. 6-2), an excess of 58 THP: R/C = (58 × 33,000)/3000 = 638 fpm, a reasonable figure at that altitude for an airplane of that Weight and THP required. (Assume IAS = CAS for this discussion.)

Some *POH*s include graphs of the best rate of climb speeds for various altitudes (IAS or CAS) (Fig. 6-3).

In cases where a graph like Fig. 6-3 is unavailable for lighter (older) planes such as trainers, which have a simplified type of *POH,* a rule of thumb may be applied: the standard sea level recommended best rate of climb speed is available in these abbreviated *Owner's Manual*s and the idea of maintaining a nearly constant TAS may be used; that is, the TAS and the CAS are the same under sea level standard conditions. You can find the indicated airspeed by *subtracting* 1% per 1000 ft from the published figure. Note that in order to maintain the same TAS at various altitudes the rule of thumb would be to subtract 2% per 1000 ft from the sea level indicated climb

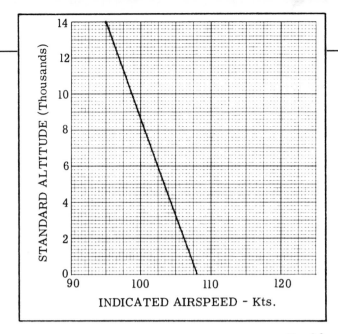

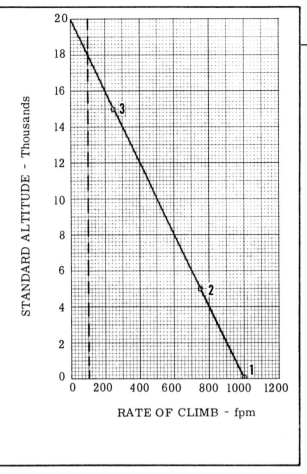

Fig. 6-3.

Fig. 6-4. Establishing a rate of climb graph.

speed but the best rate of climb *true* airspeed increases about 1% per 1000 ft (assuming no instrument error).

The 1% per 1000 ft decrease in *indicated* airspeed takes care of this. It must be repeated that this rule of thumb is for light trainers, but it also works pretty well for heavier airplanes. You couldn't go too far wrong by maintaining the same IAS throughout the climb in the trainer, although a slight loss in efficiency would result. This type of plane normally does not operate much over 5000 ft anyway.

There are two *ceilings* commonly mentioned: (1) *service ceiling* (that altitude at which the rate of climb is 100 fpm) and (2) *absolute ceiling* (the absolute altitude the plane can reach, where the rate of climb is zero). These ceilings are normally based on gross Weight but can be computed for any Weight. If you want to come right down to it, the absolute ceiling as a part of a climb schedule at gross Weight could never really be reached. In the first place, the airplane would be burning fuel and getting lighter as it climbed so wouldn't reach the absolute ceiling at the correct Weight; secondly, even if the Weight could be kept constant, the situation would be somewhat like that of the old problem of the frog 2 ft from a wall who jumps 1 ft the first time, 6 in. the second, etc., halving the length each hop. In theory, he would never reach the wall. For the airplane, that last *inch* up to the absolute ceiling would take a very long time. The rate of climb for single-engine airplanes and light twins with both engines operating is 100 fpm at the normal service ceiling but the light twin service ceiling with *one engine inoperative* is listed at the altitude at which the rate of climb is 50 fpm.

The service and absolute ceilings can be approximated by extrapolation. Measure the rate of climb at sea level and at several other altitudes and join these points (Fig. 6-4).

For instance, set your altimeter to 29.92, noting the outside air temperature and the rate of climb for several altitudes. Then convert your pressure altitude to density-altitude and, using a piece of graph paper, determine your absolute and service ceilings, correcting for the difference in Weight from the gross Weight. You're not likely to do this, but it would give you some idea of the rate of climb of your plane for various standard altitudes if you are interested. The *POH* lists the rate of climb at sea level and also the service and, in some cases, operational ceilings. You can use this information to check your rates of climb at various altitudes by making a graph such as in Fig. 6-5. Suppose your *POH* gives a rate of climb at sea level of 1000 fpm and a service ceiling of 18,000 ft. Knowing that the service ceiling rate of climb is always 100

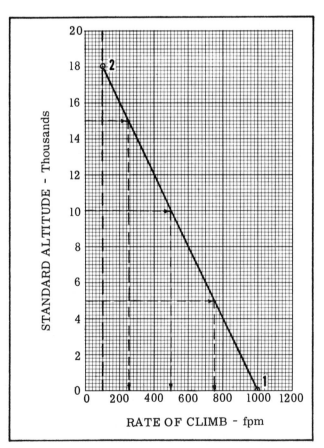

Fig. 6-5. Making an approximate rate of climb graph (gross Weight) by using the rate of climb at sea level and the published service ceiling.

fpm, you can set it up as in Fig. 6-5. Set up points 1 and 2; by connecting them with a straight line you can pick off the rate of climb for any standard altitude. (Your expected rate of climb in Fig. 6-5 is about 500 fpm at 10,000 ft.)

You can also work out a rule of thumb for your airplane. If your rate of climb drops from 1000 fpm at zero altitude to 100 fpm at 18,000 ft, it means a drop of 900 fpm in 18,000 ft. A little division shows a rate of climb drop of 50 fpm for every 1000 ft, so a good approximation of your expected rate of climb at various altitudes is 1000 fpm at sea level, 950 fpm at 1000 ft, 900 fpm at 2000 ft, etc. You can work out the figures for the plane you are flying (but it's doubtful if they would work out as evenly as this "fixed" problem).

Rate of climb varies inversely with Weight, and at first thought it would seem that variations in rate of climb could be simply calculated for variations in Weight. However, induced Drag is *also* affected by Weight change and the excess THP (and rate of climb) suffers more with added poundage than would be considered by a straight Weight ratio.

The rate of climb depends on excess THP available, and this depends on the *density-altitude*. Your rate of climb is affected by pressure altitude *and* temperature (which combine to give you density-altitude).

Two important speeds concern the climb: (1) the speed for the best rate of climb and (2) the speed for the maximum angle of climb. These speeds are obtained by flight tests. Generally the manufacturer will measure the rates of climb at various airspeeds, starting from just above the stall to the maximum level-flight speed. This is done for several altitudes and the rate of climb is plotted against the TAS and a curve drawn for each (Fig. 6-6). Corrections are made for Weight changes during the testing process.

You can see that the rate of climb would be zero at speeds near the stall and at the maximum level-flight speed because no excess HP is available. Looking back at Fig. 6-1, note that the excess THP drops off to nothing at the maximum level-

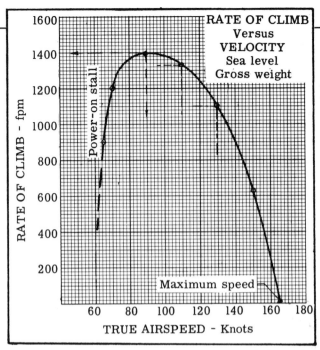

Fig. 6-6. A rate of climb curve made by noting the rate of climb at various airspeeds and joining the points.

flight speed as all the HP is being used to maintain altitude at that speed. At the lower end of the speed range the same thing occurs, but the stall characteristics of the airplane may not allow such clear-cut answers.

By looking at the resulting graph after these figures have been reduced to standard conditions and plotted, you can learn the speed for best rate of climb and for the maximum angle of climb (Fig. 6-7).

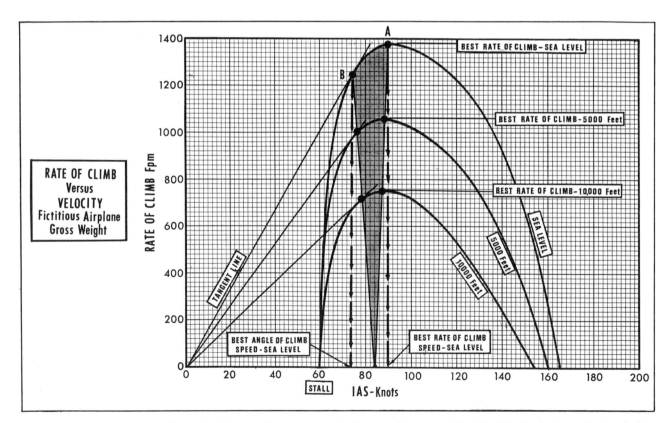

Fig. 6-7. Rate of climb versus velocity curve for several density-altitudes for a particular airplane.

The best rate of climb is at the peak of the curve. Reading the velocity below point A, you can find the speed for the best rate of climb. This is the published figure for sea level in the *POH*.

A line is drawn from the origin (0) on the graph tangent to the curve. Mathematically speaking this will give the highest ratio of climb to velocity (which means the same thing as the maximum altitude gain per foot of forward flight). The velocity directly below point B is the published figure for maximum angle of climb at sea level. Each airplane make and model is tested to find these recommended speeds. The tangent lines for the other two altitudes are shown in Fig. 6-7; note that the angle of climb decreases with altitude as might be expected. This is important to remember in that a 50-ft obstacle that can be cleared easily at the max angle climb at sea level could be a problem at airports of higher elevation (and/or higher density-altitude).

Fig. 6-7 is shown in terms of IAS to give a clearer picture of altitude effects. As shown, if the points of maximum angle are connected by a straight line and the same thing done for the points for the best rate of climb, the lines (in theory) converge at the same airspeed at the *absolute* ceiling of the airplane (zero rate of climb). In other words, the curves would get smaller and smaller until the "curve" for the absolute ceiling would be a point at some airspeed (and the rate of climb would be zero—all of the power available would be needed to keep from losing altitude at that one and only airspeed). The airspeeds for max angle and best rate get closer to each other as the altitude increases. The required IAS for best rate *decreases* with altitude and the required IAS for max angle *increases* with altitude; they will (in theory) be the same as the airplane reaches its absolute ceiling. The best rate of climb is always found at a higher airspeed than that for the max angle of climb up to that imaginary point, the absolute ceiling (Fig. 6-8).

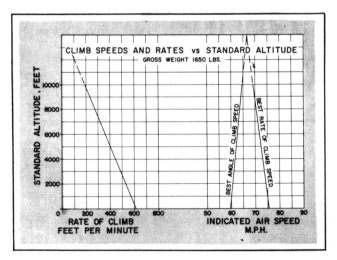

Fig. 6-8. Climb speeds and rates versus standard altitude for a two-place trainer.

For the particular airplane in Fig. 6-8, the service and absolute ceilings are given as 12,000 and 14,000 ft respectively. Note how the indicated airspeeds for best (or max) angle and best rate of climb speeds converge at the absolute ceiling. (The same condition would apply if the climb speeds were drawn in terms of TAS.)

NORMAL CLIMB

The normal climb is the best rate of climb possible without overworking the engine. The manufacturer recommends a certain airspeed and power setting for the normal climb. Pilots sometimes get impatient during a prolonged climb and start to cheat a little by easing the nose up. This does nothing more than decrease the rate of climb and strain the engine by decreasing the relative wind's cooling effects. Review Fig. 6-7 to see that when the speed is varied in either direction from the peak at A, the rate of climb is not at a maximum. You could lower the nose an equivalent amount and the rate of climb would not suffer any more than if you raised it—and the engine would be a lot better off!

After takeoff, the landing gear is raised, and as the speed approaches the best rate of climb speed, the flaps are raised and the power retarded to the recommended climb setting. As a rule of thumb for airplanes with unsupercharged engines, knock off 1% per 1000 ft from your climb *indicated* airspeed. For airplanes up through the light twins this can be considered to be up to 1 K per 1000 ft.

CRUISE CLIMB

This climb, which results in a good rate of climb as well as a high forward speed, is from 10 to 30 K faster than the recommended best rate, or normal climb speed. The cruise climb is ideal for a long cross-country where you want to fly at a certain altitude but don't want to lose much of your cruise speed getting there. Of course, if it's bumpy at lower altitudes you may want to use the best rate of climb up to smooth air and a cruise climb from that point up to your chosen altitude. An advantage to the cruise climb is that because of the higher airspeed (and higher air flow) the engine will generally be cooler during the climb.

Looking back at Fig. 6-7 (the sea level curve), note that by climbing at 110 K the rate of climb is *decreased* by about 75 fpm or about 5½%, while the forward speed (110 K, compared with the best rate of climb speed of 90 K) is *increased* by 22%—an advantage if you are interested in going places as you climb. Notice that as the climb speed increases past this value the rate of climb begins to drop off at a faster and faster rate. One method of setting up a cruise climb condition for your airplane (particularly for the cleaner, higher performance type) is to add the difference between the recommended max angle and max rate speeds to the max rate speed. In other words, if the recommended max rate speed at sea level and gross Weight is 90 K and the max angle speed (same conditions) is 75 K you add the difference (15 K) to the speed for max rate and come up with a cruise climb speed of 105 K. Speaking simply, you're operating on the opposite side of the climb curve from the max angle speed but not at such a speed that the rate of climb has dropped radically. (Notice on the curves in Figs. 6-6 and 6-7 that as the airspeed increases above that for best rate, the rate of climb decreases at a greater and greater rate per knot.) The speed for cruise climb found this way is at best an approximation and you should, as always, use the manufacturer's figure if available. Lower the cruise climb speed about 1% per 1000 ft, as was done for the max rate climb.

MAXIMUM ANGLE CLIMB

This climb usually is not an extended one and seldom continues for more than a couple of hundred feet altitude. As soon as the plane is firmly airborne, retract the landing gear and attain and maintain the recommended max angle climb speed. Keep the engine at full power. You'll need all the HP you can get, and the short length of time that full power will be used won't hurt the engine. Leave the flaps alone until the obstacle has been well cleared. After you have sufficient altitude and the adrenalin has stopped racing around, raise the flaps (if used), throttle back, and assume a normal climb. For

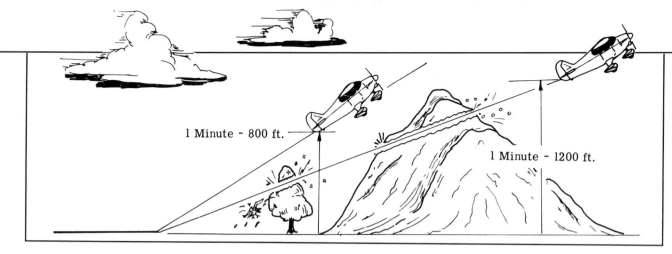

Fig. 6-9. Exaggerated comparison of max angle and best rate of climb.

1 Minute - 800 ft.

1 Minute - 1200 ft.

the best *angle of climb* add ½% per 1000 ft (about ½ K) to the *indicated* airspeed.

The max angle of climb is found at the speed at which the maximum excess Thrust is found. It will be found at the speed at which the greatest amount of Thrust component is available to move the airplane upward, compared with its forward motion. The max *rate* of climb is a function of *time* (the max angle is not) and so is dependent on the excess Thrust *horsepower* working to move the airplane upward at a certain *rate* (Fig. 6-9). Fig. 6-10 shows how the max angle climb speed is found.

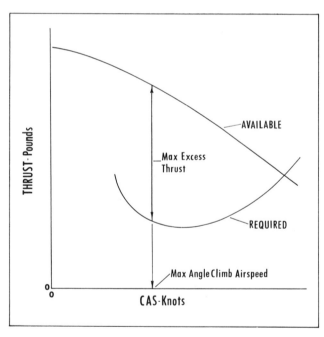

Fig. 6-10. The max angle of climb speed is found at the point of greatest excess Thrust.

The recommended *obstacle clearance* airspeed may be slightly less than the extended max angle climb because the airplane is dirty (has more parasite Drag) with the gear and flaps down.

CLIMB CHARTS

Fig. 6-11 shows the maximum rates of climb and the time, fuel, and distance needed to climb at max rate for a high-performance four-place airplane. A is pretty much self-explanatory, but you might look at B briefly.

Suppose that you are taking off from an airport at 1500 ft

(A) MAXIMUM RATE OF CLIMB

CONDITIONS:
Flaps Up
Gear Up
2700 RPM
Full Throttle
Mixture Leaned above 3000 Feet
Cowl Flaps Open

WEIGHT LBS	PRESS ALT FT	CLIMB SPEED KIAS	RATE OF CLIMB - FPM			
			-20°C	0°C	20°C	40°C
2650	S.L.	84	925	855	780	710
	2000	83	825	755	685	620
	4000	81	720	655	590	525
	6000	80	620	560	495	435
	8000	78	525	465	405	340
	10,000	77	430	370	310	- - -
	12,000	75	330	275	220	- - -

(B) TIME, FUEL, AND DISTANCE TO CLIMB

MAXIMUM RATE OF CLIMB

CONDITIONS:
Flaps Up
Gear Up
2700 RPM
Full Throttle
Mixture Leaned above 3000 Feet
Cowl Flaps Open
Standard Temperature

NOTES:
1. Add 1.4 gallons of fuel for engine start, taxi, and takeoff allowance.
2. Increase time, fuel and distance by 10% for each 10°C above standard temperature.
3. Distances shown are based on zero wind.

WEIGHT LBS	PRESSURE ALTITUDE FT	TEMP °C	CLIMB SPEED KIAS	RATE OF CLIMB FPM	FROM SEA LEVEL		
					TIME MIN	FUEL USED GALLONS	DISTANCE NM
2650	S.L.	15	84	800	0	0.0	0
	1000	13	83	760	1	0.4	2
	2000	11	83	715	3	0.8	4
	3000	9	82	675	4	1.1	6
	4000	7	81	635	6	1.6	8
	5000	5	81	590	7	2.0	10
	6000	3	80	550	9	2.4	13
	7000	1	79	510	11	2.9	16
	8000	-1	78	465	13	3.3	19
	9000	-3	78	425	15	3.8	22
	10,000	-5	77	385	18	4.3	26
	11,000	-7	76	340	21	4.9	30
	12,000	-9	75	300	24	5.5	35

Fig. 6-11. A. Maximum climb rates. B. Time, fuel, and distance to climb.

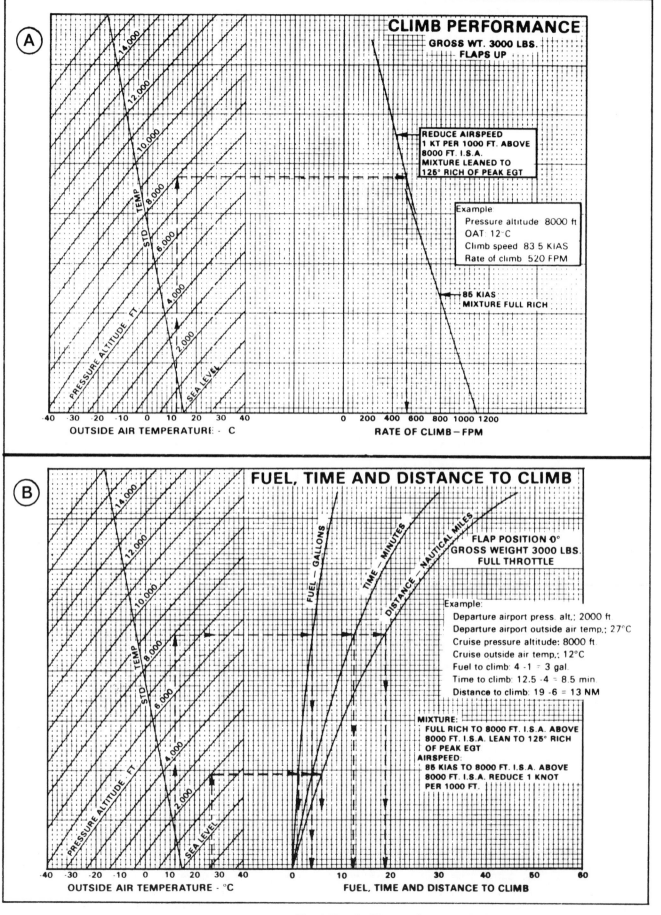

Fig. 6-12. A. Climb performance. B. Fuel, time, and distance to climb.

elevation and will level off at 7500 mean sea level (MSL). You would interpolate between 1000 and 2000 to get (1) a time of 2 min, (2) 0.6 gal fuel used (in the climb itself), and (3) a distance (no-wind) of 3 mi. To go from *sea level* to 7500 (interpolated), it would take 12 min, 3.1 gal, and 18 mi. The difference, or 10 min, 2.5 gal, and 15 mi is required to climb from 1500 ft MSL to 7500 MSL. To get total fuel used until level-off you'd add 1.4 gal for engine start, taxi, and takeoff (Fig. 6-11, Notes) for a requirement of 3.9 gal.

Note that wind will not affect time or gallons used, unless strong winds result in turbulence and performance loss. The

mileage required to reach a particular altitude depends on the wind during the climb; you could use an "average" winds aloft if you wanted to work it out that closely with your computer. The time, fuel, and distance are increased by 10% for each 10°C above standard temperature, as noted.

Fig. 6-12 is a graphical presentation of climb performance and fuel, time, and distance to climb. This example shows that, as in Fig. 6-11, the numbers (fuel, time, and distance) for the pressure altitude and temperature of takeoff must be subtracted from the cruise pressure altitude and outside air temperature. Check the example.

7 Cruise Control— Range and Endurance

CRUISE CONTROL IN GENERAL

Cruise control is an area too often ignored by pilots, and unfortunately the performance charts that come with the airplane are often classed with the writing on the walls of a Pharaoh's tomb. This chapter is a general coverage of cruise control. *Specific methods* of setting up power will be covered later.

Fig. 7-1 is a typical TAS versus standard altitude (density-altitude) curve for a high-performance retractable-gear, four-place airplane. This presentation is also known as a speed-power chart. Point 1 is the maximum level-flight speed and, like all airplanes with unsupercharged engines, is found at sea level where the maximum amount of power is available to allow the airplane to maintain altitude at such a high speed.

The normal cruise settings usually vary between 55 and 75%, with 65 and 75% being the most popular. Most engine manufacturers recommend that no continuous power settings of over 75% be used because of increased fuel consumption and added engine wear. You remember from Chap. 2 that these percentages of power are based on normal rated power, or the maximum *continuous* power allowed for the engine (brake horsepower).

Looking at Fig. 7-1, note that for the higher cruise power settings true airspeed (TAS) is gained with altitude, so that if a power setting of 75% is desired it would be best to fly at an altitude of 7000 ft (point 2) to get the most knots per HP—assuming outside factors such as ceiling, IFR-assigned altitude requirements, and winds aloft are not considered. Above 7000 ft, even full throttle will no longer furnish this airplane the required manifold pressure to maintain 75% power. If 65% power is used, this setting can be maintained to about 10,000 ft (point 3); this would be the best altitude for that setting. As the desired cruise setting decreases, the best altitude increases, but the loss of time in climbing to the optimum altitude could offset TAS gains, particularly on shorter trips. Note that as the cruise power setting decreases from 75% the TAS gain *per 1000 ft* also decreases until at 40% (point 4), there is no gain shown with altitude increase.

At the higher power settings it can also be expected that because the TAS increases with altitude for a specific power (and fuel consumption) the range is also increased with alti-

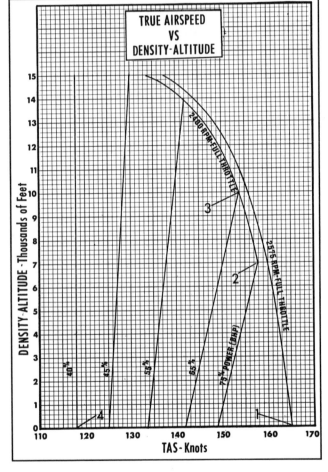

Fig. 7-1. A true airspeed versus standard altitude chart for a four-place high-performance airplane.

tude for a fixed percentage of power being used—except for one condition, that of maximum range, which will be discussed later.

Establishing the Cruise Condition. As the desired altitude is reached there are three main techniques used by pilots in establishing the cruise: (1) as soon as the altitude is reached, immediately retarding power from climb to cruise setting, (2) maintaining climb power after level-off until cruise speed is attained, and (3) climbing past the altitude 200 or so ft and diving to attain cruise speed and then setting power.

The first technique is the least effective method of attaining cruise (as far as time is concerned) and also means the resetting of power after the area of cruise speed is reached. Because the airplane is slow (at climb speed) when power is set, the increased airspeed as cruise is approached means that for the fixed-pitch propeller the rpm will have increased past that desired and, for the constant-speed type, ram effect may have increased the manifold pressure above the original setting. Acceleration to cruise speed is necessarily slow compared with maintaining climb power (the second technique), assuming a constant altitude.

Climbing past the altitude and diving down to aid in establishing cruise (technique 3) is sometimes used for cleaner airplanes. It is questionable whether this method has a perceptible advantage over leaving climb power on until cruise is reached since any comparison of the methods must include starting the timing, as the airplane initially passes through the cruise altitude in the climb-past-and-dive technique.

A phrase used by pilots is "getting the airplane on the step," an idea likely taken from seaplane operations. Pilots sometimes say, "I wasn't doing too well at first but as the flight progressed I began to get on the step." Actually they had not encountered a mysterious phenomenon but were following predictable aerodynamic laws.

The *step* is popularly defined as a condition in normal cruise in which the pilot, by lowering the nose slightly, is able to get several more knots than predicted by the manufacturer. Fig. 7-2 shows a power-required versus airspeed curve for an airplane at sea level. Note that there *are* two speeds available for most of the lower power settings but for settings used for cruise (55 to 75%) the two speeds are far enough apart so there is no question about the correct airspeed. For instance if you're carrying 55% power and are maintaining, say, 65 K—when the airplane normally cruises at 140 K at that setting—you'll know that all is not well. However, if you are carrying 35 to 40% and indicating 80 K when you *could* be indicating 90 K the problem is not so obvious.

Getting back to the idea of getting on the step as the flight progresses, Fig. 7-3 shows the power required for a particular airplane at gross Weight and when it is nearly empty of fuel. The airplane *will* indicate a higher airspeed at the lighter Weight, and this is expected and predictable. The difference in airspeeds depends on the ratio of fuel Weight to airplane Weight. Chap. 2 also discusses this idea.

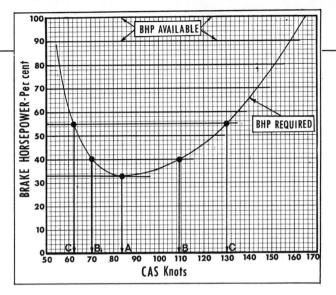

Fig. 7-2. Brake horsepower versus calibrated airspeed at a *constant* altitude for a fictitious high-performance airplane. This would be what the pilot would obtain by maintaining a constant altitude at various airspeeds, taking note of the manifold pressure and rpm necessary for each airspeed and later checking the percentage of power used after landing and referring to a power-setting chart. For instance, point C represents the two speeds available for this airplane, using 55% of normal rated power.

Down in the area of max range and max endurance, at 35 to 45% power, the speeds are not so far apart and the pilot might be flying at the low speed when it's possible to cruise several knots faster (Fig. 7-2). The principle is still the same: the pilot can fly at the higher speed rather than the low but *cannot* fly at an even higher speed than the highest airspeed allowed at one of the intersections of the power-required/power-available curve. The pilot cannot, for example, go faster than the greater of the two speeds (shown by B using 40% power) and still maintain a constant altitude. The pilot's problem is not being aware of the higher speed available, since both speeds are likely to be close together; the airplane would be quite happy to maintain that airspeed and altitude until Weight changes began to have their effect.

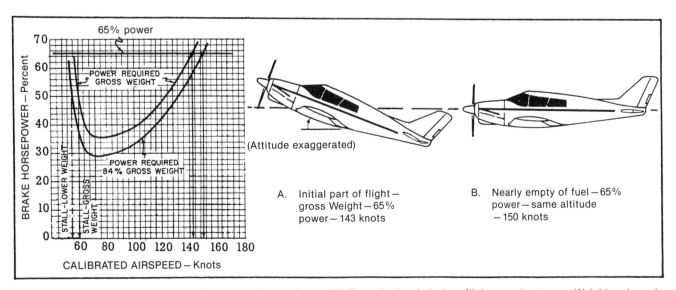

Fig. 7-3. Comparison of BHP required and airplane flight speeds at gross Weight and nearly empty of fuel at the same power setting of 65%.

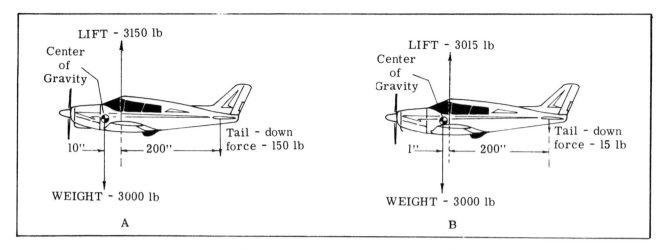

Fig. 7-4. The effects of CG position and resulting Lift (and power) required for an airplane in cruising flight.

Pilots unaware of the two available speeds may experiment by lowering the nose and, lo and behold, seem to have gotten "on the step." It might be hard to convince them they haven't beaten the game but have obtained only what is obtainable from the laws of aircraft performance.

Another fallacy of cruising flight, one often put forth by those of the "step" school of thought, is that the airplane should be loaded for a forward center of gravity (CG). One reason for this theory of loading might be the belief that with the CG forward the airplane wants to run "downhill." The pilot doesn't let it lose any altitude, goes the theory, but still benefits in added speed from this downhill-running tendency. This is close to that old theory that you don't need an engine in an automobile if the front wheels are smaller than the rear ones.

Actually, the airplane with the CG as far back as safely possible is usually faster. When two airplanes of the same model and weight carry the same power, the one with the more aft CG will cruise slightly faster. The airplane with the aft CG will also not be as longitudinally stable as the other and will be more easily disturbed from its trim. This doesn't mean that the airplane becomes unsafe; flight characteristics could be quite reasonable once the airplane is in smooth air and trimmed. If you went too far with this idea, however, serious problems of instability could arise.

Just how can aft loading add to performance? Take a look at an average high-performance airplane (Fig. 7-4). You'll find it has a tail-down force at cruise, the result of the CG location for any particular airplane-Weight combination. The center of Lift is considered to be fixed, as shown by both planes in Fig. 7-4. This produces a nose-down moment, which must be balanced by a tail-down moment furnished by the horizontal tail surfaces.

A moment is usually measured in pound-inches (lb-in.) and is the result of distance times a force or weight. For this problem, we will measure the moments around the center of Lift rather than around the CG, as was done back in Chap. 3.

Airplane A is so loaded that the CG is 10 in. ahead of the center of Lift. The airplane weighs 3000 lb, so the nose-down moment is 10 in. × 3000 lb or 30,000 lb-in. The tail-down moment must equal this (or the airplane will be wanting to do an outside loop), and the center of the tail-down force in this case is 200 in. behind the center of Lift. This calls for a force of 150 lb (the 30,000 lb-in. must equal 200 in. times the force, which is 150 lb). When the moments are equal, the airplane's nose does not tend to pitch either way. (The other moments covered in Chap. 3 will be ignored for this problem.)

If equilibrium exists and Airplane A is to maintain level flight, the *vertical* forces must also be equal; *up* must equal *down* in other words. Down forces are Weight (3000 lb) and the tail-down force (150 lb)—a total of 3150 lb down. Lift must equal this same value, so 3150 lb of Lift are required to fly a 3000-lb airplane.

Airplane B has a more aft CG. It is loaded so that the CG is 1 in. ahead of the center of Lift. The nose-down moment here is 1 in. times the 3000 lb, or 3000 lb-in. The center of the tail-down force is 200 in. behind the center of Lift, so that a down force of 15 lb is required (3000 lb-in. in this case, a product of 200 in. times the force, which must therefore be 15 lb). To sum up the vertical forces: 3000 + 15 = 3015 lb of Lift required. Airplane B has to fly at an angle of attack and airspeed to support only 3015 lb.

Both airplanes would weigh 3000 lb if placed on a scale, of course, but airplane A weighs 5% more as far as the combined angle of attack and airspeed are concerned. That airplane also requires more power to fly at a constant altitude, and as both airplanes are carrying the same power setting, the heavier airplane A would cruise more slowly. To believers riding on airplane B and noting that it flies faster than airplane A, it might well seem that their airplane is "on the step," yet all that is happening is that both airplanes are merely following predictable aerodynamic laws.

Relying solely on airspeed indicators can lead to another oversight: temperature and its effects.

Say you are flying a certain airplane on a Canadian winter morning at a pressure altitude of 4000 ft, carrying 65% power; the TAS for that power is 161 K. The outside air temperature (OAT) is −10°F (−23°C). This gives you a density-altitude of sea level. As the density-altitude is sea level, the IAS will be 161 K (assuming no instrument or position error). You could fly to Florida the next day and start operating there at the same pressure altitude of 4000 ft and the same Weight at 65%, but at an OAT of 75°F (+24°C). The density-altitude is 6000 ft, giving a TAS of 170 K. In getting this *TAS of 170*, however, you are indicating only *155 K*. By just comparing indicated airspeeds, you would come up with the fact that yesterday—at the same pressure altitude, power setting, and Weight—you were indicating *6 K more*. Yesterday, it might seem, you were "on the step"; today, you just couldn't seem to make it. Even once, perhaps, you tried to ease the nose down today to get on the step but just lost altitude, so you're more convinced than ever that the "step" is a mysterious thing only found once in a while. Quite possibly, you might have noted the variation from standard temperature in setting up your manifold pressure, but fell nevertheless into that oft-repeated trap of comparing indicated airspeeds only. *So forget the "step."*

A LOOK AT MAXIMUM RANGE CONDITIONS

It has been established that maximum range, as far as the aerodynamics of the airplane is concerned, is a function of a particular coefficient of Lift, the one at which the Lift-to-Drag ratio is at a maximum. This C_L (or angle of attack) is constant for a particular airplane (and configuration) and does not vary with Weight, as noted in Chap. 1. However, the average airplane does not have means of measuring C_L or angle of attack so the pilot must decrease the IAS (CAS) as Weight decreases in order to maintain the required optimum angle of attack. Look at the problem in terms of the power curve (Fig. 7-5).

efficiency of the engine propeller combination is only 33%, or *three* BHP is required to get *one* THP, but at a slightly higher speed the efficiency jumps up to 85%. A compromise would be in order. The same thing applies to bsfc. Fig. 7-6 illustrates that the bsfc changes with power and this might also be a factor. Basically, max range would be found at a condition at which the combination L/D × efficiency/bsfc is a maximum. You may have to fly at a *lower* Lift-to-Drag ratio in order to *increase* efficiency or *decrease* bsfc and get an overall greater range than would result from sticking to the max L/D speed and ignoring low efficiency or high bsfc at that speed. Manufacturers take this into consideration when they publish max range figures. In order to show the expected power settings for various airspeeds for max range and endurance, Figs. 7-5, 7-7, 7-8, and 7-9 are actually based on BHP as you can see by the shape of the curves.

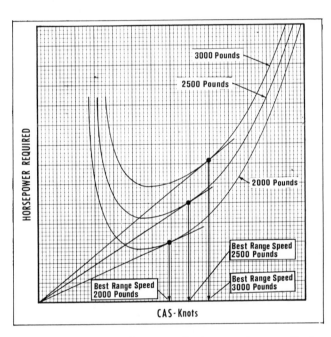

Fig. 7-5. Power-required curves for a particular airplane at various Weights. Notice that for maximum range the airspeed must be decreased as Weight decreases.

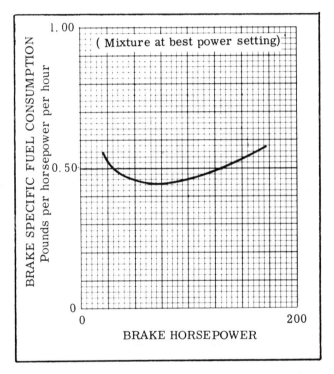

Fig. 7-6. Specific fuel consumption curve for a typical reciprocating engine as is used in light-planes.

A line drawn from the origin (0) tangent to the power-required curve gives the speed for best range at this altitude for each Weight. Assuming that the altitude remains constant, the TAS (and IAS) must be constantly decreased with decreasing Weight in order to get the absolute maximum range. This means that the power setting (brake horsepower, or BHP) is reduced from, say, 40 to 35% over the period of the flight.

From an aerodynamic standpoint the tangent line should be drawn on the *Thrust* horsepower–required curve. The speed found would be point of maximum efficiency of the airplane and, in theory at least, would coincide with the speed for the minimum Drag on the Drag versus airspeed curve for the airplane (maximum Lift-to-Drag ratio). However, other factors are involved such as propulsive efficiency (η) and brake specific fuel consumption (bsfc, or pounds of fuel used per BHP per hour). For instance, if your engine-propeller combination happened to have an extremely low efficiency at the speed found by using the THP-required curve, a compromise must be found. As an exaggeration, suppose at the speed found as the aerodynamically ideal one for best range the

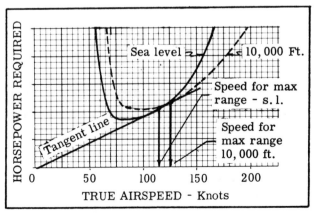

Fig. 7-7. Best range speeds (TAS) for a particular airplane at sea level and at 10,000 ft.

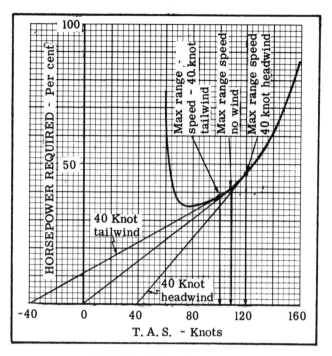

Fig. 7-8. Wind effects on best range speed.

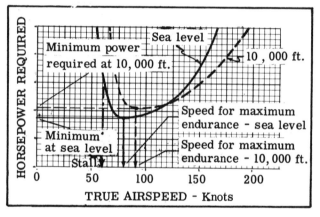

Fig. 7-9. The speed for maximum endurance (from an aerodynamic standpoint) is found at the point where power required is the least.

You can see that the normal cruise speed, which is well above that of the maximum range speed, is a compromise between speed and economy. Naturally everybody would like to get from A to B as rapidly as possible, but this is neither aerodynamically nor economically feasible.

One thing you'll find is that after careful planning for winds and other factors you may save some time en route— only to lose it at the other end by a delayed landing or ground transportation troubles. On a 200-NM trip, a plane that cruises at 150 K takes 16 min less than one that cruises at 125 K, and these savings can easily be lost at the destination. Of course the longer the trip the greater the time savings, but more time is lost at airports than is generally considered.

A study of current general aviation airplanes shows that a rule of thumb may be used to approximate the maximum range airspeeds for gross Weight. The following ratios, based on three major airplane types, are the ratio of the maximum

range speed to the flaps-up, power-off stall speeds (wings level and calibrated airspeeds). After using the ratio *you may convert to IAS* by checking the airspeed calibration chart for your airplane.

Single-engine, fixed-gear	1.5 × power-off stall speed
Single-engine, retractable-gear	1.8 × power-off stall speed
Twin-engine, retractable-gear	1.7 × power-off stall speed

Suppose you find in the *POH* or by rule of thumb that the IAS is 120 K for max range of gross Weight; how do you take care of the Weight change as fuel is burned? Looking at the Lift equation and working around to solving for V: $V = \sqrt{2W/C_L S\varrho}$. (Assume here for simplicity that Lift equals Weight.) The coefficient of Lift (C_L) is to be held constant as it is the one found for max L/D, or max range, and the wing area (S) does not change nor does the density (ϱ) for a constant altitude, so the only variable in the square root symbol is W, or Weight. (The "2" is also a constant, as always.) This means that as Weight changes, V must also change as the *square root* of the Weight change. Put in simple terms, V must change one-half the percentage of that of the Weight. If Weight decreases 20%, the V (or airspeed) must be decreased by 10% to keep the required constant C_L. If the gross Weight of the airplane is 3000 lb and the required airspeed for max range is 120 K, the airspeed at 2400 lb (a decrease in Weight of 20%) should be 108 K (a decrease in airspeed of 10%). This works for the maximum expected decrease from gross to minimum flyable Weight for most airplanes. Fig. 1-12 can be used for determining airspeed change required with Weight change, as was discussed in Chap. 1.

A higher percentage of normal rated power is required to maintain a required CAS (IAS) at higher altitudes, but the TAS will be increased so that the ratio of miles per gallon remains essentially the same (Fig. 7-7). Why do you try to use the same IAS for all altitudes (assuming equal Weights)? It goes back basically to the Lift equation of earlier chapters, L = $C_L S(\varrho/2)V^2$. The C_L is the fixed one found for max range (or max Lift-to-Drag ratio). The Weight, or Lift required, is the same for a particular time, the wing area (S) is the same, hence the final $(\varrho/2)V^2$ must be the same under all conditions if the C_L is to remain constant. The dynamic pressure q, or $(\varrho/2)V^2$, is that as measured by the airspeed instrument as IAS.

The ratios given are the approximate CAS (IAS) for maximum range for a chosen altitude. For most airplanes with unsupercharged engines, the altitude for best *normal* cruise is roughly 8000 ft standard altitude (call it 7000 to 10,000). In this altitude range wide open throttle is necessary to get the 65 to 75% recommended power setting for normal flying. But getting back to the idea of obtaining max range, once you have the ratio for your type of airplane and have found the maximum range speed for sea level you can *use this figure as an approximate IAS* for your chosen flight level. This would give you the best range under no-wind conditions for that particular altitude at gross Weight. This holds true up to the altitude where you are no longer able to get the necessary power to maintain altitude at the recommended CAS (IAS). The drawback is that you may burn some fuel getting up to this altitude, but if the trip is a long one, it might be worthwhile timewise because of the increased TAS.

For maximum range, you would climb to the chosen altitude and set up an IAS at the correct max range to stall speed ratio (1.5, 1.7, or 1.8, depending on your airplane type). You would then set up the power necessary to maintain altitude at this IAS and would lean the mixture (leaning will be discussed later).

Fig. 7-7 shows the relationship between the sea level maximum range speed and that at some altitude expressed in terms of TAS. Your project is to maintain the same IAS at higher altitudes. You are unable to maintain the *normal* cruise IAS to very high altitudes with an unsupercharged engine because you start with a high percentage of power to begin with (65 to 75%) and cannot obtain this above a certain altitude. If you start at 40 to 55%, as is required to maintain the lower maximum range speed, you will be able to use the required power at a higher altitude (Fig. 7-10).

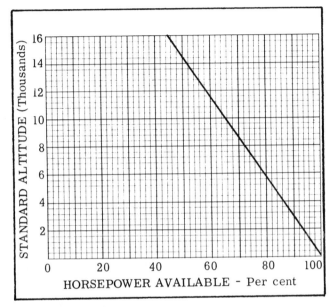

Fig. 7-10. Percentage of brake horsepower available at various altitudes, typical unsupercharged engine.

The average pilot is more interested in saving time than extending range. There is no question that the max range speed may be only 60 to 70% of the normal cruise speed. If you are interested in getting somewhere in a reasonable length of time, you are willing to operate at a higher, though costlier, speed.

These ratios are presented for you to remember in case they are needed. Suppose you are at a point where you have overestimated your range under normal cruise conditions. It's night and there is some bad country to cross before getting to a lighted airport. You can extend the remaining range by pulling the power back and judiciously leaning the mixture until you are able to maintain altitude at a CAS of 1.5, 1.7, or 1.8 times your power-off, flaps-up stall (calibrated) airspeed. You can then convert to IAS as—or if—necessary.

These ratios are not completely accurate but they do give you an approximate speed to extend your range if you have to. Propeller and engine efficiency at lower speeds, specific fuel consumption at various power settings, and other variables may result in slightly different airspeeds than given here. Fig. 7-6 shows a specific fuel consumption graph for a typical lightplane engine.

The maximum range speed at gross Weight will be found at power settings of approximately 40 to 45%, as given on the power chart in your airplane (unsupercharged engines). A variation of 5 K from these figures will make very little difference in max range.

To review: Maximum range conditions depend on the Lift-to-Drag ratio, propulsive efficiency, and brake specific fuel consumption. The speed at which the max L/D is found as far as the aerodynamics of the airplane is concerned might be one at which the propeller efficiency is low and/or bsfc is

proportionally higher. So, actually max range is found at the airspeed at which the value $C_L/C_D \times$ prop efficiency/bsfc is greatest. The max range speed for various aircraft is found by flight testing; the rules of thumb were taken from data of current airplanes, which take the above-mentioned variables into consideration.

Wind Effects on Range. There's no doubt that wind affects the range of your airplane as well as your groundspeed. Obviously, with a tailwind the range is greater than under no-wind conditions and much greater than under headwind conditions—the difference depending on the wind. So what's new?

What's new is that you can compensate for wind effects by varying airspeed for a particular altitude. Suppose you are in the situation cited previously—the night is dark and it looks like it'll be touch and go making the next available airport. After pulling the power back you remember that there is a 10- to 15-K headwind. This hurts, but there's something you can do about it. You can increase the indicated airspeed about 5% for heavy headwinds. *You will never get as much range with a headwind as under no-wind conditions but will be doing the best possible in this situation.* What you have done is decreased the time spent in this predicament.

Conversely, if you have a moderate tailwind, you can stretch your range even farther by subtracting about 5% from the speed given for maximum range under no-wind conditions (Fig. 7-8).

Summary of Range. These ideas are presented to give you a greater safety factor, not to get you to push the range of the airplane to the limit. You may never use these points but they could come in handy if you get into a bind and *have* to stretch it. It will require a great deal of willpower to throttle back when you feel like increasing power so as to "get there before you run outa gas."

The added time required to get to the airport may make you a nervous wreck, but you'll make it under conditions that wouldn't allow you to otherwise.

Incidentally, remember that you probably won't need to use max range techniques if in your preflight planning you adhere to FAR 91 (VFR fuel requirements), which basically states that no person may begin a flight under VFR unless (considering wind and forecast weather conditions) there is enough fuel to fly to the first point of intended landing and, assuming normal cruising speed (1) during the day, to fly after that for at least 30 min, or (2) at night, to fly after that for at least 45 min.

But of course, there may be unforecast wind and weather conditions that may require that you have to fly much farther than originally planned.

ENDURANCE

The maximum endurance of an airplane is seldom needed but when it is, it's *really* needed! You should be familiar with the idea of maximum endurance, particularly if you plan on getting an instrument rating, because under extreme conditions you may have to hold over a certain fix for 1 or 2 hr and then discover the destination field has gone below Instrument Flight Rules minimums and you have to go to an alternate airport. Things could get tense, particularly if you haven't tried to conserve fuel but have been boring holes in the soup all this time on full-rich mixture and cruise power settings.

Or take a VFR situation: You're coming into a large airport after a long trip. It's below VFR minimums but the weather is good enough for you to get a controlled VFR into the field; however, there's a lot of instrument traffic (and maybe other controlled-VFR pilots like yourself). The tower orders you to hold outside the control zone and control areas. The local weather is 1000 overcast and 1½ mi—good enough for you to fly underneath "elsewhere" but not to enter a control zone without clearance, so you hold just outside the control zone and "await further clearance." Here, too, would be a good place to use maximum endurance unless you have plenty of fuel.

For reciprocating engines, maximum endurance is found at sea level. Refer to the power-required versus velocity curve of Fig. 7-9.

You are interested in minimum gas consumption while still maintaining altitude. The low point of the power curve is where the least power is required and the point where gas consumption is a minimum if you properly lean the mixture. For most retractable-gear airplanes (including unsupercharged light twins), this will require a power setting of 30 to 35% of max continuous power. Few power charts go this low. The minimum BHP required (in percentages) depends on the aerodynamic cleanness and power loading of the airplane. An aerodynamically dirty, heavy airplane with comparatively little power might need a *minimum* of 50 to 55% or more of its available power to maintain altitude.

After examining Fig. 7-9 you can readily see that contrary to what might be expected, the maximum endurance speed is *not* the lowest speed possible for the airplane to fly without stalling. Many pilots, when confronted with the need for maximum endurance for the first time, automatically assume that the lower the speed, the less power required.

Horace Endsdorfer, private pilot, flew around just above a stall for 2 hr one day when he needed maximum endurance and was worn out keeping the airplane under control. Needless to say, he was one disgusted pilot when he learned that he was burning only slightly less gas than cruise—and working like heck all the time (Fig. 7-11). It should have struck him as being odd that he had to use so much power to maintain altitude in the holding pattern.

not know what this speed is and may either fly around at a speed just above stall or figure to heck with it, and circle around at cruise power. In either case, like the fellow who had his tombstone carved, "Not dead, only sleeping," the pilot isn't fooling anybody! If you have an approximate idea of, say, the ratio between the power-off, flaps-up stall speed and the maximum endurance speed, you may experiment until you find the exact speed, power setting, and mixture that will result in the lowest gas consumption. At any rate, you'll be somewhat better off.

If the information is not available in your *POH,* the following ratios give an *approximate* figure for your type of airplane. For a single-engine with fixed gear, use a 1.2 ratio of maximum endurance speed to power-off, flaps-up stall speed (calibrated airspeed given in the *POH*). As an example, if your airplane has a stall speed of 60 KCAS (flaps up) given in the *POH,* the maximum endurance speed would be 1.2 × 60 = 72 K. For a single-engine or a twin with retractable gear, use a ratio of 1.3. (These are ratios for gross Weight.)

The speeds found by this method are calibrated airspeeds and will apply at all altitudes—although the lower the better for reciprocating engines. This doesn't mean get down to 20 ft above the ground when you could be at 500 or 1000 ft. It does mean that if you have a choice, an altitude of 1000 ft is better for maximum endurance than 10,000 ft.

To set up maximum endurance, take the following steps:

1. Throttle back and slow the plane to the recommended airspeed.

2. Retard the prop control (if so equipped) until you get the lowest rpm possible and still have a reasonably smooth prop operation. In the case of a constant-speed prop this means no "hunting" by the propeller as it reaches the lower limits of governor control. Low rpm means low friction losses.

Fig. 7-11.

Manufacturers' recommended figures on speeds for maximum endurance are not always available. In many cases this is true because of the airplane's low-speed handling, and the constant-speed propeller governing characteristics at low rpm. A compromise may be desired, such as a slight loss of endurance by increasing airspeed to have smoother operation.

A few manufacturers publish the figure and the others leave it up to the pilot. The only trouble is, the pilot who does not have access to a power-required chart for the airplane may

3. Set the throttle so that the recommended speed and a constant altitude are maintained. Trim the airplane.

4. Lean the mixture as much as possible without the possibility of damaging the engine. You may then have to experiment again with the throttle to obtain the optimum setting for your particular condition (hot day, cold day, etc.).

Some of the above steps may not apply, for example, if you are flying a light trainer that has neither a mixture control nor a variable-pitch prop.

The point is that you are trying to maintain altitude with the minimum fuel consumption. This means minimum power (*not* minimum speed) and judicious leaning of the mixture. You'll be using about 30 to 35% power.

If you have to hold or "endure," it's usually over a particular spot, and this means *turns*. Keep your turns as shallow as possible, without wandering over into the next county, because steeper turns mean increased back pressure to maintain altitude—and this is a speed killer. Making steep turns usually results in constant variation of throttle as altitude or speed is lost and regained at a cost of added power and fuel consumption. Of course, if you start out high enough, you may just be lucky enough to get cleared into the airport before you run out of altitude. However, if you are on Instrument Flight Rules, it's not considered cricket to go blindly barging down into the next fellow's holding pattern.

Wind has no effect on endurance, but *turbulence decreases it.*

You may find the approximate max endurance speed for your airplane by flying at various airspeeds, maintaining a constant altitude. Fig. 7-12 shows an *actual* test of an airplane with a fixed-pitch propeller and fixed gear (flaps-up, power-off stall speed—56 K), using IAS. (In other words, the airspeeds required for various power settings were read directly off the instrument.)

Indicated Airspeed (knots)	rpm
101	2700
96	2600
90	2500
86	2400
78	2300
74	2200
70	2150
65	2075
61	2250
57	2300

Fig. 7-12.

Notice that 65 K is the indicated airspeed at which minimum power is required. The ratio of max endurance speed to flaps-up, power-off stall speed is 65/56 = 1.16, reasonably close to the predicted ratio figure of 1.20 for this type of airplane. (The 1.20 figure assumes a maximum endurance speed of 1.20 × 56 or 67 K.)

You could find the max endurance speed for an airplane with a constant-speed propeller by leaving the rpm at the lowest smooth value and making a table like Fig. 7-12, noting manifold pressure required rather than rpm. Don't use too high a manifold pressure with low rpm, as the engine could be damaged. Actually, since the max endurance speed normally falls within 50% of the stall speed, this is the only area that needs to be investigated. Make a note of the lowest manifold pressure, rpm, and airspeed at this value for future use. You may find that the airplane doesn't handle well at that speed and may want to add a few miles per hour. At any rate you'll have an approximation if needed. If the test is run at less than gross Weight, remember that the required speed should be slightly higher at gross.

In using the thumb rule multipliers in this and following chapters, if the airspeed indicator is marked as KIAS (1976 models and after), convert the bottom of the green arc to CAS, use the multiplier, and then reconvert to IAS.

More about Ratios—Why Use CAS? Back in Chap. 4 it was noted that airplanes manufactured as 1976 models and later have the airspeed indicator marked as *indicated air-*

speeds and *in knots* (KIAS). Some airplanes have a significant error between IAS and CAS near the stall and if you used the value of the bottom of the green arc (which is now IAS) your ratios would be different. For instance, one fixed-gear-airplane *POH* shows that at 4000 ft standard altitude (density-altitude) the *calibrated* airspeed should be 72 K for approximate max range conditions at gross Weight. The thumb rule multiplier for this type of airplane for max range is 1.5, as given earlier in the chapter. The stall speed is 40 KIAS and 46 KCAS. By using KIAS (the bottom of the green arc) for the later airplanes, the result would be 1.5 × 40 (IAS) = 60 K, which is too low. The proper procedure would be 1.5 × 46 (CAS) = *69 KCAS,* which would be within reason of the book figure of 72 KCAS.

A procedure that would work for all airplanes would be as follows:

Ratio (1.3, 1.5, etc), × *calibrated* stall speed = thumb rule CAS. You could then convert this to IAS for your reference to remember if you should later leave the *POH* back in the airport office. The airplane just used has an airspeed calibration table showing a CAS 1 K lower than the IAS in the 70-K area so you would add 1 K and *indicate* 70 K instead of the 69 KCAS obtained with the thumb rule.

Again, the *POH* figures, if available, are to be used for performance areas in this book. The thumb rules are basically given to show the airspeed ratios that different performance areas require.

CRUISE PERFORMANCE CHARTS

Fig. 7-13 is the cruise performance chart for a two-place trainer. You may have used this one when working on your private certificate, but a couple of points should be brought out:

CRUISE PERFORMANCE

CONDITIONS:
1670 Pounds
Recommended Lean Mixture (See Section 4, Cruise)

NOTE:
Cruise speeds are shown for an airplane equipped with speed fairings which increase the speeds by approximately two knots.

PRESSURE ALTITUDE FT	RPM	20°C BELOW STANDARD TEMP			STANDARD TEMPERATURE			20°C ABOVE STANDARD TEMP		
		% BHP	KTAS	GPH	% BHP	KTAS	GPH	% BHP	KTAS	GPH
2000	2400	---	---	---	75	101	6.1	70	101	5.7
	2300	71	97	5.7	66	96	5.4	63	95	5.1
	2200	62	92	5.1	59	91	4.8	56	90	4.6
	2100	55	87	4.5	53	86	4.3	51	85	4.2
	2000	49	81	4.1	47	80	3.9	46	79	3.8
4000	2450	---	---	---	75	103	6.1	70	102	5.7
	2400	76	102	6.1	71	101	5.7	67	100	5.4
	2300	67	96	5.4	63	95	5.1	60	95	4.9
	2200	60	91	4.8	56	90	4.6	54	89	4.4
	2100	53	86	4.4	51	85	4.2	49	84	4.0
	2000	48	81	3.9	46	80	3.8	45	78	3.7
6000	2500	---	---	---	75	105	6.1	71	104	5.7
	2400	72	101	5.8	67	100	5.4	64	99	5.2
	2300	64	96	5.2	60	95	4.9	57	94	4.7
	2200	57	90	4.6	54	89	4.4	52	88	4.3
	2100	51	85	4.2	49	84	4.0	48	83	3.9
	2000	46	80	3.8	45	79	3.7	44	77	3.6
8000	2550	---	---	---	75	107	6.1	71	106	5.7
	2500	76	105	6.2	71	104	5.8	67	103	5.4
	2400	68	100	5.5	64	99	5.2	61	98	4.9
	2300	61	95	5.0	58	94	4.7	55	93	4.5
	2200	55	90	4.5	52	89	4.3	51	87	4.2
	2100	49	84	4.1	48	83	3.9	46	82	3.8
10,000	2500	72	105	5.8	68	103	5.5	64	103	5.2
	2400	65	99	5.3	61	98	5.0	58	97	4.8
	2300	58	94	4.7	56	93	4.5	53	92	4.4
	2200	53	89	4.3	51	88	4.2	49	86	4.0
	2100	48	83	4.0	46	82	3.9	45	81	3.8
12,000	2450	65	101	5.3	62	100	5.0	59	99	4.8
	2400	62	99	5.0	59	97	4.8	56	96	4.6
	2300	56	93	4.6	54	92	4.4	52	91	4.3
	2200	51	88	4.2	49	87	4.1	48	85	4.0
	2100	47	82	3.9	45	81	3.8	44	79	3.7

Fig. 7-13. Cruise performance chart for a trainer.

1. For a fixed-pitch-propeller airplane a rule of thumb for maintaining a constant power (65%, 75%, etc.) is to add 25-rpm per 1000 ft of altitude gain. As an example, suppose you are at 2000 ft pressure altitude (standard temperature) and are carrying 75% power (BHP). The chart shows that at 2000 ft 2400 rpm is required for 75%, and at 4000 ft 2450 rpm, a required 50 rpm added for the added 2000 ft. A check of 6000 and 8000 ft at 75% shows an added 25 rpm per 1000 ft is required to maintain that percentage of power.

2. Another thumb rule, used for an airplane engine in cruise and properly leaned, is to multiply the actual BHP being used by 0.075. For most normally aspirating general aviation engines a bsfc (leaned) is in the vicinity of 0.45 lb per HP per hour. Talking in terms of 6 lb per gallon, the 0.45 is divided by 6 and the number 0.075 gal per HP per hour is derived.

The engine of Fig. 7-13 is rated at 110 BHP, so at 75% power a total of $0.75 \times 110 = 82.5$ BHP is being developed. To find the gallons per hour (gph) consumed, multiply 82.5 by the thumb rule figure of 0.075 to get 6.1875 (or 6.2) gph. This is slightly conservative, as shown by the book figure of 6.1 gph, but is close enough for a general estimate if the *POH* isn't handy at the time. Note also in Fig. 7-13 that 75% power has a fuel consumption of 6.1 gph at 2000, 4000, 6000, and 8000 ft (even though the required rpm increases with altitude), since it's assumed that judicial leaning will be used in each case.

The cruise performance charts for a higher-performance airplane at pressure altitudes of 6000 and 10,000 ft are shown in Fig. 7-14. This airplane has a 180-HP engine, and looking at the 6000-ft table you can see that, for instance, 65% power is available at several rpm–manifold pressure combinations at the different temperatures given. At 65% at 2300 rpm (standard temperature) a manifold pressure of 22 in. of mercury is required and the fuel consumption is 8.8 gph. Using the rule of thumb for finding fuel consumption at cruise: at 65%, 117 BHP is being used ($0.65 \times 180 = 117$); $117 \times 0.075 = 8.775$ gph. Things won't always work out so closely, but you'll have a fair idea of the fuel being used at various power settings for your engine if the *POH* isn't handy right then.

Look over Fig. 7-14 and make sure you can use this type of presentation. You might have to interpolate for both temperature and BHP in some cases, for example, at 6000 ft at 2400 rpm and 10°C above standard temperature if you needed the manifold pressure for 70% power.

Fig. 7-15 contains a power setting table and a speed-power graph (see Fig. 7-1 again) for a particular airplane. You decide what power setting you want to use, set it up using Fig. 7-15A, and check your expected performance at various altitudes using Fig. 7-15B. This airplane also has a speed-power graph for the mixture leaned to peak EGT (not included here).

Fig. 7-16 shows the range and endurance profiles of the airplane in Fig. 7-14. Note that at 45% power the airplane has approximately 18 min more endurance at sea level than at 11,000 ft. The range profile chart has a note that the chart "allows for the fuel used for engine start, taxi, takeoff and climb (etc.)." See Fig. 6-11 for that information.

CRUISE PERFORMANCE

PRESSURE ALTITUDE 6000 FEET

CONDITIONS:
2650 Pounds
Recommended Lean Mixture
Cowl Flaps Closed

NOTE
For best fuel economy, operate at the leanest mixture that results in smooth engine operation or at peak EGT if an EGT indicator is installed.

RPM	MP	20°C BELOW STANDARD TEMP -17°C			STANDARD TEMPERATURE 3°C			20°C ABOVE STANDARD TEMP 23°C		
		% BHP	KTAS	GPH	% BHP	KTAS	GPH	% BHP	KTAS	GPH
2500	23	---	---	---	75	136	10.0	72	136	9.6
	22	73	132	9.7	70	132	9.4	68	132	9.1
	21	68	128	9.1	66	128	8.8	63	128	8.6
	20	63	123	8.6	61	123	8.3	59	123	8.1
2400	24	---	---	---	77	137	10.2	74	138	9.9
	23	75	133	10.0	72	134	9.6	70	134	9.3
	22	70	130	9.4	68	130	9.1	66	130	8.8
	21	66	126	8.8	63	126	8.6	61	125	8.3
2300	24	77	134	10.2	74	135	9.8	71	136	9.5
	23	72	131	9.6	70	132	9.3	67	132	9.0
	22	68	127	9.1	65	128	8.8	63	127	8.5
	21	63	123	8.5	61	123	8.3	59	123	8.0
2200	24	74	132	9.9	71	133	9.5	69	133	9.2
	23	70	129	9.3	67	129	9.0	65	129	8.7
	22	65	125	8.8	63	125	8.5	61	125	8.2
	21	61	121	8.3	59	120	8.0	57	120	7.8
2100	23	67	126	8.9	64	126	8.7	62	126	8.4
	22	62	122	8.5	60	122	8.2	58	122	7.9
	21	58	118	8.0	56	117	7.7	54	117	7.5
	20	54	113	7.5	52	112	7.3	50	110	7.0
	19	50	108	7.0	48	106	6.8	46	103	6.6

PRESSURE ALTITUDE 10,000 FEET

CONDITIONS:
2650 Pounds
Recommended Lean Mixture
Cowl Flaps Closed

NOTE
For best fuel economy, operate at the leanest mixture that results in smooth engine operation or at peak EGT if an EGT indicator is installed.

RPM	MP	20°C BELOW STANDARD TEMP -25°C			STANDARD TEMPERATURE -5°C			20°C ABOVE STANDARD TEMP 15°C		
		% BHP	KTAS	GPH	% BHP	KTAS	GPH	% BHP	KTAS	GPH
2700	20	72	136	9.7	70	136	9.3	67	136	9.0
	19	67	131	9.0	65	131	8.7	62	130	8.4
2600	20	70	134	9.4	68	134	9.0	65	133	8.8
	19	65	129	8.8	63	128	8.5	61	128	8.2
	18	60	123	8.2	58	123	7.9	56	121	7.7
2500	20	68	132	9.1	66	132	8.8	63	131	8.5
	19	63	127	8.5	61	126	8.3	59	125	8.0
	18	58	121	8.0	56	120	7.7	54	119	7.5
	17	54	115	7.4	52	113	7.2	50	110	7.0
2400	20	66	130	8.9	63	129	8.6	61	129	8.3
	19	61	124	8.3	59	124	8.0	57	123	7.8
	18	56	119	7.7	54	118	7.5	52	115	7.3
	17	52	112	7.2	50	110	7.0	48	107	6.8
2300	20	64	127	8.6	61	127	8.3	59	126	8.0
	19	59	122	8.0	57	121	7.8	55	119	7.5
	18	54	116	7.5	52	114	7.3	51	112	7.1
	17	50	109	7.0	48	106	6.8	46	103	6.6
2200	20	61	125	8.3	59	124	8.0	57	123	7.8
	19	57	119	7.8	55	118	7.5	53	116	7.3
	18	52	113	7.3	50	111	7.0	49	108	6.9
2100	20	59	122	8.0	57	121	7.8	55	119	7.5
	19	55	116	7.5	52	115	7.3	51	112	7.1
	18	50	110	7.0	48	107	6.8	47	104	6.6

Fig. 7-14. Cruise performance chart for 6000 and 10,000 ft for a high-performance general aviation airplane.

POWER SETTING TABLE — AVCO LYCOMING O-540-J3A5D, 235 HP @ 2400 RPM

Press. Alt. Feet	Std. Alt. Temp. °F	129 HP - 55% Rated RPM & MAN. PRESS.				153 HP - 65% Rated RPM & MAN. PRESS.				175 HP - 75% Rated RPM & MAN. PRESS.			200 HP - 85% Rated RPM & MAN. PRESS.		
		2100	2200	2300	2400	2100	2200	2300	2400	2200	2300	2400	2200	2300	2400
SL	59	20.8	20.0	19.4	18.7	23.2	22.4	21.7	21.0	24.6	23.9	23.1	27.2	26.4	25.5
1000	55	20.5	19.8	19.2	18.5	22.9	22.2	21.5	20.8	24.3	23.6	22.9	26.9	26.1	25.3
2000	52	20.3	19.5	19.0	18.3	22.7	21.9	21.2	20.6	24.1	23.4	22.6	F.T.	25.8	25.0
3000	48	20.0	19.3	18.8	18.1	22.4	21.7	21.0	20.4	23.8	23.1	22.4		F.T.	24.7
4000	45	19.8	19.1	18.5	17.9	22.1	21.4	20.8	20.2	23.5	22.8	22.1			F.T.
5000	41	19.5	18.9	18.3	17.7	21.9	21.2	20.5	20.0	23.2	22.6	21.9			
6000	38	19.3	18.6	18.1	17.5	21.6	21.0	20.3	19.7	F.T.	22.3	21.7			
7000	34	19.1	18.4	17.9	17.3	21.3	20.7	20.1	19.5	—	F.T.	21.5			
8000	31	18.8	18.2	17.7	17.2	21.1	20.5	19.9	19.3	—	—	F.T.			
9000	27	18.6	18.0	17.5	17.0	F.T.	20.2	19.7	19.1						
10,000	23	18.3	17.7	17.2	16.8	—	F.T.	19.4	18.9						
11,000	20	18.1	17.5	17.0	16.6	—		F.T.	F.T.						
12,000	16	17.8	17.3	16.8	16.4										
13,000	13	F.T.	17.0	16.6	16.2										
14,000	9	—	F.T.	16.4	16.0										
15,000	6	—	—	F.T.	15.8										
16,000	1				F.T.										

NOTE: To maintain constant power, correct manifold pressure approximately 0.17″ Hg. for each 10°F. variation in carburetor air temperature from standard altitude temperature. Add manifold pressure for air temperatures above standard; subtract for temperatures below standard.

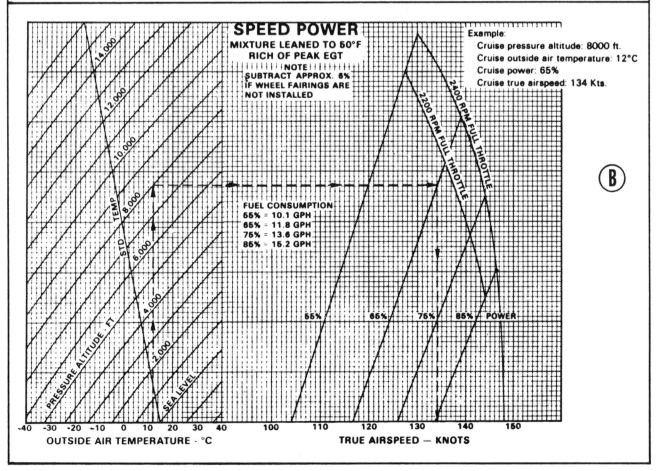

Fig. 7-15. Power-setting table and speed-power chart for a high-performance airplane.

RANGE PROFILE
45 MINUTES RESERVE
44 GALLONS USABLE FUEL

CONDITIONS:
2650 Pounds
Recommended Lean Mixture for Cruise
Standard Temperature
Zero Wind

NOTE:
This chart allows for the fuel used for engine start, taxi, takeoff and climb, and the distance during a normal climb up to 8000 feet and maximum climb above 8000 feet.

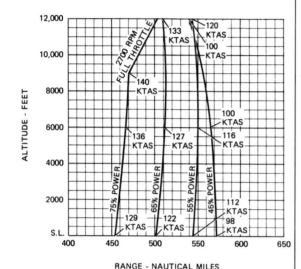

ENDURANCE PROFILE
45 MINUTES RESERVE
44 GALLONS USABLE FUEL

CONDITIONS:
2650 Pounds
Recommended Lean Mixture for Cruise
Standard Temperature

NOTE:
This chart allows for the fuel used for engine start, taxi, takeoff and climb, and the time during a normal climb up to 8000 feet and maximum climb above 8000 feet.

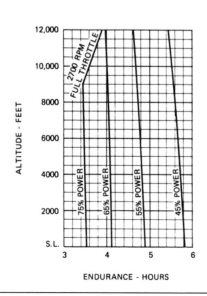

Fig. 7-16. Range and endurance profiles for a high-performance airplane.

8 GLIDES

Pilots pay comparatively little attention to the airplane's glide characteristics these days. The trend has been toward power approaches for all airplanes no matter how light, and pilots sometimes have been caught short by an engine failure.

For airplanes with higher wing loadings, power approaches are usually necessary in order to avoid steep angles of approach to landing. If the approach angle is steep and the airspeed low, you may find that the airplane will "rotate" for landing but will continue downward at an undiminished (or even greater) rate of descent, making a large airplane-shaped hole in the runway (Fig. 8-1). The stall characteristics of the swept wing make it particularly susceptible to this type of trouble.

Because of this and the fact that most jet engines give poor acceleration from idle settings, jets generally use comparatively high power during the landing approach.

This chapter discusses airplane clean glide characteristics. Back in the old days when engines were not as reliable as they are now, the pilot's knowledge of the airplane's power-off glide characteristics was of supreme importance. Nearly all approaches were at engine idle and made so that should the engine quit at some point during the process the field could still be reached. Even now, applicants for the commercial certificate are required to land beyond and within a certain distance from a point on the runway. They are allowed to use flaps, or slip to hit the spot—in earlier times even these aids were taboo. Every pilot should make occasional power-off (idle) approaches to keep in practice in case of engine failure at altitude.

Two glide speeds will be of interest to you: (1) airspeed for minimum rate of sink and (2) airspeed for farthest glide distance. The two conditions are not the same, although they might appear to be at first glance. These figures are arrived at by flight tests. Glide the airplane at various airspeeds and plot the rates of sink for each airspeed and altitude. The graph for one altitude and Weight looks like Fig. 8-2.

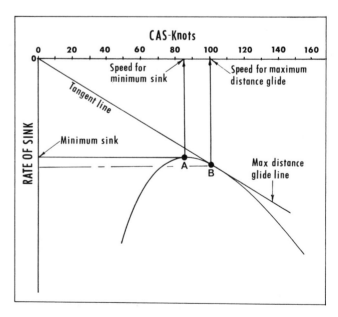

Fig. 8-2. Rate of sink versus velocity curve; a particular altitude and Weight for a fictitious airplane in the clean condition.

Fig. 8-1.

THE MINIMUM SINK GLIDE

Point A on Fig. 8-2 represents the velocity at which rate of sink is a minimum. Point B is that at which the max distance glide is found. You remember that the rate of climb is a function of excess Thrust horsepower (THP). The less HP you "require," the less the rate of sink in the power-off condition. The best velocity for this is at point A for a particular airplane. (Check Fig. 8-3 also.)

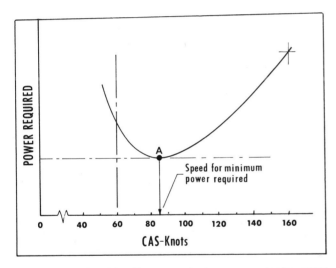

Fig. 8-3. Power-required versus velocity curve (Thrust horsepower).

You remember from Chap. 2 that the power-required curve would be moved by the effects of Weight or altitude. It can also be affected by a change in parasite Drag. So while in theory the speeds for the minimum sink and maximum distance glides should be the same as that for maximum endurance and maximum range respectively, for propeller airplanes certain practical factors are involved. When you are flying at the maximum endurance (or max range) speed you naturally have power on. Power, even the comparatively small amount used for endurance, normally increases the efficiency of the airplane by furnishing a slipstream across the wing center section. The airspeed ratios arrived at in Chap. 7 are based on power-on configurations. With the power off, Thrust and slipstream effects are missing. If the propeller is windmilling, parasite Drag increases sharply (a windmilling prop is like a barn door out front). To maintain the new, *lower* Lift-to-Drag ratio the airplane must fly at a slower airspeed in order to get the best performance in this less-efficient condition. For the light twin the props should be feathered if the engines are out of action.

Fig. 8-4 is a comparison of the rate of sink curves for an airplane in the clean condition (prop feathered or removed) and one with the prop windmilling in low pitch. By looking at the curves you can see the effects of increased parasite Drag of

the windmilling prop on the rate of sink curves. Points A and B represent respectively the speeds of minimum sink and max distance glides for the clean airplane; A′ and B′ represent the same speeds for the dirty airplane. Notice that for the dirty condition the airspeed for max distance glide must be decreased. Parasite Drag varies with airspeed so that a lower speed is necessary to help keep it to a minimum in the dirty configuration. *Incidentally, all the rate of sink curves in this chapter are exaggerated, particularly at the lower end of the speed ranges, in order to show the theory more clearly.*

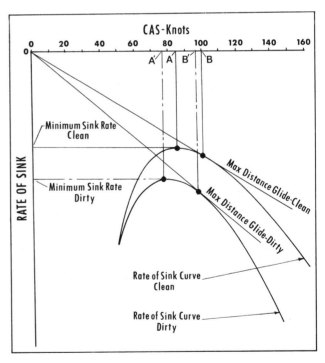

Fig. 8-4. Rate of sink curves for an airplane in the clean and dirty condition (prop windmilling in low pitch). Both curves are for the same altitude and Weight.

There's another tie-in between minimum sink and max endurance—you'll do better at low altitudes for both; the minimum sink rate will be less at lower altitudes.

The glide is one of the most difficult factors of airplane performance to pin down for rule of thumb purposes. Minimum sink speed will be in the vicinity of the speed for maximum endurance but somewhat lower because of the effects discussed earlier. The glide properties not only vary between airplanes of the same general classification (single-engine, fixed-gear, etc.) but also vary for the same airplane, depending on propeller blade setting if a variable-pitch prop is used. Here are some propeller settings and their effects on the glide:

Very bad—prop windmilling, low pitch
Better—prop windmilling, high pitch
Even better—prop stopped
Best—prop feathered (applicable to multiengine only)
Fixed-pitch prop—stopped, but read on . . .

Of course, you can usually stop the propeller by slowing up to about a flaps-down stall speed (after pulling the mixture to idle cutoff), but you may not feel like doing stalls with a dead engine at low altitudes.

For most airplanes it's difficult to slow up enough to stop the propeller and in some cases full flaps and a near-stall condition is required to accomplish it. Pilots who've deliberately stopped the prop of a single-engine airplane (at a high altitude above a very large airport) have noted that (1) the glide ratio is improved, (2) it is extremely quiet, and (3) there is some worry about getting the engine started again. Also, some pilots have been known to forget to move the mixture out of the idle cutoff before trying to start the engine, using up a considerable amount of perspiration and altitude before getting things straightened out. It is particularly interesting if, after putting your total concentration on (not) getting the engine started, you found that the large airport is now well out of gliding range.

Here are some approximations of the airspeed for minimum sink as a ratio to the flap-up, power-off stall speed (CAS) at gross Weight.

Single-engine, fixed-gear (flaps up, prop windmilling)   1.1
Single-engine, retractable-gear (gear and flaps up, prop windmilling in high pitch)   1.2
Twin-engine, retractable-gear (gear and flaps up, props feathered)   1.3

The minimum rate of sink condition will probably be used only in an emergency situation (you have engine failure at night and don't know the terrain below). This rate of sink will be low enough so that you will have a good chance in flat territory where there isn't something solid like a stone wall to hit. This would be the best approach for an engine failure at night over water, marsh grass, or snow, where altitude is hard to judge. Notice that you won't have much safety margin in gusty air.

MAXIMUM DISTANCE GLIDE

Point B on Fig. 8-2 gives the speed for the maximum glide distance (or maximum forward distance per foot down). This happens to be the airspeed for the max Lift-to-Drag ratio, which you remember was also the speed for maximum range. The speed for maximum range was with power; for the maximum glide distance, power effects are not present. Because of this, the recommended airspeed is somewhat lower.

This type of glide is used more often, particularly in a single-engine airplane where engine failure can give some small concern. *The more Drag your airplane has, the less its glide ratio,* so naturally the gear should be up (if possible) and the flaps retracted.

This maximum distance glide speed, in the case of a forced landing, is used to make sure that you get to the field and the "key point" or "key position box," after which you set up the familiar approach speed for the final part of the problem. A possible forced-landing situation might be like this: You are are on a cross-country in a single-engine plane at 3000 ft AGL when the engine quits. Carburetor heat, switching tanks, turning on the electric boost pump, or other corrective measures cannot remedy the situation and you are faced with landing whether you want to or not. There's a decent-looking field over to one side that will allow an into-the-wind landing.

The first time this happens (or the tenth, or the hundredth) you are "shook." The best procedure would be to set up the maximum distance glide speed as you turn toward the field. This will mean that you will be slowing the airplane to this speed from cruise, which will be almost automatic as you unconsciously try to maintain altitude—the trouble is that many pilots tend to overdo it. In too many cases, though, the pilot keeps the airspeed too high, losing valuable altitude too soon.

The new *POH* gives you the airspeed for maximum distance glide (some older *Owner's Manuals* do not). Use the *POH*-recommended speed if it is available. Here are some approximations for max distance glide speeds (CAS) at gross Weight for various types of airplanes taken from *POH*-recommended max distance glide speeds:

Single-engine, fixed-gear (flaps up, prop windmilling)   1.3
Single-engine, retractable-gear (gear and flaps up, prop windmilling in high pitch)   1.4
Twin-engine, retractable-gear (gear and flaps up, *props feathered*)   1.5

Notice that the single-engine, retractable-gear airplane is the most affected by the windmilling propeller. The max range speed is about 1.8 times the flaps-up, power-off stall speed, but the max glide distance speed is only 1.4 times the reference stall speed. The difference is greater for this type as it is normally cleaner than the other two groups and the windmilling propeller (parasite Drag) affects it more (Fig. 8-4).

The feathered propellers on the light twin cause its max glide distance speed to be comparatively closer to the max range speed than the other two groups because the parasite Drag is not increased so radically due to windmilling.

So while the maximum Lift-to-Drag ratio for the airplane in its cleanest condition may be 10:1 or 12:1, with a windmilling propeller the maximum ratio may be cut down to 8:1 or less. You are trying to maintain the best airspeed for this new ratio. You have to do the best with what you have. Remember that cowl flaps cause Drag, also. Fig. 8-5 shows an exaggerated comparison between a minimum sink and a maximum distance glide.

About "stretching the glide"—there is *one indicated airspeed* for maximum distance for your airplane at a given Weight and configuration. Any deviation from this means less distance per foot of altitude. The airspeed for maximum glide distance decreases with Weight decrease. *The maximum glide ratio is the maximum Lift-to-Drag ratio for the airplane in the glide condition and is independent of Weight.* This means you can glide the same distance at gross Weight as at a near empty Weight—but you'll use different airspeeds for the different Weights (Fig. 8-6). (Also see Fig. 1-12.)

As the glide ratio is that of the Lift-to-Drag ratio, cleaner airplanes will get more feet forward per foot of altitude. When a jet trainer or light jet transport weighing 12,000 lb and a J-3 Cub weighing 1200 lb each passes through 10,000 ft at its *particular max distance glide speed* (throttle at idle), which will glide farther from 10,000 ft? The jet would likely glide about 50% farther than the Cub under the conditions cited—the Weights were just put in to cloud the issue. The jet would likely have a max Lift-to-Drag ratio of 15:1 whereas the Cub would likely fall in the area of a max ratio of about 10:1. A max distance glide speed of 180 K would be reasonable for some of the earlier light jets while the Cub's best glide speed would likely be in the neighborhood of 45 K at gross Weight.

The jet's glide angle would be only about two-thirds as steep as that of the Cub, but it would be moving down the shallower slope 4 times as fast. The sum total is that the jet would reach the ground long before the Cub—but it would

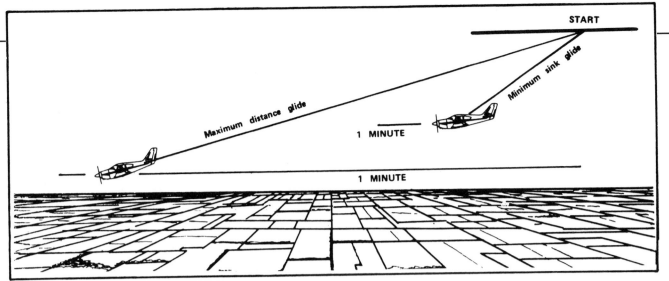

Fig. 8-5. Exaggerated view of minimum sink and maximum distance glides.

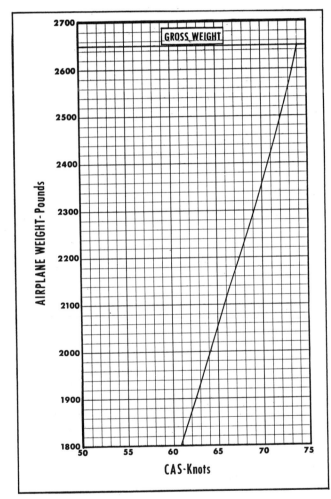

Fig. 8-6. Airspeed for maximum distance glide versus Weight for a particular airplane.

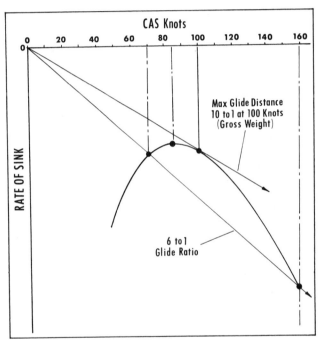

Fig. 8-7. Assume IAS = CAS at all speed ranges for all the graphs shown.

end up much farther away. (Fig. 8-5 is an example of these two airplanes, the Cub naturally being the airplane on the right.)

Take a look at Fig. 8-7, which is the rate of sink versus velocity (IAS) for a particular airplane. While it might appear that gliding too slowly is better than gliding too fast, the glide angle for 70 K is the same as that for 160 K. Fig. 8-7 shows

that for the two airspeeds, although the glide angle is the same at 70 and 160 K, there is a great deal of difference in the rates of sink. The lower airspeed gives a smaller rate of sink, but *as far as the distance covered is concerned both speeds would be bad.*

Back to stretching the glide—suppose you have an engine failure and are trying to make a field. You don't know the maximum distance glide speed for your airplane (which is 100 K—the one used for the graphs) so you use a speed of 70 K. Fig. 8-7 shows that you are definitely *not* getting the maximum distance and you soon see that it will be very close—if you're going to make the field at all.

So, like a lot of pilots, you try to stretch the glide by pulling the nose up until you're indicating 60 K. Fig. 8-8 shows that the 10-K slowdown has resulted in a much steeper glide angle and higher rate of sink—now you surely won't make it! You'd have been much better off to have *added* 10 K and held 80 K.

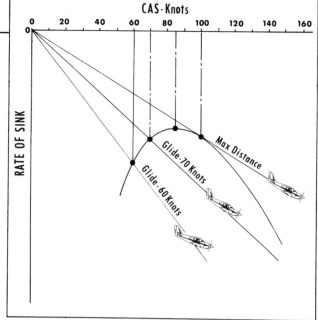

Fig. 8-8.

As the graphs show, the closer to the stall you get, the more the glide ratio and the sink rate are affected by a change in airspeed. Know the max distance glide speed(s) for your airplane and stick with it—don't try to stretch the glide.

Altitude Effects on the Glide. It was mentioned earlier that Weight has no effect on the maximum distance glide if the condition of maintaining the max L/D angle of attack is followed. (And with no angle of attack indicator your only course is to vary the airspeed with Weight change to maintain the constant angle of attack.)

Fig. 8-9 is the maximum distance glide ratio for a retractable-gear airplane in the configuration and wind condition indicated. The following is presented for those interested in the mathematics of the glide. Assume that (1) the height above terrain is also height above mean sea level on a *standard* day (that is, the heights given are also density-altitude), (2) the airplane is at a Weight of 2250 lb at the time of the start of the descent, and (3) KIAS = KCAS at 67 K.

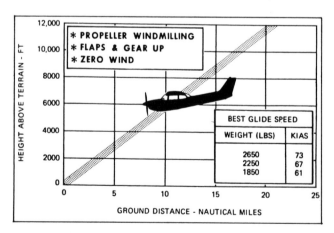

Fig. 8-9. Altitude versus maximum distance glide. Note the required decrease in IAS (CAS) with Weight decrease.

1. What is the *glide angle* of the airplane as shown on the graph in Fig. 8-9?
2. What is the *rate of descent* at 67 KCAS at 6000-ft density-altitude *at that glide angle*?

The *first* answer can be found by simply reading the graph. At 6000-ft density-altitude the glide distance is 10 NM. Apples and oranges again—convert 10 NM to feet (10 × 6080 = 60,800 ft). This problem requires a tangent function since you are working with the sides of a triangle and the tangent of the angle of glide is 6000/60,800 = 0.0987 (rounded off): tan γ = A/B′, or = 6000/60,800 = 0.0987. Looking this all up in a trig table, using Fig. 1-8 or a hand calculator, you find that the angle is 5.7° (rounded off a little). That's working strictly from the information presented. The glide ratio is a little better than 10:1. Figs. 8-10 and 8-11 show a low-wing airplane with the same glide characteristics as the airplane in Fig. 8-9.

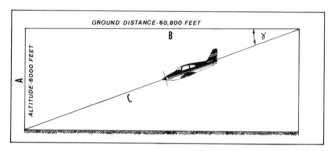

Fig. 8-10. Solving for glide angle.

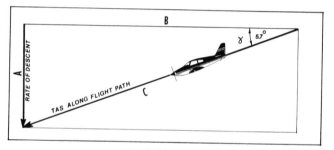

Fig. 8-11. Solving for rate of descent.

The *second* question requires a little more background (look at Fig. 8-11). It was found that the glide angle was 5.7°; now it becomes a matter of finding how fast the airplane is descending (side A) as it travels down along the hypotenuse (side C). You use the same units of speed along the flight path (C) and descent (A). Since rate of descent (RD) is usually in fpm, the move should be to convert the true *airspeed* (which is the true velocity along the flight path) to fpm. (Break out your computer.) So, 67 KCAS at 6000-ft density-altitude works out to be 73 KTAS (rounded off). Converting to fpm, you multiply it by 1.69 to convert to fps and then multiply *that* by 60 to get fpm: 1.69 × 73 × 60 = 7400 fpm TAS (rounded off), which is the rate the airplane is moving down the flight path.

The sine is involved here (opposite side and the hypotenuse—see Fig. 8-11 again); sin γ = A/C = RD/TAS; γ = 5.7°; sin 5.7° = 0.0993; RD = TAS × sin γ; RD = 7400 × 0.0993 = *735 fpm* at a density-altitude of 6000 ft.

Just out of curiosity, the rate of sink at a density-altitude of sea level would be TAS = *67 K* (CAS = TAS at sea level); TAS (fpm) = 67 × 1.69 × 60 = 6794 (call it 6800); sin γ (5.7°) = 0.0993; 6800 × 0.0993 = *675 fpm*. The rate of sink is noticeably less at sea level than at 6000 ft. (More about this later.)

To digress a little, if you're curious about the effects of a windmilling prop, take a look at Fig. 8-12, which is the maximum distance glide chart for a twin-engine airplane (clean, with the props feathered). Comparing it with the airplane in Fig. 8-9, you can see that from 10,000 ft the twin can glide 20

NM or nearly 3 mi farther than the single with its windmilling prop.

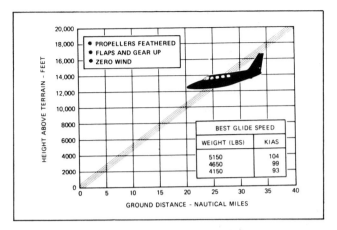

Fig. 8-12. Altitude versus maximum distance glide for a twin (propellers feathered).

Altitude does not change the maximum distance glide *angle* if the proper IAS (or CAS) is maintained for the current Weight. Fig. 8-13 shows a rate of sink versus *true* airspeed curve for an airplane at sea level and some altitude at the same Weight. The curves have been "stretched" apart for clarity. Notice that the line that represents the maximum distance glide is tangent to both curves. The difference is that the TAS is greater at altitude—the airplane, although indicating the same, is moving down the slope at a greater rate and hence has a greater rate of descent.

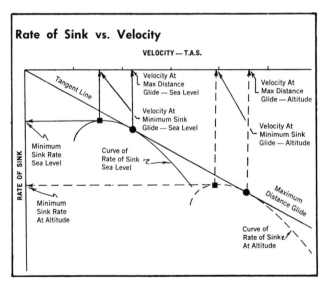

Fig. 8-13. Rate of sink versus velocity curves for a particular airplane at two altitudes (same Weight).

There have been arguments about whether a higher approach speed should be used for landings at airports of higher elevations. Assuming that the airplane weighs the same in both instances, it will stall at the same *indicated* airspeed (and calibrated airspeed) at altitude as at sea level, but its *true* airspeed will be much higher at touchdown; hence it will use more runway at the airport of higher elevation (but the landing roll is a subject for another chapter).

Now, it's agreed that the airplane will stall at the same indicated (calibrated) airspeed at higher altitude so there should be no problem—except that the rate of descent is greater for that same approach speed (IAS) (Fig. 8-13).

If you are in the habit of crossing the fence at an IAS just above a stall, you might find that at higher elevations you'd require just a touch more power than usual to sweeten the landing because of this greater rate of descent.

The chances are good that you wouldn't even notice the difference on landing except at very high altitudes and, as it's a matter of judgment or "eyeballing," would handle it with no problem. Adding airspeed would increase the landing roll (which will be covered in Chap. 9).

A problem could be encountered on a short-field approach at a higher elevation (and higher density-altitude). If you chop power and start sinking, the increased sink rate compared with sea level (for the same IAS) might fool you. Added to this is the fact that there is less HP available (for unsupercharged engines) to stop the sink rate at the higher altitude. The best thing would be to exercise care to avoid getting into such a condition at higher altitudes.

Wind Effects on the Glide. Wind affects the glide distance (and angle) for a particular airspeed—as you've noticed, particularly on power-off approaches. From a practical standpoint it is unlikely that in an engine-out emergency you would want to take the time to worry about working out a new max distance glide speed for a headwind or tailwind. The theoretical side of the problem is that you would add a few knots of IAS to the best glide speed for a moderate headwind and subtract airspeed for a moderate tailwind, basically the same idea as was discussed in Chap. 7 It has been shown that, for instance, increasing the airspeed to take care of a headwind (or decreasing for a tailwind) makes only a slight difference in glide distance in these conditions for normal winds. So you would most likely be better off in an actual emergency using the no-wind glide speed for headwind or tailwind conditions rather than further complicating an already complicated situation. You have other things to do such as picking a landing spot, trying to locate the trouble in the cockpit, and deciding whether to land gear-up or down.

Fig. 8-14 shows the effects of a headwind or tailwind on the glide angle for a particular airspeed.

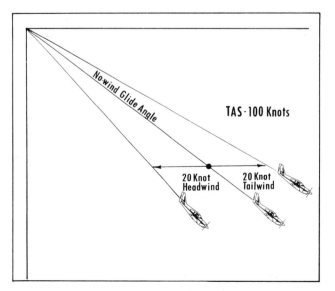

Fig. 8-14. The effects of a headwind or tailwind on the glide angle of an airplane at a particular true airspeed.

You may note the similarity to the wind triangles you did earlier in your training; here the only difference is that the vectors are in a vertical plane. The length of the no-wind glide vector represents the TAS, and others represent the glide angles and "ground speed" for the winds given. The glide angles have been exaggerated for clarity.

Speed Brakes. One company (see the Bibliography) is producing a speed brake kit for installation on some current general aviation airplanes, the principle being to provide a

means for a greater rate of descent (and steeper angle) without picking up airspeed. The speed brakes are usually located fairly well aft on the chord and are retractable. There may be one or two pairs of brakes, depending on the airplane, and each pair has an area of 55 in.². The nearly 0.4 ft² (per pair) additional area can make a significant difference.

The glide is a function of the C_L/C_D ratio, and if C_D (or Drag) is increased, the glide will be steeper and the added Drag will keep the airspeed low for that new angle of descent. (See Fig. 8-4 again.)

9 Landings

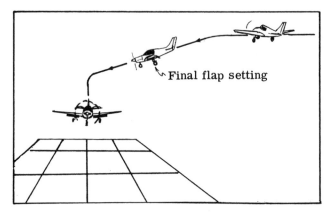

Fig. 9-1. Recommended flap setting procedure for a light trainer under normal wind and traffic conditions.

APPROACH

The Normal Approach. The rule that a good landing is generally preceded by a good approach is a true one. If you approach at too high an airspeed (adding 5 K for the wife and 2 K for each of the kids and maybe a little because it's Sunday), you'll use more runway than is necessary and won't be flying the airplane efficiently. Murgatroyd Sump, private pilot, has a beautiful wife and eleven fine children at home. It is usually necessary to shoot him down to keep him from using the whole 5000 ft of runway (Murgatroyd doesn't fly into a field any shorter). He hasn't read his *POH* for a recommended approach speed nor does he know that a rule of thumb for normal approaches is a calibrated airspeed of approximately 1.3 times stall (CAS) at the flap setting (no flaps) he uses. If he used full flaps, then it would be 1.3 times the figure given for the stall speed (calibrated) as given in the *POH*. With no flaps he would use the *POH* figure (CAS) for the flaps-up stall in setting up his approach speed. Also, although his plane has flaps, Murgatroyd originally trained in an airplane that didn't have flaps and old habits die hard. Besides, he tried using flaps once and it felt "funny."

THE USE OF FLAPS DURING THE APPROACH. *For a normal approach and landing, use as much flaps as is consistent with the wind conditions.* For strong, gusty winds use less or, perhaps, no flaps. Some airplanes have steep glide angles with no power and full flaps, and it may be preferable to use some setting of less than full flaps when planning a power-off approach.

Using flaps will help you maintain the recommended approach speed, whereas with no flaps you will nearly always be too fast on final and at the start of the landing. With flaps, you will land at a lower airspeed, using less runway and making it easier on the tires. This makes a big difference if you're operating out of an airport with a hard-surfaced runway and they are *your* tires.

Have the final flap setting completed on base and do it in one move so that you can put your attention to using wheel, rudder, and throttle—not the flap handle. Set your flaps, set up power (if necessary), trim, and fly the airplane. This means that no matter what flap setting you plan to use on the landing, from one-fourth to full, this should be completed before you reach a mid-base-leg position (Fig. 9-1).

Another reason for having the final flap setting completed on base is that airspeed is easier to control. If you are too fast on final the sudden application of flaps may result in altitude gain and the possibility of being too high. Unless you

have a very long final (and this is bad) you won't have time to get set up in attitude and airspeed. Generally the base leg is slightly faster (about 5 to 10 K) than the final. (This is no absolute law—student pilots in training airplanes should use final approach speed all the way around.)

A major area of disagreement among pilots is *when* to put the flaps down on approach. For light trainers (and low-time pilots) it's usually better under normal conditions to have the final flap setting on base so that you can direct attention to using ailerons, rudder, and throttle—and to watching the runway—rather than putting the flaps down in small increments, requiring retrimming and possible distraction from flying the airplane. In this case, no matter what flap setting you plan to use, one-fourth to full, this should be completed by the midbase position (Fig. 9-1).

As you fly heavier and more complex airplanes (particularly twins), you may not want to commit yourself to full flaps on base but would be likely to prefer making the last setting on final when you're sure the runway is made. You could put the flaps down in increments with perhaps half-flaps on base (or even less depending on the wind or whether you have one propeller feathered), but Chapter 15 goes into detail on engine-out approaches in the twin.

If you are making a power-off accuracy approach and landing, for fun or profit, it would behoove you not to be too hasty in putting down full flaps too soon in the approach. But in the case above you *would* put them down in increments and, if undershooting the spot, might stay at zero or stop at one-fourth flap deflection, as necessary.

If you have to make a go-around you'll want to clean the airplane up as expeditiously as possible. Gear and flaps create Drag (and require HP). There is an argument against raising the flaps too fast in a critical situation right at the stall, but the average pilot new to their use tends to be too timid in bringing them up in such a case. For many airplanes the addition of full power will just about offset the difference in stall speeds between flaps up and full flaps down. Some *POHs* recommend raising flaps before raising the gear in a go-around. At any rate, don't be so particular about seeing how slowly and smoothly you can raise the flaps that you fly into some object off the far end of the runway. When you check out in a new airplane do some simulated go-arounds at altitude in the full-dirty condition; pick a "base" altitude for the ground and try different techniques (flaps up slowly, then gear; gear up and then flaps slowly; flaps and gear up immediately, etc.) The check pilot will also have recommendations for the best technique for that particular airplane. Add power first in every case to stop or decrease the sink rate and then use the recommended cleanup procedure.

Traffic Pattern. Nothing looks worse or delays traffic more than a drawn-out final approach. You'll be operating into some pretty busy airports and traffic controllers don't appreciate some pilot in a lightplane with an approach speed of 70 K who happens to be making a 3-mi final. The results are cumulative. The pilot in the faster airplane will have to make an even longer final to keep from running over you and the cycle begins; each plane following must go farther before turning final and YOU are the instigator of all this.

Fig. 9-2 shows a typical landing procedure for a retractable-gear plane using flaps.

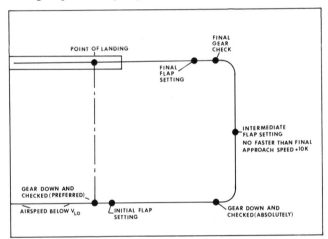

Fig. 9-2. Typical landing pattern.

There'll be times at a busy airport when you'll be rushed (there's a jet back there that looks as if it'll run into your flippers any minute). It's best to have the gear down before reaching a point opposite the spot of intended landing. *But always have the gear down before you turn on the base leg.* This must become an ingrained habit. In some cases, in order to expedite the approach, you may not use flaps and will come in "hot." The runways will be long enough at these big airports to handle you without flaps but not without landing gear. If you persist in cluttering up busy runways with airplanes resting on their bellies, you won't be welcome after a while.

THE LANDING

Landings in General. *The goal of any normal landing is to have the airplane touch down as slowly as possible, consistent with conditions.* This is sometimes forgotten by pilots who fly by themselves for many hours. When they start practicing for the commercial flight test they find that old habits are hard to break.

The most prevalent misconception about landings among private pilots, even among those who learned to fly on tailwheel airplanes, is that the tricycle-gear requires special technique in landing. Maybe it should be put the other way—

they think that *no* technique is required. They may listen to the instructor during the checkout, but sooner or later they get the habit of landing the tricycle-gear in a too-nose-low attitude. Some even go so far as to land on all three wheels at the same time on all occasions and wind conditions. This means that the airplane is not stalled and lands at a much higher speed than is necessary.

You can think of the landing distance in terms of kinetic energy that must be dissipated before the airplane is stopped: Kinetic energy = $(M/2)V^2$, where M = mass of the particular airplane (Weight in pounds divided by 32.2) and V^2 = the touchdown velocity (fps), squared.

While your landing distance is directly affected by Weight (double the Weight and you *double* the energy to be dissipated), the effect of velocity is even more pronounced (double the velocity at landing and the energy to be dissipated is *quadrupled*).

An approximation for landing roll distance can be obtained: landing roll = (landing velocity)$^2/-2a$, where $-a$ is equal to a deceleration of 7 fps, per second. This is for airplanes on a concrete runway with normal braking. Converting this to miles per hour, or knots: ground roll (no wind) = $0.225V_L^2$ (mph) or $0.3V_L^2$ (K). Fig. 9-3 shows some comparative ground roll figures for various airplanes.

Airplane	Flaps-down Stall Speed	Landing Roll	
		POH figures	Equation figures
	(knots)	*(feet)*	*(feet)*
1	43	360	565
2	49	350	705
3	53	600	835
4	48	560	680
5	42	500	540
6	47	500	655
7	37	350	415
8	54	900	870
9	49	750	710
10	64	620	1230
11	51	535	780
12	61	700	1130
13	72	1000	1530

Fig. 9-3. Landing rolls, sea level, no wind (gross Weight).

You will notice that the *POH* figures are usually lower than those arrived at using the equation. The *POH* figures come from flight tests by test pilots who are old pros. Pilot technique can make a lot of difference on takeoff and landing. Maximum range and endurance airspeeds are precomputed figures, but even there a pilot who is more skillful in leaning the engine will get more out of the airplane. Pilot technique shows up the most on takeoffs or landings. The test pilots can get these published figures for landing, but can you? Their braking may be greater than you normally use. Airplane manufacturers are in a highly competitive business and they will get the best performance possible. The given equation is an approximation—but don't cut your planning too closely.

Variables Affecting the Landing Roll

ALTITUDE EFFECTS. The landing is not affected as greatly by altitude as is the takeoff. Engine performance is not a critical factor on the landing, as it is usually at idle at touchdown, so the altitude effect generally can be more easily predicted.

In the ground roll equation, $0.225V_L^2$ (mph) or $0.3V_L^2$ (K), the V_L (landing velocity) is the true airspeed. At sea level *true airspeed* and *calibrated airspeed* are the same. Remember that the airplane will stall at the same wings-level indicated and calibrated airspeed at *all altitudes* (assuming same Weights) but the true airspeed will increase *2%* per 1000 ft. This means that if you stall the airplane at sea level and then at 10,000 ft the IAS at the "break" will be the same at both altitudes, but your actual speed with reference to the air at 10,000 ft is 20% (10 × 2%) faster than at sea level. In calm air this means that you'll also contact the ground at landing 20% faster—which results in a longer ground roll. V_L goes up 2% per 1000 ft but this figure is squared in the landing equation so that *the effect on landing roll is to add 4% per 1000 ft for density-altitude effects*. For every 1000 ft of density-altitude above sea level add 4% to the landing roll given for sea level standard conditions in the *POH*.

TEMPERATURE. Computing density-altitude and using it directly for landing computations involves the use of a conversion table. It may be easier to compute for altitude and temperature effects separately. A rule of thumb may be of some help.

If you know the pressure altitude, you know the standard temperature for this altitude (from 59°F subtract 3½°F for every 1000 ft of pressure altitude). For a pressure altitude of 6000 ft the standard temperature should be 59 − 21 = *38°F.* *For every 15°F above the standard temperature for this altitude add 4% to the landing run computed for pressure altitude effects* (subtract 4% for every 15°F below this figure). If you are working with Celsius the rule is that for every 8.5°C above or below standard, add or subtract 4% respectively.

Remember that a nonstandard temperature affects the pressure altitude indication of the altimeter. However, for the thumb rule used here it is normally ignored.

For example, suppose your airplane uses 800 ft for a landing run at sea level in no-wind conditions. You are landing at an airport at a 6000-ft pressure altitude and the last sequence report gives the surface temperature as 48°F.

The temperature (48°F) is 10° above normal for the field altitude standard (38°F). The pressure altitude is 6000 ft, which means an increased landing run of 6 × 4 = 24% for altitude effects: 1.24 × 800 = 992 ft. Added to this figure is 2⅔% (call it 3) for the extra 10° of temperature; 0.03 × 800 = *24 ft.* Your landing roll will be 216 ft longer at this airport. The 2⅔% figure was arrived at by the ratio 10°F/15°F = x%/4%; x = 2⅔% (total roll = 1016 ft).

Using an altitude conversion chart you would find that at a pressure altitude of 6000 ft and a temperature of 48°F (9°C), the density-altitude would be 6800 ft. You would then use straight altitude effects: 6.8 × 4% = 27.2%; 1.272 × 800 = *1018 ft.* In either case you are close enough to be in the ball park (or the airport).

In step 1 above you converted to the correct density-altitude the hard way by working with pressure altitude and temperature separately. You assumed the density-altitude to be 6000 ft and then corrected this assumption for temperature effects.

If you know the field elevation of the destination airport and are able to get the altimeter setting and temperature from a sequence report, you could work out your probable landing run on the way in if you think it's going to be a close squeeze on landing.

Take the same airport discussed earlier, where the pressure altitude was 6000 ft. Here's one way we could have arrived at that figure. The field elevation is 5700 ft and the latest altimeter setting for the area is 29.62. If the pressure altitude had been the same, the altimeter setting would have been 29.92 (remember that setting an altimeter to 29.92 gives the pressure altitude). But this altimeter setting is 0.30 in. *low* for the pressure altitude setting of 29.92. This means that the pressure altitude at the destination is approximately 300 ft

higher than the field elevation. The pressure altitude is 5700 plus 300, or 6000 ft (another canned problem). If you had ignored the 0.30 in., or 300 feet of pressure altitude, what would have happened? Suppose you call the field elevation the pressure altitude. The altitude effects would have been 5.7 × 4 = 22.8%; 1.228 × 800 = 982 ft. Correcting for temperature as before (plus 3%): 24 + 982 = 1006 ft, a difference of 12 ft from the first calculation. If the destination altimeter setting is within 0.50 in. of 29.92 in. (29.42 to 30.42), use the field elevation for your pressure altitude correction and then correct for temperature. The altimeter setting is nearly always within the above stated limits. Even if the corrected altimeter setting was *1 in.* off it would only mean a difference of 4% (about 40 ft) in the landing run in the above problem. You can use up 40 ft or considerably more by poor pilot technique; *so for an approximation of pressure altitude the field elevation works fine for landing.* For simplicity, the effect of temperature on the landing roll can be ignored unless the temperature is extremely high or low for the landing altitude. An approximation to correct for altitude and higher temperature effects calls for *adding 5% per 1000 ft of field elevation. This saves a lot of computing.* Actually it's pretty ridiculous to work it out to the nearest 6 ft (1006 ft) and it was done only to show the arithmetic involved.

High humidity is much less of a problem for landings than for take offs because engine power is normally not a factor when landing, as noted earlier. (Power may be increased on a soft-field landing, just before touchdown, but any humidity effects there would not be measurable.) The *aerodynamic* effects at sea level of 100°F and 100% humidity might increase the roll slightly less than 2%. On *takeoff* some reciprocating engines could lose up to 12% at full power under the temperature and moisture conditions just cited, and *that* would be a factor (see Chap. 5).

AIRPLANE WEIGHT. The effect of Weight on landing roll is generally considered to be straightforward—increase the airplane Weight 20% and the landing roll increase is close to this figure. *POH* figures show that there is a difference of about 5% between the two figures. That is, if the Weight is decreased 20%, the landing roll is decreased only about 15%. Or, if the Weight is increased 20%, the landing roll is increased about 15%. *But for estimation purposes the percentage of Weight change equals the percentage of approach and/or rolling distance change.* Landing roll is directly proportional to Weight at landing.

Assuming braking is being used, added Weight would increase the touchdown (stall) speed but would result in better braking (more Weight on the braking wheels) so it would approximately balance out. However, the brakes would be hotter at the end of the roll because of the greater energy that had to be dissipated. Braking effectiveness on dry concrete is usually considered to be from 0.4 to 0.6; that is, the coefficient of friction, μ, is that value. A 3000-lb airplane could have a braking retarding force of 0.4 × 3000 = 1200 lb if Lift is not present.

RUNWAY CONDITION. Added rolling resistance in the form of high grass, soft ground, or snow naturally shortens the landing roll. The effect of increased rolling resistance on the landing is to help in all cases—unless it becomes so great as to cause a nose-up. As you will probably be using brakes in the later part of the roll, no set figures can be given here.

WIND. The wind affects the landing roll exactly as it does the takeoff run, and a rule of thumb, 90% − wind velocity/ landing speed = percentage of no-wind runway, can be used. If the wind velocity is 20% of your landing speed, you'll use 70% of the published figure for no-wind conditions (90% −

20% = 70%). Fig. 5-9 also can be applied.

BRAKING. For normal landings, use aerodynamic braking by holding the nose wheel off (in the tricycle-gear type) and leaving the flaps down. Aerodynamic Drag (D) = $C_DS (\varrho V^2/2)$, a function of the square of the velocity. As you slow down on the roll to one-half your landing speed, the aerodynamic Drag is approximately one-fourth that at touchdown. Aerodynamic Drag is not as important as wheel braking. Use aerodynamic Drag for what you think is about one-fourth of the expected landing roll, then lower the nose and use brakes as needed (on dry concrete). In lowering the nose you increase the rolling resistance by decreasing Lift, remembering that rolling resistance = μ(Weight − Lift). The less the Lift, the greater the rolling resistance.

Some pilots start applying brakes as soon as they touch down. The brake effectiveness is not at its best because the airplane still has some Lift (though not enough to support the airplane) and this usually results in skidding and less braking effect.

Once you've lowered the nose, flaps can still give aerodynamic Drag, so for normal landings leave them down, particularly if you're using full flaps. For cleaner airplanes, *full* flaps help more in aerodynamic Drag than they hinder the braking action by furnishing Lift by being down. Leave 'em down throughout the roll and save your brakes. For short fields, get the flaps up shortly after landing, as soon as you feel you've gotten the most Drag out of them. In this case you are not interested in taking care of the brakes but want to stop in as short a distance as possible. *Hold the wheel full back as you brake. Do not retract the landing gear.*

To get the most out of your brakes, you will want to apply them as much as possible *without skidding*. Not only will skidding result in the possibility of blown tires, but it will give much less braking action than found under proper brake usage.

Some of the larger airplanes have antiskid devices so that if the wheels start to skid the brakes are automatically relaxed, even though the pilot continues to hold full force against the pedals. If the device is working properly, this may mean up to twice the braking effectiveness of braking by "feel." If it isn't working properly one or both tires may lock and blow out.

In the situation where braking action is poor, such as on frost-covered, wet, or icy runways, it's best not to count on the brakes. Although skidding sideways is not as critical for an airplane as for a car (it says here), improper brake action could result in the airplane's skidding sideways on an icy runway; if a clear spot of runway is hit, landing gear failure could result. Also, if you apply full brakes on ice, even headed straight, and suddenly hit a bare spot of runway, a tire may blow or, in the tailwheel-type airplane, a nose-up could occur.

The brake effectiveness on ice is a great deal less than that for dry concrete, so aerodynamic Drag will be the big factor for an icy or wet runway. Plan on it!

Fig. 9-4 shows some comparison of rolling resistance caused by braking and aerodynamic Drag for concrete and ice-covered runways for a particular airplane. Note that the aerodynamic Drag is the same, as it is assumed that the airplane touches down at the minimum speed and at the same Weight both times.

Some landing distance charts note that the figures are based on zero wind and a paved, level, dry runway with factors added for wind and a dry, grass runway. Fig. 9-13 at the end of this chapter indicates that distances (ground roll and total over 50 ft) should be increased by 40% of the ground roll figure if operating on a dry, grass runway. The initial thought is that since a dry, grass runway would be expected to have a higher coefficient of friction (see Chap. 5 again) the landing roll would be *less* than on pavement. You'll note, however, that the distances are based on *short-field techniques with maximum braking*. Dry grass is "slicker" than pavement as far as braking is concerned, and the airplane will use up more ground roll on dry grass.

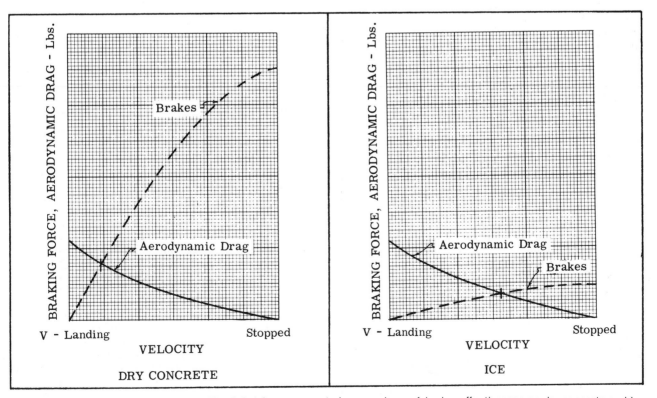

Fig. 9-4. An exaggerated comparison of brake effectiveness on dry concrete and ice.

RUNWAY SLOPE EFFECTS. Little can be said here except that if the slope is great, it is better to land uphill and downwind (unless the wind is very strong). As you saw back in Chap. 5, a 2° slope can mean a retarding component about 3½% of the Weight, which is approximately 105 lb for a 3000-lb airplane. This factor would be of significance in an off-airport landing on an upslope of 5°. (The retarding component of Weight would give a respectable 261-lb retarding force on the roll-out.)

PILOT TECHNIQUE. As in takeoffs, here is the item that can shoot all your careful computations. Landing too fast, poor brake usage, and other goof-ups can cause you to lose all you have gained. The only answer is to get an occasional check ride in your airplane with an instructor and know the variables that can affect your landings.

Short-Field Landing.
When landing area is critical you want to land as short as possible without damaging the airplane. You want a safety margin of speed, but not enough to cause floating, because every foot of runway counts.

Power is used to control your approach path at the recommended speed. Fly a wider pattern so you won't be rushed or have to make steep turns at this near-critical airspeed. The power approach angle will be 1° or 2° shallower than the normal power-off approach for your airplane and you'll need more room.

A rule of thumb for short fields uses an approach speed of no more than 1.3 times the *power-off, full flaps-down stall speed* (calibrated airspeed); you'll be using full flaps for a short-field landing, and this ratio will give a safety factor if you should think you'll be too high and suddenly chop the throttle.

For gusty air this speed should be increased by 5 to 10 K, as sudden changes in wind velocity can affect your airplane and you are interested in *not* suddenly finding yourself with a critically low airspeed at a bad time. One rule used is to add one-half the gust velocity to the approach speed. For instance, if the wind is 15 K gusting to 25 K, add one-half the difference of the 10-K gust (5 K) to the approach airspeed.

Obstacle approaches require a steeper angle of descent in that you must clear the obstacle and still land as short as possible (Fig. 9-5). The danger here is that you approach at a low airspeed, and after the obstacle is passed, a steep angle of descent is continued toward the ground. You may possibly find that there is not enough airspeed to allow you to flare. The airplane is rotated quickly but stalls. A sudden short burst of power just before touching can be used to cushion the landing if you get too slow. Don't leave the power on too long or you'll use too much runway.

1. Start the approach from a slightly wider downwind leg.

2. Have full flaps set and attain recommended short-field approach speed on base. If you plan a long final, wait until after the final turn to set up your recommended airspeed.

3. Control the approach angle with throttle after turning on final. Don't be a throttle jockey; use minor adjustments.

4. Use power as necessary to make the spot. You'll have to use power all the way to the ground if you get low and slow.

Soft-Field Landing

APPROACH. The approach for the soft-field landing is usually a normal one—only the actual touchdown is different from other landings. Of course, in an emergency situation you may be running low on fuel and have to land in a pasture—which may be both short and soft. This would require a short-field approach and a soft-field landing. Never make an approach to a soft field at a higher-than-normal approach speed because the airplane will float and usually is "put on" at a higher-than-minimum speed (pilots get impatient, it seems).

If you make a short-field type of approach to a soft field, you can pick the firmest possible landing spot. There may be parts of a muddy field where the grass cover is better or the snow is not drifted as deeply on a snow-covered field.

LANDING. The same principle applies on a soft-field landing for both tricycle-gear and tailwheel-type airplanes. Touch down as slowly as possible and with a higher nose attitude than for the normal landing. This means the use of power during touchdown (Fig. 9-6).

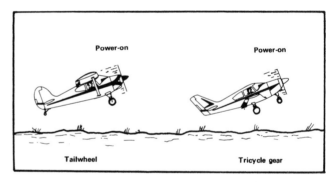

Fig. 9-6. The soft-field landing, tailwheel and tricycle-gear airplanes (attitudes exaggerated).

If you know beforehand that you'll have to land in snow or on a soft field, it would be a good idea to have the speed fairings removed before the trip. Speed fairings look good and in most cases help out on speed a little, but they get clogged up in short order on a muddy field or in snow. (If conditions are such that they are liable to get clogged up on the landing run itself, things can get pretty hairy.) The reason speed fairings weren't mentioned in more detail on the soft-field takeoff is that if the field is really soft you won't get to the takeoff area anyway.

After touching down, keep the wheel or stick *full back*. The point is to keep the tail on the ground with the tailwheel-type, and to keep as much Weight as possible *off* the nosewheel with the tricycle-gear airplane as long as possible.

You might check into the idea of retracting the flaps after touchdown to keep down damage from mud, slush, snow, etc. (This is more of a problem with low-wing airplanes.) For pete's sake don't pull the gear up by mistake.

Fig. 9-5. The obstacle approach.

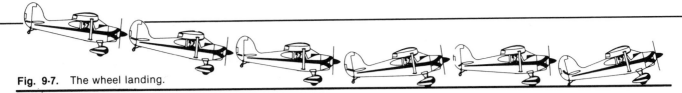

Fig. 9-7. The wheel landing.

GUSTY AND CROSSWIND LANDINGS

Approaches in Gusty Wind Conditions. In gusty wind conditions the approach must be flown 5 to 10 K faster than for a normal approach, as indicated earlier. Less flaps than normal may be used so that when the airplane is landed it won't be so apt to be lifted off again by a sudden sharp gust. If the wind is strong your landing run will be short anyway, so the higher approach speed and lack of flaps won't particularly hurt the landing roll. The approach is naturally the same for tricycle-gear or tailwheel-type airplanes.

Wheel Landings. The wheel landing is the best means of landing the tailwheel airplane in strong and/or gusty wind conditions in that the plane contacts the ground at a low angle of attack. You are literally flying the plane onto the ground.

Two-place trainers and other lightplanes of low wing loading generally do not require power to make the landing; in fact the use of power makes the problem more knotty. A "power juggler" may use up more runway than is necessary.

PROCEDURE. Make an approach about 5 K faster than for a normal glide. The landing transition is made at a lower height for two reasons: (1) the airplane must touch down at a higher speed and (2) the attitude will be only slightly tail-low—not three-point. For the lighter planes, power is only used to control the approach—not to make the landing. Make your path a curved one tangent to the runway at the touchdown point (Fig. 9-7).

The correct procedure is to land in a slightly tail-low attitude by "rounding off" the glide properly. After the plane has touched, apply slight forward pressure to keep the tail up—and maintain a low angle of attack. If you are too hasty in bringing the tail down, the chances are good of becoming airborne once more—and you will probably have to take it around again.

Impatience will be your biggest problem on the wheel landing, particularly if you're gliding too fast. The airplane is skimming a few inches above the runway and you may try to "put it on." This results in some fancy "crow hopping" and usually means you'll have to open it up and take it around. Then there are pilots who hold the plane off too long and wind up making a half-three-point, half-wheels, and all-bouncing type of landing when the plane settles fast on the front two wheels.

As the plane slows, continue to hold more forward pressure until you run out of elevator and the tail moves down and then hold the wheel (or stick) back to keep it on the ground.

Some airplanes have comparatively poor directional control at lower speeds with the tailwheel off the ground. There just may not be enough rudder effectiveness to do the job. In these airplanes it's best to maintain the forward pressure held at touchdown—don't push forward. As the speed decreases the tail will come down before you lose rudder control; then you may move the wheel smoothly back to the full aft position. This is a good technique in a strong crosswind for all types of tailwheel airplanes.

The crosswind correction for a wheel landing is the same as for the three-point landing. Lower the wing and hold opposite rudder as needed. Land on one wheel; the other will come down immediately. Hold aileron into the wind and apply rudder as needed to keep it straight. Remember that your airplane may be placarded against landing in crosswind components above a certain value.

COMMON ERRORS

1. Too fast an approach—the plane floats.
2. Too slow an approach or leveling off too high—the plane settles fast on the main gear and bounces.
3. Getting impatient—trying to put it on.

A bounce usually means taking it around, but you can lower the nose, apply power, and reland if there is enough runway left.

Keep in mind that wheel landings and soft field conditions don't mix very well.

Gusty Wind Landing for the Tricycle-Gear. The approach in gusty air is the same for both types of airplanes and the landing technique is very similar (Fig. 9-8).

You remember that the recommended procedure for normal landings for the tricycle-gear is to land on the main wheels and hold the nosewheel off during the initial portion of the landing roll. For strong, gusty wind conditions, however, holding the nose up may result in a sudden gust lifting the airplane off again. The best technique for this wind condition is to touch down in a nearly level flight attitude. If you used flaps get them up immediately after touchdown to lessen any chance of a gust picking you up. The objection to picking up the flaps during the landing roll is that in a retractable-gear airplane you could inadvertently pull up the *landing gear*. This would preclude a sudden gust picking you up as you would slow down very quickly, but it's more expensive than pulling up the flaps.

After you touch down, lower the nose immediately to decrease the angle of attack, and raise the flaps. If the wind is very strong, you may not want to use flaps for landings. Check the *POH*.

COMMON ERRORS

1. Flying the airplane on and "slamming" it on the ground with the possibility of damaging the nosewheel.
2. Failure to take into consideration the gusty conditions and holding the nosewheel off after landing.

Crosswind Landings. As in the gusty wind landings, the approach is the same for the two types of landing gear. You have four choices in making the approach and landing for either type of landing gear.

1. *The wing-down method*—This was probably the method taught you as it is the simplest for light-to-moderate crosswinds. It's easy because you do not need to raise the wing or kick rudder to straighten the airplane at the last second. You hold the wing down with aileron and use opposite rudder all through the final approach and landing as necessary to

NORMAL LANDING

GUSTY WINDS

Fig. 9-8. Landing attitudes.

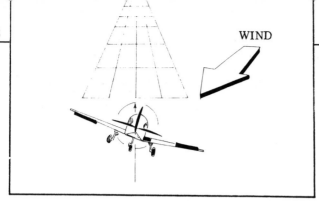

Fig. 9-9. Wing-down method of crosswind correction.

keep the nose lined up with the runway (Fig. 9-9). With strong crosswind components the wing may be down to such a degree that the slipping approach is uncomfortable to the passengers. In extreme cases, the lowered wing may be in danger of striking the ground, particularly in a low-wing airplane. Chances are in such conditions you wouldn't land at that airport, but would find one having a runway more into the wind. If you are low on fuel and must land, this method may limit your correction for strong crosswind.

Common errors: Probably the most common error committed by private pilots in this type of correction is using too much top rudder, yawing the nose away from the runway. The nose should be lined up with the runway during the approach and landing. Also, some pilots try to raise the down wing at the last instant. This isn't necessary.

2. *Crab method*—This makes for a comfortable approach as the plane is not slipping, but it has the disadvantage of requiring fine judgment in knowing when to kick the airplane straight. Also, if the crosswind is strong, the crab angle will have to be so great as to make it doubtful that you would have enough rudder effectiveness left to completely straighten the airplane before it touched—and this makes for a possible ground loop. If the airplane hits in a crab, you'll have a weathercocking tendency. In the tailwheel-type airplane, forces will be set up to aggravate the ground loop once it has started. So, the crab method also is limited to moderate crosswind components (Fig. 9-10).

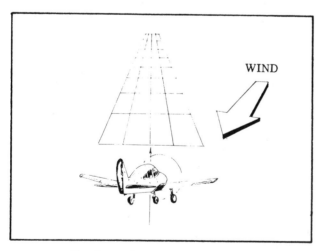

Fig. 9-10. Crab method of crosswind correction.

Common errors: Not straightening the airplane at the right time. Gusts may cause the airplane to float and start drifting after you've kicked it straight, or you may touch down before you're ready, still in a crab.

3. *Combination crab and wing-down.* —The limitations of the previous methods may be overcome by combining the two. If you are able to comfortably correct for 15 K of crosswind component by either method outlined above, chances are you'll find the results additive if they are combined and you will be able to correct for nearly double the crosswind component (Fig. 9-11).

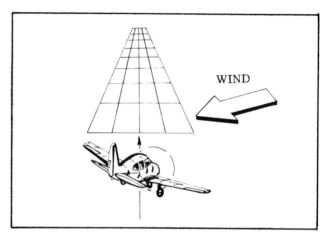

Fig. 9-11. Combination wing-down and crab methods.

You'll be crabbed *and* have the wing down, which means that the wing is not uncomfortably low and the crab is not such that the plane cannot be yawed straight as it touches. The idea is to yaw the plane straight, not to bother trying to raise the wing. Land on the upwind wheel as was done in the wing-down method.

Common errors: Getting so engrossed in one of the corrections that the other is neglected. Usually you forget you're in a crab as well as having the wing down.

4. *Crab approach and wing-down landing*—This makes a comfortable approach for light to moderate crosswinds. The crab is used during the final approach and, as the landing flare is begun, the nose is straightened and the wing lowered. From this point on it is the wing-down method. This avoids the long slipping approach, but it may require a couple of practice periods to make a smooth transition from the crab to the wing-down attitude.

Common errors: —Poor transition from crab to wing-down attitude, with some frantic scrambling around and poor use of controls.

The Ground Roll. Here's where tricycle-gear pays for itself. The CG is ahead of the main wheels, which tends to straighten the airplane out. The tailwheel-type reacts just the opposite. The ground roll is the toughest part of the problem in strong crosswinds. Keep that aileron into the wind to help fight wing-lifting tendencies and to also utilize the down aileron Drag to help keep you straight. The aileron is more important for the tailwheel airplane during the ground roll because of the airplane's attitude, but use it for both types.

Tailwheel-type—Keep that wheel back (if you made a three-point landing) because this will allow the tailwheel to get a good grip and help fight the weathercocking tendency.

Tricycle-gear—Ease the nosewheel on but don't hold forward pressure; you may wheelbarrow.

Hydroplaning. As you progress to faster airplanes with their higher-speed ground rolls and fly in more adverse weather conditions, hydroplaning will be more of a problem.

There are three types of hydroplaning:

LANDING DISTANCE

SHORT FIELD

CONDITIONS:
Flaps 30°
Power Off
Maximum Braking
Paved, Level, Dry Runway
Zero Wind

NOTES:
1. Short field technique as specified in Section 4.
2. Decrease distances 10% for each 9 knots headwind. For operation with tailwinds up to 10 knots, increase distances by 10% for each 2 knots.
3. For operation on a dry, grass runway, increase distances by 40% of the "ground roll" figure.
4. If a landing with flaps up is necessary, increase the approach speed by 9 KIAS and allow for 35% longer distances.

WEIGHT LBS	SPEED AT 50 FT KIAS	PRESS ALT FT	0°C		10°C		20°C		30°C		40°C	
			GRND ROLL	TOTAL TO CLEAR 50 FT OBS	GRND ROLL	TOTAL TO CLEAR 50 FT OBS	GRND ROLL	TOTAL TO CLEAR 50 FT OBS	GRND ROLL	TOTAL TO CLEAR 50 FT OBS	GRND ROLL	TOTAL TO CLEAR 50 FT OBS
2650	63	S.L.	590	1290	615	1325	635	1355	660	1390	680	1425
		1000	615	1325	635	1355	660	1395	680	1425	705	1460
		2000	635	1355	660	1395	685	1430	705	1465	730	1500
		3000	660	1395	685	1430	710	1470	735	1505	760	1545
		4000	685	1430	710	1470	735	1510	760	1545	785	1585
		5000	710	1470	740	1515	765	1550	790	1590	815	1630
		6000	740	1515	765	1555	795	1595	820	1635	850	1680
		7000	770	1560	795	1600	825	1645	850	1685	880	1725
		8000	800	1605	825	1645	855	1690	885	1735	915	1780

Fig. 9-13. Landing distance chart (short-field techniques).

1. *Dynamic.* In total dynamic hydroplaning, water standing on the runway exerts pressures between the tires and the runway. The tires are lifted and are not in contact with the runway surface. The rolling coefficient of friction (and also brake effectiveness) is reduced to nearly nothing. This means also that steering is not effective. A strong crosswind can cause added problems of control. *Dynamic hydroplaning starts at high speeds and in standing water on the runway.*

A thumb rule for predicting the minimum dynamic hydroplaning speed (knots) is $8.6 \sqrt{\text{tire pressure, psi}}$. At a tire pressure of 25 lb the expected minimum dynamic hydroplaning speed is 43 K ($8.6 \times \sqrt{25} = 8.6 \times 5 = 43$). You could expect problems above this speed. See Fig. 9-12.·

2. *Viscous hydroplaning.* When the runway has painted areas or rubber deposits that make it smooth, the tire can't

Fig. 9-12. Tire pressure versus minimum hydroplaning speed (72 K at 70 psi).

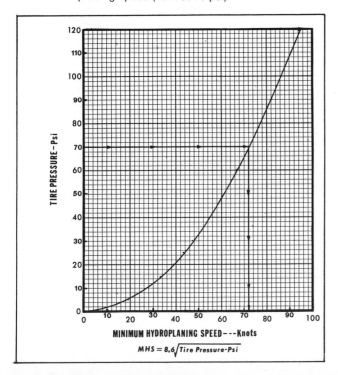

MINIMUM HYDROPLANING SPEED---Knots

$$MHS = 8.6 \sqrt{\text{Tire Pressure-Psi}}$$

fully displace the moisture *film.* You can feel this effect in driving a car when your car slips momentarily as you cross an extra thick painted highway centerline covered with rain or dew. When a large area of the runway or taxiway is involved, you could lose steering and braking ability. *This can occur at a much lower speed than dynamic hydroplaning.*

3. *Reverted rubber hydroplaning.* Suppose you are touching down on a wet runway and (wrongly) apply brakes immediately after touchdown. The airplane starts dynamic hydroplaning because the brakes are locked. The airplane slows, the dynamic hydroplaning decreases, and the locked tires heat up because of added friction. A layer of steam occurs between the tires and the runway and the rubber melts. This prevents water dispersal because the tire is riding on a layer of steam and molten rubber.

This is the worst of the hydroplaning variations because it can happen down to zero speed. *Locking the brakes for prolonged periods causes reverted (melted) rubber hydroplaning.*

Some of the newer runways are grooved to cut down on hydroplaning effects, but you should be ready for it anytime you are taking off or landing on a wet runway. Think of braking or directional control problems, and avoid excessive use of the rudder pedals or brakes. You might assume that the liquid water will have the friction properties of ice (which it will, under the conditions just mentioned).

References for further reading: (1) *ATP.* K. T. Boyd, Iowa State University Press; (2) You vs. Hydroplaning (article), *Aerospace Safety.* Norton AFB, Calif.

As was indicated earlier in this chapter, a dry, grass runway doesn't allow as good braking as pavement (wet grass is even worse) so that the ground roll and total distances for a given pressure altitude and temperature are to be increased by 40% of the ground roll figure. Looking at 2000 ft and 10°C in Fig. 9-13 you'll see that the ground roll is 660 ft with a *total* distance of 1395 ft required to clear a 50-ft obstacle. When landing on dry grass the distance required will be 0.40 × 660 = 264 ft. Add 264 ft to both values: 924 ft ground roll and 1659 ft total over the 50-ft obstacle.

Fig. 9-14 is a graphical presentation of two landing performance charts. The examples show the procedure for using the charts.

Fig. 9-14. Landing distance charts. A. Distance over 50-ft barrier. B. Landing ground roll.

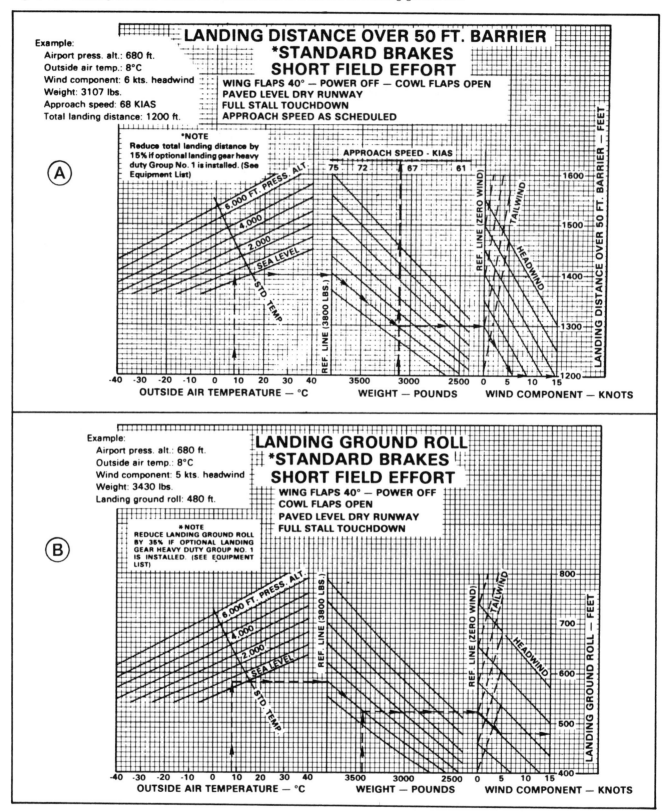

10 Airplane Stability and Control

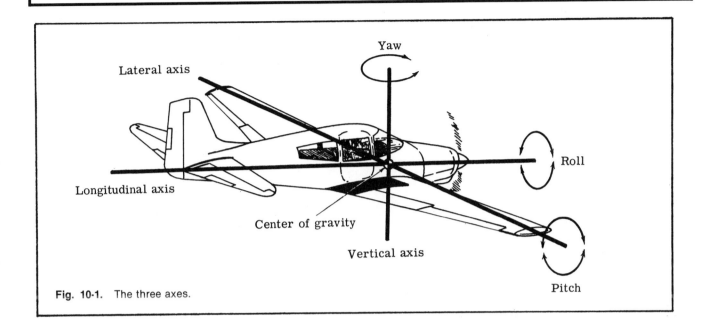

Fig. 10-1. The three axes.

THE THREE AXES

There are three axes around which the airplane moves. These axes pass through the airplane's center of gravity, or the point where the airplane Weight is considered to be concentrated (Fig. 10-1).

An airplane that is stable requires little pilot attention after it is trimmed for a certain airspeed and power setting. Airplanes certificated by the FAA for use in private and commercial flying must meet certain stability requirements around all three axes — otherwise the pilot could get into a dangerous situation because of a momentary lapse of attention. All the airplanes you have flown to date certificated as "normal" or "utility" category can be trimmed to maintain prescribed limits within certain airspeed ranges.

STABILITY IN GENERAL

Stability, as defined by the dictionary, means "fixedness, steadiness, or equilibrium." An object that is *positively stable* resists any displacement. One that is *negatively stable* does not resist displacement; indeed, it tends to displace itself more and more if acted upon by an outside force. An object that is *neutrally stable* doesn't particularly care what happens to it. If acted on by a force it will move, but it does not tend to return to its position or to move farther after the force is removed.

Static Stability. Static (at rest) stability is the initial tendency of a body to return to its original position after being disturbed. An example of positive static stability is a steel ball sitting inside a perfectly smooth hubcap (Fig. 10-2). You can see that the ball has an initial tendency to return to its original position if displaced.

Fig. 10-3 is an example of negative static stability. The ball is carefully balanced on the peak of the hubcap, and the application of outside force results in its falling. It does *not* tend to return to its original position; on the contrary, it gets farther and farther from the original position as it falls.

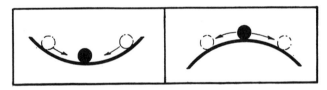

Fig. 10-2. Positive static stability.   **Fig. 10-3.** Negative static stability.

Neutral static stability can be likened to a steel ball on a perfectly flat smooth surface. If a force is exerted on it, the ball will move and stop at some new point after the force is removed (Fig. 10-4).

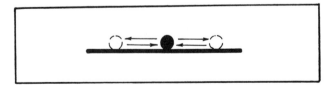

Fig. 10-4. Neutral static stability.

Dynamic Stability. The actions a body takes in response to its static stability properties show its dynamic (active) stability. This dynamic stability usually is considered to be the time history of a body's response to its inherent static stability.

Take the example of the steel ball and the hubcap. Fig. 10-2 shows that the ball when inside tends to stay in the center of the hubcap, it has *positive static stability*. It requires force to displace it up the side, and it returns immediately to its original position.

Now suppose you push the steel ball well up the side of the hubcap and quickly release it. The ball will roll toward the center position, overshoot, and return, keeping this up with ever shortening oscillations until finally it returns to rest in the center. The ball has positive *static* stability because it resists your pushing it up the side and has positive *dynamic* stability because its actions tend to return it to the original position. *That is, the oscillations about its original position become less and less until it stops at the original point.* This is called *periodic motion;* the ball makes a complete oscillation in a given interval of time or period. These periods remain approximately the same length (exactly the same under theoretical conditions) even though the *amplitude* (movement) is less and less.

You can also see periodic motion by suspending a heavy weight on a string, making a homemade pendulum. The pendulum at rest has positive *static* stability—it resists any attempt to displace it. It has positive *dynamic* stability in that it finally returns to its original position through a series of periodic (equal time) oscillations of decreasing amplitude.

The ball in the hubcap could be given the property of *aperiodic* (nontimed) positive dynamic stability by filling the hubcap with a heavy liquid such as oil (Fig. 10-5). The liquid would damp the oscillations to such an extent that the ball would probably return directly, though more slowly, to the original position with no overshooting and hence no periodic motion. Through manipulation of the system (adding oil), you have caused its motions to be aperiodic.

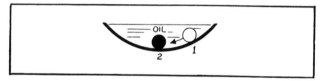

Fig. 10-5. Aperiodic positive dynamic stability.

Unlike the steel ball *inside* the hubcap, which is statically stable, resists any displacement, and has positive dynamic stability, a properly designed airplane does not necessarily have positive dynamic stability under all conditions (see the section Longitudinal Dynamic Stability of the Airplane later in the chapter). And the fact that an airplane sometimes has positive static stability does not mean that its dynamic stability is also positive. Outside forces may act on the airplane so that the oscillations stay the same or even become greater.

Back to the ball inside the hubcap. Suppose you start the ball rolling and then rock the hubcap with your hand so that the oscillations do *not* decrease. Because of the outside force you set up, the ball's oscillations retain the same amplitude. The system has positive static stability but neutral dynamic stability—the ball's oscillations continue without change. The airplane may also be affected by outside (aerodynamic) or inside (pilot-induced) forces that result in undiminishing oscillations, or neutral dynamic stability, even though it is properly balanced, or statically stable.

Now suppose you rock the hubcap even more violently. The ball's oscillations get greater and greater until it shoots over the side. You introduced an outside factor that resulted in negative dynamic stability—the oscillations increasing in size until *structural damage* occurred (the ball went over the side).

Thus the system (or airplane) with positive *static* stability may have positive, neutral, or negative *dynamic* stability. *A system that is statically stable will have some form of oscillatory behavior.* This tendency may be so heavily damped (the oil in the hubcap) that it is not readily evident. The oscillations show that the system is statically stable; the ball (or airplane) is trying to return to the original position. Outside forces may continually cause it to equally overshoot this position or may be strong enough to cause the oscillations to increase until structural damage occurs.

For a system that has *neutral* static stability such as a ball on a smooth flat plate, there are no oscillations because the ball isn't trying to return to any particular position. It's displaced and stays displaced.

A system that has *negative* static stability or is statically *unstable* (the terms mean the same thing) will have no oscillations; there will be a steady divergence. Let's use the ball and hubcap again. This time turn the hubcap over and balance the ball carefully on the peak (sure you can) and take another look at the statically unstable system (Fig. 10-6).

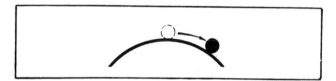

Fig. 10-6. A statically unstable system.

If even a small force is applied, the ball rolls down the side of the hubcap. The ball does not resist any force to offset it from its position—on the contrary, it wants to leave in the first place and when displaced leaves its original position at a faster and faster rate. There are no oscillations as there is no tendency to return at all. *The statically unstable system has no dynamic (oscillatory) characteristics but continually diverges.* The action this system takes in diverging is not always that simple, but *that* we'll leave for the slide rule boys. A *statically stable system (or airplane) may have either positive, neutral, or negative dynamic stability characteristics.*

How this applies to you as a pilot will be shown shortly.

LONGITUDINAL OR PITCH STABILITY

The elevators control the *pitch* (the movement around the lateral axis) (Fig. 10-7). The pilot's ability to control the airplane about this axis is very important. In designing an airplane a great deal of effort is spent in making it stable around all three axes. But *longitudinal stability* (stability about the pitch axis) is considered to be the most affected by variables introduced by the pilot, such as airplane loading.

Lateral axis

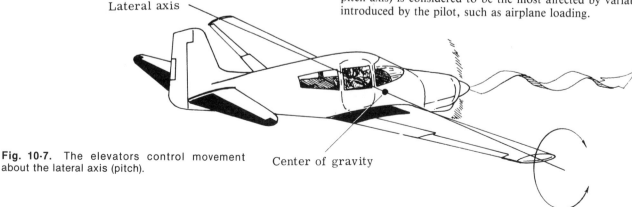

Fig. 10-7. The elevators control movement about the lateral axis (pitch).

Center of gravity

Pitch

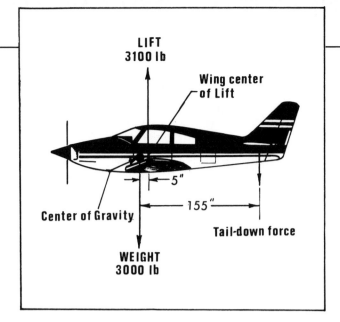

Fig. 10-8. Airplane in balanced, straight and level flight.

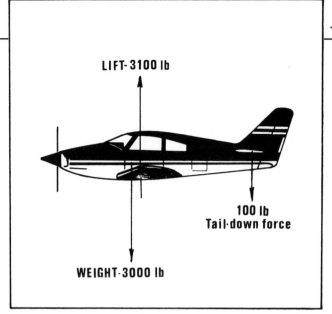

Fig. 10-9. Summation of vertical forces: total up force 3100 lb and total down force 3100 lb — forces balanced.

Take a look at an airplane in balanced, straight and level flight (Fig. 10-8). Making calculations from the center of gravity (CG), you find the *moment* (force times distance) about the CG caused by the wing's Lift is 5×3100 or 15,500 lb-in. This is a nose-down moment. To maintain straight and level flight there must be an equal moment in the opposite direction or the airplane would be attempting to do an outside loop. This opposite moment is furnished by a down force on the tail. Its moment must be 15,500 lb-in. in a tail-down direction. The distance shown from the CG to the center of tail lift is 155 in.; therefore the down force at the tail must be 100 lb (force $\times$ distance = 100 lb $\times$ 155 in.). The tail-down moment is also 15,500 lb-in., which balances the nose-down moment. The airplane is statically balanced.

In order for the airplane to maintain level flight the upward forces must balance the downward forces, as was covered in Chap. 3 (Fig. 10-9).

The down forces are the airplane's weight (3000 lb) and the tail-down force (100 lb), which total 3100 lb. In order to balance this, the up force (Lift) must be 3100 lb. The wing itself contributes some pitching effects, as was mentioned in Chap. 3.

For airplanes with fixed, or nonadjustable, stabilizers, the stabilizer is set by the manufacturer at an angle that furnishes the correct down force at the expected cruising speed and CG position.

The tail-down force is the result of propeller slipstream, downwash from the wing, and the free stream velocity (airspeed) (Fig. 10-10).

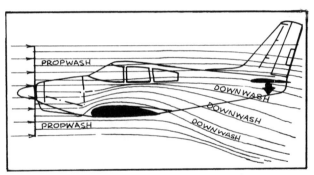

Fig. 10-10. Factors contributing to the tail-down force.

Suppose you're flying straight and level (hands-off) at the design cruise speed and power setting and suddenly close the throttle. The slipstream force suddenly drops to practically nothing; the airplane starts slowing as Thrust is no longer equal to Drag, and the free stream velocity also drops. You've suddenly lost some of the tail-down force. The result is that the nose drops. This is a healthy situation; the airplane is trying to pick up speed and reestablish the balance (Fig. 10-11).

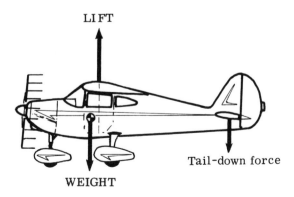

STRAIGHT AND LEVEL
CRUISING POWER

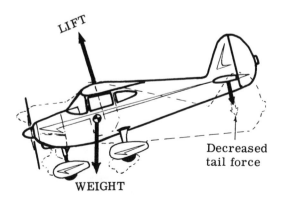

THROTTLE CLOSED,
AIRPLANE NOSES DOWN **Fig. 10-11.**

Of course, as the airplane slows, Lift decreases and the airplane starts to accelerate downward for a very short time, but this is not so noticeable to you as the nosing-down action.

We'll disregard the airplane settling and think only in terms of the rotational movement caused by closing the throttle. One way of looking at it is to return to the seesaw of your earlier days. When the kid on the other end suddenly jumped off you set up your own "nose down" (the moments were no longer balanced).

You set the desired tail force for various airspeeds by either holding fore or aft wheel pressure or setting the elevator trim. If you are trimmed for straight and level flight, closing the throttle means more up-elevator trim if you want to glide hands-off at the recommended glide speed. A propeller-driven airplane will always require less up-elevator trim for a given airspeed when using power than when under power-off conditions. You can see this for yourself the next pretty day when you're out just flying around. Trim the airplane to fly straight and level at the recommended glide speed and use whatever power is necessary to maintain altitude. Then close the throttle and keep your hands off the wheel. You'll find that the airspeed is greater in the power-off condition—the airplane's nose drops until it picks up enough free stream velocity to compensate for the loss of slipstream. This may be up to about cruise speed, depending on the airplane.

The arrangement of having the CG ahead of the center of Lift, and an aerodynamic tail-down force, results in the airplane always trying to return to a safe condition. Pull the nose up and the airplane slows and the tail-down force decreases. The nose will soon drop unless you retrim it or hold it up with increased back pressure. Push the nose down and it wants to come back up as the airspeed increases the tail-down force. The stable airplane wants to remain in its trimmed conditions, and this *inherent* (built-in) *stability* has gotten a lot of pilots out of trouble.

Another arrangement is shown in Fig. 10-12. A lifting tail is necessary on this airplane in order to maintain balance. From a purely aerodynamic standpoint the two lifting surfaces (wing and tail) are a good idea; from a stability standpoint this type of configuration is not so good.

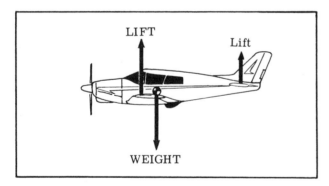

Fig. 10-12.

When you throttle back, the tail Lift decreases and the nose tends to go up! This is not conducive to easy pilot control. The engineers would rather have a little less aerodynamic efficiency and more stability. So this arrangement is avoided—although it is not nearly as critical in a jet airplane. Actually, in some conditions (high C_L), a tail upload may be present, even for the "standard" airplane that has a tail-down force at cruise.

The *canard* (horizontal-tail-first) designs have appeared again in the past few years. Some of these airplanes are quite efficient because both the wings and horizontal tail are lifting,

as in the more conventional arrangement in Fig. 10-9. One advantage of the canard-type is that it is stall and spin resistant if the forward surface is designed to lose its Lift (and pitch the nose down to decrease the angle of attack of the main wing before it reaches the critical angle). The canard arrangement is not new (see photos of the Wright brothers' first powered flight), but the state of the art has improved so much that the newer designs are making a strong impact on the industry.

POWER EFFECTS ON STABILITY. Power is considered to be destabilizing; that is, the addition of power tends to make the nose rise. The designer may offset this somewhat by having a high thrust line. The line through the center of the propeller disk passes above the CG so that as Thrust is increased a moment is produced to counteract slipstream effects on the tail (Fig. 10-13). Or the designer may offset the thrust line so that it passes above the CG (Fig. 10-14).

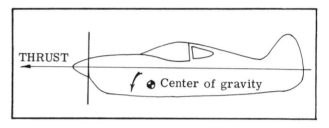

Fig. 10-13. Exaggerated view of a high thrust line as an aid to stability.

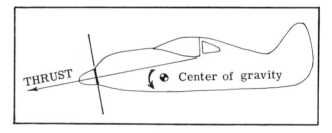

Fig. 10-14. Offset thrust line.

A very low thrust line would be bad as it would tend to add to the nose-up effect of the slipstream on the horizontal tail surfaces (Fig. 10-15).

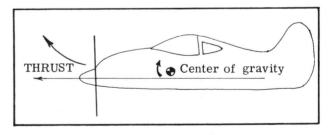

Fig. 10-15. Low thrust line effects with application of power.

The thrust line of your airplane is fixed and there's nothing you can do about it; this has been presented only for your interest. All these factors have been taken into consideration in the certification. No airplane will be certificated in the normal or utility categories if it has dangerous tendencies.

HOW LOADING AFFECTS LONGITUDINAL STATIC STABILITY

You can affect the longitudinal static stability of your airplane by the way you load it. If you stay within the loading limitations as given by the *POH* you'll always have a statically stable airplane.

The properly loaded airplane is analogous to the steel ball inside the hubcap. It will tend to stay in the attitude and airspeed at which it was trimmed (Fig. 10-16). If the CG is moved aft, the airplane becomes less statically stable and does not have as strong a tendency to return to its original position. It is as if our hubcap were made shallower (Fig. 10-17).

The CG can be moved aft to a point where the airplane has *no* tendency to return but remains offset if displaced. It is as if the hubcap had been completely flattened (Fig. 10-18). By moving the CG even farther aft, the area of *negative* static stability is encountered (Fig. 10-19). The hubcap has been turned inside out.

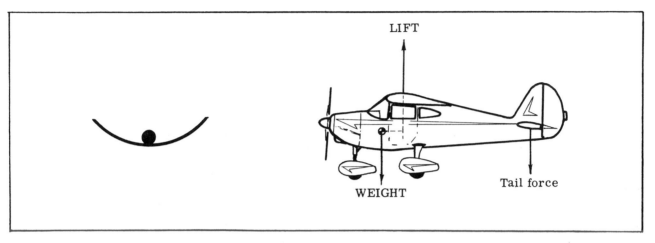

Fig. 10-16.   The properly loaded airplane—positive static stability (tail force exaggerated).

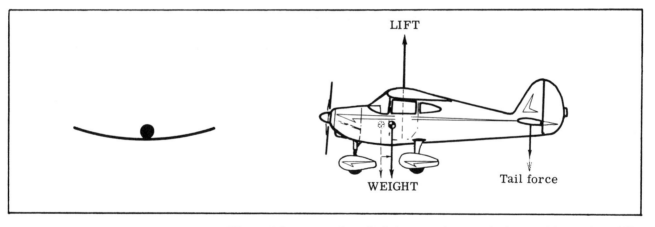

Fig. 10-17.   Effects of the center of gravity being moved rearward—less positive static stability.

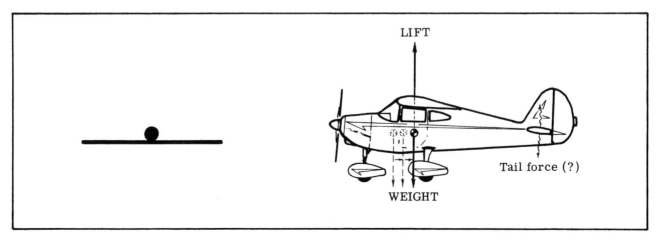

Fig. 10-18.   Neutral static stability.

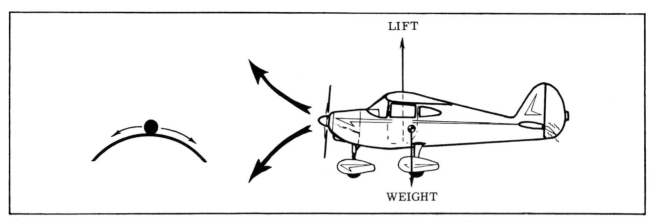

Fig. 10-19. Negative static stability.

It would seem at first glance that the more statically stable an airplane is made, the better its flight characteristics. This is true—up to a point. If an airplane is so stable that a great deal of force is needed to displace it from a certain attitude, control problems arise. The pilot may not be able to maneuver the airplane and make it do its job. This is more of a problem for fighters than for transports, however.

The problem with neutral static stability is that the plane does not tend to return to its trimmed state. If you load the airplane to such a condition you might get into trouble. In a plane with neutral static stability the feel is changed considerably. After takeoff you may ease the nose up using normal back pressure and find that the nose attitude has overshot and is too high. You ease it down and again overshoot because you have been used to fighting the airplane's natural stability, and in this case it isn't there. *This type of situation causes accidents.* Particularly dangerous is the fact that the airplane could become unstable during the flight as the fuel is burned. Designers always place the fuel tanks as near to the CG as possible. But in a neutral stability condition, a rearward movement of the CG could put you into negative static stability. It's possible that the airplane could become uncontrollable or at least be in a very dangerous condition.

LONGITUDINAL DYNAMIC STABILITY

Learn your plane's actions (*dynamic stability*) in response to its *static stability.* The next time you are flying cross-coun-

try, ease the nose up until the airspeed is about 20 K below cruise and slowly release it. The nose will slowly drop past the cruise position and the airplane will pick up excess speed and slowly rise again. If the airplane has *positive* dynamic stability, it may do this several times, each time the nose moving less distance from the cruise position until finally it is again flying straight and level at cruise. The same thing would have occurred if you had eased the nose down (Fig. 10-20). This is like the steel ball in the hubcap as cited earlier. It was dynamically stable and finally resumed its normal position.

An airplane that has *neutral* dynamic stability as a result of some design factor would react to being offset (Fig. 10-21). This is as if some outside unknown force were rocking the hubcap, keeping the ball constantly oscillating.

The airplane with *negative* dynamic stability would have oscillations of increasing magnitude (Fig. 10-22). You see that the system (hubcap and ball) and the airplane are statically stable, but other factors may be introduced that create neutral or negative dynamic stability. The oscillations shown in Figs. 10-20, 10-21, and 10-22 are called *phugoid* or *long mode* oscillations. They are long enough that they can be easily controlled by the pilot and are considered of relatively little importance. The airplane you are flying may have a neutrally or negatively stable phugoid and still be completely safe. (So don't be disappointed or worried if, when trying the experiment at the beginning of this section, you find these slow oscillations do *not* decrease in amplitude.) An airplane with neutral or negative dynamic stability in these long modes can

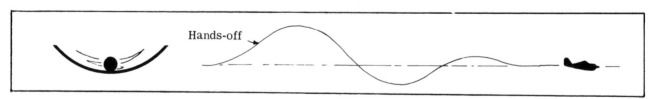

Fig. 10-20. Flight path of a dynamically stable airplane (hands-off).

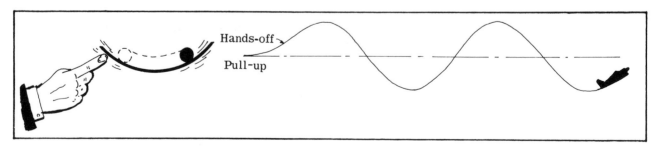

Fig. 10-21. Flight path of an airplane with neutral dynamic stability (hands-off); no decrease in oscillations.

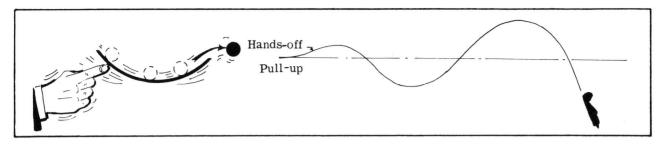

Fig. 10-22. Flight path of an airplane with negative dynamic stability (hands-off); oscillations increase in amplitude.

be flown quite safely with little or no effort, as the periods may be many seconds or even minutes in length.

Of primary importance is the *short mode* (rapid) oscillation. The periods of the short mode may be in fractions of seconds. You can see that if the short mode is unstable the oscillations could increase dangerously before the pilot realizes what is happening. Even if the oscillations are being damped, it's possible that the pilot, in trying to "help" stop the oscillations, could get out of phase and reinforce them to the point where g forces could cause structural failure. Usually such problems are caused by poor elevator design or balancing, and they are always solved by the manufacturer before the airplane is certificated. Airplanes certificated by the FAA have *positive dynamic stability* in the short mode. If the plane is offset from its path abruptly, it will return in a series of rapid, converging oscillations. (You can see this when flying hands-off on a gusty day.) An airplane that is *statically unstable* would have no oscillations at all but would continually diverge (the hubcap is upside down as in Fig. 10-19).

The point to remember is to keep your airplane statically stable by correct placement of Weight and you won't have any stability problems.

The dynamic longitudinal stability of an airplane is affected by *stick-fixed* or *stick-free* conditions. This means that the airplane's response is different if the elevators are "locked" by the pilot (wheel, stick, or elevators fixed) or are allowed to float free (hands off stick or wheel—or elevators free). As you probably have already guessed, the *elevator-fixed* condition is more stable and the airplane's oscillations would be more likely to dampen (Fig. 10-20). Aerodynamics texts sometimes use pages of calculations to show why it is so, but it all boils down to common sense. Look at Fig. 10-23, which shows the elevator free and fixed. In Fig. 10-23A the pilot has pulled the nose up sharply and immediately released (freed) it. As you can see, the aerodynamic loads tend to make the elevator position itself parallel to the air flow instead of staying parallel to the chord line (where it belongs) to help straighten the airplane out. As the airplane pitches up and down in its oscillation, the elevator follows the line of least resistance and moves itself out of the airflow.

In Fig. 10-23B the pilot or autopilot has returned the elevator to the neutral position and has locked it there so that more surface is available to stabilize the situation. You might consider that the elevator-fixed condition is like an arrow with the proper amount of feather area; the elevator-free one is as if some of the area was clipped off, allowing the arrow to wobble more in flight. Aerodynamicists would rightly note that the elevator normally does not float the full angles shown here, but moves up or down to a lesser degree.

Fig. 10-24 is an actual trace of an airplane's dynamic stability (phugoid) at cruise power in the clean condition. Note that the elevator-free condition is basically neutrally stable while the elevator-fixed oscillations are heavily damped.

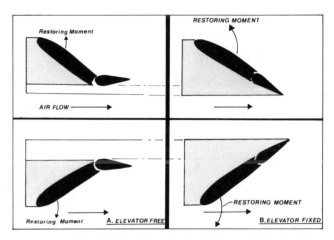

Fig. 10-23. Exaggerated effects of elevator free and fixed on dynamic longitudinal stability. A. The elevator floats up (or down, as also shown) out of the airstream, decreasing the damping (stabilizing) effect. B. The elevator is "locked" (fixed) and presents more stabilizing area to damp the oscillations. Compare the shaded areas for A and B.

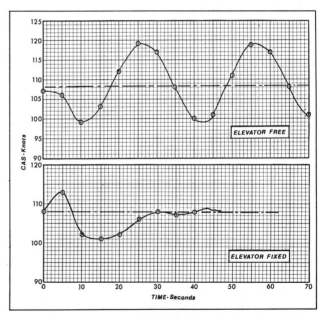

Fig. 10-24. Elevator-free and -fixed oscillation (airspeed versus time) for a particular airplane in the cruise configuration.

The periods from peak to peak are 30 sec in the elevator-free configuration.

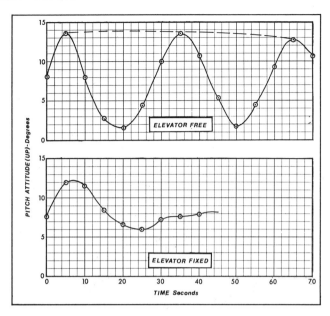

Fig. 10-25. Pitch attitude versus time for the airplane in Fig. 10-24.

Fig. 10-25 is an analysis of the airplane in Fig. 10-24 showing a trace of the nose pitch attitude (degrees) versus time. In this case, the exercise started at 107 K (Fig. 10–24) and a nose-up attitude of 8°. Note that in the *elevator-fixed condition the pitch attitude settled down to a value very close to the original.* The dashed line in the elevator-free condition in Fig. 10-25 shows that the airplane might "some day" settle back down to the original pitch attitude but, as indicated earlier, the oscillations can be quickly and easily stopped by the pilot (by "fixing" the elevators), so there's no problem.

Longitudinal Control

ELEVATOR. You are familiar with elevators as a means of longitudinal control; airplanes also have been designed utilizing a *stabilator.* You may have trained on such an airplane. Let's review the stabilizer-elevator system.

You use the elevator to change the camber of the horizontal tail system, which changes the tail force. For the design cruise airspeed, the elevators are designed to "float" parallel with the stabilizer. Any change from this speed and power setting must be compensated for by elevator deflection. The normal airplane requires that forward pressure be held for speeds above this, and back pressure held for any speeds below cruise. You rotate the airplane to the desired attitude by exerting fore or aft pressure on the wheel. If an airplane is too stable longitudinally, the elevator control may not be effective enough for good control. One problem that airplane manufacturers face is the too-stable airplane, although to be truthful, it's not as much of a problem to them as the unstable type. It has been found through experience that the total horizontal tail area should be 15 to 20% of the effective wing area and the elevator should make up about 35 to 45% of the total horizontal tail surface area. The farther the horizontal tail is from the CG, the less area is necessary for the required stability (tail moment = distance × force).

The stabilizer-elevator combination is an airfoil, and you vary the tail force by positioning the elevators with the wheel or elevator trim.

The properly designed airplane requires forward pressure for airspeed above the trim speed you have selected, and back pressure for speeds below the trim speed (this applies whether you trim it for a speed 30% above stall or at the airplane's

maximum speed). This indicates *positive static stability.*

You can see that this is what you've been encountering all along in your flights in FAA-certificated airplanes. A happy medium should be found; the airplane must be stable but not be too hard to displace, or maneuvering problems may arise. The more variation in velocity, the more pressure is required, because the airplane is stable and resists your efforts to vary its airspeed from trim speed.

As you move the CG aft you may find you can't set any particular speed as trim speed.

Stick or Wheel Forces. Fig. 10-26 shows the stick (or wheel) force required to pitch the nose up (or down) at two CG positions at a particular chosen trim speed. A fictitious airplane is used but the numbers are reasonable for a general aviation airplane (clean) trimmed for approach or holding. Assuming that push or pull forces are zero at the trim speed of 90 K, you'll notice that the back pressure required to slow it up and hold it at 75 K is 8 lb at forward CG and 4 lb at a more aft CG. The stick or wheel forces will become even lighter as the CG is moved aft (dashed line) and at some point could approach zero. (The airplane may pitch up or down without help from the pilot.) The lines are curved because the dynamic pressure, q, goes up as the *square* of the airspeed. With a forward CG the forces required to pull up or push over are much higher and the airplane would lack maneuverability. More about forward CG later in the chapter.

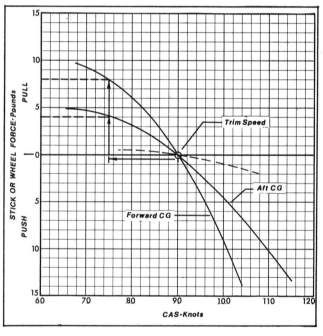

Fig. 10-26. Effects of CG position on stick or wheel forces at a particular trim speed.

Suppose you are indicating 90 K and have the elevator trim tab set at what you think is the correct position. In the normal airplane this would mean that if you applied fore or aft pressure on the wheel the pressure necessary to hold this nose position would increase as the airspeed changed — not so the neutrally stable airplane. You are fooling yourself by even trying to trim the airplane.

When you pull the nose up and the speed decreases, the airplane isn't fighting the back pressure and will continue in this attitude without any help from you. Wheel pressure is *not* a function of airspeed in this case and the airplane could

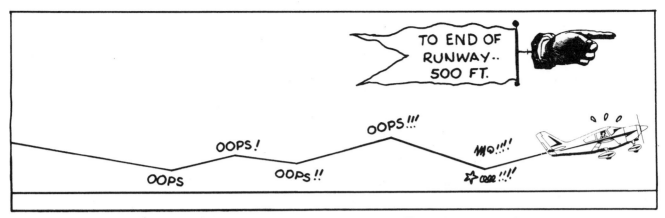

Fig. 10-27. Landing (?) a neutrally stable airplane.

continue to a stall, the nose would then drop, and it would maintain this nose-down attitude. This is, of course, assuming you are flying hands-off. Naturally you'll be flying the airplane and will ease the nose back down before the stall occurs. This is not to imply that the airplane is uncontrollable, but it does mean you'll have to make a conscious effort to return the nose to the proper position if it is displaced—and on a bumpy day this could get mighty tiresome. On landing, you will not be fighting the plane's stability. When you flare for the landing you will probably overdo it because of the very light back pressure required, compared with what you've been used to. You'll probably get the nose too high, then consciously have to ease it over and may set up a cycle (Fig. 10-27).

If you've trimmed the airplane for a glide, you'll normally expect the required back pressure to increase as the plane slows during the landing—that's why you could get into trouble in this situation.

The airplane with *negative* longitudinal stability will aggravate any displacement. If the nose is raised in the neutrally stable airplane, it stays at that attitude until you (or some other force) lower it. The airplane that is negatively stable tends to get an even more nose-high attitude.

If you load the airplane with too much weight in the rear and get into an unstable condition, a serious accident is almost certain to occur. Take an extreme situation: You've loaded the airplane until the CG is much too far aft. You realize that there's quite a bit of weight back there and set the elevator tab to what you think is about the right amount of nose-down trim. You go roaring down the runway, ease the nose up—and it just keeps going up. This is neither the time, place, or altitude to be practicing stalls. It may require more down elevator than you have available—and that's that.

STICK FORCE PER G. One measure of an airplane's maneuverability is its *stick-force-per-g* factor, which is basically the pounds of pull or push necessary to change by 1 g the acceleration acting parallel to the vertical axis. A fighter or aerobatic airplane should have comparatively light control forces so that pull-ups, loops, steep turns, and other maneuvers requiring extended pilot input would not be fatiguing. The stick forces must not be so light, however, as to easily allow the pilot to overstress the airplane. In WW II, before hydraulically boosted controls were in wide use, the stick-force-per-g limits were 3 to 8 lb for fighters and a maximum of 35 lb for transports. This meant, for instance, that a fighter having a stick force per g of 5 lb would require 20 lb of stick force to pull an added 4 g's. The pilot on a transport of that era who wanted to pull those 4 extra g's from cruise could be required to exert up to 140 lb back pressure, which discouraged an impulse to do loops in that airplane.

As far as CG position is concerned, the stick-force-per-g

idea follows that of the unaccelerated longitudinal stability reactions. *As the CG is moved aft, the stick forces become lighter* and the airplane can have more g's exerted on it with less effort by the pilot. With a CG near, or at, the aft limit, what starts out as a 3-g loop pull-up could end up as a 6- or 7-g "serious situation" as the airplane continues to pitch up with little or no additional back pressure.

For a given CG position the stick force required to pull, say, 3 g's is *higher in a turn* than in a wings-level pull-up. In a wings-level pull-up, the added Lift being produced by back pressure is acting directly against Weight. The pilot would not have to exert quite as much control force as in a bank where the vertical *component* of Lift is acting directly against Weight.

Altitude reduces the stick force per g. The airplane at a higher altitude, all other factors equal, will require less push-pull force to get a certain g loading.

Manufacturers may affect the longitudinal stability and stick (or wheel) forces of the airplane by adding a weight either ahead of or behind the stick pivot point. This "bob-weight," if placed ahead of the pivot point, under normal conditions will tend to move the stick or wheel forward, providing a nose-down effort to provide more positive stability. With increasing g forces, the weight becomes "heavier," increasing the back pressure required to pull more g's. As can be seen, a bobweight *behind* the stick or wheel pivot point would have an opposite effect in both accelerated and nonaccelerated flight conditions.

LONGITUDINAL TRIM. There are several methods of longitudinal trim for the airplane. The most familiar is the elevator trim tab, which acts as a control surface on a control surface and has been put to good use by you for many flying hours. When you trim "nose-up" the tab goes down and the force of the relative wind moves the elevator up (Fig. 10-28).

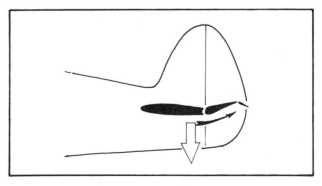

Fig. 10-28. Elevator trim tab, set for nose-up.

You've found this very handy for nose-heavy conditions and for help during the glide. You may have found that the tab set this way caused trouble, too. Some pilots use almost full up-trim for landing, as this makes for light back pressure during the landing process. If they should suddenly have to take it around, the application of power may result in a severe tendency for the nose to rise. The slipstream hits the trim tab and elevator, which are greatly displaced at the low-speed, power-off condition; this is particularly dangerous if the elevator tab control is geared so that it requires many turns to get back to a more nose-down setting. If the airplane were not so close to the ground, it would be amusing to watch the pilot, who can't decide whether to take one hand off the wheel (pushing forward with both hands) and make a grab for the trim control, or hold the nose down with both hands and try to get altitude first. The usual result is that the pilot does both, frantically moving the right hand from wheel to trim control and gradually getting things under control. Seen from outside the airplane, the maneuvering looks like a whale with a severe case of hiccups. This problem usually is not quite so critical in multiengine planes, as the elevators are not so much in the slipstream. In any airplane—single, multi, prop, or jet—the nose is harder to keep down as the speed increases, though the single-engine, high-powered prop plane gives the most trouble under these conditions. The airplane with an adjustable stabilizer can give the same problems, so don't think that the trim tab alone is the culprit.

Another method of elevator trimming is the use of bungees. These consist of springs that tend to hold the elevator in the desired position when you set the trim control (Fig. 10-29). The spring also acts as a damper for any forces that might be working through the system. You set the spring tension with the trim control. Actually you couldn't care less what the spring tension is—you move the trim handle or wheel until you get the desired result. It's doubtful that you could tell by "flight feel" that the airplane had a bungee instead of a trim tab unless you noticed it during the preflight check (and you should have).

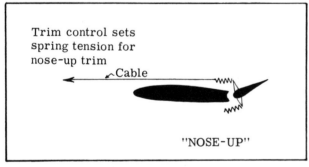

Fig. 10-29. Bungees as a method of elevator trim.

Another method of longitudinal trimming is the movable or controllable stabilizer (Fig. 10-30). The cockpit control merely turns a jack screw to position the stabilizer.

Fig. 10-30. Stabilizer trim, nose-up.

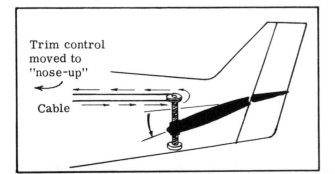

SPECIAL TYPES OF TABS. *Link balance tab*—If an airplane is found during flight tests to have heavy control forces it may require a *link balance tab,* which is a tab mechanically linked so that it moves opposite to the control surface and makes the control forces much lighter. For instance, the link balance tab on an elevator moves down as the elevator moves up—a sort of mutual aid society. These tabs, by the way, also can act as trim tabs when variable length linkage is used. (You vary the linkage length when you move the trim control in the cockpit. This type of arrangement, called a *lagging tab,* is shown in Fig. 10-31.

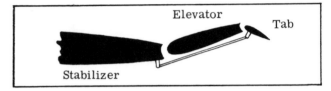

Fig. 10-31. Link balance tab, lagging.

In some instances the control forces may be too light—that is, the elevator or stabilator may move so easily that in extreme conditions the pilot could inadvertently overstress the airplane. The manufacturer may use a leading link balance tab (Fig. 10-32) in order to increase the control forces necessary to displace the control surface.

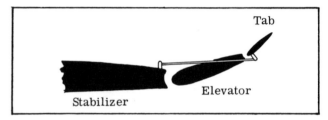

Fig. 10-32. Link balance tab, leading.

Servo tab—It'll probably be a long time before you use this system, as only large planes have them. The control wheel is connected to the tab rather than to the elevator itself. When the pilot moves the wheel back the tab is deflected downward. The impact air pressure strikes the tab and the elevator is deflected upward. The elevator is free floating and moves in accordance with the tab deflection.

The principle of the trim tab is simple. It uses a small area, long arm, and greater angular deflection to deflect a control surface of greater area to a lesser deflection. (Got it?)

STABILATOR. The stabilator is popular as a means of longitudinal control for general aviation airplanes. It's, in effect, no more than an airfoil whose angle of attack is controlled by the control wheel and trim control. The stabilator is hinged at its aerodynamic center. In computing the tail force you could use the Lift equation for a wing of the stabilator's airfoil and area. You would have a C_L versus angle of attack curve and could use the equation $L = C_L S(\varrho/2)V^2$; the problem would be complicated by the fact that the downwash and slipstream effects are hard to predict. But the principle is exactly the same as that for the wing.

The stabilator was first used as an effective means of control for jets in the transonic region (Mach 0.8 to 1.2). The elevator system lost effectiveness in this speed range due to shock wave effects on the stabilizer, and severe nose-down tendencies were encountered—with little control to offset these forces. In effect, the elevator was "blanketed" behind the shock wave. It was found that by moving the entire stabilizer-elevator (or stabilator) system, longitudinal control could be maintained in this critical range.

The stabilator control, when properly balanced, is quite sensitive at low speeds. (The pilot who has been flying an elevator-equipped airplane usually tends to slightly overcontrol in moving the nose up or down for the first few minutes.) Because the stabilator has more movable area it usually does not use as much angular travel. Whereas an elevator may have a travel of 30° up and 20° down, the stabilator may move less than half this amount. One system has limits of 18° up and 2° down. The trim tab for the stabilator works in the same way—impact pressure on the tab holding the stabilator in the desired position.

FORWARD CG CONSIDERATIONS

It would seem, from the discussion of the aft CG position, that the farther forward the CG, the better off you are. (Okay now, everybody run to the front of the airplane.) This is true for longitudinal stability but not from a control standpoint.

Let's start out with a longitudinally balanced airplane (Fig. 10-8). Note in Fig. 10-8 that there is no elevator deflection; the airplane is at design cruise speed and properly balanced weightwise. For our hypothetical situation suppose that during the flight Weight is moved forward, so the CG also is moved forward another 5 in. (Fig. 10-33). In order to maintain balance the tail force must be increased, and this is done by back pressure or use of the trim tab.

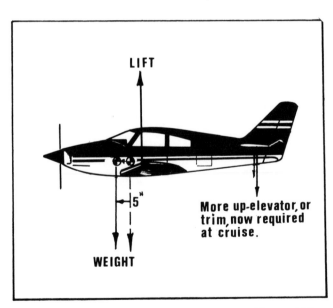

Fig. 10-33. Center of gravity moved forward 5 in.

Of course, you don't give a hang for the value of the tail force but would trim it until the nose stays where it belongs. If you move the CG forward another 5 in., the required tail force would be further increased and more up-elevator would be necessary. By moving the CG forward you would soon reach a point where full up-elevator would be required. If the throttle were chopped, the loss in effectiveness of the elevators would result in a definite nosing down of the airplane. You'd be in the unhappy situation of being unable to slow down because you'd be using full elevator to maintain level flight and would have none left to ease the nose up. Of course, you couldn't chop power because control would be lost. In this

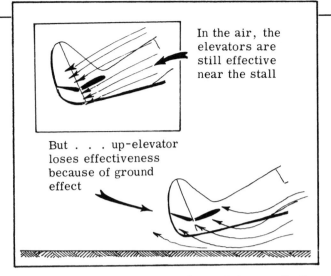

Fig. 10-34. Ground effect and elevator effectiveness.

exaggerated situation you'd have a tiger by the tail. The manufacturer sets forward CG limitations strict enough so that if you comply you'll never get into a dangerous situation.

You have seen that power nearly always results in a nose-up tendency, so the airplane can have a more forward CG with power on. A critical condition could exist at very low airspeeds (approaching a stall) in the power-off condition, where the elevators are relatively inefficient due to lack of slipstream and airspeed. Such a condition would limit the most forward CG location in flight. This would also seem to be the same condition for the landing, but this is not the case. *The ground effect on landing results in a further decrease in elevator control effectiveness* (as can be seen in Fig. 10-34). *In fact, it could take up to 15° more elevator deflection to get the stall (same configuration) in ground effect as at altitude, depending on the make and model. This, then, is the most limiting factor in establishing the forward CG of the airplane.*

AIRPLANE WEIGHT AND BALANCE

The CG of an airplane must remain within certain limits for stability and control reasons. These limits are expressed by designers in terms of percentage of the mean aerodynamic chord (Fig. 10-35).

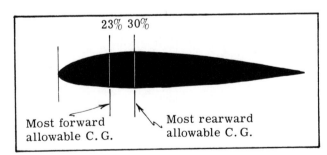

Fig. 10-35. Allowable center of gravity range, expressed as percentage of mean aerodynamic chord (average wing chord).

The airplane's *Weight and Balance Form* usually expresses these limits in the form of inches from the *datum* (the point from which the measurements are taken). This datum is at different points for different airplane makes and models. Some airplanes use the junction of the leading edge of the wing with the fuselage as the datum; others use the front face of the firewall. The allowable CG range is expressed in inches aft of this point, such as "allowable center of gravity range— from 13.1 to 17.5 in. aft of datum" (Fig. 10-36).

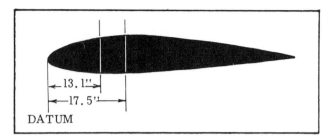

Fig. 10-36. Allowable center of gravity range, expressed as inches aft of datum.

Sometimes the datum is an imaginary point ahead of the airplane. This is easier to compute, in that all the moment arms are positive. The datum usually is picked so that it is an even distance ahead of a well-defined position such as the junction of the wing's leading edge with the fuselage.

Measurements are taken from a reference point and added to or subtracted from the datum to get the proper arm. In Fig. 10-37 you see that the wing's leading edge is 70 in. aft of the datum. If object A weighing 10 lb is placed at a point 10 in. behind the junction of the leading edge of the wing and the fuselage, its Weight (10 lb) would be multiplied by 70 + 10, or 80 in. Its moment would be 800 lb-in. Object B, also weighing 10 lb, 10 in. ahead of the leading edge point, would have a moment of 70 − 10, or 60 in. times its Weight, or 600 lb-in.

The CG limits for the airplane in Fig. 10-37 are expressed as "CG allowable range from 80 to 87 in. aft of datum."

Here's how you might run a Weight and Balance for the above-mentioned airplane: the manufacturer will give its Basic Empty Weight (the Weight at which the airplane is actually ready to fly except for usable fuel, pilots, passengers, and baggage—in other words, with full oil and unusable fuel and not lacking any mechanical parts). Its empty CG position and/or moment are also given.

To find the empty Weight and CG position for the hypothetical airplane you would place each of the three wheels on a scale and level the airplane, using a bubble level on the points (usually protruding screws) on the fuselage marked

LEVEL. Because you'd want the Basic Empty Weight of a particular airplane, before putting it on the scales you'd do the following:

1. Be sure that items checked in the equipment list are installed in the proper location in the airplane.

2. Remove excessive dirt, grease, moisture, and foreign items such as rags, tools, sleeping passengers, or dead horses from the airplane before weighing.

3. Defuel the airplane, then open all fuel drains until all remaining fuel is drained. Operate the engine on each tank until all undrainable fuel is used and the engine stops. Then add the unusable fuel (given in the *POH*) to each tank.

4. Fill with oil to full capacity.

5. Place pilot and copilot seat in fourth (4th) notch aft of the forward position. (Use the seat placement given in the *POH*.)

6. Put the flaps in the full-up position and all control surfaces in the neutral position. The towbar should be in the proper location and all entrance and baggage doors closed.

7. Weigh the airplane inside a closed building to prevent errors in scale reading because of wind.

8. Leveling—with the airplane on scales, block the main gear oleo pistons in the fully extended position and level the airplane by deflating the nosewheel to center the bubble in the level.

9. With the airplane level and brakes released, record the Weight on each scale. Deduct the tare Weight, if any, from the scale reading.

The term *tare* may be new to you; it means any extraneous equipment on the scale, such as chocks, or in the case of a tailwheel airplane (which must be weighed in the level flight attitude), the ladder or brace placed under the tailwheel.

The Weight at the nosewheel would be multiplied by its arm (44 in. in Fig. 10-37) and the two totals of the main wheel weights by their arms (arm = 100 in.); the total moment is divided by the total net Weight to get the Basic Empty Weight CG.

As an example, after the preparation for weighing is complete the airplane in Fig. 10-37 has a nosewheel weight of 643 lb and the combined weight of the main gear is 1157 lb. Computing, the nosewheel weight (643 lb) is multiplied by the arm of 44 in. to get a moment of 28,292 lb-in.

The total weight of the main gear is 1157 lb, and this is multiplied by 100 in. to get a moment of 115,700 lb-in. Adding the two, a total moment of 143,992 lb-in. is obtained (round it off to 144,000 for simplicity). Dividing this total moment by the total Weight of 1800 lb, the Basic Empty

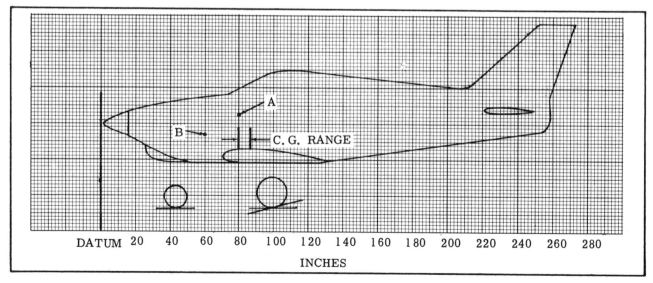

Fig. 10-37. Weight and balance diagram.

Item	Weight, lb	Arm Distance, in.	Moment, lb-in.
Basic Empty Weight	1800	× 80 =	144,000
Fuel—70 gal@ 6 lb	420	× 82 =	34,400
Pilot	180	× 80 =	14,400
Passenger (front seat)	160	× 80 =	12,800
Passenger (rear seat)	170	× 115 =	19,550
Passenger (rear seat)	170	× 115 =	19,550
Baggage	100	× 135 =	13,500
Total	3000 lb		258,240

Fig. 10-38. Weight and balance table with fuel, oil, occupants, and baggage located.

Item	Weight, lb	Arm Distance, in.	Moment, lb-in.
Basic Empty Weight	1015		12,640
Fuel (in wing)—20 gal	120	× +15 =	+1,800
Pilot	170	× +13 =	+2,210
Passenger	170	× +13 =	+2,210
Baggage	100	× +40 =	+4,000
Total	1575 lb		+22,860

Fig. 10-39. Weight and balance table for a two-place, side-by-side trainer. Incidentally, for positions ahead of the datum a minus sign is used, for positions behind the datum a plus sign.

Weight CG is found to be at 80 in. aft of datum (Fig. 10-38).

This airplane is a high-performance, low-wing type that carries four persons. The basic Empty Weight is 1800 lb and the empty CG position is 80 in. aft of datum. The airplane has an allowable gross Weight of 3000 lb, leaving a useful load of 1200 lb (fuel, pilot, passengers, baggage). See Fig. 10-38 for the calculations.

The average arm (or CG position) can then be found by dividing the total moment (258,240 lb-in.) by the total Weight (3000 lb), getting an answer of 86.1 in., which is within the allowable flying range of 80 to 87 in. Use the above information to find the CG for various combinations, such as half fuel, pilot only, pilot and passengers, no baggage, etc. (rounded off to nearest 0.1 in.).

Following is an example of an airplane that uses the junction of the wing's leading edge with the fuselage as a datum. The airplane is a two-place side-by-side trainer with a Basic Empty Weight of 1015 lb and a gross Weight of 1575 lb. The manufacturer has found that the empty moment is 12,640 lb-in. The allowable CG travel is from 12 to 16 in. aft of the datum (Fig. 10-39). Allowable baggage is 100 lb and usable fuel 20 gal.

The CG = +22,860/1575 = +14.5 in., or 14.5 in. aft of the datum. This is well within the 12- to 16-in. CG range

limitation. The moment of 22,860 lb-in. was found by adding all the moments. You could call all distances behind the datum negative and those forward positive and still arrive at the same answer. Your answer would then be a minus number, meaning that the CG is behind the datum under your new set of rules for the calculations. Or you could pick a point 10, 20, or 50 ft behind the tail as a datum and still arrive at a proper answer. The principle applies to any airplane or datum point: Weight times distance equals moment. You can use feet or yards for distance, but inches are the usual measurement so that you get moments in pound-inches. When heavier components are added to or taken from your airplane (such as radar and radios) the mechanic will show this on the airplane *Major Alteration and Repair Form*.

SOME SAMPLE PROBLEMS. (While in the sample problems that follow the numbers are rounded off to show the principle more easily, you'll find in actual conditions you'll be multiplying Weight numbers like 1736 times arm numbers like 43.95 so a calculator might be useful.)

Figure 10-40 is the loading graph for a four-place, high-performance airplane. A sample Basic Empty Weight of this airplane is 1670 lb with a moment of 63,300 lb-in. Add people, fuel, and baggage.

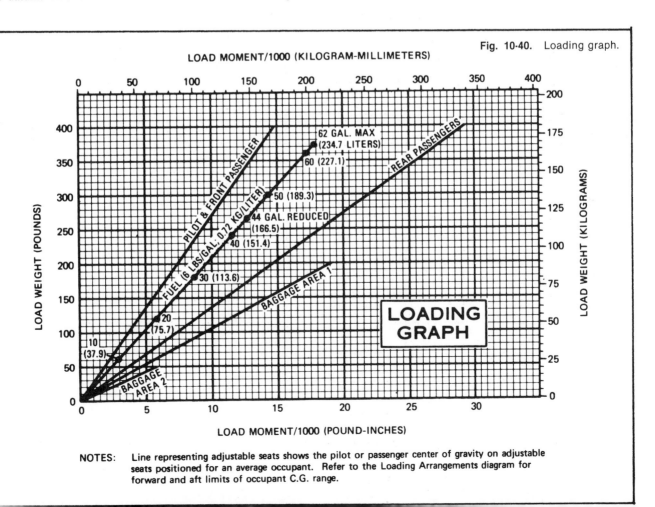

Fig. 10-40. Loading graph.

NOTES: Line representing adjustable seats shows the pilot or passenger center of gravity on adjustable seats positioned for an average occupant. Refer to the Loading Arrangements diagram for forward and aft limits of occupant C.G. range.

In Fig. 10-40 the line representing the adjustable seats shows the pilot or passenger CG with the seat positioned for an average occupant, which is an arm of 37 in. (Fig. 10-41). (The CG of some people is lower than others, although this would have comparatively little effect when they are sitting.)

You might work a problem using the following data (refer to Fig. 10-40):

Item	Weight, lb	Moment, lb-in.
Basic Empty Weight	1670	63,300 (or 63.3/1000)
Pilot	175	6.6
Front passenger	160	6.2
Rear passenger	130	9.5
Rear passenger	120	8.7
Fuel (30 gal)	180	8.7
Baggage (area 1)	120	12.5
	2555	115.5 (115,500 lb-in.)

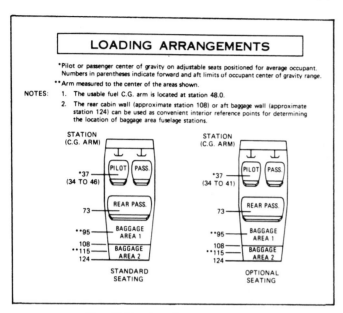

Fig. 10-41. Loading arrangements. The notes are self-explanatory. This may answer some of your questions as to how the arms are derived for adjustable seats.

Look at Fig. 10-42 to see if the results fall within the moment envelope. Fig. 10-43 is a CG limit envelope for the same airplane. You would check to see the CG location on it by dividing the total moment by the total Weight: 115,500/2555 = 45.2 in. aft of datum (which is the front face of the firewall).

One question you might run into is how much Weight may be added at a particular station to move the CG rearward a certain distance. For instance, a question about the problem just worked might be, How much weight can now be added to baggage area 2 without exceeding the rearward CG limit? Looking back at Fig. 10-41 you see that the midpoint of baggage area 2 is 115 in. aft of datum. Checking Fig. 10-43 you see that the CG can move rearward from its present position of 45.2 to the rear CG limit of 46.5 in., for a total of 1.3 in. Use this equation:

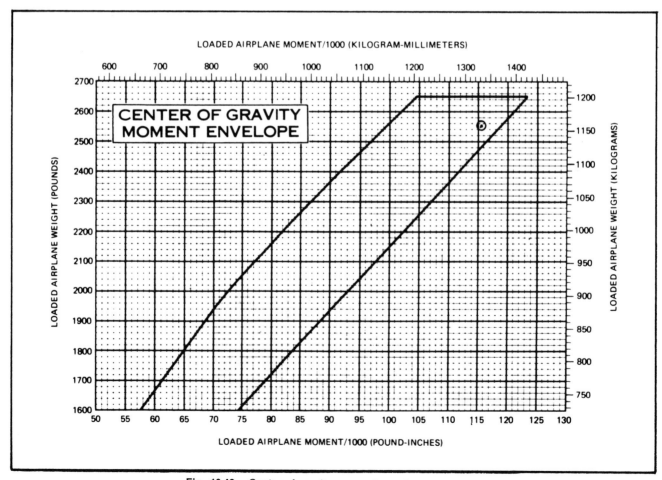

Fig. 10-42. Center of gravity moment envelope. Note that moments may also be found by using the metric scale. The dot indicates that the airplane in the sample problem in the text is within the envelope.

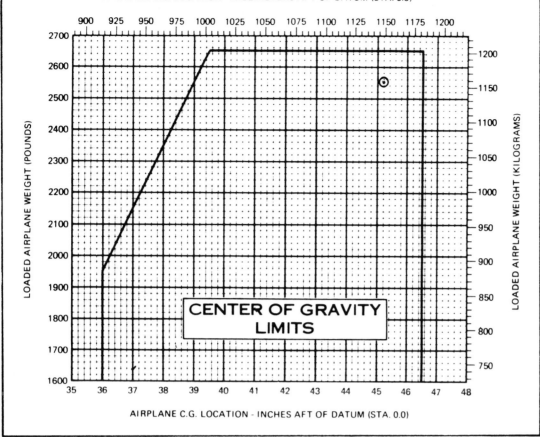

AIRPLANE C.G. LOCATION - MILLIMETERS AFT OF DATUM (STA. 0.0)

CENTER OF GRAVITY LIMITS

AIRPLANE C.G. LOCATION - INCHES AFT OF DATUM (STA. 0.0)

LOADED AIRPLANE WEIGHT (POUNDS)

LOADED AIRPLANE WEIGHT (KILOGRAMS)

Fig. 10-43. Center of gravity limit envelope. The dot indicates the airplane Weight and the position of the CG for the sample problem in the text.

$$\frac{\text{added Weight}}{\text{present Weight}} = \frac{\text{CG change}}{\text{new Weight arm} - \text{new CG position}}$$

$$\frac{\text{AW}}{\text{PW}} = \frac{\text{CG}}{\text{NW}_{\text{arm}} - \text{NCG}}$$

The added Weight is x (to be solved), the current Weight is 2555 lb, the change in CG is 1.3 in., the new Weight arm is 115.0 in., and the new CG position is 46.5 in.: x/2555 = 1.3/(115.0 − 46.5) = 1.3/68.5. Cross multiplying you'd get 68.5x = 3321.5, x = 3321.5/68.5 = *48.5 lb* (rounded off). This addition does not exceed the maximum allowed Weight.

Doublechecking and going back to the original problem, the final figures there were a Weight of 2555 lb and a moment of 115,500 lb-in. Add the Weight and moment of the added baggage: 2555 + 48.5 = 2603.5 lb. The added moment of the baggage is 48.5 × 115.0 = 5577 lb-in.; 115,500 + 5577 = 121,077 lb-in., the new total moment. Divide the new moment (121,077 lb-in.) by the new total Weight: 121,077/2603.5 = *46.5 in*. The aft limit is 46.5 in. and the result just obtained was the result of rounding off some five- and six-figure numbers during the process. To repeat:

$$\frac{\text{AW}}{\text{PW}} = \frac{\text{CG}}{\text{NW}_{\text{arm}} - \text{NCG}}$$

Here are some more problems:
1. Given:
    total Weight − 4037 lb
    CG location − station 67.8
    fuel consumption − 14.7 gph
    fuel CG − station 68.0.
After 1 hr 45 min flying time the CG would be located at station
    1 − 67.79
    2 − 68.79
    3 − 69.78
    4 − 70.78
Airplane total moment = 4037 × 67.8 = 273,709 lb-in. (including the fuel at the beginning of the problem).

The Weight change in fuel in 1.75 hr (1 hr 45 min) × 14.7 × 6 (pounds per gallon) = 154 lb (rounded off).

The change in the total moment is the fuel Weight (154 lb) multiplied by the fuel arm (68.0): 154 × 68.0 = 10,472 lb-in.

Subtract the fuel Weight and moment from the airplane's "old" Weight and moment to find the airplane's Weight and moment after 1 hr 45 min of flying: 273,709 − 10,472 = 263,237 lb-in; 4037 − 154 = 3883 lb. The new CG = 263,237/3883 = 67.79 in. (or answer 1).

2. If the total airplane loaded Weight is 8900 lb, how far will the CG shift forward if a 200-lb passenger moves from a seat at station 210 (in.) to a seat at station 168 (in.)?
    1 − 2.1 in.
    2 − 1.4 in.
    3 − 0.9 in.
    4 − 0.4 in.
This problem is slightly different from the last one in that the airplane Weight is not changed, but the general principle is still the same. The passenger will move *forward* 42 in.

The relationship between the passenger weight and the airplane Weight and the passenger's movement and its effect on the airplane's CG change have a close relationship: 200/8900 = CG shift (in.)/passenger shift (in.) = 200/8900 = x/42. Cross multiplying: 8900x = 8400, x = 0.944 in. The airplane CG will move forward 0.944 in.

To check this, assume that the airplane's original CG is at station 100.0 (in.): airplane moment = 8900 × 100.0 = 890,000 lb-in.

The 200-lb passenger, who is still part of the 8900 lb and has moved *forward* 42 in., would subtract from the moment but not from the Weight. The passenger moment to be subtracted from the total moment is 200 × 42 = 8400 lb-in. To find the new CG, the new, smaller total moment is divided by the total Weight: new moment = 890,000 − 8400 = 881,600 lb-in., 881,600/8900 = 99.056. The *new* airplane CG is at 99.056 in., or has moved *forward* by 100.000 − 99.056 = 0.944 in. This is closest to answer 3.

Using an airplane original CG of 80.0 in. as a check: 80.0 × 8900 = 712,000 lb-in.; 42 × 200 = −8400 lb-in.; total new moment = 703,600.

The new CG = 703,600/8900 = 79.056 in. The CG has moved *forward* 0.944 in. (80.000 − 79.056 = 0.944).

3. Your airplane is loaded to a gross Weight of 5000 lb with 3 pieces of luggage in the rear baggage compartment. The CG is 98 in. aft of datum, which is *2 in. aft of limits.* If you move two pieces of luggage that together weigh 100 lb from the rear baggage compartment (145 in. aft of datum) to the front compartment (45 in. aft of datum), what is the new CG (inches aft of datum)?

1 − 95.8
2 − 96.0
3 − 96.5
4 − 97.0

The airplane's total moment = 98 × 5000 ≐ 490,000 lb-in. Subtracting the moment resulting from the luggage being moved forward: 490,000 − 10,000 = 480,000 lb-in.; the baggage is moved forward 100 in. (145 − 45 = 100); 100 × 100 = 10,000 lb-in. Dividing the new moment by the weight: 480,000/5000 = 96.0 in. (answer 2).

The *POH* of your airplane has an equipment list describing the various items (engine, propeller, battery, etc.) with their weights and arms from the datum. Each piece of equipment has a code letter indicating whether it is *required* (for certification), *optional,* or *standard* installation. You'll find that in some cases the spinner is required equipment, not because of any weight and balance factors, but because the airplane's cooling tests were done with the spinner installed and poor cooling airflow might result without it. By looking over the equipment list you can get some idea of the weights of various items; for instance, a heavy-duty battery for a particular light twin weighs nearly 42 lb and an ammeter hits the scale at 0.5 lb.

The baggage compartment has Weight limitations for two reasons: (1) you might move the CG too far aft by overloading it and (2) you could cause structural failure of the compartment floor if you should pull g's during the flight (Fig. 10-44). For instance, you are flying a four-place airplane and are the only occupant, and the boss asks you to deliver some anvils to another town. You figure that there'll be no sweat on the CG and throw 400 lb of anvils in the 200-lb-limit baggage

compartment. For the sake of the example let's say there is no CG problem and away you go.

Enroute, you suddenly see another airplane coming head-on and without thinking, pull up abruptly. You could send 400 pounds of anvils through the bottom of the airplane down through somebody's greenhouse—or worse (Fig. 10-45).

Fig. 10-45.

The baggage compartment floor is designed to withstand a certain number of g's with 200 lb in it. If you pull this number of g's with 400 lb in there, something will give.

You have a couple of early indications that maybe things are not as they should be and that maybe a dangerous condition is developing. (1) After loading a tricycle-gear airplane heavily you will see that the airplane is in an extremely tail-low position on the ground and that taxiing is very sloppy because the nosewheel doesn't have enough weight on it for effective directional control. The nosewheel "bounces" slowly as you taxi—it doesn't know whether it wants to stay on the ground or not. (2) In the tailwheel-type airplane the tail may be extremely hard to raise during the takeoff run, even with a farther-than-normal nose-down trim setting. If this happens, chop the power before you've gone too far to stop the process.

This is all common sense. Even if you ignore rear baggage compartment placards and other rear loading limitations, maybe the fact that the airplane "just doesn't feel right, even taxiing" may give that extra warning. *But—heed those loading limitations and don't depend on "feel" to save your neck.*

Fig. 10-44.   "I dunno, do you think we might have put too much stuff in the baggage compartment?"

You won't always run a Weight and balance calculation on the airplane every time you fly it, but this discussion will give you an idea of the principles involved. Stay within the limitations on passengers and baggage as given in the *POH* and you'll have no fear of exceeding the CG limits or suffering in performance. *Excessive Weight, poorly placed,* will result in a dangerous situation both from a performance *and* a stability and control standpoint. *Stall and spin recovery becomes more critical as the CG moves aft.* (See Fig. 10-46 for a summary.)

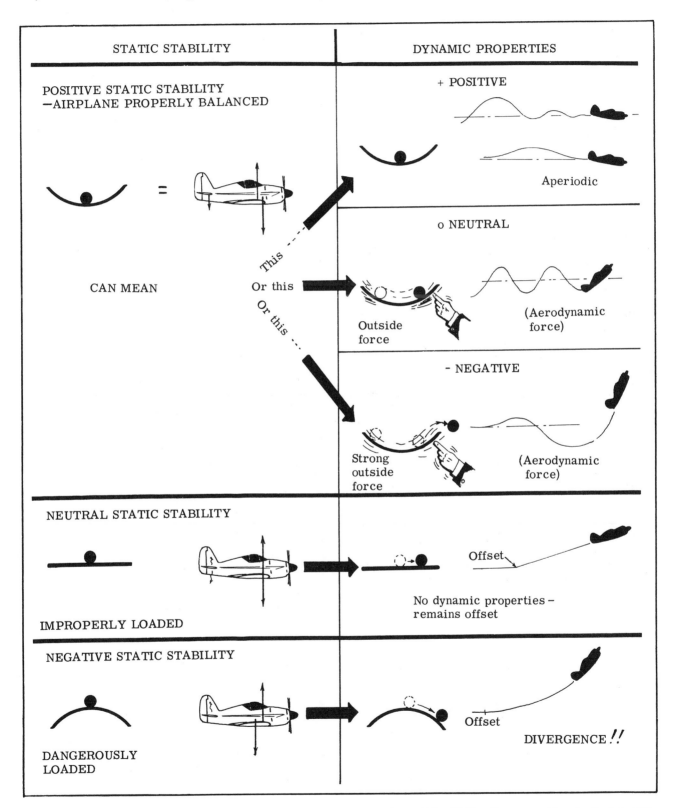

Fig. 10-46. Summary of longitudinal stability.

DIRECTIONAL STABILITY

Directional stability, unlike longitudinal stability, is not greatly affected by the pilot's placement of Weight in the airplane. An airplane is designed with either good or less than good directional stability. For simplification, let's consider an airplane with no fin or rudder (Fig. 10-47).

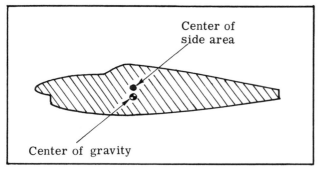

Fig. 10-47. Center of side area, fuselage only.

You can see that if the center of side area is even with the CG, little or no directional stability is present. If this airplane were displaced in a yaw by turbulence it would not tend to return to its original heading. If the offsetting force were strong enough, the airplane might pivot on around and fly backward for a while.

The designer must insure positive directional static stability by making sure that this center of side area is behind the CG. This is done through the addition of a fin (Fig. 10-48). You can see that a restoring moment is produced if the airplane is yawed (Fig. 10-49).

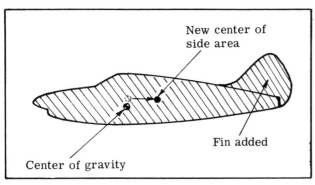

Fig. 10-48. Center of side area, fin added.

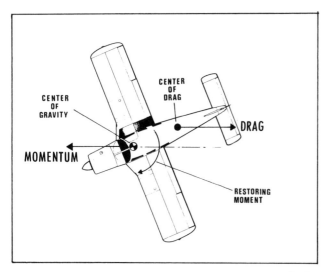

Fig. 10-49. Restoring moment of a properly designed fuselage-fin combination.

The fin (like the horizontal stabilizer) acts like the feather on an arrow in maintaining stable flight. Naturally the farther aft this fin is placed and the larger its size, the greater the airplane's directional stability.

The rudder, as a part of this area, is furnished to give the pilot control in yaw. If the fin is too large in comparison with the rudder area and deflection limits, poor yaw control results. The airplane may be so directionally stable that the pilot is unable to make forward or sideslips or safe crosswind landings and takeoffs.

The rudder effectiveness, or "rudder power" as it is called by engineers, is very important in the event of an engine failure on a multiengine airplane at low airspeeds. The pilot must be able to offset the asymmetric thrust of the working engine(s) at full power. For multiengine airplanes this rudder power governs the minimum controllable speed with one engine out, or in the case of a four-engine plane, two engines out on the same side. Lateral control also enters into consideration in establishing the minimum controllable speed, but this will be covered more thoroughly in Part 2, Checking Out in Advanced Models.

Rudder deflections usually are held below 30°, as the effectiveness falls off past this amount. Another factor in rudder design is the requirement for spin recovery. However, normal category airplanes are restricted against spinning and also it's very rare these days that deliberate spinning is required (only on the flight test for the instructor's certificate).

A properly designed airplane requires more and more rudder force to be exerted as the yaw angle is increased at any given airspeed. You've found this to be the case when steepening a forward or sideslip to land. You found that you were limited in steepness of slip by the rudder more than by the ailerons.

The rudder is considered to be an auxiliary control in flight, and in newer airplanes is losing even this value. Its primary purpose is to overcome adverse aileron yaw and correct for torque. With the advent of differential aileron movement and other means of overcoming adverse yaw, it is becoming less important for normal coordinated flight. It's still mighty handy in slipping and other unbalanced conditions, though!

Steerable tailwheels, nosewheels, and separate wheel brakes have even decreased the rudder's importance for ground control. When airplanes had tail skids or free-swiveling tailwheels, the slipstream and relative wind on the rudder were the only means of turning on the ground. The rudder is still of primary importance for tailwheel-type airplanes during takeoffs and wheel landings—and particularly so in a crosswind!

A swept-back wing contributes to directional stability but very few lightplanes use this idea any more. However, a wing with double taper does help, as there is some sweep effect (Fig. 10-50).

Although there are cross effects between lateral and directional stability, for simplicity's sake sweepback will be discussed here only as it affects directional stability. Take a look at an airplane in a yaw (Fig. 10-51); the plane is yawed and you can see that there is a difference in Drag that results in a restoring moment. Of course the fin area would be helping, too.

It's hard to separate lateral and directional control effects even though we did it to discuss sweepback. You know yourself that kicking a rudder yaws the airplane, but it also causes reactions in a roll. You also know that abrupt application of aileron alone normally results in adverse yaw.

Directional Dynamic Stability. With directional dynamic stability, a maneuver called Dutch roll may result when a rudder pedal is pushed and released.

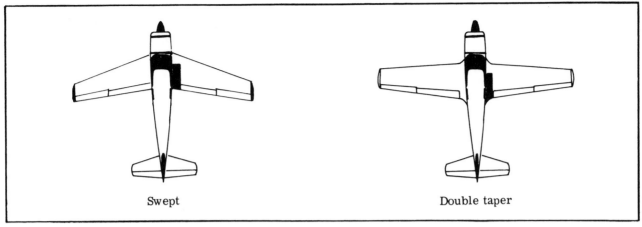

Fig. 10-50. Swept-back and double-tapered wing.

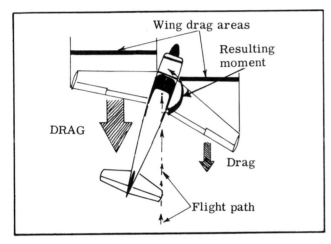

Fig. 10-51. Effects of sweepback in a yaw. Sweepback increases dihedral effect and can decrease roll maneuverability.

Suppose you kick right rudder and quickly release it. The nose of the airplane yaws to the right initially. This speeds up the left wing (and slows down the right wing) so that a rolling motion is effected. The airplane, having dynamic or oscillatory properties (assuming positive static directional stability), will return and overshoot, speeding up the right wing, which raises, etc. You get a combination yawing and rolling oscillation which, putting it mildly, is somewhat disconcerting. An airplane that Dutch rolls is miserable to fly in choppy air (Fig. 10-52).

The manufacturer tries to reach a happy medium between too great and too little directional stability (called "weathercock stability" in some texts).

Such factors as rudder balance and design have strong effects on the dynamic properties of directional stability. An airplane certificated by the FAA has positive directional stability (both dynamic and static). It's hard to separate lateral and directional control effects. Dihedral, which helps assure positive *lateral* static stability, may result in cross effects and give the airplane Dutch roll problems.

Because it is better to have a situation known as *spiral instability* than Dutch roll, nearly all airplanes are designed this way. You will note in your own airplane that if a wing lowers (controls free) and a spiral is allowed to develop, the bank increases and the spiral tightens if no effort is made by the pilot to stop it. However, the rate of increase of bank is normally slow and causes no problem in VFR conditions. This is the lesser of two evils, compared with the annoyance of Dutch roll. In situations where visual references are lost by the pilot who is not instrument qualified and/or doesn't have proper instrumentation, the tendency of the airplane is to get into a spiral of increasing tightness. (Check it sometime under VFR conditions—at a safe altitude and in an area clear of other airplanes, of course.)

SUMMARY OF DIRECTIONAL STABILITY

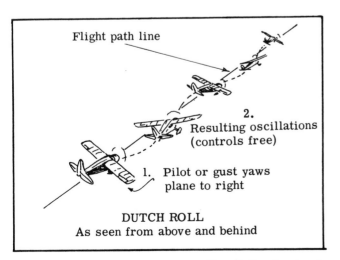

DUTCH ROLL
As seen from above and behind

Fig. 10-52. Dutch roll.

STATIC STABILITY	DYNAMIC PROPERTIES
POSITIVE STATIC STABILITY Airplane with sufficient fin area. (Ball inside hubcap)	POSITIVE DYNAMIC STABILITY Airplane returns to straight flight after several decreasing oscillations (yaw). Rudder properly balanced.
Three Possibilities....	NEUTRAL DYNAMIC STABILITY Airplane oscillates from side to side (yaws) when offset, neither increasing nor decreasing in amplitude.
	NEGATIVE DYNAMIC STABILITY Airplane, when offset, oscillates (yaws) with increasing amplitude. Poor rudder balance.
NEUTRAL STATIC STABILITY Airplane with small fin. (Ball on flat plate)	NO OSCILLATIONS When yawed, the airplane tends to stay in that position. No tendency to return to straight flight.
NEGATIVE STATIC STABILITY Airplane with critical shortage of fin area. (Ball on top of hubcap)	NO OSCILLATIONS When yawed, the airplane tends to increase the yaw. Divergence occurs.

LATERAL STABILITY

Dihedral. The most common design factor for insuring *positive static lateral stability* is dihedral. Dihedral is considered to be positive when the wing tips are higher than the roots (Fig. 10-53). The effect of dihedral is to produce a rolling moment tending to return the airplane to a balanced flight condition if sideslip occurs.

Fig. 10-54 shows what forces are at work in a sideslip. You can see that a rolling moment is produced, which tends to correct the unbalanced condition.

A high-wing airplane, even though it may actually have zero dihedral, has a tendency to return to balanced condition because of its wing position. A low-wing airplane with zero dihedral will generally have negative lateral stability because of its CG position. A midwing airplane with zero dihedral usually exhibits neutral stability (Fig. 10-55).

Understanding this idea, you can see that two airplanes of similar design in all other respects, but one having a high wing and the other a low wing, will have different dihedral angles for the same lateral stability requirements (Fig. 10-56).

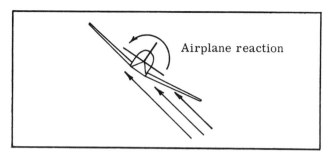

Fig. 10-54. Dihedral effect in a sideslip.

Excessive dihedral makes for poor rolling qualities. The airplane is so stable laterally that it is fighting any rolling motion where slipping might be introduced (such as in a slow roll). For this reason, airplanes requiring fast roll characteristics usually have less dihedral than a less-maneuverable airplane. A fighter pilot doesn't go around doing slow rolls in

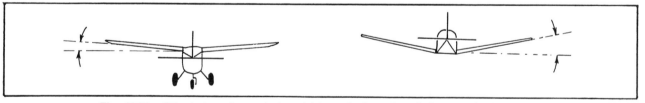

Fig. 10-53. Dihedral.

Positive   Zero dihedral   Negative

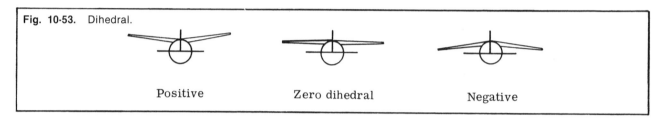

POSITIVE STABILITY   NEUTRAL STABILITY   NEGATIVE STABILITY

Fig. 10-55. The effects of various wing positions on lateral stability; zero dihedral in each case.

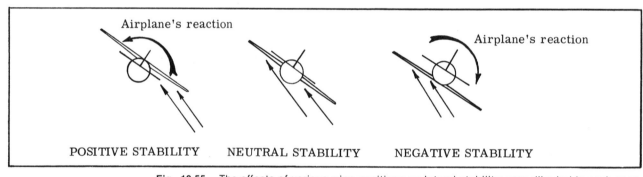

Fig. 10-56. Dihedral requirements for a high- and a low-wing airplane to obtain equivalent lateral stability.

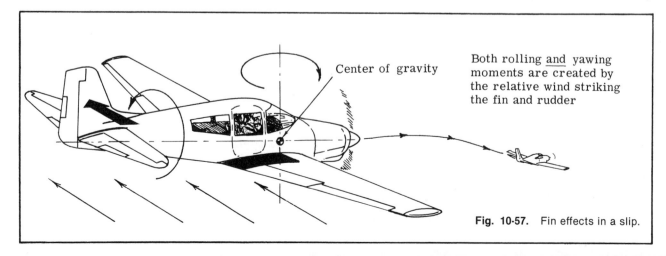

Center of gravity

Both rolling _and_ yawing moments are created by the relative wind striking the fin and rudder

Fig. 10-57. Fin effects in a slip.

combat but does need to have a high rate of roll in order to turn quickly—and sometimes in the heat of the moment may not coordinate perfectly. If the airplane has a great deal of dihedral, it may be hard to maneuver laterally, particularly if sideslipping is a factor in the roll.

Lateral and directional stability are hard to separate. For instance, the fin, which is primarily designed to aid in directional stability, may contribute to lateral stability as well. Fig. 10-57 shows that the fin and rudder contribute a rolling moment as well as a yawing moment in a sideslip. In a slipping turn the effect of the fin is to stop the slip and balance the turn, which it does through yaw *and* roll effects.

Power Effects on Lateral Stability. Power is destabilizing in a sideslip for a propeller-driven airplane; that is, it may tend to counteract the effects of dihedral (Fig. 10-58).

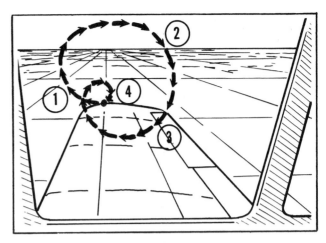

Fig. 10-59. Apparent movement of a point on the wing tip during Dutch roll (damped oscillations). The pilot pressed left rudder pedal and released it.

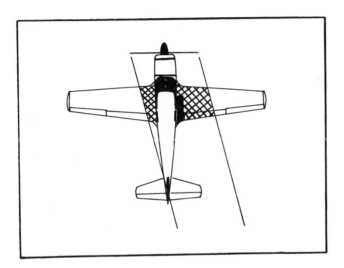

Fig. 10-58. Slipstream effects on lateral stability in a left slip with power. Note that the slipstream tends to increase the Lift of the high wing.

You can visualize that in an accidental slip the slipstream will tend to make the bank steeper, whereas the dihedral effect is to recover from the unnatural position. This effect is aggravated in the flaps-down condition.

Loading Effects. Usually the airplane loading has no effect on lateral static stability, as the fuselage is too narrow to allow offset loads. However, planes with wing tanks may present slight wing-down tendencies with asymmetric fuel load, but usually the only result is a tired arm, if there's no aileron trim.

Lateral Dynamic Stability. Dynamic stability is not a major concern in lateral stability. You recall that control surface balancing and other design factors introduced aerodynamic effects that furnished the outside force acting on the system, and the principles apply in the same way. The ailerons, if *mass balanced* (balanced around the hinge line by Weight) and if comparatively free in movement, usually assure that the pure lateral movements are heavily damped. However, cross effects of yaw displacement may result in lateral oscillations, and also Dutch roll (Fig. 10-59).

Lateral Control. The aileron is the most widely known form of lateral control, although spoiler-type controls have been used to some extent.

A problem with ailerons is that they introduce cross effects between lateral and directional movement. You were

taught from the beginning that aileron and rudder go together 99.99% of the time in the air. You were also shown that the ailerons are the principal banking control, with rudder used as an auxiliary to overcome adverse yaw (Fig. 10-60). Well, everybody's been busy trying to decrease aileron yaw and no doubt you've flown airplanes with Frise ailerons (Fig. 10-61) and ailerons with differential movement (Fig. 10-62).

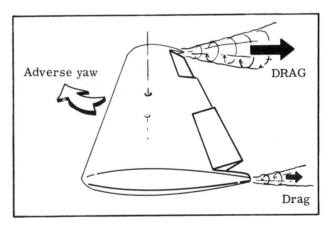

Fig. 10-60. Adverse yaw.

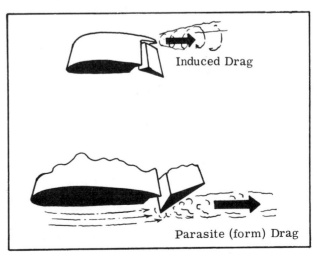

Fig. 10-61. Frise-type ailerons.

The reason for this adverse yaw is simple. You remember from Chap. 2 that induced Drag is caused by Lift. When you deflect the ailerons, the down aileron causes a higher C_L and higher induced Drag, which results in yaw.

You can see in Fig. 10-61 that the up aileron has some area hanging down, which causes Drag—and helps overcome the Drag of the down aileron. The design also helps the pilot—as soon as the aileron is deflected up, aerodynamic forces help deflect it so that the pilot's stick force is small. A disadvantage of the Frise-type aileron can be seen in the burbling and separation (Fig. 10-61). Another disadvantage is that at high speeds the aileron may tend to overbalance. The pilot's stick force may become too light and the ailerons don't tend to return to neutral, but, if deflected, tend to deflect to the stop. You can imagine the discomfiture of your passengers when you start a nice turn and suddenly do a couple of aileron rolls. The Frise aileron usually is modified to get rid of overbalance or aileron buffet by rounding off the leading edge or making other minor shape changes.

DIFFERENTIAL AILERON MOVEMENT. This is the most popular method today of overcoming adverse yaw, and though the control system is slightly more complicated, there are not as many aerodynamic problems to cope with. The principle involved is to balance induced Drag with flat plate or form Drag (Fig. 10-62).

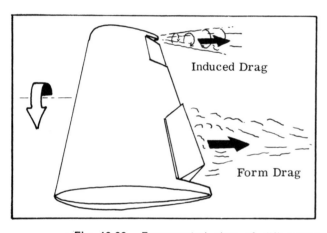

Fig. 10-62. Exaggerated view of differential aileron movement.

SPOILER-TYPE CONTROL. This method of control has been used on some jets and heavier prop planes but at present is not on any lightplanes. The resulting force lowers the wing as well as adding Drag to that side—a desired combination. These spoilers usually are hydraulically actuated for use at high speeds (Fig. 10-63).

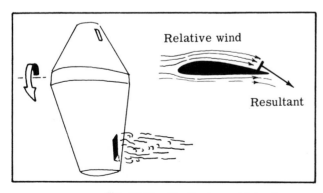

Fig. 10-63. Spoiler type of lateral control.

AILERON REVERSAL. This is presented more for interest than anything else, as you won't be affected by it in the airplane you are flying. But earlier it was a problem for high-speed airplanes with thin wings and hydraulic (or irreversible) control systems. If an aileron is deflected by hydraulic power, the aileron may act as a trim tab and the wing will be twisted the opposite direction by aerodynamic forces (Fig. 10-64). The application of right stick could result in a roll to the left!

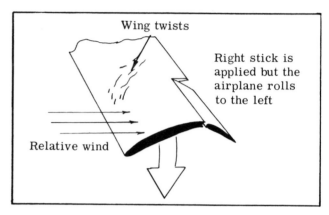

Fig. 10-64. Aileron reversal for a high-speed airplane with irreversible controls.

Another use of the term *aileron reversal* applies to some planes—the reaction of the airplane to the sudden sharp application of ailerons near the stall. The down aileron causes added induced Drag that results in that wing slowing and dropping—which further increases its angle of attack and stalls it. Aileron application in this case also results in the opposite effect desired. This problem will be covered more thoroughly in Chap. 21.

Fig. 10-65 shows a plot of rate of roll versus calibrated airspeed for a fictitious airplane. Assuming full deflection of the ailerons, the rate of roll increases in a straight line until the point at which aerodynamic forces are such that the pilot's strength is no longer sufficient to maintain full deflection. There must be some standard of comparison between airplanes, so the FARs establish a maximum force (with a wheel control) of 50 lb "exerted on opposite sides of the wheel and in opposite directions." Note in Fig. 10-65 that the max rate of roll is 90° per second at 130 K and drops above that speed because the forces required for full aileron deflection exceed the 50-lb maximum. The rate of roll at the probable approach speed of 80 K is only slightly greater than *one-half* the maximum rate, something of interest if wing tip vortices are encountered there and you need to recover from an induced roll.

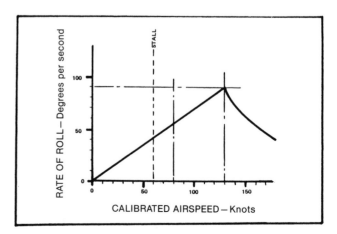

Fig. 10-65. Rate of roll versus velocity for a fictitious airplane. (*Flight Instructor's Manual*)

FLUTTER

Control surfaces (and other components of the airplane) have natural frequencies that are a function of mass and stiffness. Aerodynamic forces of certain values may act on the structure so as to excite or negatively damp those natural modes and allow flutter. Basically, a particular control surface has a natural frequency and the designer must keep it damped in the normal flight envelope or construct it so as to have a flutter mode well above the design dive speed (V_D).

The control surface must be aerodynamically and mass balanced or restricted so that the chances of inducing flutter are negligible (or better, impossible) in the operating range. The rigidity of the control surface may be increased to avoid flutter tendencies. Generally speaking, damping of control-surface flutter increases with increase in airspeed—at lower ranges. (That makes sense—the increasing dynamic pressure tends to keep the control surface in line.) The problem is that at a particular higher airspeed the damping decreases rapidly. At the point of critical flutter speed for a particular airplane, the resulting oscillation maintains itself with a steady amplitude. (For a much longer period of steady oscillation of a whole airplane, check the elevator-free condition in Fig. 10-24.) It's possible that the airplane might ease up past the critical flutter speed without damage at the edge of flutter, but accidental disturbances, such as turbulence or other factors, could trigger full-scale destructive flutter. In many cases, the onset of flutter happens so fast that damage (or destruction) occurs before the pilot can take action.

The surface, including wing or tail, can be subject to both flexing and torsional moments and this can start or add to the aileron, elevator, or rudder flutter (Fig. 10-66). Fig. 10-67 shows what can occur when three factors in flutter are working on a wing. (It can get as busy as an after-Christmas sale.)

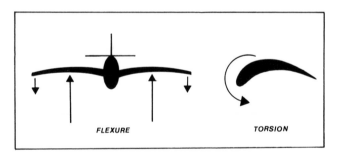

Fig. 10-66. Flexure and torsion (twist) of a wing. These will not be in phase with each other, which is one cause for onset of flutter.

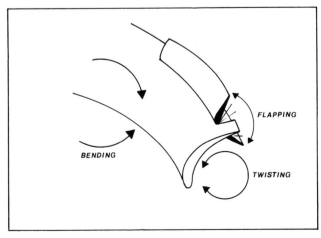

Fig. 10-67. Three forces working on a wing in flutter.

An elevator or stabilator trim tab can be an instigator of flutter, and as part of your preflight check you should check the tab for excessive play, particularly the nut and bolt attaching the actuating rod to the tab arm. Some mention has been made of a maximum play of ⅛ in. at the trailing edge of the tab (relative to the main surface). The point is that after a period of time the aerodynamic forces working on the tab can cause the hinge pin or other components to wear and flutter could occur at airspeeds well down in the cruise area—or below.

Control Surfaces. It was noted earlier that a control surface (aileron, rudder, and elevator) must be mass balanced or have some other method to avoid flutter in the operating range. It depends on the airplane and control surface design, but generally a surface should not have its chordwise CG behind the hinge line (Fig. 10-68 is an example).

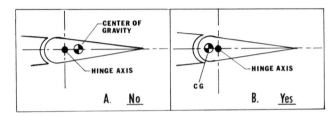

Fig. 10-68. Centers of gravity for a control surface. A. The CG is at a bad position. B. A better arrangement.

Look at a particular elevator designed with the CG behind the hinge line (Figure 10-69). If a gust or disturbance accelerates the *tail* of the airplane *downward,* inertia of the CG of the surface causes it to move upward in relation to the fixed surfaces. The same *type* of reaction would result if the airplane tail moved upward due to a gust; the inertia of the CG of the surface would cause it to move *downward* in relation to the fixed surfaces.

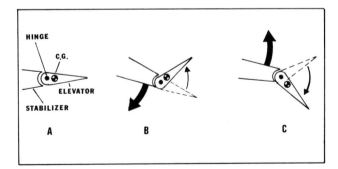

Fig. 10-69. A. The CG of the elevators is behind the hinge line. B. A gust or disturbance moves the *airplane's tail down.* Because of the inertia effects of the elevators', CG, it stays "up" relative to the rest of the tail and *increases* the tail-down motion. C. The elevator may then tend to "catch up" and overshoot, exaggerating any recovery pitch motions (overrebound).

If the CG is *ahead* of the hinge line such problems will tend to be damped. If the CG is on the hinge line, no inertia effects will be noted. This idea can be used for the rudder and ailerons as well.

There have been incidents of ice creating a mass imbalance of control surfaces (ailerons) when water worked its way into the interior and froze there. The pilots were extremely surprised when flutter (and wing loss) occurred right after takeoff at a speed where flutter problems aren't supposed to exist.

Another factor, sometimes overlooked, is that excess coats of paint (applied when a control surface has been repainted) may throw off the mass balance to such a degree that flutter could occur in the normal flight regime. Owners who have refurbished airplanes have discovered this.

The mass overhang or "horn" balance is one way of keeping the control surface CG at or ahead of the hinge line and can act as a surface to decrease control forces since the surface area ahead of the hinge line is pressed on by aerodynamic forces (Fig. 10-70). You may have seen some older type airplanes that used the balance system shown in Fig. 10-71. This is an external balance weight for a control surface.

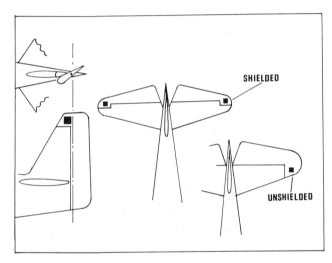

Fig. 10-70. Horn-type mass and aerodynamic balancing.

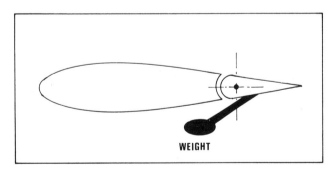

Fig. 10-71. A type of control-surface balance that was normally used on older, slower airplanes because the parasite Drag would be very high at higher speeds.

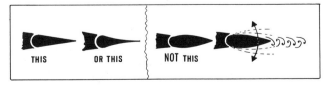

Fig. 10-72. Cross sections of control surfaces should be flat or concave, not convex.

The *cross-section shape* of the control surface also has an effect on flutter possibilities. The surfaces should be concave or flat, not convex (Fig. 10-72). The curvature of the convex surface may allow flow past the trailing edge, setting up vortices that induce flutter. Control surfaces must be built strong enough to retain the flat or concave cross section in aerodynamic forces. This is very important to the owner of a home-built airplane (Fig. 10-73).

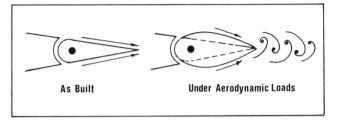

Fig. 10-73. Control-surface contours may be deformed under aerodynamic loading.

If a control surface lacks torsional stiffness or does not have enough hinges, it may not be rigid enough along its span and flutter may be induced as it "bows" up and down.

In some cases, ice may be more of a problem on stabilators than on the stabilizer-elevator system. Fig. 10-74 shows a stabilator system, both clean and with ice.

It's important that you be aware of possible flutter problems and during the preflight check to take an extra look at the control surfaces, balance weights, and trim systems for wear plus ice accumulation after a rain and freeze. You may be doing some charter work under some bad weather conditions and should be aware of these factors. It's very tempting on those extra-cold days to make only a cursory inspection. The main idea is for you to be alert to possible control problems if the airplane has picked up a load of ice and you are making an instrument approach when you're tired and pushing minimums.

SUMMARY OF THE CHAPTER

Static stability is the measure of the *initial tendency* of a body to return to its original position. This initial tendency to return may further be broken down into positive, neutral, or negative static stability.

Dynamic stability is the *action* of a body caused by its static stability properties. To have oscillations, the system must have *positive* static stability. A system that has *neutral* static stability has no initial tendency to return and therefore has no oscillatory properties. Likewise, a system that has *negative* static stability diverges—it tends to leave the original position at a faster and faster rate—it cannot have oscillatory properties but diverges if offset.

The ball inside the hubcap is statically stable, but outside forces may act on the system so that it may have neutral or negative dynamic stability. This outside force can be compared to aerodynamic forces set up by improper control balance or design, even though the airplane itself is properly loaded and the overall design is good.

Longitudinal stability is the most important, as it is most affected by airplane loading. If the airplane is loaded properly, as recommended by the *POH*, it will fall well within safe limits for longitudinal static stability.

Entire texts have been written on both airplane stability and flutter; this chapter merely hits the high points. For more thorough coverage you are referred to the references at the end of this book.

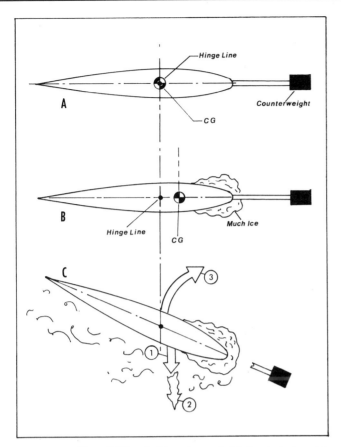

Fig. 10-74. A. The clean stabilator is balanced on the hinge line and has no over- or undershooting tendencies if the airplane's tail is deflected up or down by gusts. B. The added weight of ice may move the CG of the system ahead of the hinge line, which is stabilizing for outside forces such as gusts but could cause overshoots of the stabilator position when pilot-induced forces are involved (the CG wants to "keep going"). C. In some cases, the ice could decrease the critical angle of attack (stall angle) so that, for example, when the pilot tries to raise the nose (move the tail down) as on an approach, a too-abrupt movement causes the stabilator to stall (1) and causes the tail down force to decrease radically (2) so a nose pitch-down results (3).

When you run into turbulent air in VFR conditions, you slow the airplane down and probably also change altitude to try to find smoother air. In extreme conditions (such as over mountainous terrain), you might also decide to make a 180° turn. If you're on an instrument flight plan and actually on instruments, you don't have this immediate freedom of choice. You'll have to slow the airplane down to the recommended speed and notify ATC that your true airspeed has changed. Changing altitude or making a 180° turn has to be cleared with ATC, and you could be in turbulent conditions for some time without relief.

Interestingly, most pilots tend to *overrate* the amount of stress put on the airplane in rough air. A bump that is just about to tear the airplane apart (it seems) may register a miserable 2 g's on an accelerometer. Anyway, this is sort of like locking the barn after the horse is gone, and checking an accelerometer after the fact could result in notification by that instrument (if you had one) that you had just pulled 9 g's and the wings (or other parts) have departed your airplane.

LOAD FACTORS—A REVIEW

Befoe getting too deeply into the subject of stress, the idea of g's might be reviewed. A g is a unit of acceleration. Your body, as you read this, has 1 g acting on it (that is, if you're just sitting motionless somewhere—if you are reading this while on a carnival ride, doing loops, etc., then this statement doesn't apply).

For an airplane, the usual measure of g (or G) forces is the Lift-to-Weight ratio. In straight and level flight, Lift is considered to equal Weight, or more properly, the up forces equal the down forces, and the airplane (and the occupants) have 1 positive g working on them. In any steady-state maneuver (climb, descent, straight and level) this is the case, except in the turn. In the turn you make Lift greater, to have its vertical component equal to the Weight of the airplane (Fig. 11-1). (You might also review Chaps. 1 and 3.)

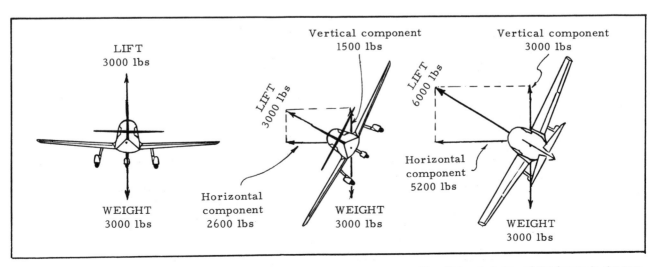

Fig. 11-1. A review of the forces in the turn.

145

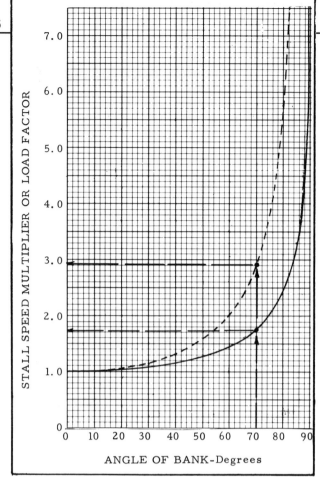

Fig. 11-2. Load factors and their effects on stall speed at various bank angles. The dashed line is the load factor, the solid line the stall speed multiplier. At a 70° bank the load factor is 2.92, the stall speed multiplier 1.71. (Old stall speed 60 K, stall speed in 70° bank = 1.71 × 60, or 103 K.) Notice the sharp increase in both load factor and stall speed at higher bank angles. This applies to all airplanes and airspeeds.

As shown in Fig. 11-1, the Lift vector is broken down into horizontal and vertical components. The horizontal component balances the centrifugal force created by the turn, and the vertical component balances the component of Weight.

In a 30° banked, balanced, level turn, the Lift required for a 3000-lb airplane is 3460 lb, or the Lift-to-Weight ratio is approximately 1.15 (the airplane is pulling about 1.15 g's). At a 60° bank (Fig. 11-1), the Lift required (6000 lb) is *twice* the weight, and the airplane is pulling 2 g's. The stall speed increases as the *square root* of the load factor (or g's pulled). The square root of 2, 1.414, is the multiple of the stall speed existing in 1-g flight. If the plane stalls at 60 K at gross Weight in wings-level 1-g flight, it will stall at 1.414 × 60, or 85 K, in a 60°-banked, constant-altitude turn. Fig. 11-2 indicates the effects of bank on stall speed and also shows the number of g's (positive) being pulled in a level turn at a particular angle of bank.

You can check the effects of positive g's on stall speed, or if you prefer, check in terms of bank angle. The effects of load factor on stall speed are the same for a straight pull-up as for turning flight. If you are pulling out of a dive and have a load factor of 4, your stall speed is twice normal (Fig. 11-2). Or if you try to pull 4 g's in straight and level flight at 115 K (normal stall speed is 60 K at the Weight in question), the airplane will stall first. Why? Because the stall speed is *doubled* at 4 g's: 2 × 60 K = 120 K. The speed of 120 K is the minimum

this airplane can fly at 4 g's without stalling, and if you try to do the job at 115 K, the airplane will stall before you get the 4 g's.

Suppose your airplane normally stalls at 60 K at the Weight at which you are flying, and you decide to do an accelerated stall at 150 K. You horse back on the wheel, and the stall breaks at that speed. It's likely that the stall is not the only thing that will break because you'll pull 6.25 g's, more than the limit load factor on an acrobatic airplane. Your normal stall speed at 1 g is 60 K, and the stall speed multiplier is 150/60 = 2.5. The load factor is the square of the multiplier (this is working backward now) so the $(2.5)^2 = 6.25$ g's. (See also Fig. 11-2.)

A stall at 180 K (9 g's) would result in structural failure. You can see that the pilot who comes spiraling out of the clouds at 200 to 250 K and suddenly pulls back on the wheel will put stress on the airplane that even fighter planes might find hard to handle.

Another thing—a *rolling* sharp pull-up is actually much worse than a straight pull-up. Even if a g meter (accelerometer) indicates that you are within limits, one wing will have a higher load factor although the "average" load on the airplane still may not be critical.

In addition to the fact that the wing Lift loads are not equal, the deflection of the ailerons exerts torsional forces on the wing. If the wing is close to the limit of its endurance when the torsional forces are introduced, you may witness an exciting event.

It's best on a rolling pull-up if you keep the load factor to a *maximum* of two-thirds of the limit load factor. For instance, if the limit load factor is 6.0 (acrobatic airplane) the rolling pull-up should not exceed 4.0 on the g meter. It's hard to judge, however, *without* an accelerometer.

The point to remember is that the *airplane always stalls at a certain angle of attack for a given flap setting (from 0° to full), regardless of Weight, dynamic pressure, or bank angle,* and that's why the stall airspeeds and load factors vary.

Negative g's would result if the stick or wheel were shoved briskly forward. If you ease forward on the wheel, you approach or reach the zero-g condition. Pencils, maps, and other objects may float, and you and your passengers feel light or tend to leave the seat.

Increased forward pressure could result in the aircraft and occupants having negative g's acting on them. Cockpit equipment, such as computers and map cases, slam to the ceiling, and the occupants are forced against the seat belts. There is a sudden awareness among the group of that chili and hot dog lunch of an hour or so ago. The airplane is designed to take less negative-g than positive-g forces.

The average healthy human usually "greys out" (loses vision) at a positive 4 g's and "blacks out" (loses consciousness) above 6 g's. These average reactions are based on load factors sustained over a period of several seconds; the length of time has a lot to do with the effects. Negative acceleration (or negative g's), as mentioned earlier, is harder on the pilot, and the average person gets pretty uncomfortable at −2g's.

The physical symptoms of excessive negative acceleration (minus g) are called "red out." The blood rushes to the head and small blood vessels in the eyes may hemorrhage, leaving the eyes looking like road maps for several days after the occurrence.

The pilot's positive-g tolerance may be raised by wearing a *g-suit,* a tight-fitting flight suit with air bladders at the stomach and thighs. The suit is plugged into a pressure source in the airplane and the bladders are automatically inflated when positive-g forces are encountered.

The problem of raising the negative-g tolerance remains unsolved. Of course, an automatic tourniquet around the pilot's neck might stop the flow of blood to the head but this would result in a high turnover of pilots, to say the least.

The airplane, because of the physical limitations of the pilots, is designed to withstand a higher positive than negative load factor.

AIRPLANE CATEGORIES

Just how much stress is your airplane able to take, anyway? This depends on the category in which it is certificated. The *normal* category airplane is restricted from aerobatics (acrobatics) and spins. The *utility* category may do limited aerobatics, and spins. The *acrobatic* category may do full aerobatics, and spins. The airplane categories you'll be working with during your instrument training are most likely to be *normal* and *utility*. An *acrobatic* category airplane normally is not used in straight VFR flying or instrument work but will be mentioned here as a comparison with the others. The FAA minimum limit load factor requirements for lighter airplanes (gross Weights below 12,500 lb) are as follows:

Airplane Category	Positive g's Required	Negative g's Required
Normal	2.5 to 3.8	40% of the positive g's or −1.0 to −1.52
Utility	4.4	40% of the positive g's or −1.76
Acrobatic	6.0	50% of the positive g's or −3.0

Notice under the normal category that the minimum positive required g's are 2.5 to 3.8. Actually, the requirement states that the positive limit maneuvering load factor shall not be less than 2.5 g's and need not be higher than 3.8 g's. Most manufacturers design for the 3.8 figure (it actually depends on the gross Weight of the model). *This means that the pilot can pull up to 3.8 positive g's without causing permanent deformation or structural damage to the airplane.* In addition to this, a safety factor of 1.5 is built in.

A typical normal category airplane might be designed for the following load factors:

Limit load factor (no deformation): +3.8 g's and −1.52 g's.

Ultimate load factor (1.5 safety factor): +5.7 g's and −2.28 g's. When the limit is reached, *primary* structure (wings, engines, etc.) will start to leave the airplane. The secondary structures will have long gone. In other words, if you exceed the limit load factor, you can expect some damage to occur to the airplane. Just how *much* damage will depend on how far you exceed it. If the airplane has been damaged previously, you don't have even a 1.5 safety factor any more.

MORE ABOUT LIMIT AND ULTIMATE LOAD FACTORS

Take a look at Fig. 11-3 and the *limit* and *ultimate* load factors.

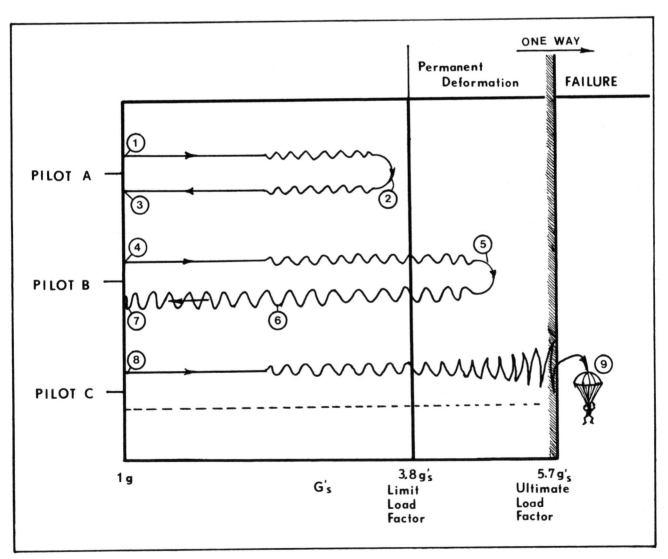

Fig. 11-3. Limit and ultimate load factors for the Zephyr Six as "tested" by three pilots.

Pilot A. Fig. 11-3 is for the Zephyr Six, a four-place, high-performance, low-wing airplane certificated in the normal category. Suppose that Pilot A decides to try a loop. He's not supposed to do aerobatics in a normal category airplane, but he figures he's so skillful that he won't pull over 3.8 g's.

He dives to what he thinks is a good speed for a loop and pul-l-l-ls *very* carefully up. His route along the g trail starts at point 1. As the loop continues, he sees that the wings are wrinkled. He immediately starts easing off the back pressure. (The loop goes to pot and the airplane sort of falls out of it, but that's not his worry right now.) The airplane is at point 2 as he relaxes back pressure and the airplane moves back to the 1-g (normal) flight situation at point 3. He notices that the wrinkles disappear as the g forces are relaxed. The plane has no accelerometer and he didn't know that he had gone close to the limit load factor. It wasn't exceeded, so no permanent deformation occured (the wrinkles disappeared). *Whew!*

Several days later in a hangar-flying session, his equanimity regained, he advises that in doing a loop in the Zephyr Six, "you can expect to see wrinkles during the loop, and you're only in trouble if they're still there after the loop is finished — ha ha." Nearly everyone is impressed.

Pilot B. Pilot B, who has visions of being an international aerobatic champion, didn't hear the last sentence of A's discussion, or it made no impression. Anyway, at the first opportunity, remembering A's description of the loop ("dive to *x* K and pull"), B does a loop in the Zephyr Six, starting at point 4 in Fig. 11-3. Since he knows that the aircraft owner wouldn't approve of aerobatics in his normal category, favorite charter airplane, he flies well out to the far edge of the practice area before doing the loop.

He dives to *x* K (well, *x* + 15 K, because Pilot A did mention that he'd sorta fallen out of it, being in the process of watching the wings wrinkle and all, so maybe an extra 15 K would be better) and pulls back on the wheel with a goodly tug.

Yep, the wings start wrinkling, just like A said. (A also said that he'd heard somewhere that engineers required that they wrinkle or the wing would break off at the root.) Pilot B continues his mighty tugging and the airplane continues the loop. He doesn't know it, but he went as far as point 5. He eases the back pressure off and figures that the wrinkles ought to disappear as he comes back to point 6. They don't, and he realizes as he comes back to point 7 that, as the engineers would put it, "permanent deformation has occurred." With a large knot in his stomach he flies *carefully* back to the airport thinking of how to explain this to the owner. Maybe he could say he hit an air pocket, or something. The airplane has aged considerably in the last few minutes.

Pilot C. Sometime after the airplane has been repaired, Pilot C, having heard Pilot A's talk about the loop and wings wrinkling but not knowing of B's problems, also decides to do aerobatics in it. He thinks he's read somewhere that parachutes are required for aerobatics (he also should have read that he shouldn't do aerobatics in this airplane). So he gets one, and goes out to practice for the demonstration he promised the local citizens for July Fourth. He also decides to do his practicing at a high altitude for "safety's sake."

C starts out at point 8 and decides to do a square loop as a starter. He starts his dive and pull-up (yes, the wings start wrinkling as expected). This first pull-up will have to be sharp, if the corner is going to be square. To make a long story short, C exceeds the ultimate load factor and is fortunate enough to have both a parachute and altitude. He can't fly back in the airplane to explain. But he telephones home base as soon as he is on the ground and has the parachute gathered up.

Obviously, these three stooges were lucky—no one got hurt. (Things were rounded off a bit here to avoid complications and maybe stretched a mite to make a point.) The airplane may have been previously damaged, and components would fail before reaching the ultimate load factor. Also, the airplane might not get permanent deformation at exactly 3.8001 g's. But the point is, if you *suspect* that you may have exceeded the limit load factor (not having an accelerometer on board), ease back to the airport and have a mechanic look things over. It would be very bad to find out later that some other pilot and his family were killed in an airplane you possibly overstressed but kept quiet about.

AIRSPEED INDICATOR MARKINGS AND IMPORTANT AIRSPEEDS

In Chap. 4, it was noted that the airspeed markings gave clues to important speeds. You may have wondered just how the speeds were arrived at and *why* a gust could affect the airplane above or below certain speeds.

You won't need to memorize the following speeds, but they are listed for reference for your information or for ammunition in a hangar argument and are all termed *equivalent airspeed* (EAS). You remember from Chap. 4 that *indicated airspeed* (IAS) is that registered by the airspeed indicator—and it could be a far-out reading. *Calibrated airspeed* (CAS) is the dynamic pressure or "real" indicated airspeed (with the instrument and system error corrected). At lower airspeeds and altitudes, the CAS is an actual measure of the dynamic pressure acting on the airplane, but at higher speeds and/or altitudes where the airplane might be nudging into compressibility effects, certain corrections must be made. This results in EAS, or CAS corrected for compressibility effects on the airspeed system.

So, to repeat a little: If the airspeed system of your airplane were perfect the indicated and calibrated airspeeds would be the same at all times. Assume that your airplane is capable of flying at speeds and altitudes where compressibility is encountered. The effect is of "packing" in the pitot tube—the static pressure within the pitot tube and airspeed diaphragm is increased above normal, but the static pressure *outside* the diaphragm (in the instrument case) remains "normal," and therefore, the two static pressures do not cancel out. The result is an airspeed that shows a higher reading than is a measure of the actual dynamic pressure working on the airplane structure. The FAA requirements are based on EAS, which covers all areas of flight and indicates the *real* forces working on the airplane. CAS is good enough for slower, lower-flying airplanes and is to be considered the same as EAS in this book.

While we're on the subject, the stresses imposed on the airplane are a function of the dynamic pressure acting on it, so the stress envelopes are based on indicated (or calibrated or equivalent, as applicable) airspeeds, which are measurements of q ($\rho V^2/2$) working on the structure. True airspeed or groundspeed doesn't enter the picture. (For instance, a satellite in orbit has a "true airspeed" of approximately 15,200 K, but because of the extremely low density, the combination of $\rho V^2/2$, or dynamic pressure, is not enough to make a flag move.)

Don't be like the private pilot who, while flying in an easterly direction at normal cruise (indicating in the green airspeed range), checked the progress with a computer and found that because of an exceptionally strong tailwind, the *groundspeed* was well over the red line speed given in the *POH,* throttled back, and landed immediately, thankful for the escape. Although you shouldn't exceed the red line speed, red line speed is *indicated or calibrated* (depending on the age of the airplane) *airspeed,* not true airspeed or groundspeed.

The airspeed indicator hand tells you if you're in trouble in this sort of situation.

Here are some of the design airspeeds (CAS or EAS) that are important in this chapter:

1. V_c — *Design cruising speed.* In designing an airplane, the manufacturer must plan for the following minimum V_c speeds in knots of at least:

a. $33\sqrt{W/S}$ for normal and utility category airplanes. The term W/S is the wing loading (gross Weight divided by area), so that an airplane with a wing loading of 16 lb per square foot (psf) would have a V_c of $33 \times \sqrt{16} = 33 \times 4 = 132$ K.

b. $36\sqrt{W/S}$ for acrobatic category airplanes. A manufacturer wanting to make a plane with a wing loading of 16 psf in the acrobatic category would have to make sure the airplane meets certain strength requirements at $36\sqrt{W/S} = 36 \times \sqrt{16} = 36 \times 4 = 144$ K.

2. V_{NO} — *Maximum structural cruising speed.* This is the limit of the green arc, where the green and yellow arcs meet. It must be no less than the minimum value of V_c just discussed. For the purpose of this book, it is shown to be the *exact* value of V_c in the markings and requirements of the figures shown.

3. V_D — *Design dive speed.* The manufacturer must prove that the airplane is capable of diving to certain speeds without coming unglued. The minimums are

a. $1.40 V_c$ (min) for *normal* category airplanes. This means that the airplane of 16-psf wing loading ($V_c = 132$ K) would have a minimum V_D of $1.40 \times 132 = 185$ K.

b. An airplane of the same wing loading, if in the *utility* category, would have a minimum V_D of $1.50 \times 132 = 198$ K.

4. V_{NE} — *Never exceed speed.* This is the red line on the airspeed indicator and is not more than 0.9 of the V_D speed. *A test pilot flying up to the V_D speed wears a parachute, in an airplane with a quick-jettison door. If you exceed the red line*

(V_{NE}) *and search for V_D, you may discover a vital need for such equipment. Do not exceed the red line.*

5. V_A — *The maneuvering speed.* This is the maximum speed at a particular Weight at which the controls may be fully deflected without overstressing the airplane. This one will be covered in more detail in sections following.

THE MANEUVER ENVELOPE

For the normal category airplane, the *maneuver envelope* basically shows the limits of load factor and airspeed allowed for that airplane at a particular Weight. Fig. 11-4 is for a fictitious normal category airplane at its maximum certificated Weight. Maneuver (and gust) envelopes are made up for Weights down to the *minimum design Weight,* which is defined as the empty Weight of the airplane with standard equipment, plus crew, plus fuel of no more than the quantity necessary to operate for ½ hr at max continuous power, plus a full load of oil. Fig. 11-4 matches some airspeeds with the maneuver envelope. The maneuver envelope for flaps-extended flight is drawn in with hatched lines. (The *maneuver* envelope is considered to cover the limits of *pilot-induced* load factors at various speeds.)

FAR 23 covers the strength requirements for normal and utility (and acrobatic) category airplanes, and the requirements are reasonable enough: you are not to exceed the limit load factors of $+3.8$ g's or -1.52 g's for the normal category airplane at any time. When flying between V_A (the maneuvering speed) and V_{NE} (the red line speed), just make sure that your handling of the elevators does not break this rule. Note in Fig. 11-4 that above V_{NO} the negative g's are further restricted in this range.

V_A, the maneuvering speed, is the dividing line between exceeding the limit load factor and stalling the airplane *before*

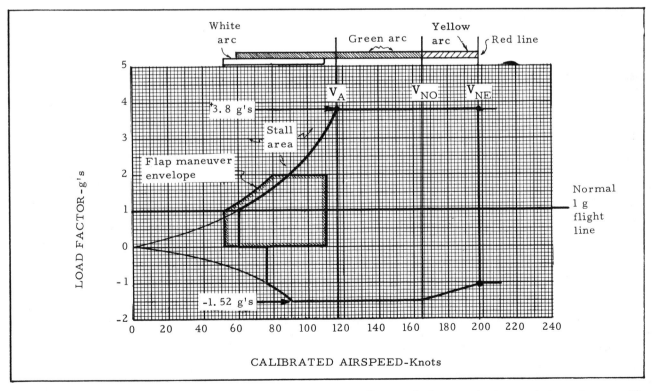

Fig. 11-4. The maneuver envelope for a particular normal category airplane at max certificated Weight. The envelope for flight with the flaps extended (white arc on the airspeed indicator) is shown.

getting into such a problem. Looking back a little earlier in the chapter, if you wanted to pull 4 g's in flight (and no more) with the plane that normally stalls at 60 K, you would stall the airplane at 120 K—and no faster. By pulling back abruptly at any speed less than 120 K, you'll never pull 4 g's. If you pull back abruptly at 90 K, you'll put 2.25 positive g's on the airplane (and occupants). It's the old story of squaring the ratio of stall speeds: (accelerated stall speed/normal stall speed)^2 = $(90/60)^2$ = 1.5^2 = 2.25 g's. That's how the curved line running from the normal stall at 1 g (60 K) up to the maneuvering speed was developed. The stall speeds at various load factors were worked out. However, instead of 4 g's, the positive limit load factor for this normal category airplane is 3.8 g's, so the maneuvering speed is $\sqrt{3.8} \times 60$ K = 1.95×60 = 117 K. If you are at the maximum certificated Weight, you'd slow down to this airspeed (or below) in rough air so that a sharp-edged vertical gust would result in a stall rather than exceeding the limit load factor. Vertical gusts will be covered later.

So, it's agreed that at the max certificated Weight (3000 lb in this example), the example airplane will stall before running into stress problems if the airspeed is kept below 117 K.

The stress imposed is a function of the Lift-to-Weight ratio. The amount of Lift an airplane can suddenly produce depends on the coefficient of Lift (proportional to angle of attack), wing area, air density, and TAS (L = $C_L S(\varrho/2)V^2$). Since the wing area is constant for a particular airplane and its wing can only develop a certain maximum coefficient of Lift before stalling, the amount of Lift available varies with the square of the airspeed. Since the maneuvering speed for this fictitious airplane is established as 117 K at a gross Weight of 3000 lb, it would be able to develop a maximum of 11,400 lb of Lift at 117 K without stalling or pulling over 3.8 g's (3.8 × 3000 = 11,400 lb). Check back to Fig. 2-8 and note that the C_L drops rapidly after the angle of attack for stall so that a peak Lift is made available by suddenly increasing the angle of attack at a specific airspeed. The peak Lift at 117 K for this airplane is 11,400 lb, which gives a load factor of 3.8, resulting from the combination of C_{Lmax}, wing area (S), air density (ϱ), and TAS squared (V^2). The C_L used here will be C_{Lmax} (clean) since this is the factor at the stall. (You might review the section on Lift in Chap. 2 if this is hazy right now.) The load factor as checked by the engineers is 11,400 (Lift)/3000 (Weight) = 3.8 g's if the airplane is stalled at 117 K. So this is the maneuvering speed—or is it? It's *the* maneuvering speed for the gross Weight of 3000 lb *but not for lower Weights*. The maneuvering speed must decrease with the square root of the Weight decrease, as introduced in Chap. 1.

Take the airplane at a near empty Weight of 1500 lb. Admittedly, it's unusual for an airplane to be able to fly at a Weight one-half its gross Weight, but there are some models capable of this ratio and it makes for easier figuring.

Assume again that the airplane is abruptly stalled at 117 K at the light Weight of 1500 lb. Since the maximum *Lift* developed depends only on the Lift factors just mentioned and has no bearing on the Weight of the airplane, 11,400 lb will be developed as before. The positive load factor will be 11,400/1500 = 7.6 g's. The first impression is that the occupants will have 7.6 g's working on them and will probably black out (it depends on the length of time they are subjected to the load factor; this abrupt movement would result in only a very short period of 7.6 g's before the stall occurs, so let's forget them).

Okay, you say, the wings have the same load as before (11,400), so what's the problem except for a brief discomfort on the part of the pilot and passengers? The wings are all right, but there *are* "fixed-Weight components," such as the engine(s), baggage, retracted landing gear, etc. The airplane's limit load factor here of 3.8 g's is based on an overall analysis

of the aircraft components. The engine has gotten no lighter during the flight, and it is, as mentioned, a fixed-Weight component. Because of the lighter overall Weight of the airplane, the engine and other fixed-Weight components are subjected to greater acceleration forces. The engine mounts may not be able to support an engine and accessories that weigh nearly 8 times normal, and the same thing might be said about retracted landing gear, batteries, and baggage. You recall from Chap. 10 that the baggage compartment is placarded for max Weight for *two* reasons: (1) the CG could be moved to a dangerous position and (2) the baggage compartment floor is only stressed to take a certain number of g's with the placarded Weight. For instance, the example airplane, which has a limit load factor of 3.8 positive g's, has a limit of 200 lb Weight in the baggage compartment and could have a total force up to 3.8 × 200 lb, or 760 lb acting on the floor without structural damage. The pilot who stalled the airplane at the light Weight at the 117-K speed has caused a force of 7.6 × 200 lb, or 1520 lb, to be exerted on the floor. Fig. 11-5 shows that the lighter Weight at the old maneuvering speed results in load factors that can cause problems for the fixed-Weight components.

Fig. 11-5. Using the maneuvering speed for max certificated Weight at lighter Weights can put extra stress on the fixed-Weight components.

If you put *400* lb in the baggage compartment and pulled the legal 3.8 g's, the result would also be illegal, immoral, and disappointing: 1520 lb (temporarily) acting on a compartment floor that is stressed for 760 lb. An effort of this nature probably will allow the taking of aerial photographs through the hole where the bottom of the compartment *used* to be. This is a separate matter from the problem of the maneuvering speed change but is a factor to be watched also.

A *new* maneuvering speed is necessary for the lighter Weight. Since the overall limit for this fictitious airplane is 3.8 g's, the maneuvering speed must be such that that load factor cannot be exceeded—the airplane will stall first. Again, since the load factor is the Lift-to-Weight ratio, the airplane at the Weight of 1500 lb must be flown at such an airspeed that the limit load factor will not be exceeded by suddenly increasing the angle of attack to the maximum. The maximum allowable Lift with this lighter Weight is 5700 lb because 5700/1500 = 3.8 g's. The variable is airspeed, and since airspeed is a *squared* function, the new airspeed (V_2) can be found: L_1 = $C_{Lmax}S(\varrho/2)V_1^2$, L_2 = $C_{Lmax} S(\varrho/2)V_2^2$. If L_1 = 11,400 lb, L_2 = 5700 lb, and V_1 = 117 K, V_2 = ?.

The maximum C_L attainable is fixed, as is the wing area,

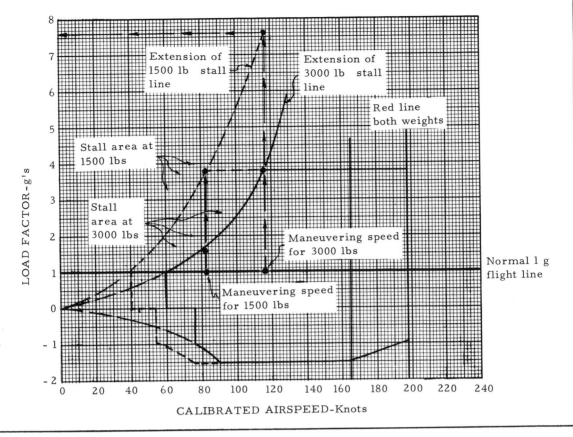

Fig. 11-6. The maneuver envelope for two aircraft Weights showing the two maneuvering speeds. The dashed lines show how the maneuver envelope is extended back to lower speeds as the Weight decreases. (See also Fig. 11-13 at the end of the chapter for Weight effects on V_A for a particular airplane.)

so what it boils down to is that the ratio of the two maneuvering speeds is proportional to the *square root* of the ratio of Weights (because the two fixed factors of wing area and air density cancel each other): $V_2^2/V_1^2 = L_2/L_1$; $V_2/V_1 = \sqrt{L_2/L_1}$; $V_2/V_1 = \sqrt{5700/11,400} = \sqrt{0.5} = 0.7$, or $V_2 = 0.7V_1$.

The second (lighter Weight) maneuvering speed is seventenths of the original. As the original was 117 K, the new one (at 1500 lb) is 82 K. Fig. 11-6 compares the maneuvering envelopes at both Weights. Notice that the only changes occur at the lower end of the speed range; the red line speed is the same, and the limit load factors have not changed.

The extension of the dashed curved line shows that if the airplane is abruptly stalled at the higher maneuvering speed of 117 K, a load factor of 7.6 g's will result—which is another way of looking at the comparison just discussed (Fig. 11-6).

In-Flight Failures. Airplanes are still being flown into IFR conditions by pilots who aren't qualified, and witnesses still report hearing an "explosion" in the clouds and seeing parts of an airplane falling out of the bases to the ground. Or, in VFR conditions, the pilot may let the airplane get into an area of airspeed and/or g's beyond its design limits. Many times witnesses hear—and see—the break-up and the noise and breakup convince them that an internal explosion did occur and they may even convince themselves there was a fiery blast with accompanying smoke. This may throw off accident investigators for a while until a check of the wreckage shows no scorching.

Taking a hypothetical situation, assume that a normally configured airplane is in a high-speed, uncontrolled spiral. The pilot is pulling back on the wheel to pull the nose up (not realizing that the wings should be leveled first) and is increasing the download on the horizontal tail.

In this case, the wings have a very high *upload,* while the tail is being overstressed by the added download induced by the pilot's attempt to bring the nose up. If the tail fails first (it will break off "downward"), the nose will pitch down immediately and the wings, which were probably about to break off upward (and may have already been permanently bent in that direction), are now subjected to an instantaneous force in the opposite direction and fail downward. It's possible, too, that a wing (or both wings) could fail first, taking the tail with it.

The accident investigator doesn't take anything for granted but a wings-downward failure *usually* means that the horizontal tail went first and a wing-upward failing *usually* means that that item failed first. In the earlier scenario, where the wings had high positive loads during the pull-up and then failed downward the instant the tail failed, the spars may have been deformed by the high positive (up) load before they failed downward and this might be the *first* clue seen. It's fairly unusual for both wings to fail simultaneously but it has happened.

The current retractable-gear airplanes are very clean and can build up excess speed very quickly. Keep it in mind.

THE GUST ENVELOPE

The maneuver envelope is very interesting, you say, but who's going to fly around yanking back on the wheel and putting load factors on the airplane? Probably nobody, but vertical gusts can do just about the same thing. Fig. 11-7 shows the effects of a sharp-edged gust on the airplane. The term *sharp-edged* means that the transition from smooth air to the gust is instantaneous—this is a safer approach in computing stress, rather than thinking in terms of a more gradual transition during which the airspeed and aircraft structure would "adjust" to the stress.

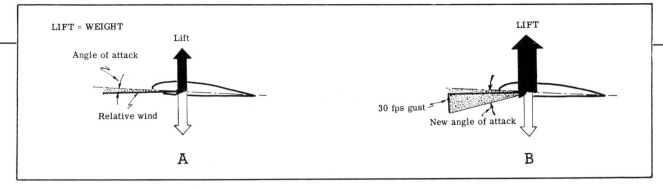

LIFT = WEIGHT

Lift

Angle of attack

Relative wind

A

LIFT

30 fps gust

New angle of attack

B

Fig. 11-7.   The effects of a vertical (upward) gust.

In Fig. 11-7A, the airplane is flying straight and level at cruise, and 1 g is acting upon it. Suddenly, a vertical gust is encountered (Fig. 11-7B), which increases the angle of attack (and C_L) and results in much added Lift—and load factor. The wing doesn't know the difference between your control handling and a natural phenomenon, so the effect on it is the same. Again, looking back to Fig. 2-8, you will note that the increase in the C_L is a straight line with increase of angle of attack. The sudden increase in load factor is because the other factors (air density, wing area, and airspeed) remain the same for an instantaneous action.

Normal and utility category airplanes must be able to withstand vertical gusts of 30 fps at the maximum structural cruising speed (the junction of the green and yellow arcs on the airspeed) and 15-fps sharp-edged vertical gusts up to the design dive speed (models certificated under FAR 3).

New criteria have been established in FAR 23 concerning the effects of gusts on the airplane. The gusts in the design specifications are stronger but the requirements include a "gust alleviation" factor that brings the result back pretty close to the 15- and 30-fps *sharp-edged* gusts. The idea of an instant change is easier to see in an example, so it is used here.

Fig. 11-8 shows a gust envelope for the fictitious airplane discussed earlier (at max certificated Weight). Assume the airplane is flying straight and level in 1-g flight at a CAS of 140

K (Fig. 11-8, point 1). It suddenly encounters a 15-fps upward gust and is moved up to point 2 and has 2 g's imposed on it. The conditions would be such that the airplane would return to its original 1-g flight, but the load factor would have already worked on the airframe.

Suppose the airplane is flying straight and level in slow flight at 70 K at 1 g (point 3). (The pilot is expecting turbulence and has slowed down to take care of it.) A 30-fps upward gust is encountered, and the airplane is suddenly at point 4—or it should be said that the airplane moves *toward* point 4 but enters the stall area. As another example, the airplane is flying at the red line when the 30-fps gust is encountered at point 5, it will be out of the envelope (point 6). While a stall is better than losing part of the airplane, it could still cause a problem when you are on the gages.

The idea is that you want to fly in an area of airspeeds where there is no danger of stall *or* overstress, and for operating in situations where 30-fps gusts are expected, the airplane should be flown at a speed between 117 K and the maximum structural cruising speed of 165 K (Fig. 11-8). (This is for the airplane at max certificated Weight.)

The effects of gusts, like the earlier example of sudden full-elevator deflection, are increased at lighter Weights so that the lines representing the gusts are "spread apart," and a 30-fps gust may actually result in stresses greater than that

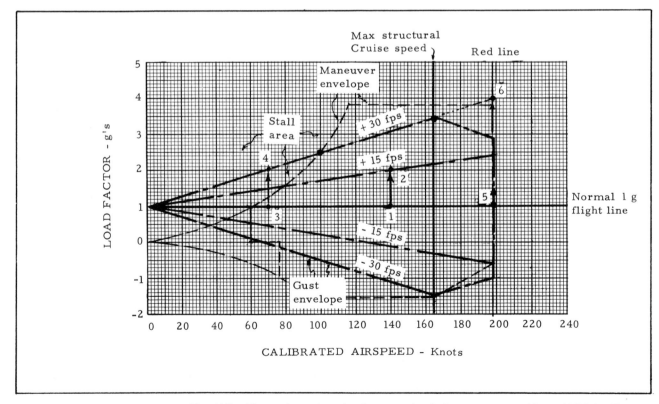

Fig. 11-8.   The gust envelope for the example airplane at max certificated Weight. The maneuver envelope is indicated by the dashed line.

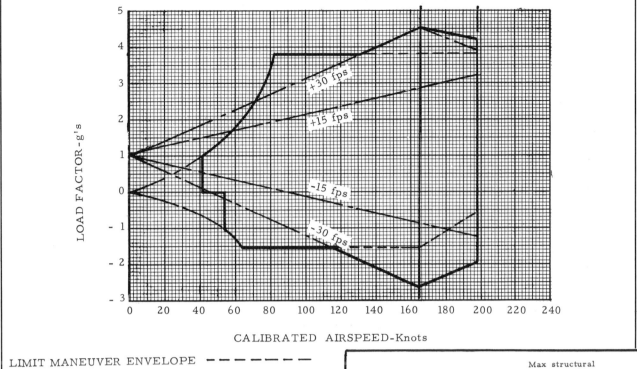

LIMIT MANEUVER ENVELOPE ――― ――― ―
LIMIT GUST ENVELOPE ― · ―― · ― ―― ·
LIMIT COMBINED ENVELOPE ―――――――

Fig. 11-9. The gust envelope for the example airplane at a near-empty Weight.

indicated by the maneuvering envelope (Fig. 11-9).

The 30-fps gust has put the load factor up to 4.5 g's, but
this has been justified by the manufacturer, as shown by the
solid line, which indicates the *limit combined envelope boundary.* Just a minute, you say — back in the section discussing
the maneuvering envelope, it was noted that the pilot was not to
handle the elevators in such a way that the airplane could
exceed the limit load factor (in this case 3.8 g's); now, all of a
sudden, the airplane can hit a 30-fps gust and exceed 3.8 g's,
and it's okay. The answer is that the elevators must not be
fully deflected above the maneuvering speed (it may not require full deflection at the higher speed to get the 4.5 g's). The
manufacturer assumes that the airplane is flying straight and
level with fixed elevators, and a vertical gust changes the angle
of attack of the wings without elevator deflection. To get the
same load factor by elevator deflection, strong twisting moments are introduced, and the horizontal tail could be the first
part to leave your company. The manufacturer plays it safe as
far as elevator usage is concerned.

Notice the range of airspeeds between exceeding the maneuvering limit load factor of 3.8 g's and stalling (even at the
lower stall speed). The effect is moving the "safe" speed range
back and narrowing it as the Weight decreases. Some manufacturers list the recommended flight speed ranges for gross
and minimum Weights at various expected gust velocities in
the *POH.*

Fig. 11-10 shows the "safe speed range" (no stall *or* overstress) for the fictitious airplane discussed earlier at Weights
of 3000 and 1500 lb. Assume for simplicity that the manufacturer wants to give the pilot information for flying in areas
where 30-fps vertical gusts are expected and wants to make
sure that the airplane does not (1) exceed the limit load factor

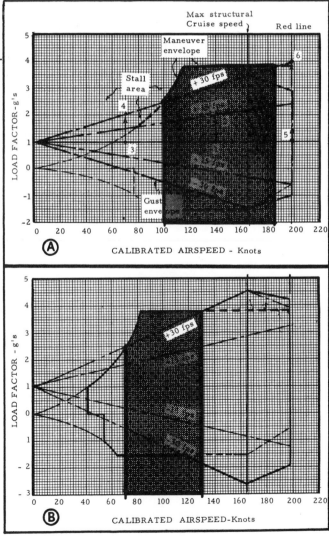

Fig. 11-10. The range of operations (airspeed)
for 30-fps gusts at gross Weight of 3000 lb (A) and
1500 lb (B). A 45-fps gust would cut the safe area
even thinner.

of 3.8 g's or (2) stall at these Weights. (Disregard the earlier comment that the manufacturer justified the 4.5-g load factor at the lighter weight of 1500 lb for this example.)

In Fig. 11-10A the 30-fps gust would cause the airplane, at a Weight of 3000 lbs, to exceed the limit load factor at speeds above 185 K. The gust would cause a stall at a speed of 100 K (or less). The extreme range of safe operation here is 85 K.

In Fig. 11-10B, at a lighter Weight of 1500 lb, the 30-fps gust would cause the airplane to exceed the 3.8-g load factor at 130 K and cause it to stall at a speed of 70 K (or less). The spread of airspeed would be 60 K.

At 3000 lb, your best operating speed in expected 30-fps vertical gust conditions would be 142.5 K. (*Sure,* you could maintain this exactly.) For the light Weight condition the mid-point speed would be 100 K, which is the lowest safe speed for the airplane at the max certificated Weight of 3000 lb (Fig. 11-10A).

The manufacturer may show graphs of several gust values and airplane Weights and may also take into consideration any justifications of stress required in certification of the air-plane. Also, the graph may have a certain (center) area of the safe airspeeds shown in green, with yellow caution areas at each end (and red lines to show the stall and overstress points).

Fig. 11-11 shows a turbulent air penetration graph for an airplane at a particular Weight when encountering 30- and 45-fps gusts. You might sketch in an estimated 45-fps gust line in Figs. 11-8 and 11-9 to see how much leeway in airspeed you'd have at each Weight. You'd have maybe 3 to 5 K at the heavy Weight of 3000 lb as the line cuts across the V_A corner but might miss the maneuver envelope altogether at the lighter Weight. You could make a graph like that in Fig. 11-11 by using various airspeeds (marking them in yellow for caution etc.).

Another factor in stress on the airplane is how the load is distributed. Fig. 11-12 shows the effects of a vertical gust on airplanes of different wing load distributions. You can see that full tip tanks might give a better lateral Weight distribution effect in gusts.

You can consider that 30-fps gusts are found *in the vicinity of* thunderstorms, 45-fps gusts are found *near* thunder-

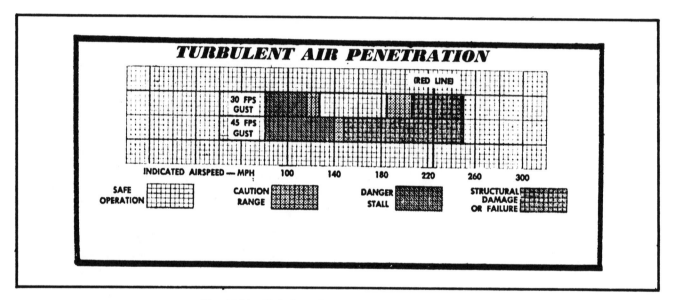

Fig. 11-11. Turbulent air penetration graph. (You could make up such a chart using the gust and maneuver envelopes of the fictitious airplane of Figs. 11-8, 9, and 10.) (*FAA–T–8080–2.*)

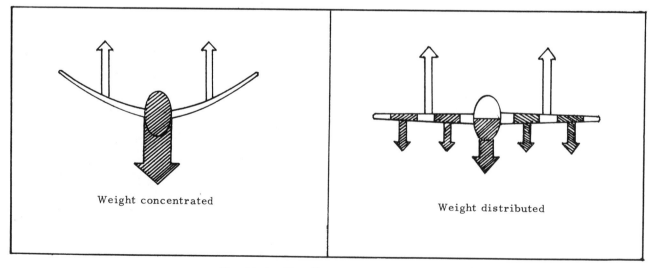

Fig. 11-12. The effects of lateral Weight distribution on gust- or pilot-induced stress.

storms, and *inside* a cell these values can be exceeded by a wide margin.

The up gusts were discussed first because gusts acting in this direction are more readily understood. But the down-acting gusts are more uncomfortable on the pilot and airframe. A vector system of the type illustrated in Fig. 11-7 could be drawn for the down-acting gust, and the result would be a sharp decrease in angle of attack (and Lift), accompanied by the sound of seat belts being stretched and heads contacting the head liner.

Summary

1. *Don't exceed the limit load factors—positive or negative.*

2. *In moderately turbulent air keep the airspeed in the green arc.* You don't know when you may encounter severe turbulence. Stay out of the yellow arc when it's bumpy.

3. *In severe turbulence slow the airplane below the maneuvering speed.* Use 1.5 times the flaps-up, power-off stall speed (CAS) as a rule of thumb for *all* Weights.

4. *If you want to do aerobatics, rent an aerobatic airplane* (chandelles and lazy eights are not considered to be acrobatics, or *aerobatics*).

5. *Read your POH.* It may have recommendations for turbulent air penetration.

6. *Check the placards on the instrument panel, and keep the airspeed within reason for the conditions under which you are flying* (Fig. 11-13).

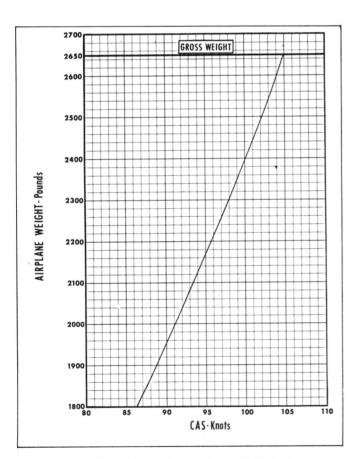

Fig. 11-13. Change of V_A with Weight decrease for a particular airplane, developed from Fig. 1-12. Yours may have the airspeeds in tabular form for several lighter Weights.

THE CHECKOUT

When you first check out in an airplane with a constant-speed propeller things can be pretty hectic. In the first place, it's a new airplane to you and the addition of the propeller control further complicates matters. After all, it's only *one* more control you say to yourself, but juggling the throttle and prop to get the right combination of power may cause some consternation for the first few tries. The check pilot who's sitting so calmly in the right seat once had the same problem. If he's grinning at your workout, it's probably because he's remembering his first struggle with throttle *and* prop controls.

The constant-speed prop allows you to get more efficiency out of the engine-propeller combination in all speed ranges. That extra control is not just put there to complicate matters, although it does impress the nonpilot to see you making adjustments with those mysterious knobs. One of the major factors is the ability to get max power on takeoff without compromising other performance.

The discussion of throttle and propeller controls in this chapter will cover their use with the unsupercharged or normally aspirated engine. Superchargers will be covered in Chap. 19.

The HP developed by a particular engine depends on the manifold pressure and rpm. For instance, 65% power, often used for cruise, may be set up in several combinations of manifold pressure (mp) and rpm. The manufacturer furnishes a power setting table that allows the pilot to establish the desired HP for a particular altitude (Fig. 12-1).

Another thing you might look at in Fig. 12-1 — the mp required at a particular rpm becomes less as altitude increases. At sea level, at 2200 rpm, 23.3 in. of mp are required to develop 65%. At 5000 ft, only 22 in. are required for 65% power at 2200 rpm. There are two main reasons for this apparent inconsistency. (1) The exhaust gases have less outside pressure (back pressure) to fight at higher altitudes. Remember that the "explosion" in the cylinder is sealed, and power is used to expel the waste gases. Less back pressure means less power used to eliminate this waste (there's better scavenging)—power that can be used in making the airplane go. (2) The air is cooler at higher altitudes. If you use the same mp as you carried at sea level, the mixture density and the HP developed would be greater (lower temperature means greater density if the pressure remains the same). Therefore, in order to maintain the same power, less mp is used for a given rpm with altitude increase, as Fig. 12-1 shows.

The figures given in the table are for standard pressure altitudes. The footnote shows how to correct for deviations from standard temperature, though in actual practice this is seldom done as the mp gage can't be read that closely.

While we're on the subject of the power table, notice that you are unable to maintain the various percentages of power above certain altitudes. Naturally you won't be able to hold 75% power at as high an altitude as you could hold 65% — the engine can't maintain the required mp.

For a given rpm the higher the mp, the more power developed. Of course you can ruin an engine very quickly by thinking that this is the way it should be operated. At low rpm and high mp the engine could suffer damage, which is an expensive as well as a dangerous problem. Manufacturers generally do not recommend power settings of over 75% for cruise for reciprocating engines, as the fuel consumption and extra engine wear preclude use above this value.

USING THE THROTTLE AND PROPELLER CONTROLS

The mp gage tells you of the potential power going to the engine; the tachometer tells how much is being used. With the proper throttle and prop setting you have ideal potential *and* use of the power.

A part of the measure of an engine's power output is bmep (brake mean effective pressure) in the cylinders at the instant of combustion. If this internal pressure is too great the engine can be damaged.

The engine can efficiently use a maximum amount of fuel-air mixture at a certain rpm. A high mp means that a lot of fuel and air is available for the engine. When this higher compressed charge is shoved into the cylinders, more power should be produced. But if the prop control is set at too low an rpm, it's like putting the powder load for a cannon into a shotgun (well, maybe not quite).

If you have trouble remembering which goes first in a

Fig. 12-1.

Power Setting Table — Lycoming Model O-540-A1B5, 250 HP Engine

Press. Alt. 1000 Feet	Std. Alt. Temp. °F.	138 HP 55% Rated Approx. Fuel 10.3 Gal. Hr. RPM AND MAN. PRESS.				163 HP 65% Rated Approx. Fuel 12.3 Gal. Hr. RPM AND MAN. PRESS.				188 HP 75% Rated Approx. Fuel 14.0 Gal. Hr. RPM AND MAN. PRESS.		
		2100	2200	2300	2400	2100	2200	2300	2400	2200	2300	2400
SL	59	21.6	20.8	20.2	19.6	24.2	23.3	22.6	22.0	25.8	25.1	24.3
1	55	21.4	20.6	20.0	19.3	23.9	23.0	22.4	21.8	25.5	24.8	24.1
2	52	21.4	20.4	19.7	19.1	23.7	22.8	22.2	21.5	25.3	24.6	23.8
3	48	20.9	20.1	19.5	18.9	23.4	22.5	21.9	21.3	25.0	24.3	23.6
4	45	20.6	19.9	19.3	18.7	23.1	22.3	21.7	21.0	24.8	24.1	23.3
5	41	20.4	19.7	19.1	18.5	22.9	22.0	21.4	20.8	—	23.8	23.0
6	38	20.1	19.5	18.9	18.3	22.6	21.8	21.2	20.6	—	—	22.8
7	34	19.9	19.2	18.6	18.0	22.3	21.5	21.0	20.4	—	—	—
8	31	19.6	19.0	18.4	17.8	—	—	20.5	19.9			
9	27	19.4	18.8	18.2	17.6	—	21.3	20.7	20.1			
10	23	19.1	18.6	18.0	17.4	—	—	—	19.6			
11	19	18.9	18.3	17.8	17.2	—	—	—	—			
12	16	18.6	18.1	17.5	17.0	—	—	—	—			
13	12	—	17.9	17.3	16.8							
14	9	—	—	17.1	16.5							
15	5	—	—	—	16.3							

To maintain constant power, correct manifold pressure approximately 0.17″ Hg for each 10° F. variation in carburetor air temperature from standard altitude temperature. Add manifold pressure for air temperatures above standard; subtract for temperatures below standard.

Fig. 12-2. "I guess I should have eased the prop control forward before opening the throttle." (Improper use of the throttle and prop control can cause engine indigestion.)

power change—throttle or prop—remember this. *Keep the propeller control forward more than the throttle.* If you're increasing power, the propeller control is moved forward first; in decreasing power the propeller control is moved back last. In normal usage, if it were timed, the propeller control would be forward more than the throttle (by seconds). Don't slam the throttle or prop control—the engine and propeller have inertia to overcome in changing speeds and if you get too hasty you could damage the engine this way, too. Abrupt opening of the throttle at low speeds can cause *detonation* (Chap. 13). Rapid throttle changes in heavy engines may cause overstress.

The propeller control may be thought of as similar to an automobile (manual) gearshift. However, whereas the car just has a few set positions, you can set any "gear" combination you want with the prop control. Flat pitch, or high rpm, is comparable to low gear in a car. You set it before takeoff (prop control full forward) and "step on the gas" (open the throttle all the way). After getting off the ground you throttle back to the climb mp setting and *then* pull the prop control back to the recommended rpm setting (a slightly higher pitch) for climb.

About decreasing power: if you pull the prop control back *before* the throttle, the mp will increase because the engine isn't taking the mixture as fast any more—you're giving it more bmep than it can efficiently use, which can be bad if the difference becomes too great.

There are some geared (unsupercharged)-engine-equipped airplanes that require the pilot to reduce the rpm after takeoff and continue to use full throttle. (Pulling the throttle back with this engine would lean the mixture, a condition not conducive to long engine life in a climb.) Since the original takeoff rpm is 3400 and the METO (maximum except take-off) rpm was (is) 3000, the normally aspirated engine was not overboosted (28–29 in. mp and 3000 rpm). The example engine is geared at a 120:77 ratio, or the engine turns 120 rpm to the propeller's 77 rpm. (This was mentioned so that you know that such procedures may be required for a few models of airplanes. But you'll find that in most cases the power-changing procedures are as mentioned earlier. In any event, use the manufacturer's recommended procedure.)

To increase power, the order of engine control use is
(1) Richen mixture
(2) Propeller control forward
(3) Increase manifold pressure—throttle forward

To reduce power (say, to level off from a climb to assume cruising flight):
(1) Throttle back
(2) Decrease rpm (retard the prop control)
(3) Set mixture as necessary

Sometimes there's confusion concerning the prop setting.

For takeoff you'd set the prop control forward for *low pitch—high rpm.* For cruise, the setting would be *high pitch—low rpm.* This confusion most often occurs on an FAA written test where you know which is which but misread the question.

Some Items about Takeoff. Your first takeoff in the new airplane almost can be predicted. You take off, feeling strange and maybe a little tense as you want to be sure to do a good job. You have the prop full forward in high rpm and the throttle wide open. Fine. The airplane lifts off and you're naturally pretty busy. Watching the runway and the area ahead you prepare to throttle back. Glancing at the mp gage you see it hasn't moved so you pull the power back some more. There's a power loss felt but the mp gage hasn't moved. Is it broken? The screams of the check pilot (and maybe a groan or two from the engine) direct your attention to the tachometer. Oops—it's back below cruising rpm. You pulled the prop control back first, *instead* of the throttle. You hastily shove it back up—the prop overspeeds for a couple of seconds—and you have to start the power reduction process anew for the climbout, this time pulling the throttle back *first* and *then* the prop control, as it should be. You'll feel about 6 in. high. Well, welcome to the club; you've joined a group of several hundred thousand other pilots who've done the same thing (and this includes the one in the right seat over there, who's hollering so loudly).

However, just because you didn't mean to do it doesn't lessen punishment to the engine in a deal like this. The proper procedure will come with practice.

Some pilots use their knowledge of this fact—at a constant throttle position the mp will increase if the rpm decreases—to save themselves the extra manipulation of the prop and throttle on takeoff. Suppose your airplane uses 28 in. and 2700 rpm for takeoff at sea level, and the manufacturer recommends 24 in. and 2400 rpm for climbout. The old pro will throttle back to about 23 in. Then when the prop is pulled back to 2400 rpm (moving the prop into higher pitch), the mp will be up to 24 in. and no further adjustment will be required. If the throttle had been set to 24 in., it would have eased up to, say, 25 in. when the prop was pulled back, which would require resetting the mp. You will soon note the rise in mp with decrease in rpm after takeoff for your airplane and will do this automatically. The 1-in. rise used here is an illustration; the exact rise will depend on the difference between takeoff and climb rpm for your engine.

The Climb. You've set the power to the recommended value of 24 in. and 2400 rpm (or whatever is set up for your particular airplane) and now feel you can relax a little. On your first flight in the new airplane you'll want to get some altitude and just get used to it before doing anything exotic like takeoffs and landings.

As you climb it seems that after 2000 or 3000 ft the airplane has lost quite a bit of its go and if the check pilot hasn't already brought it to your attention, a glance at the mp gage shows that the mp has dropped 2 (or 3) in. A creeping throttle? No, the atmospheric pressure drops about 1 in. of mercury per 1000 ft at lower altitudes, and the engine just isn't able to get the same amount of mp at the old throttle setting. You'll have to open the throttle of the unsupercharged engine as altitude is gained.

At the beginning of the chapter, it was mentioned that the engine of the example needed about ¼ in. less mp per 1000 ft to maintain the same percentage of power. The mp drops 1 in. so this puts you about ¾ in. in the hole for each 1000 ft. Some engine manufacturers recommend a constant mp for a particular engine for the climb at *all* altitudes (if you can maintain it), while for engines having limits of continuous power they furnish tables for recommended maximum mp at various altitudes. Maintaining a constant mp to higher altitudes does mean that more power is being developed up there; this power may exceed the manufacturer's recommendation for longtime use for some engines.

Cruise. On leveling off leave the power at climb setting until the expected cruising speed is reached. This is done for two reasons: (1) the transition from climb to cruise is shorter and (2) you'll only have to set cruise power once. If you throttle back and set the power to, say, 23 in. and 2300 rpm for cruise (or whatever the power setting chart recommends for your altitude and chosen power) immediately upon reaching the altitude, you'll find that as the airspeed picks up from climb to cruise the mp may also increase due to "ram effect" (increased dynamic pressure of the air entering the intake). You'll have to reset the mp, then lean the mixture.

Assume that you have set the prop control to maintain, for example, 2400 rpm; if you open the throttle the initial tendency will be for the rpm to increase (as would be the case for a fixed-pitch propeller). The propeller governor senses this and makes the pitch angle greater (higher pitch), and the added drag stops the rpm increase. Conversely, pulling the throttle back will tend to decrease the rpm, so the governor flattens the pitch as necessary so the lesser blade drag will allow the rpm to be maintained. As will be discussed shortly, if the throttle is closed the blades reach the low pitch limit and cannot maintain the preset rpm.

Landing Notes. Another problem you may have the first few times is remembering to move the prop control forward to a high rpm (low pitch) during the approach to prepare for the possibility of a go-around. Some *POH*s recommend that the rpm be set to high cruise or climb rpm rather than for takeoff in this case, as there is a possibility of engine overspeed if throttle is suddenly applied. Others may recommend a full-high rpm setting for the landing approach.

For airplanes in which a high cruise or climb rpm is recommended for an approach, this is best done on the downwind leg when you have cruise power on. Even the constant-speed prop cannot maintain the preset rpm when you've throttled back for landing. If you have it set for 2400 rpm at cruise, when you close or nearly close the throttle, the rpm may drop down to 2000, or well below, when you slow up. Of course, as soon as you open the throttle past a certain mp, the rpm will increase and hold your preset value. Actually what happens when you throttle back to idle is this: the prop tries to maintain the preset rpm, and as you throttle back the blade angle (pitch) decreases—trying to maintain the required rpm. Finally you throttle back so far that the blades are as flat as they can go but can't keep up the rpm. Moving the prop controls forward won't help—you'll have to increase power (mp pressure) before getting a reaction.

On the other hand, if the recommendation for your airplane is to set the prop to full-high rpm for the approach, *don't* do it on the downwind leg where you are developing power in the engine. The result would be a probable rpm overshoot and, at best, a noisy announcement of your presence in the area. The usual practice is to move the prop control (or controls) forward on base or after turning on final, when you're not using a lot of power. Of the four main items for landing (gear, flaps, mixture, and prop) the propeller is normally set last if a full-high-rpm setting is recommended for landing.

At any rate, you haven't been setting a propeller for landing before now and may have to be reminded by the check pilot a couple of times. Remember this: If you have to go around, you may need full power quickly and will be in bad shape if you shove the throttle wide open with the prop control back in a low-cruise setting.

Prop Controls. The prop control is somewhat similar to the throttle. It works the same way and may resemble the throttle, although the handle itself is usually a different shape for quick recognition by feel. The prop control for the single-engine airplane usually projects out of the instrument panel, whereas the multiengine airplane throttles, prop controls, and mixtures are on a quadrant. The single-engine airplane prop control usually can be moved either of two ways: (1) by pressing a manual release (lock) button and moving the control in or out in the same manner as for the throttle or (2) by using the vernier adjustment, screwing the control in (clockwise) to increase rpm and turning it counterclockwise to decrease rpm. The vernier method allows for a finer setting and is used for making adjustments when the engine is developing power, such as after takeoff, cruise, or setting rpm on the downwind leg. The button lock push-pull method is good for quickly setting full-high rpm when the engine is not developing a great deal of power (before opening the throttle for takeoff or on final). See Fig. 12-3.

The end result is the same. Naturally, it will take longer, for instance, to go to full-high rpm using the vernier, but many pilots prefer it and never use the button release. The *throttles* for some airplanes also may use a combination vernier and button release. *One thing to remember, the prop control moves the same way as the throttle—for more power (rpm) it's forward, for less power (rpm) it's back.*

Throttles for some *fixed-pitch* propeller planes are also of the vernier type.

MORE BACKGROUND ABOUT PROPELLER OPERATION

In Chap. 2, operating theory of constant-speed propellers was covered briefly. Following is more information that will be of direct interest to you as a pilot.

There are three main types of constant-speed propellers in use today. You will probably get to fly all three types (including some featherable variations) as you progress to more complex airplanes.

If you know what type of propeller you're using on your airplane you will be better able to analyze problems, both in flight and on the ground. Also, you should know that the constant-speed propeller needs overhauls, as does the engine. (The suggested overhaul period for some props is 1500 hr of operation or 4 yr in-service time, but more about that later.) In some cases, the prop overhaul coincides with the engine overhaul, and if it's your responsibility you should get a factory-approved shop to do the job.

The Oil-Counterweight Propeller. This type uses oil pressure from the engine, passed through a governor to move the propeller into low pitch. Centrifugal force acting on the counterweight attached to the inner portion of each blade tends to cause the blade to twist in the hub to a higher angle of attack (higher pitch). When you select a specific rpm setting with the prop control you're balancing oil pressure (acting on the prop piston-cylinder assembly in the hub, which moves actuating arms to "twist" the blades) against the centrifugal force acting on the prop counterweights. A loss of oil pressure in this system would have the propeller tending to increase pitch.

The Governor. The job of the governor is to make sure that the selected rpm is maintained, and without going into detail about the many parts involved in its construction, you might take a look at Fig. 12-4. The governor is normally mounted on the front of, and geared to, the engine. The flyweights in the governor are in a constant rpm position (Fig. 12-4A); the rpm is steady.

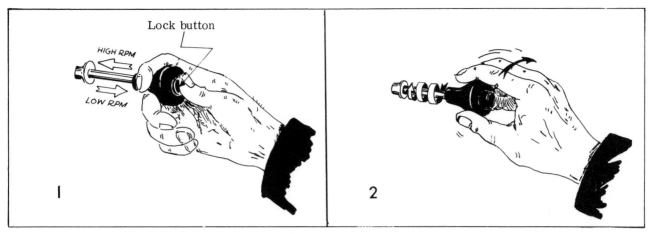

Fig. 12-3. 1. Using the lock button for large rpm adjustments. 2. Using the vernier for smoother, minor adjustments. The propeller control is being turned to obtain higher rpm in the illustration.

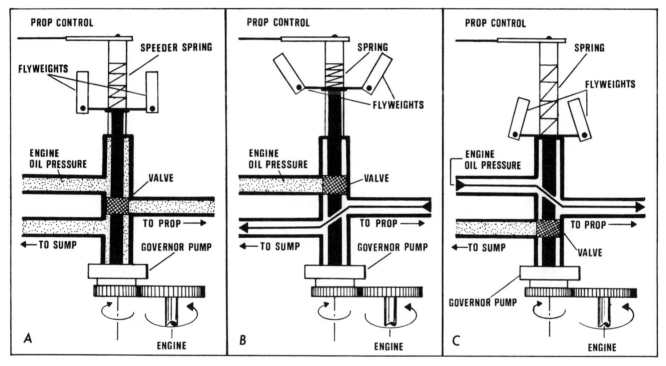

Fig. 12-4. A schematic diagram of the prop governor for an oil-counterweight propeller. The flyweights are connected to the valve and shaft and are rotated by the engine through gearing. Assume that the rpm has been set to, for instance, 2200 rpm by the prop control (which isn't moved during the sequence shown — A, B, and C). By setting the prop control the pilot has set the compression of the speeder spring and the counterweights (trying to increase the pitch or moving it to a *low*-rpm position) are balanced by the oil pressure (acting to decrease pitch or increase rpm), and as you will note in A, nothing is happening.

B. The airplane is dived, the prop gets windmilling effect, and the engine (and flyweight) rpm increases. The valve, which was doing very well earlier (in A, having shut off oil *to* or *from* the prop), is now raised as the flyweights are moved out by centrifugal force. Oil now moves from the prop hub and the counterweights (on the prop) move the prop toward a higher pitch to increase drag and knock off the excess rpm, until equilibrium is again established at 2200 rpm.

C. If the airplane is slowed, the engine (and flyweight) rpm decreases and the valve is lowered so that engine oil (boosted by the governor pump) goes to the hub piston assembly to *decrease* pitch and increase rpm back to the preset 2200 figure.

For clarity, the *governor pump* is shown well down out of the way of the lines and valve, but it's actually boosting the engine oil pressure to the prop in (C). Also, numerous springs, valves, and other esoteria are not shown, probably causing prop engineers seeing this diagram to have a sharp rise in blood pressure; but maybe this approach will help you as a pilot to remember what's happening.

After you've read the section on *noncounterweight* props, you can see in the simplified diagram here that by reversing the sump and engine oil pressure lines to the governor the actions in B and C could be reversed.

The governor has its own gear-type pump, which, like the flywheel, is geared to and driven by the engine. The governor pump boosts the oil pressure at the prop to give quick and positive response by the propeller. One type of governor pump, for example, boosts the engine oil pressure of 60 psi to 275 psi.

Possible indications of governor trouble are seen by a constant hunting for the prechosen rpm or difficulty in setting a specific rpm. The governor controls the propeller through a particular upper range of rpm (say, 2000 to 2600 rpm).

Some governors may be set up for single-acting operation in either direction, or double action. Governor oil pressure can be used either to increase or decrease pitch, or both. In looking at the counterweight-equipped propeller the governor oil pressure was used to decrease, or flatten, the pitch. In the noncounterweight type it would be used to increase the pitch. *This type of system is now used on featherable propellers (not on single-engine airplanes);* further results of a loss of oil pressure will be covered in that section.

Noncounterweight Propellers. This is a system with no counterweights in which oil pressure, working through the prop governor (and into the piston-cylinder system), moves the actuator arms to *increase* the pitch, opposing (1) the natural "down" pitching moment of the airfoil (blade) and (2) a spring, to maintain a prechosen rpm set by you.

So what, you ask. What can I do about it in the air anyway, if something goes wrong? If you have an idea beforehand of what a certain type of prop will do (if, for instance, all governor oil pressure was lost), you'd be able to figure how it would affect your flight now and in the immediate future. In this type of propeller, sudden and complete loss of oil pressure *in the prop hub system* at cruise would mean that the blades would go to low pitch and you'd have a noisy, high-rpm situation. You'd have no control over the propeller but the high-rpm condition would be very handy if a go-around during that approach to the airport was required. So, the point about reviewing the system is that if the rpm suddenly goes to astounding numbers you will know what's happening and won't hit the panic button but instead make moves to correct the situation and plan for an approach (and landing) at the nearest reasonable airport. (Assume for discussion purposes that the lack-of-oil problem is in the prop alone and the engine itself is still getting plenty of oil.) What could be done to help the situation as you head for the airport? One thing you could do is called "putting a load on the prop," or pulling the nose up to slow the airplane up (plus throttling back to decrease the power input). Basically in this condition (overspeed) you are flying a fixed-pitch prop and it would be as if the throttle on that (very low) fixed-pitch-prop airplane were *locked* full open at a high airspeed. How could you get the rpm back down to a reasonable, low figure in that case? You'd have to slow the airplane up since you couldn't throttle back to get the rpm to decrease.

Feathering Propellers

OIL-COUNTERWEIGHT TYPE. There are a couple of types of feathering propellers, and you'll have more practical interest in them when you start flying twins (Chap. 15). But the theory and operation of the system will be covered here with the other types of constant-speed props.

One type of feathering propeller has the counterweights and spring discussed earlier. You recall that in that type, oil pressure is used to put the prop into low pitch, and the counterweights (and a spring) work to increase the pitch. In the older, nonfeathering types, when the prop control was pulled back to the full-aft position, oil was let out of the hub cylinder and the pitch increased to the high-pitch limit stop, as the

counterweights and spring were then in command. The high pitch was still in a "normal flying regime" but rpm was low in this setting.

The feathering prop uses the same idea only more so. (The prop, when feathered, goes to a very high pitch—going from, say, 15° to 80° to the plane of rotation.) The normal high- and low-pitch limits still stand as long as the propeller control is being moved in the normal range. But when you move the control into the feathering detent a mechanical linkage overrides the flyweights and speeder spring. In the feather setting, the governor lever and shaft are turned beyond the normal high pitch and the pilot valve is lifted. Oil flows out of the propeller, oil pressure is lost, and it moves to feather pitch.

To unfeather (without an accumulator system) the prop control is moved to the full-forward position and the starter engaged. When the engine is turning over, oil pressure will come up to bring the prop blades out of feather. The accumulator, which stores oil pressure for unfeathering, will be discussed in Chap. 15.

The question arises as to why the feathering props don't feather every time the engine is shut down (and the oil pressure goes to zero). The props *would* feather except that a spring-loaded centrifugal latch is inside each propeller hub system. The latch is held out of engagement by centrifugal force. When the engine is shut down in the air, the windmilling prop holds the latch *out* and the prop can be moved into feather pitch. When the prop is shut down on the ground the propellers are in low pitch and after shutdown there is no windmilling. As soon as the propeller slows down to about 600 rpm, the spring pulls the latch into engagement before oil pressure is lost. The latch holds the blades at an angle a few degrees above low pitch so that there will be no problems with the next start.

AIR-OIL TYPE. One type of feathering propeller uses governor oil pressure *and* the twisting movement of the blade to move the prop into low pitch (high rpm); these factors are opposed by compressed air or nitrogen trapped between the cylinder head and the piston. The compressed air takes the place of the counterweights on other types and furnishes the force for feathering when the control is moved into the feather detent.

For one air-oil propeller, the air chamber is charged with dry air or dry nitrogen gas at 175 psi at 70°F and the pressure is decreased ⅓ psi for each 1°F reduction in temperature. (A placard giving charge pressure versus temperature is attached to the propeller cylinder.) The main reason for using *dry* air or nitrogen is that excessive moisture could cause the piston to freeze in place in very cold weather.

You can see that if the air pressure is lost or not kept up, the propeller could tend to go to and stay in flat pitch and feathering could be difficult or impossible. This type of propeller, because no counterweights are required, saves a significant amount of Weight.

With the air-oil feathering type, if engine oil pressure is lost the propeller will automatically feather. This would be better for twin performance than to have the prop going into full *flat* pitch in that situation.

With a feathering propeller with an air system and *counterweights* or *springs*, a loss of air charge may result in

1. The pretakeoff feathering check being sluggish or slow

2. Rpm control being sluggish in flight, particularly when moved in the direction of reduced rpm.

3. A slight overspeed (or poor synchronization) in multiengine airplanes at the upper end of the prop speed range

4. The prop overspeeding when the throttle is opened rapidly, accompanied with poor rpm recovery

Your job, when you become a commercial pilot (or a

private pilot flying more complex airplanes), will be to keep up with what is required in checking or service of the constant-speed prop. The fixed-pitch type you've been using only required checking for nicks and security and safetying of the nuts holding it on. Now you'll also look for oil or grease leaks at the hub area and ensure that the air pressure, if your plane has that type of prop, is kept up. The spinner will cover more of the mechanism than you'd like for easy preflight inspection, but centrifugal force will move oil or grease leaks out along the blades where they can be seen.

To sum up some ideas for keeping the prop in good shape, a leading propeller manufacturer suggests the following as a guide for service instructions:

1. *Propeller care* — Be careful about where you run up the engine; loose stones and cinders can be sucked up into the prop. When starting a takeoff on an area having loose gravel or stones, allow the airplane to build up speed before you open the throttle fully. A nick in the leading edge of the propeller can be a stress raiser. Cracks can start, with the possibility of losing a tip and big problems to follow. The critical area is 5 to 9 in. from the tip where the highest vibratory stresses are found. The mechanic can file (round out) the nicks and polish the surface with fine emery cloth to assure that stresses wouldn't be concentrated at the point of the nick. Steel hub parts shouldn't be allowed to rust; use aluminum paint to touch them up as necessary, or they may be replated during the prop overhaul.

2. *Daily inspection* — Check the blade, spinner, and visible hub parts for damage or cracks. Check for grease or oil leakage.

3. *100-hr inspection* — Generally the following is to be done on the 100-hr and/or annual inspection:

a. Remove spinner

b. Check for nicks and cracks in the blades. Remove leading edge nicks.

c. Inspect the hub parts for cracks and all visible parts for wear and safety.

d. Check for oil and grease leaks.

e. Check the air pressure in the cylinder of air-oil feathering propellers. Use manufacturer's recommended figure for pressure and use dry nitrogen gas if available.

4. *1000- or 1500-hr inspection* (this is normally coincided with the engine overhaul and is done at an authorized repair station) — The following steps are listed:

a. Remove prop and completely disassemble.

b. Magnetic inspect all steel parts. Inspect aluminum parts by the dye penetrate method.

c. Inspect and refinish blades and if eroded or nicked, anodize.

d. Inspect all parts for wear. Replace worn parts and replace steel parts if necessary. After plating, bake parts in oven at 375° for 3 hr.

e. Reassemble the prop and grease and balance it.

Talk to the local mechanics and read the *Propeller Owner's Manual* for a specific guide to the care of your propeller(s).

Pretakeoff Check of Controllable-Pitch-Propeller Airplane.

Maybe this seems to be a little late in the chapter to discuss the preflight check of the propeller since the takeoff, cruise, and landing procedures have been covered, but you should have an idea of its use so you know what to look for during the check.

It's best *not* to check the magnetos of a constant-speed-prop-equipped airplane when the rpm setting is in the constant-speed operating range. If you switch to a bad magneto and the rpm starts to drop, the governor will sense it and automatically flatten pitch to keep the tachometer hand at its old reading. The constant-speed prop will, because of its inherent design, tend to mask fouled plugs, bad mags, etc. You will check the magnetos before takeoff *below* the governor operating range to get a true picture. Usually this is done somewhere between 1700 and 2000 rpm with the prop control full forward (high rpm).

You will want to check the propeller operation before takeoff. Run the prop control through its range, starting with the prop in full-high rpm and at the tachometer reading recommended by the manufacturer (usually around 2000 rpm). Pull the prop control aft to reduce rpm. Don't leave it back too long as the mp will be too high for the rpm. Most pilots pull the prop control back and immediately move it forward before the rpm drops off too far. With practice you can check the response of the propeller the instant the control is moved aft.

In really cold weather you won't get a good response the first time or two you cycle the prop. The oil that's been sitting in the hub overnight, or longer, will be thick and will need to be replaced by the warm engine oil as you cycle it. If you don't get good workable oil in the prop system there may be problems with "hunting" (the prop not holding the preset rpm) or poor response to prop-control-setting changes. This also could be a problem if you are flying a long time in very cold weather at a constant-prop control setting. The prop wants to hunt because the oil in the hub has thickened in the cold. Periodically changing rpm (up and down) within allowed mp and rpm combination limits can help this problem. (Using multiviscosity oil or special lubricants makes matters much better in this regard.)

SUMMARY

When you decide to check out in the airplane with a controllable-pitch prop and manifold pressure gage, give yourself a few days. Sit in the cockpit and become familiar with the new controls. Go over in your mind the various steps for takeoff, climb, cruise, and landing. Ask questions. It's hard to jump cold into a new airplane and do a good job the first time. The professional pilots realize this and spend time in the cockpit before actually flying a new type or model. You might also review Chaps. 2 and 4 concerning controllable-pitch propellers and the mp gage if you plan on checking out in an airplane so equipped.

Review the *POH, Engine Manual,* and *Propeller Manual* so that you'll be familiar with possible problems. As always, you'll want to keep surprises to a minimum.

13 New and Advanced Fuel Systems

The information given here, of course, is general. For specifics, consult the *POH* for the airplane you are flying.

THE FUEL BOOST PUMP

Maybe most of your flying to date has been done in high-wing airplanes using one or at most two fuel tanks and a gravity fuel system. When you start flying low-wing airplanes with wing tanks, the need for an engine-driven fuel pump will become evident. Very few cases of airplane engine–driven fuel pump failures are on record. But it *could* happen, so means are furnished to provide fuel pressure in the event of a failure. High-wing airplanes having fuel-injected engines (and also some using carburetors) require an engine-driven (constantly operating) fuel pump because of the high fuel pressure requirements, which will be discussed shortly.

In earlier days backup was provided by a "wobble pump," a mechanical lever used to pump up fuel pressure for starting and in flight if necessary. The handle usually was placed so that maximum muscle strain was needed to work it. After a long siege of pumping, the pilot "wobbled" when leaving the cockpit. (Actually the name is derived from the movement of the handle.) In older multiengine airplanes equipped with a wobble pump, the copilot stood by to use it should one of the engine-driven pumps fail on takeoff.

People being what they are—lazy—the electric boost pump came into use. It is turned on to aid in starting and again turned on to standby during the takeoff when a loss of fuel pressure is most serious. Of course, it could always be turned on should the engine-driven pump fail, but the delay during takeoff could cause serious problems. The boost pump also is turned on before landing, as it would be most embarrassing to lose the engine-driven pump if you were too low to make the runway without power. Your big problem for the first few flights will be remembering to turn it on or off at the right times.

After takeoff, turn the boost pump off as soon as a safe altitude has been reached—a lot of pilots use 500 ft as a minimum; your check pilot may have recommendations. *Always look at the fuel pressure gage as you turn the boost pump off after takeoff.* If the pressure starts going down to zero, better get the boost pump back on and get back to the airport because the indications are that the engine-driven pump has failed and the boost pump has been carrying the load. Don't just automatically flick the switch off without looking, as that way the first warning you'll have will be the engine stopping—and it may be hard to get going, even with the boost pump on again.

Assuming you use the boost for starting, turn it off temporarily sometime between starting and takeoff to see if the engine-driven pump is operating. In some airplanes with carburetors it's hard to tell the difference in fuel pressure with the boost pump on or off with the engine running; that is, its pressure is not noticeably additive to the engine-driven pump pressure. On others, it's noticeable right away. Check the operation of the boost pump (or pumps) for the carburetor-type engine *before* the engine is started, after turning the master battery switch and boost pump on. The boost pump should give a pressure reading in the normal operation range

for the engine-driven pumps. This prestart check is not recommended for fuel injection engines as it will likely cause flooding if the engine is hot.

Some boost pumps have three-position switches: ON, OFF, and PRIME. The PRIME position is a low-pressure position for priming and starting. The ON position also runs the pumps at low speed as long as the engine-driven pump is running. If the engine-driven pump fails with the boost pump switch ON, the boost pump will automatically switch to high-speed operation. This system, because of its complexity, normally is used on multiengine airplanes.

The *POH*s for some airplanes require the use of boost pumps throughout the start. Others recommended their use to build up pressure *before* the start and turning them off during the actual starting process. Still others don't suggest using boost pumps for starting.

Some boost pumps are located in the fuel line system; others are "submerged." The submerged boost pumps are normally only in the main fuel tanks. This is one reason why takeoffs and landings are made on the main tanks for most airplanes.

The boost pump may seem to be an additional problem to cope with, but if you remember its purpose—to furnish fuel pressure when the engine isn't running (before the start) or when the engine-driven pump has failed, or may fail—you'll have no problem with its use. Remember, it is a starting aid or a safety standby.

TANK SYSTEMS AND FUEL MANAGEMENT

The airplane may have both main and auxiliary tanks. Naturally the manufacturer would prefer to have all the fuel in one tank as this would simplify the fuel system. Unfortunately, this is not possible from either a structural or a space standpoint for larger airplanes.

When you first look at the fuel system diagram of the new airplane you'll wonder how you'll ever learn which tank should be used at what time (Fig. 13-1). It may not be clear until you have actually used the tank system. After the check pilot has described the fuel management and you have flown the airplane, go back to the *POH* again—it'll be a lot clearer. Ask yourself WHY certain tanks are used at certain times and not at others.

Fig. 13-1. Sometimes the fuel system seems a little complicated at first glance.

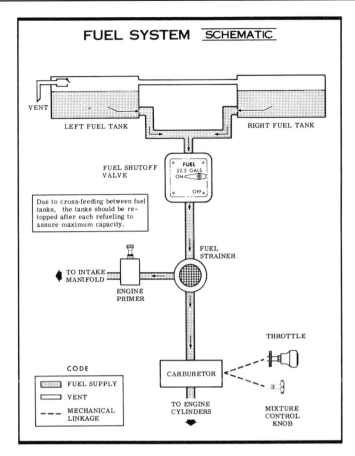

Fig. 13-2. Fuel schematic.

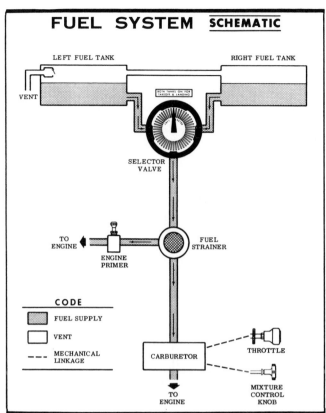

Fig. 13-3. Fuel schematic.

Fuel Systems. Figs. 13-2 through 13-8 show some representative types of fuel systems, in a generally ascending order of complexity.

Fig. 13-2, the simplest type of system, uses gravity to feed the carburetor simultaneously from both tanks. The selector (or fuel shutoff valve) in this case has two positions, ON and OFF. Note that a vent system is needed, basically for the same reason that you punch that extra hole in a can of oil to expedite the flow. (No vent would mean no fuel flow after a while.) In this case the tanks are vented together with the outlet at the left strut wing junction.

Fig. 13-3 is the next step in complexity. In this high-wing, gravity-fed carburetor system, the pilot has BOTH, LEFT, RIGHT, and OFF selections available. The *POH* advises that the selector be on BOTH for takeoff and landing. The two tanks in this system are vented together here (as in Fig. 13-2). (Note the one-way vent valves for the two airplanes.) The individual tank selections allow the pilot to compensate for unequal flow and lateral trim on longer flights.

Fig. 13-4 is the fuel system for a carbureted high-wing airplane equipped with an engine-driven pump and an auxiliary (boost) pump. Fuel from each wing tank flows through the selector valve small reservoir and a fuel shutoff valve to the fuel strainer. From there it's routed to the engine-driven pump, which delivers fuel under pressure to the carburetor. The electric aux pump, which parallels the engine-driven pump, is used when the fuel pressure drops below 2 psi. It's not necessary to have the auxiliary pump operating during normal takeoff and landing since gravity feed supplies adequate fuel flow to the carburetor with the engine-driven pump inoperative. However, this airplane has a comparatively low "high wing," and gravity flow is considerably reduced at maximum performance takeoff and climb attitudes. The aux fuel

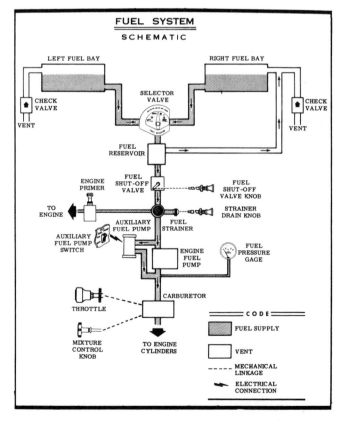

Fig. 13-4. Fuel system. Note the separate fuel shut-off valve.

pump *would* be needed if the engine-driven pump should fail during those maneuvers.

Fig. 13-5 shows the system for a popular low-wing trainer (carburetor). The fuel selector has three settings, LEFT, RIGHT, and OFF. The vast majority of low-wing airplanes (fuel injected or carburetor) and some high-wing airplanes with fuel injection don't have a BOTH selection. The fuller tank is used for takeoff and landing, and the selector is switched as necessary in cruise for lateral trim.

The electric fuel pump in this system is used as a standby for takeoff and landing and whenever the engine-driven pump fails.

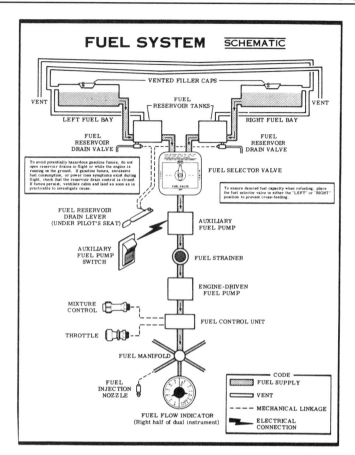

Fig. 13-6. Fuel system.

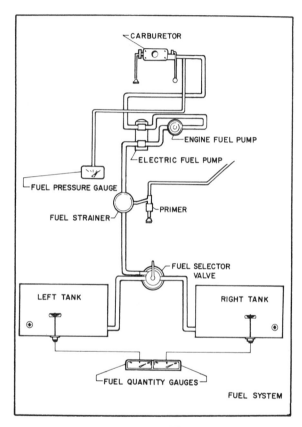

Fig. 13-5. Fuel system.

Fig. 13-6 is the system for a high-wing airplane (fuel injected) with two wing tanks. It looks complicated but a close study shows that everything makes sense. This is the first system shown with two reservoir tanks. This system is one method of assuring constant fuel flow for a predetermined time in fairly radical pitch or bank (slip) conditions where one of the main tank outlets might be exposed and fuel is not getting to the line when the fuel level is low.

This airplane is cross-vented (and the reservoir tanks are also vented to the system). The size of the vents in *any* fuel system depends on the fuel flow requirement for the engine. This is a fuel injection–equipped engine (*Lycoming* IO-360A1B6D—more about the designation later in the chapter) and has a fuel control unit rather than a carburetor. Basically, in any system, you'll have a tank drain for each tank (this equipment should not be, but often is, *optional*) and a drain at the fuel strainer.

Fig. 13-7 is a schematic for a high-wing airplane using a different fuel injection system from the one just discussed. This system design furnishes more fuel to the fuel control unit than needed and has a return line for vapor and excess fuel.

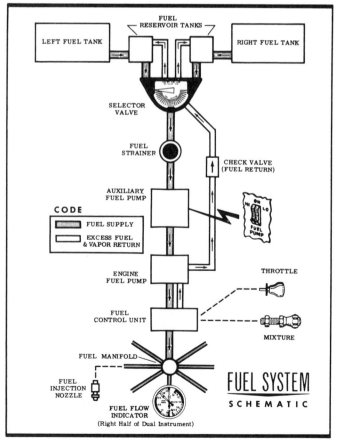

Fig. 13-7. Fuel system schematic.

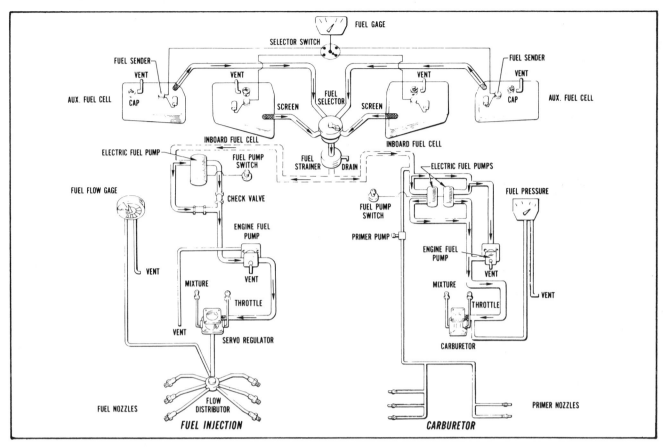

Fig. 13-8. Fuel injection and carburetor fuel systems.

(The system in Fig. 13-6 is a demand-type system; it furnishes fuel as needed to mix with the air and does not require a return line. This type will be covered later in the chapter.) The returned fuel goes to the reservoir tank of the tank selected (left or right), which means that the engine is really only taking a predictable amount of fuel since what isn't used is put back into the same tank. Some earlier makes and models of single-engine airplanes returned excess fuel to the left (main) tank only.

The fuel system represented by Fig. 13-8 shows two options for fuel distribution. The tanks are the same, but you'll note that following the fuel strainer a carburetor or fuel injection system may be used. Compare Figs. 13-5, -6, -7, and -8. Note that the fuel pressure is taken from a point between the fuel pump(s) and the carburetor for the carburetor-equipped engine, and at the fuel manifold (or fuel distributor, depending on the manufacturer's term for it) for the fuel-injected engine. In effect, the gage measures the pressure available to the carburetor (which is normally a constant for all power settings, say, 3 to 5 lb) for the that type. In the injected engine the gage measures the relative amount of fuel going through the flow distributor and so varies with mixture *and* power being used. The electric fuel pump on a carburetor engine may be energized indefinitely with the engine not running (with the fuel ON and mixture rich) without flooding (loading up) the engine. Turn on the electric fuel pump in a fuel injection engine under the conditions just cited and you'll pump fuel out on the ground.

The systems just covered include some on airplanes that are no longer in production as well as current types. In Chap. 15, the fuel systems of twins will be covered.

Fuel management includes the use of crossfeed for multi-engine airplanes as well. The use of the crossfeed control will be covered in that chapter.

Some airplanes have an amber LOW FUEL warning light

(or two lights, as required) on the annunciator panel in full view of the pilot. These are usually set to illuminate at a reasonably low fuel quantity but with enough warning for you to make other plans, such as finding a nearby convenient airport instead of completing the last thousand miles of your trip.

LEANING

As an all-around figure, gasoline engine mixtures for combustion are about 1:15, that is, about 1 lb fuel to every 15 lb air—or about 7% fuel and 93% air by weight. For richer mixtures an 8 to 10% fuel-air ratio is found.

For takeoff, a mixture setting of "full rich" is used. This setting assures the best combination of power *and* cooling. The full-rich setting will be slightly richer than best power, but as engine cooling also depends on a richer mixture a compromise must be made.

With the mixture in the full-rich position you'll be using a predetermined mixture of fuel and air. As you climb, naturally the air becomes less dense (weighs less per unit volume). On the full-rich setting your carburetor is putting out about the same amount of fuel but there's less air to mix with it, so the mixture gets richer and richer. In fact, you may climb so high in full-rich that the engine will start to run rough; the fuel-air ratio is too great for smooth operation. So, you not only are losing power but are using fuel like there's no tomorrow (compared with what you should be consuming). After reaching the desired cruise altitude, you'll level off, set cruise power, and lean the mixture. Your job with the mixture control is to establish the optimum fuel-air ratio for all conditions.

Fig. 13-9 takes a general look at the effects of mixture on power, specific fuel consumption (pounds per horsepower per hour), and exhaust gas and cylinder head temperatures.

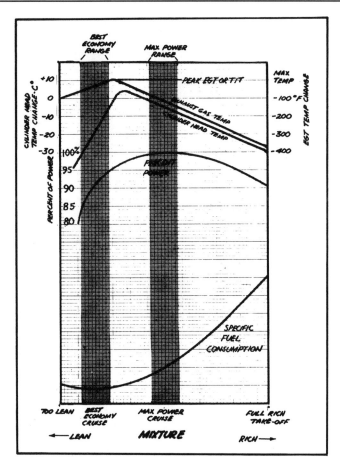

Fig. 13-9. Effect of leaning on cylinder head temperature, exhaust gas temperature (EGT), engine power, and specific fuel consumption at a constant engine rpm and manifold pressure. (*Avco Lycoming Flyer*)

Mixture Control with Carburetor. There will be times when handling the mixture control will be very important. In Chap. 7 you learned that proper leaning of the mixture is vital for both best range and max endurance. There are nearly as many techniques for leaning as there are pilots. A couple of the less complicated ones will be discussed here.

First, it is assumed that you have neither a fuel mixture indicator (very likely you won't), a cylinder head temperature gage, or an EGT gage. In other words, you'll be leaning the mixture more or less by feel.

After leveling off and establishing the desired power setting, ease the mixture control back until the engine begins to roughen slightly. Ease it forward just until the engine smooths. This is the system most used for airplanes not equipped with an excess of gages for engine information.

A variation of the above technique is to lean the mixture with the engine operating on one magneto, as a too-lean mixture will show up more quickly than it would on BOTH. (Of course, as soon as you've set the mixture you'll go back to BOTH mags.) Most pilots don't bother to do this, and it's doubtful if a noticeable advantage is gained by using this technique.

If a cylinder head temperature gage is available, many pilots prefer to use it in leaning the mixture, particularly with a constant-speed propeller. The first method above will work with a constant-speed propeller but sometimes requires more experience because the actions of the governor tend to mask the roughness caused by the too-lean mixture.

Here is a typical method of leaning a carburetor engine using the cylinder head temperature. Set power at desired rpm and manifold pressure for cruise. Leave the mixture rich and allow the cylinder head temperature to stabilize. Begin leaning in increments, observing the cylinder head temperature. When the cylinder head temperature peaks, this is your final mixture setting for that altitude. Don't permit the cylinder head temperature to exceed the limit given in the *POH* or *Engine Manual*. If a sudden temperature rise should occur during the process, move the mixture control back to the position before the temperature increase. (You overdid it a little.) Let the engine stabilize for at least 5 min before leaning the mixture for a further cylinder head temperature reading. If the cylinder head temperature lead is on a lean cylinder, you may get a drop in temperature as you lean it out (you are decreasing power at that cylinder and decreasing the temperature for the engine as indicated by the gage).

The exhaust gas temperature gage (EGT) is an excellent aid in properly setting the mixture. The system is composed of an instrument on the panel connected to a probe in the exhaust stack(s) so that the EGT may be taken and indicated. Since excess fuel or excess air in the mixture produces a cooling effect (lowering the exhaust temperature), the EGT gage may be used to find the optimum for cruise and other conditions.

As an example for one engine, to set up a cruise-leaned situation (at 75% power or less) using one of these instruments, lean the mixture until the EGT needle peaks. Then richen the mixture until the needle shows at least a 25°F temperature drop (this puts the mixture on the rich side of the highest EGT). The 25°F drop is best for fuel economy. A drop of 100°F (on the rich side) is in the area for best power. If your airplane has one of these systems you should read the accompanying literature and talk with pilots who've used it before using it on your own. The *POH* for a particular airplane is the ultimate guide for EGT use.

A common erroneous idea is that an engine should not be leaned under 5000 ft *under any circumstances*. One engine manufacturer notes that their normally aspirated, direct-drive engines with a manual mixture control should be leaned at cruise powers of 75% or less at any altitude while cruising. The 5000-ft rule is only for climbing. In other words, in the climb use full rich to 5000 MSL, then lean for added power and smoothness. Other airplanes have a lower limit of 3000 ft for lean in the climb. If you're flying the type of engine(s) just described at, say, 1500 ft MSL at 74% power at cruise, go ahead and lean; there's no need to burn fuel you could use later. As will be noted in Chap. 19, turbocharged and other more complex engines have specified operating procedures.

To lean the carburetor-type engine at *cruise*, a leading engine manufacturer suggests the following:

1. Fixed-pitch prop—Lean to a maximum increase in rpm, or just before engine roughness.

2. Controllable prop—Lean until roughness is encountered, then richen slightly to eliminate roughness for smooth operation.

Suppose you are taking off from a field at high altitude and/or temperature (you are at a high density-altitude). It is likely that with the mixture control in the full-rich setting the weight of fuel going into the engine is too great for the weight of the air mixed with it; that is, the mixture at that setting and altitude is so rich that the engine is not developing full power (Fig. 13-10).

Under these conditions, particularly if the field is short and power is needed badly, some pilots run the engine up to some point just below prop-governor operating speed and move the mixture control back until there is a definite pickup of rpm. The peak indicates the best power mixture setting for the density-altitude. The mixture control should be moved

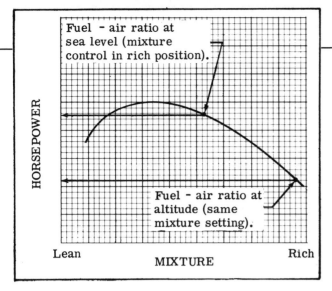

Fig. 13-10. A high density-altitude and a full rich setting mean a power loss.

slightly forward of this maximum power point so the mixture will be a little on the rich side to ensure proper cooling. The mixture is normally preset to be slightly richer than best power for this reason when in the full-rich position, even at sea level conditions. It is better to be slightly on the rich side to avoid possible engine damage — even if it means a small deviation from best power. The density-altitude has to be fairly high before leaning has very much effect in increasing takeoff power.

A common error made by the pilot new to the mixture control is, after setting the mixture for best cruise at some fairly high altitude, starting the descent to the destination airport and forgetting about the mixture. During descent, the air density increases but the carburetor is still putting out the same amount of fuel that worked so well at the higher altitude. Finally the comparable amount of fuel-air becomes so lean that the engine starts running rough and gives every sign of quitting any second. The simple remedy is to richen the mixture and all is well again. You actually have two choices in the matter of the descent. (1) You can push the mixture control all the way forward to full rich and not have to worry about it, or (2) you can richen the mixture in increments by guess as you go down. In (1) if you are very high the engine operation may roughen slightly (it's assumed that you plan on using cruise power during the descent) but will soon smooth out as you lose altitude and you won't be as apt to forget to move it into full rich for landing.

VAPORIZATION. It would seem that, all other things being equal, the colder the air entering the carburetor, the denser it is and the more power would be developed. However, fuel particles do not mix as well with cold air, and fuel may be wasted.

For best vaporization a carburetor air inlet temperature of 90° to 100°F is ideal. This could mean using carburetor heat. If you are interested in maximum economy, *after* setting power, use carburetor heat to establish this temperature and then lean the mixture in one of the ways mentioned earlier. Your airplane may not have a carburetor inlet temperature gage (measuring the air temperature just *before* it goes into the carburetor), so another technique may be used.

In order to find the probable best heat setting for vaporization, lean the engine until it just starts to run rough — then apply enough carburetor heat to smooth it out (the less-dense warm air will result in a comparatively richer mixture, hence the smoothness). This is the probable heat control setting for best vaporization. *The addition of carburetor heat usually means higher engine temperatures and could be overdone in*

warmer weather, perhaps leading to detonation at high power settings.

There's some confusion between *detonation* and *surface ignition* or *preignition* (people sometimes say one when they mean the other):

Detonation — As noted by FAA AC 65–9 *Airframe and Powerplant Mechanics General Handbook*, in an engine operating in a normal manner, the flame front in the cylinder traverses the charge at a *steady* velocity of about 100 ft per second. When *detonation* occurs, the first portion of the charge burns in a normal manner but the last portion burns almost instantaneously, creating an excessive momentary pressure imbalance in the combustion chamber. The cylinder head temperature will rise, engine efficiency decreases, and structural damage occurs to the piston or cylinder head. You can hear the "knock" in an automobile engine but other sounds cover it in an aircraft engine, so you'll have to depend on the instruments for indications. Normal burning or detonation might be compared with smoothly pushing the piston down with your hand or hitting the piston with a hammer to move it down.

If you suspect that detonation is occurring, throttle back, make sure the mixture is rich, open cowl flaps, and *ease* the nose down to assure that good cooling can occur.

Surface ignition or *preignition* — This is caused by hot spots or surfaces in the chamber igniting the fuel-air mixture. If this happens before the spark plugs get the chance to do their thing, it's called *preignition*. Power loss and roughness occur. It's generally attributed to overheating of spark plug electrodes (glow plugs in model airplane engines use this principle for *normal* ignition) and exhaust valves and to carbon deposits. In the days before idle shutoff systems were used for trainers, preignition was sometimes a problem and the engine would continue to run after the ignition switch was turned off. Usually opening the throttle as the switch was cut helped cool off matters, but in extreme cases the fuel had to be shut off to stop the engine.

Some mixture controls have AUTO LEAN setting positions. The more complex carburetor has an automatic altitude compensator. It contains a bellows that senses the incoming air pressure and controls the fuel metering accordingly. If you set the mixture at best economy at 5000 ft and climb to 10,000 ft, the mixture will also be at best lean at the higher altitude — even though you haven't touched the mixture control. It is assumed here that you used a *cruise climb* and didn't need to increase the richness for the climb.

FUEL INJECTION

The big advantage of fuel injection is that carburetor icing is no longer present. The fuel is injected into the intake manifold just before going into the cylinder; hence there is no temperature drop in the carburetor due to vaporization. The air temperature drops in the carburetor for two reasons: (1) vaporization and (2) the lowered pressure caused by the venturi effect — these two effects being additive.

Of course, you can get impact icing in freezing rain, etc., in either type of fuel system, but this is not the kind caused by invisible moisture.

A particular advantage of fuel injection lies in the pilot's ability to lean the mixture accurately by use of the fuel pressure gage. This gage measures metered fuel pressure or the pressure of the fuel going to the spray nozzles — this being a direct measure of fuel flow. The gage usually is marked with proper fuel pressures for various power settings and/or altitudes. The lower pressure range is for various cruise power settings (45, 55, 65, or 75%). The altitude is automatically compensated for by a bellows or diaphragm within the control unit that regulates the fuel flow from the nozzles in proportion to the air pressure (volume) passing through the unit.

In addition, the gage may be marked for best power for takeoff and climb for various altitudes (this will be in the higher pressure range). Whereas the fuel pressure gage in the carburetor-equipped airplane remains constant at all power settings (it measures the pressure of the fuel from the pumps to the carburetor), the pressure gage for fuel injection varies with mixture setting. To lean this engine you merely move the mixture control until the fuel pressure or fuel flow indicates that you have the correct mixture for the power setting and/or altitude.

Another advantage of fuel injection is that it theoretically gives a better fuel-air distribution to the cylinders. This does not always occur but should if the system is properly operating, because the fuel-air is mixed in a carburetor at one place for all cylinders. By the time this mixture reaches each cylinder some variation in mixture may occur among cylinders. This is not apt to occur in the fuel injection engine because the mixing is done just before entering each cylinder.

Disadvantages of fuel injection are

1. At low power settings on hot days (such as during prolonged taxiing) vapor lock may occur and the engine may quit.

2. A hot fuel-injected engine is often very hard to start.

3. It normally takes longer for the fuel-injected engine to get power back if a tank is run dry (more about this in Chap. 16).

Leaning the Mixture. If you've leaned a carburetor-type engine, you've noticed that when the mixture is overleaned the engine will start to get rough. This is because of the initial difference in mixtures in each of the cylinders. You are leaning them all the same rate, but some cylinders were leaner to begin with and will be too lean, while the other cylinders are still operating smoothly. Naturally the engine will run rough if only part of the cylinders are getting enough fuel. This is the idea you used in manual leaning of the carburetor.

The fuel injection system, having better fuel distribution, will not react this way. As all the cylinders are getting an equal amount of fuel (theoretically), when you lean the mixture excessively there will be no initial roughness but the engine will quietly and smoothly die. Therefore it is a great deal harder to set the mixture by "feel" so a pressure gage or fuel flow gage is helpful.

Fig. 13-11 is a fuel flow indicator used on a current four-place airplane. Most indicators are of this type. The outside numbers on the meter indicate the fuel flow in gallons per hour. The following procedures are used:

STARTING. This is the starting procedure for this particular airplane (cold):

1. Set fuel selector on the proper tank.
2. Open the throttle approximately ½ in.
3. Turn on the master switch and electric auxiliary fuel pump.
4. Move the mixture control to full rich until an indication of 4 to 6 gph is indicated on the flow meter; then turn the pump off (the engine is primed).
5. Move the mixture control to idle cutoff.
6. Switch ignition ON and engage starter.
7. When the engine fires, move the mixture control to full rich.

For starting hot or flooded engines the flow meter is not used, but the engine is started with the mixture in idle cutoff and fuel pump off. (The throttle is cracked ½ in. or open respectively.) When the engine fires, move the mixture control to full rich (and retard the throttle as necessary).

TAKEOFF. For this fuel-injected airplane during a normal take-

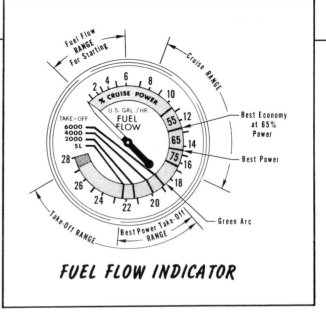

Fig. 13-11. Fuel flow indicator for a single-engine, fuel-injected airplane.

off with full-rich mixture the pointer on the fuel flow meter will stabilize between the sea level mark and the red line (Fig. 13-11). This is slightly rich to aid in fuel cooling and is recommended for normal takeoffs at sea level.

When taking off from a high-altitude field (say 4000 ft density-altitude), the mixture should be leaned to maximum power during the pretakeoff check. Full throttle is applied and the mixture control is moved toward the lean position until the pointer has stabilized at the 4000-ft mark (between the 19.5- and 20.0-gph marks). The takeoff is made with this mixture. The same technique can be used for obtaining maximum power at sea level, using the sea level mark. (Don't overheat the engine with prolonged climbs; richen it again after clearing any obstacles.)

CRUISE. The flow meter is a good aid in setting up a cruise mixture. The example of 65% power in Fig. 13-11 indicates that the two widest variations are 14.5 gph (best power) and 12.6 gph (best economy); settings should be between these limits. As you can see, 55 and 75% settings also have a range of possible settings. The EGT gage is a more precise method of leaning, however.

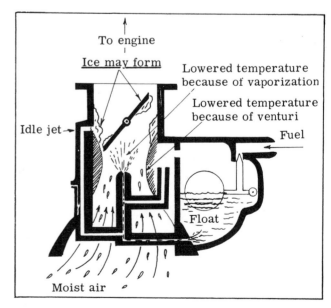

Fig. 13-12. Float carburetor, showing how ice can form.

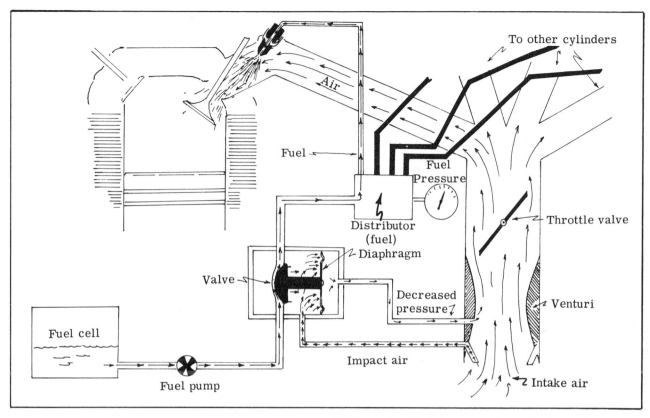

Fig. 13-13. A simplified view of one type of fuel injection system.

APPROACH AND LANDING. Set the mixture to full rich. (No reference to fuel flow meter for a *precise* setting.) The *POH* may have some suggestions on mixture settings for approaches to high-elevation (high-density-altitude) airports.

Figs. 13-12 and 13-13 show the basic differences between the three fuel-metering systems just discussed.

FUEL AND OIL FACTS

Fuel. Never use fuel rated below the minimum octane or performance numbers. You may go above the rating as a temporary arrangement, but even then try to stay as close to the recommended octane as you can. Using a lower-than-recommended-rate fuel can result in high operating (oil and cylinder head) temperatures. If your engine normally uses 100/130 octane and only 80/87 and 115/145 fuel are available, use 115/145.

The numbers are the antiknock quality of the fuel—the higher the number, the better the antiknock qualities. Take, for instance, 100/130 fuel; the first number (100) is the minimum antiknock quality of the fuel in a lean mixture, the last (130) the minimum antiknock quality in a rich mixture.

The American Society for Testing and Materials has recommended that the double figure (80/87, 100/130, etc.) be dropped for puposes of simplification and the term *grade* be substituted for the octane or performance numbers. The ratings (100 for lean and 130 for rich mixtures) still stand however.

The various octanes and performance numbered fuels are dyed different colors for easy identification.

Grade	Fuel Color
80	Red
100LL (low lead)	Blue
100	Green
115/145	Purple

The grade 100LL is used as a common fuel for airplanes requiring 80 or the 100 (higher-leaded) grade minimums. Grade 80 fuel is becoming more difficult to find in the United States.

Oil. A chapter on fuel systems may seem a rather strange place to talk about oil, but you usually check the oil when you check the fuel and should have some information on it.

The viscosity of the oil may be given in one of three ways. You are probably the most familiar with the SAE (Society of Automotive Engineers) number.

Notice that in every case except one, the commercial aviation number is exactly twice the SAE "weight." A rule of thumb to get the SAE equivalent is to divide the aviation number by two and go to the nearest number divisible by 10: $65/2 = 32\frac{1}{2}$, or 30 (the nearest number divisible by 10); $80/2 = 40$ (which is the nearest number divisible by 10, etc.).

There are two main types of aviation oil in use today for reciprocating engines:

1. *Straight mineral oil*—This oil is without any dispersant additives. It is a more or less inert lubricating medium.

2. *Ashless dispersant oils*—This type of detergent or compound oils (with additive) keep the foreign particles in solution without the disadvantages of ash-forming detergent additives.

Engine manufacturers generally recommend that new or newly overhauled engines should be operated on straight mineral oil during the first 50 hr of operation, or until oil consumption has stabilized. If an additive oil is used in these engines, high oil consumption might result, since the antifriction additive of some of these oils will retard the break-in of piston rings and cylinder walls.

Okay, what if you've been using straight mineral oil for several hundred hours and decide that it's to your advantage to start using a compounded oil? The least you'd better do is the following, according to one major engine manufacturer (making sure the compounded oil is approved for your engine):

1. Don't add the additive oil to straight mineral oil. Drain the straight mineral oil and then fill with additive oil.

2. Don't operate the engine longer than 5 hr before the first oil change.

3. Check all oil screens for evidence of sludge or plugging. Change oil every 10 hr if sludge conditions are evident. Resume normal oil drain periods after the sludge conditions improve.

If you are fairly close to overhaul you might not want to go to all that trouble. The real point is that putting additive oils in an engine that has been using straight mineral oil for several hundred hours can cause problems unless you are careful.

Along these same lines, *don't* put special "antifriction" additives in the oil; the manufacturer's warranty could be voided. Don't use automotive oil in an airplane engine. In short, follow the engine manufacturer's recommendations or make a phone call to check, if you're not sure. A couple of bucks for the call sure beats damaging an engine (and maybe damaging you and your passengers).

Since you are an "advanced pilot" and will be flying more powerful and complex engines, you should know *exactly* the type of fuel and oil to be used during servicing. A crew member should be available to oversee the fuel and oil servicing. Jet fuel *has* been mistakenly put in the tanks of airplanes with piston engines—with fatal accidents resulting in some cases.

SOME ADDED POINTS

You will have more responsibility and authority as an advanced pilot, and will have to know more things about the airplane and its maintenance requirements. This seems like a good place to follow on with some general information (courtesy of Avco Lycoming *Flyer*), particularly in the area of engine operations.

To most private pilots, the letters and numbers that describe the engine they are using are meaningless, but you can learn a lot about your engine by looking at the model code. Fig. 13–14 shows designations used.

Definitions of Engine Maintenance and Repair. You may later need to oversee the maintenance and repair of engine(s) in the airplane you're flying and so should know the types of repair or replacement services available.

NEW ENGINE. As defined by Avco Lycoming, a new engine is the original product with all new parts and accessories, meeting all production test specifications, quality control tests, and regulations for a production certificate issued by the FAA. By the time the ultimate purchaser gets the airplane, the engine will have had the airframe manufacturer's production test time plus ferry time. The engine will have a new engine warranty and will be accompanied by an *Engine Logbook*.

REMANUFACTURE. The factory remanufactured engine gives the benefits of a new engine at a price savings. The definition of a factory remanufactured engine is one originally designed and manufactured by a company and disassembled, repaired or altered, and inspected in accordance with that company's service bulletins, mandatory engineering changes, and any airworthiness directives (more about ADs later).

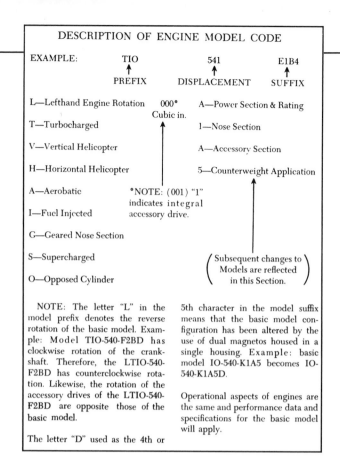

Fig. 13-14. Engine model code. (*Avco Lycoming Flyer*)

To summarize, the factory-remanufactured engine is a zero-time power plant with the same warranty as a new one. It's *re*manufactured at the same place and by the same personnel who worked on it originally.

MAJOR OVERHAUL. An engine may have a major overhaul done on it by an approved repair agency, as noted in FAR 43. Without going into details here, this FAR goes basically into the who, what, and how of major overhaul responsibilities. A major overhaul consists of the *complete* disassembly of the engine and its repair, reassembly, and testing to ensure proper operation. Engines are overhauled in the field and not by the manufacturer. One disadvantage of overhauling an engine is that the airplane is grounded during the process unless there's a spare available. Many owners trade in a run-out engine for a new or remanufactured one (getting credit for the old engine), thus saving a lot of downtime.

TOP OVERHAUL. A top overhaul is defined as repair or overhaul of parts on the outside of the crankcase without completely disassembling the engine. It includes the removal of the cylinders and deglazing the cylinder walls; inspections of pistons, valve operating mechanisms, and valve guides; and replacing of piston rings. This is done in the field; engines in earlier days had one or more top overhauls between majors.

NITRIDED AND CHROME CYLINDERS. The engine cylinders get quite a workout and the walls have to withstand friction plus the heat of combustion, and the harder the surface, the less the wear.

In 1960 Lycoming started the nitriding process to combat wear problems. This process consists of introducing an ammonia gas (NH_3) atmosphere to the practically finished part. This is done in special heat-treating, airtight furnaces at 975°F for a period of 25 to 80 hr, depending on what's required. The ammonia gas is broken down into elements of nitrogen and hydrogen. The nitrogen joins the steel and makes a very hard, wear-resistant surface. (All crankshafts and some gears are nitrided by Lycoming.) Nitrided cylinder walls increase piston ring life, giving better sealing and increased fatigue strength, compared with regular steel barrels. You can tell if your engine has nitrided barrels by (1) reading the engine manual or (2) checking for an *azure* painted band around the cylinder base (if they are painted black) or on the edges of the top cylinder head fins between the two valve push rod tubes (if the engine is painted all gray).

Some barrel walls may be chrome plated instead of nitrided (also for longer wear); the color code is orange at the places mentioned in the last paragraph.

Repair or Maintenance Notifications.

The FAA states that whenever an aircraft or engine manufacturer determines through service experience that a modification is needed to extend the life of the product or for safety purposes, the manufacturer may let the owners know of impending problems or needed (or suggested) repairs. Suppose you, an owner or operator of an airplane, get a service letter—do you have to ground the airplane immediately? There are different levels of notifications by the manufacturer, and these may apply to the airplane *and/or* the engine.

SERVICE LETTER. A service letter is product information that is optional for the owner/operator, who may decide that the changes would be nice but would be too expensive.

SERVICE INFORMATION. This is product information that the manufacturer definitely recommends compliance with. While it isn't mandatory, you'd be very wise to take advantage of the manufacturer's knowledge gained by inputs from the field.

SERVICE BULLETIN. A service letter or service instruction may be followed by a service bulletin. The bulletin outlines the trouble and tells how to remedy it. A service bulletin is technically not mandatory unless there is a time limit requirement, in which case it becomes virtually mandatory.

AIRWORTHINESS DIRECTIVE (AD NOTE). If an unsafe condition arises for an airframe or engine, the FAA issues an AD note, which specifies the component found to be unsafe and any conditions, limitations, or inspections under which the aircraft may continue to be operated. It's the aircraft owner/operator's mandatory responsibility to assure compliance with *all* AD notes. Some ADs are recurrent or repetitive, requiring certain inspections, say, every 100 hr. This must be done and recorded in the logbook each time, with the signature and certificate number of the mechanic or repair agency involved.

An AD note may have a date of effectiveness and a flight time limit for compliance. For instance, as well as giving the serial numbers of the aircraft/engines involved and referring to a service bulletin for repair procedures, the AD may basically state that "within 25 flight hours [such and such] must be done, this AD becoming effective July 10, 19____."

Know your airplane.

BACKGROUND

The biggest single step forward in decreasing airplane Drag was the improved design of retractable landing gear. At first the retracting systems were so complex and heavy that only large airplanes could use them. Now, through the use of electrical motors or very light hydraulic systems, nearly all high-performance, single-engine airplanes and all the light twins have retractable gear.

The advantages in speed and economy are obvious. You have no doubt already figured out the main disadvantage—the landing gear is sometimes retracted at what might be termed an "inopportune moment." Pilots also forget to put the landing gear *down* at the opportune moment. You usually can get away with forgetting to shove the prop control forward or forgetting to use flaps (you can take care of the prop on the sly as you taxi in), *but* you won't get away with forgetting to put the gear down. Three things are certain about gear-up landings: (1) they are definitely more noisy than the gear-down type; (2) the airplane does not "roll" as far; and (3) expenses are somewhat higher.

At some time in your flying career you will come close to landing gear-up—and you may go all the way if you aren't careful. The purpose of this chapter is to help keep you from going all the way.

So here's a *general* look at retractable-gear airplanes.

Pilot Stress.

Believe it or not, the danger period for the pilot of a retractable-gear plane normally is not the first few hours after checkout. If you are like most new checkouts, you'll spoil the enjoyment of the first few flights by muttering to yourself over and over, "Mustn't forget to put the gear down, mustn't forget the gear, mustn't...etc." After a while you'll consider yourself an old pro and the gear check will be important but not the *only* item on the checklist as it seemed to be at first.

Back to the idea of stress: One day you'll be going into Chicago O'Hare or Atlanta Hartsfield or some other busy airport. There'll be a lot of traffic and the tower will be giving instructions at a machine gun rate. Suppose you aren't able to finish the approach because of conflicting traffic and are advised by the tower to "take it around." You pull the gear up and try to work back into the downwind leg. The traffic is heavy and the pressure is on. The tower people may seem unsympathetic but their job is to expedite traffic flow with safety. You are cleared to land again and are very busy, looking for other airplanes and setting up the pattern. *In this stress situation you could forget to put the gear down again.* In the daytime the tower operators will probably catch you before you land gear-up. Many a pilot has been saved from a dangerous or embarrassing situation by an alert tower controller. But don't count on their doing a job that is rightfully yours. They're very busy.

At night you don't even have the possibility of a tower controller spotting the results of your memory lapse. The shower of sparks when you land will reveal your problem.

Always have the gear down before turning on base leg under normal conditions. If the tower clears you to enter base leg, have the gear *down* and *locked* before starting the *descent* on base. *Always check the gear indicators again after turning on final.* Some pilots point to the gear indicators so that they're sure their attention is directed there. Of course, it's possible to point to a gear-*up* light absentmindedly.

Checklist. The checklist is a valuable aid if used correctly. The trouble is that after a while you'll "know" it so thoroughly that using it becomes just a ritual done at certain times. Some pilots glance at it and don't read it. It's very easy to skip an item this way. A checklist is a liability if not used correctly—a quick glance at it may lead you to believe you've done what's necessary, giving a false sense of security. On the other hand, if you use the checklist religiously and always put the gear down at the same point, habit may save you embarrassment some time when your conscious mind is out to lunch.

GUMP (gas, undercarriage, mixture, prop) is a good back-up check, too, for landing.

Remember—just because you went through the motions and moved the right lever doesn't mean the gear is down. CHECK IT! Mechanical devices have their off-days too.

Landing Gear Systems. Fig. 14-1 is a schematic for a landing gear system that uses an electric pump to provide pressure for the hydraulic system. The system normally operates at pressures from 1000 to 1500 psi. The electrical portion of the power pack is protected by a 35-amp pull-off-type circuit breaker switch (labeled GEAR PUMP) on the left switch and control panel. (See Fig. 4-70, Chap. 4.) This CB may be pulled if the pump continues to run longer than 1 min (the

usual time for a cycle—up or down—is 5 to 7 sec) so as to avoid pump overheating.

Fig. 14-2 is a landing gear system for a twin that has an engine-driven hydraulic pump on each engine. Note that a hand pump is provided in addition to the two engine-driven pumps. Usually a hydraulic system uses a standpipe in the fluid reservoir to prevent the engine—or electric pumps—from pumping all the fluid overboard in the event of a leak. The remaining fluid may be utilized by the hand pump (Fig. 14-3).

An added point: when you first go out to the airplane to start the preflight check, confirm that the gear handle or switch is DOWN and then turn on the master switch to check for down indications.

EMERGENCY PROCEDURES

Next to the fear that you'll forget to put the gear down will be the thought, "What if it just won't come down?" The newspapers, movies, and television have probably milked more drama out of this situation than any other phase of flying. If it won't come down, you'll probably bend the prop and scrape some paint off the belly. But the cases of pilots of general aviation planes being physically unable to lower the gear by any means are extremely rare. Manufacturers frown on people belly-landing their products. This makes their airplanes look bad, and they try to arrange it so gear-up landings aren't necessary. Actuating arms and other mechanical parts

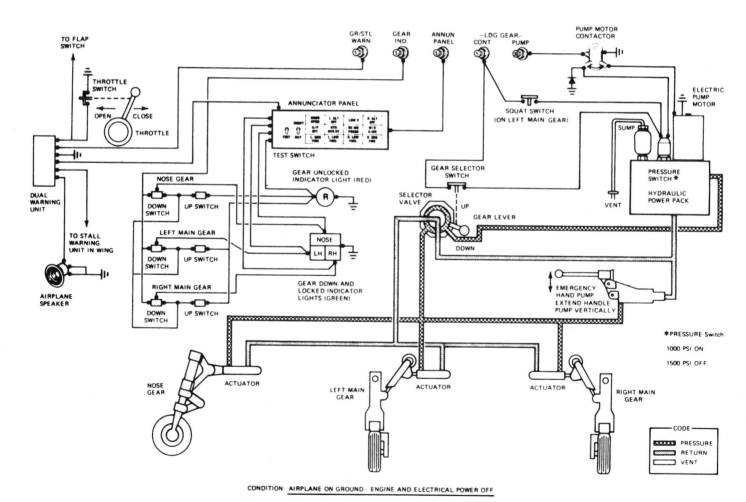

Fig. 14-1. Electrical-hydraulic landing gear system. Note the emergency hand pump for lowering the gear. The *POH* Emergency Procedures section and the checklist detail the procedures.

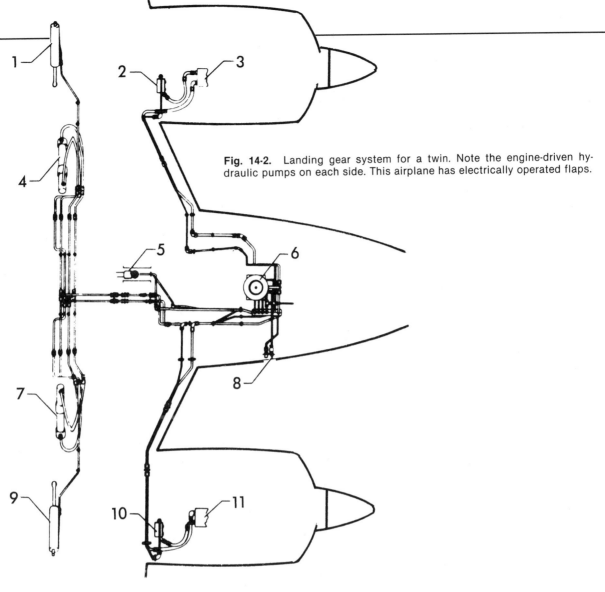

Fig. 14-2. Landing gear system for a twin. Note the engine-driven hydraulic pumps on each side. This airplane has electrically operated flaps.

1. LEFT MAIN GEAR ACTUATING CYLINDER
2. LEFT HYDRAULIC PUMP FILTER
3. LEFT HYDRAULIC PUMP
4. LEFT GEAR DOOR ACTUATING CYLINDER
5. EMERGENCY HAND PUMP
6. POWER PACK ASSEMBLY

7. RIGHT GEAR DOOR ACTUATING CYLINDER
8. CHECK VALVES
9. RIGHT MAIN GEAR ACTUATING CYLINDERS
10. RIGHT HYDRAULIC PUMP FILTER
11. RIGHT HYDRAULIC PUMP

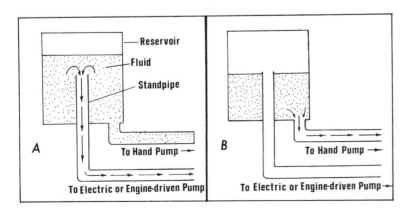

Fig. 14-3. A simplified look at a standpipe principle. A. Under normal conditions (plenty of hydraulic fluid), the standpipe is the route of the fluid to the pump(s) and system. The hand pump line is essentially closed off. B. When a leak occurs the engine-driven or electric pump(s) may pump the fluid overboard until it gets down to the top of the standpipe. The remaining fluid is available for use when the hand pump system is used. The hand pump is considered a carefully planned one-shot operation (gear-down only) because the leak may be at a point such that much or all of the remaining fluid could be lost during the hand pumping process.

have been known to fail, but the majority of the belly landings made by general aviation planes are due to pilot oversight, not structural failure.

While in flight suppose you put the gear handle or switch down and can see no green light? You probably got in, started the airplane, and went about your business — overlooking the fact that there was no down-light when you taxied out and not noticing that there was no up-light after you pulled the gear up. Here's where the ball is dropped at the beginning of the flight. *As soon as you get in the airplane, check the position of the gear handle or switch. When the master switch is turned on for start, check for a down-light.* Somebody might have tinkered around in the cockpit and moved the control to the up position. If the safety lock isn't working, the plane could slowly sink to the ground as you start to taxi. This is unlikely, but there's no need to take a chance.

In some airplanes, when the navigation lights are on, the landing gear indicator lights are dimmed because the bright lights are disconcerting at night. If the navigation lights are on in the daytime, the gear indicator lights may be so dim as to appear to be off. There have been many cases of newly checked-out pilots calling on Unicom to state that the gear isn't down. One of the first things old pilots in the airport office ask is, "Are your navigation lights off?" This usually is answered by a long pause and a rather weak, "Uh, Roger." The embarrassed pilot comes in and lands, the gear having been down all the time but the lights dimmed.

The new pilot has a red face, but this is far better than taking a chance on bellying it in. In cases like this, new pilots have been known to use the normal *and* emergency means of lowering the gear and still not seeing a down indication (naturally).

Some airplanes with electrically operated landing gear have a three-position switch (UP, OFF, and DOWN), and it's possible to stop in the middle or OFF position instead of DOWN.

Suppose you've put the gear switch or handle down and instead of three green lights (nose and both main gears down and locked) you see that there is no green light for the left main gear (the other two greens are bright and clear). Should you put passengers on the right side of the airplane and prepare for a two-wheel landing? Get the runway foamed? Recycle the gear several times to try to get the left main gear extended? *Not yet. It could be a bulb problem* (the gear is down but the left gear light bulb isn't working). In a four-bulb setup (three green for *down* and one amber for *all up*), you should first take out the amber up-bulb and use it to replace the left main bulb. It would be foolish to get everybody in a dither when a bulb worth a few cents is the cause of your concern. (A pilot in this situation *could* decide, since the left main wasn't "down," to get them all back up and make a belly landing, only to discover afterward that everything had been fine except for a burned-out bulb.)

You might think, "Why not transfer one of the other green bulbs to the left main indicator?" You know each of the others *had* been showing green, but it's better to be able to confirm just before landing that all three show a *down* indication than to assume the blank bulb socket would still be showing a green light if the bulb was in it.

If you have landing gear problems in flight, get yourself some altitude where you can think — get out of the traffic pattern.

The FAA requires that the *POH* or its equivalent be in the airplane at all times — and this is one of the main reasons why. It's funny how blank a usually sharp mind can get sometimes. You no doubt learned the emergency gear-down procedures until you could say them in your sleep, but now the steps have eluded you. *Take your time.* Get the *POH* out and read the emergency procedures if you have to. Some airplanes have the

step-by-step instructions printed near or on the cover plate of the emergency gear handle or switch. Follow them carefully.

Slowing the airplane down makes the landing gear extension a lot easier. Don't fly it around just above stall, but have the airspeed well below maximum gear-down speed.

In most airplanes with hydraulically actuated gear, the emergency procedure requires the gear handle to be placed in the *down* position before going on to the extension of the gear. Pilots have forgotten this and, when using a CO_2 bottle emergency extender, have wasted their one shot by having the gear handle up. They got in a hurry and didn't bother to follow the step-by-step procedure, or thought they knew the emergency procedure and didn't need to reread it. The recommendations for the emergency extension of electrically operated landing gear call for the switch to be in the DOWN position.

Getting out of the traffic pattern allows you to analyze the situation. It may be just a popped CB for electrical gear or a problem requiring a little hand pumping for hydraulic gear.

Don't use the emergency procedure until you are ready to land. This sounds like a rather inane statement but what it means is that the emergency gear *extension* is usually a one-way affair. Once the gear is put down by emergency means you have to leave it there.

There's the case of the curious private pilot who suspected after takeoff from a strange field that he might have trouble getting the gear down by normal means because it didn't act right coming up — so he did everything wrong. Home field with a good repair station for his airplane was only 1 hr away (gear up) and he had 5 hr of fuel. On the way home he started thinking "Will it go down?" until he couldn't stand the suspense any longer and used the emergency procedure. Of course, the gear came down but he had a mighty slow trip and almost got an overheated engine.

Then there was the private pilot who did the same thing, but, being heavily loaded over mountainous terrain, decided that he had to get the gear back up. By clean living and hard work he managed to get the gear started back up (where it stuck halfway, naturally) and did a fine job of messing up his new Zephyr Six when he landed.

If you have trouble getting the gear up after takeoff, don't force the issue — leave it down. *Make sure it's down,* return, and land, unless it would be wiser to fly (gear down) to a nearby airport where the trouble can be more easily fixed after you land.

Gear-up Landing. If the emergency procedure doesn't work (you forgot to have the gear handle down when you pulled the CO_2 bottle as a last resort), or there has been a mechanical failure or damage that won't allow the gear to come down by any means, you might remember a few points on gear-up landings. In the majority of belly landings, (1) comparatively little damage will be done and (2) the plane's occupants won't even be shaken up (physically, that is). A quick summary of your probable procedure:

1. Tighten seat belt and shoulder harness.
2. Make a normal approach; then after the field is made —
3. Battery and alternators OFF.
4. Chop the power and turn off all fuel system switches.
5. Ignition switch(es) OFF.
6. Make a normal landing.

If the runway is long enough, don't extend the flaps on the low-wing airplane. This will save a few more dollars, as extended flaps can be damaged. If the terrain is rough it would be better, though, to extend the flaps to further decrease the touchdown speed.

Figure on the prop being damaged. It will still be windmilling when you touch if you cut off the engine after the field is made. If you have any idea of killing the engine at altitude, slowing the plane up until the prop stops, and making it horizontal with the starter, forget it unless the runway is extremely long (say, 10,000 or 12,000 ft). This is no time to be practicing dead stick landings. *A bent prop is a small price to pay for assurance that the field is made.*

Your *POH* will cover the procedures for various gear problems, but here's an item you might consider if you have a flat nosewheel tire or the nosewheel remains up (and the main gear is down and locked). After touchdown, as you're holding the nosewheel off as long as possible, if it's not distracting you might roll in nose *down* trim to help keep the nose up to as slow an airspeed as possible. (Logical reasoning would assume that the elevator-stabilator trim should be rolled to a nose-*up* setting but if you check the positions for nose-up or nose-down trim you'll see that for most airplanes more *area* is available in the latter condition.)

Summary of Emergency Procedures.

(The *exact* emergency procedures vary, as some airplanes use electrical power for gear actuation and others use hydraulic means.)

1. Take your time and analyze.
2. Know your emergency procedures.
3. Keep the *POH* handy to help you remember each step.
4. Again, *take your time.*

SOME MORE POINTS ABOUT RETRACTABLE GEAR. Some pilots get the idea that the sooner they get the gear up on takeoff the better they look to the airport crowd. 'Tain't so!

The landing gear has a safety switch (electric gear) or a by-pass valve (hydraulically actuated gear) on one of the oleos to ensure against inadvertent retraction on the ground. As long as the weight is on this gear (the oleo is compressed), the landing gear can't be retracted (oh yeah?). Don't depend on this safety switch—it might not be working that day. Curiosity can cost money, so don't test the antiretraction safety features.

Even if the safety mechanism is working normally, don't get any ideas of putting the gear handle up during the takeoff run to "look sharp," because a gust might lift the plane enough temporarily to extend the oleo and the gear would start up before you're ready. Don't raise the gear before you are definitely airborne *and* no longer land gear-down on the runway should the engine quit.

Apply the brakes after takeoff before retracting the gear. Otherwise the wheels will be spinning at a good clip when they enter the wheel wells and can burn rubber that you might want to use later. Most manufacturers have buffer blocks on strips in the main wheel wells to stop the spinning, but you might as well save the tires as much as possible. Of course there's nothing you can do about a nosewheel. For larger airplanes with high takeoff speeds, this braking is frowned upon, as the rapidly spinning heavy wheel has a great deal of inertia and the sudden stopping of the wheel may cause the tire to slip around the rim.

Know your maximum gear extension speed (Fig. 14-4).

Fig. 14-4.

If you're taking off through puddles or slush and the temperature is near freezing, leave the gear down for a while after takeoff to allow the airflow to dry the landing gear. You may want to cycle the gear a time or two to clear it before leaving it up. If the landing gear has a lot of water on it and this freezes, it might cause problems in extending the gear later.

Some retractable-gear airplanes have "automatic" gear-lowering systems designed to help the pilot who *inadvertently forgets* to put the wheels down where they belong. These systems are not intended to replace good headwork. The pilot who flies airplanes so equipped and automatically relies on the systems, could be unpleasantly surprised sometime when landing the usual type of retractable-gear airplane.

15 Checking Out in the Light Twin

airplane and its systems in detail, and you'll spend a great deal of time with the *POH*.

This chapter takes a general look at the factors involved in checking out in the light twin; it is not intended to replace the information given by the *POH* and/or your instructor for a particular airplane.

If you're like many single-engine pilots, you may have sold yourself on the idea that twin-engine flying is strictly for people with thousands of hours and skills seldom found in lesser mortals.

Remember when you first started flying and you sometimes wondered if you'd ever really solo? (Particularly after one of those flights where everything went wrong.) Also, maybe there for a while it looked as though you'd never get the private certificate because you had to take the written again, and then had checkitis for days before the flight test. That's all behind, and now you've found a new subject to worry about—whether you'll be able to fly one of those light twins you've been drooling over.

Under normal conditions the airplane is flown *exactly* as if it were a single-engine airplane. Many new pilots don't believe this even after being told by the check pilot. It *looks* more complicated than the single-engine airplane, so they convince themselves that they'll be working a lot harder all the time.

Although there are two of each of the engine controls (throttle, prop, and mixture), think of each pair of controls as one handle—at least at the beginning. The check pilot will allow you to get well familiarized with the airplane before starting into engine-out procedures. You'll find that after a while you'll be using the controls separately as needed without any trouble.

Before flying, you and the check pilot will discuss the

PREFLIGHT CHECK

1. a. Ignition and master switches OFF (Fig. 15-1).
   b. Check that the landing gear selector and the other controls are in their proper positions.
2. a. Check for external damage or operational interference to the control surfaces, wings, or fuselage.
   b. Check for snow, ice, or frost on the wings or control surfaces.
3. a. Visually check fuel supply.
   b. Check fuel cell caps and covers for security (adjust caps to maintain tight seal).
   c. Fuel system vents open.
4. a. Landing gear shock struts properly inflated (approximately 3 in. of piston exposed).
   b. Tires satisfactorily inflated and not excessively worn.
   c. Fuel strainers and lines drained.
   d. Cowling, landing gear doors, and inspection covers properly attached and secured.
   e. Propellers free of detrimental nicks.
   f. No obvious fuel or oil leaks.
   g. Engine oil at the proper level.
5. a. Windshield clean and free of defects.
   b. Tow bar and control locks detached and properly stowed; baggage doors secured.
6. a. Upon entering the airplane, all control operation checked.
   b. Landing gear selector and the other controls in their proper position.
   c. Required papers in order and in the airplane.

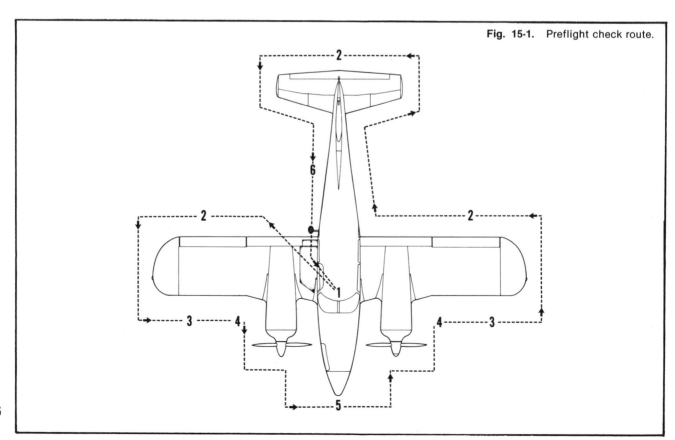

Fig. 15-1. Preflight check route.

CHECK BEFORE STARTING ENGINES:

1. Baggage secured.
2. Weight and CG computed.
3. Performance computed.
4. Aircraft papers in order.
5. Maps and charts checked.
6. Cabin door locked.
7. Seat belts secured.
8. Crew seats adjusted.
9. Parking brake set.
10. Altimeter set.
11. Control response checked.
12. Oxygen pressure checked for adequate supply.
13. Fuel valves ON.
14. Circuit breakers checked.
15. Switches (radio, etc.) OFF.
    Except: Main voltage regulator ON.
    Alternators ON.

The check pilot may give you a ground briefing several days before flying to give you a chance to learn the various control locations and their use. Spend some time in the cockpit by yourself after the ground check, using the *POH* to mentally review the steps for starting, takeoff, etc. This generally makes the first flight a little easier for both you and the check pilot.

In addition to checking the *POH* for operating procedures, you should also become familiar with the various system schematics. Samples will be included as they come up for discussion in this chapter.

STARTING

Normally the left (number one) engine is started first in the light twins (originally because many of the earlier light twins had a generator only on the left engine, and it could then be working to help start the right engine). Many light twin airplane manufacturers now recommend starting the left engine first because the cable from the battery to that engine is shorter, permitting more electrical power to be available. Check the boost pumps before starting, as was discussed back in Chap. 13 (carburetor engines).

Safety is still the big item in starting. Make sure that the areas around the props are clear before engaging the starter. The tendency for new pilots is to be so busy with procedures that they sometimes forget to shout "Clear!" and get an acknowledgment before starting the engine.

After one engine has started, run it at a high enough rpm to ensure that the alternator has cut in to aid in starting the other engine. It's sometimes more than a weak battery can do to start two engines in close succession. If it's wintertime you may not want to run the engine at higher rpm right away. If this is the case, don't be in too big a hurry to start the second engine. A short wait will allow the battery to build up again—plus the fact that you can soon run the operating engine up until it's helping.

If the engine you are starting first is cantankerous, you'd better forget it and start the other one. The alternator of the second engine can help give the boost needed to start the laggard one.

Leave all unnecessary electrical equipment OFF. This goes for starting any airplane (single- or multiengine) with an electrical system. The sudden surge of power required for starting may damage avionics equipment. Pitot heat also causes very strong current drain and, unlike the radios and other electrically powered equipment, is less noticeable when on. Unless you happen to check the switch directly or notice the ammeter gasping at the lower end of the discharge range, the fact that the pitot heat is on may be overlooked.

If you *really* want to give the battery (or batteries) the supreme test, turn on the landing lights also. With the pitot heat, radios, and landing lights on, the chances of the engine getting started are very slim indeed (Fig. 15-2).

Fig. 15-2. Joshua Barnslogger, private pilot, sometimes seems to have trouble getting the prop to turn over for starting (lousy electrical system design, he figures).

A lot of people are awed by the idea of starting a twin-engine airplane. One way of looking at it is that you are starting a single-engine airplane twice.

Following is a checklist for starting one type of twin (fuel injected):

1. Master switch ON.
2. Cowl flaps open to proper position.
3. Throttle controls open ½ in.
4. Propeller controls forward.
5. Electric fuel pumps ON.
6. Mixture controls set at rich until indication on fuel flow gage, then at idle cutoff.
7. Magneto switches ON.
8. Propellers clear.
9. Engage starters.
10. Check oil pressure.

If engine does not fire within 5 to 10 sec, disengage starter and reprime.

Starting engine when hot:

1. Master switch ON.
2. Magneto switches ON.
3. Electric fuel pump OFF.
4. Throttle opened ½ in.
5. Mixture in idle cutoff.
6. Engage starter.
7. Mixture at full rich when engine fires.
8. Oil pressure checked.

Starting engine when flooded:

1. Master switch ON.
2. Magneto switches ON.
3. Electric fuel pump OFF.
4. Throttle full open.
5. Mixture in idle cutoff.
6. Engage starter.
7. Retard throttle and advance mixture when engine fires.
8. Check oil pressure.

Cranking periods should be limited to 30 sec with a 2-min interval between. Longer cranking periods shorten the life of the starter.

Remember that for twins as for the single-engine airplanes, after each engine has started, check for proper oil pressures within 30 sec (it will take longer if outside temperatures are 10°F or lower) and make sure the flight instruments are working and the radios are on as needed.

If you have to use an auxiliary power unit (APU) to start the engine, be sure that the avionics switches are OFF and the master switch is ON or OFF during APU use (as indicated by the *POH*). Don't assume because the airplanes you flew earlier required the master switch to be OFF during APU-assisted starts that this is the case for any twin you are checking out in. Of two current twins examined in writing this chapter, one required the master ON for APU use and the other required it OFF. In the latter case, after removal of APU plug, you'd make sure that the master switch is ON.

TAXIING

Before taxiing, check your radios for proper functioning (this goes for single- *or* multiengine airplanes).

In earlier times, when nearly all multiengine airplanes had tailwheels, one of the biggest problems was learning to taxi. The new pilot was taught that the use of asymmetric power was helpful in steering the airplane. This is true, but it was sometimes overemphasized to the extent that both the check pilot and the pilot checking out became discouraged. It always started about like this: the new pilot starts taxiing and maybe the plane begins to turn to the left a little; overdoing a touch of power on the left engine to help straighten matters out, of course, then requires use of right engine power. This seesaw usually goes on until the airplane is thundering down the taxiway at ever increasing speed and in sharper and sharper S-turns. The check pilot finally has to take over and slow the airplane down, the new pilot is given back the controls, and the same procedure occurs again.

Taxi the airplane as if it were a single-engine type. It's very likely that the twin you are checking out in has a nosewheel, and the separate use of throttles will have much less effect. However, you'll soon be subconsciously using extra power on one engine whenever it's needed to make a sharper turn, so don't worry about using it right away as it only complicates matters. One good thing about tricycle-gear and nosewheel steering—as was stated above, if you do overuse either of the throttles, the plane isn't as apt to get away from you.

Check the brakes as the airplane starts to move; you don't need any surprises when taxiing at a normal speed toward that other expensive twin (or the hangar, etc.).

PRETAKEOFF CHECK

A good checklist pays off. The same checks that applied to an advanced single-engine airplane apply here. You'll run the engines at a setting that allows the alternators to be charging well and, in the airplane with augmenter cooling, gives efficient exhaust venturi action (usually 1200 to 1400 rpm). Check for freedom and proper movement of controls, and check the instruments and other items as required by the checklist.

Following are some general checklist items concerning light twins:

1. *Controls free*—This is nothing new to you. Make sure the ailerons, elevators, and rudder(s) move in the right direction (it's hard to check rudder movement in some nosewheel airplanes when they're sitting still, but you can check the rudder pedal and nosewheel action while taxiing).

2. *Fuel on proper (main) tank or tanks*—*Always*, repeat, *always* make your run-up on the tanks you plan to use on takeoff. This gives you a chance to discover if they are furnishing fuel properly. If you make a run-up on one set of tanks and just before takeoff switch to another set, you may find that the last tank or tanks selected are not working properly. This discovery usually occurs at the most inconvenient point shortly after takeoff. It's an old aviation truism that after unknowingly switching to a dry or bad tank, there'll be just enough fuel in the fuel lines to get you into a compromising position during takeoff. Always run the engines for at least a minute at moderate (1400 to 1600) rpm before takeoff if you see the need for changing tanks during or after the run-up.

3. *Electric fuel pumps OFF temporarily*—This is to check the action of the engine-driven pumps. *After the check make sure they are both ON for the takeoff.*

4. *Crossfeed checked and then OFF for takeoff*—Here's a new control for you. Normally each engine will use fuel from the tanks in its own wing. However, in the event of an engine failure there would be a great deal of unusable fuel on the dead engine side, limiting single-engine range as well as causing lateral trim problems as fuel is used from the operating-engine side. The crossfeed valve allows the working engine to draw fuel from the dead engine's tanks. Fig. 15-3 shows a simplified schematic of the normal operation of a typical light twin fuel system.

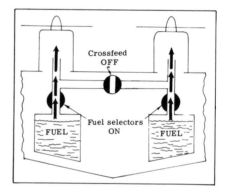

Fig. 15-3. Schematic of fuel system under normal conditions, crossfeed OFF.

Some airplanes do not have a separate valve for crossfeed but have a selector position on each of the two main fuel valves. If you needed to shut down the right engine in flight, for instance, you would "secure it" by throttling back, feathering it, pulling the mixture back to idle cutoff, turning off ignition switches, and putting the fuel selector to the OFF position. If you begin to run low on left-wing fuel for the good engine, you can select the crossfeed setting to allow the good engine to draw fuel from the opposite tank (Fig. 15-4).

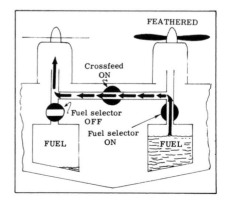

Fig. 15-4. The use of crossfeed.

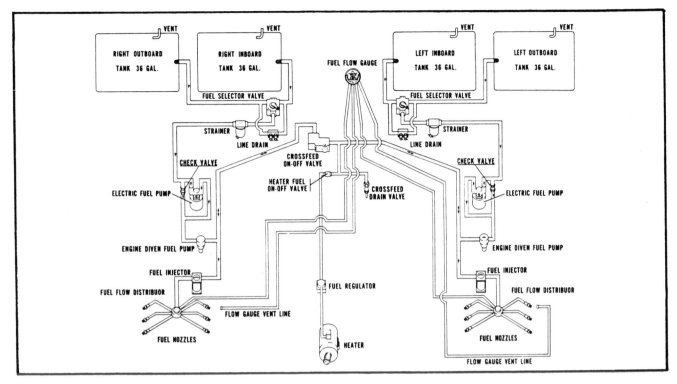

Fig. 15-5. Fuel system schematic.

Other manufacturers have a setup whereby the pilot merely selects the tank to use fuel from—and no particular mention is made of crossfeed—which results in a great deal less confusion.

You could, under normal conditions on some airplanes, run the left engine from the right tank and vice versa. This is frowned upon, on general principles, as it could cause confusion at a time when instantaneous selection is necessary. The setup on most airplanes is that each engine uses its own fuel and only turning off the fuel valve and selecting crossfeed allows you to operate an engine from an opposite tank (both engines running from the same wing tank). There are several combinations, and you will learn your airplane's particular fuel system.

You might especially check which tanks the crossfeed can be operated on. The crossfeed on some airplanes works only for the main fuel tanks—auxiliary fuel in one wing cannot be used by the other engine. No matter how complicated it sounds, remember that the only purpose for crossfeed is to enable you to use fuel that would otherwise be dead weight and/or cause lateral trim problems.

Fig. 15-5 shows a fuel system schematic, including the crossfeed system. This is a next step in the fuel systems discussed in Chap. 13. Inboard or outboard tanks may be used for crossfeeding. In effect, all four tanks are "main" tanks for this airplane. The crossfeed system shown is a *pressure* crossfeed, which means the fuel is "pushed" from the dead-engine side. Since the engine-driven fuel pump isn't working with the engine stopped and the prop feathered, the *electric* boost pump on that engine must be ON to push the fuel over (the *right* engine electric pump in the situation shown in Fig. 15-4).

Fig. 15-6 is another light twin fuel system with a close-up of its fuel selector panel.

5. *Tabs set*—You may have aileron tabs to contend with (the airplane will certainly have elevator and rudder trim controls). Make sure there's no wild setting on any of the trim controls.

6. *Flap operation checked*—If flaps are required for takeoff, or if you plan on using them, it might be better to wait until after the engine run-up before putting them down. The props, being run at high rpm on the ground, may pick up gravel and bat it into the flaps. You might find that for your particular airplane you would prefer setting the flaps just before taxiing onto the runway.

7. *All instruments checked*—You've been doing this for the single-engine airplane but now have two of each of the engine instruments to check. Be sure that oil and fuel pressures, cylinder head temperatures, and other gages are operating normally.

8. *Engine run-up*—Make sure the mixtures are full rich and the propellers are full forward (low-pitch, high-rpm). Run each engine up individually. The required rpm for prop and mag check varies with each airplane.

a. *Check the magnetos*—Here's the place where you'll realize that there are two engines instead of your usual one. It seems that checking the four mags is a good day's work. In fact, single-engine pilots have been known to have gotten writer's cramp, or its aeronautical equivalent, checking the mags of a multiengine airplane that first time. The usual maximum allowable drop for some light twins is 150 rpm, but you might check to confirm this for your airplane. The usual maximum allowed difference in drop between the two magnetos is 50 rpm.

b. *Exercise the propellers*—This goes for either air-oil or oil-counterweight types. At a recommended rpm move the propeller controls through the range from high rpm to low rpm several times (Chap. 12).

c. *Check the propeller feathering*—Multiengine airplanes have featherable propellers because it was discovered that turning the propeller blades of a dead engine edgewise to the airflow means much better engine-out performance. Naturally you'll be interested in making sure that you can feather a prop if necessary. A windmilling propeller on a dead engine cuts performance to such a degree that a critical condition could

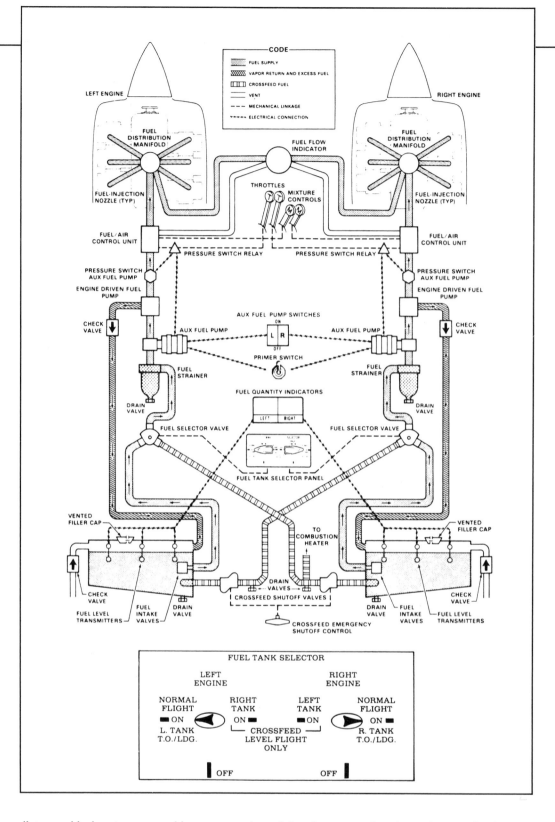

Fig. 15-6. Light twin fuel system with fuel selected for normal operation. Note the system of selecting crossfeed.

result. Most multiengine pilots would almost as soon skip checking the mags as not check the feather system. As the check pilot will tell you, don't let the prop stay in the feathered setting too long; the comparatively high manifold pressure and low rpm are not good for the engine. (One twin *POH* recommends a maximum drop of 500 rpm during the feather check.)

d. *Carburetor heat (carburetor engines)*—Use the carburetor air temperature gage if available, or check for a drop in manifold pressure (mp) as heat is applied. You remember that with the fixed-pitch-prop airplane you checked for an rpm drop when the carburetor heat was applied. A drop in

rpm showed that the warmer, less-dense air was going into the engine, proof that the carburetor heat was working normally.

The constant-speed propeller, when in its operating range, will tend to cover any rpm drop. So lacking a carburetor air temperature gage, the mp is the most positive indication that the system is working. In fact, the mp gives an *immediate* indication, whereas the carburetor air temperature gage needs a short period to indicate temperature. The mp gage is the primary indicator of the presence of carburetor ice, as you can no longer rely on rpm drop as a warning with a constant-speed propeller. You may be able to notice a very brief rpm drop, but it will immediately recover if the rpm indication is in the constant-speed-prop operating range. Remember that you'll be getting unfiltered air, and some manufacturers frown on using carburetor heat or alternate air systems during the ground run-up.

If you apply the carburetor heat with the rpm below the constant-speed operating range, you'll get an mp *and* an rpm drop that remains as long as the heat is on. The mp drop with application of full carburetor heat is not as great as you might think from the power loss involved, in some cases being about ½ in.

Most light twins in use today have fuel-injected engines so carburetor heat, as such, isn't part of those installations. But you should know how to use alternate air systems (see Chap. 16) for your airplane.

Alternate air or carburetor heat OFF for takeoff.

e. *Electrical system* — A look at the diagram of the electrical system that first time can be pretty discouraging.

Current twins have two things going for them electrically, compared with the first light twins manufactured:

(1) Alternators, not generators, are used. As you are probably aware from your other flying, alternators produce voltage at lower engine rpm than do generators. (You may have never flown an airplane with a generator.)

(2) *Two* alternators, one for each engine, are used on nearly all twins these days. Back in the old days, the left engine had the only *generator*. Losing that one could mean that electrical problems would be added to your other obvious problem. In most cases, loss of one of the alternators means husbanding your electrical equipment, but you'll normally have enough voltage produced for the fundamentals. Before takeoff, check that each alternator is working properly, using the procedure suggested by the *POH* and your instructor.

f. Suction or pressure systems — Check both sources to see that the engine-driven pumps are properly operating and providing the correct suction, or pressure, in inches of mercury. It's likely that the single-engine airplanes you've been flying have been using a vacuum system; that is, the engine-driven vacuum pump *pulls* the air past the vanes on the gyro wheels in the attitude and heading indicators and you check the suction gage for the proper reading. Many twins use a pressure or pneumatic pump (which in effect means that the air is *pushed* past the gyro wheels from the opposite direction). This system can be used also for de-icer boots, autopilots and cabin pressurization (see Chap. 19).

TAKEOFF AND CLIMB

See the takeoff chart in Fig. 15-7. There is very little difference in the takeoff of a single- or multiengine airplane because the throttles are normally treated as one control. However, if there is a strong crosswind you may increase the power on the upwind engine first and carry more power on that side during the initial part of the run to help offset weathercocking tendencies (Fig. 15-8). As the airspeed picks up and steering improves, increase to full power on both engines. This is helpful even for airplanes with a steerable nosewheel.

You'll have to watch your throttle handling if the engines are supercharged — you might overboost them — and the check pilot will remind you to check the mp gage as power is applied. Most instructors recommend keeping the airplane on the ground until you reach a speed of V_{MC} (single-engine minimum controllable speed) + 5 K.

Shortly after takeoff the fun begins. You raise the landing gear and set climb power (throttles back first, then props!). One of your most frustrating experiences will be trying to synchronize the propellers when you are busy getting set up for the climb. (Wait until you have 500-ft altitude before reducing power.)

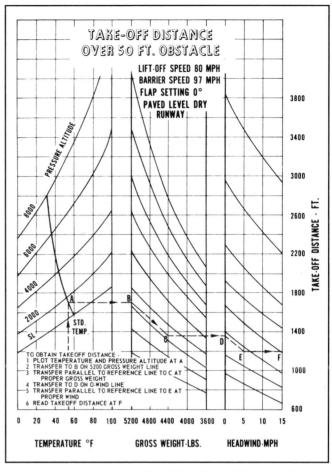

Fig. 15-7. Takeoff distance chart.

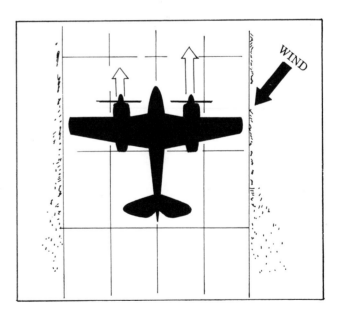

Fig. 15-8. The use of asymmetric power during the beginning of a crosswind takeoff.

One tip for synchronization is to use sound as much as possible. After throttling back to the climb mp, move the propeller controls back to the proper rpm setting. Some twins use a single tachometer with two hands, which makes the problem a little easier. In addition there may be a "synchronizing wheel," or indicator, which tells if one engine is turning faster than the other. Other twins use two separate tachometers. When moving the prop controls back, try to keep them in the same relative position to each other (don't worry—you won't the first few times). Use one tachometer hand as a "master" and note the relative position of the other. If the other hand is at a higher rpm, ease its prop control back until the "throb" sound has disappeared. This throb is your indication of degree of synchronization—the faster the pulse, the greater the difference between the rpm of the two props. Use common sense, of course; you could pull one prop so far back that it is in feather and would have no pulsating noise at all—performance would suffer though. You'll soon be able to smooth out the props with a flick of the wrist (Fig. 15-9).

Fig. 15-9. Sometimes poor prop synchronization can drive a check pilot to distraction.

An expression for the maximum climbing power, or maximum continuous power, is METO (maximum except take-off). Many engines are limited in time for full-power operations; this is given in the *POH* and *Engine Manual*.

Some of the engines in this class have unlimited time allowed for full-power operation. The engine manufacturer usually states that while there is no danger of failure or immediate damage the overhaul period may be made shorter by abuse of this privilege.

Know the max rate and max angle climb speeds for your airplane—both multiengine and engine-out.

The airplane will be cleaned up and power set for proper climb, using the recommended best rate of climb speed. After reaching a safe altitude the flaps will be retracted, if used, and shortly afterward the boost pumps will be turned OFF. *Check the fuel pressure as you turn off each pump individually.*

Here is a sample checklist for takeoff and climb:
1. Parking brake OFF.
2. Mixture controls forward.
3. Propeller controls forward.
4. Throttle controls forward.
5. Accelerate to 80 K (prior to climb).
6. Retract landing gear.
7. Accelerate to best rate of climb speed.
8. Climb power set at approximately 400 AGL.
9. Electric fuel pumps OFF (one at a time)
10. Cowl flaps set (maintain cylinder head temperature at or below maximum).
11. Oxygen ON (above 10,000 ft or lower, as required).

CRUISE AND AIRWORK

After reaching the practice altitude, the check pilot will show you the proper cruise power setting and leaning procedure. You may have a little trouble with synchronization again, but this is to be expected. A good procedure for leveling is to ease the nose over to cruise attitude, using trim as

necessary and leaving the power at climb setting to help acceleration. As the cruise airspeed is approached, throttle back to cruise mp and set the props. After getting the airplane trimmed to your satisfaction, switch tanks and lean the mixtures using the technique(s) described in Chap. 13 or those recommended by the check pilot, who may have a method particularly effective for your airplane.

The check pilot will have you do shallow, medium, and steep turns (up to 45° bank) to get the feel of the airplane. You will stall the airplane in various combinations: gear-up or -down, flaps at various settings, and at different power settings. The check pilot will probably demonstrate the effects of the loss of an engine when you are making a power-on stall. The best thing is to pull the power back on the other engine and lower the nose to pick up V_{MC} before reapplying full power.

The check pilot will throttle back or feather one engine and have you continue to slow up the airplane to V_{MC} so that you will have a graphic demonstration of the required rudder force and what can happen when you get too slow on one engine.

Single-Engine Minimum Controllable Speed. FAR 23 gives the requirements for V_{MC} as follows:

23.149 Minimum control speed.
(a) V_{MC} is the calibrated airspeed, at which, when the critical engine is suddenly made inoperative, it is possible to recover control of the airplane with that engine still inoperative, and maintain straight flight either with zero yaw or, at the option of the applicant, with an angle of bank of not more than five degrees. The method used to simulate critical engine failure must represent the most critical mode of powerplant failure with respect to controllability expected in service.

(b) For reciprocating engine–powered airplanes, V_{MC} may not exceed 1.2 V_{S1} (where V_{S1} is determined at the maximum takeoff weight) with—
(1) Takeoff or maximum available power on the engines;
(2) The most unfavorable center of gravity;
(3) The airplane trimmed for takeoff;
(4) The maximum sea level takeoff weight (or any lesser weight necessary to show V_{MC});
(5) Flaps in the takeoff position;
(6) Landing gear retracted;
(7) Cowl flaps in the normal takeoff position;
(8) The propeller of the inoperative engine—
    (i) Windmilling;
    (ii) In the most probable position for the specific design of the propeller control; or
    (iii) Feathered, if the airplane has an automatic feathering device; and
(9) The airplane airborne and the ground effect negligible.

You will normally want to attain this speed before taking off so that should an engine fail you'll have directional control. V_{MC} is marked as a red radial line on the airspeed indicator.

Later you will have a chance to feather and unfeather a propeller and to fly around on one engine to check the performance. If possible, you should fly the airplane at gross Weight and, at a safe altitude, simulate or actually feather a propeller to see what effect Weight has on performance.

There have been cases where a plane was damaged or destroyed because commonsense rules weren't followed during a simulated engine failure. It would be mighty embarrassing to clamber from the wreckage and try to explain to an irate operator/owner that you "were just practicing single-engine flight so as to avoid damaging the airplane should the real thing occur."

You'll probably practice slow flight and will slow the airplane to about 10 K above the stall warning or buffeting point for the configuration used, at a constant altitude. You will also fly at landing configuration to demonstrate your ability to fly the airplane safely, maintaining altitude, speed, and a constant direction through proper use of power and the flight controls. You'll fly it long enough in each configuration to demonstrate the acceleration and deceleration characteristics of your airplane. You'll do straight and level flight, level flight turns, and climbing and gliding turns at slow flight speeds. The check pilot will be particularly interested in your transitions to and from slow flight. You will avoid accidental stalls, of course.

In general, this phase of your transition to multiengine flying is quite similar to the checkout in an advanced single-engine airplane (except for the engine-out demonstration). You'll be finding out how the airplane reacts under normal conditions. The full treatment on engine-out procedures comes later.

The procedures for leaning at cruise, rough air penetration, and use of the prop and throttle controls have been covered in earlier chapters. You might have a little problem with prop synchronization at cruise but will soon work it out. You should be able to do a good job of synchronization manually before using the automatic synchronizer installed in some airplanes.

APPROACH AND LANDING

You'll have a few more items to check than you've been used to and should use the checklist religiously, pointing to each item as you check it. Everything mentioned about mixtures, boost pumps, gear, flaps, and props for the advanced single-engine airplane still applies except that you'll have two of some of the controls to move. But, again, under normal conditions the two controls can be handled as one. (Use the main tanks for landing unless the manufacturer recommends differently.)

Note the gear- and flap-down speed and give yourself plenty of time and room on the downwind leg and approach, particularly the first few landings. Check the gear again on final.

The approach and landing will be just like a single-engine airplane except that you must keep in mind one thing: It's best to maintain an approach speed above the single-engine minimum controllable speed (V_{MC}). As the airplane has a comparatively high wing loading, you will be making the majority of your approaches with some power. This means that should you have a complete power failure (both engines) you probably wouldn't make the runway. The chances of both engines quitting are practically nonexistent (although it's not impossible), but one engine *could* quit on you. Suppose you get low and slow (below V_{MC}) and are dragging it in from way back. An engine fails, and as the plane starts sinking you apply full power on the operating engine. You'll find that you made a bad mistake by being too slow—because the directional control is nil with full power on the good engine. You are too low to nose over and pick up V_{MC} (and then go to best single-engine climb speed). You might also find that the only thing to do is to chop the other throttle, turn all the switches off, and hit something soft and cheap. You can get caught in a trap of your own making.

Even if you are at or slightly above V_{MC}, you'll have to accelerate to best single-engine climb speed, so take this into consideration on the approach. Avoid dragged out finals (this goes for any airplane).

Many *POH*s suggest an approach speed above best single-engine climb speed (V_{YSE}). More about this later.

For short fields you still should have no reason to get

below V_{MC}, as that speed is usually low enough to assure that you won't float before touching down. Again, dragging it around close to or below V_{MC} is taking a calculated risk, as with the short-field takeoff.

You'll be given plenty of chances to shoot normal and short-field takeoffs and landings before making single-engine approaches or go-arounds.

The landing roll, taxi, and shutdown procedures of the light twin follow closely those of advanced single-engine airplanes. The check pilot will cover any peculiarities of the checkout airplane.

Following is a landing checklist for a fictitious twin:
1. Oxygen OFF (below 10,000 ft).
2. Seat belts fastened.
3. Electric fuel pumps ON.
4. Mixture controls forward.
5. Fuel valves ON, fullest cells.
6. Landing gear (under 150 K) extended, check green.
7. Propellers set.
8. Cowl flaps as required.
9. Flaps set:
   Full flap—125 K (max)
   ½ flap—140 K (max)
   ¼ flap—160 K (max)
10. Heater (if used) fan ON.

And a postlanding checklist:
1. Wing flaps retracted.
2. Cowl flaps open.
3. Electric fuel pump OFF.
4. Prop controls forward.
5. When completely stopped in a parking spot, check the following items for shutdown:
   a. Radio and electrical equipment OFF.
   b. Heater (if used) fan OFF.
   c. Mixture controls at idle cutoff.
   d. Magneto switches OFF.
   e. Master switch OFF.
   f. Parking brake OFF.
   g. Main volt regulator OFF
   h. Alternators OFF.

If control locks are not available and the airplane is to be left for more than a few minutes, secure the control wheel with the safety belt strap. Chock the wheels and secure tie-downs at appropriate places.

Figs. 15-10 and 15-11 (on the next page) are typical landing distance charts. Fig. 15-11 is a graphical presentation using mph. The light twin you'll be flying will use basically the same types of performance charts as were covered in earlier chapters and you should be able to use them with little trouble. Later in this chapter are a couple of figures for twins only (accelerate and stop distance chart and area of decision—go or no go).

EMERGENCY PROCEDURES

The nonpilot may feel that loss of an engine on a multiengine airplane is either a terrifying disaster or nothing to be concerned about. Experienced pilots know that the multiengine airplane, if properly flown with an engine out, has a strong safety factor. They also know that at certain times the airplane must be flown precisely, and in some cases it is safer to chop the other engine(s) than to try to continue. New pilots have been killed by the loss of an engine on takeoff or approach when they believed they could go around. Ironically enough, they might have survived had the engine quit at the same place in a single-engine airplane. They would have landed straight ahead in the single-engine airplane but instead attempted the impossible because of overconfidence in or ignorance of the single-engine performance of their twin.

LANDING DISTANCE

SHORT FIELD

CONDITIONS:
Flaps 30°
Power Off
Maximum Braking
Paved, Level, Dry Runway
Zero Wind

NOTES:
1. Short field technique as specified in Section 4.
2. Decrease distances 10% for each 11 knots headwind. For operation with tailwinds up to 10 knots, increase distances by 10% for each 2.5 knots.
3. For operation on a dry, grass runway, increase distances by 40% of the "ground roll" figure.
4. If a landing with flaps up is necessary, increase the approach speed by 10 KIAS and allow for 35% longer distances.
5. This chart may be used for any landing weight with either standard or heavy duty main wheels, tires and brakes. (See Section 2 for landing weight limitation with standard main wheels, tires and brakes.)

WEIGHT LBS	SPEED AT 50 FT KIAS	PRESS ALT FT	0°C		10°C		20°C		30°C		40°C	
			GRND ROLL FT	TOTAL FT TO CLEAR 50 FT OBS	GRND ROLL FT	TOTAL FT TO CLEAR 50 FT OBS	GRND ROLL FT	TOTAL FT TO CLEAR 50 FT OBS	GRND ROLL FT	TOTAL FT TO CLEAR 50 FT OBS	GRND ROLL FT	TOTAL FT TO CLEAR 50 FT OBS
5150	81	S.L.	775	1395	805	1430	835	1470	865	1505	890	1545
		1000	805	1430	835	1470	865	1510	895	1550	925	1590
		2000	835	1470	865	1510	895	1555	930	1595	960	1635
		3000	865	1515	900	1555	930	1595	965	1640	995	1680
		4000	900	1555	935	1600	965	1645	1000	1690	1030	1730
		5000	935	1600	970	1650	1005	1695	1035	1740	1070	1785
		6000	970	1650	1005	1695	1040	1745	1075	1790	1110	1840
		7000	1005	1700	1045	1750	1080	1800	1120	1845	1155	1895
		8000	1045	1750	1085	1800	1125	1855	1160	1905	1200	1955

Fig. 15-10. A tabular presentation of a landing distance chart for a light twin.

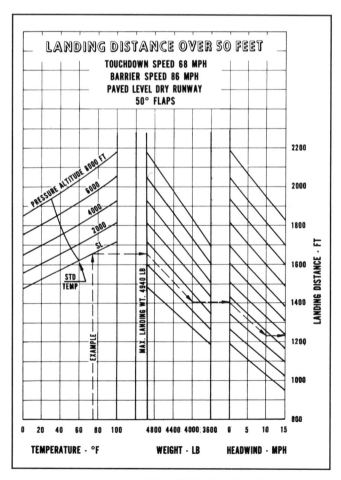

Fig. 15-11. Landing distance chart.

Here's where you'll start running into the age-old problem of decisions. You may end up like the orange sorter who finally went berserk because "although the work was easy, the decisions finally got me down." As a single-engine pilot noted, one advantage to the plane with just one fan is that when the engine quits you don't have to make the decision whether to go around or not.

So, although multiengine flight is safer—you'll feel more comfortable flying over rough terrain and at night—you must realize that you earn this increased safety by learning what to do in an emergency.

One of the first things you'll find is that a windmilling prop can cause a great reduction in performance, and that gear and flaps cause a problem on a single-engine go-around.

Another point: Because you've lost half your power with one engine out doesn't mean that you'll have half the performance. *You'll have considerably less than half the performance and must take this into consideration.* For instance, you remember that the rate of climb is dependent on *excess* HP. When you cut power being produced you'll be losing nearly all that excess HP—what you'll have left will be enough to fly the airplane plus some small amount of excess power. So, the excess HP is what suffers. (Unfortunately, there is no way for you to lose the power required to fly the airplane and keep the *excess* HP.)

A study of 11 current reciprocating-engine light twins comparing multi- and single-engine climb rates at sea level has reported differences in rate of 10 to 22%. That is, the worst performance was a rate of climb on one engine only 10% of that with both engines running; the best single-engine performer had a rate of climb 22% of that with both engines running. The others fell in between, with the average single-engine climb rate for the group about 16.5% of the multiengine rate.

Your enroute performance will not suffer nearly as much as the climb or acceleration characteristics, but all phases will be affected. The single-engine rate of climb is based on a clean airplane with the inoperative prop in the minimum Drag position—feathered if possible, or in high pitch (low rpm). Fig. 15-12 is a Thrust horsepower available and required versus airspeed curve for the light twin in Fig. 2-50, with both engines operating and with one feathered at gross Weight and sea level. Notice that even with a prop feathered the THP required is greater than normal because of control deflection, loss of efficiency, etc.

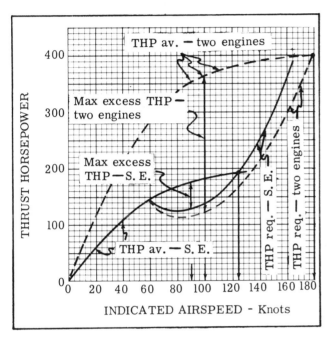

Fig. 15-12. Thrust horsepower available and required versus airspeed for a light twin in both twin and single-engine flight. Gross Weight at sea level.

Looking at the excess HP in Fig. 15-12, you can see that with both engines operating there is about 240 THP in excess of that required at the best rate of climb speed of 100 K. Using the equation for rate of climb and assuming an airplane Weight of 5000 lb, the rate of climb = (EHP × 33,000)/Weight = (240 × 33,000)/5000 = 1584 fpm.

Checking the single-engine situation in Fig. 15-12, you can see that about 45 excess THP is available at the speed for max rate of climb (90 K) in that condition: (45 × 33,000)/5000 = 297 fpm.

You can climb 297 fpm in this airplane at gross Weight *at sea level under ideal conditions.* (Turbulent air and/or a higher density-altitude can wreak havoc.) This gives a single-engine rate of climb of 18.75% of the rate with both engines operating. You can imagine what percentage of normal rate of climb you'd have at gross Weight on a hot day with an engine out, the gear and flaps down, and a windmilling prop. You would likely end up with a negative rate of climb.

The lighter the airplane's load, the better the single-engine performance. But even an airplane at light weight doesn't have much get-up-and-go with a lot of garbage hanging out in the slipstream.

SINGLE-ENGINE CONTROL

More about V_{MC}. Single-engine minimum control speed means just that; V_{MC} has to do with control, not performance. Pilots new to twins sometimes think that as long as they maintain V_{MC} the airplane will have climb performance. As will be shown shortly, holding the published V_{MC} does not always mean that *control* is maintained, either.

First, take a look at a situation where an airplane is clean and loses an engine. The pilot is determined to maintain control with the wings level (it seems more orderly that way) and Fig. 15-13 shows some of the yawing forces and moments involved.

Looking at A in Fig. 15-13, you see that the airplane yaws around its CG. The moment created by the thrust of the operating engine must be balanced by the moment the pilot created by (fully?) deflecting the rudder. In B, when the CG is moved aft, the arm is shortened and the airspeed required for directional control increases. (V_{MC} *gets higher with a rearward movement of CG.*) The rudder is producing sidewise "Lift" when deflected, and the shorter arm requires a higher rudder "Lift" (more airspeed) to maintain the same moment.

Fig. 15-14 shows that banking the airplane about 5° into the operating engine results in a slip. This has the relative wind hitting the fin and rudder at a greater angle, increasing the control effectiveness.

Note that earlier in the chapter, in the FAR 23 requirements, the manufacturer had the option of banking not more than 5° when establishing V_{MC}. Since the manufacturer would like a low V_{MC}, you can pretty well be assured that the test pilot used a bank in establishing that figure.

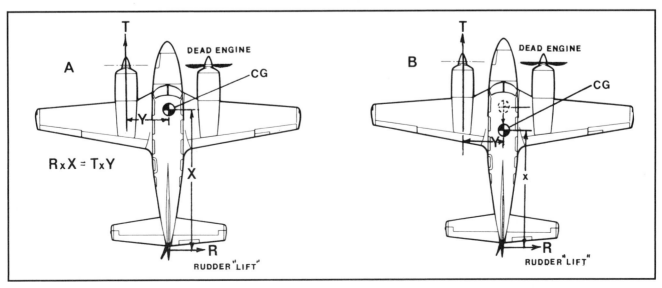

Fig. 15-13. A. Yawing moments in wings-level flight. B. Note that moving the CG rearward hurts directional control (raises the minimum control speed).

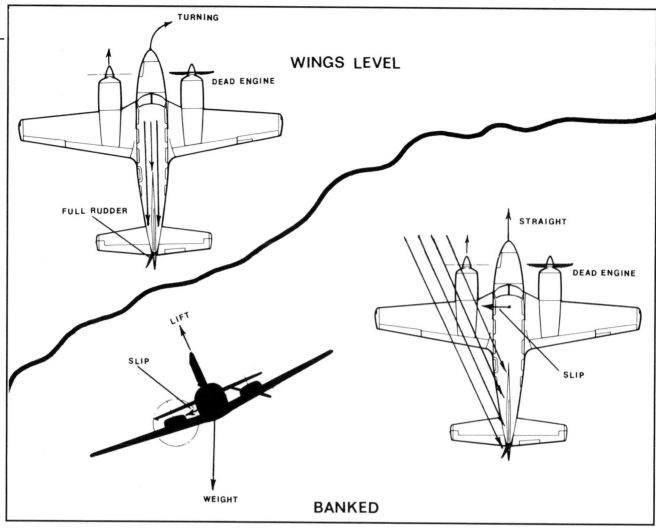

Fig. 15-14. Banking into the good engine about 5° can increase control effectiveness (lower V_{MC}) – a simplified look at what happens. (Bank and slip effects exaggerated.)

When the airplane is banked, the slip occurs because a component of Weight is acting along the wing (similar to the idea of a wing-down crosswind approach). *The heavier an airplane, for a given angle of bank, the greater the Weight effect and the lower the V_{MC}.* You'd figure that the lighter you fly the airplane, the lower the V_{MC}, but it doesn't work that way. Of course, the discussion here is about *control;* added Weight would hurt performance.

Figure 15-15 shows an exaggerated example of the effects of added Weight on V_{MC}. As far as the 5° bank is concerned, the greater the Weight, the larger the component of Weight acting toward the operating engine and the greater the sideslip (and more effective rudder and fin to help fight the turning into the dead engine). The added Weight shown helps *control* but performance will suffer. *Best control and best performance are separate items requiring different banks.* (After the airplane is under control, you'll shallow the bank as necessary to maintain a *zero sideslip,* but more about that later.)

Increased altitude lowers V_{MC}. This makes sense because the nonsupercharged engine loses power (and Thrust) with altitude, and the moment created by that operating engine is less. If you deflect the rudder fully you'll need less dynamic pressure (lower airspeed) to counter the yawing moment created by the less-powerful engine. This, however, can be a trap. Fig. 15-16 shows that while V_{MC} (IAS) decreases with altitude, the single-engine stall speed (IAS) stays the same for a given Weight. The airplane will stall at the same IAS at 10,000 ft density-altitude as at sea level (see Chap. 4).

The decreasing V_{MC} soon meets and crosses the power-on stall line. You may find that at some higher altitudes (usually 3000 to 4000 ft MSL) the airplane will stall before getting to V_{MC}. When you and the instructor are up there with one feath-

ered, and are slowing the airplane up looking for V_{MC}, you could get a stall with very bad rolling tendencies. Fatal accidents have occurred on training flights when people got surprised. The main thing to do is get the power off that operating engine and use rudder opposite to the roll and also brisk forward wheel.

V_{SSE}. The manufacturers have established an "intentional one-engine inoperative speed, V_{SSE}," which can be remembered as a *safe single-engine speed.* V_{SSE} is several knots above V_{MC} and is

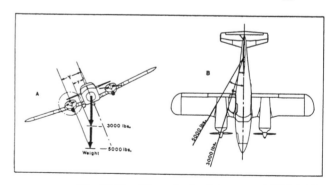

Fig. 15-15. The effect of increased Weight in lowering V_{MC} (constant bank). (A) The spanwise component of Weight and sideslip effect is greater at 5000 pounds (Y) than at 3000 pounds (y). (B) The angle of sideslip is greater at the higher Weight. (Angles of bank and sideslip exaggerated.) Note that the added Weight *hurts performance* as does too much (or any) sideslip. (*The Flight Instructor's Manual*)

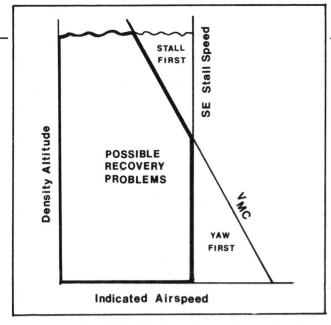

Fig. 15-16. Single-engine stall speed and V$_{MC}$ (IAS) versus density-altitude for a fictitious twin.

propeller or the power was reduced to simulate the feather. You could be holding hard rudder and aileron as necessary to keep the airplane under control, and if the throttle of the operating engine is abruptly closed, the prop flattens out and radically increases Drag on that side. *Now* you have a strong yawing force in the *same direction in which you are holding rudder!* You can see that the contrast would be greater if the propeller of the inoperative engine were feathered, or at its lowest Drag condition, compared with having that engine carrying *some* power.

V$_{SSE}$. The manufacturers have established an "intentional one-engine inoperative speed, V$_{SSE}$," which can be remembered as a *safe single-engine speed*. V$_{SSE}$ is several knots above V$_{MC}$ and is listed in the *POH*. Different twins have different safety margins for V$_{SSE}$ (one twin uses 12 K and another uses 6 K above V$_{MC}$, so you should check the *POH* for each airplane). Your instructor will limit deliberate engine cuts to V$_{SSE}$ and above, when demonstrating V$_{MC}$. Max continuous power will be set on the operating engine, reducing the airspeed at about 1 K per second until directional control starts being lost or a stall nibble occurs.

Roll Factors. Fig. 15-17 shows the approximate Lift distribution across a twin with an engine windmilling and max continuous power on the other. Induced flow from the operating engine adds to the freestream velocity. A windmilling propeller can disturb the airflow over the wing behind it.

Okay, so you'll use aileron (with rudder) to counteract the roll and also to establish the 5° bank into the good engine, as

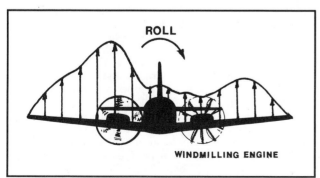

Fig. 15-17. Lift distribution of a fictitious light twin with a windmilling right engine.

noted earlier. This may take a fair amount of aileron deflection, and you get the problem of adverse yaw. This tends to turn the airplane into the dead engine, requiring more rudder. But banking into the operating engine certainly helps in maintaining directional control. It's possible, though, to get a bank so steep, with a resulting increased angle of flow, that the rudder and fin "stall" and you'd lose control that way. Dihedral effect also will work against the bank.

Another factor working against the bank you set up is the fin and rudder above the centerline of the fuselage. You then have the airflow "striking" the side of those surfaces, tending to roll the airplane out in the opposite direction (see Fig. 10-57).

SINGLE-ENGINE PERFORMANCE

Performance. Performance will suffer from the directional and lateral *control* requirements because asymmetrical flight, such as the sideslip used for *best control,* greatly increases Drag and hurts climb performance.

The bank required for best performance (climb) may be approximately half of the 5° example used for control, depending on the airplane. (Remember, get the bank in immediately to maintain control when that engine fails, because if you lose control, there won't be a need for performance.) After lateral/directional control is established, the bank is shallowed as necessary to get a zero sideslip for performance.

Your instructor might demonstrate the following at a safe altitude. Put a yaw string on center of the nose where you both can see it. (It's best to do this on the ground *before* the flight.) Feather or set zero thrust on one of the engines. After looking around for other airplanes, set up a climb at the single-engine best rate of climb speed (V$_{YSE}$), starting *about 200 ft below* your chosen altitude of, say, 4000 ft MSL. Use max continuous power on the operating engine. The extra 200 ft allow the climb to stabilize, so that as you reach the reference altitude you can start timing with a stopwatch or a sweep second hand. *Keep the ball centered and the wings level if possible.* Don't pay any attention to the yaw string. Maintain V$_{YSE}$, and after 200 ft of climb or 3 minutes, whichever you prefer, check the rate of climb.

Descend back to 200 ft below the starting altitude used before and start the climb sequence. Use V$_{YSE}$, and time the same climb segment, only this time set up a bank about one-half ball width into the operating engine and keep the yaw string centered. The immediate reaction of the ball in the turn and slip, or turn coordinator, is to move away from the dead engine as the yaw starts, and you'll be fighting this. The chances are that this second time you'll see a measurable improvement in the single-engine rate of climb. With the zero sideslip, you have set up a cleaner condition, so that Drag (and required HP) is at a minimum for existing conditions.

Engine Failure Enroute. This is usually the least critical place for engine failure (except during taxiing or warm-up) but can lead to trouble if things are allowed to progress too far.

The check pilot will usually pull an in-flight emergency on you after you've had a chance to get the feel of the airplane. The procedure to follow in the event of an engine failure will be demonstrated and, after you have had a chance to run through it several times, the check pilot may quietly turn the fuel off on one engine in order to catch you by surprise. This is not done to see how badly you can foul up but, like the primary instructor who used to give simulated emergencies at unexpected times, it's realistic training. It's a lot different to watch the check pilot pull back one of the throttles (you'll know immediately which engine is going to be "bad") than suddenly to have one of the engines quit (which one?). You'll find that no matter how hard you've practiced or memorized the procedure, you'll be all thumbs and feet in the cockpit the first time one stops when you aren't ready for it.

Some instructors, however, argue against turning off the fuel because of possible restarting problems. They say that the check pilot can cover the power control quadrant with a chart and pull one of the mixtures.

The biggest problem at first is knowing which engine is out. In flight you'll have more time to judge and make a decision. If you feather the wrong prop on the check ride—well, you can always take the flight test again. What is needed is caution with some speed of action, but make sure that the decision is a good one. Better to be a little slow and be right, than to be fast but wrong.

To go through a typical case: an engine fails. You can't tell which one immediately by looking at the tachometers. Remember the constant-speed prop will tend to flatten pitch and maintain the chosen rpm. As long as the prop is windmilling the engine is still acting as a pump and the mp will tend to stay at the former indication. Although a slight change may immediately occur, it's hard to tell at a quick glance just which mp hand did the moving. However, as the airplane begins to slow down, the constant-speed propeller of the dead engine can no longer maintain rpm. (The governor continually flattens the blades to maintain rpm, but the low pitch limit is finally reached.) Because the dead engine is still "making the motions," movement of that throttle will still result in mp change but no feel of power variation as would normally be expected. One visual indicator is the ball in the turn and slip or turn coordinator. The ball, because things are amiss, will tend to move *away* from the engine that's causing the problem. But to be on the safe side, you should take the following steps before feathering.

Advance the engine controls for both engines in this order: mixtures, props, throttles. You will be needing more power on the good engine and, as you have not definitely ascertained which is good or bad, will move all engine controls forward. Some engines are limited in the time allowed for full power, and you will not want to leave the power up too long. But get in the habit of increasing power on both engines (of course, you will actually only be increasing the power of one engine but you'll be sure this way).

Now the problem becomes one of definitely isolating the bad engine.

So, an engine has quit. Remember, *working foot—working engine.*

This means that the airplane will yaw when power is lost on one engine. You will consciously or unconsciously try to hold it straight, which requires the use of rudder—and that foot is the *working foot.* Therefore, that engine is working okay. You can use this idea: *loafing foot—loafing engine.* This is a better memory aid because it automatically directs your attention to the engine that will be needing the procedures.

For instance, let's say it requires right rudder to keep the airplane straight (it wants to yaw to the left). Your left foot and the left engine are not working. Do you feather the left prop as soon as you can get your grubby little hand on the control? You do not! First, you pull the left throttle back. If the left engine *is* dead as you figured, nothing will happen—no change in power effects or sound or feel of the airplane. If somehow you made an error in feel of the rudder and the left engine is the working engine, you'll feel and see the loss of power and discover the mistake before feathering the good engine.

FEATHERING. The order of engine control usage for feathering varies among airplanes but may generally be given as this: (1) throttle back to idle, (2) mixture at idle cutoff, (3) prop control into the feather detent.

In an actual engine failure at cruise, don't be in too big a hurry to feather. After you've discovered which engine is the culprit, you might turn on the boost pump for that engine (or better still, turn on the boost pumps for both engines to make sure). You can also switch tanks and check for other problems (carburetor or ram icing will generally hit both engines more or less equally). You richened the mixture when the engine controls were moved forward.

Okay, so you've checked everything, but the problem still exists and it looks like you'll have to feather it. If you make a thorough check during the simulated failure you might discover that the check pilot has turned the fuel off, but you'll go ahead with the feathering procedure for practice.

The oil-counterweight propeller must be rotating in order to be feathered. If the engine "freezes up" before the prop is feathered, you'll have some flat blades out there giving lots of Drag and there won't be anything you can do about it. If, under actual conditions, the oil pressure is dropping or has gone to zero and the oil and cylinder head temperatures are going up out of sight, you'd better feather while you can.

After the prop has stopped, trim the airplane, secure the dead engine mag and boost pump switches, and turn off the fuel to that engine.

Under actual conditions you will want to land at the nearest airport that will safely take your plane. This is no time to be landing at an extremely short field with poor approaches to the runway. On the other hand, don't figure on finishing the last 400 mi of your trip either.

CARE OF THE OPERATING ENGINE. Now that you have feathered the propeller, you are once again a single-engine pilot. You are interested in taking care of the operating engine—you don't want to be the pilot in command of the only twin-engine glider in the area.

There are two ways to combat possible engine abuse: *airflow* and *richer mixture.* If you throttle back and slow down, you're decreasing the airflow and *in some light twins, throttling back automatically leans the mixture as well.*

Watch the cylinder head temperature (if available) and the oil temperature carefully. It's a lot easier to keep the engine temperature within limits than to cool it *after* things have gone too far. Open the cowl flaps on the operating engine as necessary.

If you are above the single-engine ceiling, you will lose altitude after the failure of one engine. If the engine gets too hot, you also may have to ease some power and make a slight dive to get increased airflow if altitude permits. Manufacturers check their engines for cooling at gross Weight, best rate of climb speed, full power, and full rich, so unless you really get wild with the good engine, you'll have no problem with it.

LANDING WITH ONE ENGINE (ACTUAL EMERGENCY). A twin-engine airplane with an engine out is an airplane in distress, no matter how glowingly the manufacturer describes its single-engine performance. You'll certainly let the tower know your status. They may see it as you enter the pattern but give them a little advance notice so they can do some traffic planning. You'll certainly have the right-of-way—unless somebody else has *both* engines out. At an uncontrolled field you might let Unicom know that you have one out—other pilots in the pattern on that frequency will give you plenty of room. It's a sad fact that many pilots would literally rather die than let anybody know that they may have a problem. There have been many cases of serious or fatal accidents being caused purely by stubbornness. Don't be afraid of being joshed by fellow pilots for asking for precedence or preference in an unusual situation. Your passengers have more or less blindly entrusted their lives to YOU and you have no right to risk them to save your pride. The pros will congratulate you for recognizing an unusual situation; the amateurs are the ones who scoff.

Enough of the philosophizing. You are interested in landing on the *first* approach. Don't fly in such a manner that you get low and slow and have to apply full power to get to the runway. You might find that it will take more power than you have available to drag the airplane up to the landing area—which brings up another point: *don't lower the gear and flaps until you are pretty well assured you'll make the field.*

Some older light twins that use hydraulic pressure for actuating the gear and flaps may have only one engine-driven hydraulic pump (usually on the left engine). Should this engine be the one that is secured, you'll have to remember to hand pump the gear and flaps down. This may take some time, so give yourself plenty of leeway on final. Forgetting to do this is one of the most common errors of the new twin pilot during simulated engine-out maneuvers at altitude. You make a good pattern and use good headwork until the time comes to lower the gear and flaps. You've got a good final, so you push the gear lever down but forget about the necessity for hand pumping. Valuable seconds go by before your realize that in an actual approach you would have to start pumping—and pronto! Many a new pilot, making a simulated approach at altitude with the propeller feathered on the engine-driven hydraulic pump side has "landed gear-up" at 3,000 ft. This could cause certain inconveniences in an actual landing—so do it right the first time to avoid a potentially dangerous situation.

Keep your approach speed above the single-engine minimum controllable speed (V_{MC}) until landing is assured. You can get yourself into "coffin corner" by slowing it up too soon below V_{MC}; if full power is needed for any reason, you may lose control of the airplane. *Most twin-engine instructors and POHs recommend that the approach be made at least V_{YSE} for best chances of a successful go-around if needed.* (Not *too* fast, though.)

A good single-engine approach is one that requires gradual throttling back of the good engine as you approach the field. As you throttle back, take care of the rudder trim so that when the power is off the airplane will be in trimmed flight. Some pilots neutralize the rudder trim on final and hold the required rudder pressure with one foot. This is good except that if a sudden go-around is required things could get complicated, as the pilot will get no help at all on the rudder and must quickly trim the airplane while executing the required steps.

Another common mistake for the new twin pilot is being much too high on a single-engine approach. If you overdo the idea of not being low, you can be so high and fast that when the flaps are extended you balloon to new heights of glory and have to take it around—*on one engine.* (This makes for problems!)

The perfect single-engine approach is one that allows the pilot plenty of time to correct for crosswinds and to get the airplane in the landing configuration. So, an approach that requires a slight amount of power (with gradual reduction) all the way around is much better than a high, hot, and overshot one. You'll do better if the pattern is close to normal (gear down on downwind leg), but flying a *slightly* closer pattern and delaying flap extension as compared to a two-engine approach. *No radical maneuvering!*

This is a time when the checklist is most important. The good engine should be taken care of, so make sure that the mixture is rich, boost pump on, and fuel on best tank. A double check of the gear is important. In the stress of the moment you may overlook it if the checklist isn't used. Make sure the prop is in high rpm (low pitch) in case you should have to go around.

As noted earlier in the chapter, abrupt throttle closing on the operating engine could cause loss of control in an *unexpected direction.* Figure 15-18 shows what could happen with a *feathered* propeller. The airplane is heavily loaded and has lost an engine. The pilot is carrying full power on the operating (right) engine and is holding full rudder and/or trim to cope with the problem (Fig. 15-18A). The pilot makes the approach and sees that the plane is *too* high and jerks the operating engine abruptly to idle. The right propeller goes to the flat-pitch limit in an attempt to maintain the earlier rpm, and now the Drag on that side is very high. The sudden high Drag plus the rudder or trim being to the right (probably *full* right) can cause an instantaneous and uncontrollable roll to the *right,* opposite to the earlier tendency. The chances of recovery in this situation would be very slim indeed.

TAKING IT AROUND ON ONE ENGINE. It may be that after careful planning on your part somebody taxis out on the runway just

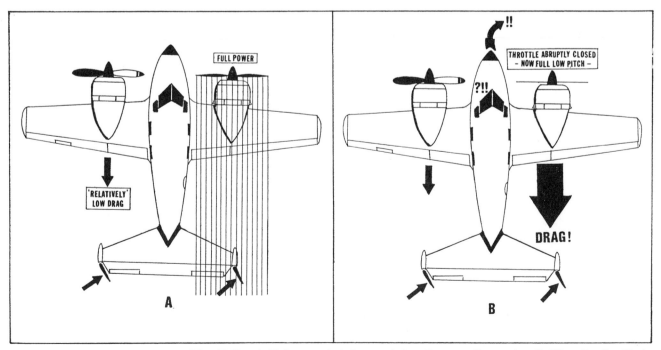

Fig. 15-18. A. Full power is being carried on the operating engine. B. When the throttle is abruptly closed the prop flattens into full low pitch and the Drag situation is as shown. This could set up an uncontrollable roll to the right with fatal results.

as you are on final, or for some other reason you must go around. Once you've decided to make the big move—the sooner the better! The sooner that power is applied on final, the more airspeed and altitude you'll have.

Don't ram the throttle open, as this will cause directional trim problems. Ease it open and retract the landing gear (you may have to pump it up). Flaps up gradually. Don't try to climb too soon—remember that you must attain and maintain the best single-engine climb speed. If you start the go-around early on final, you may use a small amount of altitude—after opening the throttle and cleaning it up—to help attain the best single-engine climb speed if you've dropped below that number. Remember that flaps require the use of vital HP, so don't be *too* slow about getting them up. The makers of several light twins recommend that the flaps be retracted *before* the gear in a go-around. Check the recommended sequence of cleaning up for your airplane. One-engine go-arounds are extremely risky, no matter what light twin you are flying. Obstructions ahead might make it better to land anyway, even if you did forget to lower the gear (and realize it at the last second).

One *POH* notes the following approximate *penalties* in rate of climb:

Landing gear extended—350 fpm
Flaps extended 10°—50 fpm
Flaps extended fully—450 fpm
Inoperative engine propeller windmilling—250 fpm

You can see that with gear and full flaps extended and a windmilling propeller the penalty can be 1050 fpm.

Engine Failure on Takeoff. You may wonder why we've waited so long to be talking about engine failures on takeoff. It might seem more logical to talk about this *first* and then go into the in-flight emergencies. The fact is that you won't cover takeoff engine-out procedures until you've had plenty of practice in the air and have a good idea of the principles of single-engine flight.

There's no doubt about it, during takeoff is the most critical time to lose an engine. The plane is at its heaviest and the airspeed and altitude are low. This is the time for cautious haste. You won't have a great deal of time but will have enough to make a decision.

Lower the good-engine wing as soon as possible to maintain control (Fig. 15-14). *Control is first*, performance next. In fact, if you had a yaw string on the nose, a 15° sideslip into the good engine (the string deflected about 15° from center, toward the inoperative engine) results in *best control*—but not best performance—for some light twins. When things are under control, *then* set up zero sideslip (your string straight and ball deflected approximately one-half width toward the good engine) for best performance, as in the single-engine climb experiment discussed earlier.

The check pilot will give you a single-engine emergency on takeoff by throttling one engine back to zero Thrust and you will go through the necessary recovery actions. You will probably be given simulated takeoff emergencies and engine-out approaches at altitude, where you can actually feather a prop, before simulating one close to the ground with zero Thrust.

Always pick up the best single-engine climb speed as soon as possible after lift-off and then assume the best twin-engine climb speed. Don't accelerate above the twin-engine climb speed; altitude is much more valuable than *added* airspeed.

V_{YSE}, the best single-engine climb speed, is a blue radial *line* on the airspeed indicator for airplanes type-certificated earlier. Future certificated airplanes may require a blue *sector* showing an IAS for V_{YSE} at sea level and extending to the IAS for V_{YSE} at 5000 ft density-altitude or higher, as required by FAR 23. V_{XSE}, the best single-engine *angle* of climb speed, is *not* marked on the airspeed indicator. You'd use this until obstacles were cleared and then assume V_{YSE}.

One thing is sometimes overlooked—if an engine quits on takeoff you do not always take it around. Most new pilots have drilled themselves so thoroughly on what *to* do that they forget that there are things *not* to do, also:

1. If an engine quits before leaving the ground, close the throttle on the good one, taxi back to the hangar, and complain.

2. If an engine quits after you become airborne and there is enough runway left (and your gear is still down), *always* close the throttle on the good engine, land, go back to the hangar, and complain. Light twins on a standard sea level day at gross Weight need 2000 to 4000 ft of runway (depending on the make and model) to accelerate to a particular airspeed and stop. Check your *POH* for the accelerate and stop distance information. If you are taking off from a 2000-ft strip and your airplane requires 3000 ft to accelerate to a predetermined engine failure speed and then stop, you are pretty well committed to go around after getting much above that speed. Remember too, that the accelerate and stop distance will *increase* with an increase in temperature and/or altitude (higher density-altitude) and wet runways (Fig. 15-19).

Also included in some *POH*s is accelerate and *go* information for the airplane, if an engine is lost during takeoff. Like the accelerate and stop chart, data is given for various Weights, engine failure speeds, pressure altitudes, and temperatures. The numbers given note the total distance (feet) to clear a 50-ft obstacle under the various combinations. For instance, one twin, taking off at a particular Weight, at a 6000-ft pressure altitude, at a temperature of 50°F (10°C) with an engine failure at 100 K, will take nearly 16,000 ft (3 mi) to clear a 50-ft obstacle. At sea level standard pressure and temperature, this airplane requires approximately 1 mi to clear 50 ft. It's likely that there will be obstacles 50 ft (or higher) within a mile of any decision point—think about it.

3. If you have lifted off above V_{MC} but have not attained best single-engine climb speed and the runway is rapidly disappearing—

a. Use aileron and rudder to maintain a bank of 5° against the initial roll and yaw.

b. Clean the airplane up.

c. Keep the nose down, keep all engine controls forward, and accelerate to best single-engine climb speed as soon as possible.

d. Remember, loafing foot—loafing engine.

e. Throttle back to check, and after making sure which engine is the culprit, feather that prop.

f. Maintain the recommended best single-engine climb speed and return and land (no low, tight patterns).

Covering all possibilities for an engine failure on takeoff would take a set of encyclopedias. For instance, rough terrain or obstructions well off the end of the runway might mean it's better to belly it in, even though you have best single-engine climb speed.

Pilots have been killed when they overrated their ability and their airplanes' single-engine performance—and forgot about such things as temperature, turbulence, and altitude effects.

Fig. 15-20 is a simplified look at the accelerate-stop versus accelerate-go decision. The *POH* for the twin you are using may have a diagram like this with specific airspeeds noted.

One thing overlooked in light twin flight training is that you *don't always immediately feather* an engine that has lost power on takeoff. You may need any power it's still producing for obstacle clearance. To exaggerate, if that sick engine is producing *one* THP, that's one more than would be working if the prop was feathered. You may decide that even though the engine is giving you some power, the sounds coming from it indicate imminent total failure and problems in feathering later and it's best to feather right away and get on with the traffic pattern. The main things are to (1) maintain control,

ACCELERATE-STOP DISTANCE

CONDITIONS:
Flaps 10°
2400 RPM, 32.5 Inches Hg and
   Mixtures Set at 160 PPH Prior to Brake Release
Cowl Flaps Open
Throttles Closed at Engine Failure
Maximum Braking During Deceleration
Paved, Level, Dry Runway
Zero Wind

Fig. 15-19. Accelerate-stop distance table. At a Weight of 4800 lb at a pressure altitude of 4000 ft and 10°C, the airplane will require 3340 ft to accelerate to 74 K and then stop.

NOTE:
Decrease distances 10% for each 11 knots headwind. For operation with tailwinds up to 10 knots, increase distances by 10% for each 2.5 knots.

WEIGHT LBS	ENGINE FAILURE SPEED KIAS	PRESS ALT FT	ACCELERATE - STOP DISTANCE - FEET				
			0°C	10°C	20°C	30°C	40°C
5150	77	S.L.	2965	3110	3260	3420	3595
		1000	3085	3235	3395	3570	3755
		2000	3210	3370	3540	3725	3925
		3000	3345	3515	3695	3895	4105
		4000	3490	3670	3865	4075	4305
		5000	3645	3840	4050	4275	4515
		6000	3815	4020	4245	4485	4745
		7000	3990	4210	4450	4710	4990
		8000	4180	4415	4670	4950	5250
4800	74	S.L.	2725	2845	2975	3115	3260
		1000	2830	2955	3095	3240	3400
		2000	2940	3075	3220	3375	3545
		3000	3055	3200	3355	3520	3700
		4000	3185	3340	3505	3680	3870
		5000	3320	3485	3660	3850	4055
		6000	3465	3640	3830	4030	4250
		7000	3620	3805	4010	4225	4460
		8000	3785	3985	4200	4435	4685
4400	71	S.L.	2475	2575	2680	2790	2915
		1000	2560	2670	2780	2900	3030
		2000	2655	2770	2890	3015	3155
		3000	2760	2875	3005	3140	3285
		4000	2865	2995	3130	3270	3425
		5000	2980	3120	3260	3415	3580
		6000	3105	3250	3400	3565	3745
		7000	3235	3390	3555	3730	3920
		8000	3375	3540	3715	3905	4110

(2) clear any immediate obstacles, and (3) set up the best configurations for a pattern and landing.

UNFEATHERING IN FLIGHT. Generally, if an engine is so rough that it must be shut down, it should remain so. Sometimes restarting an engine that's cutting up is asking for a fire or a situation where the prop can not be feathered again. However, for practice purposes, it would be wise to try as much actual feathering and unfeathering as possible. Again, this will be done with the check pilot and at a safe altitude. Although you may be leery of the whole idea at first, you'll find that your confidence in single-engine flight will be immeasurably raised if *you* feather and unfeather the propeller several times and do a considerable amount of flying on one engine.

The method of unfeathering varies between models. Some use normal starting procedures (turning it over with the starter, the oil pressure unfeathering the prop as the engine starts) while others have an accumulator that stores oil or nitrogen pressure for unfeathering.

Whatever method used (which will be outlined in detail in the *POH*), remember that the secured engine will be cold because of the airstream passing over it. If properly primed, the engine will make an easier start in the air than on the ground because engine oil pressure will start to build up as the

propeller starts turning, and the prop will move farther and farther out of feather and start windmilling.

You should take it easy in getting full power back on the engine that was shut down, particularly if you've been flying in cold conditions. Don't immediately add full power after getting it started.

After you've read the procedure and done it yourself several times it will be quite clear.

THE CRITICAL ENGINE. You may hear the term *critical engine* and will probably be asked about it when you take the check ride for the multiengine rating. First, in light twins that have both propellers turning clockwise as seen from the cockpit (which pretty well covers the U.S. light twins) the left engine is the critical one. This is because of "asymmetric disk loading" (see Chap. 2). Fig. 15-21 shows that the yawing force is greater when the left engine is out, and therefore directional control is more critical with the loss of that engine. Remember that asymmetric disk loading is popularly called the *P-factor*.

Don't be like some pilots who, when asked by the check pilot why the left engine is the critical one, answer, "It's because the hydraulic pump is on that engine on some light twins."

Some light twins have counterrotating propellers, a de-

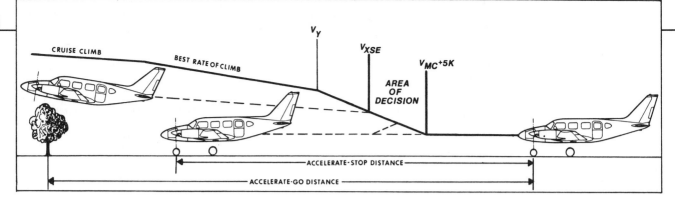

Fig. 15-20. The rotation for lift-off is usually done at V_{MC} + 5 K. The area of decision is between lift-off speed and V_{XSE} (*and* height) and your actions in that area depend on the runway length and heights of obstacles ahead.

sign that eliminates the problem of a critical engine. (This does not mean that there is no longer a yaw when an engine quits but that single-engine performance is the same for either engine.) When both engines are operating normally (and equally), the "torque" forces are cancelled, with no need for rudder trim change for climbs, cruise, or dives.

Learning the Systems and Procedures. So far in this chapter attention has been directed only to items directly concerned with flying the airplane on local flights with you and the checkout pilot and a light load of fuel. When you go up for the multiengine flight test and later when you get out on your own, you'll have to know about the electrical, hydraulic, and de-icing systems as avionics of your airplane, plus be able to run an accurate weight and balance, cope with electrical fires, and know engine fire control procedures. Also, the heating and ventilation system is more complicated than for the singles you've been flying. You might even find yourself unable to start the cabin gasoline heater some cold morning when you and your passengers are turning blue.

Also, you should again take some time to really cope with flying the airplane and to start expanding your knowledge of the avionics and other systems. You might sit down in the airplane with the *POH* and identify various items that you've been too busy to look at closely. "Fly" a flight from start to finish in your mind, using normal procedures (but not moving any controls). Simulate start, taxi, pretakeoff check, takeoff, power change to climb, level-off with power setting and leaning, descents, patterns, approaches, landings, postlanding procedures, taxi, and shutdown. You can later (again not moving any controls) simulate an engine failure on takeoff and during climb and cruise, and go through feathering and restart procedures, plus single-engine approaches and landings. It will help you to feel at ease in the airplane if you can sit in it and make these "dry runs." (If no one is listening, you might want to make engine noises.)

If you're planning to go on and fly with the military or try for the airlines, you can set up some good attitudes about learning these more complicated systems. A light twin hydraulic system no doubt looks very complicated at this point but, compared with that of a 767, it's simple. *But* you can, by studying your system (and maybe reading a little on hydraulics and asking questions of the local mechanics), get information that can be used later. This is not to say that you'll have to memorize all the parts and know exactly where each line goes in order to be a good pilot (since you probably couldn't do a repair job in flight anyway), but you might have some alternate ideas for system use should a problem arise.

SOURCES

Thanks to Mr. Les Berven, engineer and test pilot, for his permission to use notes from his lecture on multiengine aero-dynamics at the University of Tennessee Space Institute in June 1978.

Also, thanks are extended to Capt. M. R. Byington, Jr. (USN, retired), of Embry-Riddle Aeronautical University, Daytona Beach, Florida, whose report, *Optimized Engine Out Procedures for Multi Engine Airplanes,* has helped revise downward earlier estimates of the angles of bank required for zero sideslip (and best climb performance). His flight tests of the single-engine performances of a Cessna Crusader, Piper Seminole, and Beech Baron 58 at various banks have shed much light on a subject that needs to be resolved for *all* multi-engine airplanes.

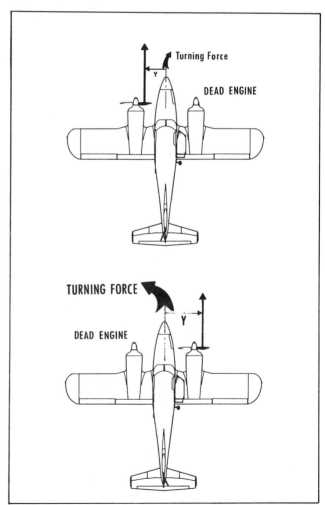

Fig. 15-21. An exaggerated comparison of forces showing that from a control standpoint it's worse to lose the left engine.

16 Problems and Emergencies

When you became a private pilot you were "on your own"—no more check rides or sweating out sessions with an instructor. You became free to establish as many bad habits as you pleased—and like most of us, probably set about it very soon. If you fly your own airplane and keep up the minimum take-offs and landings in the required period, you may legally fly for 24 mo and hundreds of hours without benefit of dual. Your passengers have blind faith in your ability; they don't know whether you've been up recently with an instructor or that you haven't had a check ride since your Curtis Robin was new way back when. If everything goes normally there's no sweat, but if it *doesn't,* you may have a hard time finding passengers to share the expenses on your trips. If your flying is shaky enough, even the uninitiated will begin to suspect that all is not well. Gone are the days when pilots boasted of the number of planes they'd damaged during their careers.

Sure, you've been shooting landings every chance you get, and this is particularly enjoyable in the late afternoon when the air is calm. Takeoffs and landings are fun, and you can learn a lot in a good session. But there are other phases of flying, too. For instance, when was the last time you made a power-off approach? Do you have a good idea of the airplane's approximate glide ratio, clean *and* dirty?

Every once in a while you should drag out the *POH* and go over the emergency procedures again. You'll be surprised how much you have forgotten since the last time you reviewed them.

This chapter will bring up a few points on both low- and high-altitude emergencies and enroute problems.

ROUGH OPERATION OR LOSS OF POWER

The rough running discussed here is not the "automatic rough" that the engine always jumps into when you're flying over water or rough terrain.

Okay, so the engine really starts to run rough—now what? It's a complicated piece of machinery and the trouble could be caused by any one of a thousand things—but a large percentage of problems are caused by a very few items—namely, carburetion, fuel management, and ignition. You'll want to analyze the problem and, if possible, correct it.

Carburetion. This term covers the fuel-air mixture delivered to the engine cylinders—whether using a carburetor or fuel injection.

CARBURETOR ICE. One of the most common problems for carburetors is plain old-fashioned ice. However, if you've let icing go so far as to cause the engine to start running rough, you've really been asleep. You know that carburetor ice gives warning by (1) a decrease in manifold pressure (mp) in an airplane with a constant-speed prop or (2) a decrease in rpm for the fixed-pitch prop. It's quite possible that carburetor icing in a light trainer can progress to a point that *full* carburetor heat won't undo the damage. It's a vicious cycle: the heat capacity naturally depends on the engine, but the engine is sick because of the ice and the carburetor heat suffers. The engine may quit and there you sit with a windmilling propeller. So you fell asleep and now must pick a field. *Leave the carburetor heat full on as you try for the field.* There may be enough residual heat getting into the carburetor to clear out the ice before you have to land. You pulled it on and nothing happened right away, so what may be needed is a little time. This doesn't mean that you won't be picking a field and preparing for an unscheduled landing—because the residual heat may *not* do the trick. Don't count on it and sit up there with your head up and locked.

One thing of importance about carburetor ice if you don't have a carburetor air temperature gage—when you discover you have ice, use *full* carburetor heat to get the garbage cleaned out. It's suggested by a major engine manufacturer that if the airplane doesn't have any sort of induction air temperature gage (and carburetor ice is suspected) you'd best use either full heat or none, since you don't know the temperature you're setting up for the carburetor. Icing can be induced at low temperatures where moisture in the air is in crystalline form. These particles would pass on through the carburetor without problems except that partial heat melts them and they refreeze on the cold metal of the throttle plate. At temperatures of 14°F and below, any moisture in the outside air is frozen and heat shouldn't be used.

On some of the older higher-performance lightplanes the carburetor or manifold heat is very effective, and the air going into the carburetor may be raised up to 200°F by application of full heat. *The use of full heat will cause a power loss and could cause detonation at high power settings.*

Remember that the ice will collect around the butterfly and jets of the float carburetor.

Your job will be to use carburetor heat and open the throttle if it looks as though the ice is getting ahead. When you open the throttle you've made sure that the butterfly valve is opened so that the fuel-air mixture has a better chance of getting through to the engine. Icing can give you more trouble at part- or closed-throttle operation—it will take less ice to cut off the fuel-air mixture from the engine. You remember this from your student pilot days when you used carburetor heat before closing the throttle for a glide. More power means more carburetor heat available for use.

Normally, though, you'll apply heat as needed and won't increase the power. With a constant-speed propeller you don't want to just ram the throttle wide open without thinking you might overboost the engine.

As you know, carburetor ice is not as much a function of low temperature as it is of high humidity. If the outside air temperature is quite low the air will be so dry that carburetor ice will be a lesser problem.

Anytime you are more or less smoothly losing mp or rpm, use carburetor heat or alternate air (assuming you don't have a creeping throttle). Here's the typical situation: You notice that the mp is lower than it should be, you haven't climbed, and it looks as though you might have ice. Suppose that you were carrying 24 in. of mercury for cruise, but it has dropped to 22 in. You apply heat and the mp drops to 21 in. because of the less-dense air introduced. After a few seconds the mp picks up the 2 in. it lost so that the gage registers 23 in. When you push the heat off it will again be up to 24 in. But if it iced once it will do it again; you'll have to experiment to get the right setting. (It may be full heat if there's no CAT gages.)

When you use full carburetor heat and send the warm, less-dense air through the engine, the mixture will be richer. *At cruise* you'll lean the mixture to smooth out operations. (*Don't* use heat for *takeoff* or *climb* except in Arctic operations. You'd be checked out about the proper procedure if you were flying in that area.) After you ease the heat off, you readjust the mixture to a richer setting, as the denser cold air starts coming through again.

Some trainers' *POHs* suggest the use of carburetor heat throughout the approach and landing. You know by now that a go-around with full heat cuts down noticeably on perform-

ance. It's possible, too, that detonation could occur on a climb with full heat, so get heat off as full power is being applied.

If a carburetor air or induction air temperature gage is available, maintaining a minimum of 90°F CAT at cruise or letdown is seen as one way to prevent icing.

IMPACT ICING. The fuel injection system has the advantage of doing away with carburetor ice, but both types of systems may suffer from impact icing.

Saturated air is the culprit here. Whenever you're flying in rain, clouds, or fog, and the outside air is near freezing, impact icing may occur. As the air enters the induction system it may be condensed and cooled to the point that ice will form at the 90° bend where the air scoop turns to enter the carburetor or fuel injection control.

Another problem is structural icing on the air intake screen. You may run into this when flying instruments later. Structural icing on the airplane may not be serious but could cause a power loss. Fig. 16-1 shows a simple method of taking care of this problem. When the intake is iced over, the engine suction will open the spring-loaded trap door and the warm air from around the engine is drawn into the intake system. Naturally some power will be lost, as the warmer air is less dense than the cold outside air. But better to lose some power than all of it.

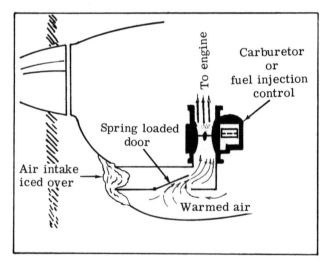

Fig. 16-1. An alternate air source.

Freezing rain or drizzle may glaze over the intake also, but you will be busy trying to see through a glazed windshield and keep a logy airplane flying and won't have any time to appreciate the automatic features of your airplane.

Very heavy (nonfreezing) rain may close off the air intake screen so that the engine loses partial or complete power. If this is encountered, carburetor heat or alternate air will get most of the power back. (Reset the mixture as necessary for efficient operation after using carb heat.)

MIXTURE. Occasionally an engine runs rough because pilots abuse the mixture control—but usually they're aware of this misdemeanor. The two main problems are (1) a too-rich mixture at altitude and (2) descending with the mixture set for a high-altitude cruise. Occasionally there will be those who descend and try to apply full power when in the best economy setting.

You might check to see that the primer is in *and locked.* This is an often-overlooked cause of rough running, particularly at lower power settings. Notice in the fuel system schematics (carburetors) in Chap. 13 that the primer furnishes fuel to the engine at a different point. The primer fuel doesn't go through the carburetor but goes directly to the engine at the intake manifold. If the primer control (or primer pump as it's sometimes called) is not locked, the engine may pull fuel from this source in addition to that furnished by the carburetor. The engine will run rich even though the mixture control is set properly. In rare cases, such as overenthusiastically pulling back on the mixture control and finding it pulling out in your hand (and the engine in idle cutoff at 5000 ft AGL), the primer may be used to stretch the glide, if somewhat erratically. You leave the throttle at cruise or slightly less, pull the primer out, and give "shots" to the engine. The power will increase with each shot and decrease to a windmilling condition when you're pulling the control out for the next try. Such power surging could be pretty rough on some engines. This technique shouldn't be used for fun, but it might give you a few hundred (or thousand) feet of distance needed to make it to an airport in a jam. Check on the schematic of your airplane fuel system to see the tie-in.

If you have carburetor ice, it is not advisable to richen the mixture. Carburetor ice tends to cause a richer mixture. You may be heaping coals on the engine's head if you move the mixture control to full rich and throw on full carburetor heat (which further tends to richen the mixture because the warm air has less weight per unit volume). There for a split second, you have the richest mixture in town—and the engine may not like it.

For all other occasions of engine roughness, moving the mixture control forward is a good idea. A richer mixture means cooler running and more power, particularly at lower altitudes. You may have overleaned the engine.

Fuel Management

> Breathes there a soul so dead,
> Who has not shook his head and said,
> "Cripes, I forgot to switch tanks!"

There's one thing about running a tank dry—you won't get 5 min of frantic warning beforehand. In fact, if you haven't been watching the fuel pressure, your first warning will be a hiccup from the engine—followed by a loud silence. There is a no more active group than four pilots in a four-place airplane when a tank unexpectedly runs dry. The front-seat occupants are both scrambling for the tank selector (getting in each other's way and tripling the required time to switch tanks) while the back-seat occupants are shouting advice and maybe trying to get *their* hands into the act. Running a tank dry is a particularly effective attention getter if the three pilot-passengers are dozing when it happens. Funny as it may seem, nonpilots are not as affected by such a practice—they just sit back and quietly tremble. It's best to throttle back to prevent overspeeding of the engine when the tank change is made.

Keep up with the flying time on each tank—gages can be wrong. If the engine quits abruptly or starts losing power, you may have had a leak or perhaps a stoppage. Don't get the idea because the tank(s) started at full and the consumption time isn't up that it won't do any good to switch tanks—it's worth a try. There have been too many accident reports stating, "In the wreckage it was found that the fuel selector was on an empty tank—the other tank was full." (Admittedly, it's hard to imagine a tank remaining full after the solid impact of a crash, but it has happened.)

FAR 23 states, "If a reciprocating engine can be supplied with fuel from more than one tank, it must be possible, in level flight, to regain full power and fuel pressure to that engine in not more than 10 seconds (for single-engine airplanes) or 20 seconds (for multiengine airplanes) after switching to any fuel tank after engine malfunctioning due to fuel depletion becomes apparent while the engine is being supplied from any other tank."

Some *POH*s advise that should it be necessary to run a tank dry, it's best to switch at the first indication of fuel flow fluctuation or power loss and give steps for best recovery of power (fuel boost ON, etc.). Other *POH*s may suggest that running a tank dry be avoided. Refer to your specific handbook for suggestions as to whether a tank should be run dry and the procedures involved.

It has been found that several carburetor-equipped single-engine airplanes start 1 to 2 sec *after* the fuel selector is switched from an empty to a full tank. Fuel-injected engines of the same general-type airplane took 6 to 8 sec after the new tank was selected. While the time variance seems small, a pilot who is used to the carburetor-type reaction *could* decide that the fuel-injected engine won't regain power again, start switching back and forth, and get out of phase with the fuel system; 8 sec can seem a long time—particularly if the engine has lost power and you delay analyzing the problem. The point is, the single-engine airplane must regain power within 10 sec in either type of fuel-metering system. In the case of simply running out of fuel on one tank, you'd use the *POH* procedure (which may call for throttling back, turning on the boost pump, and richening the mixture) and give it a chance to work.

Ignition Problems

PLUG FOULING. The most common ignition problem on the ground and at very low power settings in the air (extended glides, etc.) is plug fouling. This often occurs when using a fuel of higher lead content than recommended. The bottom plugs on a horizontally opposed engine may tend to be fouled after starting, especially if the plane has been sitting for several days. Your indication is an excessive rpm drop during a mag check. This usually can be corrected by leaning the mixture at a fairly high power setting (1500 to 2000 rpm). Move the mixture back until the first signs of roughness appear and leave it there for 30 to 60 sec. You are raising the cylinder head temperature to such an extent that the illegal oil or lead on the plug tip is burned off. Naturally it doesn't do the engine any good to be run on the ground in this way, but it's simpler than going back and getting the plugs cleaned. Normally, fouled plugs will clean themselves out with operation, *but* it may be in the magneto and you just think it's in the plugs. If the treatment just described doesn't work, don't abuse the engine; richen the mixture and taxi back to the hangar to find out what's up.

This chapter is about in-flight problems. For plugs to suddenly start fouling in flight is unusual. In-flight fouling may mean serious piston ring problems and it's best to land at the nearest airport.

MAGNETO PROBLEMS. If you start getting a bum mag when you're right over the center of Gitchygoomy Swamp, there's little you can do in the way of repairs. Plug or mag problems usually are characterized by almost instantaneous rough running (or not running). The engine may run smoothly and then abruptly cut in and out. Unfortunately this instantaneous change is sometimes a characteristic of certain carburetion, as well as governor, problems. Generally speaking though, the ignition, by its very principle of operation, is more apt to cause immediate changes in engine characteristics.

If the engine starts running rough and you are unable to clear up the problem, start a shallow climb and head for the nearest cleared area or airport—altitude is very comforting on these occasions.

Sometimes the engine will start raising a fuss because the rotor in one of the mags has broken down and is allowing the spark plugs for that mag to fire at random. This is bad because in a sense there is a continual spark and every time the fuel-air is injected into the cylinders it gets fired—ready or not. In effect, the timing has broken down. There's a time for everything and this ain't it, as the young lady said when discouraging an ardent admirer during church services.

In this situation (talking about the magneto again), it would be better to turn off the one mag completely and run on one—that's why you have two magnetos. If the engine really sounds bad, check the mags to see if this is the problem.

Loss of Oil Pressure. The average pilot tends to neglect scanning the engine instruments during flight, looking at them before takeoff and then checking them once an hour, if that often. It's quite a jarring experience to look casually at the oil pressure and find that it's gone—the hand is nestled up against ZERO and you don't know how long it's been there.

Well, take heart; for every instance of actual oil pressure loss, there are several cases where the instrument is the culprit. There's one way of telling if you're in trouble: watch the oil temperature gage (and cylinder head temperature if available). Usually a couple of minutes will tell the tale. If the temperature doesn't start up it's just the instrument and you can relax—a little. In other words, just because you have low (or no) oil pressure doesn't mean that all is lost. But if the temperature starts a rapid rise into the red, you'd better look for a field in a single-engine plane or start feathering that engine in a twin. No oil means engine seizure in a very short while.

FIRE IN FLIGHT

The smell of "unauthorized" smoke in the cockpit (no one is smoking) can get your attention even more quickly than a rough engine. You'll be checked on your knowledge of what to do in such a case on the commercial or multiengine flight tests, but you should review the procedures for your own benefit, even if you plan to stay a private pilot for the next 50 yr. When a real emergency happens you won't have time to set up a procedure—it should be already laid out in your mind.

Electrical Fires. You're climbing out of the local airport with a full load of passengers and baggage. Suddenly you smell insulation burning and/or see smoke in the instrument panel area. Some pilots panic in this situation. Airplane control is pretty much forgotten and screaming steep turns are made back to the airport with gear-up landings following—all because maybe 20 cents worth of insulation burned. *The first requirement is to maintain control of the airplane.* Stalling and spinning at low altitudes is no way to resolve the problem.

Turn off the master switch in the case of an electrical fire for most airplanes. Then turn off all electrical and avionics equipment. If you've just lifted from an uncontrolled airport, return and land, watching for other aircraft. (Before turning off the master switch you might make a quick call to local traffic or Unicom to let your intentions be known.) At a busy, controlled field you'd want to leave the Master and one transceiver on until off the active runway. Otherwise you'd be gambling the possibility of expanding the fire against a possible midair collision because no one knows your intentions.

Enroute, you'd turn the master switch off, turn avionics and other electrical switches off, and check circuit breakers to see if one popped as the fire started (leave the CB out). Turn the master switch back on and (if no CB had been popped) turn on items one by one with a short pause each time.

There are two schools of thought on opening the cabin ventilators:

1. Keep the cabin ventilators closed to avoid fanning the flames. Open them only after the fire is burned out and the system isolated.

2. Open the ventilators immediately to clear out possible toxic fumes and also to get the smoke out to expedite the isolation of the culprit. (For instance, if you turn on transceiver number two and smoke comes back, there's your problem.)

There are good arguments for both procedures; it depends on the amount of smoke and whether it is beginning to get to you. The main thing is to have considered some alternatives beforehand.

Engine Fires. Probably one of the worst situations you could encounter would be a full-fledged engine fire while on solid IFR over mountainous terrain in a single-engine airplane. One manufacturer recommends some steps in the event of an engine fire:

1. Turn mixture control to idle cutoff.
2. Turn fuel selector OFF.
3. Turn master switch OFF.
4. Establish the best glide distance airspeed.
5. Close cabin heat and cabin air controls. (Open overhead adjustable ventilators or cabin windows to get ventilation.)
6. Select a field suitable for a forced landing.
7. If the fire is not extinguished, increase the glide speed to try to find a speed at which combustion cannot occur. The usual recommendation is not to restart the engine. If one engine of a twin catches on fire you'd naturally go through the feathering procedure. Fortunately, engine fires are extremely rare, but that doesn't help when it happens to you. Review the *POH*.

HIGH-ALTITUDE FORCED LANDINGS

Picking a Field. Here's where you wish you'd practiced more power-off approaches. Set up the max distance glide speed, use carburetor heat, switch tanks, and go through the other steps previously mentioned.

Naturally you'll pick the best field available and land into the wind if possible. Maneuver so that you have a "Key Position" at a point opposite the point of intended landing, similar to the spot on the downwind leg where you've been starting the 180° side approaches at the airport. You are trying to turn an unusual situation into a more familiar one. The Key Position altitude should be somewhat higher above the ground than the traffic altitude you've been flying. You can S-turn or spiral to reach this position, but don't give yourself such a high margin of altitude that you overshoot—you may be so high that flaps and/or slipping won't be enough. Establish an imaginary box at the Key Position; the bottom of the box will be *at least* traffic pattern altitude and the top no more than 300 ft higher. The center of the Key Position box should be at approximately the abeam position on the downwind leg (Fig. 16-2).

You may have been shooting power-on approaches throughout your recent flying career—this means that your downwind and base legs may have been much farther from the field than could be allowed for a power-off approach. *This, and the fact that a windmilling or stopped prop gives more drag than you may have counted on, could result in undershooting.* If you have a controllable-pitch prop, pull the propeller control full back to high pitch (low rpm).

If the wind is strong the downwind leg or Key Position box should be moved in slightly, as you would do for any power-off approach.

After you've hit the Key Position, the rest is pretty well

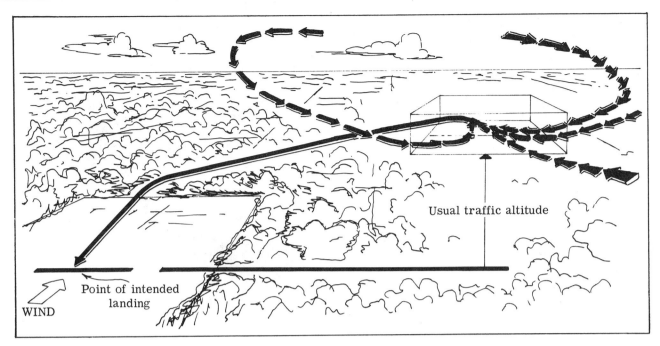

Fig. 16-2. The Key Position box.

up to you. Hitting a spot is a matter of experience and practice, and there are no printed "cribs" or "gouges" to help you. Your judgment is especially important the last 90° of turn into the field. If you are low on base, naturally you'll "cut across"; if high, you may S-turn past the wind line (Fig. 16-3).

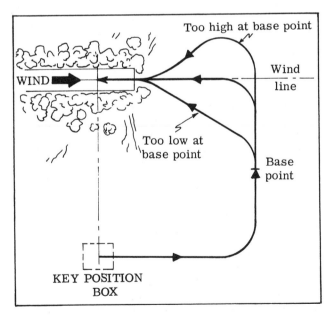

Fig. 16-3. Playing the final turn.

What you definitely do *not* want to do is get the airplane slow and wrapped up. That's the best possible way to get into serious trouble. It's a lot better to fly into something (a rougher field or bushes) with the plane under some semblance of control than to spin at a low altitude. Many fatal accidents have occurred when a pilot, under the pressure of an actual emergency, got slow and tried to rack the plane around. Some

of the higher-performance planes you'll be flying are not as forgiving as the trainer you flew earlier.

There'll be times when a righthand pattern will be better.

If you don't have shoulder harnesses, have your front seat passenger hold a map case or a folded coat in front of his or her face, with the feet back—just in case. *Seats locked.* Some *POH*s recommend cracking the door(s) before touchdown so that they don't jam shut on impact.

Gear and Flaps. With a fixed-gear airplane there is no decision to be made as to whether the gear should be up or down. It's down and you can like it or lump it.

For the retractable-gear airplane, you'll have to decide whether it'll be gear-up or -down on the forced landing. There's a story that some years ago at a large military training base the cadets were admonished always to land gear-up in the event of an engine failure—unless they could land on a "designated military field." This rule was to ensure that the cadets did not try to land gear-down in pastures or the short civilian fields in the area; there would be less over-all damage done by landing gear-up. One day on a cross-country a cadet had an engine failure right over a busy civilian field (with 8000-ft runways). You guessed it—he made a perfect approach and landed gear-up in the middle of the busiest runway. Needless to say, the runway wasn't of much use until the airplane was dragged off. The cadet's story? "But sir, the rules—this wasn't a designated *military* field." This left a very frustrated accident board chewing their nails and trying to broaden the regulations.

You won't have any hard-and-fast rules to go by. If the surface is either firm and smooth or extremely rough (large rocks, stumps, etc.) you'd probably be better off to put the gear *down*. If there are stumps and large rocks, the down gear will take a large amount of the shock before being torn off. You remember that the kinetic energy of your airplane is $(M/2)V^2$, or one-half the mass (Weight divided by 32.2) times the square of the velocity. The longer you take to stop, the better off you are, even if it's a matter of a split second's difference. If you land gear-up on the rocky or stump-strewn field, it's possible that the obstacles may start ripping through the belly while you're at a high speed. In such a situation forget the rest of the airplane—you'll be wanting to keep the cabin intact, so leave the gear down. As has been stated about jumping off a roof, "It's not the fall that hurts, it's the sudden stop."

The following table gives examples of impact speed versus approximate stopping distance and the longitudinal deceleration forces (g's) resulting (with g's rounded off to the nearest one-half). The stopping (skid) distance is *20 ft* in each case:

Impact Speed (K)	g's
20	1
40	3½
60	8
80	14
100	20

In another example, the stopping distance (skid) is *40 ft* in each case:

Impact Speed (K)	g's
20	Less than 1
40	2
60	4
80	7
100	10

Doubling the distance to stop cuts down on the deceleration forces by about one-half. (An airplane impacting at 100 K and stopping in 1 ft would be the victim of over 400 g's.) The old idea in a forced landing, hitting the softest, cheapest object in the area as slowly as possible, still stands.

If you think the chosen field will be soft, generally it's a good idea to keep the gear up. And naturally for a water landing (ditching) the gear should be up.

Your decision for gear-up or -down will be based on what you see at the time. If in doubt about the firmness of a field the usual decision is to leave the gear up. If it is soft and the wheels sink in, high deceleration forces will result.

All these considerations, of course, depend on whether you are *able* to get the gear down. You should have enough residual hydraulic pressure or electric power for one cycle anyway (and you may change your mind on the way down).

FLAPS. Proper use of flaps can mean the difference between success or failure. A common error in practice emergencies is for the pilot to put down the gear and use full flaps right away—resulting in an undershoot. Taking off some of the flaps when undershooting may be too late to do any good—plus the fact that the sudden upping of flaps causes a temporarily increased sink rate, especially at low airspeeds.

Use the flaps in this situation in increments; put a little down as you feel they are needed. If it looks as though the flaps will have to be put down by emergency means because of the no-power condition, you might be better off forgetting about them—this is no time to be fumbling around in the cockpit.

SLIPS. For airplanes without flaps, the slip is the big aid in hitting the field. If you are on a close base leg and are high, waiting until after turning final to slip may be too late—you may miss the field because the final leg will be too short to give you time to get set for a slip.

If it looks as though you'll be crowded, a slipping turn comes in handy. It's a good way to lose altitude in the turn without picking up excessive airspeed. You're holding a touch of top rudder and a little aileron into the turn. Don't hold so much top rudder that the turn is stopped—you still want to land in the field you picked originally (Fig. 16-4).

Fig. 16-4.   The slipping turn.

Flaps and slips don't always mix well. Some airplanes are unforgiving this way, as the flaps may blanket the tail surfaces in a slip. You might go to altitude and try the reaction of your airplane to a flaps-down slip and also talk with some of the local pros. Check your *POH,* too.

Ditching. Plan your approach into the wind if the wind is high and seas are heavy. If the swells are heavy but the wind is light, land parallel to the swells. *If you are uncertain of wind direction, remember that the white caps appear to move into the wind.* Land the way the white caps are moving (unless the swells are heavy).

Obviously the best ditching can be made with landing gear up. A fixed-gear airplane is not good for ditching, but it is too late to switch airplanes. In this case you can make the impact as light as possible under the conditions by the following steps:

1. Use full flaps. It has been suggested that for low-wing airplanes an intermediate flap setting be used to avoid digging in. The digging-in characteristics depend on the airplane. The *POH* may give some advice on this.

2. Set up a minimum descent glide (power-on or -off as your situation dictates).

3. Unlatch the door so that it doesn't jam on impact.

4. *Don't* try to second-guess and flare when you think it's time. You may level off too high and drop in at a nose-down attitude—this will generally ensure an unsuccessful ditching. Also if the tail is too low on impact, the result may be a pitching forward and digging in. It is very hard to judge altitude over water, particularly in a slick sea.

5. Make sure all the passengers' seat belts are snug (and yours too). If the airplane is equipped with shoulder harnesses, so much the better. It would be wise to have your front-seat passenger cover his or her face with a folded coat if there are no shoulder harnesses available—and you might do the same at the last second.

Expect more than one impact shock. The airplane may skip once or more before the final hard shock. You will swear that the airplane has gone straight to the bottom as nothing but spray will be visible for several seconds. In witnessing a ditching from the air, the airplane may be completely hidden in spray for a few seconds (you, of course, won't be particularly interested in how it looks from the air at this time).

As soon as all forward motion has stopped, leave the

airplane (it is assumed that you planned on flying over water and have flotation gear—or that you are a strong swimmer). The length of time the airplane will float depends on how empty the tanks are and how much the airplane is damaged.

It's important to have the wings level when you hit the water—this is no time to be cartwheeling.

It is very important that you get on the radio as soon as you know you'll have to ditch. Broadcast "Mayday" and your position on the Emergency frequency (121.5 MHz). You might also transmit on regular communications frequencies because you seldom transmit on 121.5 MHz and don't know if it's working or not. This is definitely an emergency, so your transponder should be on 7700. Since the transponder depends on line of sight for pickup, the higher you are when 7700 is initiated, the better the chance of being seen. Then get back to flying the airplane. A wise move, if you plan on flying an extended overwater trip, is to make sure that the Emergency and other important transmitter frequencies are working, and above all—*file a flight plan*.

AIM—Basic Flight Information and ATC Procedures has a very good section on ditching, with illustrations of swell and wind combinations, and you should read it thoroughly before making that long overwater flight. The best time to consider emergency procedures is *before* the flight.

PRECAUTIONARY LANDINGS

In the event of imminent fuel exhaustion, fast-deteriorating weather, or engine problems, it may be necessary to make an off-airport landing. It's always best, naturally, to be able to pick your spot while the picking is good. You should know what to do when you have to land in the hinterlands; the technique of "dragging the area" is valuable for this situation.

Basically, this technique consists of picking a field that appears to be able to take your airplane (gear-down, if possible) and flying a normal pattern and approach to the area of the field on which you plan to land. Add power and level off at about 100-ft altitude on final and fly to the right side and parallel to the landing area. Look over the landing area for holes, ditches, field condition (high grass, soft,,etc.), and in general look for items that couldn't have been seen from altitude. If everything looks okay, open the throttle, climb out, and make a pattern with a short-field approach and landing. If you see that the field isn't for you on the first pass, repeat this technique at another one.

During the approach and pass, watch for wires or other obstructions of that nature. You can't always see the wires but if there are poles check which way they are running. In the case of wires, look for other poles well to both sides of the pole line; there may be other wires that would cause you trouble if you were landing parallel to the known wires.

Your decision whether to land gear-up or -down depends on the points mentioned earlier in the chapter. You'll have to decide whether things have gone so far that you may be better off to belly it in to a fairly bad field rather than take the time to find another one (if you have only a couple of minutes of fuel left, or if it looks as if the weather will soon go to zero-zero and you're practically at rock bottom altitude).

If you're not going to be able to make it to an airport, it's better to land at a field of *your* choice. After you're down, get to a telephone and let the proper offices or people know of your plight.

LOW-ALTITUDE PROBLEMS

Engine Failure on Takeoff (Single-Engine Airplane).
One thing that has been discussed in many ways throughout this book and during your flying career is worth repeating: *Keep the airplane under control!* You can make a

minor turn but keep it shallow. If you have time, cut the mixture, ignition, and fuel. Turn off the master switch after you've used flaps (electric). Have the airplane as slow as possible when you touch down. If you are going into trees, don't stall it out above them but fly into them at the lowest possible speed, still with control.

If the engine starts running rough after passing the airport boundary (or any point where it's too late to try to land again), fly straight ahead (if the terrain and populated area allow) and try to gain altitude without getting too slow. The engine may quit at any time and at least you'll be headed more or less into the wind. *Ease* your way back to the airport. Maintain a safe airspeed.

Open Door. A door opening suddenly during takeoff or in flight is quite an experience. There is a loud bang as it opens, and the noise of the air moving past the crack is enough to set up a good case of combat fatigue in a short while. In addition to the sundry noises associated with such a problem, the airplane may have tail buffeting or the wing on that side may tend to drop because of the disturbed airflow.

The usual situation is that the pilot has forgotten to lock the door (it should be on the checklist) and no problem occurs until the airspeed is such that the drop in pressure caused by the air moving past the door is enough to pull it from the latching mechanism—then the fun begins. It seems that the airspeed required for this is reached just after lift-off; the usual setting for a door opening episide is on a short runway, in turbulent air, with obstacles ahead, the airplane at gross Weight, and your nervous maiden aunt sitting by the door.

If the door opens on the takeoff run and there is room to stop, naturally this is the thing to do. If it opens after lift-off and there isn't room left to land, keep *full* power on climb at the normal climb airspeed. In most cases performance will suffer but the airplane can be flown. Fly a normal pattern (don't wrack it around), make your approach at a slightly faster airspeed, and carry the airplane closer to the ground before starting the transition—more or less fly it on. As was mentioned, the wing on that side may tend to drop out early. It would help if your passenger would hold the door as closely shut as possible to minimize the effects.

Your biggest problem will be plain old-fashioned fear. It's a nerve-shattering occurrence and between the noise and the buffeting, plus occasional screams from distraught passengers, you could be fatally distracted. Fatalities have occurred in airplanes that were perfectly capable of flying with the door open, when the pilot tried to cut corners and spun in.

If you're at altitude and your Aunt Minerva catches her knitting bag on the handle and suddenly presents you with fresh air in copious quantities, you may be able to shut the door in flight. Generally, the procedure is to throttle back to idle, slow and trim the airplane to a speed just above the stall, open the small storm window on the pilot's side to help equalize the pressure, and shut the door—and lock it. On some airplanes the storm window can be held open with your left elbow while holding the control wheel with your left hand. You can reach over and shut the door with your right hand if you're by yourself. Needless to say, these gymnastics could be hairy at lower altitudes.

You may have to land the airplane with the door ajar and should expect some buffeting during the approach and landing. Usually, of its own accord, the door will settle on a position of 3 to 6 in. open. If there isn't a passenger available to hold it shut add 5 to 10 K to the approach speed *using a normal approach pattern*.

There may be different techniques for your airplane; the main idea is to bring this possible problem to your attention. Check on your airplane with other pilots and/or your *POH* and go over in your mind what to do in such an event. Better to set up a plan now than to have to work something out in all that noise and confusion.

Seat Belt and Shoulder Harness. There may be a time when you lift off and are committed (the runway is behind you) and you suddenly hear what sounds like the engine destroying itself. There is a bang, bang, bang, and you're sure that a complete power loss is imminent. Check the engine instruments and maintain control of the airplane as you gain altitude and decide what might be the problem.

There have been instances of pilots chopping power at the end of the runway and landing in bad terrain (damaging their airplanes and injuring themselves) when the only problem was the right seat belt or shoulder harness hanging out the door and whacking against the fuselage. Such noises could be engine problems, of course, but you want to maintain control of the airplane while you check things. When you are flying solo, fasten that empty seat belt and harness so that this can't happen. (If you have passengers you should certainly oversee fastening their belts and harnesses.)

The sound of a rampaging seat belt or harness is usually a steady banging that may sound like an engine problem but is isolated as to its general position. Sure, the straps will probably cause minor paint or fabric damage, but you'd be a lot better flying a normal pattern and landing rather than opening the door and pulling the straps and/or belt in. The main point, anyway, is to remind you that control of the airplane is primary in case you hear such sounds.

Gusty Air, Turbulence, and Gradient Winds. Wind velocities and directions vary with altitude—this is expected—but what's not always expected is the fact that the wind may change velocity and/or direction with only a small altitude change. On a gusty day the wind velocity may change almost instantly; you might be in a tight spot if you're flying the airplane too close to the stall.

A problem to watch closely is the effect on the wind of obstacles such as trees or buildings on the windward side of the runway (Fig. 16-5).

Even if the wind is steady and you've been holding the

same crosswind correction all the way down on final, things can go to pot pretty fast when you get close to the ground. Not only obstacles cause trouble—but the wind itself could change velocity abruptly. The airplane feels as if the bottom were dropping out and the air may be extremely choppy. Adding power (fast!) usually keeps things under control.

There may be a time when you are racing a thunderstorm to the field. Remember something here, too—the wind may shift abruptly; it can be very strong one way and when you get all set up for landing, you find that you are now trying to land cross-downwind. Keep a close eye on the wind indicator on final when there are thunderstorms in the vicinity or a cold front passage is expected momentarily.

Wake Turbulence. You may not have had the dubious pleasure of encountering wake turbulence, but chances are good that sometime you will.

Naturally, the most critical place to fly into wake turbulence is at a low altitude and the most likely place for trouble is on takeoff or landing. Give the big planes plenty of room. Take it around again or ask for another runway if you think there might be wake turbulence hanging around; the turbulence may be around for several minutes after the instigator has made its getaway.

If there is a crosswind, always take off or land on the upwind side of the runway. After taking off, stay off to one side of the big airplane that's causing the problem. One hazard in a light crosswind condition (3 to 7 K) is that one of the vortices is kept over the same position relative to the runway. (The downwind vortex will be moved even faster laterally.) One vortex may move over to a parallel runway and cause mischief over there.

If the wind is straight down the runway or calm and you *must* take off, the following steps are best: (1) don't lift the airplane off until you have plenty of flying speed—hold it on a little longer than usual but plan to get off before the point of the big plane's lift-off, since its vortices will begin at the point of rotation for lift-off and (2) after lifting off make a shallow turn to one side and then turn back to parallel the runway (Fig. 16-6).

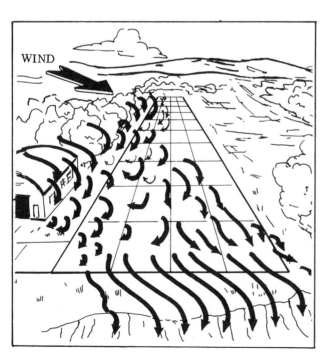

Fig. 16-5. The effects of obstacles on the wind.

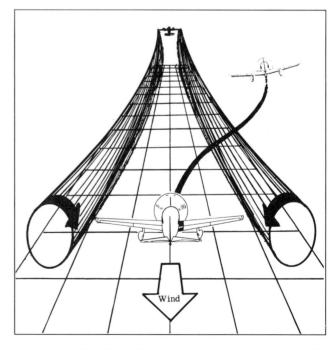

Fig. 16-6. Clearing wake turbulence on takeoff.

Even clearing the runway will be dangerous if you take off directly behind the other plane with no waiting time. Though you will get out of the way as soon as possible there may be a period when you will be in the turbulence. Whether you'll have airspeed enough to get through it safely is a matter for conjecture—so it's best to wait.

If you are landing behind another plane and the wind is directly down the runway or calm, you'd be better off to land past the spot it touched down, making a slightly steeper approach than usual. Of course, if it overshoots and lands so far down the runway that reversible thrust was the only thing that saved it, you'd better take your airplane around rather than land long.

The best thing is to avoid wake turbulence, but you may be caught unprepared. Again, the most exciting place to get caught is during takeoff or landing; you're low and slow and don't have ideal control response.

WAKE TURBULENCE ON TAKEOFF OR LANDING. You've just lifted off and suddenly turbulence makes the airplane go berserk; it rolls violently, and opposite aileron and rudder have little effect in stopping it. In addition to the roll the turbulence may try to pick the airplane up or slam it back on the ground.

Keep full power on and do not try to climb up through it. Keep the nose down. You need airspeed. If you are slow when hitting the disturbance you'll make more trouble by hauling back on the wheel. Don't let it put you into the ground (if you can help it), but don't get to thinking that you can pop up through it either—you might end up on your back at 20 ft and get socked with a violation of Federal Aviation Regulations for putting on an airshow without permission. Besides, you wouldn't want to land this way as there are no wheels on the top of the airplane.

When the airplane rolls, try to stop the bank from becoming too steep but don't attempt to level the wings completely. A turn is needed right now, and some bank will help you get out of the choppy area. Turn in the direction that the turbulence tends to roll you.

You may cut some fancy capers at a low altitude and end up flying 45° from your takeoff heading for a few seconds but you want to get into smooth air—and stay there. After doing all sorts of graceful and not so graceful rolling and maneuvering right off the ground because of wake turbulence one day, a private pilot was asked by the tower if he were in trouble. His answer became a classic in radio communication, although it resulted in an FCC violation for "improper language over the air." Tower operators realize that wake turbulence is a definite menace to lightplanes and warn pilots if there is a chance of it during takeoff or landing.

On takeoff or landing, airspeed is insurance when wake turbulence is encountered. You may have to deliberately fly a few feet off the ground for a few seconds until clear of the disturbance.

Wake turbulence is unpredictable; the airplane's reaction will depend on how you fly into it. Seen from behind, its motion is rotational, but you may fly into only one side of the vortex.

If turbulence is encountered on approach, the best answer is full power. Keep the nose down, turn out of the area, and go around.

If you suspect there will be wake turbulence during an approach and landing, keep your airspeed up and literally fly the airplane on. *Better yet, if you suspect that there'll be turbulence on approach or landing, take it around—always.* When you take off or land into a known area of turbulence you're betting a large repair bill against a couple of minutes saved. Anytime you think there may be wake turbulence on landing you can request another runway—a crosswind usually is much easier to cope with.

Wingtip vortices have a direct tie-in with induced Drag. You remember that induced Drag was a function of a high coefficient of Lift. This means that induced Drag is greatest at low airspeeds (high angles of attack). Wingtip vortices are the worst for an airplane with a high span loading (pounds of weight per foot of span) and at low speeds with flaps up.

Avoid flying into wake turbulence at high speeds—enough stress may be imposed on the airplane to cause structural failure. Avoid crossing directly behind a large airplane. If you should encounter wake turbulence at altitude, *don't pull up sharply to climb out of it.* Throttle back but don't try to slow up too quickly, as you will be adding stress to the airplane. The most aggressive maneuver you should try is a *shallow* climbing turn. If you are crossing the turbulence at a 90° angle, you'll probably be through it before you have a chance to do anything.

You can see that at altitude the greatest danger is at high speeds where the sudden encountering of turbulence results in overstressing the airplane. On takeoff and landing the problem is that the airspeed is low and control may be marginal.

If you must cross directly behind a large airplane, go above it if possible (this is assuming that you have time to make up your mind) because (1) the downwash of the wings tends to carry the disturbances downward and (2) you'll be slowing up as you start to climb (Fig. 16-7). There's no need to add further stress on the airplane by sharp pull-ups or other radical maneuvers.

Fig. 16-7. If you have time to decide, when crossing behind a large airplane always go above it.

Wake turbulence moves downward (and outward as it gets close to the ground). You may encounter downward flows of several hundred feet per minute. Here's an excerpt from the AIM on the subject:

AIM—BASIC FLIGHT INFORMATION AND ATC PROCEDURES—VORTEX AVOIDANCE PROCEDURES

a. Under certain conditions, airport traffic controllers apply procedures for separating aircraft from heavy jet aircraft. The controllers will also provide VFR aircraft, with whom they are in communication and which in the tower's opinion may be adversely affected by wake turbulence from a large aircraft, the position, altitude and direction of flight of the large aircraft followed by the phrase "CAUTION—WAKE TURBULENCE." WHETHER OR NOT A WARNING HAS BEEN GIVEN, HOWEVER, THE PILOT IS EXPECTED TO ADJUST HIS OPERATIONS AND FLIGHT PATH AS NECESSARY TO PRECLUDE SERIOUS WAKE ENCOUNTERS.

b. the following VORTEX avoidance procedures are recommended for the various situations:

(1) Landing behind a large aircraft—same runway: Stay at or above the large aircraft's final approach flight path—note his touchdown point—land beyond it.

(2) Landing behind a large aircraft—when parallel runway is closer than 2,500 feet: Consider possible drift to your runway. Stay at or above the large aircraft's final approach flight path—note his touchdown point.

(3) Landing behind a large aircraft—crossing runway: Cross above the large aircraft's flight path.

(4) Landing behind a departing large aircraft—same runway: Note the large aircraft's rotation point—land well prior to rotation point.

(5) Landing behind a departing large aircraft—crossing runway: Note the large aircraft's rotation point—if past the intersection—continue the approach—land prior to the intersection. If the large aircraft rotates prior to the intersection, avoid flight below the large aircraft's flight path. Abandon the approach unless a landing is assured well before reaching the intersection.

(6) Departing behind a large aircraft: Note the large aircraft's rotation point—rotate prior to large aircraft's rotation point—continue climb above and stay upwind of the large aircraft's climb path until turning clear of his wake. Avoid subsequent headings which will cross below and behind a large aircraft. Be alert for any critical takeoff situation which could lead to a VORTEX encounter.

(7) Intersection takeoffs—same runway: Be alert to adjacent large aircraft operations particularly upwind of your runway. If intersection takeoff clearance is received, avoid subsequent heading which will cross below a large aircraft's path.

(8) Departing or landing after a large aircraft executing a low approach, missed approach or touch-and-go landing: Because vortices settle and move laterally near the ground, the VORTEX hazard may exist along the runway and in your flight path after a large aircraft has executed a low approach, missed approach or a touch-and-go landing, particularly in light quartering wind conditions. You should assure that an interval of at least 2 minutes has elapsed before your takeoff or landing.

(9) En route VFR (thousand-foot altitude plus 500 feet): Avoid flight below and behind a large aircraft's path. If a large aircraft is observed above on the same track (meeting or overtaking) adjust your position laterally, preferably upwind.

The FAA is continually updating information on wake turbulence; Advisory Circular AC 90-23D (or 23E or 23F by the time you read this) covers the actions of wake turbulence and suggests the best ways of avoiding it. Order a copy (it's free). The *Basic Flight Information and ATC Procedures Manual* has a full section on wake turbulence, also.

Wake turbulence can be a menace to your health.

SUMMARY

Every so often break out the *POH* of the airplane(s) you are flying, and look through Section 3, Emergency Procedures, to review the steps to take in the event of various problems. You'll be surprised how procedures may have slipped a bit in your mind. You're on the way to becoming a professional pilot and need to be able to make the right moves when needed.

17 Advanced Navigation

A REVIEW

You may have been flying cross-country primarily by use of nav-aids since getting the private certificate (and some pilots carry nothing but IFR enroute low altitude charts on VFR cross-countries—which could pose a problem if the avionics fail), but as an aspiring advanced or professional pilot you should have more than just the bare bones of VFR navigation. This chapter discusses some points that will help with the commercial certificate written test as well as some techniques to use in actual operations.

It's assumed here that you remember the factors of variation (East is Least and West is Best) and can still read a compass deviation card, but you might get your computer and review a couple of wind triangle problems. For instance,

GIVEN:
True course (TC)—150°
True airspeed (TAS)—120 K
Wind—340° at 15 K (winds aloft are given in knots and true directions.)
Find the true heading and groundspeed:
True heading (TH)—149°
Groundspeed (GS)—135 K

The wind is about 10° from being directly on the tail and, remembering the trigonometry from Chap. 1, you can see that the tailwind component is 98.5% (the cosine of 10°) of the wind's value, or 14.77 K (call it 15 K).

Here's another problem:

GIVEN:
True course—276°
True airspeed—157 K
Wind—from 170° at 20 K
Find the true heading and groundspeed:
True heading—269°
Groundspeed—161 K

When you're working a wind triangle try to visualize the situation. The true course is 276° and the wind is from 170° (true), giving about a 16° advantage behind the wing (Fig. 17-1).

The wind triangle is three legs (naturally), consisting of (1) the E-W (earth-wind) line (the wind's path in relation to the earth), the (2) E-P (earth-plane) line, or the true course and groundspeed (what the airplane is doing in relation to the earth), and (3) the W-P (wind-plane) line, or the true airspeed and true heading (what the airplane is doing in relation to the air mass it is flying through). If you know the values of two of the lines, the third may be found (Fig. 17-2).

The usual navigation problem is like the two just worked: given the true course and wind, you have to find the true heading and groundspeed. As you'll see, in some problems you may be required to work backward to find the wind.

Finding the Wind. For instance, you are on a cross-country and, having no knowledge of the wind, keep the heading indicator (corrected to the compass) exactly on the selected TC of 083°. The TAS at your altitude is 148 K and after exactly 1 hr of flight you find yourself over a town 20 nautical miles (NM) north of the course line at a distance of 156 NM from the point of departure. The wind can be found as shown in Fig. 17-3.

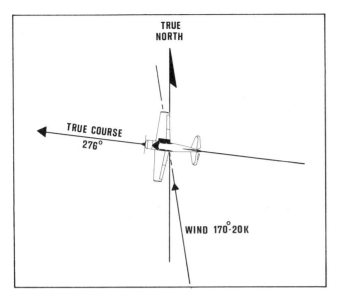

Fig. 17-1. Visualizing the problem just cited, you'll note that you'll have a slight tailwind component and will have to correct to the left. The computer can find the details.

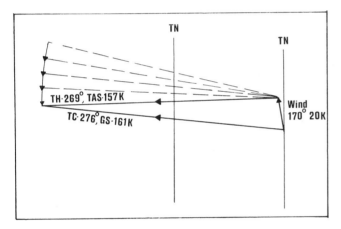

Fig. 17-2. The wind triangle. The TAS value (157 K) is swung down to intersect the TC line to get the TH and GS.

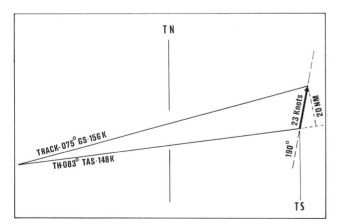

Fig. 17-3. Finding the wind — the graphical solution. The implication here is that you've been sitting with your head in the cockpit and haven't looked out since departing an hour ago, but for Pete's sake, it's only an example. TS means True South.

PART **4**

ADVANCED NAVIGATION

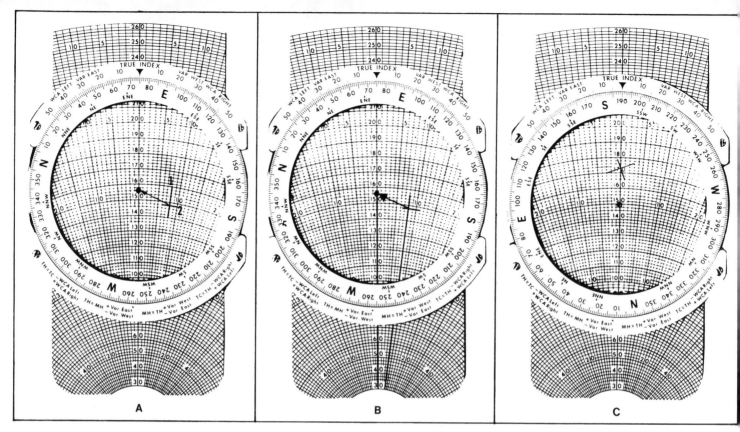

Fig. 17-4. Finding the wind speed and direction on the Safetech E-6B, model FDF-57-B. A. Set up the true course (075°) and groundspeed (156 K) and then draw in the lines representing the drift correction (8° right, 1) and true airspeed (148 K, 2). Their intersection (the cross) is the wind's origin. B. You are "filling out" the third side of the triangle when the wind is inserted. C. Turn the compass rose until the intersection is lined up with the TRUE INDEX to read the wind speed and direction (190° at 23 K).

Naturally, you can use your electronic computer, or E-6B computer to find the wind; here is how the problem might look on the written test:

(Question) 01.   GIVEN:

True course (track) . . . . .075°
Groundspeed. . . . . .156 knots
True heading . . . .·. . . . . .083°
True airspeed. . . . . .148 knots
Determine the approximate wind direction and speed:
1 — 240° at 25 knots.
2 — 140° at 12 knots.
3 — 190° at 23 knots.
4 — 320° at 22 knots.

You will note that the TH is 8° to the right of the true course, or track, and the GS is 8 K greater than the TAS, so the wind is from the right and slightly behind the airplane. This would eliminate answers 2 and 4 immediately, but the best way to get the answer is to work the problem (Fig. 17-4).

You would set up the GS and TC using the permanent-etched circle on the E-6B. To more easily remember: The permanent circle on the wind side of the computer always has to do with the factors that apply to the (solid) ground, such as TC and GS. *You* draw in the penciled circle for the more nebulous air factors such as TAS and TH. The TH is 8° more (right) than the true course, so somewhere along line 1 will be the wind's origin. Also, the TAS is 148 K and where value 2 intersects the drift line is the origin of the wind. Looking at both the drift correction angle and TAS you can keep the length of the intersecting lines to a minimum. The arrow drawn in represents the relative bearing and wind velocity.

Rotate the compass rose until the line intersections are lined up with the TRUE INDEX and slide the grommet to an

even number (150 K in Fig. 17-4C) to be able to read the wind speed more easily. The result is 190° at 23 K (answer 3).

In any navigation problems be sure the various factors use the same criteria (knots with nautical miles; true headings with other true directions, etc.).

Looking at another problem:

02.   GIVEN:

True course. . . . . .155°
Groundspeed. . . . . .174 knots
True heading . . . .·. . . . . .163°
True airspeed. . . . . .182 knots
Determine the approximate wind direction and speed:
1 — 050° at 20 knots.
2 — 080° at 24 knots.
3 — 230° at 26 knots.
4 — 260° at 28 knots.

The TC is 155° and the TH is 8° farther right (163°). The GS is 8 K less than the TAS so that a headwind component exists (Fig. 17-5).

Fig. 17-5. A quick sketch shows that the wind is probably from the southwest (around 230°).

If you are sharp at trigonometry you could probably figure out a rough answer before using the computer. For instance, an airplane's GS is 174 K and it has to correct 8° for wind. The ratio between the correction angle (8°) and 60° is the same as the relationship between the GS and the component of wind acting perpendicular to the flight path.

For a rule of thumb in finding angles, use the "rule of 60"—for every mile the airplane is off course at 60 mi, it will be 1° off the course line. (Or for every degree off course at 60 mi, it will be a 1-mi distance from the centerline.) Fig. 17-6 shows the idea. (Your navigation problems don't usually come out in even 60s but the relationship still stands.) (See Fig. 17-5 again: 8°/60 (the correction in degrees) = x/174 K, or, cross-multiplying, the component is 60x = 8 × 174; 60x = 1392; x = 23.2 K (call it 23 K).

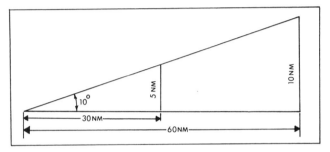

Fig. 17-6. The rule of 60: the angle = (10/60) × 60 = 10°, 10° = (10/60) × 60; for 30 miles, 10° = (5/30) × 60 (the angle is exaggerated).

The headwind component is the difference between the TAS and GS, as given, or 8 K. You could solve for the hypotenuse (the wind speed) in the manner shown back in Fig. 1-3—squaring the two sides, adding the results, and then taking the square root of that: $(23)^2 + (8)^2 = (\text{wind speed})^2$; 529 + 64 = 593; wind speed = $\sqrt{593}$ = 24+ K. As far as the wind *speed* is concerned it splits answers 2 and 3, but only 3 requires a correction to the right.

The tangent of the angle is 8/23.2 = 0.3448. Fig. 1-8 or a trig table would give an answer, but you can use the rule of 60 again and *approximate* the *small* angle (α): $\alpha = 0.3448 \times 60 = 20.7°$ (call it 21°). The large angle (β) is $90 - \alpha = 90 - 21 = 69°$. The wind is from approximately 69° to the right, or based on the thumb rule, 155° (TC) + 69° = 224°. The triangle shown in Fig. 17-5 is a right triangle (one of the angles is 90°), and since any triangle has interior angles totaling 180°, the two other angles must add up to 90°. One angle (α) is 21°, so the other angle (β) must be 69° (rounded off).

The answer by the rule of thumb is wind from 224° at 24+ K, which is closest to answer 3. The rule of thumb becomes less and less accurate as an angle of 30° is approached, but works well for smaller angles as a quick estimate.

Of course, this method is for background purposes and too long and involved for working in a practical situation, but as will be shown later in the chapter, the rule of 60 may be used to quickly find the time required to fly inbound to a VOR or NDB and solve off-course correction problems. Using a computer to solve the problem just discussed, Fig. 17-7 shows the steps to take.

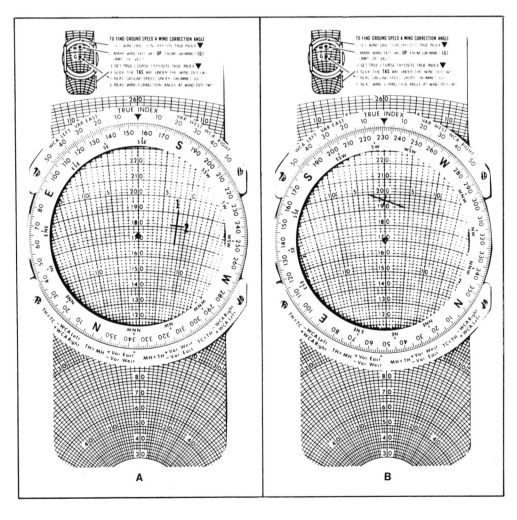

Fig. 17-7. Solving for wind. A. The TC (155°) and GS (174 K) are set under the grommet and the lines representing an 8° right correction (1) and a TAS of 182 K (2) are drawn in. B. The compass rose is rotated to center the cross on the TRUE INDEX to get a wind from 231° at 26 K, which is closest to answer 3. (*Safetech, Inc.*)

A   B

Solving another problem for finding the wind:

03. GIVEN:

True course..027°
Groundspeed..............................138 knots
True heading ....018°
True airspeed............................146 knots
Find the approximate wind direction and speed:
1—040° at 22 knots.
2—100° at 24 knots.
3—150° at 22 knots.
4—312° at 24 knots.

An analysis shows that the TH (018°) is *less* than the TC (027°), so that a left correction for wind is required. This would eliminate the first three answers since in each of those choices the wind is from the *right* of the TC.

Also, since the GS is *less* than the TAS a headwind component exists, which could be either 1 or 4. Since the wind of 040° is too close on the nose to require 9° correction (and it's on the wrong side to require a left correction), the answer must be 4.

Sketch and then work the following problems. Answers to all the numbered problems are at the end of this chapter.

04. GIVEN:

TC..230°
GS.....................................168 knots
TH..221°
TAS...................................162 knots
Determine the approximate wind direction and speed:
1—100° at 28 knots.
2—123° at 27 knots.
3—135° at 24 knots.
4—335° at 28 knots.

05. GIVEN:

TC..335°
GS.....................................144 knots
TH..324°
TAS...................................158 knots
The wind is from approximately
1—190° at 36 knots.
2—220° at 30 knots.
3—280° at 34 knots.
4—265° at 32 knots.

06. GIVEN:

TC..295°
GS.....................................174 knots
TH..308°
TAS...................................164 knots
Determine the approximate wind direction and speed:
1—046° at 40 knots.
2—150° at 35 knots.
3—185° at 40 knots.
4—350° at 35 knots.

RADIUS OF ACTION (FIXED BASE)

The problem is basically to determine the time to turn back to the point of departure after flying outbound as far as possible, as might be done on a search or intercept mission. The simplest problem is that of a no-wind situation: an airplane cruising at 150 K TAS (and GS) with a fuel supply for 4 hr (plus reserve) can fly how far out before turning back? The simple answer is that the airplane can fly out for 2 hr (300 NM) and fly back the same distance. Of course, the wind complicates the matter somewhat.

The point is that the airplane must fly the same ground distance out and back (it's still the same distance from "here" to "there" as it is from "there" to "here"). The relationship is that of GS out to distance out and GS back to distance back; for the times required outbound and back (without hitting the details), the formula turns out to be

$$TO = \frac{TT \times GSB}{GSO + GSB}$$

(TO = time out, TT = total time, GSO = groundspeed out, GSB = groundspeed back, TB = time back, which equals TT minus TO).

In the following example, the wind, TAS, and total fuel (or total time) are given. The GS is solved for both legs, and the problem is set up:

TT—4 hr of fuel (not including reserves)
GSO—146 K
GSB—166 K
Departure time—1107Z

Problem: Find the time to turn back toward the departure point (home base) and the distance of that point from the base: TO = (TT × GSB)/(GSO + GSB) = (240 min × 166)/(146 + 166) = 39840/312 = 127.7 min (call it 128 min). The time to turn back is 2 hr and 8 min (2:08) after takeoff, or 1315Z.

You might prefer to work the problem using hours and tenths of hours: TO = (4.0 × 166)/312 = 664/312 = 2.128 hr, = 2 hr and 8 min (rounded off). You would fly out for 2.128 hr at 146 K (GSO) for a distance of 311 NM. Since the distance back should be the same, a check would be as follows: 4.0 hr (TT) − 2.128 hr = 1.872 hr back at 166 K = 311 NM. (The out and back distances don't always come out exactly because of rounding off.)

If you use hours and tenths of hours for time, instead of minutes, be sure to convert the decimal to minutes. One of the following questions has a departure time of 1440 and an answer of 2.27 hr (rounded off) for time outbound. One of the choices is 1707Z (2 hr and 27 min later). The 2.27 hr should be converted to 2:16 (0.27 × 60 = 16.2 min) for an answer of 1656Z.

07. GIVEN:

TC out ....065°
TAS...................................180 knots
Fuel available......................3 hours plus reserve
Wind velocity.......................290° at 30 knots
Takeoff time.............................1021Z
Determine the time to turn back toward the departure point:
1—1128Z.
2—1140Z.
3—1152Z.
4—1216Z.

Fig. 17-8 shows the procedure: TO = (TT × GSB)/(GSO + GSB) = (180 min × 158)/(200 + 158) = 28440/358 = 79.44 min (call it 79 min, or 1 hr and 19 min). Departing at 1021Z, the turn should be made at 1140Z (answer 2). As a double check see that the distances out and back are the same: time out = 79 min at 200 K = 263 NM; time back = 3:00 − 1:19 = 1:41 min at 158 K = 265 NM. The slight difference is caused by rounding off to the nearest minute earlier, but you can tell that the answer is correct.

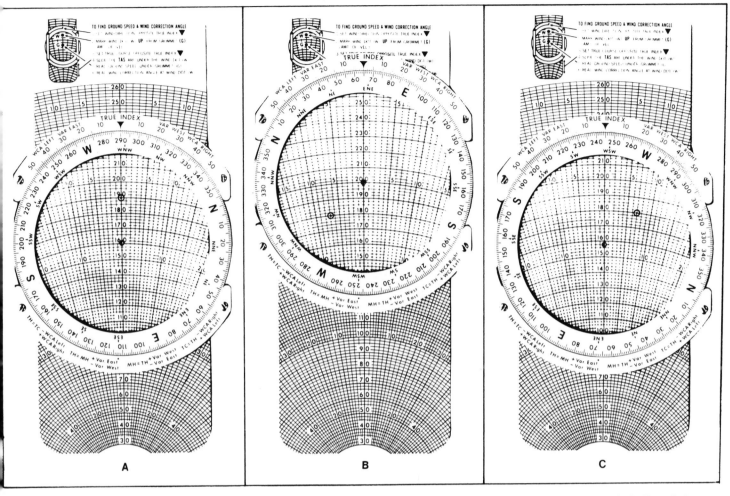

Fig. 17-8. Radius of action from a fixed base. A. Set up the wind (290° at 30 K). B. The wind triangle is solved for the outbound leg (065° TC), getting a TH of 058° and a GS of 200 K. C. The return leg, the reciprocal of the outbound leg, is 245°. The TH back is 252° and the GS 158 K.

One more example:

08. GIVEN:

TC out ....300°
TAS ....150 knots
Fuel available ....4 hours plus reserve
Wind velocity ....250° at 30 knots
Takeoff time 1323Z
Determine the time to turn back toward the departure point:
1 — 1453Z.
2 — 1507Z.
3 — 1539Z.
4 — 1545Z.

Fig. 17-9 illustrates the solution: The GS is found to be 129 K outbound and 168 K inbound. Solving: TO = (TT × GSB)/ (GSO + GSB) = 40320/297 = 135.76 min (rounded off to 136 min). Takeoff time = 1323 + 2:16 = 1539Z (answer 3). A double check on distances: distance out = 2 hours 16 minutes (or 2.27 hours) at 129 K = 293 mi; distance back = 1:44 at 168 K = 291 mi. Again, the slight difference is caused by rounding off to the nearest minute.

09. GIVEN:

TC out ....215°
TAS ....190 knots
Fuel available ....4 hours 30 minutes plus reserve
Wind velocity ....130° at 20 knots
Takeoff time 1440Z
Determine the time to turn back toward the departure point:
1 — 1549Z.
2 — 1618Z.
3 — 1656Z.
4 — 1707Z.

10. GIVEN:

TC out ....155°
TAS ....200 knots
Fuel available ....3 hours 30 minutes plus reserve
Wind velocity ....100° at 15 knots
Takeoff time 0940Z
Determine the time to turn back toward the departure point:
1 — 1129Z.
2 — 1159Z.
3 — 1217Z.
4 — 1243Z.

Fig. 17-9. Solving for time to turn back toward the departure point. The wind of 250° at 30 K has already been set in. A. The groundspeed out (GSO) is 129 K. B. The groundspeed back is 168 K. TO = $\dfrac{240 \times 168}{129 + 168}$ = $\dfrac{40320}{297}$; TO = 136 minutes (rounded off); TO = 2 hours and 16 minutes.

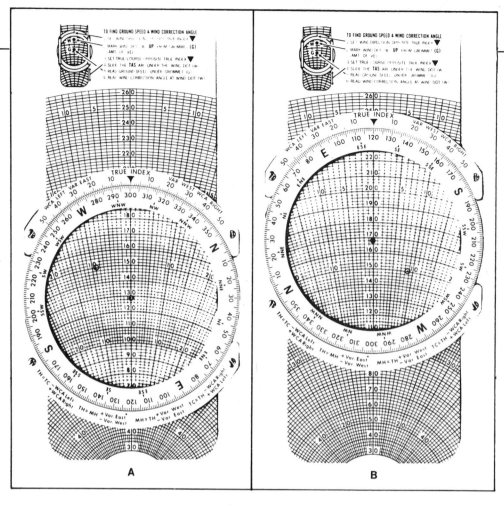

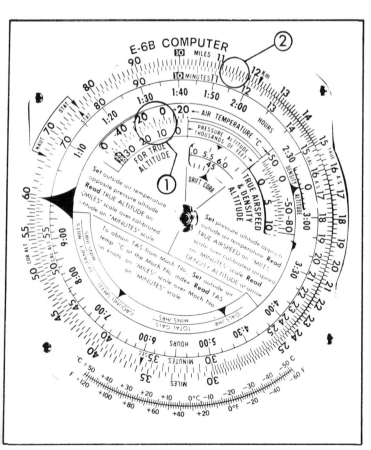

Fig. 17-10. Finding the true and absolute altitudes. (*Safetech, Inc.*)

Correcting for True and Absolute Altitude.

Using the circular slide rule side of the E-6B you can solve for true and absolute altitudes (*true altitude = height above sea level; absolute altitude = height above terrain*).

Several problems follow (indicated altitude equals calibrated altitude for these problems).

11. GIVEN:

Pressure altitude ....12,000 feet
Indicated altitude............................11,500 feet
Free air temperature (OAT) ....−10°C
Terrain elevation ....10,500 feet

From the conditions given, determine the approximate absolute altitude:

1 − 500 feet.
2 − 950 feet.
3 − 1000 feet.
4 − 1500 feet.

Refer to Fig. 17-10:

1. Set up the pressure altitude (12,000 ft) opposite the OAT (−10°C).

2. Read the *true* altitude (11,450 ft) on the outer scale opposite the indicated (calibrated) altitude of 11,500 ft on the inner scale.

3. Subtract the terrain elevation (10,500 ft) from the true altitude (11,450 ft) to get 950 absolute altitude (answer 2).

Another problem of the same type:

12. GIVEN:

Pressure altitude ....10,000 feet
Indicated (and calibrated) altitude................8500 feet
Free air temperature (OAT) ....+20°C
Terrain elevation ....6500 feet
Determine the approximate absolute altitude:
1 — 1500 feet.
2 — 2795 feet.
3 — 3150 feet.
4 — 3375 feet.

Refer to Fig.17-11:
1. Set up the pressure altitude (10,000 ft) opposite the OAT (+20°C).
2. Read the *true* altitude of 9300 ft (outer scale) opposite the indicated (calibrated) altitude of 8500 ft.
3. Subtract the terrain elevation (6500 ft) from the true altitude (9300 ft) to get 2800 ft (answer 2). You could read the true altitude closer (9295 ft) to come up with the *exact* answer.

13. GIVEN:

Pressure altitude ....11,000 feet
Indicated (calibrated) altitude...................9500 feet
Free air temperature (OAT) ....−15°C
Terrain elevation ....8300 feet
Determine the absolute altitude:
1 — 920 feet.
2 — 1200 feet.
3 — 1500 feet.
4 — 2700 feet.

14. GIVEN:

Pressure altitude ....13,000 feet
Indicated (calibrated) altitude ....11,500 feet
Free air temperature (OAT) ....−25°C
Terrain elevation ....9600 feet
Determine the absolute altitude:
1 — 970 feet.
2 — 1300 feet.
3 — 2600 feet.
4 — 3400 feet.

Off-Course Problems. The rule of 60 is a good aid for solving this type of problem in its simplest form. For instance, consider a situation as follows:

15. GIVEN:

An airplane is 15 NM off course from the 125-NM enroute course position. The distance from that original enroute position to the destination is 200 NM. Determine the approximate heading change necessary to fly to the destination (Look at Fig. 17-12).
1 — 5° correction.
2 — 7° correction.
3 — 12° correction.
4 — 14° correction.

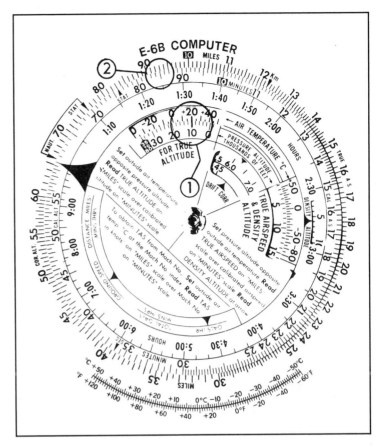

Fig. 17-11. Another true altitude problem. (*Safetech, Inc.*)

Using the rule of 60, the angle at which the airplane has departed the original course line can be found. Remember that at 60 NM, 1° = 1 NM (and vice versa), and though the numbers here are not even factors of 60, the rule applies. Therefore, if the airplane was 15 NM off the course line at 60 NM, the angle would be 15°, or $\alpha = (15/60) \times 60 = 15°$. However, it's off 15 NM in 125 NM, so the equation would be $(15/125) \times 60 = 7.2°$. This makes sense because if it were off 15 NM at the 120-NM point the angle would be 7.5°, or $(15/120) \times 60 = 7.5°$. The airplane is off 15 NM at 125 NM so the angle would be slightly less than 7.5°, or in this case 7.2°. The airplane would have to turn this amount *toward* the course to *parallel* it. To return to the course at the destination (or fly direct to the destination), the airplane would have to turn another angle in addition to the 7.2° (Fig. 17-13).

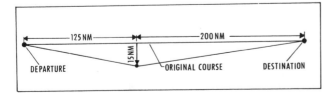

Fig. 17-12. An off-course correction problem. The airplane is 15 NM off course from the 125-NM course position (drawing not to scale).

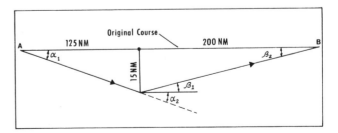

Fig. 17-13. Angle α_1 is the off-course angle. Angle α_2, the change in heading required to parallel the original course, equals α_1. Angle β_1 is the additional change in heading to fly to the destination (angles exaggerated and not to scale). $\beta_1 = \beta_2$.

To find α_1 (α_1 and α_2 are equal in Fig. 17-13 so you can work backward from α_2 if you prefer), the same rule of 60 procedure is applied. Angle β_1 is a function of the ratio of the distance off course (15 NM) to the distance to the destination (200 NM) times 60: $\beta_1 = (15/200) \times 60 = 4.5°$. The total heading change required is $\alpha_2 + \beta_1 = 7.2 + 4.5 = 11.7°$. The correct answer from the four choices listed earlier would be 3.

FOR MATH BUFFS ONLY. You could work it out trigonometrically using a calculator and/or trig table: $\tan \alpha_2 = 15/125 = 0.12 = 6.8427734°$; $\tan \beta_1 = 15/200$, $\beta_1 = 4.2891534°$; total change $= 11.131927°$. You would, of course, change the airplane's heading by this exact amount. The answer is closest to choice 3.

At small angles the sine and tangent are very close and the argument might be that, because of the way the question is stated (leg x is 125 NM), the other leg distance should be found by using the sine of the angle: $\sin \alpha_1 = 15/125$, $\alpha_1 = 6.8921026°$; $\sin \beta_1 = 15/200$, $\beta_1 = 4.301224°$; total heading change $= 11.193325°$, which is still the closest answer to choice 3. Okay, fun's fun—but let's get back to the practical side.

USING THE NAVIGATION COMPUTER. You can set up the off-course problem on the circular slide rule side of the computer (Fig. 17-14):

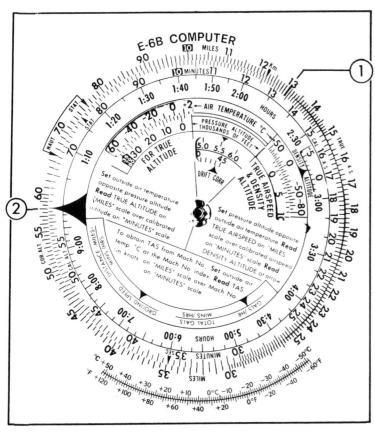

Fig. 17-14. Setting up an off-course problem: Set up the distance (134, on the inner scale) opposite the off-course value (13, on the outer scale); then read the degrees (5.8) at the 60 index.

16. GIVEN:

At the point where you should be 134 NM along the true course line you find that you are 13 NM off course.

1. How many degrees correction are required to *parallel* the course?

2. If the destination is 104 mi farther, what additional correction is required to fly to the destination?

Set up the problem with the distance (134 NM) on the inner scale opposite the distance off course (13 NM) on the outer scale. The answer, which is read at the 60 index, is approximately 5.8°. How do you know that the answer shouldn't be 58° or 580° or 0.58°? The answer can be approximated by the rule of 60. The 13 NM is slightly less than one-tenth of 134 NM so the angle should be 60/10, or roughly 6° (slightly less). Doing the same for the remaining distance of 104 NM, you find that the angle is 7.5°, for a total of 13.3° heading change to fly to the destination.

Checking it with the rule of 60: $(13/134) \times 60 = 5.8°$ and $(13/104) \times 60 = 7.5°$; $5.8 + 7.5 = 13.3°$. It's not likely that you'll fly this close an angle.

One last off-course problem:

17. GIVEN:

Distance flown ....160 NM
Distance off course...........................20 NM
Distance to destination ....220 NM
Determine the total heading correction necessary to fly to the destination:
1 — 5° correction.
2 — 8° correction.
3 — 13° correction.
4 — 17° correction.

Using the rule of 60: to parallel the course, $(20/160) \times 60 = 7.5°$; additional heading change required, $(20/220) \times 60 = 5.5°$; total heading change, $7.5 + 5.5 = 13°$ (answer 3).

A variation on this is the computation of wind correction required to fly from the point off course to the destination. For instance (a simple approach):

TC from A to B is 090°, TAS is 120 K, total distance (straight line) from A to B is 230 NM.

The wind was predicted to be calm at the (lower) altitude of cruise. After carefully holding the compass heading required to maintain the TH *and* TC of 090° you find 55 min after takeoff that you are over the town of Shiloh, which is 10 mi south of course and a straight line distance of 90 NM from the departure point A (Fig. 17-15).

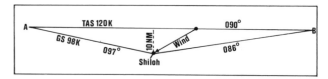

Fig. 17-15. Off-course wind correction problem.

Using the rule of 60 you can estimate that the ground track flown is angled south of the TC by a certain number of degrees. First solve for the GS (using the circular slide rule: In 55 min the airplane has traveled 90 NM, for a GS of 98 K.

Next solve for the track or "new" TC you flew, which will be added (in *this* problem) to the original TC: degrees off course $= (10/90) \times 60 = 6.67°$ (call it 7°). The track or TC was $090 + 7° = 097°$. You can solve for the heading required to get to B (no-wind) by using the same method used earlier.

The distance from the correction point is 230 − 90 = 140 NM to go. The *added* angle would be (10/140) × 60 = 4.3°. The new TC to get to B is 90° − 4.3° = 86° (rounded off). In real life, with a sectional chart you could draw a new TC from Shiloh to B, measure it as 086°, and go on from there.

First solve for the wind as was done earlier in this chapter. You have the following information:

GS = 98 K, TC = 097°, TAS = 120 K, TH = 090°.

Putting this into your computer, you find that the *wind is from 062° at 26 K*.

The next problem is compute the TH and GS to the destination (B). If you were over Shiloh at 1107Z, at what time should you be over the destination? Putting the wind of 062° at 26 K into the computer, using a TC of 086° and a TAS of 120K, you find the TH and GS in flying to B: TH = 081°, GS = 96 K.

At what time, assuming no change in TAS, should you be over B? The straight-line distance from Shiloh to B is 140 NM. (Working out the trigonometry you'd find that it's really 140.35 mi from Shiloh to B; the angle from the original course is so shallow that the new distance is practically the same.)

The time required at 96 K to travel 140 NM is 88 min, or 1:28; 1107Z + 1:28 = 1235Z. You'd be over B at 1235Z.

You can see that over- or undercorrecting for wind could be worked out the same way.

Summing it all up, look at Fig. 17-16. If the off-course angle is 10° or less, for practical purposes assume that leg 1 and leg 2 are equal—and the same applies for legs 3 and 4. In the problem just worked, the angles are 7° and 4° respectively (rule of thumb) so the assumption could be used. (The computer would give closer tolerances than these estimates.)

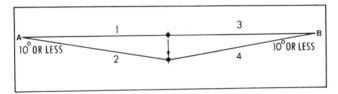

Fig. 17-16. Legs 1 and 2 are considered equal here, as are legs 3 and 4.

Computing Climb and Descent Factors

THE CLIMB. There's nothing complicated about computing climb factors (time, fuel, miles covered, TH, GS, magnetic heading, compass heading). Climbs were discussed in Chap. 5, and the *Student Pilot's Flight Manual*, Chap. 24, covers just such a problem as follows:

18. GIVEN:

An airplane departs an airport under the following conditions:

Airport elevation...............................900 feet
Cruise altitude................................8500 feet
Rate of climb ....500 fpm
Average TAS (during climb)....................130 knots
True course....................................220°
Average wind velocity....................300° at 30 knots
Variation.......................................3°W
Deviation ....−2°
Average fuel consumption during climb.....14 gallons/hour
Determine the approximate time, compass heading, distance, and fuel consumption during the climb:

1—15 minutes, 242°, 31 NM, 3.5 gallons.
2—15 minutes, 234°, 31 NM, 3.5 gallons.

3—15 minutes, 234°, 26 NM, 3.9 gallons.
4—12 minutes, 234°, 31 NM, 4.2 gallons.

First, start at the beginning (always a good idea, if slightly overstated here). The time required to climb from 900 ft to 8500 ft at 500 fpm is (8500 − 900)/500 = 7600/500 = 15.2 min. Let that sit for a while.

Work the wind triangle with the known facts and find the TH and GS. The computer finds that TH = 233° and GS = 121 K. The magnetic heading (MH) is TH ± variation = 233° + 3° = 236°. The compass heading is MH ± deviation = 236° − 2° = 234°. The *time in climb = 15.2 min*, the *compass heading = 234°*, the *distance* = 15.2 min at 121 K = *31 NM* (rounded off), and *fuel consumption* = 15.2 min at 14.0 gph = *3.5 gal*. It looks like *choice 2* of the answers gets the nod.

DESCENT FACTORS. The descent problem is basically the same except that you must realize that the descent is normally made to the traffic pattern; you might have a set-up such as cruising altitude = 6500 ft, airport elevation = 700 ft, and traffic pattern altitude = *800 ft*.

You'll be letting down to 1500 MSL (700 + 800) for a descent of 5000 ft at a given descent rate. You'll be given the average wind and will work a wind triangle to find the time, compass heading, distance, and fuel consumption during the descent (as was done for the climb problem).

Time between Bearings. It's likely that you will have an instrument rating before getting the commercial certificate and will have worked on time-and-distance problems using the VOR and/or ADF, but a review might be in order.

The rule of 60 works for both time and distance, since the ratios would be the same in a given situation. Here's a typical problem: Find the time and fuel required to fly to the station after flying perpendicularly through a certain number of degrees of bearing change (Fig. 17-17). Using the rule of 60 you'd find that if the airplane in Fig. 17-17 took 7 min to fly the 10° from A to B, it would require (60/10) × 7 = 42 min to fly from B to C, or time between bearings/time to station = bearing change (degrees)/60.

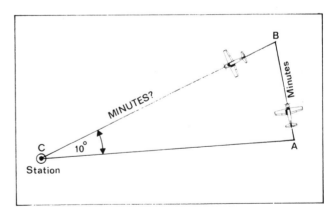

Fig. 17-17. Time-to-station problem.

As an example: an airplane changes bearing 10° (Fig. 17-17) in 7 min. Substituting the numbers in the above formula: 7 min/time to station = 10/60. Cross-multiplying: 42 min = time to station × 10 = 420/10 = 42 min; time to station = 42 min.

It's easier to divide 60 by degrees of bearing change and multiply by the result: 60°/10 = 6; 6 × 7 min = 42 min. For a 15° bearing change, the time multiplier is 60/15 = 4. For a

20° bearing change, the multiplier is 3, etc. Accuracy is lost as angles reach 30°, as indicated earlier.

An airplane using 14.3 gph, flying a time-and-distance problem, has a bearing change of 10° in 8 min and 36 sec. It has just completed its turn and has just headed into the station at exactly 1122:00Z. When is station passage expected and how much fuel will be required to fly to the station under *no-wind conditions*?

The multiplier is 60°/10° = 6. It will take 6 times as long to fly into the station as it did to fly the 10° bearing change (no-wind): 6 × 8.6 = 51.6 = 51 min and 36 sec. At a fuel consumption of 14.3 gph, 52 min (rounded off) would require 12.4 gal of fuel. The time over the station would be 1122:00 + 51:36 = 1213:36Z (1213 + 36 sec) Z.

There's a lot wrong with calling the time to the station to the nearest second with a wind, and that's why *no-wind* conditions were cited earlier. Fig. 17-18 shows why there might be a discrepancy between the predicted and actual time to station. In Fig. 17-18 the wind effect shortens the time required to fly the 10° bearing change (because of tailwind) and lengthens the time-to-station figure (because of headwind). You'd get there later than predicted.

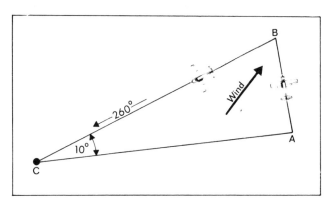

Fig. 17-18. The wind can affect time-to-station predictions.

Using the rule of 60, if the airplane in Fig. 17-18 takes 6 min to fly the 10° bearing change, it should get to the station in (60/10) × 6 = 36 min. This is the estimate for no-wind conditions, or if the wind is not known. Looking at Fig. 17-18, you can see that with a wind from the opposite direction, the time required to fly the bearing change would be greater and hence the time to fly to the station would be *over*estimated. (You'd get there earlier than predicted.)

Here's a problem from an advanced written test:

19. GIVEN:
Time between bearings . . . . .8 minutes
Bearing change . . . . .5°
Rate of fuel consumption . . . . .14 gallons per hour
Calculate the approximate fuel required to fly to the station: 60/5 = 12; 12 × 8 min = 96 min to the station at 14.0 gal per hour; fuel consumed = 22.4 gal.

The ADF and Relative Bearings. As you know, ADF problems are usually tougher than VOR work because of the need to include the *relative* bearing of the station in solving magnetic bearings *to* or *from* the station.

A typical problem: You are inbound to VOR A on the 270 radial. (This first sentence is enough to shoot some people out of the saddle when they think that they are inbound on a *course* of 270.) Your magnetic heading = 078°, your relative

bearing to NDB B = 070°. Using the information given, determine the magnetic bearing *to* (italics added) NDB B.

The situation is shown in Fig. 17-19. The magnetic heading and relative bearing are added together to get a magnetic bearing *to* the station of 078° + 070° = 148°.

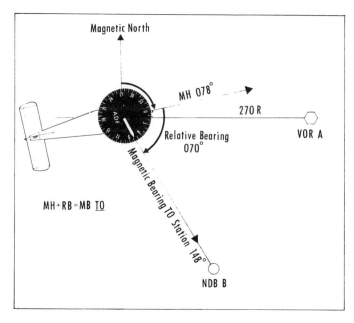

Fig. 17-19. Visualizing an ADF problem.

Remember, if you add the magnetic heading and relative bearing and the answer is greater than 360° then 360° must be subtracted to get the magnetic bearing *to* the station.

Here's another problem:

20. GIVEN:
Inbound to VOR A . . . . .130 radial
Magnetic heading . . . . .317°
Relative bearing to NDB B (fixed dial ADF) . . . . .215°
Using the information given, determine the magnetic bearing from NDB B (sketch it).
1 — 165°.
2 — 172°.
3 — 345°.
4 — 352°.

The magnetic heading 317° plus the relative bearing 215° = 532°. Subtracting 360°, 532 − 360 = 172° to the NDB. Looking at the answers, 2 has this value, so problem solved — *not at all*!

The requirement was to find the bearing *from* the station as might be used in getting cross-bearings for locating the airplane's position. It's necessary to add or subtract 180° to or from the airplane's bearing *to* the station to get the answer: 172° + 180° = 352°. Answer 4 is correct.

Carefully read all questions on written tests.

OTHER NAVIGATION TECHNIQUES

No-Wind Plot. If a number of course changes are required during a flight (say, on an overwater search) it would be inconvenient to run a wind triangle for each short leg; a log should be kept of true headings and true airspeeds, however, so that the *air track* may be combined with the known or estimated wind to find the ground position.

Your log might read as follows (Fig. 17-20):

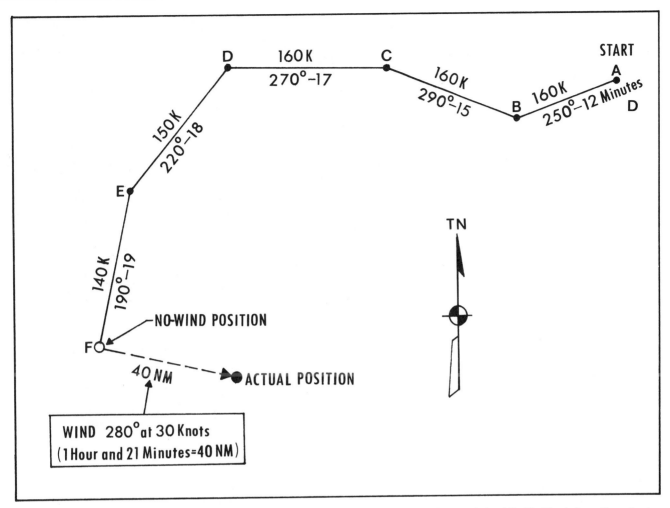

Fig. 17-20. No-wind or air plot. The numbers on each leg (12, 15, 17, etc.) are the minutes.

| | | WIND—280°/30 K | | |
Leg	TH	KTAS (K)	Min	Air Distance (NM)
A–B	250°	160	12	32
B–C	290°	160	15	40
C–D	270°	160	17	45
D–E	220°	150	18	45
E–F	190°	140	19	44
			81	

You would note the compass heading for each leg and then convert it to TH. After laying out the legs of the air plot to point F, you would extend the wind *from* there 100° for a distance of 40 NM. The wind (air mass) of 280° at 30 K has been acting on the airplane for 81 min and has moved the airplane 40 NM, 100° from the no-wind (air) plot at F. If you had worked a wind triangle for each leg and plotted the ground points on the chart the answer should have been the same. (Distances are rounded off to the nearest mile here.)

Landfall Navigation. This is the technique used if fuel is an important consideration and there are no airports near the destination. During WW II airplanes ferried from Brazil to Dakar (Africa) didn't have enough fuel for an extended search up and down the barren coastline if landfall was made out of sight of the destination airport. After a very long flight over the ocean with generally poor wind information, at landfall with no references the question was, Which way should I turn to go to the airport—north or south? A wrong turn could

mean fuel exhaustion and bellying in on a deserted beach with its attendant problems. One answer was to *make sure* that the airplane was north (or south, as the crew chose) of the desired landfall (Fig. 17-21).

The problem was either turning downwind in a strong wind (A) and drifting so far (south in Fig. 17-21) that the flight up the coast or river (leg B) was slow (so that the airplane runs out of fuel before getting to the destination), or turning upwind in a strong wind and *not* compensating enough for the wind (leg C) (so that the airplane still makes landfall south—out of sight—of the airport and the pilot, because of the "northerly" heading change, turns south and flies away from it). The choice of which way to make the cut would depend on best wind or drift information.

You can use this procedure in finding an airport by a road or river in lowered visibility and in strange territory: Turn to one side or the other, and then after hitting the road or river turn and fly up or down it until reaching the airport (Fig. 17-21, right). Keep the road or river in sight.

SUMMARY

Once in a while review the aspects of navigation you don't normally use, such as making one of your shorter cross-countries using sectional charts and keeping the nav radios turned off. Also, one of these nights when there's nothing on TV you might break out the instruction book for your E-6B or electronic computer and work some of the "other" types of

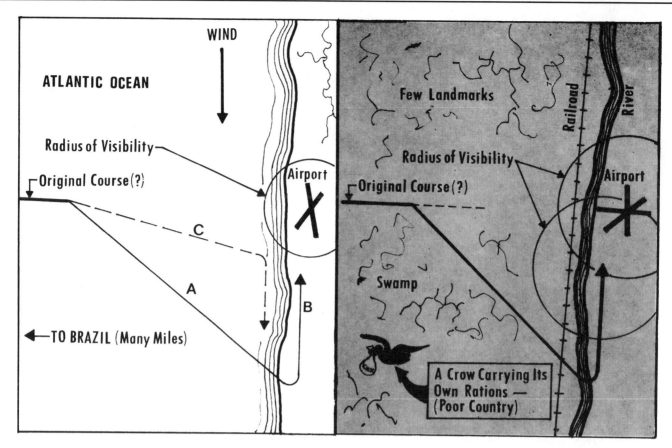

Fig. 17-21. Landfall navigation. This is particularly important in periods of poor visibility (right).

navigation problems that you skipped when working on the private certificate. As a professional pilot you may need that extra knowledge in a tight situation.

As a naval aviator this writer worked problems involving radius of action from a moving base (which could also be an alternate airport problem) on a Mark III plotting board. The current computers do not lend themselves so well to this problem but a graphical solution is described in *Practical Air Navigation* by Lyons (see the Bibliography); though the knowledge is useful at times, it is not critical for the commercial aspirant and is left for study in that book.

It has been noted over the past few years that the basic navigation skills of the average U.S. pilot have slipped and should a nav-radio failure occur, in some cases a bona fide emergency would exist even in good VFR conditions. You, of course, are not included with that group. I've used four choices for these problems, unlike the A, B, C choices you'll run into for the FAA written test in Chapter 20.

ANSWERS TO PROBLEMS IN THIS CHAPTER. (Answers to problems here include those answers already given as a part of the explanation process.)

01.	3	08.	3	15.	3
02.	3	09.	3	16.	5.8°, 7.5°
03.	4	10.	1	17.	3
04.	2	11.	2	18.	2
05.	4	12.	2	19.	22.4 gal
06.	1	13.	1	20.	4
07.	2	14.	2		

18 Altitude and the pilot

PART 5

HIGH-ALTITUDE OPERATIONS

Most of the world's population lives somewhere between 6000 ft and sea level. While residents of the Himalayas and Andes perform well above 10,000 ft, most persons' physical and mental performances deteriorate as that altitude is approached and passed. The rate of deterioration naturally depends on the physical condition of the individual.

As Fig. 18-1 shows, the troposphere goes up to an average of about 35,000 ft. It varies from about 28,000 ft at the geographic poles to 55,000 ft at the equator and varies with the seasons, being highest in the summer. The troposphere provides most of the weather problems because it contains moisture and has temperature changes and turbulence.

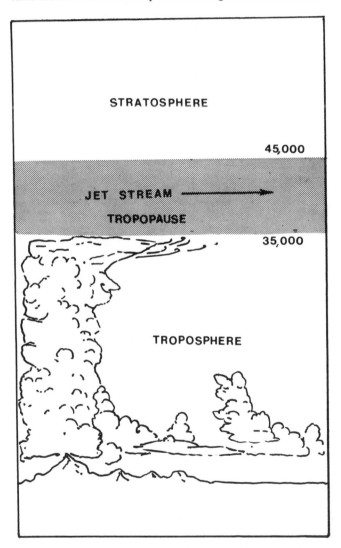

Fig. 18-1. The atmosphere.

The tropopause is a comparatively narrow band between the troposphere and the stratosphere, and its lower altitude boundary naturally varies with that of the troposphere. The tropopause, on average, is considered to extend from approximately 35,000 to 45,000 ft and be approximately 10,000 ft thick.

Above the tropopause lie the stratosphere and ionosphere, as yet relatively uncrowded with flight traffic. There the normal temperature lapse rate of 3½°F or 2°C no longer exists, and the temperature remains a constant −67°F above 35,000 ft. The jet stream is found in the upper tropopause and in the stratosphere.

OXYGEN REQUIREMENTS

Oxygen makes up about 21% of the atmosphere, nitrogen is 78%, and various inert gases such as argon fill out the rest of the mixture.

This ratio of gases remains constant up to about 70,000 ft. However, the physiology people are more interested in the partial *pressures* of the air acting on the pilot. At sea level the total pressure is 760 mm of mercury. The lung air sacs are 100% saturated with water vapor at a body temperature of 98.6%F. Physiologists have determined that a water vapor pressure of 47 mm of mercury is present in the lungs with this body temperature and does not vary with the altitude at which the pilot is operating. This vapor pressure has to be subtracted from the pressure of inhaled air. The available atmospheric pressure at sea level is 760 mm. When the lung water vapor pressure is considered there will be a loss of about 6.2% of the available intake (47/760 = 6.2%). At 12,000 ft the available atmospheric air pressure is 483 mm and the constant lung water vapor pressure of 47 mm takes a relatively bigger bite out of the available air pressure (about 9.8%).

Fig. 18-2 shows a good summary of the usable atmosphere oxygen (O_2) at sea level and at 12,000 ft pressure altitude. (The O_2 pressure available is rounded off to 20% for each altitude.)

UTILIZABLE ATMOSPHERIC OXYGEN		
	Sea Level	*12,000 feet*
Available Atmospheric Air Pressure	760 mm Mercury	483 mm Mercury
Lung Air Sac Water Vapor	−47	−47
Pressure of Remaining Lung Gases	713	436
Oxygen Portion (20%)	x0.20	x0.20
Oxygen Pressure in Air Sac	143	87
Minus Air Sac Carbon Dioxide	40	40
Oxygen Pressure in Lung Air Sacs	103 mm Mercury	47 mm Mercury
Provides Arterial Blood Oxygen % of	96%	87%

Fig. 18-2. Utilizable atmospheric oxygen. (*FAA AM 66-28 Oxygen in General Aviation, Stanley R. Mohler, M.D.*)

The lungs clear the blood of carbon dioxide (CO_2), which is the gaseous by-product of metabolism. Under resting conditions the lung air sacs contain 40 mm CO_2 pressure. Note that this is another constant regardless of altitude and takes a comparatively greater amount of the available atmospheric pressure at 12,000 ft.

The brain needs a continuous irrigation of 96% O_2 saturation for peak mental function. A saturation of 87% allows acceptable mental performance in a normal individual but is getting close to marginal. (Sometimes it feels as if you're mentally operating at 18,000 ft when sitting on the ground if you've had a full day of flying or not enough rest lately.) So 12,000 ft is as high as you should go without supplemental O_2.

The CO_2 pressure (40 mm) is in an at-rest condition. When you're flying you'll be performing some activity, if only adjusting the autopilot, and the CO_2 level might be higher than 40 mm. Your physical condition has a great deal to do with your reaction to altitude operations. If you're tired, have been partying too much the last few nights, are a heavy smoker, or have been taking antihistamines, you can expect that your tolerance to altitude operations will be lowered, at least

temporarily. You should consider your passengers' health also; they may have heart disease, poor circulation, or lung problems such as emphysema or asthma. If you do charter work after getting your commercial certificate you'll find that a dependable O_2 system can not only give you more flexibility in choice of altitude but also can be a valuable aid if one of your passengers finds that 8000 or 9000 ft is *his* or *her* limit without supplemental O_2. Of course, it depends on the size of the airplane and the type of trips you'd be making as to the economics of installing a permanent type of O_2 system, but portable systems are available for specific trips.

FAR 91 (Supplemental Oxygen) states:

(a) *General.* No person may operate a civil aircraft of U.S. registry—

(1) At cabin pressure altitudes above 12,500 feet (MSL) up to and including 14,000 feet (MSL), unless the required minimum flight crew is provided with and uses supplemental oxygen for that part of the flight at those altitudes that is of more than 30 minutes duration;

(2) At cabin pressure altitudes above 14,000 feet (MSL), unless the required minimum flight crew is provided with and uses supplemental oxygen during the entire flight time at those altitudes; and

(3) At cabin pressure altitudes above 15,000 feet (MSL), unless each occupant of the aircraft is provided with supplemental oxygen.

(b) *Pressurized cabin aircraft.*

(1) No person may operate a civil aircraft of U.S. registry with a pressurized cabin—

(i) At flight altitudes above flight level 250, unless at least a 10-minute supply of supplemental oxygen, in addition to any oxygen required to satisfy paragraph (a) of this section, is available for each occupant of the aircraft for use in the event that a descent is necessitated by loss of cabin pressurization; and

(ii) At flight altitudes above flight level 350, unless one pilot at the controls of the airplane is wearing and using an oxygen mask that is secured and sealed, and that either supplies oxygen at all times or automatically supplies oxygen whenever the cabin pressure altitude of the airplane exceeds 14,000 feet (MSL), except that the one pilot need not wear and use an oxygen mask while at or below flight level 410 if there are two pilots at the controls and each pilot has a quick-donning type of oxygen mask that can be placed on the face with one hand from the ready position within five seconds, supplying oxygen and properly secured and sealed.

(2) Notwithstanding subparagraph (1) (ii) of this paragraph, if for any reason at any time it is necessary for one pilot to leave his station at the controls of the aircraft when operating at flight altitudes above flight level 350, the remaining pilot at the controls shall put on and use his oxygen mask until the other pilot has returned to his station.

If your airplane is unsupercharged, operations above 12,000 ft will be rather disappointing anyway. (Note that the regulations say *12,500* up to 30 min.)

Some Physiological Facts. Okay, now you're convinced that it's not wise to fly in an environment higher than 12,000 ft pressure altitude without supplemental oxygen. (Note the use of the term *environment*—if your cabin is pressurized to an altitude of 12,000 ft or below you can be flying at an actual altitude of, say, 45,000 ft and doing just fine as long as the system works—but more about the airplane systems requirements in the next chapter.)

Each time you *inhale* (at 12 to 16 times per minute) you pull in about 1 pt of air (500 cc), bringing O_2 into your body. Each *exhalation* is getting rid of CO_2. The inhaled O_2 passes into the blood, and CO_2 is released, moving from the blood to the lung air sacs. The blood continually takes the fresh O_2 to the tissues and carries the CO_2 back to the lungs for exhalation.

Gases tend to move from high to low pressures. Blood entering the lung has a comparatively high CO_2 pressure, so the CO_2 is passed out through the lung membrane and exhaled. The incoming air has a high O_2 pressure and is absorbed through the membrane to join the blood.

The balance between O_2 and CO_2 in the body is maintained by sensing devices in the brain that react to CO_2 partial pressure. If the CO_2 partial pressure is too high the rate of breathing (and the volume of air intake) is increased so that more CO_2 is exhaled. If the CO_2 partial pressure is too low the opposite occurs. Another system located in the large arteries near the heart checks the partial pressure of O_2.

If you get anxious or scared you could develop hyperventilation—breathing too fast or too deeply and losing an excessive amount of CO_2. You might feel dizzy, drowsy, or lightheaded and experience tingling of the fingers and toes, increased feelings of body heat, blurring of vision, a rapid heart rate, muscle spasm, nausea, and even unconsciousness. Except for the last two items, hyperventilation has much the same symptoms as an extreme case of teenage love, but hyperventilation is the more dangerous of the two when flying an airplane. The word is to slow down your rate of breathing. In extreme cases, breathing into a paper bag will build up the CO_2 again, reusing the CO_2 you just breathed out.

Oxygen Equipment Types. *Continuous flow*—This is considered the simplest system and is normally used from ground level to 25,000 ft (or higher, with more advanced mask and regulator designs, according to the FAA pamphlet "O_2 over 10.") This system may consist of a carry-on O_2 bottle with a control knob for setting a predetermined O_2 flow rate,

and, of course, an oxygen mask. Much of the O_2 was lost around the edges of the earlier general aviation "disposable" masks, but later designs have improved considerably.

The continuous-flow system could be a fixed-type regulator with the console in the cabin (the O_2 bottle is Usually in the baggage compartment or an area where it can easily be replenished on the ground). The regulator may have several outlets for plugging in hoses and masks (Fig. 18-3).

The *diluter-demand system*, which was first widely used in WW II fighters, is designed to give different amounts of air and O_2, as required by altitude (Fig. 18-4). As the cabin altitude increases (cabin air pressure, without pressurization, is the same as that outside) or the atmospheric pressure decreases, whichever way you want to look at it, the pilot's inhalation will bring in a higher percentage of O_2 until at 30,000 ft it reaches 100% O_2. Usually the system has two settings: NORMAL, for the condition just discussed, and 100% OXYGEN, for use anytime the pilot thinks it's necessary (for instance, getting fumes through the cabin air–O_2 mix on the normal setting). There is usually an emergency valve on the system that turns on a steady flow of O_2 for emergency use (if you're about to pass out from lack of O_2 on the other two settings and need to get perked up before it's too late—but more about that later).

The *pressure-demand* system is used for operations in the 35,000- to 45,000-ft level (unpressurized cabin) where the diluter-demand system is unable to keep up the pressure for O_2 absorption into the lungs and also blood O_2 saturation (Fig. 18-5). You'd need this type of equipment in case of decompression when operating a pressurized airplane at this altitude range.

You don't necessarily have to use all three systems for sea level to 45,000-ft operations. But the top altitude listed for each is the maximum at which it would normally be used.

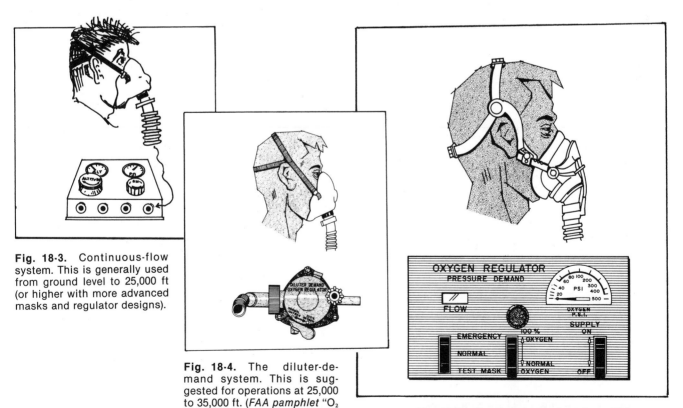

Fig. 18-3. Continuous-flow system. This is generally used from ground level to 25,000 ft (or higher with more advanced masks and regulator designs).

Fig. 18-4. The diluter-demand system. This is suggested for operations at 25,000 to 35,000 ft. (*FAA pamphlet "O_2 over 10"*)

Fig. 18-5. Pressure-demand system. This system is for operations from 35,000 to 45,000 ft. (*FAA pamphlet "O_2 over 10"*)

In breathing normally without an oxygen mask, or using the demand-diluter O₂ system, you do the work when you inhale; the air is pulled in and the normal elasticity of the lungs forces it out. The first time you use a pressure-demand system, you almost have to learn to breathe again, consciously breathing out against the pressure coming into the mask. For some people the first encounter can be claustrophobic. One pilot describing his introduction to the system said, "It seemed that every time I relaxed a little, I got a lungful of oxygen, whether I needed it or not!" Some of your passengers may get a closed-in feeling or one of being unable to get their breath when using the oxygen mask the first time with *any* system. You may have to do some extra reassuring and tell them that this feeling does happen to some people and with familiarity the feeling should pass. Their worry should be whether they are getting sufficient (or any) O₂; depending on the type or model of equipment you're using, an indicator showing that O₂ is flowing can be an aid.

If your airplane has permanent O₂ equipment, it should be a part of the preflight check even if you are only planning a trip on a CAVU day at lower altitudes. If you make checking it a habit, you won't get caught short sometime when you need to go high to avoid turbulent weather.

Carbon monoxide (CO) is produced by incomplete burning of the engine exhaust and is most commonly found in aircraft cockpits when there is a leak in the exhaust manifold inside the cabin heater shroud. If the cabin heat is on, the CO is piped into the cockpit and, since it has no smell, it can be detected only by special equipment.

CO is concentrated in the blood as a carboxyhemoglobin complex that cannot transport oxygen. Since CO binds the hemoglobin 200 times greater than oxygen, it is essential to avoid toxic levels. One of the first symptoms (a slight headache) of CO intoxication occurs at 10% blood level; at 20% you develop a throbbing headache, and at 30% a severe headache. Vision starts to decrease and you become irritable, dizzy, or nauseous.

The possibility of detecting these symptoms before they impair your judgment on a long high-altitude flight are slight. If, however, you are on 100% oxygen you shorten the half-life of carboxyhemoglobin from 6 hours to 1 hour. Furthermore, if the mask is tight fitting you will not be breathing any CO. So if your passengers complain of headaches, dizziness, and/or nausea you should all go on 100% oxygen at once.

Know your O₂ system. A full bottle won't do you any good at altitude if the valve is OFF—and it's in the baggage compartment or some other inaccessible place.

Know the hours of O₂ available for the number of passengers for various pressures for your system. Fig. 18-6 is a table of the duration of a particular full system for various pilot and passenger combinations.

PROBLEMS AT HIGH ALTITUDES

Your general health should be good if you are going to fly at high altitudes; a person who is overweight and never exercises can expect problems.

Tobacco and alcohol can raise your "apparent" altitude by several thousand feet:

Actual Altitude (Ft)	Physiological Altitude (Ft)
Sea level	7,000 (+7000)
10,000	14,000 (+4000)
20,000	22,000 (+2000)

From this information it would seem that smokers and nonsmokers are the same at altitudes above 20,000 ft, but physiological evidence doesn't back this up.

For night flying it's suggested that O₂ be used from 5000

Crew	Passengers	Oxygen Supply Range in Hours
1	0	25.76
1	1	14.72
1	2	10.30
1	3	7.93
1	4	6.44
1	5	5.42
1	6	4.68
1	7	4.12
2	0	12.88
2	1	9.37
2	2	7.36
2	3	6.07
2	4	5.15
2	5	4.48
2	6	3.96

Fig. 18-6. Oxygen duration chart.

ft for better vision. (Night fighters go on 100% O₂ from the surface up.)

If you're tired or shook-up or using certain drugs, your tolerances to hypoxia will be low or practically nonexistent.

Hypoxia. The problem you'd most expect is hypoxia, or lack of O₂ at the tissue level. There are several types of hypoxia. One is caused by an *anemic* condition, so an individual can have trouble even at sea level. Anemia may be caused by a disease or by loss of blood through accident or overenthusiastic blood donating. The average healthy person recovers from a blood donation in a few hours, but as a rule 72 hr is the minimum time after a donation before flying as pilot in command.

Hypoxic hypoxia is the type that could occur at high altitudes. Some of your passengers might need more O₂ than you are using because of lung problems such as emphysema, bronchitis, or other conditions.

If your O₂ system goes haywire or pressurization is lost, you'll have a certain amount of useful-consciousness time in which to put on an oxygen mask or open another valve, descend, etc. (Fig.18-7). The *rate* of change for useful-consciousness time starts to level off as higher altitudes are reached. For instance, the 3000-ft change between 22,000 and 25,000 ft shortens the time by about 180 sec, whereas the 25,000-ft change from 40,000 to 65,000 ft only shortens it an additional 6 sec.

Altitude	Useful Consciousness
22,000 feet	5 minutes
25,000 feet	2 minutes
28,000 feet	1 minute
30,000 feet	45 seconds
35,000 feet	30 seconds
40,000 feet	18 seconds
65,000 feet	12 seconds

Fig. 18-7. Time of useful consciousness at various altitudes, based on O₂ circulation time plus the amount necessary in the brain to keep it functioning. (*Aircraft Division United States Steel*)

How do you recognize the symptoms of hypoxia (Fig. 18-8)? People react differently, but a person's particular symptoms are much the same each time, so once you've experienced hypoxia you can recognize it later (assuming, of course, that the first time was under controlled conditions

Symptoms of Hypoxia

Altitude	Time of Exposure	Symptoms
10,000 to 14,000 ft.	several hours	Headache, fatigue, listlessness, nonspecific deterioration of physical and mental performance.
15,000 to 18,000 ft	30 minutes	Impairment of judgment and vision, high self-confidence, euphoria, disregard for sensory perceptions, poor coordination, sleepiness, dizziness, personality changes as if intoxicated, cyanosis (bluing).
20,000 to 35,000 ft	5 minutes	Same symptoms as "15,000 to 18,000 feet" only more pronounced with eventual unconsciousness.
35,000 to 40,000 ft.	15 to 45 seconds	Immediate unconsciousness (with little or no warning!)

Fig. 18-8. Some common symptoms of hypoxia. (*Aircraft Division United States Steel*)

such as in an altitude chamber so you survived to experience it again.)

The problem is that once hypoxia is well developed, a feeling of lethargy or well-being may cause you to ignore the warning signs such as added difficulty in computing ETAs or reading back clearances. One jet fighter pilot who had a close shave at 35,000 ft when his oxygen hose inadvertently became disconnected noted that he saw the "blinker" (the indicator of proper O₂ flow) wasn't working but "it didn't seem to make much difference." His erratic flying showed problems, his wingman's radio calls alerted him to go on emergency O₂, and things then got back to normal. There have been cases of fighter pilots in an advanced stage of hypoxia who haven't responded to such calls and crashed. While you can make a rapid recovery from hypoxia after the proper O₂ flow is established (15 sec), there may be some disorientation and dizziness for a time. A person who has had a bad case of hypoxia may not remember being unconscious.

If you are going to be pilot in command of an airplane capable of operating a high altitudes, it's a good idea to get a checkout in the altitude chamber at the FAA Center at Oklahoma City or a military installation near you. Check with your local Flight Standards District Office for a list of these military facilities and the procedure in scheduling a checkout.

If possible, while under supervision in the chamber take off your mask and see the effects of hypoxia on *you*. The supervisors may have you name the suits of various playing cards or have you write your name and address several times in succession to check the deterioration of your mental and physical processes. (You'll start well but soon will forget how

to spell your name or will stare at a big black ace of spades trying to figure out the suit.) The supervisor will put your mask on before things go too far. The thing about hypoxia is that generally it's not an uncomfortable feeling and can induce a euphoria that interferes with the instinct for survival. You'll have to *reason* that O₂ is needed, even though you "feel fine."

Hypoxia increases fatigue even after recovery.

Dysbarism. Dysbarism is a big word for body gas problems, whether trapped in the blood or in body cavities, such as sinuses, intestines, stomach, or middle ear. Aeroembolism is a term used for gas bubbles in the blood.

You've probably had some trouble at one time or another with clearing your ears on a letdown, particularly if you had a cold. In extreme conditions you may have had trouble in a climb, even in the low-powered types of airplane you flew as a student or private pilot. You can well imagine the ear problem if decompression occurred in a pressurized airplane. It has been said that the Stuka pilots of WW II had their eardrums pierced to facilitate pressure equalization. The U.S. dive bomber pilots did not follow suit but made sure the passages (eustachian and ear tubes) were clear when diving. Pilots with colds or other sources of stoppages have had ruptured eardrums in glide or dive bombing on the first run and then the "pleasure" of making several more runs in this condition—it is extremely painful.

Aeroembolism (the bends)— is the result of nitrogen and other gases being dissolved in the blood and other fluids. When the surrounding pressure fails (as would be the case in failure of cabin pressure or flying at an altitude of 35,000 to 45,000 ft without any pressurization), these gases—nitrogen mostly—form gas bubbles, particularly in the joints. The pain is severe. Although advice is often given to "not exercise the area, it makes more bubbles form," you'll find yourself bending your wrists or other joints in an attempt to ease the pain. Bubble formation in the lungs can also cause pain and disability. Bends can be fatal. Scuba and other divers who've been down to depths of 35 ft or more (where the pressure on them is at least twice that of the sea level atmosphere) and come up too fast can suffer the bends, as can a pilot in an unpressurized airplane at high altitudes.

Bends at altitude (35,000 to 40,000 ft) may take up to 20 min to develop severe symptoms. But if you were scuba diving and then flew within a few hours, it's possible that you could get the bends at 10,000 ft cabin altitude.

SUMMARY

Know your O₂ equipment and pressurization system thoroughly. Work out beforehand the procedures to be used in the event of O₂ system failures, loss of pressurization, or other problems. Get a checkout on altitude effects in a chamber before acting as pilot in command of an airplane capable of operating at high altitudes.

19 Turbocharging and Pressurization

BACKGROUND

This chapter is intended only to give some general information on supercharging (turbocharging). You'll get a thorough checkout when you start to fly any new turbo system because of the different pilot techniques and requirements, compared with normally aspirated engines.

You'll find that some systems have a separate control for the turbo waste gate (more about that later) and others are automatic; in the latter, the pilot uses the throttle(s) alone to set up the desired manifold pressure (mp).

Turbocharging allows the engine to develop more HP at sea level (ground-boosted engines) and at altitude (ground-boosted and altitude-turbocharged). But the primary purpose of such systems is to develop and maintain better high-altitude engine operations at a small cost in weight.

Some of the superchargers used in the older light twins with radial engines are driven by the crankshaft, but at a much higher speed through gearing. These superchargers are single-stage, single-speed. The single compressor always operates at the same gear ratio, and the pilot does not "shift gears" as altitude is gained.

The number of "stages" of an engine supercharging system indicates the number of compressing cycles it goes through. The air, or mixture, may be compressed several times through a series of compressor sections, but most light general aviation airplane systems have only one stage. The terms *single-speed* or *two-speed* are used in conjunction with mechanically driven superchargers (part of the original engine, hooked up with the crankshaft through a gear train). The single speed is at a fixed-gear ratio, and there's nothing the pilot can do about it. The two-speed type allowed the system to change from low blower to high blower as altitude was gained (this shifting was done at altitudes varying from 7000 to 12,000 ft, depending on the airplane/engine combinations). (See the FAA *A&P Mechanics Powerplant Handbook*.)

TURBOSUPERCHARGING

Basically, *turbocharging* is accomplished by using the exhaust gases of the engine to turn a turbine wheel directly connected to a compressor wheel that compresses intake air and routes it to the carburetor for mixing with the fuel. In the fuel injection engine, the compressed air is sent on to the engine for mixing at the cylinder intake. If you were going to design a system, you might start as shown in Fig. 19-1. The turbo is always "on" in that example. At sea level the internal pressures in the engine (brake mean effective pressure) could be too high.

Altitude Turbocharging. Assuming that an engine being turbocharged is not allowed to exceed, say, 29 in. of mp at its maximum rpm, some means of getting the compressed air at altitude is needed. In other words, in order to get 29 in. of mp at 16,000 ft might require starting off with 43 in. at sea level. This won't work for our fictitious engine—it may not take the pressure.

The best thing is to add a "waste gate" to the system so that a choice *is* available (Fig. 19-2). The pilot can control the waste gate position as altitude is gained, finally closing it com-

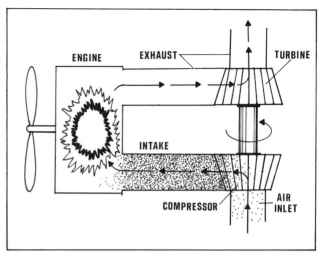

Fig. 19-1. A view of the turbocharging principle. There are, of course, a *few* other factors to consider.

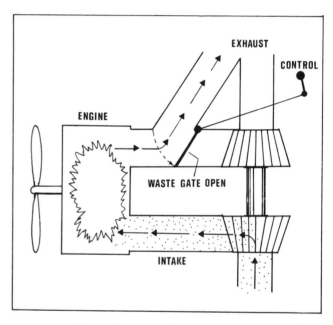

Fig. 19-2. A simplified view of a system with a waste gate added. The gate is open so the engine is normally aspirated (the turbo isn't working).

pletely to route all the exhaust gases through the turbine wheel. When the waste gate is completely closed the available mp drops with further altitude gain (Fig. 19-3).

In Chap. 12 it was noted that as altitude is increased, the cooler outside air and lower exhaust back pressure result in more HP per inch of mp. This was also shown in Fig. 12-1, a power-setting chart. But, another practical consideration is involved in the operation of the turbocharger. As the air is compressed in the process it becomes hotter. As the airplane goes higher the turbo wheel must turn faster to do the job and so some heat (and loss of efficiency) is involved. With some models of equipment a *higher* mp is required to get the same HP at altitude to offset this. This is mentioned because some turbocharged airplanes you'll be flying may have power-setting charts that call for relative manifold pressures that don't jibe with your previous experience with nonboosted engines (as discussed in Chapter 12) (Fig. 19-4).

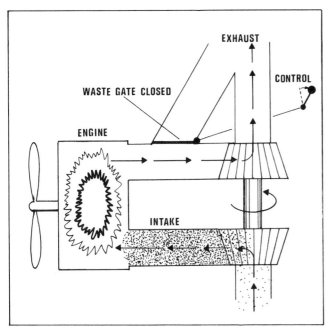

Fig. 19-3. The waste gate is completely closed; any further increase in altitude will result in a drop in manifold pressure.

Fig. 19-4. (below) Power setting charts for (A) a normally aspirated engine and (B) the boosted version. Comparing manifold pressures for long-range cruise power settings for both types, you can see (underlined) that the boosted engine requires higher manifold pressure for a given rpm. The full chart carries information on mp limits for various altitudes for different propellers and corrective factors. (Example only, not to be used for flight purposes.)

(A) Power Setting Table (Cruise) - Lycoming Model IO-540-C4B5, 250 HP Engine

Normal Cruise Approx 210 HP		Intermediate Cruise Approx 190 HP		Economy Cruise Approx 175 HP		Long Range Cruise Approx 140 HP	
RPM	MP	RPM	MP	RPM	MP	RPM	MP
2400	26.0	2200	26.0	2200	24.0	2100	21.0
		2300	25.0	2300	23.2	2200	20.0
		2400	24.0	2400	22.4	2300	19.3

(B) Power Setting Table (Cruise) - Lycoming Model TIO-540-C1A, 250 HP Engine

Turbo Cruise Approx 232 HP		Intermediate Cruise Approx 200 HP		Economy Cruise Approx 173 HP		Long Range Cruise Approx 140 HP	
RPM	MP	RPM	MP	RPM	MP	RPM	MP
2400	34.0	2300	31.0	2200	28.0	2100	25.0
		2400	30.0	2300	27.0	2200	24.0
		2500	29.0	2400	26.0	2300	23.0

Ground-boosted Engines. The Lycoming TIO-541 model engine, which permits 38 in. to 43 in. for takeoff, has a larger and stronger crankshaft, lower compression ratio to protect the combustion chamber, special exhaust valves and guides to protect against hotter exhaust gas temperatures (EGTs), and oil squirts in the crankcase that direct a stream of oil at the pistons to help cool them.

It's extremely important that the proper octane fuel be used — detonation can be much more of a menace for boosted engines.

Waste Gates Again. To get back to the turbocharging system you're designing, look again at Figs. 19-2 and 19-3. You've decided that the waste gate idea is the best way to go,

and now need to design a way to control it. Oil pressure from the engine could be used to actuate the waste gate and also lubricate the turbine shaft.

Like a constant-speed propeller (which has a combination of oil pressure and counterweight, oil versus air pressure, or oil versus the normal pitching moment of the prop), maybe here an oil pressure and spring combination would be a good system for controlling the waste gate operation. The most logical approach would be to use oil pressure to *close* the waste gate, fighting a spring that wants to open it. The waste gate control, which is separate from the other engine controls in the manual system, is adjusted for the desired mp altitude. This control is usually a vernier type, and in the multi there'll be one for each engine. With this oil pressure spring arrange-

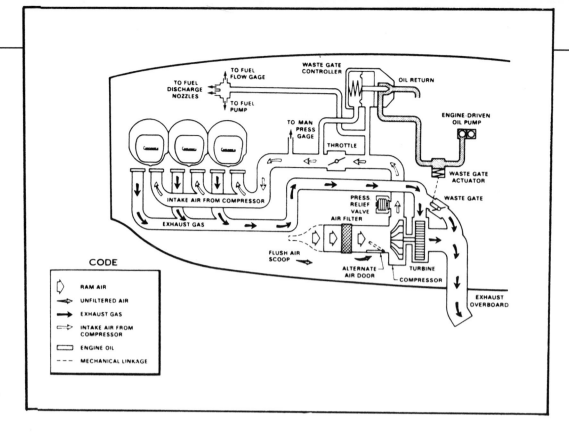

Fig. 19-5. Turbocharger system.

ment, a loss of oil pressure in the system would result in the spring opening the waste gate and the engine becoming normally respirating—unboosted—again. The airplane, if at altitudes requiring boosting to sustain flight, would descend until power was available for straight and level and other operations. Better this setup than having the waste gate *closed* when oil pressure is lost in the turbo system, which could mean, at low altitudes, overboosting an engine designed for a maximum of 29 in. of mercury or thereabouts. Fig. 19-5 shows a schematic of a turbocharged engine.

The next step is to install an *automatic absolute pressure control system*. With it the pilot uses the throttle at altitude to set up the mp desired without adjusting a separate control. The automatic control system adjusts for pressure, and the supercharger is operated so that the mp follows throttle movements. This automatic feature is normally set at the factory and shouldn't be worked on in the field.

Operation of a Turbocharged Engine.
You'll naturally use the *POH* for the exact word on the particular airplane/engine setup, but a few general items on operations should be covered.

First, while you're careful in changing power with the nonboosted constant-speed prop, even more care must be taken with the turbocharged engine. An abrupt or improper sequence of power adjustment can damage the engine. The following items apply to both manual and automatic systems when in operation:

1. The throttle(s) must be operated smoothly or the engines will surge. Since the turbo(s) will react to power input this is bad for the turbocharger(s) and the engine(s).

2. Fig. 12-2 (engine indigestion) shows what can happen if you get out of sequence in using the prop control and throttle in a nonboosted engine. So, to increase power, increase rpm first. To decrease power, decrease mp first. Handle the power controls very carefully.

3. The cylinder head temperatures (CHTs) will run hotter at high altitudes because of the higher turbine speeds. You'll need to closely monitor that instrument. Keep temperatures within prescribed limits. (The CHT will tend to average at least 30°F higher at altitude.)

4. Cruise control at altitude is to be in accordance with specific instructions for that airplane and engine combination.

5. Because of the higher temperatures and operating limits, turbocharged engines use 100-octane fuel as a *minimum*.

6. A power setting of 75% is used by most pilots for cruise. Consult charts for the most utility.

Manually Controlled Turbocharger.
The waste gate(s) will be open (turbo turned OFF) for takeoffs at field density-altitudes below 4000 to 5000 ft. Always make sure that the manual control is in the waste-gate-open position before starting the engine. *You* may have brought things back to normal as you descended on that last flight, but somebody might have closed the waste gate in the meantime. Using 60+ in. of mp on takeoff or go-around, in an engine limited to 29 in. or so, could get everybody's attention and cost you several thousand dollars.

TAKEOFF AND CLIMB. This type of system is left OFF (waste gate open) for takeoff and climb until 4000 to 5000 ft (density-altitude) is reached, at which point you'll be using full throttle to maintain required climb mp. (Takeoff and climb at *full rich* mixture.) As altitude is gained, the manual waste gate control, usually a vernier type, is gradually closed to maintain the required mp.

CRUISE CONTROL. Use the power chart for your airplane/engine to set power at the particular altitude chosen. As far as leaning by reference to the EGT is concerned, use the recommended proper leaning procedures.

Temperatures, particularly CHT, are higher at altitude and can be a critical factor, if ignored. One of the first light twins equipped with turbochargers could not fly level on one engine above a certain altitude because *cooling was the critical factor*. It could maintain altitude on one engine at 90- to 100-mph CAS but 120-mph CAS was necessary to keep the temperatures down, and it was going downhill at that speed. Some manufacturers use a turbine inlet temperature (TIT) gage as standard equipment.

Fig. 19-6. Pressurized cabin area for a light twin. The floor is the bottom part of the pressurized cabin area.

DESCENT. Descent with a *manually* controlled turbocharger is the reverse of the climb in that the waste gates are gradually opened as altitude is lost, so the airplane passes through the 4000- to 5000-ft level as a normal aspirating engine type. Suppose you *forget* to open the waste gates (after closing the throttle to make a fast descent) and then suddenly apply full throttle(s) for a quick go-around. The ensuing noise and activity would be very interesting to those on the ground observing, but you would probably be so busy trying to land a no-powered airplane that you wouldn't appreciate it.

Always reduce power with the turbo controls first.

Automatic Control. One type of automatic turbocharging system is described as follows:

1. Engine induction air taken in through a flush scoop on the inboard side of the nacelle is dusted through a filter and passes into the compressor.

2. The compressed (or pressurized) air then passes through the throttle system and induction manifold into the engine. (The air and fuel are mixed as normally for a fuel injection system.)

3. The exhaust is routed to the turbine, which drives the compressor, and the cycle continues (Figs. 19-1, -2, and -3).

To avoid exceeding the maximum allowed manifold pressure, the waste gate in this system allows some of the exhaust to bypass the turbine and exit via the tailpipe. The waste gate position changes to hold a constant compressor discharge pressure.

When the waste gate is *fully closed* (as might be the case at or above the critical altitude—see Fig. 19-3), any change in turbine speed will directly affect the mp (the more turbine rpm, the more mp, etc.).

When the waste gate is *fully open* (see Fig. 19-2), the engine will respond as does a normally aspirated engine in rpm changes. If you move the prop control forward (*increase* rpm) the mp will *decrease* slightly and vice versa, just like that constant-speed-prop-equipped, normally aspirating engine you've been flying. When the *waste gate is fully closed* (see Fig. 19-3 again) the mp reacts the opposite of a normally aspirated engine. An increase in rpm (and the resulting increase in turbine and compressor speed) *increases* the mp. A decrease in rpm decreases mp because of these factors.

When the waste gate is closed the mp will vary with airspeed (impact air). The turbocharger operates with pressure ratios of up to 3:1, and any change in intake pressure is multiplied—with a result that the exhaust and turbine (and compression) are affected.

Check the *POH* for details on how the turbocharging system works on *your* airplane.

CABIN PRESSURIZATION

Turbocharged airplanes may also use the system for cabin pressurization. Probably the optimum shape for pressurization would be a sphere, which would have no sharp angles or possible stress areas. Since crowding crewmen and passengers into such an arrangement would be uncomfortable, the next best and most logical move is to pressurize a cylindrical section (Fig. 19-6). Note that some variation from a pure sealed cylinder is necessary because of the airplane's geometry, but that basically the pressure cabin might be considered an environment cylinder in the airplane. Sealing of windows and particularly the door is of great importance.

Turbo-prop airplanes or jets usually take air from the earlier stages of the compressor section. This would seem simple enough except that the air is very hot (normally much too hot for a comfortable cabin) and must be routed through the airplane's air conditioning system. The pilot sets the cabin temperature controls. The result is the mixture of pressurized (hot) air from the compressor and cold air from the air conditioner necessary to get the right temperature. In some cases, a failure of the air conditioner means that depressurization (to get some cooler outside air so that the people in the airplane don't get dehydrated) and descent (so that those same people don't get hypoxia) are necessary.

Some cabin pressurization systems are tied in with the engine gear–driven pneumatic pumps (as opposed to vacuum pumps). To review a little, you've had plenty of experience with flight instruments being operated by the engine-driven vacuum pumps. You know that in some twins each of the two vacuum pumps has the capacity to operate the flight instruments, plus the de-icer boots on the wings and horizontal tail. Since the instrument gyro wheels operate because of air moving across the vanes, how this flow is obtained (whether by suction at one end of the system or pressure at the other) doesn't matter. A pneumatic pump, or pumps, may be tied in with pressure from the turbocharger compressor section(s) so that each may supplement the other for cabin pressurization or running the de-icers or flight instruments. A series of check valves and controls are used to make sure that each system is contributing as necessary. For instance, you'd need the instruments and maybe the de-icers at lower altitudes during IFR operations when neither turbocharging nor cabin pressurization is required—and the engine-driven pneumatic pumps are then doing the job. At higher altitudes, air from the compressor section(s) may be working hard to pressurize and do the other chores required by the various systems.

The pressurization system for one current reciprocating-engine twin depends totally on the pneumatic pumps for cabin pressurization when the manifold pressures are below 17 to 18 in. There is no turbocharger pressure used in this power regime. In cruise conditions the cabin pressurization is split 50–50 between the pneumatic pump and the turbochargers.

If it comes to which system (de-icers or cabin pressurization) has first choice with the pneumatic pump(s), the de-icers get the nod.

A detailed description of the various high-altitude systems would take up too much space here. Besides, the *POH* will give all the operating details needed. The idea here is to take an overall look so that you can understand the principles of systems for different airplanes and so can make better use of them. If you memorize the operating steps (push button 1, pull button 2, etc.) without knowing how the system works generally, you wouldn't be as apt to correct serious problems at, say, 29,000 ft when action is needed *now*. Or if you have a gripe about the system and need to talk to a mechanic, it's not considered professional to say something like, "Gee, it sure doesn't work right"—if that's all you can contribute.

Basically, when introduced to a system new to you, ask *what, why,* and *how*.

What is the system? Think about its description. *What* should it do? This will help start you thinking about how it works.

Why is it needed, or *why* is its addition advantageous? This also pins down the idea of its principle of operation.

How should it work? How will you make it function both normally and under emergency conditions?

You might find that the approach used in the beginning of the chapter—designing a turbocharging system—will work for other systems as well. Remember that most of the complicated systems are based on simple principles. Fig. 19-7 shows the pressurization controls for a pressurized twin. If you were handed this illustration or sat down in the airplane with no explanation or preparation, the dials and controls would probably not make much sense. Of course, you aren't likely to be put on the spot this way but would likely go to a factory school and get a good checkout in the system.

To continue with our example—in looking at Fig. 19-7

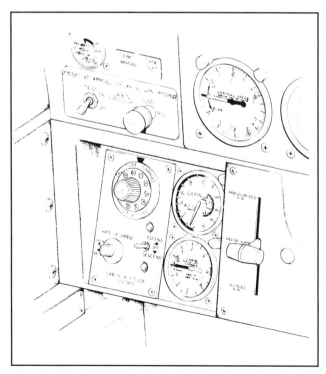

Fig. 19-7. Pressurized cabin console.

you might examine the various items and ask, *why?* For example, it would be useful to know the cabin altitude when you are well above the altitude requiring O_2 for survival. The gage is handier and more accurate than turning around to check the various shades of blue in the passengers' faces. Don't be afraid to ask *why* something is a part of the system.

If you design your "own" system for a turbocharged, pressurized airplane, you might at first come up with a very simple one. You'd then expand it for various component controls. The first design would be close to the one in Fig. 19-1. You'd soon see that a continuously operating turbocharging, pressurizing, and de-icing system wouldn't work. You would then start adding controls to operate the de-icers, or turbochargers, or pressurization when needed. While you'd like to avoid any unauthorized cabin air leaks, you'd have to provide *controlled* leakage in order to get the desired cabin pressure. Besides, who wants to breathe the same air over and over?

You'd soon find yourself adding all the "complicated" controls and instruments as you progressed in designing a system. When each is added as necessary, it's easy to understand, but if you are faced with the whole conglomerate at once it can be overpowering.

SUMMARY

This chapter has taken a general look at turbocharging and cabin pressurization so that you'll understand the principles when you are first introduced to the systems (and the controls) for a specific airplane. Once you understand what the system is to do, the *POH* instructions will make more sense.

Following are some terms you should be familiar with concerning turbocharging (as given by the Lycoming *Flyer*):

Supercharge and *supercharger*—The term *supercharge* means to increase the air pressure (density) above or higher than ambient conditions. A *supercharger* is any device that accomplishes this.

Turbo-supercharger—More commonly referred to as a *turbocharger*, this device is a supercharger driven by a turbine. The turbine is spun by energy extracted from engine exhaust gas.

Compressor—A compressor is the portion of a turbocharger that takes in ambient air and compresses it before discharging it to the engine. This compressor is a high-speed radial outflow wheel that accelerates the air as it passes through the wheel passages. Then the collector around the wheel transforms the velocity energy to a pressure head.

Turbine—A turbocharger turbine operates almost in reverse of the compressor. Hot exhaust gases of the engine are ducted into the turbine housing where the velocity is increased prior to passing through the turbine wheel. The expansion of these gases releases energy to drive the turbine wheel.

Waste gate and *waste gate actuator*—In a turbocharger system the term *waste gate* refers to a valve (usually a butterfly type) that dumps engine exhaust gases before they reach the turbocharger. The valve may be actuated by a hydraulic piston and cylinder with the piston linked to an arm on the butterfly valve shaft.

Absolute pressure controller—This is an automatic control that senses compressor discharge pressure in an aneroid bellows attached to a poppet valve. This poppet valve in turn controls the amount of hydraulic fluid bled to the crankcase, thereby modulating the waste gate as necessary to maintain a constant compressor discharge pressure.

Adjustable absolute pressure controller—This controller is similar to the absolute pressure controller except that the desired compressor discharge pressure can be varied by the pilot. Each time a new pressure is selected, that pressure will hold automatically.

Manual controls—With manual controls the waste gate position and subsequent turbocharger output are controlled and modulated by the pilot rather than by an automatic control device.

Automatic controls—Unlike manual controls, the automatic controls perform the necessary functions to maintain preselected operating conditions without the pilot's attention.

Density controller—This device has the same general construction as an absolute pressure controller, except the bellows are filled with a temperature-sensitive dry nitrogen. These bellows will cause the controller to maintain a constant density, rather than pressure, by allowing the pressure to increase as the temperature increases, holding a constant of pressure over the square root of a temperature: $C = P/\sqrt{T}$, where C = constant, P = pressure, and T = temperature).

Ground-boosted or *ground turbocharged*—These phrases indicate that the engine depends on a certain amount of supercharging at sea level to produce the advertised HP. An engine that is so designed will usually include a lower compression ratio to avoid detonation.

Deck pressure—This is the pressure measured in the area downstream of the turbo compressor discharge and upstream of the engine throttle valve. This should not be confused with manifold pressure.

Manifold pressure—This is the pressure measured downstream of the engine throttle valve. It is almost directly proportional to the engine power output.

Differential pressure controller—This controller uses a diaphragm rather than the bellows found in the absolute pressure controller. It is usually used in conjunction with a density controller. Its function is to override the density controller so that the compressor discharge pressure is not held at an unnecessarily high level when lower manifold pressures are being used. The differential controller will usually maintain a compressor discharge approximately 2 in. to 4 in. of mercury above the selected mp. In this system, the density controller is only effective at wide-open engine throttle conditions.

Normalizing—If a turbocharger system is used only to regain power losses caused by decreased air pressure of high altitude, it is considered that the engine has been *normalized*.

Overboost—An overboost condition means that mp is exceeding the limits at which the engine was tested and FAA certified. This can be detrimental to the life and performance of the engine. Overboost can be caused by malfunctioning controllers or an improperly operating waste gate in the automatic system or by pilot error in a manually controlled system.

Overshoot—This is a condition in which the automatic controls do not have the ability to respond quickly enough to check the inertia of the turbocharger speed increase with rapid engine throttle advance. Overshoot differs from overboost in that the high mp lasts for only a few seconds. This condition can usually be overcome by smooth throttle advance.

Sonic nozzle—Sonic nozzles are used in turbocharger systems where bleed air is used for cabin pressurization. This is a flow-limiting device that works on the principle of controlling flow by passing the air through a smooth orifice. They are sized so that, at sonic velocity, the maximum desired flow is achieved. The sonic nozzle prevents too much air going to the cabin and thereby starving the engine of its needed supply.

Bootstrapping—This is a term used in conjunction with turbo machinery. If you were to take all the air coming from a turbocharger compressor and duct it directly back into the turbine of that turbocharger, it would be called a *bootstrap system*. If no losses were encountered, it theoretically would run continuously. It would also be very unstable because if for some reason the turbo speed changed, the compressor would pump more air to drive the turbine faster, etc. A turbocharged engine above critical altitude (waste gate closed) is similar to the example mentioned above, except there is an engine placed between the compressor discharge and turbine inlet. Slight system changes cause the exhaust gas to change slightly, which causes the turbine speed to change slightly, which causes the compressor air to the engine to change slightly, which in turn again affects the exhaust gas, etc.

Critical altitude—A turbocharged engine's (auto) waste gate is in a partially open position at sea level. As the aircraft is flown to higher altitudes (lower ambient pressures), the waste gate closes gradually to maintain the preselected mp. At the point where the waste gate reaches its full closed position, the preselected mp starts to drop. This is the critical altitude for that engine.

PART 6

6

PREPARING FOR THE COMMERCIAL WRITTEN AND PRACTICAL TESTS

20 The Written Test

You have, at this stage, taken the private written (and maybe others) and so have a good idea of what to expect in getting ready for an FAA written. It could be that it's been a little while since you really hit the theory so this chapter has some suggestions for home study plus a sample written test at the end. It's suggested that you fly more complex airplanes and, if possible, actually use oxygen systems and turbocharged airplanes before taking the written—it will help you remember.

HOME STUDY AND REVIEW

You may prefer to study at *your* pace rather than attend a formal ground school. Get your own copy of the *Commercial Pilot Written Test Book* (FAA-T-8080-16B) and use it as a review and preparation for the written test. There are questions on weather in the *Written Test Book,* but this book does not include material on that subject because it is available and well covered in *Aviation Weather*—AC 00-6A (it may be AC 00-6B or -C when you read this). *Aviation Weather* should be in the library of every pilot; all the weather questions in the *Commercial Pilot Written Test Book* are based on *Aviation Weather* and *Aviation Weather Services*—AC 00-45C. The Appendix of this book includes aviation weather services cited in the *Airman's Information Manual—Basic Flight Information and ATC Procedures,* and you should review this information there. The weather books noted are well written and complete.

You should know the weather information available, such printed data as Hourly Weather Reports, Terminal and Area Forecasts, Pilot Reports, and Winds and Temperatures Aloft Forecasts.

Be familiar with charted data and their symbols as given on Radar Summary Charts, Low and High Level Significant Weather Prognosis Charts, Tropopause Wind Shear Prog Charts, Constant Pressure Prog Charts, Observed Winds and Temperature Aloft Charts, Weather Depiction Charts, and Stability Charts.

In weather theory, know the various types of fog and how they are formed. What are the initial indications of wind shear? Know the various stages of thunderstorms and the charactristics of each. On the commercial test you'll be expected to know much more about high-altitude meteorology and jet stream theory.

You should be able to estimate the height of the bases of local convective type (summertime) clouds when given the surface temperature and dewpoint. The dry air lapse rate is 5½°F and the dewpoint drops 1°F per 1000 ft; the two are approaching each other at 4½°F per 1000 ft (the cloud base problems in the written test call for a 4°F difference). Remember that 59°F and 15°C are sea level standard temperatures, and the normal lapse rates are −3½°F and −2°C per 1000 ft.

There are copies of FARs and AIM available from commercial publishers and you should have the latest copies to study for the questions in the written test here (as well as references for your day-to-day operations).

Following are some suggested study areas that not only apply as a review for the commercial written test but also as a review of the material covered in this book.

Chapter 2

Laws of motion—Newton's laws of motion should be reviewed and understood.

Principles of airfoils—As noted in this chapter, Bernoulli's theorem and Newton's law (for every action there is an equal and opposite reaction) go here. Have a good knowledge of the general pressure distribution around an airfoil and what happens to the center of pressure as angle to attack is increased (Fig. 2-3). Make sure that you have a good picture of coefficient of Lift versus angle of attack, and the effects of flaps on the coefficient of Lift and Drag (and how pitch and trim are affected by the use of flaps). Review the effects of ice, snow, or frost on airfoils. Also know the effects of air density on Lift and Thrust.

Wing planforms—The planform of the wing affects stall characteristics (rectangular planforms give best lateral control characteristics if other factors are equal). Be familiar with such terms as aspect ratio, taper, sweep, span, and area, and how they affect airplane aerodynamics and performance.

Drag—Review the types of Drag and how airspeed and/ or angle of attack affect each.

Gyroscopic precession—This and the other factors of torque should be well familiar to you.

Stalls—What happens to the airflow when the critical (stall) angle of attack is reached? Stalls are a function of angle of attack, not airspeed. Know the effects of CG position on stall speed and recovery characteristics. What are the effects of flaps on stall speed? Of Weight?

Power—Brake and Thrust horsepower and the effect of THP on performance (climbs, descents, and straight and level) should be understood. Be aware of the airplane's actions on the front and back sides of the power curve and how a change in airspeed requires more (or less) power to maintain a constant altitude.

Ground effect—Know that ground effect is the result of a change in downwash and a decrease in induced drag and be able to analyze its effects on the airplane performance and longitudinal stability during takeoff or landing. What happens to induced Drag as the airplane flies out of ground effect?

Chapter 3

The four forces—Know that the axis of reference in flight mechanics is the airplane's flight path and that the Four Forces are measured parallel and perpendicular to that axis. Weight must be broken down into two components in climbing or descending flight, in order to see what proportion is acting perpendicular or parallel to the line of flight. Analyze the forces at level slow flight and at cruise, climbs, descents, and turns.

Particularly review Figs. 3-15, -16, and -17. Check these equations (The V is in knots):

$$\text{radius (r)} = \frac{V^2}{11.26 \tan \phi}$$
$$\text{rate of turn} = \frac{1091 \tan \phi}{V}$$

The point is not necessarily to memorize the equations but to realize that the radius goes up as a function of the velocity squared for a given bank angle (ϕ). (If you double the airspeed when flying at a particular angle of bank, the radius goes up 4 times.) For turn rate, the slower the airspeed, the greater the rate of turn for a particular bank angle (halve the airspeed and the turn rate doubles).

Chapter 4. Be sure that you can answer questions on the flight instruments and their errors. Be well versed on vacuum and pressure pump systems, including the principles of gyroscopic operations and aircraft acceleration effects on the attitude indicator. Review the pitot/static system and how those instruments may be affected by icing and other factors. (Also know the effects on the instruments of using the alternate air source.) You should take another very good look at the magnetic compass and its operational errors, including acceleration (ANDS), northerly turning (NOSE), deviation, and vari-

ation. Know the various types of altitudes (indicated, density, pressure, true, and absolute) and how pressure and temperature affect the indicated-altitude and true-altitude relationships. Understand how the various engine instruments obtain their readings. Know the various airspeeds (IAS, CAS, EAS, and TAS) and how each is found. (Be able to work both ways through each type of airspeed and understand what a Mach number is.) What are the airspeed indicator markings (V speeds)?

Chapter 5. Be able to work with the various types of takeoff and obstacle-clearance charts, as given in the chapter and for airplanes you're flying. Know the effects of headwind component (and crosswind component limits), Weight, runway surface, density-altitude (pressure altitude, temperature, and humidity) and approximate runway slope effects. Remember that *H*igh, *H*ot, and *H*umid *H*urt (takeoff performance). Be able to use a crosswind/headwind component chart. Also be able to answer questions on normal and crosswind takeoff techniques, and short- and soft-field takeoffs and landings Review in your mind the techniques you use in taxiing in strong surface winds.

Chapter 6. Review this chapter well and understand the difference between max rate and max angle climbs and how they are derived. Wind affects *angle* of climb but *not rate* (assume no turbulence). Be able to read—quickly and accurately—the various rate of climb charts available. Know that excess *Thrust horsepower* controls the *rate* of climb and excess *Thrust* controls *angle* of climb. Be able to accurately use time, fuel, and distance-to-climb information—both tabular and graphic.

Chapter 7. Review this chapter, with emphasis on being able to read cruise power setting charts; understand that the maximum range speeds and power settings are lower than for "normal" cruise (65 to 75%) and that maximum endurance is found at even lower speed/power settings. Max endurance is greatest at lower altitudes. Note that airplanes close to the max range airspeed can fly at a "high" or "low" airspeed and pilots may not realize that they are flying the lower one and may think they've gotten it "on the step" (Fig. 7-2).

Chapter 8. Understand how max distance and minimum sink glides are different. Note that the wind affects the glide angle but not the *rate* of sink. (This is the same condition as max angle and max rate climbs and, like them, it's assumed that there is no turbulence to affect performance.)

Review how density-altitude affects the maximum distance glide angle and sink rate, and how the indicated (calibrated) airspeed for the max distance glide must be reduced with Weight decrease. Look at the maximum glide distance charts again.

Chapter 9. The theory and techniques of normal and crosswind landings and short- and soft-field approaches and landings should be well established in your mind. This is a good time to review the various flap operations and systems you've encountered in your practical flying experience (electrical, hydraulic, and manual systems and their idiosyncrasies) so that you'll be able to answer any questions from a pilot's standpoint. Know the factors (wind, density-altitude, slope, runway surface, and braking) that affect the landing roll. Check out your use of graphic and tabular landing distance data. Read about the different types of hydroplaning and the minimum hydroplaning speed.

Chapter 10. As a commercial pilot you'll be expected to go more deeply into the theory of stability and control so that you can generally predict an airplane's reaction to a new Weight placement or a design change.

Take a good look at Fig. 10-46 and be sure that you are knowledgeable about the principles of longitudinal static and dynamic stability. Know what effects sweepback and dihedral have on directional and lateral stability. It should go without saying that you will be expected to be familiar with the various types of Weight and balance envelopes and be able to accurately work any Weight and balance problems on the test. Also know the effects that Weight and balance have on performance (forward CG means a higher stall speed in most cases because the down force on the tail makes it "weigh" more—see Fig. 7-4). What is gross Weight and useful load? What is included in the Basic Empty Weight of the airplane? How can the pilot affect the longitudinal stability of the airplane? As you fly larger airplanes with greater cargo capacity, you'll have to be aware of such factors as cargo shifting and complete management of Weight and balance. Know how ground effect affects longitudinal stability.

Chapter 11. Take another good look at this chapter for aircraft limitations (airspeeds, load factors, and Weights). Remember that the definition of the maneuvering speed is that maximum airspeed (calibrated) at which abrupt and complete control travel may be accomplished without exceeding the limit load factor. The maneuvering speed (CAS) is a multiple of the stall speed times the square root of the limit load factor. Since the stall speed decreases with the square root of the Weight (the limit load factor is required to be constant), the maneuvering speed used must decrease with the *square root* of the Weight change. Note that stresses due to gusts depend on the Weight, lift slope of the airfoil, velocity of the airplane, and the gust velocity. Review Figs. 11-8 and 11-9 and be able to find on similar charts the load factor imposed by a 15- or 30-psf (vertical) gust at a chosen airspeed. Know the limit (design) and ultimate positive and negative load factors for normal, utility, and acrobatic category airplanes. Remember that the load factor is the Lift to Weight ratio (LF = L/W), and these can be shuffled around to solve for each value (if you know the other two). Be able to find the increase in stall speed and/or load factors for a given angle of bank as shown in Fig. 11-2. *The load factor imposed in a balanced, constant-altitude turn is the same at a given bank for all airplanes at all airspeeds.* In a 60° bank the C-152 pilot will have the same 2 g's imposed as will an F-16 pilot at that bank.

What are the *differences* in stall speed and load factors as a bank is changed?

Chapter 12. Know the basics of manifold pressure/rpm relationships and the theory of the constant-speed propeller (review also Chap. 2 in the section on Thrust to see *why* the constant-speed propeller is more efficient than the fixed-pitch type). Remember the different types of constant-speed propellers and their principles of operation (also covered in Chap. 2).

Chapter 13. There will be questions on fuel injection and carburetor principles and the use of mixture/throttle and boost pumps. And, elementary as it may seem, know the principles of the reciprocating engine (general ideas of carburetion, ignition, and the fuel and oil types available and how they are designated). Understand detonation and preignition, including their causes and effects, and general engine starting and shutdown procedures. You might also review the operations of the various fuel systems you've used. Know the point(s) in the carburetor where icing would most likely occur. Be able to describe the symptoms of carburetor icing in fixed-pitch-prop and constant-speed-prop airplanes. Remember that the term *induction icing* covers both carburetor and fuel injection systems. What temperatures are "best" (worst?) for carb ice? Fuel vaporization and lowered pressure in the venturi are the two big factors in forming carb ice. What are the

advantages and disadvantages of carburetor and fuel injection systems? Note that the carburetor or air mixture temperature gage becomes more important for high-powered and turbocharged engines. What does carburetor heat do to the mixture?

Chapter 14. Know the various types of retractable landing gear systems used, plus safety additions and general emergency procedures for the two main types (electrically and hydraulically actuated). Also review the systems you've had practical experience with.

Chapter 15. Look at this chapter for the definition of the single-engine minimum controllable speed and for a further review of airplane performance as indicated by the graph of twin- and single-engine THP available and required. You might review the section on engine starting for some reminders on general engine starting and run-up procedures. How are V_{YSE} and V_{MC} shown on the airspeed indicator?

Chapter 16. There will likely be questions on the written test on emergency landings. You should go over some general ideas on rough-running engines, fire in flight (both engine and electrical), and techniques for landing on various types of terrain and on water. For further study, order NTSB Report No. AAS-72-3, *Emergency Landing Techniques in Small Fixed Wing Aircraft*.

Wake turbulence and procedures to avoid it should be gone over in your mind again, both for this test *and* for your day-to-day flying, in case you hadn't thought about it for a while. Have you worked out a procedure for your airplane if a door comes open on takeoff or enroute? Run over in your mind the possible effects of turbulence and gradient winds.

Chapter 17. Rework some of the navigation and performance problems in this chapter and affirm that your work with the computer is quick and accurate. Review the equation for radius of action from a moving base, time out (TO) = (TT × GSB)/(GSO + GSB), and if you use hours and tenths be sure that you don't confuse fractions of hours with minutes (2.28 hr is *not* 2 hr and 28 min but 2 hr and 16.8 min). In the off-course problems, the flight to the destination will require two steps in heading corrections: (1) the change required to parallel the original course plus (2) the turn to fly to the destination. Review the "rule of 60" so that you can double-check your computer work on off-course and time- or fuel-to-station problems.

Chapter 18. You'll have some questions on the physiological effects of high-altitude flying. Know the general theory of the three types of O_2 systems. Be able to recognize the symptoms of hypoxia, dysbarism (and aeroembolism), and hyperventilation (the latter is not a problem caused by altitude, but it could happen at altitude and be confused with hypoxia, which might result in more anxiety and more hyperventilation). Review the FAR 91 O_2 requirements in this chapter.

Chapter 19. Have a good grasp of the theory and operation of turbocharged engines and how cabin pressurization is generally used. Some people get confused as to whether the waste gate is open or closed when the turbocharger is in action. Review the illustrations, and, if your mind goes blank on the written, "redesign" a system.

Federal Aviation Regulations. Be familiar with FAR 1, 61, 71, 91, and 135, plus National Transportation Safety Board Part 830. You'll be expected to have a very good knowledge of these parts and the following FAA Advisory Circulars:

Series 00—General

Series 20—Aircraft
Series 60—Airmen
Series 70—Airspace
Series 90—ATC and General Operations
Series 120—Air Carrier and Commercial Operators
Series 150—Airports
Series 170—Air Navigation Facilities

AIM and Other Publications. Review the *AIM—Basic Flight Information and ATC Procedures,* Notices to AIRMEN (Class II), and *Airport/Facilities Directories* to bring yourself up to date on the latest requirements.

Summary of the Home Study and Review. Don't try to memorize a lot of information, but use your time to cover the required areas. It's better if you use a couple of weeks for review (a comparatively small amount each evening) than to try to cram at the last minute.

THE WRITTEN TEST

Because the written test questions included here are for airplanes only, you'll see gaps in the question numbers and several of the reference figures that don't apply to airplanes have been deleted.

CONTENTS

GENERAL INSTRUCTIONS

MAXIMUM TIME ALLOWED FOR TEST: 4 HOURS

Maximum time allowed for each test is based upon previous experience and educational statistics. This time is considered more than adequate for applicants with proper preparation and instruction.

MATERIALS

Materials to be used with this written test book when used for airman certification testing:

1. AC Form 8080-3, Airman Written Test Application, which includes the answer sheet.

2. Question selection sheet which identifies the questions to be answered.

3. Plastic overlay sheet which can be placed over performance charts for plotting purposes.

TEST INSTRUCTIONS

1. Read the instructions on page 1 of AC Form 8080-3, and complete page 4 of the form. Incomplete or erroneous personal information entered on this form delays the scoring process.

2. The questions in this written test book are numbered consecutively beginning with 5001. Refer to the question selection sheet to determine which questions to answer.

3. For each question number on the answer sheet, find the appropriate question in the written test book.

4. Mark your answer in the space provided for each question number on the answer sheet. Spaces 1, 2, or 3 left unmarked will be counted by the computer scanner as a miss.

5. The test questions are of the multiple-choice type. Until revised, answer sheets contain selections listed as 1, 2, 3, and 4 and should be interpreted as A, B, and C respectively. Selection 4 should never be used.

6. The supplementary material required to answer the questions will be found in appendix 2.

7. Read each question carefully and avoid hasty assumptions. Do not answer until you understand the question. Do not spend too much time on any one question. Answer all of the questions that you readily know and then reconsider those you find difficult. Be careful to make necessary conversions when working with temperatures, speeds, and distances.

8. If a regulation or operations procedure is changed after this written test book is printed, you will receive credit for the affected question.

THE MINIMUM PASSING GRADE IS 70.

WARNING

§61.37 Written tests: Cheating or other unauthorized conduct.

(a) Except as authorized by the Administrator, no person may—

(1) Copy, or intentionally remove, a written test under this part;

(2) Give to another, or receive from another, any part or copy of that test;

(3) Give help on that test to, or receive help on that test from, any person during the period that test is being given;

(4) Take any part of that test in behalf of another person;

(5) Use any material or aid during the period that test is being given; or

(6) Intentionally cause, assist, or participate in any act prohibited by this paragraph.

(b) No person whom the Administrator finds to have committed an act prohibited by paragraph (a) of this section is eligible for any airman or ground instructor certificate or rating, or to take any test therefor, under this chapter for a period of 1 year after the date of that act. In addition, the commission of that act is a basis for suspending or revoking any airman or ground instructor certificate or rating held by that person.

INTRODUCTION TO THE COMMERCIAL PILOT WRITTEN TEST BOOK

This written test book presents the FAA commercial pilot written tests. These testing materials relate to the applicant who seeks the commercial pilot certificate. Any question requiring the problem-solving process is considered to be academic in nature and is not predicted upon any commercial operator's operating specifications, procedures, or policies. Fundamentals of Instruction subject matter is included in this book for use by lighter-than-air applicants. Instrument approach charts and IFR en route charts are included in this book for use by airship applicants.

Question selection sheets are used in conjunction with this written test book to administer the proper written test to each applicant. Each test is constructed from the questions included in this written test book.

The written test book is scheduled for revision each 24 months. Associated question selection sheets will be revised periodically, as required.

Testing and Scoring

The written test may be taken at FAA testing centers, FAA written test examiner's facilities, or other designated places.

The applicant is issued a "clean copy" of this written test book, an appropriate question selection sheet indicating the specific questions to be answered, and AC Form 8080-3, Airman Written Test Application, which includes the answer sheet. The written test book contains all supplementary material required to answer the questions. Supplementary material is located in appendix 2.

Instructions for completing the test are contained on page vii of this written test book.

Upon completion of the test, the applicant must surrender the issued written test book, question selection sheet, answer sheet, and any papers used for computations or notations to the monitor before leaving the test room.

The answer sheet is sent to the Mike Monroney Aeronautical Center in Oklahoma City, Oklahoma, where it is scored by computer. The applicant is then issued AC Form 8080-2, Airman Written Test Report. This form will list the test score and subject matter knowledge codes referencing the subjects in which the applicant is deficient. Retain AC Form 8080-2 to be presented for the practical test, or for retesting in the event of written test failure.

The written test subject matter knowledge codes are then matched to the corresponding subject matter knowledge areas published in appendix 1 of this written test book. The applicant should review those subject areas until proficient.

The applicant should be aware that a subject matter code on AC Form 8080-2 appears only once even though more than one question may have been missed in that subject area. Therefore, the number of subject matter codes on AC Form 8080-2 may not represent the number of questions missed on the test.

When taking the test, the applicant should keep the following points in mind:

1. Answer each question in accordance with the latest regulations and procedures.

2. Read each question carefully before looking at the possible answers. You should clearly understand the problem before attempting to solve it.

3. After formulating an answer, determine which of the alternatives most nearly corresponds with that answer. The answer chosen should completely resolve the problem.

4. From the answers given, it may appear that there is more than one possible answer; however, there is only one answer that is correct and complete. The other answers are either incomplete or are derived from popular misconceptions.

5. If a certain question is difficult for you, it is best to proceed to other questions. After you answer the less difficult questions, return to those which gave you difficulty. Be sure to indicate on your question selection sheet the questions to which you wish to return.

6. When solving a calculator problem, select the answer nearest your solution. The problem has been checked with various types of calculators; therefore, if you have solved it correctly, your answer will be closer to the correct answer than to any of the other choices.

7. To aid in scoring, enter personal data in the appropriate spaces on the test answer sheet in a complete and legible manner. Be sure to enter the test number exactly as printed on the question selection sheet.

Retesting after Failure—[FAR Section 61.49]

An applicant for a written or practical test who fails that test may not apply for retesting until 30 days after the date the test was failed. However, in the case of a first failure, the applicant may apply for retesting before the 30 days have expired provided the applicant presents a logbook or training record endorsement from an authorized instructor who has given the applicant remedial instruction and finds the applicant competent to pass the test.

DEPARTMENT OF TRANSPORTATION   FEDERAL AVIATION ADMINISTRATION

AIRMAN WRITTEN TEST APPLICATION

DATE OF TEST	TITLE OF TEST	TEST NO
MONTH DAY YEAR	COMMERCIAL PILOT - AIRPLANE	254615
08 169 -		

PLEASE PRINT ONE LETTER IN EACH SPACE LEAVE A BLANK SPACE AFTER EACH NAME

NAME (LAST, FIRST, MIDDLE)	DATE OF BIRTH
DOE JOHN ROCHESTER	MONTH DAY YEAR
	06 29 48

MAILING ADDRESS   NO AND STREET, APT. #, P.O. BOX, OR RURAL ROUTE

1810 SOUTH MOTLOW AVENUE

CITY, TOWN OR POST OFFICE AND STATE	ZIP CODE	DESCRIPTION
HANDLEY TENNESSEE	37352	HEIGHT 72 WEIGHT 170 HAIR BR EYES BR

BIRTHPLACE (City and State or foreign country) DOVER, TN	CITIZENSHIP USA	SOCIAL SECURITY NO. 408402427	IF A SOCIAL SECURITY NUMBER HAS NEVER BEEN ISSUED CHECK THIS BLOCK ☐

Is this a retest? ☒ No ☐ Yes, date of last test   Have you taken or are you taking an FAA approved course for this test? ☒ No ☐ Yes (if yes give details below)

Graduation date   NAME OF SCHOOL   CITY AND STATE

CERTIFICATION   I CERTIFY that all of the statements made in this application are true, complete and correct to the best of my knowledge and belief and are made in good faith Signature *John R. Doe*

DO NOT WRITE IN THIS BLOCK	FOR USE OF FAA OFFICE ONLY	Applicant's identity established by
CARD A	CARD B	FIELD OFFICE DESIGNATION

TEST NUMBER	TAKE NO	SECTIONS 1 2 3 4 5 6 7	EXPIRATION MONTH DAY YEAR	CERTIFICATED SCHOOL NUMBER	MECH EXP DATE BY SECTION 1 2 3	SIGNATURE of FAA Representative

INSTRUCTIONS FOR MARKING THE ANSWER SHEET. Completely darken only one circle for each question. DO NOT USE (X) OR (✓). Use black lead pencil furnished by examiner. To make corrections, open answer sheet so erasure marks will not show on page 2. Then erase incorrect response on page 4. On page 2 (copy) mark the incorrect response with a slash ( ). Questions are arranged in VERTICAL sequence as indicated by the arrows

1 ①②③④ 23 ①②③④ 45 ①②③④ 67 ①②③④ 89 ①②③④ 111 ①②③④ 133 ①②③④
2 ①②③④ 24 ①②③④ 46 ①②③④ 68 ①②③④ 90 ①②③④ 112 ①②③④ 134 ①②③④
3 ①②③④ 25 ①②③④ 47 ①②③④ 69 ①②③④ 91 ①②③④ 113 ①②③④ 135 ①②③④
4 ①②③④ 26 ①②③④ 48 ①②③④ 70 ①②③④ 92 ①②③④ 114 ①②③④ 136 ①②③④
5 ①②③④ 27 ①②③④ 49 ①②③④ 71 ①②③④ 93 ①②③④ 115 ①②③④ 137 ①②③④
6 ①②③④ 28 ①②③④ 50 ①②③④ 72 ①②③④ 94 ①②③④ 116 ①②③④ 138 ①②③④
7 ①②③④ 29 ①②③④ 51 ①②③④ 73 ①②③④ 95 ①②③④ 117 ①②③④ 139 ①②③④
8 ①②③④ 30 ①②③④ 52 ①②③④ 74 ①②③④ 96 ①②③④ 118 ①②③④ 140 ①②③④
9 ①②③④ 31 ①②③④ 53 ①②③④ 75 ①②③④ 97 ①②③④ 119 ①②③④ 141 ①②③④
10 ①②③④ 32 ①②③④ 54 ①②③④ 76 ①②③④ 98 ①②③④ 120 ①②③④ 142 ①②③④
11 ①②③④ 33 ①②③④ 55 ①②③④ 77 ①②③④ 99 ①②③④ 121 ①②③④ 143 ①②③④
12 ①②③④ 34 ①②③④ 56 ①②③④ 78 ①②③④ 100 ①②③④ 122 ①②③④ 144 ①②③④
13 ①②③④ 35 ①②③④ 57 ①②③④ 79 ①②③④ 101 ①②③④ 123 ①②③④ 145 ①②③④
14 ①②③④ 36 ①②③④ 58 ①②③④ 80 ①②③④ 102 ①②③④ 124 ①②③④ 146 ①②③④
15 ①②③④ 37 ①②③④ 59 ①②③④ 81 ①②③④ 103 ①②③④ 125 ①②③④ 147 ①②③④
16 ①②③④ 38 ①②③④ 60 ①②③④ 82 ①②③④ 104 ①②③④ 126 ①②③④ 148 ①②③④
17 ①②③④ 39 ①②③④ 61 ①②③④ 83 ①②③④ 105 ①②③④ 127 ①②③④ 149 ①②③④
18 ①②③④ 40 ①②③④ 62 ①②③④ 84 ①②③④ 106 ①②③④ 128 ①②③④ 150 ①②③④
19 ①②③④ 41 ①②③④ 63 ①②③④ 85 ①②③④ 107 ①②③④ 129 ①②③④
20 ①②③④ 42 ①②③④ 64 ①②③④ 86 ①②③④ 108 ①②③④ 130 ①②③④
21 ①②③④ 43 ①②③④ 65 ①②③④ 87 ①②③④ 109 ①②③④ **THIS IS A SAMPLE FORMAT OF A COMMERCIAL PILOT WRITTEN TEST ANSWER SHEET WITH ALL QUESTIONS CREATED BY THE AUTHOR.**
22 ①②③④ 44 ①②③④ 66 ①②③④ 88 ①②③④ 110 ①②③④

Fig. 20-1. Airman Written Test Application.

QUESTIONS

5001. Notification to the NTSB is required when there has been substantial damage

A— which requires repairs to landing gear.
B— to an engine caused by engine failure in flight.
C— which adversely affects structural strength or flight characteristics.

5002. NTSB Part 830 requires an immediate notification as a result of which incident?

A— Engine failure for any reason during flight.
B— Damage to the landing gear as a result of a hard landing.
C— Any required flight crewmember being unable to perform flight duties because of illness.

5003. Which incident would require that the nearest NTSB field office be notified immediately?

A— In-flight fire.
B— Ground fire resulting in fire equipment dispatch.
C— Fire of the primary aircraft while hangered which results in damage to other property of more than $50,000.

5004. While taxiing for takeoff, a small fire burned the insulation from a transceiver wire. What action would be required to comply with NTSB Part 830?

A— No notification or report is required.
B— A report must be filed with the avionics inspector at the nearest FAA field office within 48 hours.
C— An immediate notification must be filed by the operator of the aircraft with the nearest NTSB field office.

5005. During flight a fire which was extinguished burned the insulation from a transceiver wire. What action is required by regulations?

A— No notification or report is required.
B— Report must be filed with the avionics inspector at the nearest FAA field office within 48 hours.
C— An immediate notification by the operator of the aircraft to the nearest NTSB field office.

5006. When should notification of an aircraft accident be made to the NTSB if there was substantial damage and no injuries?

A— Immediately.
B— Within 10 days.
C— Within 30 days.

5007. The operator of an aircraft that has been involved in an incident is required to submit a report to the nearest field office of the NTSB

A— within 7 days.
B— within 10 days.
C— only if requested to do so.

5008. Within how many days of an accident is an accident report required to be filed with the nearest NTSB field office?

A— 2 days.
B— 7 days.
C— 10 days.

5009. What designated airspace associated with an airport becomes inactive when the control tower at that airport is not in operation?

A— Class D, which then becomes Class C.
B— Class D, which then becomes Class E.
C— Class B.

5010. Regulations which refer to commercial operators relate to that person who

A— is the owner of a small scheduled airline.
B— for compensation or hire, engages in the carriage by aircraft in air commerce of persons or property, as an air carrier.
C— for compensation or hire, engages in the carriage by aircraft in air commerce of persons or property, other than as an air carrier.

5011. Regulations which refer to operate relate to that person who

A— acts as pilot in command of the aircraft.
B— is the sole manipulator of the aircraft controls.
C— causes the aircraft to be used or authorizes its use.

5012. Regulations which refer to the operational control of a flight are in relation to

A— the specific duties of any required crewmember.
B— acting as the sole manipulator of the aircraft controls.
C— exercising authority over initiating, conducting, or terminating a flight.

5013. Which is the correct symbol for the stalling speed or the minimum steady flight speed in a specified configuration?

A— V_S.
B— V_{S1}.
C— V_{SO}.

5014. Which is the correct symbol for the stalling speed or the minimum steady flight speed at which the airplane is controllable?

A— V_S.
B— V_{S1}.
C— V_{SO}.

5015. FAR Part 1 defines V_F as

A— design flap speed.
B— flap operating speed.
C— maximum flap extended speed.

5016. FAR Part 1 defines V_{LE} as

A— maximum landing gear extended speed.
B— maximum landing gear operating speed.
C— maximum leading edge flaps extended speed.

5017. If the operational category of an airplane is listed as utility, it would mean that this airplane could be operated in which of the following maneuvers?

A— Limited acrobatics, excluding spins.
B— Limited acrobatics, including spins.
C— Any maneuver except acrobatics or spins.

5018. Commercial pilots are required to have a current and appropriate pilot certificate in their personal possession when

A— piloting for hire only.
B— carrying passengers only.
C— acting as pilot in command.

5019. Which of the following is considered aircraft class ratings?

A— Transport, normal, utility, and acrobatic.
B— Airplane, rotorcraft, glider, and lighter-than-air.
C— Single-engine land, multiengine land, single-engine sea, and multiengine sea.

5020. Does a commercial pilot certificate have a specific expiration date?

A— No, it is issued without an expiration date.
B— Yes, it expires at the end of the 24th month after the month in which it was issued.
C— No, but commercial privileges expire if a flight review is not satisfactorily completed each 12 months.

5021. A second-class medical certificate issued to a commercial pilot on April 10, this year, permits the pilot to exercise which of the following privileges?

A— Commercial pilot privileges through April 30, next year.
B— Commercial pilot privileges through April 10, 2 years later.
C— Private pilot privileges through, but not after, March 31, next year.

5022. When is the pilot in command required to hold a category and class rating appropriate to the aircraft being flown?

A— All solo flights.
B— Flight tests given by the FAA.
C— Flights for compensation or hire.

5023. Unless otherwise authorized, the pilot in command is required to hold a type rating when operating any

A— aircraft that is certificated for more than one pilot.
B— aircraft of more than 12,500 pounds maximum certificated takeoff weight.
C— multiengine aircraft having a gross weight of more than 6,000 pounds.

5024. To act as pilot in command of an airplane that is equipped with a retractable landing gear, if no pilot-in-command time in such an airplane was logged prior to November 1, 1973, a person is required to

A— hold a multiengine airplane class rating.
B— make at least six takeoffs and landings in such an airplane within the preceding 6 months.
C— receive flight instruction in such an airplane and obtain a logbook endorsement of competency.

5025. What flight time may a pilot log as second in command?

A— All flight time while acting as second in command in aircraft requiring more than one pilot.
B— Only that flight time during which the second in command is the sole manipulator of the controls.
C— All flight time while acting as second in command regardless of aircraft crew requirements.

5026. What flight time must be shown, in a reliable record, by a pilot exercising the privileges of a commercial certificate?

A— Flight time showing aeronautical training and experience to meet requirements for a certificate or rating.
B— All flight time flown for compensation or hire.
C— Only flight time for compensation or hire with passengers aboard which is necessary to meet the recent flight experience requirements.

5027. If a pilot does not meet the recency of experience requirements for night flight and official sunset is 1800 CST, the latest time passengers should be carried is

A— 1759 CST.
B— 1829 CST.
C— 1859 CST.

5028. Prior to carrying passengers at night, the pilot in command must have accomplished the required takeoffs and landings in

A— any category aircraft.
B— the same category and class of aircraft to be used.
C— the same category, class, and type of aircraft to be used.

* * *

5031. To act as pilot in command of an aircraft under FAR Part 91, a commercial pilot must have satisfactorily accomplished a flight review or completed a proficiency check within the preceding

A— 6 months.
B— 12 months.
C— 24 months.

5032. Pilots who change their permanent mailing address and fail to notify the FAA Airmen Certification Branch of this change, are entitled to exercise the privileges of their pilot certificate for a period of

A— 30 days.
B— 60 days.
C— 90 days.

5033. To act as pilot in command of an airplane towing a glider, a certificated airplane pilot is required to have

A— a logbook record of having made at least 3 flights as sole manipulator of the controls of a glider being towed by an airplane.
B— a logbook endorsement for receipt of ground and flight instruction in gliders and familiarity with techniques and procedures for glider towing.
C— at least a private pilot certificate with a glider rating and made and logged at least 3 flights as pilot or observer in a glider being towed by an airplane.

5034. To act as pilot in command of an airplane towing a glider, the tow pilot is required to have a pilot certificate and

A— a glider rating, and pass a written test on the techniques and procedures essential for safe towing of gliders.
B— a logbook record of having made at least 3 flights in a glider, and be familiar with the techniques and procedures essential for safe towing of gliders.
C— have received and logged ground and flight instruction in gliders, and be familiar with the techniques and procedures essential for safe towing of gliders.

* * *

5039. What limitation is imposed on a newly certificated commercial airplane pilot if that person does not hold an instrument pilot rating? The carrying of passengers

A— or property for hire on cross-country flights at night is limited to a radius of 50 NM.
B— for hire on cross-country flights is limited to 50 NM for night flights, but not limited for day flights.
C— for hire on cross-country flights is limited to 50 NM and the carrying of passengers for hire at night is prohibited.

* * *

5041. What is the maximum amount of flight instruction an authorized instructor may give in any 24 consecutive hours?

A— 4 hours.
B— 6 hours.
C— 8 hours.

* * *

5043. Excluding Hawaii, the vertical limits of the Federal Low Altitude airways extend from

A— 700 feet AGL up to, but not including, 14,500 feet MSL.
B— 1,200 feet AGL up to, but not including, 18,000 feet MSL.
C— 1,200 feet AGL up to, but not including, 14,500 feet MSL.

5044. One of the major differences between Class D airspace and Class E airspace is that Class D airspace

A— is located at tower-controlled airports and Class E airspace is at uncontrolled airports.
B— always begins at 700 feet AGL while Class E always begins at 1,200 feet above the surface.
C— begins at the surface, while Class E always begins at an altitude of 700 feet or 1,200 feet above the surface.

5045. The Continental Control Area

A— does not exist anymore.
B— extends upward from 10,000 feet MSL.
C— extends upward from 14,500 feet MSL.

5046. Within the contiguous U.S., the vertical limit of Class D airspace normally extends from the surface upward to

A— infinity.
B— but not including the base of Class A airspace.
C— 2,500 feet AGL or indicated within a square depicted within that airspace on aeronautical charts.

5047. Which is true regarding Class E airspace?

A— The basic VFR minimums are greater than those associated Class D airspace.
B— Class E airspace may start at the surface, but usually begins at an altitude of 700 feet or 1,200 feet above the surface.
C— Class E airspace begins at the surface and extend upward to Flight Level 600.

* * *

5049. The required preflight action relative to alternatives available, if the planned flight cannot be completed, is applicable to

A— IFR flights only.
B— any flight not in the vicinity of an airport.
C— any flight conducted for hire or compensation.

5050. Before beginning any flight under IFR, the pilot in command must become familiar with all available information concerning that flight. In addition, the pilot must

A— be familiar with all instrument approaches at the destination airport.
B— list an alternate airport on the flight plan and confirm adequate takeoff and landing performance at the destination airport.
C— be familiar with the runway lengths at airports of intended use, and the alternatives available if the flight cannot be completed.

5051. Required flight crewmembers' seatbelts must be fastened

A— only during takeoff and landing.
B— while the crewmembers are at their stations.
C— only during takeoff and landing when passengers are aboard the aircraft.

5052. The use of seatbelts, with certain exceptions, during takeoffs and landings is

A— required for all occupants.
B— required during commercial operations only.
C— a good operating practice, but not required by regulations.

* * *

5055. Which is required to operate an aircraft towing an advertising banner?

A— Approval from ATC to operate in Class E airspace.
B— A certificate of waiver issued by the Administrator.
C— A safety link at each end of the towline which has a breaking strength not less than 80 percent of the aircraft's gross weight.

5056. Portable electronic devices which may cause interference with the navigation or communication system may not be operated on aircraft being flown

A— along Federal airways.
B— within the U.S.
C— in commercial operations.

* * *

5059. If weather conditions are such that it is required to designate an alternate airport on your IFR flight plan, you should plan to carry enough fuel to arrive at the first airport of intended landing, fly from that airport to the alternate airport, and fly thereafter for

A— 30 minutes at slow cruising speed.
B— 45 minutes at normal cruising speed.
C— 1 hour at normal cruising speed.

5060. A coded transponder equipped with altitude reporting equipment is required for

A— Class A, Class B, and Class C airspace areas.
B— all airspace of the 48 contiguous U.S. and the District of Columbia at and above 10,000 feet MSL (including airspace at and below 2,500 feet above the surface).
C— both answer A and B.

5061. In the contiguous U.S., excluding the airspace at and below 2,500 feet AGL, an operable coded transponder equipped with Mode C capability is required in all airspace above

A— 10,000 feet MSL.
B— 12,500 feet MSL.
C— 14,500 feet MSL.

5062. What is the maximum tolerance (+ or -) allowed for an operational VOR equipment check when using a VOT?

A— 4°.
B— 6°.
C— 8°.

5063. In accordance with FAR Part 91, supplemental oxygen must be used by the required minimum flightcrew for that time exceeding 30 minutes while at cabin pressure altitudes of

A— 10,500 feet MSL up to and including 12,500 feet MSL.
B— 12,000 feet MSL up to and including 18,000 feet MSL.
C— 12,500 feet MSL up to and including 14,000 feet MSL.

5064. What are the oxygen requirements when operating above 15,000 feet MSL?

A— Oxygen must be available for the flightcrew.
B— Oxygen is not required at any altitude in a free balloon.
C— The flightcrew must use and passengers must be provided oxygen.

5065. Which is required equipment for powered aircraft during VFR night flights?

A— Anticollision light system.
B— Gyroscopic direction indicator.
C— Gyroscopic bank-and-pitch indicator.

5066. Which is required equipment for powered aircraft during VFR night flights?

A— Flashlight with red lens if the flight is for hire.
B— A landing light if the flight is for hire.
C— Sensitive altimeter adjustable for barometric pressure.

5067. Approved flotation gear, readily available to each occupant, is required on each aircraft if it is being flown for hire over water,

A— in amphibious aircraft beyond 50 NM from shore.
B— beyond power-off gliding distance from shore.
C— regardless of the distance flown from shore.

* * *

5069. The carriage of passengers for hire by a commercial pilot is

A— not authorized in utility category aircraft.
B— not authorized in limited category aircraft.
C— authorized in restricted category aircraft.

5070. The maximum cumulative time that an emergency locator transmitter may be operated before the rechargeable battery must be recharged is

A— 30 minutes.
B— 45 minutes.
C— 60 minutes.

5071. No person may operate a large civil U.S. aircraft which is subject to a lease, unless the lessee has mailed a copy of the lease to the FAA Mike Monroney Aeronautical Center within how many hours of its execution?

A— 24.
B— 48.
C— 72.

* * *

5073. Which is true with respect to formation flights? Formation flights are

A— authorized when carrying passengers for hire with prior arrangement with the pilot in command of each aircraft in the formation.
B— not authorized when visibilities are less than 3 SM.
C— not authorized when carrying passengers for hire.

5074. While in flight a helicopter and an airplane are converging at a 90° angle, and the helicopter is located to the right of the airplane. Which aircraft has the right-of-way, and why?

A— The helicopter, because it is to the right of the airplane.
B— The helicopter, because helicopters have the right-of-way over airplanes.
C— The airplane, because airplanes have the right-of-way over helicopters.

5075. Two aircraft of the same category are approaching an airport for the purpose of landing. The right-of-way belongs to the aircraft

A— at the higher altitude.
B— at the lower altitude, but the pilot shall not take advantage of this rule to cut in front of or to overtake the other aircraft.
C— that is more maneuverable, and that aircraft may, with caution, move in front of or overtake the other aircraft.

5076. Airplane A is overtaking airplane B. Which airplane has the right-of-way?

A— Airplane A; the pilot should alter course to the right to pass.
B— Airplane B; the pilot should expect to be passed on the right.
C— Airplane B; the pilot should expect to be passed on the left.

5077. What is the maximum indicated airspeed allowed in the airspace underlying Class B airspace?

A— 156 knots.
B— 200 knots.
C— 230 knots.

5078. Unless otherwise authorized or required by ATC, the maximum indicated airspeed permitted when at or below 2,500 feet AGL within 4 NM of the primary airport of a Class B, C, or D airspace is

A— 180 knots.
B— 200 knots.
C— 230 knots.

5079. What is the minimum altitude and flight visibility required for acrobatic flight?

A— 1,500 feet AGL and 3 miles.
B— 2,000 feet MSL and 2 miles.
C— 3,000 feet AGL and 1 mile.

5080. If not equipped with required position lights, an aircraft must terminate flight

A— at sunset.
B— 30 minutes after sunset.
C— 1 hour after sunset.

* * *

5082. Which is true regarding VFR operations in Class B airspace?

A— Area navigation equipment is required.
B— Flight under VFR is not authorized unless the pilot in command is instrument rated.
C— Solo student pilot operations are allowed if certain conditions are satisfied.

5083. The minimum flight visibility for VFR flight increases to 5 miles beginning at an altitude of

A— 14,500 feet MSL.
B— 10,000 feet MSL if above 1,200 feet AGL.
C— 10,000 feet MSL regardless of height above ground.

5084. When flying a glider above 10,000 feet MSL and more than 1,200 feet AGL, what minimum flight visibility is required?

A— 3 NM.
B— 5 SM.
C— 7 SM.

5085. What is the minimum flight visibility and proximity to cloud requirements for VFR flight, at 6,500 feet MSL, in Class C, D, and E airspace?

A— 1 mile visibility; clear of clouds.
B— 3 miles visibility; 1,000 feet above and 500 feet below.
C— 5 miles visibility; 1,000 feet above and 1,000 feet below.

5086. Which minimum flight visibility and distance from clouds is required for a day VFR helicopter flight in Class G airspace at 3,500 feet MSL over terrain with an elevation of 1,900 feet MSL?

A— Visibility-3 miles; distance from clouds-1,000 feet below, 1,000 feet above, and 1 mile horizontally.
B— Visibility-3 miles; distance from clouds-500 feet below, 1,000 feet above, and 2,000 feet horizontally.
C— Visibility-1 mile; distance from clouds-500 feet below, 1,000 feet above, and 2,000 feet horizontally.

5087. Basic VFR weather minimums require at least what visibility for operating a helicopter within Class D airspace?

A— 1 mile.
B— 2 miles.
C— 3 miles.

5088. When operating an airplane for the purpose of landing or takeoff within Class D under special VFR, what minimum distance from clouds and what visibility are required?

A— Remain clear of clouds, and the ground visibility must be at least 1 SM.
B— 500 feet beneath clouds, and the ground visibility must be at least 1 SM.
C— Remain clear of clouds, and the flight visibility must be at least 1 SM.

5089. At some airports located in Class D airspace where ground visibility is not reported, takeoffs and landings under special VFR are

A— not authorized.
B— authorized by ATC if the flight visibility is at least 1 SM.
C— authorized only if the ground visibility is observed to be at least 3 SM.

5090. To operate an airplane under SPECIAL VFR (SVFR) within Class D airspace at night, which is required?

A— The pilot must hold an instrument pilot rating, but the airplane need not be equipped for instrument flight, as long as the weather will remain at or above SVFR minimums.
B— The Class D airspace must be specifically designated as a night SVFR area.
C— The pilot must hold an instrument pilot rating and the airplane must be equipped for instrument flight.

5091. VFR cruising altitudes are required to be maintained when flying

A— at 3,000 feet or more AGL; based on true course.
B— more than 3,000 feet AGL; based on magnetic course.
C— at 3,000 feet or more above MSL; based on magnetic heading.

5092. Except when necessary for takeoff or landing or unless otherwise authorized by the Administrator, the minimum altitude for IFR flight is

A— 3,000 feet over all terrain.
B— 3,000 feet over designated mountainous terrain; 2,000 feet over terrain elsewhere.
C— 2,000 feet above the highest obstacle over designated mountainous terrain; 1,000 feet above the highest obstacle over terrain elsewhere.

5093. Who is primarily responsible for maintaining an aircraft in an airworthy condition?

A— The lead mechanic responsible for that aircraft.
B— Pilot in command.
C— Operator or owner of the aircraft.

5094. Assuring compliance with an Airworthiness Directive is the responsibility of the

A— pilot in command and the FAA certificated mechanic assigned to that aircraft.
B— pilot in command of that aircraft.
C— owner or operator of that aircraft.

5095. After an annual inspection has been completed and the aircraft has been returned to service, an appropriate notation should be made

A— on the airworthiness certificate.
B— in the aircraft maintenance records.
C— in the FAA-approved flight manual.

5096. The validity of the airworthiness certificate is maintained by

A— performance of an annual inspection.
B— performance of an annual inspection and a 100-hour inspection prior to their expiration date.
C— an appropriate return to service statement in the aircraft maintenance records upon the completion of required inspections and maintenance.

5097. If an aircraft's operation in flight was substantially affected by an alteration or repair, the aircraft documents must show that it was test flown and approved for return to service by an appropriately-rated pilot prior to being operated

A— by any private pilot.
B— with passengers aboard.
C— for compensation or hire.

5098. Which is correct concerning preventive maintenance, when accomplished by a pilot?

A— A record of preventive maintenance is not required.
B— A record of preventive maintenance must be entered in the maintenance records.
C— Records of preventive maintenance must be entered in the FAA-approved flight manual.

5099. An aircraft carrying passengers for hire has been on a schedule of inspection every 100 hours of time in service. Under which condition, if any, may that aircraft be operated beyond 100 hours without a new inspection?

A— The aircraft may be flown for any flight as long as the time in service has not exceeded 110 hours.
B— The aircraft may be dispatched for a flight of any duration as long as 100 hours has not been exceeded at the time it departs.
C— The 100-hour limitation may be exceeded by not more than 10 hours if necessary to reach a place at which the inspection can be done.

5100. Which is true concerning required maintenance inspections?

A— A 100-hour inspection may be substituted for an annual inspection.
B— An annual inspection may be substituted for a 100-hour inspection.
C— An annual inspection is required even if a progressive inspection system has been approved.

5101. An ATC transponder is not to be used unless it has been tested, inspected, and found to comply with regulations within the preceding

A— 30 days.
B— 12 calendar months.
C— 24 calendar months.

5102. Aircraft maintenance records must include the current status of the

A— applicable airworthiness certificate.
B— life-limited parts of only the engine and airframe.
C— life-limited parts of each airframe, engine, propeller, rotor, and appliance.

5103. Which is true relating to Airworthiness Directives (AD's)?

A— AD's are advisory in nature and are, generally, not addressed immediately.
B— Noncompliance with AD's renders an aircraft unairworthy.
C— Compliance with AD's is the responsibility of maintenance personnel.

5104. A new maintenance record being used for an aircraft engine rebuilt by the manufacturer must include previous

A— operating hours of the engine.
B— annual inspections performed on the engine.
C— changes as required by Airworthiness Directives.

5105. If an ATC transponder installed in an aircraft has not been tested, inspected, and found to comply with regulations within a specified period, what is the limitation on its use?

A— Its use is not permitted.
B— It may be used when in Class G airspace.
C— It may be used for VFR flight only.

5106. Which of these operations could fall under the jurisdiction of FAR Part 125?

A— Operations in U.S. registered civil airplanes having a seating capacity of more than 10 but less than 20 passenger seats.
B— Scheduled commercial operations (not an air carrier) using an airplane having a seating capacity of 20 or more passenger seats.
C— Nonscheduled commercial operations (not an air carrier) using an airplane having a maximum payload of 6,000 pounds or more.

5107. FAR Part 125 could apply to which of these operations?

A— Nonscheduled commercial operations (not an air carrier) using an airplane having a maximum payload of less than 6,000 pounds.
B— Nonscheduled commercial operations (not an air carrier) using an airplane having a seating capacity of 20 or more passenger seats.
C— U.S. registered civil airplanes operating outside the U.S. by persons who are not U.S. citizens.

5108. To obtain relief from any specified section of FAR Part 125, an operator holding an FAR Part 125 certificate should request

A— an "authorization waiver" from the FAA district office holding that certificate.
B— an appropriate waiver from the Administrator for Aviation Standards.
C— a "letter of deviation authority" from the nearest Flight Standards District Office.

5109. An FAR Part 125 certificate holder must display a true copy of the

A— FAR Part 125 "letter of deviation authority."
B— address of its principal operations base in each of its aircraft.
C— FAR Part 125 certificate in each of its aircraft.

5110. No person is eligible for a certificate to operate under FAR Part 125 if that person

A— conducts pilot training under FAR Part 61.
B— conducts ferry flights under FAR Part 135.
C— "holds out" to the public to furnish transportation.

5111. No person is eligible to operate under FAR Part 125 if that person already holds an appropriate operating certificate under

A— FAR Part 103.
B— FAR Part 121 or FAR Part 135.
C— FAR Part 141.

5112. Each person operating an airplane inside the U.S. under FAR Part 125 shall also operate under

A— FAR Part 91.
B— FAR Part 121.
C— FAR Part 135.

5113. No person may serve as pilot in command of an airplane under FAR Part 125 operations unless that person

A— holds at least an airline transport pilot certificate and a type rating for the airplane to be flown.
B— holds at least a commercial pilot certificate, an appropriate category, class, and type rating, and an instrument rating.
C— has logged at least 700 hours of flight time as pilot, including 100 hours of night flight time.

5114. To act as second in command under an FAR Part 125 operation, a person is required to hold at least a

A— U.S. commercial pilot or commercial pilot certificate issued on the basis of a valid foreign senior commercial pilot license.
B— commercial pilot certificate with appropriate category, class, and instrument rating.
C— commercial pilot certificate with appropriate category and class.

5115. Select the pilot action listed below that meets the recent experience requirement for a person to serve as pilot in command of an airplane for an FAR Part 125 operation.

A— Passed a written test within the preceding 6 calendar months, covering FAR Parts 61, 91, and 135, and the operations specifications and manual of the certificate holder.
B— Completed 3 takeoffs and 3 landings within the preceding 90 days in an approved visual simulator.
C— Passed a written EQUIPMENT test, in at least one of the aircraft operated, within the preceding 6 calendar months.

5116. FAR Part 135 applies to which operation?

A— Aerial work including crop dusting and spraying.
B— Carrying weekend skiers for hire to another state.
C— Student instruction for hire at an approved school.

5117. When operating an airplane with a maximum payload capacity of 7,500 pounds or less as a scheduled commercial operator (not an air carrier) in common carriage solely between points within a state, the operation is governed by the provisions of

A— FAR Part 121.
B— FAR Part 133.
C— FAR Part 135.

*   *   *

5120. FAR Part 135 applies to which operation?

A— Nonstop sightseeing flights that begin and end at the same airport, and are conducted within a 25 SM radius of that airport.
B— Aerial operations for compensation, such as aerial photography, pipeline patrol, rescue, and crop dusting.
C— Commercial operations (not an air carrier) in an aircraft with less than 20 passenger seats and a maximum payload capacity of less than 6,000 pounds.

5121. Under FAR Part 135 operations, who is responsible for keeping copies of the ATCO manual up to date with approved changes or additions?

A— Supervising FAA district office and the certificate holder.
B— Each district office employee responsible for that manual.
C— Each employee of the certificate holder who is furnished a manual.

5122. For FAR Part 135 operations, which document(s) contain(s) procedures that explain how the pilot in command knows that the required return-to-service conditions have been met?

A— Daily flight log and operation specifications.
B— Certificate holder's manual.
C— Mechanical deviation summary guide.

5123. For FAR Part 135 operations, which document specifically authorizes a person to operate an aircraft in a particular geographic area?

A— Letter of authorization.
B— Operations specifications.
C— Air taxi operating certificate.

5124. An aircraft may be operated in a foreign country by an FAR Part 135 operator if authorized to do so by

A— that country.
B— the supervising district office.
C— the FAA International Field Office in that country.

5125. In accordance with FAR Part 135, what period of time is the minimum flightcrew required to use supplemental oxygen while cruising at 13,500 feet MSL for 3 hours 45 minutes in an unpressurized aircraft?

A— 1 hour 30 minutes.
B— 2 hours 30 minutes.
C— 3 hours 45 minutes.

5126. Which person may be carried aboard an aircraft without complying with the passenger-carrying requirements of FAR Part 135?

A— A crewmember or employee of another certificate holder.
B— A member of the U.S. diplomatic corps on an official courier mission.
C— An individual who is necessary for the safe handling of animals on the aircraft.

5127. For FAR Part 135 operations, what restrictions must be observed regarding the carrying of cargo in the passenger compartment? Cargo must be

A— carried directly above the seated occupants in overhead bins.
B— properly secured by a seatbelt or other approved tiedown.
C— separated from seated passengers by a partition capable of withstanding specified stresses.

5128. Under FAR Part 135, which is a requirement governing the carriage of carry-on baggage?

A— Carry-on baggage must be stowed ahead of all seated occupants.
B— All carry-on baggage must be restrained so that its movement is prevented during turbulence.
C— Any piece of carry-on baggage, regardless of size, must be properly secured by a seatbelt or tiedown device.

5129. In accordance with FAR Part 135, what period of time is the minimum flightcrew required to use supplemental oxygen while cruising at 12,500 feet MSL for 1 hour 50 minutes in an unpressurized aircraft?

A— 55 minutes.
B— 1 hour 20 minutes.
C— 1 hour 50 minutes.

5130. In accordance with FAR Part 135, what use of supplemental oxygen is required, if any, of a pilot when cruising at 12,500 feet MSL in an unpressurized aircraft? Supplemental oxygen is

A— not required at that altitude.
B— to be used during the entire flight while at that altitude.
C— required for that portion of the flight that is more than 60 minutes in duration while at that altitude.

5131. For FAR Part 135 operations, the airplane flight manual specifies a maximum altitude loss of 75 feet for malfunction of the autopilot under cruise conditions. What is the lowest altitude above the terrain the autopilot may be used during en route operations?

A— 500 feet.
B— 1,000 feet.
C— 1,500 feet.

5132. A commuter air carrier certificate holder plans to assign a pilot as pilot in command of an airplane to be used in passenger-carrying operations. Which experience requirement must that pilot meet if the airplane is to be flown with an autopilot and no second in command?

A— 150 hours as pilot in command in category and type.
B— 100 hours in the category, class, and type.
C— 100 hours as pilot in command in the make and model.

5133. For FAR Part 135 operations, in which airplanes is a flight attendant crewmember required?

A— Any airplane being operated in commuter air carrier service with a gross weight in excess of 12,500 pounds, regardless of the seating capacity.
B— All turbine-engine-powered airplanes having a total seating capacity of 19 or more.
C— Any airplane having a passenger seating configuration, excluding any pilot seat, of 20 or more.

5134. The oral preflight briefing required on FAR Part 135 passenger-carrying airplanes shall be

A— substituted by printed cards carried in locations convenient for use by each passenger in aircraft with 9 seats or less.
B— conducted by the pilot in command or a crewmember and supplemented by printed cards for the use of each passenger.
C— presented in person by the pilot in command while another flight crewmember demonstrates the operation of emergency equipment.

5135. In which aircraft, operating under FAR Part 135, is a third gyroscopic pitch-and-bank indicator required?

A— All turbojet airplanes.
B— All transport category airplanes.
C— All airplanes where a pilot in command and second in command is required.

5136. For which airplanes, under FAR Part 135 operations, must each flight crewmember station have a shoulder harness installed?

A— All airplanes operated in commuter air carrier service.
B— Any airplane being operated under FAR Part 135, regardless of weight and seating configuration.
C— All airplanes having a passenger seating configuration, excluding any pilot seat, of 10 seats or more.

*   *   *

5138. To operate an airplane over water with passengers aboard, except for takeoff and landing, what is the minimum altitude requirement (FAR Part 135)?

A— There is no minimum altitude if flotation devices are aboard.
B— There is no minimum altitude requirement under FAR Part 135.
C— An altitude that allows land to be reached in the event of an engine failure.

5139. A pilot is en route over designated mountainous terrain at night in an airplane under VFR. Under FAR Part 135, what is the minimum altitude requirement above the highest obstacle within 5 miles of the course to be flown?

A— 1,000 feet.
B— 1,500 feet.
C— 2,000 feet.

5140. A pilot is en route at night in an airplane under VFR. Under FAR Part 135, what is the minimum altitude requirement above the highest obstacle within 5 miles of the course to be flown?

A— 500 feet.
B— 1,000 feet.
C— 1,500 feet.

*   *   *

5142. Except for takeoffs and landings, what is the minimum altitude requirement to operate an airplane under FAR Part 135 during day VFR?

A— 1,500 feet AGL.
B— 1,000 feet AGL.
C— 500 feet AGL.

5143. Except for takeoffs and landings, what is the minimum horizontal distance from any obstacle requirement for an airplane under FAR Part 135 during day VFR?

A— 1,500 feet.
B— 1,000 feet.
C— 500 feet.

*   *   *

5146. Under FAR Part 135, what is the minimum visibility requirement for airplane VFR operations in Class G airspace when the ceiling is less than 1,000 feet?

A— Day - 1/2 mile; night - 1 mile.
B— Day - 2 miles; night - 3 miles.
C— Day - 2 miles; night - 2 miles.

*   *   *

5148. To operate an airplane VFR over-the-top while carrying passengers, what operating limitations, in part, are required by FAR Part 135 operations?

A— Two appropriately rated pilots must be aboard; autopilot not authorized.
B— Weather conditions that allow descent under VFR in the event of an engine failure.
C— Radar approach facilities must be in operation at the destination point 1 hour before to 1 hour after ETA.

*   *   *

5150. To act as pilot in command during IFR operations under FAR Part 135, how many hours of previous instrument time in actual flight is required? At least

A— 50 hours.
B— 75 hours.
C— 100 hours.

5151. The ratio between the total airload imposed on the wing and the gross weight of an aircraft in flight is known as

A— load factor and directly affects stall speed.
B— aspect load and directly affects stall speed.
C— load factor and has no relation with stall speed.

5152. Load factor is the lift generated by the wings of an aircraft at any given time

A— divided by the total weight of the aircraft.
B— multiplied by the total weight of the aircraft.
C— divided by the basic empty weight of the aircraft.

5153. For a given angle of bank, in any airplane, the load factor imposed in a coordinated constant-altitude turn

A— is constant and the stall speed increases.
B— varies with the rate of turn.
C— is constant and the stall speed decreases.

5154. Airplane wing loading during a level coordinated turn in smooth air depends upon the

A— rate of turn.
B— angle of bank.
C— true airspeed.

5155. In a rapid recovery from a dive, the effects of load factor would cause the stall speed to

A— increase.
B— decrease.
C— not vary.

5156. If an aircraft with a gross weight of 2,000 pounds was subjected to a 60° constant-altitude bank, the total load would be

A— 3,000 pounds.
B— 4,000 pounds.
C— 12,000 pounds.

5157. While maintaining a constant angle of bank and altitude in a coordinated turn, an increase in airspeed will

A— decrease the rate of turn resulting in a decreased load factor.
B— decrease the rate of turn resulting in no change in load factor.
C— increase the rate of turn resulting in no change in load factor.

5158. Lift on a wing is most properly defined as the

A— force acting perpendicular to the relative wind.
B— differential pressure acting perpendicular to the chord of the wing.
C— reduced pressure resulting from a laminar flow over the upper camber of an airfoil, which acts perpendicular to the mean camber.

5159. While holding the angle of bank constant, if the rate of turn is varied the load factor would

A— remain constant regardless of air density and the resultant lift vector.
B— vary depending upon speed and air density provided the resultant lift vector varies proportionately.
C— vary depending upon the resultant lift vector.

5160. The need to slow an aircraft below V_A is brought about by the following weather phenomenon:

A— High density altitude which increases the indicated stall speed.
B— Turbulence which causes an increase in stall speed.
C— Turbulence which causes a decrease in stall speed.

5161. In theory, if the airspeed of an airplane is doubled while in level flight, parasite drag will become

A— twice as great.
B— half as great.
C— four times greater.

5162. As airspeed decreases in level flight below that speed for maximum lift/drag ratio, total drag of an airplane

A— decreases because of lower parasite drag.
B— increases because of increased induced drag.
C— increases because of increased parasite drag.

5163. If the airspeed is increased from 90 knots to 135 knots during a level 60° banked turn, the load factor will

A— increase as well as the stall speed.
B— decrease and the stall speed will increase.
C— remain the same but the radius of turn will increase.

5164. Baggage weighing 90 pounds is placed in a normal category airplane's baggage compartment which is placarded at 100 pounds. If this airplane is subjected to a positive load factor of 3.5 G's, the total load of the baggage would be

A— 315 pounds and would be excessive.
B— 315 pounds and would not be excessive.
C— 350 pounds and would not be excessive.

5165. (Refer to figure 1.) At the airspeed represented by point A, in steady flight, the airplane will

A— have its maximum L/D ratio.
B— have its minimum L/D ratio.
C— be developing its maximum coefficient of lift.

5166. (Refer to figure 1.) At an airspeed represented by point B, in steady flight, the pilot can expect to obtain the airplane's maximum

A— endurance.
B— glide range.
C— coefficient of lift.

5167. Which statement is true relative to changing angle of attack?

A— A decrease in angle of attack will increase impact pressure below the wing, and decrease drag.
B— An increase in angle of attack will decrease impact pressure below the wing, and increase drag.
C— An increase in angle of attack will increase impact pressure below the wing, and increase drag.

*   *   *

5169. Before shutdown, while at idle, the ignition key is momentarily turned OFF. The engine continues to run with no interruption; this

A— is normal because the engine is usually stopped by moving the mixture to idle cut-off.
B— should not normally happen and indicates a dangerous situation.
C— is an undesirable practice, but indicates that nothing is wrong.

5170. Leaving the carburetor heat on while taking off

A— leans the mixture for more power on takeoff.
B— will decrease the takeoff distance.
C— will increase the ground roll.

5171. A way to detect a broken magneto primary grounding lead is to

A— idle the engine and momentarily turn the ignition off.
B— add full power, while holding the brakes, and momentarily turn off the ignition.
C— run on one magneto, lean the mixture, and look for a rise in manifold pressure.

5172. Fouling of spark plugs is more apt to occur if the aircraft

A— gains altitude with no mixture adjustment.
B— descends from altitude with no mixture adjustment.
C— throttle is advanced very abruptly.

5173. The most probable reason an engine continues to run after the ignition switch has been turned off is

A— carbon deposits glowing on the spark plugs.
B— a magneto ground wire is in contact with the engine casing.
C— a broken magneto ground wire.

5174. If the ground wire between the magneto and the ignition switch becomes disconnected, the engine

A— will not operate on one magneto.
B— cannot be started with the switch in the BOTH position.
C— could accidently start if the propeller is moved with fuel in the cylinder.

5175. For internal cooling, reciprocating aircraft engines are especially dependent on

A— a properly functioning cowl flap augmenter.
B— the circulation of lubricating oil.
C— the proper freon/compressor output ratio.

5176. The pilot controls the air/fuel ratio with the

A— throttle
B— manifold pressure
C— mixture control

5177. Which airspeed would a pilot be unable to identify by the color coding of an airspeed indicator?

A— The never-exceed speed.
B— The power-off stall speed.
C— The maneuvering speed.

5178. Which statement is true about magnetic deviation of a compass? Deviation

A— varies over time as the agonic line shifts.
B— varies for different headings of the same aircraft.
C— is the same for all aircraft in the same locality.

5179. (Refer to figure 2.) Select the correct statement regarding stall speeds.

A— Power-off stalls occur at higher airspeeds with the gear and flaps down.
B— In a 60° bank the airplane stalls at a lower airspeed with the gear up.
C— Power-on stalls occur at lower airspeeds in shallower banks.

5180. (Refer to figure 2.) Select the correct statement regarding stall speeds. The airplane will stall

A— 10 knots higher in a power-on 60° bank with gear and flaps up than with gear and flaps down.
B— 35 knots lower in a power-off, flaps-up, 60° bank, than in a power-off, flaps-down, wings-level configuration.
C— 10 knots higher in a 45° bank, power-on stall than in a wings-level stall.

5181. Which is true regarding the use of flaps during level turns?

A— The lowering of flaps increases the stall speed.
B— The raising of flaps increases the stall speed.
C— Raising flaps will require added forward pressure on the yoke or stick.

5182. One of the main functions of flaps during the approach and landing is to

A— decrease the angle of descent without increasing the airspeed.
B— provide the same amount of lift at a slower airspeed.
C— decrease lift, thus enabling a steeper-than-normal approach to be made.

5183. Which statement best describes the operating principle of a constant-speed propeller?

A— As throttle setting is changed by the pilot, the prop governor causes pitch angle of the propeller blades to remain unchanged.
B— A high blade angle, or increased pitch, reduces the propeller drag and allows more engine power for takeoffs.
C— The propeller control regulates the engine RPM and in turn the propeller RPM.

5184. In aircraft equipped with constant-speed propellers and normally-aspirated engines, which procedure should be used to avoid placing undue stress on the engine components? When power is being

A— decreased, reduce the RPM before reducing the manifold pressure.
B— increased, increase the RPM before increasing the manifold pressure.
C— increased or decreased, the RPM should be adjusted before the manifold pressure.

5185. Detonation may occur at high-power settings when

A— the fuel mixture instantaneously ignites instead of burning progressively and evenly.
B— an excessively rich fuel mixture causes an explosive gain in power.
C— the fuel mixture is ignited too early by hot carbon deposits in the cylinder.

5186. The uncontrolled firing of the fuel/air charge in advance of normal spark ignition is known as

A— instantaneous combustion.
B— detonation.
C— pre-ignition.

5187. Fuel/air ratio is the ratio between the

A— volume of fuel and volume of air entering the cylinder.
B— weight of fuel and weight of air entering the cylinder.
C— weight of fuel and weight of air entering the carburetor.

5188. The mixture control can be adjusted, which

A— prevents the fuel/air combination from becoming too rich at higher altitudes.
B— regulates the amount of air flow through the carburetor's venturi.
C— prevents the fuel/air combination from becoming lean as the airplane climbs.

5189. Which statement is true concerning the effect of the application of carburetor heat?

A— It enriches the fuel/air mixture.
B— It leans the fuel/air mixture.
C— It has no effect on the fuel/air mixture.

5190. Detonation occurs in a reciprocating aircraft engine when

A— there is an explosive increase of fuel caused by too rich a fuel/air mixture.
B— the spark plugs receive an electrical jolt caused by a short in the wiring.
C— the unburned charge in the cylinders is subjected to instantaneous combustion.

5191. Name the four fundamentals involved in maneuvering an aircraft.

A— Power, pitch, bank, and trim.
B— Thrust, lift, turns, and glides.
C— Straight-and-level flight, turns, climbs, and descents.

5192. To increase the rate of turn and at the same time decrease the radius, a pilot should

A— maintain the bank and decrease airspeed.
B— steepen the bank and increase airspeed.
C— steepen the bank and decrease airspeed.

5193. Which is correct with respect to rate and radius of turn for an airplane flown in a coordinated turn at a constant altitude?

A— For a specific angle of bank and airspeed, the rate and radius of turn will not vary.
B— To maintain a steady rate of turn, the angle of bank must be increased as the airspeed is decreased.
C— The faster the true airspeed, the faster the rate and larger the radius of turn regardless of the angle of bank.

5194. Why is it necessary to increase back elevator pressure to maintain altitude during a turn? To compensate for the

A— loss of the vertical component of lift.
B— loss of the horizontal component of lift and the increase in centrifugal force.
C— rudder deflection and slight opposite aileron throughout the turn.

5195. To maintain altitude during a turn, the angle of attack must be increased to compensate for the decrease in the

A— forces opposing the resultant component of drag.
B— vertical component of lift.
C— horizontal component of lift.

5196. Stall speed is affected by

A— weight, load factor, and power.
B— load factor, angle of attack, and power.
C— angle of attack, weight, and air density.

5197. A rectangular wing, as compared to other wing planforms, has a tendency to stall first at the

A— wingtip, with the stall progression toward the wing root.
B— wing root, with the stall progression toward the wing tip.
C— center trailing edge, with the stall progression outward toward the wing root and tip.

5198. By changing the angle of attack of a wing, the pilot can control the airplane's

A— lift, airspeed, and drag.
B— lift, airspeed, and CG.
C— lift and airspeed, but not drag.

5199. The angle of attack of a wing directly controls the

A— angle of incidence of the wing.
B— amount of airflow above and below the wing.
C— distribution of pressures acting on the wing.

5200. In theory, if the angle of attack and other factors remain constant and the airspeed is doubled, the lift produced at the higher speed will be

A— the same as at the lower speed.
B— two times greater than at the lower speed.
C— four times greater than at the lower speed.

5201. An aircraft wing is designed to produce lift resulting from relatively

A— negative air pressure below and a vacuum above the wing's surface.
B— a vacuum below the wing's surface and greater air pressure above the wing's surface.
C— higher air pressure below the wing's surface and lower air pressure above the wing's surface.

5202. On a wing, the force of lift acts perpendicular to and the force of drag acts parallel to the

A— chord line.
B— flight path.
C— longitudinal axis.

5203. Which statement is true, regarding the opposing forces acting on an airplane in steady-state level flight?

A— These forces are equal.
B— Thrust is greater than drag and weight and lift are equal.
C— Thrust is greater than drag and lift is greater than weight.

5204. The angle of attack at which a wing stalls remains constant regardless of

A— weight, dynamic pressure, bank angle, or pitch attitude.
B— dynamic pressure, but varies with weight, bank angle, and pitch attitude.
C— weight and pitch attitude, but varies with dynamic pressure and bank angle.

5205. In light airplanes, normal recovery from spins may become difficult if the

A— CG is too far rearward and rotation is around the longitudinal axis.
B— CG is too far rearward and rotation is around the CG.
C— spin is entered before the stall is fully developed.

5206. The inclinometer is mounted on the left side of the instrument panel. A spin to the left would displace the ball in which direction?

A— To the right.
B— No displacement, it will remain centered.
C— To the left.

5207. If an airplane is loaded to the rear of its CG range, it will tend to be unstable about its

A— vertical axis.
B— lateral axis.
C— longitudinal axis.

5208. At higher elevation airports the pilot should know that indicated airspeed

A— will be unchanged, but groundspeed will be faster.
B— will be higher, but groundspeed will be unchanged.
C— should be increased to compensate for the thinner air.

5209. An airplane leaving ground effect will

A— experience a reduction in ground friction and require a slight power reduction.
B— experience an increase in induced drag and require more thrust.
C— require a lower angle of attack to maintain the same lift coefficient.

5210. If airspeed is increased during a level turn, what action would be necessary to maintain altitude? The angle of attack

A— and angle of bank must be decreased.
B— must be increased or angle of bank decreased.
C— must be decreased or angle of bank increased.

5211. The stalling speed of an airplane is most affected by

A— changes in air density.
B— variations in flight altitude.
C— variations in airplane loading.

5212. An airplane will stall at the same

A— angle of attack regardless of the attitude with relation to the horizon.
B— airspeed regardless of the attitude with relation to the horizon.
C— angle of attack and attitude with relation to the horizon.

5213. (Refer to figure 3.) If an airplane glides at an angle of attack of 10°, how much altitude will it lose in 1 mile?

A— 240 feet.
B— 480 feet.
C— 960 feet.

5214. (Refer to figure 3.) How much altitude will this airplane lose in 3 miles of gliding at an angle of attack of 8°?

A— 440 feet.
B— 880 feet.
C— 1,320 feet.

5215. (Refer to figure 3.) The L/D ratio at a 2° angle of attack is approximately the same as the L/D ratio for a

A— 9.75° angle of attack.
B— 10.5° angle of attack.
C— 16.5° angle of attack.

5216. If the same angle of attack is maintained in ground effect as when out of ground effect, lift will

A— increase, and induced drag will decrease.
B— decrease, and parasite drag will increase.
C— increase, and induced drag will increase.

5217. What performance is characteristic of flight at maximum lift/drag ratio in a propeller-driven airplane? Maximum

A— gain in altitude over a given distance.
B— range and maximum distance glide.
C— coefficient of lift and minimum coefficient of drag.

5218. Which is true regarding the forces acting on an aircraft in a steady-state descent? The sum of all

A— upward forces is less than the sum of all downward forces.
B— rearward forces is greater than the sum of all forward forces.
C— forward forces is equal to the sum of all rearward forces.

5219. Which is true regarding the force of lift in steady, unaccelerated flight?

A— At lower airspeeds the angle of attack must be less to generate sufficient lift to maintain altitude.
B— There is a corresponding indicated airspeed required for every angle of attack to generate sufficient lift to maintain altitude.
C— An airfoil will always stall at the same indicated airspeed; therefore, an increase in weight will require an increase in speed to generate sufficient lift to maintain altitude.

5220. During the transition from straight-and-level flight to a climb, the angle of attack is increased and lift

A— is momentarily decreased.
B— remains the same.
C— is momentarily increased.

5221. (Refer to figure 4.) What is the stall speed of an airplane under a load factor of 2 G's if the unaccelerated stall speed is 60 knots?

A— 66 knots.
B— 74 knots.
C— 84 knots.

5222. (Refer to figure 4.) What increase in load factor would take place if the angle of bank were increased from 60° to 80°?

A— 3 G's.
B— 3.5 G's.
C— 4 G's.

5223. To generate the same amount of lift as altitude is increased, an airplane must be flown at

A— the same true airspeed regardless of angle of attack.
B— a lower true airspeed and a greater angle of attack.
C— a higher true airspeed for any given angle of attack.

5224. To produce the same lift while in ground effect as when out of ground effect, the airplane requires

A— a lower angle of attack.
B— the same angle of attack.
C— a greater angle of attack.

5225. As the angle of bank is increased, the vertical component of lift

A— decreases and the horizontal component of lift increases.
B— increases and the horizontal component of lift decreases.
C— decreases and the horizontal component of lift remains constant.

5226. If the airplane attitude remains in a new position after the elevator control is pressed forward and released, the airplane displays

A— neutral longitudinal static stability.
B— positive longitudinal static stability.
C— neutral longitudinal dynamic stability.

5227. Longitudinal dynamic instability in an airplane can be identified by

A— bank oscillations becoming progressively steeper.
B— pitch oscillations becoming progressively steeper.
C— Trilatitudinal roll oscillations becoming progressively steeper.

5228. Longitudinal stability involves the motion of the airplane controlled by its

A— rudder.
B— elevator.
C— ailerons.

5229. What changes in airplane longitudinal control must be made to maintain altitude while the airspeed is being decreased?

A— Increase the angle of attack to produce more lift than drag.
B— Increase the angle of attack to compensate for the decreasing lift.
C— Decrease the angle of attack to compensate for the increasing drag.

5230. If the airplane attitude initially tends to return to its original position after the elevator control is pressed forward and released, the airplane displays

A— positive dynamic stability.
B— positive static stability.
C— neutral dynamic stability.

5231. (Refer to figure 5.) The horizontal dashed line from point C to point E represents the

A— ultimate load factor.
B— positive limit load factor.
C— airspeed range for normal operations.

5232. (Refer to figure 5.) The vertical line from point E to point F is represented on the airspeed indicator by the

A— upper limit of the yellow arc.
B— upper limit of the green arc.
C— blue radial line.

5233. (Refer to figure 5.) The vertical line from point D to point G is represented on the airspeed indicator by the maximum speed limit of the

A— green arc.
B— yellow arc.
C— white arc.

5234. The performance tables of an aircraft for takeoff and climb are based on

A— pressure/density altitude.
B— cabin altitude.
C— true altitude.

5235. Propeller efficiency is the

A— ratio of thrust horsepower to brake horsepower.
B— actual distance a propeller advances in one revolution.
C— ratio of geometric pitch to effective pitch.

5236. A fixed-pitch propeller is designed for best efficiency only at a given combination of

A— altitude and RPM.
B— airspeed and RPM.
C— airspeed and altitude.

5237. The reason for variations in geometric pitch (twisting) along a propeller blade is that it

A— permits a relatively constant angle of incidence along its length when in cruising flight.
B— prevents the portion of the blade near the hub from stalling during cruising flight.
C— permits a relatively constant angle of attack along its length when in cruising flight.

5238. A propeller rotating clockwise as seen from the rear, creates a spiraling slipstream that tends to rotate the airplane to the

A— right around the vertical axis, and to the left around the longitudinal axis.
B— left around the vertical axis, and to the right around the longitudinal axis.
C— left around the vertical axis, and to the left around the longitudinal axis.

5239. When the angle of attack of a symmetrical airfoil is increased, the center of pressure will

A— have very limited movement.
B— move aft along the airfoil surface.
C— remain unaffected.

* * *

5268. What is an operational difference between the turn coordinator and the turn-and-slip indicator? The turn coordinator

A— is always electric; the turn-and-slip indicator is always vacuum-driven.
B— indicates bank angle only; the turn-and-slip indicator indicates rate of turn and coordination.
C— indicates roll rate, rate of turn, and coordination; the turn-and-slip indicator indicates rate of turn and coordination.

5269. What is an advantage of an electric turn coordinator if the airplane has a vacuum system for other gyroscopic instruments?

A— It is a backup in case of vacuum system failure.
B— It is more reliable than the vacuum-driven indicators.
C— It will not tumble as will vacuum-driven turn indicators.

5270. If a standard rate turn is maintained, how long would it take to turn 360°?

A— 1 minute.
B— 2 minutes.
C— 3 minutes.

5271. A detuning of engine crankshaft counterweights is a source of overstress that may be caused by

A— rapid opening and closing of the throttle.
B— carburetor ice forming on the throttle valve.
C— operating with an excessively rich fuel/air mixture.

5272. How can you determine if another aircraft is on a collision course with your aircraft?

A— The nose of each aircraft is pointed at the same point in space.
B— The other aircraft will always appear to get larger and closer at a rapid rate.
C— There will be no apparent relative motion between your aircraft and the other aircraft.

* * *

5298. The best power mixture is that fuel/air ratio at which

A— cylinder head temperatures are the coolest.
B— the most power can be obtained for any given throttle setting.
C— a given power can be obtained with the highest manifold pressure or throttle setting.

5299. Detonation can be caused by

A— too lean a mixture.
B— low engine temperatures.
C— using a higher grade fuel than recommended.

5300. What effect, if any, would a change in ambient temperature or air density have on gas turbine engine performance?

A— As air density decreases, thrust increases.
B— As temperature increases, thrust increases.
C— As temperature increases, thrust decreases.

5301. Every physical process of weather is accompanied by or is the result of

A— a heat exchange.
B— the movement of air.
C— a pressure differential.

5302. What is the standard temperature at 10,000 feet?

A— - 5 °C.
B— - 15 °C.
C— + 5 °C.

5303. What is the standard temperature at 20,000 feet?

A— - 15 °C.
B— - 20 °C.
C— - 25 °C.

5304. Which conditions are favorable for the formation of a surface based temperature inversion?

A— Clear, cool nights with calm or light wind.
B— Area of unstable air rapidly transferring heat from the surface.
C— Broad areas of cumulus clouds with smooth, level bases at the same altitude.

5305. What are the standard temperature and pressure values for sea level?

A— 15 °C and 29.92" Hg.
B— 59 °F and 1013.2" Hg.
C— 15 °C and 29.92 Mb.

5306. GIVEN:

Pressure altitude . . . . 12,000 ft
True air temperature . . . . +50 °F

From the conditions given, the approximate density altitude is

A— 11,900 feet.
B— 14,130 feet.
C— 18,150 feet.

5307. GIVEN:

Pressure altitude . . . . 5,000 ft
True air temperature . . . . +30 °C

From the conditions given, the approximate density altitude is

A— 7,800 feet.
B— 8,100 feet.
C— 8,800 feet.

5308. GIVEN:

Pressure altitude . . . . 6,000 ft
True air temperature . . . . +30 °F

From the conditions given, the approximate density altitude is

A— 9,000 feet.
B— 5,500 feet.
C— 5,000 feet.

5309. GIVEN:

Pressure altitude . . . . 7,000 ft
True air temperature . . . . +15 °C

From the conditions given, the approximate density altitude is

A— 5,000 feet.
B— 8,500 feet.
C— 9,500 feet.

5310. What causes wind?

A— The Earth's rotation.
B— Air mass modification.
C— Pressure differences.

5311. In the Northern Hemisphere, the wind is deflected to the

A— right by Coriolis force.
B— right by surface friction.
C— left by Coriolis force.

5312. Why does the wind have a tendency to flow parallel to the isobars above the friction level?

A— Coriolis force tends to counterbalance the horizontal pressure gradient.
B— Coriolis force acts perpendicular to a line connecting the highs and lows.
C— Friction of the air with the Earth deflects the air perpendicular to the pressure gradient.

5313. The wind system associated with a low-pressure area in the Northern Hemisphere is

A— an anticyclone and is caused by descending cold air.
B— a cyclone and is caused by Coriolis force.
C— an anticyclone and is caused by Coriolis force.

5314. With regard to windflow patterns shown on surface analysis charts; when the isobars are

A— close together, the pressure gradient force is slight and wind velocities are weaker.
B— not close together, the pressure gradient force is greater and wind velocities are stronger.
C— close together, the pressure gradient force is greater and wind velocities are stronger.

5315. What prevents air from flowing directly from high-pressure areas to low-pressure areas?

A— Coriolis force.
B— Surface friction.
C— Pressure gradient force.

5316. While flying cross-country, in the Northern Hemisphere, you experience a continuous left crosswind which is associated with a major wind system. This indicates that you

A— are flying toward an area of generally unfavorable weather conditions.
B— have flown from an area of unfavorable weather conditions.
C— cannot determine weather conditions without knowing pressure changes.

5317. Which is true with respect to a high- or low-pressure system?

A— A high-pressure area or ridge is an area of rising air.
B— A low-pressure area or trough is an area of descending air.
C— A high-pressure area or ridge is an area of descending air.

5318. Which is true regarding high- or low-pressure systems?

A— A high-pressure area or ridge is an area of rising air.
B— A low-pressure area or trough is an area of rising air.
C— Both high- and low-pressure areas are characterized by descending air.

5319. When flying into a low-pressure area in the Northern Hemisphere, the wind direction and velocity will be from the

A— left and decreasing.
B— left and increasing.
C— right and decreasing.

5320. Which is true regarding actual air temperature and dewpoint temperature spread? The temperature spread

A— decreases as the relative humidity decreases.
B— decreases as the relative humidity increases.
C— increases as the relative humidity increases.

5321. The general circulation of air associated with a high-pressure area in the Northern Hemisphere is

A— outward, downward, and clockwise.
B— outward, upward, and clockwise.
C— inward, downward, and clockwise.

5322. Virga is best described as

A— streamers of precipitation trailing beneath clouds which evaporates before reaching the ground.
B— wall cloud torrents trailing beneath cumulonimbus clouds which dissipate before reaching the ground.
C— turbulent areas beneath cumulonimbus clouds.

5323. Moisture is added to a parcel of air by

A— sublimation and condensation.
B— evaporation and condensation.
C— evaporation and sublimation.

5324. Ice pellets encountered during flight normally are evidence that

A— a warm front has passed.
B— a warm front is about to pass.
C— there are thunderstorms in the area.

5325. What is indicated if ice pellets are encountered at 8,000 feet?

A— Freezing rain at higher altitude.
B— You are approaching an area of thunderstorms.
C— You will encounter hail if you continue your flight.

5326. Ice pellets encountered during flight are normally evidence that

A— a cold front has passed.
B— there are thunderstorms in the area.
C— freezing rain exists at higher altitudes.

5327. When conditionally unstable air with high-moisture content and very warm surface temperature is forecast, one can expect what type of weather?

A— Strong updrafts and stratonimbus clouds.
B— Restricted visibility near the surface over a large area.
C— Strong updrafts and cumulonimbus clouds.

5328. What is the approximate base of the cumulus clouds if the temperature at 2,000 feet MSL is 70 °F. and the dewpoint is 52 °F?

A— 3,000 feet MSL.
B— 4,000 feet MSL.
C— 6,000 feet MSL.

5329. If clouds form as a result of very stable, moist air being forced to ascend a mountain slope, the clouds will be

A— cirrus type with no vertical development or turbulence.
B— cumulus type with considerable vertical development and turbulence.
C— stratus type with little vertical development and little or no turbulence.

5330. What determines the structure or type of clouds which will form as a result of air being forced to ascend?

A— The method by which the air is lifted.
B— The stability of the air before lifting occurs.
C— The relative humidity of the air after lifting occurs.

5331. Refer to the excerpt from a surface weather report:

ABC ...194/89/45/2115/993...

At approximately what altitude AGL should bases of convective-type cumuliform clouds be expected? (Use most accurate method.)

A— 4,400 feet.
B— 10,000 feet.
C— 17,600 feet.

5332. What are the characteristics of stable air?

A— Good visibility; steady precipitation; stratus clouds.
B— Poor visibility; steady precipitation; stratus clouds.
C— Poor visibility; intermittent precipitation; cumulus clouds.

5333. Which would decrease the stability of an air mass?

A— Warming from below.
B— Cooling from below.
C— Decrease in water vapor.

5334. From which measurement of the atmosphere can stability be determined?

A— Atmospheric pressure.
B— The ambient lapse rate.
C— The dry adiabatic lapse rate.

5335. What type weather can one expect from moist, unstable air, and very warm surface temperatures?

A— Fog and low stratus clouds.
B— Continuous heavy precipitation.
C— Strong updrafts and cumulonimbus clouds.

5336. Which would increase the stability of an air mass?

A— Warming from below.
B— Cooling from below.
C— Decrease in water vapor.

5337. The conditions necessary for the formation of stratiform clouds are a lifting action and

A— unstable, dry air.
B— stable, moist air.
C— unstable, moist air.

5338. Which cloud types would indicate convective turbulence?

A— Cirrus clouds.
B— Nimbostratus clouds.
C— Towering cumulus clouds.

5339. The presence of standing lenticular altocumulus clouds is a good indication of

A— lenticular ice formation in calm air.
B— very strong turbulence.
C— heavy icing conditions.

5340. The formation of either predominantly stratiform or predominantly cumuliform clouds is dependent upon the

A— source of lift.
B— stability of the air being lifted.
C— temperature of the air being lifted.

5341. Which combination of weather-producing variables would likely result in cumuliform-type clouds, good visibility, and showery rain?

A— Stable, moist air and orographic lifting.
B— Unstable, moist air and orographic lifting.
C— Unstable, moist air and no lifting mechanism.

5342. What is a characteristic of stable air?

A— Stratiform clouds.
B— Fair weather cumulus clouds.
C— Temperature decreases rapidly with altitude.

5343. A moist, unstable air mass is characterized by

A— poor visibility and smooth air.
B— cumuliform clouds and showery precipitation.
C— stratiform clouds and continuous precipitation.

5344. When an air mass is stable, which of these conditions are most likely to exist?

A— Numerous towering cumulus and cumulonimbus clouds.
B— Moderate to severe turbulence at the lower levels.
C— Smoke, dust, haze, etc., concentrated at the lower levels with resulting poor visibility.

5345. Which is a characteristic of stable air?

A— Cumuliform clouds.
B— Excellent visibility.
C— Restricted visibility.

5346. Which is a characteristic typical of a stable air mass?

A— Cumuliform clouds.
B— Showery precipitation.
C— Continuous precipitation.

5347. Which is true regarding a cold front occlusion? The air ahead of the warm front

A— is colder than the air behind the overtaking cold front.
B— is warmer than the air behind the overtaking cold front.
C— has the same temperature as the air behind the overtaking cold front.

5348. Which are characteristics of a cold air mass moving over a warm surface?

A— Cumuliform clouds, turbulence, and poor visibility.
B— Cumuliform clouds, turbulence, and good visibility.
C— Stratiform clouds, smooth air, and poor visibility.

5349. The conditions necessary for the formation of cumulonimbus clouds are a lifting action and

A— unstable, dry air.
B— stable, moist air.
C— unstable, moist air.

5350. Fog produced by frontal activity is a result of saturation due to

A— nocturnal cooling.
B— adiabatic cooling.
C— evaporation of precipitation.

5351. What is an important characteristic of wind shear?

A— It is present at only lower levels and exists in a horizontal direction.
B— It is present at any level and exists in only a vertical direction.
C— It can be present at any level and can exist in both a horizontal and vertical direction.

5352. Hazardous wind shear is commonly encountered

A— near warm or stationary frontal activity.
B— when the wind velocity is stronger than 35 knots.
C— in areas of temperature inversion and near thunderstorms.

5353. Low-level wind shear may occur when

A— surface winds are light and variable.
B— there is a low-level temperature inversion with strong winds above the inversion.
C— surface winds are above 15 knots and there is no change in wind direction and windspeed with height.

5354. If a temperature inversion is encountered immediately after takeoff or during an approach to a landing, a potential hazard exists due to

A— wind shear.
B— strong surface winds.
C— strong convective currents.

5355. GIVEN:

Winds at 3,000 feet AGL . . . . 30 kts
Surface winds . . . . Calm

While approaching for landing under clear skies a few hours after sunrise, one should

A— allow a margin of approach airspeed above normal to avoid stalling.
B— keep the approach airspeed at or slightly below normal to compensate for floating.
C— not alter our approach airspeed, these conditions are nearly ideal.

5356. Convective currents are most active on warm summer afternoons when winds are

A— light.
B— moderate.
C— strong.

5357. When flying low over hilly terrain, ridges, or mountain ranges, the greatest potential danger from turbulent air currents will usually be encountered on the

A— leeward side when flying with a tailwind.
B— leeward side when flying into the wind.
C— windward side when flying into the wind.

5358. During an approach, the most important and most easily recognized means of being alerted to possible wind shear is monitoring the

A— amount of trim required to relieve control pressures.
B— heading changes necessary to remain on the runway centerline.
C— power and vertical velocity required to remain on the proper glidepath.

5359. During departure, under conditions of suspected low-level wind shear, a sudden decrease in headwind will cause

A— a loss in airspeed equal to the decrease in wind velocity.
B— a gain in airspeed equal to the decrease in wind velocity.
C— no change in airspeed, but groundspeed will decrease.

5360. Which situation would most likely result in freezing precipitation? Rain falling from air which has a temperature of

A— 32 °F or less into air having a temperature of more than 32 °F.
B— 0 °C or less into air having a temperature of 0 °C or more.
C— more than 32 °F into air having a temperature of 32 °F or less.

5361. Which statement is true concerning the hazards of hail?

A— Hail damage in horizontal flight is minimal due to the vertical movement of hail in the clouds.
B— Rain at the surface is a reliable indication of no hail aloft.
C— Hailstones may be encountered in clear air several miles from a thunderstorm.

5362. Hail is most likely to be associated with

A— cumulus clouds.
B— cumulonimbus clouds.
C— stratocumulus clouds.

5363. The most severe weather conditions, such as destructive winds, heavy hail, and tornadoes, are generally associated with

A— slow-moving warm fronts which slope above the tropopause.
B— squall lines.
C— fast-moving occluded fronts.

5364. Of the following, which is accurate regarding turbulence associated with thunderstorms?

A— Outside the cloud, shear turbulence can be encountered 50 miles laterally from a severe storm.
B— Shear turbulence is encountered only inside cumulonimbus clouds or within a 5-mile radius of them.
C— Outside the cloud, shear turbulence can be encountered 20 miles laterally from a severe storm.

5365. If airborne radar is indicating an extremely intense thunderstorm echo, this thunderstorm should be avoided by a distance of at least

A— 20 miles.
B— 10 miles.
C— 5 miles.

5366. Which statement is true regarding squall lines?

A— They are always associated with cold fronts.
B— They are slow in forming, but rapid in movement.
C— They are nonfrontal and often contain severe, steady-state thunderstorms.

5367. Which statement is true concerning squall lines?

A— They form slowly, but move rapidly.
B— They are associated with frontal systems only.
C— They offer the most intense weather hazards to aircraft.

5368. Select the true statement pertaining to the life cycle of a thunderstorm.

A— Updrafts continue to develop throughout the dissipating stage of a thunderstorm.
B— The beginning of rain at the Earth's surface indicates the mature stage of the thunderstorm.
C— The beginning of rain at the Earth's surface indicates the dissipating stage of the thunderstorm.

5369. What visible signs indicate extreme turbulence in thunderstorms?

A— Base of the clouds near the surface, heavy rain, and hail.
B— Low ceiling and visibility, hail, and precipitation static.
C— Cumulonimbus clouds, very frequent lightning, and roll clouds.

5370. Which weather phenomenon signals the beginning of the mature stage of a thunderstorm?

A— The start of rain.
B— The appearance of an anvil top.
C— Growth rate of cloud is maximum.

5371. What feature is normally associated with the cumulus stage of a thunderstorm?

A— Roll cloud.
B— Continuous updraft.
C— Beginning of rain at the surface.

5372. During the life cycle of a thunderstorm, which stage is characterized predominately by downdrafts?

A— Mature.
B— Developing.
C— Dissipating.

5373. What minimum distance should exist between intense radar echoes before any attempt is made to fly between these thunderstorms?

A— 20 miles.
B— 30 miles.
C— 40 miles.

5374. Which in-flight hazard is most commonly associated with warm fronts?

A— Advection fog.
B— Radiation fog.
C— Precipitation-induced fog.

5375. Which is true regarding the use of airborne weather-avoidance radar for the recognition of certain weather conditions?

A— The radarscope provides no assurance of avoiding instrument weather conditions.
B— The avoidance of hail is assured when flying between and just clear of the most intense echoes.
C— The clear area between intense echoes indicates that visual sighting of storms can be maintained when flying between the echoes.

5376. A situation most conducive to the formation of advection fog is

A— a light breeze moving colder air over a water surface.
B— an air mass moving inland from the coastline during the winter.
C— a warm, moist air mass settling over a cool surface under no-wind conditions.

5377. Advection fog has drifted over a coastal airport during the day. What may tend to dissipate or lift this fog into low stratus clouds?

A— Nighttime cooling.
B— Surface radiation.
C— Wind 15 knots or stronger.

5378. What lifts advection fog into low stratus clouds?

A— Nighttime cooling.
B— Dryness of the underlying land mass.
C— Surface winds of approximately 15 knots or stronger.

5379. In what ways do advection fog, radiation fog, and steam fog differ in their formation or location?

A— Radiation fog is restricted to land areas; advection fog is most common along coastal areas; steam fog forms over a water surface.
B— Advection fog deepens as windspeed increases up to 20 knots; steam fog requires calm or very light wind; radiation fog forms when the ground or water cools the air by radiation.
C— Steam fog forms from moist air moving over a colder surface; advection fog requires cold air over a warmer surface; radiation fog is produced by radiational cooling of the ground.

5380. With respect to advection fog, which statement is true?

A— It is slow to develop, and dissipates quite rapidly.
B— It forms almost exclusively at night or near daybreak.
C— It can appear suddenly during day or night, and it is more persistent than radiation fog.

5381. Which feature is associated with the tropopause?

A— Constant height above the Earth.
B— Abrupt change in temperature lapse rate.
C— Absolute upper limit of cloud formation.

5382. A common location of clear air turbulence is

A— in an upper trough on the polar side of a jet stream.
B— near a ridge aloft on the equatorial side of a high-pressure flow.
C— south of an east/west oriented high-pressure ridge in its dissipating stage.

5383. The jet stream and associated clear air turbulence can sometimes be visually identified in flight by

A— dust or haze at flight level.
B— long streaks of cirrus clouds.
C— a constant outside air temperature.

5384. During the winter months in the middle latitudes, the jet stream shifts toward the

A— north and speed decreases.
B— south and speed increases.
C— north and speed increases.

5385. The strength and location of the jet stream is normally

A— weaker and farther north in the summer.
B— stronger and farther north in the winter.
C— stronger and farther north in the summer.

* * *

5398. During preflight preparation, weather report forecasts which are not routinely available at the local service outlet (FSS or WSFO) can best be obtained by means of the

A— request/reply service.
B— air route traffic control center.
C— pilot's automatic telephone answering service.

5399. The most current en route and destination weather information for an instrument flight should be obtained from

A— the FSS or WSO.
B— the ATIS broadcast.
C— NOTAM's (Class II).

5400. FSS's in the conterminous 48 U.S. having voice capability on VOR's or radiobeacons (NDB's) broadcast

A— AIRMET's and SIGMET s at 15 minutes past the hour and each 15 minutes thereafter as long as they are in effect.
B— AIRMET's and Nonconvective SIGMET's at 15 minutes and 45 minutes past the hour for the first hour after issuance.
C— hourly weather reports at 15 and 45 minutes past each hour for those reporting stations within approximately 150 NM of the broadcast stations.

5401. Transcribed Weather Broadcasts (TWEB's) may be monitored by tuning the appropriate radio receiver to certain

A— NDB, but not VOR frequencies.
B— VOR and NDB frequencies.
C— VOR, but not NDB frequencies.

5402. The remarks section of the hourly aviation weather report contains the following coded information:

RADAT 87045

What is the meaning of this information?

A— Radar echoes with tops at 45,000 feet were observed on the 087 radial of the VORTAC.
B— A pilot reported thunderstorms 87 DME miles distance on the 045 radial of the VORTAC.
C— Relative humidity was 87 percent and the freezing level (0 °C) was at 4,500 feet MSL.

5403. What is meant by the entry in the remarks section of this Surface Aviation Weather Report for BOI?

BOI SP 1854 -X M7 OVC 1 1/2R+F 990/63/61/
3205/980/RF2 RB12

A— Rain and fog obscuring two-tenths of the sky; rain began at 1912.
B— Rain and fog obscuring two-tenths of the sky; rain began at 1812.
C— Runway fog, visibility 2 miles; base of the rain clouds 1,200 feet.

5404. The station originating the following weather report has a field elevation of 3,500 feet MSL. If the sky cover is one continuous layer, what is its thickness?

M5 OVC 1/2HK 173/73/72/0000/002/OVC 75

A— 2,500 feet.
B— 3,500 feet.
C— 4,000 feet.

5405. What wind conditions would you anticipate when squalls are reported at your destination?

A— Rapid variations in windspeed of 15 knots or more between peaks and lulls.
B— Peak gusts of at least 35 knots combined with a change in wind direction of 30° or more.
C— Sudden increases in windspeed of at least 15 knots to a sustained speed of 20 knots or more for at least 1 minute.

5406. What significant cloud coverage is reported by a pilot in this SA?

MOB...M9 OVC 2LF 131/44/43/3212/991/UA/OV
15NW MOB 1355/SK OVC 025/045 OVC 090

A— Three separate overcast layers exist with bases at 2,500, 7,500, and 13,500 feet.
B— The top of lower overcast is 2,500 feet; base and top of second overcast layer is 4,500 and 9,000 feet, respectively.
C— The base of second overcast layer is 2,500 feet; top of second overcast layer is 7,500 feet; base of third layer is 13,500 feet.

5407. To best determine observed weather conditions between weather reporting stations, the pilot should refer to

A— pilot reports.
B— Area Forecasts.
C— prognostic charts.

5408. Which is true concerning this radar weather report for OKC?

OKC 1934 LN 8TRW+/+ 86/40 164/60 199/115
15W 2425 MT 570 AT 159/65 2 INCH HAIL
RPRTD THIS ECHO

A— There are three cells with tops at 11,500, 40,000, and 60,000 feet.
B— The line of cells is moving 080° with winds reported up to 40 knots.
C— The maximum top of the cells is 57,000 feet located 65 NM south-southeast of the station.

5409. What is the meaning of the term MVFR, as used in the categorical outlook portion of Terminal and Area Forecasts?

A— A ceiling less than 1,000 feet, and/or visibility less than 3 miles.
B— A ceiling of 1,000 to 3,000 feet, and/or visibility of 3 to 5 miles.
C— A ceiling of 3,000 to 5,000 feet, and visibility of 5 to 7 miles.

5410. The contraction WND in the 6-hour categorical outlook in the Terminal Forecast means that the wind during that period is forecast to be

A— 15 to 20 knots.
B— less than 25 knots.
C— 25 knots or stronger.

5411. Which statement pertaining to a Terminal Forecast is true? The term

A— WND in the categorical outlook implies surface winds are forecast to be 10 knots or greater.
B— CHC TRW VCNTY in the remarks section pertains to an area within a 5-mile radius of the airport.
C— VFR CIGS ABV 100 in the categorical outlook implies ceilings above 10,000 feet and visibility more than 5 miles.

5412. The absence of a visibility entry in a Terminal Forecast specifically implies that the surface visibility is expected to be more than

A— 3 miles.
B— 6 miles.
C— 10 miles.

5413. Terminal Forecasts are issued how many times a day and cover what period of time?

A— Three times daily and are valid for 24 hours including a 6-hour categorical outlook.
B— Four times daily and are valid for 18 hours including a 4-hour categorical outlook.
C— Six times daily and are valid for 12 hours with an additional 6-hour categorical outlook.

5414. Which information is contained in the HAZARDS section of the Area Forecast?

A— A summary of general weather conditions for the entire region covered in the Area Forecast.
B— A brief list of weather phenomena that meet AIRMET and/or SIGMET criteria and the location of each.
C— A brief summary of significant weather and clouds that do not meet AIRMET, but meet SIGMET criteria.

5415. The section of the Area Forecast entitled SGFNT CLOUD AND WX contains a summary of

A— forecast sky cover, cloud tops, visibility, and obstructions to vision along specific routes.
B— only those weather systems producing liquid or frozen precipitation, fog, thunderstorms, or IFR ceilings.
C— sky condition, cloud heights, visibility, weather and/or obstructions to visibility, and surface winds of 30 knots or more.

5416. In the HAZARDS AND FLIGHT PRECAUTIONS section of an Area Forecast, what is indicated by the forecast term - - FLT PRCTNS...IFR...TX AR LA MS TN AL AND CSTL WTRS?

A— IFR conditions which meet in-flight advisory criteria are forecast for the states listed.
B— Each state and geographic area listed is reporting ceilings and visibilities below VFR minimums.
C— IFR conditions, turbulence, and icing are all forecast within the valid period for the listed states.

5417. In the Area Forecast (FA), what method is used to describe the location of each icing phenomenon?

A— VOR points outline the affected area(s) within the designated FA boundary, but not beyond the FA boundary.
B— State names and portions of states, such as northwest and south central, are used to outline each affected area.
C— VOR points are used to outline the area of icing, including VOR points outside the designated FA boundary, if necessary.

5418. What single reference contains information regarding expected frontal movement, turbulence, and icing conditions for a specific area?

A— Area Forecast.
B— Surface Analysis Chart.
C— Weather Depiction Chart.

5419. The National Aviation Weather Advisory Unit prepares FA's for the contiguous U.S.

A— twice each day.
B— three times each day.
C— every 6 hours unless significant changes in weather require it more often.

5420. Which forecast provides specific information concerning expected sky cover, cloud tops, visibility, weather, and obstructions to vision in a route format?

A— Area Forecast.
B— Terminal Forecast.
C— Transcribed Weather Broadcast.

5421. To obtain a continuous transcribed weather briefing including winds aloft and route forecasts for a cross-country flight, a pilot could monitor

A— a TWEB on a low-frequency radio receiver.
B— the regularly scheduled weather broadcast on a VOR frequency.
C— a high-frequency radio receiver tuned to En Route Flight Advisory Service.

5422. SIGMET's are issued as a warning of weather conditions which are hazardous

A— to all aircraft.
B— particularly to heavy aircraft.
C— particularly to light airplanes.

5423. Which correctly describes the purpose of convective SIGMET's (WST)?

A— They consist of an hourly observation of tornadoes, significant thunderstorm activity, and large hailstone activity.
B— They contain both an observation and a forecast of all thunderstorm and hailstone activity. The forecast is valid for 1 hour only.
C— They consist of either an observation and a forecast or just a forecast for tornadoes, significant thunderstorm activity, or hail greater than or equal to 3/4 inch in diameter.

5424. What values are used for Winds Aloft Forecasts?

A— True direction and MPH.
B— True direction and knots.
C— Magnetic direction and knots.

5425. On a Surface Analysis Chart, the solid lines that depict sea level pressure patterns are called

A— isobars.
B— isogons.
C— millibars.

5426. Dashed lines on a Surface Analysis Chart, if depicted, indicate that the pressure gradient is

A— weak.
B— strong.
C— unstable.

5427. Which chart provides a ready means of locating observed frontal positions and pressure centers?

A— Surface Analysis Chart.
B— Constant Pressure Analysis Chart.
C— Weather Depiction Chart.

5428. On a Surface Analysis Chart, close spacing of the isobars indicates

A— weak pressure gradient.
B— strong pressure gradient.
C— strong temperature gradient.

5429. The Surface Analysis Chart depicts

A— frontal locations and expected movement, pressure centers, cloud coverage, and obstructions to vision at the time of chart transmission.
B— actual frontal positions, pressure patterns, temperature, dewpoint, wind, weather, and obstructions to vision at the valid time of the chart.
C— actual pressure distribution, frontal systems, cloud heights and coverage, temperature, dewpoint, and wind at the time shown on the chart.

5430. Which provides a graphic display of both VFR and IFR weather?

A— Surface Weather Map.
B— Radar Summary Chart.
C— Weather Depiction Chart.

5431. When total sky cover is few or scattered, the height shown on the Weather Depiction Chart is the

A— top of the lowest layer.
B— base of the lowest layer.
C— base of the highest layer.

5432. What information is provided by the Radar Summary Chart that is not shown on other weather charts?

A— Lines and cells of hazardous thunderstorms.
B— Ceilings and precipitation between reporting stations.
C— Areas of cloud cover and icing levels within the clouds.

5433. Which weather chart depicts conditions forecast to exist at a specific time in the future?

A— Freezing Level Chart.
B— Weather Depiction Chart.
C— 12-Hour Significant Weather Prognostication Chart.

5434. What weather phenomenon is implied within an area enclosed by small scalloped lines on a U.S. High-Level Significant Weather Prognostic Chart?

A— Cirriform clouds, light to moderate turbulence, and icing.
B— Cumulonimbus clouds, icing, and moderate or greater turbulence.
C— Cumuliform or standing lenticular clouds, moderate to severe turbulence, and icing.

5435. The U.S. High-Level Significant Weather Prognostic Chart forecasts significant weather for what airspace?

A— 18,000 feet to 45,000 feet.
B— 24,000 feet to 45,000 feet.
C— 24,000 feet to 63,000 feet.

5436. What is the upper limit of the Low Level Significant Weather Prognostic Chart?

A— 30,000 feet.
B— 24,000 feet.
C— 18,000 feet.

* * *

5438. A freezing level panel of the composite moisture stability chart is an analysis of

A— forecast freezing level data from surface observations.
B— forecast freezing level data from upper air observations.
C— observed freezing level data from upper air observations.

5439. The difference found by subtracting the temperature of a parcel of air theoretically lifted from the surface to 500 millibars and the existing temperature at 500 millibars is called the

A— lifted index.
B— negative index.
C— positive index.

5440. Hatching on a Constant Pressure Analysis Chart indicates

A— hurricane eye.
B— windspeed 70 knots to 110 knots.
C— windspeed 110 knots to 150 knots.

5441. What flight planning information can a pilot derive from Constant Pressure Analysis Charts?

A— Winds and temperatures aloft.
B— Clear air turbulence and icing conditions.
C— Frontal systems and obstructions to vision aloft.

5442. From which of the following can the observed temperature, wind, and temperature/dewpoint spread be determined at a specified altitude?

A— Stability Charts.
B— Winds Aloft Forecasts.
C— Constant Pressure Analysis Charts.

5443. The minimum vertical wind shear value critical for probable moderate or greater turbulence is

A— 4 knots per 1,000 feet.
B— 6 knots per 1,000 feet.
C— 8 knots per 1,000 feet.

5444. A pilot reporting turbulence that momentarily causes slight, erratic changes in altitude and/or attitude should report it as

A— light chop.
B— light turbulence.
C— moderate turbulence.

5445. When turbulence causes changes in altitude and/or attitude, but aircraft control remains positive, that should be reported as

A— light.
B— severe.
C— moderate.

5446. Turbulence that is encountered above 15,000 feet AGL not associated with cumuliform cloudiness, including thunderstorms, should be reported as

A— severe turbulence.
B— clear air turbulence.
C— convective turbulence.

5447. Which type of jetstream can be expected to cause the greater turbulence?

A— A straight jetstream associated with a low-pressure trough.
B— A curving jetstream associated with a deep low-pressure trough.
C— A jetstream occurring during the summer at the lower latitudes.

5448. A strong wind shear can be expected

A— in the jetstream front above a core having a speed of 60 to 90 knots.
B— if the 5 °C isotherms are spaced between 7° to 10° of latitude.
C— on the low-pressure side of a jetstream core where the speed at the core is stronger than 110 knots.

5449. Low-level wind shear is best described as a

A— violently rotating column of air extending from a cumulonimbus cloud.
B— change in wind direction and/or speed within a very short distance in the atmosphere.
C— downward motion of the air associated with continuous winds blowing with an easterly component due to the rotation of the Earth.

5450. One of the most dangerous features of mountain waves is the turbulent areas in and

A— below rotor clouds.
B— above rotor clouds.
C— below lenticular clouds.

5451. (Refer to figure 8.)

GIVEN:

Fuel quantity . . . . 47 gal
Power-cruise (lean) . . . . 55 percent

Approximately how much flight time would be available with a night VFR fuel reserve remaining?

A— 3 hours 8 minutes.
B— 3 hours 22 minutes.
C— 3 hours 43 minutes.

5452. (Refer to figure 8.)

GIVEN:

Fuel quantity . . . . 65 gal
Best power (level flight) . . . . 55 percent

Approximately how much flight time would be available with a day VFR fuel reserve remaining?

A— 4 hours 17 minutes.
B— 4 hours 30 minutes.
C— 5 hours 4 minutes.

5453. (Refer to figure 8.) Approximately how much fuel would be consumed when climbing at 75 percent power for 7 minutes?

A— 1.82 gallons.
B— 1.97 gallons.
C— 2.15 gallons.

5454. (Refer to figure 8.) Determine the amount of fuel consumed during takeoff and climb at 70 percent power for 10 minutes.

A— 2.66 gallons.
B— 2.88 gallons.
C— 3.2 gallons.

5455. (Refer to figure 8.) With 38 gallons of fuel aboard at cruise power (55 percent), how much flight time is available with night VFR fuel reserve still remaining?

A— 2 hours 34 minutes.
B— 2 hours 49 minutes.
C— 3 hours 18 minutes.

5456. (Refer to figure 9.) Using a normal climb, how much fuel would be used from engine start to 12,000 feet pressure altitude?

Aircraft weight . . . . 3,800 lb
Airport pressure altitude . . . . 4,000 ft
Temperature . . . . 26 °C

A— 46 pounds.
B— 51 pounds.
C— 58 pounds.

5457. (Refer to figure 9.) Using a normal climb, how much fuel would be used from engine start to 10,000 feet pressure altitude?

Aircraft weight . . . . 3,500 lb
Airport pressure altitude . . . . 4,000 ft
Temperature . . . . 21 °C

A— 23 pounds.
B— 31 pounds.
C— 35 pounds.

5458. (Refer to figure 10.) Using a maximum rate of climb, how much fuel would be used from engine start to 6,000 feet pressure altitude?

Aircraft weight . . . . 3,200 lb
Airport pressure altitude . . . . 2,000 ft
Temperature . . . . 27 °C

A— 10 pounds.
B— 14 pounds.
C— 24 pounds.

5459. (Refer to figure 10.) Using a maximum rate of climb, how much fuel would be used from engine start to 10,000 feet pressure altitude?

Aircraft weight . . . . 3,800 lb
Airport pressure altitude . . . . 4,000 ft
Temperature . . . . 30 °C

A— 28 pounds.
B— 35 pounds.
C— 40 pounds.

5460. (Refer to figure 11.) If the cruise altitude is 7,500 feet, using 64 percent power at 2,500 RPM, what would be the range with 48 gallons of usable fuel?

A— 635 miles.
B— 645 miles.
C— 810 miles.

5461. (Refer to figure 11.) What would be the endurance at an altitude of 7,500 feet, using 52 percent power?

NOTE: (With 48 gallons fuel-no reserve.)

A— 6.1 hours.
B— 7.7 hours.
C— 8.0 hours.

5462. (Refer to figure 11.) What would be the approximate true airspeed and fuel consumption per hour at an altitude of 7,500 feet, using 52 percent power?

A— 103 MPH TAS, 7.7 GPH.
B— 105 MPH TAS, 6.1 GPH.
C— 105 MPH TAS, 6.2 GPH.

5463. (Refer to figure 12.)

GIVEN:

Pressure altitude . . . . 18,000 ft
Temperature . . . . -21 °C
Power . . . . 2,400 RPM - 28" MP
Recommended lean mixture
   usable fuel . . . . 425 lb

What is the approximate flight time available under the given conditions? (Allow for VFR day fuel reserve.)

A— 3 hours 46 minutes.
B— 4 hours 1 minute.
C— 4 hours 31 minutes.

5464. (Refer to figure 12.)

GIVEN:

Pressure altitude . . . . 18,000 ft
Temperature . . . . -41 °C
Power . . . . 2,500 RPM - 26" MP
Recommended lean mixture
   usable fuel . . . . 318 lb

What is the approximate flight time available under the given conditions? (Allow for VFR night fuel reserve.)

A— 2 hours 27 minutes.
B— 3 hours 12 minutes.
C— 3 hours 42 minutes.

5465. (Refer to figure 12.)

GIVEN:

Pressure altitude . . . . 18,000 ft
Temperature . . . . -1 °C
Power . . . . 2,200 RPM - 20" MP
Best fuel economy
   usable fuel . . . . 344 lb

What is the approximate flight time available under the given conditions? (Allow for VFR day fuel reserve.)

A— 4 hours 50 minutes.
B— 5 hours 20 minutes.
C— 5 hours 59 minutes.

5466. An airplane descends to an airport under the following conditions:

Cruising altitude . . . . 6,500 ft
Airport elevation . . . . 700 ft
Descends to . . . . 800 ft AGL
Rate of descent . . . . 500 ft/min
Average true airspeed . . . . 110 kts
True course . . . . 335°
Average wind velocity . . . . 060° at 15 kts
Variation . . . . 3°W
Deviation . . . . +2°
Average fuel consumption . . . . 8.5 gal/hr

Determine the approximate time, compass heading, distance, and fuel consumed during the descent.

A— 10 minutes, 348°, 18 NM, 1.4 gallons.
B— 10 minutes, 355°, 17 NM, 2.4 gallons.
C— 12 minutes, 346°, 18 NM, 1.6 gallons.

5467. An airplane descends to an airport under the following conditions:

Cruising altitude . . . . 7,500 ft
Airport elevation . . . . 1,300 ft
Descends to . . . . 800 ft AGL
Rate of descent . . . . 300 ft/min
Average true airspeed . . . . 120 kts
True course . . . . 165°
Average wind velocity . . . . 240° at 20 kts
Variation . . . . 4°E
Deviation . . . . -2°
Average fuel consumption . . . . 9.6 gal/hr

Determine the approximate time, compass heading, distance, and fuel consumed during the descent.

A— 16 minutes, 168°, 30 NM, 2.9 gallons.
B— 18 minutes, 164°, 34 NM, 3.2 gallons.
C— 18 minutes, 168°, 34 NM, 2.9 gallons.

5468. An airplane descends to an airport under the following conditions:

Cruising altitude . . . . 10,500 ft
Airport elevation . . . . 1,700 ft
Descends to . . . . 1,000 ft AGL
Rate of descent . . . . 600 ft/min
Average true airspeed . . . . 135 kts
True course . . . . 263°
Average wind velocity . . . . 330° at 30 kts
Variation . . . . 7°E
Deviation . . . . +3°
Average fuel consumption . . . . 11.5 gal/hr

Determine the approximate time, compass heading, distance, and fuel consumed during the descent.

A— 9 minutes, 274°, 26 NM, 2.8 gallons.
B— 13 minutes, 274°, 28 NM, 2.5 gallons.
C— 13 minutes, 271°, 26 NM, 2.5 gallons.

5469. If fuel consumption is 80 pounds per hour and groundspeed is 180 knots, how much fuel is required for an airplane to travel 460 NM?

A— 205 pounds.
B— 212 pounds.
C— 460 pounds.

5470. If an airplane is consuming 95 pounds of fuel per hour at a cruising altitude of 6,500 feet and the groundspeed is 173 knots, how much fuel is required to travel 450 NM?

A— 248 pounds.
B— 265 pounds.
C— 284 pounds.

5471. If an airplane is consuming 12.5 gallons of fuel per hour at a cruising altitude of 8,500 feet and the groundspeed is 145 knots, how much fuel is required to travel 435 NM?

A— 27 gallons.
B— 34 gallons.
C— 38 gallons.

5472. If an airplane is consuming 9.5 gallons of fuel per hour at a cruising altitude of 6,000 feet and the groundspeed is 135 knots, how much fuel is required to travel 490 NM?

A— 27 gallons.
B— 30 gallons.
C— 35 gallons.

5473. If an airplane is consuming 14.8 gallons of fuel per hour at a cruising altitude of 7,500 feet and the groundspeed is 167 knots, how much fuel is required to travel 560 NM?

A— 50 gallons.
B— 53 gallons.
C— 57 gallons.

5474. If fuel consumption is 14.7 gallons per hour and groundspeed is 157 knots, how much fuel is required for an airplane to travel 612 NM?

A— 58 gallons.
B— 60 gallons.
C— 64 gallons.

5475. GIVEN:

True course .... 105°
True heading .... 085°
True airspeed .... 95 kts
Groundspeed .... 87 kts

Determine the wind direction and speed.

A— 020° and 32 knots.
B— 030° and 38 knots.
C— 200° and 32 knots.

5476. GIVEN:

True course .... 345°
True heading .... 355°
True airspeed .... 85 kts
Groundspeed .... 95 kts

Determine the wind direction and speed.

A— 095° and 19 knots.
B— 113° and 19 knots.
C— 238° and 18 knots.

5477. You have flown 52 miles, are 6 miles off course, and have 118 miles yet to fly. To converge on your destination, the total correction angle would be

A— 3°.
B— 6°.
C— 10°.

5478. GIVEN:

Distance off course .... 9 mi
Distance flown .... 95 mi
Distance to fly .... 125 mi

To converge at the destination, the total correction angle would be

A— 4°.
B— 6°.
C— 10°.

5479. True course measurements on a Sectional Aeronautical Chart should be made at a meridian near the midpoint of the course because the

A— values of isogonic lines change from point to point.
B— angles formed by isogonic lines and lines of latitude vary from point to point.
C— angles formed by lines of longitude and the course line vary from point to point.

* * *

5481. GIVEN:

Wind .... 175° at 20 kts
Distance .... 135 NM
True course .... 075°
True airspeed .... 80 kts
Fuel consumption .... 105 lb/hr

Determine the time en route and fuel consumption.

A— 1 hour 28 minutes and 73.2 pounds.
B— 1 hour 38 minutes and 158 pounds.
C— 1 hour 40 minutes and 175 pounds.

5482. (Refer to figure 13.)

GIVEN:

Aircraft weight .... 3,400 lb
Airport pressure altitude .... 6,000 ft
Temperature at 6,000 feet .... 10 °C

Using a maximum rate of climb under the given conditions, how much fuel would be used from engine start to a pressure altitude of 16,000 feet?

A— 43 pounds.
B— 45 pounds.
C— 49 pounds.

5483. (Refer to figure 13.)

GIVEN:

Aircraft weight .... 4,000 lb
Airport pressure altitude .... 2,000 ft
Temperature at 2,000 feet .... 32 °C

Using a maximum rate of climb under the given conditions, how much time would be required to climb to a pressure altitude of 8,000 feet?

A— 7 minutes.
B— 8.4 minutes.
C— 11.2 minutes.

5484. (Refer to figure 14.)

GIVEN:

Aircraft weight .... 3,700 lb
Airport pressure altitude .... 4,000 ft
Temperature at 4,000 feet .... 21 °C

Using a normal climb under the given conditions, how much fuel would be used from engine start to a pressure altitude of 12,000 feet?

A— 30 pounds.
B— 37 pounds.
C— 46 pounds.

5485. (Refer to figure 14.)

GIVEN:

Weight .... 3,400 lb
Airport pressure altitude .... 4,000 ft
Temperature at 4,000 feet .... 14 °C

Using a normal climb under the given conditions, how much time would be required to climb to a pressure altitude of 8,000 feet?

A— 4.8 minutes.
B— 5 minutes.
C— 5.5 minutes.

5486. (Refer to figure 15.)

GIVEN:

Airport pressure altitude .... 4,000 ft
Airport temperature .... 12 °C
Cruise pressure altitude .... 9,000 ft
Cruise temperature .... -4 °C

What will be the distance required to climb to cruise altitude under the given conditions?

A— 6 miles.
B— 8.5 miles.
C— 11 miles.

5487. (Refer to figure 15.)

GIVEN:

Airport pressure altitude .... 2,000 ft
Airport température .... 20 °C
Cruise pressure altitude .... 10,000 ft
Cruise temperature .... 0 °C

What will be the fuel, time, and distance required to climb to cruise altitude under the given conditions?

A— 5 gallons, 9 minutes, 13 NM.
B— 6 gallons, 11 minutes, 16 NM.
C— 7 gallons, 12 minutes, 18 NM.

5488. An airplane departs an airport under the following conditions:

Airport elevation .... 1,000 ft
Cruise altitude .... 9,500 ft
Rate of climb .... 500 ft/min
Average true airspeed .... 135 kts
True course .... 215°
Average wind velocity .... 290° at 20 kts
Variation .... 3°W
Deviation .... -2°
Average fuel consumption .... 13 gal/hr

Determine the approximate time, compass heading, distance, and fuel consumed during the climb.

A— 14 minutes, 234°, 26 NM, 3.9 gallons.
B— 17 minutes, 224°, 36 NM, 3.7 gallons.
C— 17 minutes, 242°, 31 NM, 3.5 gallons.

5489. An airplane departs an airport under the following conditions:

Airport elevation .... 1,500 ft
Cruise altitude .... 9,500 ft
Rate of climb .... 500 ft/min
Average true airspeed .... 160 kts
True course .... 145°
Average wind velocity .... 080° at 15 kts
Variation .... 5°E
Deviation .... -3°
Average fuel consumption .... 14 gal/hr

Determine the approximate time, compass heading, distance, and fuel consumed during the climb.

A— 14 minutes, 128°, 35 NM, 3.2 gallons.
B— 16 minutes, 132°, 41 NM, 3.7 gallons.
C— 16 minutes, 128°, 32 NM, 3.8 gallons.

5490. Which is true about homing when using ADF during crosswind conditions? Homing

A— to a radio station results in a curved path that leads to the station.
B— is a practical navigation method for flying both to and from a radio station.
C— to a radio station requires that the ADF have an automatically or manually rotatable azimuth.

5491. Which is true regarding tracking on a desired bearing when using ADF during crosswind conditions?

A— To track outbound, heading corrections should be made away from the ADF pointer.
B— When on the desired track outbound with the proper drift correction established, the ADF pointer will be deflected to the windward side of the tail position.
C— When on the desired track inbound with the proper drift correction established, the ADF pointer will be deflected to the windward side of the nose position.

5492. An aircraft is maintaining a magnetic heading of 265° and the ADF shows a relative bearing of 065°. This indicates that the aircraft is crossing the

A— 065° magnetic bearing FROM the radio beacon.
B— 150° magnetic bearing FROM the radio beacon.
C— 330° magnetic bearing FROM the radio beacon.

5493. The magnetic heading is 315° and the ADF shows a relative bearing of 140°. The magnetic bearing FROM the radiobeacon would be

A— 095°.
B— 175°.
C— 275°.

5494. The magnetic heading is 350° and the relative bearing to a radiobeacon is 240°. What would be the magnetic bearing TO that radiobeacon?

A— 050°.
B— 230°.
C— 295°.

5495. The ADF is tuned to a radiobeacon. If the magnetic heading is 040° and the relative bearing is 290°, the magnetic bearing TO that radiobeacon would be

A— 150°.
B— 285°.
C— 330°.

5496. If the relative bearing to a nondirectional radiobeacon is 045° and the magnetic heading is 355°, the magnetic bearing TO that radiobeacon would be

A— 040°.
B— 065°.
C— 220°.

5497. (Refer to figure 16.) If the aircraft continues its present heading as shown in instrument group 3, what will be the relative bearing when the aircraft reaches the magnetic bearing of 030° FROM the NDB?

A— 030°.
B— 060°.
C— 240°.

5498. (Refer to figure 16.) At the position indicated by instrument group 1, what would be the relative bearing if the aircraft were turned to a magnetic heading of 090°?

A— 150°.
B— 190°.
C— 250°.

5499. (Refer to figure 16.) At the position indicated by instrument group 1, to intercept the 330° magnetic bearing to the NDB at a 30° angle, the aircraft should be turned

A— left to a heading of 270°.
B— right to a heading of 330°.
C— right to a heading of 360°.

5500. Which situation would result in reverse sensing of a VOR receiver?

A— Flying a heading that is reciprocal to the bearing selected on the OBS.
B— Setting the OBS to a bearing that is 90° from the bearing on which the aircraft is located.
C— Failing to change the OBS from the selected inbound course to the outbound course after passing the station.

5501. To track outbound on the 180 radial of a VOR station, the recommended procedure is to set the OBS to

A— 360° and make heading corrections toward the CDI needle.
B— 180° and make heading corrections away from the CDI needle.
C— 180° and make heading corrections toward the CDI needle.

5502. To track inbound on the 215 radial of a VOR station, the recommended procedure is to set the OBS to

A— 215° and make heading corrections toward the CDI needle.
B— 215° and make heading corrections away from the CDI needle.
C— 035° and make heading corrections toward the CDI needle.

5503. When diverting to an alternate airport because of an emergency, pilots should

A— rely upon radio as the primary method of navigation.
B— climb to a higher altitude because it will be easier to identify checkpoints.
C— apply rule-of-thumb computations, estimates, and other appropriate shortcuts to divert to the new course as soon as possible.

5504. To use VHF/DF facilities for assistance in locating your position, you must have an operative VHF

A— transmitter and receiver.
B— transmitter and receiver, and an operative ADF receiver.
C— transmitter and receiver, and an operative VOR receiver.

5505. Which maximum range factor decreases as weight decreases?

A— Altitude.
B— Airspeed.
C— Angle of attack.

5506. (Refer to figure 17.) Which illustration indicates that the airplane will intercept the 360 radial at a 60° angle inbound, if the present heading is maintained?

A— 3.
B— 4.
C— 5.

5507. (Refer to figure 17.) Which statement is true regarding illustration 2, if the present heading is maintained? The airplane will

A— cross the 180 radial at a 45° angle outbound.
B— intercept the 225 radial at a 45° angle.
C— intercept the 360 radial at a 45° angle inbound.

5508. (Refer to figure 17.) Which illustration indicates that the airplane will intercept the 060 radial at a 75° angle outbound, if the present heading is maintained?

A— 4.
B— 5.
C— 6.

5509. (Refer to figure 17.) Which illustration indicates that the airplane should be turned 150° left to intercept the 360 radial at a 60° angle inbound?

A— 1.
B— 2.
C— 3.

5510. (Refer to figure 17.) Which is true regarding illustration 4, if the present heading is maintained? The airplane will

A— cross the 060 radial at a 15° angle.
B— intercept the 240 radial at a 30° angle.
C— cross the 180 radial at a 75° angle.

5511. (Refer to figure 18.) To intercept a magnetic bearing of 240° FROM at a 030° angle (while outbound), the airplane should be turned

A— left 065°.
B— left 125°.
C— right 270°.

5512. (Refer to figure 18.) If the airplane continues to fly on the heading as shown, what magnetic bearing FROM the station would be intercepted at a 35° angle outbound?

A— 035°.
B— 070°.
C— 215°.

5513. (Refer to figure 19.) If the airplane continues to fly on the magnetic heading as illustrated, what magnetic bearing FROM the station would be intercepted at a 35° angle?

A— 090°.
B— 270°.
C— 305°.

5514. (Refer to figure 19.) If the airplane continues to fly on the magnetic heading as illustrated, what magnetic bearing FROM the station would be intercepted at a 30° angle?

A— 090°.
B— 270°.
C— 310°.

5515. The relative bearing on an ADF changes from 265° to 260° in 2 minutes of elapsed time. If the groundspeed is 145 knots, the distance to that station would be

A— 26 NM.
B— 37 NM.
C— 58 NM.

5516. The ADF indicates a wingtip bearing change of 10° in 2 minutes of elapsed time, and the TAS is 160 knots. What is the distance to the station?

A— 15 NM.
B— 32 NM.
C— 36 NM.

5517. With a TAS of 115 knots, the relative bearing on an ADF changes from 090° to 095° in 1.5 minutes of elapsed time. The distance to the station would be

A— 12.5 NM.
B— 24.5 NM.
C— 34.5 NM.

5518. GIVEN:

Wingtip bearing change . . . . 5°
Time elapsed between bearing change . . . 5 min
True airspeed . . . . 115 kts

The distance to the station is

A— 36 NM.
B— 57.5 NM.
C— 115 NM.

5519. The ADF is tuned to a nondirectional radiobeacon and the relative bearing changes from 095° to 100° in 1.5 minutes of elapsed time. The time en route to that station would be

A— 18 minutes.
B— 24 minutes.
C— 30 minutes.

5520. The ADF is tuned to a nondirectional radiobeacon and the relative bearing changes from 270° to 265° in 2.5 minutes of elapsed time. The time en route to that beacon would be

A— 9 minutes.
B— 18 minutes.
C— 30 minutes.

5521. The ADF is tuned to a nondirectional radiobeacon and the relative bearing changes from 085° to 090° in 2 minutes of elapsed time. The time en route to the station would be

A— 15 minutes.
B— 18 minutes.
C— 24 minutes.

5522. If the relative bearing changes from 090° to 100° in 2.5 minutes of elapsed time, the time en route to the station would be

A— 12 minutes.
B— 15 minutes.
C— 18 minutes.

5523. The ADF is tuned to a nondirectional radiobeacon and the relative bearing changes from 090° to 100° in 2.5 minutes of elapsed time. If the true airspeed is 90 knots, the distance and time en route to that radiobeacon would be

A— 15 miles and 22.5 minutes.
B— 22.5 miles and 15 minutes.
C— 32 miles and 18 minutes.

5524. GIVEN:

Wingtip bearing change . . . . 10°
Elapsed time between bearing change . . . 4 min
Rate of fuel consumption . . . . 11 gal/hr

Calculate the fuel required to fly to the station.

A— 4.4 gallons.
B— 8.4 gallons.
C— 12 gallons.

5525. GIVEN:

Wingtip bearing change . . . . 5°
Elapsed time between bearing change . . . 6 min
Rate of fuel consumption . . . . 12 gal/hr

The fuel required to fly to the station is

A— 8.2 gallons.
B— 14.4 gallons.
C— 18.7 gallons.

5526. GIVEN:

Wingtip bearing change . . . . 15°
Elapsed time between bearing change . . . 6 min
Rate of fuel consumption . . . . 8.6 gal/hr

Calculate the approximate fuel required to fly to the station.

A— 3.44 gallons.
B— 6.88 gallons.
C— 17.84 gallons.

5527. GIVEN:

Wingtip bearing change . . . . 15°
Elapsed time between bearing change . . 7.5 min
True airspeed . . . . 85 kts
Rate of fuel consumption . . . . 9.6 gal/hr

The time, distance, and fuel required to fly to the station is

A— 30 minutes; 42.5 miles; 4.80 gallons.
B— 32 minutes; 48 miles; 5.58 gallons.
C— 48 minutes; 48 miles; 4.58 gallons.

5528. While maintaining a constant heading, a relative bearing of 15° doubles in 6 minutes. The time to the station being used is

A— 3 minutes.
B— 6 minutes.
C— 12 minutes.

5529. While maintaining a constant heading, the ADF needle increases from a relative bearing of 045° to 090° in 5 minutes. The time to the station being used is

A— 5 minutes.
B— 10 minutes.
C— 15 minutes.

5530. While cruising at 135 knots and on a constant heading, the ADF needle decreases from a relative bearing of 315° to 270° in 7 minutes. The approximate time and distance to the station being used is

A— 7 minutes and 16 miles.
B— 14 minutes and 28 miles.
C— 19 minutes and 38 miles.

5531. While maintaining a constant heading, a relative bearing of 10° doubles in 5 minutes. If the true airspeed is 105 knots, the time and distance to the station being used is approximately

A— 5 minutes and 8.7 miles.
B— 10 minutes and 17 miles.
C— 15 minutes and 31.2 miles.

5532. When checking the course sensitivity of a VOR receiver, how many degrees should the OBS be rotated to move the CDI from the center to the last dot on either side?

A— 5° to 10°.
B— 10° to 12°.
C— 18° to 20°.

5533. An aircraft 60 miles from a VOR station has a CDI indication of one-fifth deflection, this represents a course centerline deviation of approximately

A— 6 miles.
B— 2 miles.
C— 1 mile.

5534. (Refer to figure 20.) Using instrument group 3, if the aircraft makes a 180° turn to the left and continues straight ahead, it will intercept which radial?

A— 135 radial.
B— 270 radial.
C— 360 radial.

5535. (Refer to figure 20.) Which instrument shows the aircraft in a position where a 180° turn would result in the aircraft intercepting the 150 radial at a 30° angle?

A— 2.
B— 3.
C— 4.

5536. (Refer to figure 20.) Which instrument shows the aircraft in a position where a straight course after a 90° left turn would result in intercepting the 180 radial?

A— 2.
B— 3.
C— 4.

5537. (Refer to figure 20.) Which instrument shows the aircraft to be northwest of the VORTAC?

A— 1.
B— 2.
C— 3.

5538. (Refer to figure 20.) Which instrument(s) show(s) that the aircraft is getting further from the selected VORTAC?

A— 4.
B— 1 and 4.
C— 2 and 3.

5539. While maintaining a magnetic heading of 270° and a true airspeed of 120 knots, the 360 radial of a VOR is crossed at 1237 and the 350 radial is crossed at 1244. The approximate time and distance to this station are

A— 42 minutes and 84 NM.
B— 42 minutes and 91 NM.
C— 44 minutes and 96 NM.

5540. (Refer to figure 21.) If the time flown between aircraft positions 2 and 3 is 13 minutes, what is the estimated time to the station?

A— 13 minutes.
B— 17 minutes.
C— 26 minutes.

5541. (Refer to figure 22.) If the time flown between aircraft positions 2 and 3 is 8 minutes, what is the estimated time to the station?

A— 8 minutes.
B— 16 minutes.
C— 48 minutes.

5542. (Refer to figure 23.) If the time flown between aircraft positions 2 and 3 is 13 minutes, what is the estimated time to the station?

A— 7.8 minutes.
B— 13 minutes.
C— 26 minutes.

5543. (Refer to figure 24.) If the time flown between aircraft positions 2 and 3 is 15 minutes, what is the estimated time to the station?

A— 15 minutes.
B— 30 minutes.
C— 60 minutes.

5544. Inbound on the 040 radial, a pilot selects the 055 radial, turns 15° to the left, and notes the time. While maintaining a constant heading, the pilot notes the time for the CDI to center is 15 minutes. Based on this information, the ETE to the station is

A— 8 minutes.
B— 15 minutes.
C— 30 minutes.

5545. Inbound on the 090 radial, a pilot rotates the OBS 010° to the left, turns 010° to the right, and notes the time. While maintaining a constant heading, the pilot determines that the elapsed time for the CDI to center is 8 minutes. Based on this information, the ETE to the station is

A— 8 minutes.
B— 16 minutes.
C— 24 minutes.

5546. Inbound on the 315 radial, a pilot selects the 320 radial, turns 5° to the left, and notes the time. While maintaining a constant heading, the pilot notes the time for the CDI to center is 12 minutes. The ETE to the station is

A— 10 minutes.
B— 12 minutes.
C— 24 minutes.

5547. Inbound on the 190 radial, a pilot selects the 195 radial, turns 5° to the left, and notes the time. While maintaining a constant heading, the pilot notes the time for the CDI to center is 10 minutes. The ETE to the station is

A— 10 minutes.
B— 15 minutes.
C— 20 minutes.

5548. (Refer to figures 25 and 25A.) During the ILS RWY 13L procedure at DSM, what altitude minimum applies if the glide slope becomes inoperative?

A— 1,420 feet.
B— 1,360 feet.
C— 1,121 feet.

5549. What does the absence of the procedure turn barb on the plan view on an approach chart indicate?

A— A procedure turn is not authorized.
B— Teardrop-type procedure turn is authorized.
C— Racetrack-type procedure turn is authorized.

5550. When making an instrument approach at the selected alternate airport, what landing minimums apply?

A— Standard alternate minimums.
B— The IFR alternate minimums listed for that airport.
C— The landing minimums published for the type of procedure selected.

5551. How should the pilot make a VOR receiver check when the aircraft is located on the designated checkpoint on the airport surface?

A— Set the OBS on 180° plus or minus 4°; the CDI should center with a FROM indication.
B— Set the OBS on the designated radial. The CDI must center within plus or minus 4° of that radial with a FROM indication.
C— With the aircraft headed directly toward the VOR and the OBS set to 000°, the CDI should center within plus or minus 4° of that radial with a TO indication.

5552. When using VOT to make a VOR receiver check, the CDI should be centered and the OBS should indicate that the aircraft is on the

A— 090 radial.
B— 180 radial.
C— 360 radial.

5553. When the CDI needle is centered during an airborne VOR check, the omnibearing selector and the TO/FROM indicator should read

A— within 4° of the selected radial.
B— within 6° of the selected radial.
C— 0° TO, only if you are due south of the VOR.

* * *

5556. Which is true regarding the use of a Standard Instrument Departure (SID) chart?

A— At airfields where SID's have been established, SID usage is mandatory for IFR departures.
B— To use a SID, the pilot must possess at least the textual description of the approved standard departure.
C— To use a SID, the pilot must possess both the textual and graphic form of the approved standard departure.

5557. Which is true regarding STAR's? STAR's are

A— used to separate IFR and VFR traffic.
B— established to simplify clearance delivery procedures.
C— used at certain airports to decrease traffic congestion.

5558. While being radar vectored, an approach clearance is received. The last assigned altitude should be maintained until

A— reaching the FAF.
B— advised to begin descent.
C— established on a segment of a published route or instrument approach procedure.

5559. Flight Service Stations in the conterminous 48 United States having voice capability on VOR's or radiobeacons (NDB's) broadcast

A— AIRMET's and SIGMET's at 15 minutes past the hour and each 15 minutes thereafter as long as they are in effect.
B— AIRMET's and Nonconvective SIGMET's upon receipt and at 15 minutes and 45 minutes past the hour for the first hour after issuance.
C— hourly weather reports at 15 and 45 minutes past each hour for those reporting stations within approximately 150 NM of the broadcast stations.

5560. To obtain a continuous transcribed weather briefing including winds aloft and route forecasts for a cross-country flight, a pilot could monitor

A— a TWEB on a low-frequency radio receiver.
B— the regularly scheduled weather broadcast on a VOR frequency.
C— a high-frequency radio receiver tuned to En Route Flight Advisory Service.

5561. (Refer to figures 26 and 26A.) The final approach fix for the precision approach is located at

A— DENAY Intersection.
B— Glide slope intercept.
C— ROMEN Intersection/Locator outer marker.

* * *

5564. Which is true relating to the blue and magenta colors used to depict airports on Sectional Aeronautical Charts?

A— Class E airports are shown in blue; Class C and D are magenta.
B— Class B airports are shown in blue; Class D and E are magenta.
C— Class E airports are shown in magenta; Class B, C, and D are blue.

5565. (Refer to figure 52, point A.) The floor of the Class E airspace above Georgetown Airport (Q61) is at

A— the surface.
B— 3,788 feet MSL.
C— 700 feet AGL.

5566. (Refer to figure 52, point G.) The floor of Class E airspace over the town of Woodland is

A— 700 feet AGL over part of the town and no floor over the remainder.
B— 1,200 feet AGL over part of the town and no floor over the remainder.
C— both 700 feet and 1,200 feet AGL.

5567. (Refer to figure 52, point E.) The floor of the Class E airspace over University Airport (O05) is

A— the surface.
B— 700 feet AGL.
C— 1,200 feet AGL.

5568. (Refer to figure 52, point H.) The floor of the Class E airspace over the town of Auburn is

A— 1,200 feet MSL.
B— 700 feet AGL.
C— 1,200 feet AGL.

5569. (Refer to figure 53, point A.) This thin black shaded line is most likely

A— an arrival route.
B— a military training route.
C— a state boundary line.

5570. (Refer to figure 53, point B.) The 16 indicates

A— an antenna top at 1,600 feet AGL.
B— the maximum elevation figure for that quadrangle.
C— the minimum safe sector altitude for that quadrangle.

* * *

5572. (Refer to figure 54, point A.) What minimum altitude is required to avoid the Livermore Airport (LVK) Class D airspace?

A— 2,503 feet MSL.
B— 2,901 feet MSL.
C— 3,297 feet MSL.

* * *

5574. (Refer to figure 54, point A.) Flight over Livermore Airport (LVK) at 300 feet MSL

A— requires a transponder, but ATC communication is not necessary.
B— does not require a transponder or ATC communication.
C— cannot be accomplished without meeting all Class B airspace requirements.

5575. (Refer to figure 52, point I.) The rectangular blue box depicted is airspace within which

A— there is a high volume of pilot training activities or an unusual type of aerial activity, neither of which is hazardous to aircraft.
B— the flight of aircraft is prohibited.
C— the flight of aircraft, while not prohibited, is subject to restriction.

5576. (Refer to figure 54, point D.) The thinner outer blue circle depicted around San Francisco International Airport is

A— the outer segment of Class B airspace.
B— an area within which an appropriate transponder must be used from outside of the Class B airspace from the surface to 10,000 feet MSL.
C— a Mode C veil boundary where a balloon may penetrate without a transponder provided it remains below 8,000 feet.

5577. When fixed wing Special Visual Flight Rules (SVFR) operation is prohibited at an airport, the sectional aeronautical chart will

A— depict "TTTT" symbols in a circular fashion around that airport.
B— State "No SVFR" near the airport symbol.
C— not depict this information.

* * *

5581. (Refer to figure 52, point D.) The highest obstruction with high intensity lighting within 10 NM of Lincoln Airport (O51) is how high above the ground?

A— 1,254 feet.
B— 662 feet.
C— 299 feet.

* * *

5583. (Refer to figure 52, point F.) Mosier Airport is

A— an airport restricted to use by private and recreational pilots.
B— a restricted military stage field within restricted airspace.
C— a nonpublic use airport.

* * *

5585. (Refer to figure 52, point D.) The terrain at the obstruction approximately 8 NM east southeast of the Lincoln Airport is approximately how much higher than the airport elevation?

A— 376 feet.
B— 835 feet.
C— 1,135 feet.

* * *

5587. (Refer to figure 54, point F.) The Class C airspace at Metropolitan Oakland International (OAK) which extends from the surface upward has a ceiling of

A— both 2,100 feet and 3,000 feet MSL.
B— 8,000 feet MSL.
C— 2,100 feet AGL.

5588. (Refer to figure 53.)

GIVEN:
Altitude . . . . 1,000 ft AGL
Position . . . . 7 NM north of point E
Time . . . . 3 p.m. local
Flight visibility . . . . 1 SM

You are VFR approaching Madera Airport (point E) for a landing from the north. You

A— are in violation of the FAR's; you need 3 miles of visibility under VFR.
B— are required to descend to below 700 feet AGL before entering Class E airspace and may continue for landing.
C— may descend to 800 feet AGL (Pattern Altitude) after entering Class E airspace and continue to the airport.

* * *

5591. (Refer to figures 55 and 55A.) En route on V112 from BTG VORTAC to LTJ VORTAC, the minimum altitude crossing GYMME intersection is

A— 6,400 feet.
B— 6,500 feet.
C— 7,000 feet.

5592. (Refer to figures 55 and 55A.) En route on V448 from YKM VORTAC to BTG VORTAC, what minimum navigation equipment is required to identify ANGOO intersection?

A— One VOR receiver.
B— One VOR receiver and DME.
C— Two VOR receivers.

5593. (Refer to figures 55 and 55A.) En route on V468 from BTG VORTAC to YKM VORTAC, the minimum en route altitude at TROTS intersection is

A— 7,100 feet.
B— 10,000 feet.
C— 11,500 feet.

5594. (Refer to figures 27 and 27A.) In the DEN ILS RWY 35R procedure the FAF intercept altitude is

A— 7,488 feet MSL.
B— 7,500 feet MSL.
C— 9,000 feet MSL.

5595. (Refer to figures 27 and 27A.) The symbol [8100] in the MSA circle of the ILS RWY 35R procedure at DEN represents a minimum safe sector altitude within 25 NM of

A— Denver VORTAC.
B— Gandi outer marker.
C— Denver/Stapleton International Airport.

5596. (Refer to figures 28 and 28A.) During the ILS RWY 31R procedure at DSM, the minimum altitude for glide slope interception is

A— 2,365 feet MSL.
B— 2,500 feet MSL.
C— 3,000 feet MSL.

5597. (Refer to figures 28 and 28A.) If the glide slope becomes inoperative during the ILS RWY 31R procedure at DSM, what MDA applies?

A— 1,157 feet.
B— 1,320 feet.
C— 1,360 feet.

5598. (Refer to figures 29 and 29A.) When approaching the ATL ILS RWY 8L, how far from the FAF is the missed approach point?

A— 4.8 NM.
B— 5.2 NM.
C— 12.0 NM.

5599. (Refer to figures 30 and 30A.) When approaching the VOR/DME-A, the symbol [2800] in the MSA circle represents a minimum safe sector altitude within 25 NM of

A— DEANI intersection.
B— White Cloud VORTAC.
C— Baldwin Municipal Airport.

5600. (Refer to figures 30 and 30A.) What minimum navigation equipment is required to complete the VOR/DME-A procedure?

A— One VOR receiver.
B— One VOR receiver and DME.
C— Two VOR receivers and DME.

5601. During a night operation, the pilot of aircraft 1 sees only the green light of aircraft 2. If the aircraft are converging, which pilot has the right-of-way? The pilot of aircraft

A— 2; aircraft 2 is to the right of aircraft 1.
B— 1; aircraft 1 is to the right of aircraft 2.
C— 2; aircraft 2 is to the left of aircraft 1.

5602. A pilot flying a single-engine airplane observes a multiengine airplane approaching on a collision course from the left. Which pilot should give way?

A— Each pilot should alter course to the right.
B— The pilot of the single-engine airplane should give way; the other airplane is to the left.
C— The pilot of the multiengine airplane should give way; the single-engine airplane is to its right.

5603. You are flying an airship under an IFR flight plan and experience two-way communications radio failure while in VFR conditions. In this situation, you should continue your flight under

A— VFR and land as soon as practicable.
B— VFR and proceed to your flight-plan destination.
C— IFR and maintain the last assigned route and altitude to your flight-plan destination.

5604. Why should flight speeds above V_{NE} be avoided?

A— Excessive induced drag will result in structural failure.
B— Design limit load factors may be exceeded, if gusts are encountered.
C— Control effectiveness is so impaired that the aircraft becomes uncontrollable.

5605. Maximum structural cruising speed is the maximum speed at which an airplane can be operated during

A— abrupt maneuvers.
B— normal operations.
C— flight in smooth air.

5606. Applying carburetor heat will

A— not affect the mixture.
B— lean the fuel/air mixture.
C— enrich the fuel/air mixture.

5607. An abnormally high engine oil temperature indication may be caused by

A— a defective bearing.
B— the oil level being too low.
C— operating with an excessively rich mixture.

5608. What will occur if no leaning is made with the mixture control as the flight altitude increases?

A— The volume of air entering the carburetor decreases and the amount of fuel decreases.
B— The density of air entering the carburetor decreases and the amount of fuel increases.
C— The density of air entering the carburetor decreases and the amount of fuel remains constant.

5609. Unless adjusted, the fuel/air mixture becomes richer with an increase in altitude because the amount of fuel

A— decreases while the volume of air decreases.
B— remains constant while the volume of air decreases.
C— remains constant while the density of air decreases.

5610. The basic purpose of adjusting the fuel/air mixture control at altitude is to

A— decrease the fuel flow to compensate for decreased air density.
B— decrease the amount of fuel in the mixture to compensate for increased air density.
C— increase the amount of fuel in the mixture to compensate for the decrease in pressure and density of the air.

5611. At high altitudes, an excessively rich mixture will cause the

A— engine to overheat.
B— fouling of spark plugs.
C— engine to operate smoother even though fuel consumption is increased.

5612. In the Northern Hemisphere, if a sailplane is accelerated or decelerated, the magnetic compass will normally indicate

A— correctly, only when on a north or south heading.
B— a turn toward south while accelerating on a west heading.
C— a turn toward north while decelerating on an east heading.

5613. When flying on a heading of west from one thermal to the next, the airspeed is increased to the speed-to-fly with the wings level. What will the conventional magnetic compass indicate while the airspeed is increasing?

A— A turn toward the south.
B— A turn toward the north.
C— Straight flight on a heading of 270°.

5614. What effect does an uphill runway slope have on takeoff performance?

A— Increases takeoff speed.
B— Increases takeoff distance.
C— Decreases takeoff distance.

5615. (Refer to figure 31.) Rwy 30 is being used for landing. Which surface wind would exceed the airplane's crosswind capability of 0.2 V_{SO}, if V_{SO} is 60 knots?

A— 260° at 20 knots.
B— 275° at 25 knots.
C— 315° at 35 knots.

5616. (Refer to figure 31.) If the tower-reported surface wind is 010° at 18 knots, what is the crosswind component for a Rwy 08 landing?

A— 7 knots.
B— 15 knots.
C— 17 knots.

5617. (Refer to figure 31.) The surface wind is 180° at 25 knots. What is the crosswind component for a Rwy 13 landing?

A— 19 knots.
B— 21 knots.
C— 23 knots.

5618. (Refer to figure 31.) What is the headwind component for a Rwy 13 takeoff if the surface wind is 190° at 15 knots?

A— 7 knots.
B— 13 knots.
C— 15 knots.

5619. (Refer to figure 32.)

GIVEN:

Temperature . . . . 75 °F
Pressure altitude . . . . 6,000 ft
Weight . . . . 2,900 lb
Headwind . . . . 20 kts

To safely take off over a 50-foot obstacle in 1,000 feet, what weight reduction is necessary?

A— 50 pounds.
B— 100 pounds.
C— 300 pounds.

5620. (Refer to figure 32.)

GIVEN:

Temperature . . . . 50 °F
Pressure altitude . . . . Sea level
Weight . . . . 2,700 lb
Wind . . . . Calm

What is the total takeoff distance over a 50-foot obstacle?

A— 550 feet.
B— 650 feet.
C— 750 feet.

5621. (Refer to figure 32.)

GIVEN:

Temperature . . . . 100 °F
Pressure altitude . . . . 4,000 ft
Weight . . . . 3,200 lb
Wind . . . . Calm

What is the ground roll required for takeoff over a 50-foot obstacle?

A— 1,180 feet.
B— 1,350 feet.
C— 1,850 feet.

5622. (Refer to figure 32.)

GIVEN:

Temperature . . . . 30 °F
Pressure altitude . . . . 6,000 ft
Weight . . . . 3,300 lb
Headwind . . . . 20 kts

What is the total takeoff distance over a 50-foot obstacle?

A— 1,100 feet.
B— 1,300 feet.
C— 1,500 feet.

5623. (Refer to figure 33.)

GIVEN:

Weight . . . . 4,000 lb
Pressure altitude . . . . 5,000 ft
Temperature . . . . 30 °C

What is the maximum rate of climb under the given conditions?

A— 655 ft/min.
B— 702 ft/min.
C— 774 ft/min.

5624. (Refer to figure 33.)

GIVEN:

Weight . . . . 3,700 lb
Pressure altitude . . . . 22,000 ft
Temperature . . . . -10 °C

What is the maximum rate of climb under the given conditions?

A— 305 ft/min.
B— 320 ft/min.
C— 384 ft/min.

5625. (Refer to figure 34.)

GIVEN:

Pressure altitude . . . . 6,000 ft
Temperature . . . . +3 °C
Power . . . . 2,200 RPM - 22" MP
Usable fuel available . . . . 465 lb

What is the maximum available flight time under the conditions stated?

A— 6 hours 27 minutes.
B— 6 hours 39 minutes.
C— 6 hours 56 minutes.

5626. (Refer to figure 34.)

GIVEN:

Pressure altitude . . . . 6,000 ft
Temperature . . . . -17 °C
Power . . . . 2,300 RPM - 23" MP
Usable fuel available . . . . 370 lb

What is the maximum available flight time under the conditions stated?

A— 4 hours 20 minutes.
B— 4 hours 30 minutes.
C— 4 hours 50 minutes.

5627. (Refer to figure 34.)

GIVEN:

Pressure altitude . . . . 6,000 ft
Temperature . . . . +13 °C
Power . . . . 2,500 RPM - 23" MP
Usable fuel available . . . . 460 lb

What is the maximum available flight time under the conditions stated?

A— 4 hours 58 minutes.
B— 5 hours 7 minutes.
C— 5 hours 12 minutes.

5628. (Refer to figure 35.)

GIVEN:

Temperature . . . . 70 °F
Pressure altitude . . . . Sea level
Weight . . . . 3,400 lb
Headwind . . . . 16 kts

Determine the approximate ground roll.

A— 689 feet.
B— 716 feet.
C— 1,275 feet.

5629. (Refer to figure 35.)

GIVEN:

Temperature	85 °F
Pressure altitude	6,000 ft
Weight	2,800 lb
Headwind	14 kts

Determine the approximate ground roll.

A— 742 feet.
B— 1,280 feet.
C— 1,480 feet.

5630. (Refer to figure 35.)

GIVEN:

Temperature	50 °F
Pressure altitude	Sea level
Weight	3,000 lb
Headwind	10 kts

Determine the approximate ground roll.

A— 425 feet.
B— 636 feet.
C— 836 feet.

5631. (Refer to figure 35.)

GIVEN:

Temperature	80 °F
Pressure altitude	4,000 ft
Weight	2,800 lb
Headwind	24 kts

What is the total landing distance over a 50-foot obstacle?

A— 1,125 feet.
B— 1,250 feet.
C— 1,325 feet.

5632. When computing weight and balance, the empty weight includes the weight of the airframe, engine(s), and all items of operating equipment permanently installed. Empty weight also includes

A— the unusable fuel, hydraulic fluid, and undrainable oil or, in some aircraft, all of the oil.
B— all usable fuel, maximum oil, hydraulic fluid, but does not include the weight of pilot, passengers, or baggage.
C— all usable fuel and oil, but does not include any radio equipment or instruments that were installed by someone other than the manufacturer.

5633. If all index units are positive when computing weight and balance, the location of the datum would be at the

A— centerline of the main wheels.
B— nose, or out in front of the airplane.
C— centerline of the nose or tailwheel, depending on the type of airplane.

5634. The CG of an aircraft can be determined by which of the following methods?

A— Dividing total arms by total moments.
B— Multiplying total arms by total weight.
C— Dividing total moments by total weight.

5635. The CG of an aircraft may be determined by

A— dividing total arms by total moments.
B— dividing total moments by total weight.
C— multiplying total weight by total moments.

5636. GIVEN:

Weight A — 155 pounds at 45 inches aft of datum
Weight B — 165 pounds at 145 inches aft of datum
Weight C — 95 pounds at 185 inches aft of datum

Based on this information, where would the CG be located aft of datum?

A— 86.0 inches.
B— 116.8 inches.
C— 125.0 inches.

5637. GIVEN:

Weight A — 140 pounds at 17 inches aft of datum
Weight B — 120 pounds at 110 inches aft of datum
Weight C — 85 pounds at 210 inches aft of datum

Based on this information, the CG would be located how far aft of datum?

A— 89.11 inches.
B— 96.89 inches.
C— 106.92 inches.

5638. GIVEN:

Weight A — 135 pounds at 15 inches aft of datum
Weight B — 205 pounds at 117 inches aft of datum
Weight C — 85 pounds at 195 inches aft of datum

Based on this information, the CG would be located how far aft of datum?

A— 100.2 inches.
B— 109.0 inches.
C— 121.7 inches.

5639. GIVEN:

Weight A — 175 pounds at 135 inches aft of datum
Weight B — 135 pounds at 115 inches aft of datum
Weight C — 75 pounds at 85 inches aft of datum

The CG for the combined weights would be located how far aft of datum?

A— 91.76 inches.
B— 111.67 inches.
C— 118.24 inches.

* * *

5646. GIVEN:

Total weight .... 4,137 lb
CG location .... station 67.8
Fuel consumption .... 13.7 GPH
Fuel CG .... station 68.0

After 1 hour 30 minutes of flight time, the CG would be located at station

A— 67.79.
B— 68.79.
C— 70.78.

5647. An aircraft is loaded with a ramp weight of 3,650 pounds and having a CG of 94.0, approximately how much baggage would have to be moved from the rear baggage area at station 180 to the forward baggage area at station 40 in order to move the CG to 92.0?

A— 52.14 pounds.
B— 62.24 pounds.
C— 78.14 pounds.

5648. An airplane is loaded to a gross weight of 4,800 pounds, with three pieces of luggage in the rear baggage compartment. The CG is located 98 inches aft of datum, which is 1 inch aft of limits. If luggage which weighs 90 pounds is moved from the rear baggage compartment (145 inches aft of datum) to the front compartment (45 inches aft of datum), what is the new CG?

A— 96.13 inches aft of datum.
B— 95.50 inches aft of datum.
C— 99.87 inches aft of datum.

5649. GIVEN:

Total weight .... 3,037 lb
CG location .... station 68.8
Fuel consumption .... 12.7 GPH
Fuel CG .... station 68.0

After 1 hour 45 minutes of flight time, the CG would be located at station

A— 68.77.
B— 68.83.
C— 69.77.

5650. (Refer to figure 38.)

GIVEN:

Empty weight (oil is included) .... 1,271 lb
Empty weight moment (in-lb/1,000) 102.04
Pilot and copilot .... 400 lb
Rear seat passenger .... 140 lb
Cargo .... 100 lb
Fuel .... 37 gal

Is the airplane loaded within limits?

A— Yes, the weight and CG is within limits.
B— No, the weight exceeds the maximum allowable.
C— No, the weight is acceptable, but the CG is aft of the aft limit.

5651. (Refer to figure 38.)

GIVEN:

Empty weight (oil is included) . . . . 1,271 lb
Empty weight moment (in-lb/1,000) 102.04
Pilot and copilot . . . . 260 lb
Rear seat passenger . . . . 120 lb
Cargo . . . . 60 lb
Fuel . . . . 37 gal

Under these conditions, the CG is determined to be located

A— within the CG envelope.
B— on the forward limit of the CG envelope.
C— within the shaded area of the CG envelope.

5652. (Refer to figure 38.)

GIVEN:

Empty weight (oil is included) . . . . 1,271 lb
Empty weight moment (in-lb/1,000) 102.04
Pilot and copilot . . . . 360 lb
Cargo . . . . 340 lb
Fuel . . . . 37 gal

Will the CG remain within limits after 30 gallons of fuel has been used in flight?

A— Yes, the CG will remain within limits.
B— No, the CG will be located aft of the aft CG limit.
C— Yes, but the CG will be located in the shaded area of the CG envelope.

5653. Frequent inspections should be made of aircraft exhaust manifold-type heating systems to minimize the possibility of

A— exhaust gases leaking into the cockpit.
B— a power loss due to back pressure in the exhaust system.
C— a cold-running engine due to the heat withdrawn by the heater.

5654. To establish a climb after takeoff in an aircraft equipped with a constant-speed propeller, the output of the engine is reduced to climb power by decreasing manifold pressure and

A— increasing RPM by decreasing propeller blade angle.
B— decreasing RPM by decreasing propeller blade angle.
C— decreasing RPM by increasing propeller blade angle.

5655. When taxiing during strong quartering tailwinds, which aileron positions should be used?

A— Neutral.
B— Aileron up on the side from which the wind is blowing.
C— Aileron down on the side from which the wind is blowing.

5656. While taxiing a light, high-wing airplane during strong quartering tailwinds, the aileron control should be positioned

A— neutral at all times.
B— toward the direction from which the wind is blowing.
C— opposite the direction from which the wind is blowing.

5657. (Refer to figure 51.) The pilot generally calls ground control after landing when the aircraft is completely clear of the runway. This is when you

A— pass the red symbol shown at the top of the figure.
B— are on the dashed-line side of the middle symbol.
C— are on the solid-line side of the middle symbol.

5658. (Refer to figure 51.) The red symbol at the top would most likely be found

A— upon exiting all runways prior to calling ground control.
B— where a roadway may be mistaken as a taxiway.
C— near the approach end of ILS runways.

5659. (Refer to figure 51.) While clearing an active runway you are most likely clear of the ILS critical area when you pass which symbol?

A— Top red.
B— Middle yellow.
C— Bottom yellow.

5660. (Refer to figure 51.) Which symbol does not directly address runway incursion with other aircraft?

A— Top red.
B— Middle yellow.
C— Bottom yellow.

5661. With regard to the technique required for a crosswind correction on takeoff, a pilot should use

A— aileron pressure into the wind and initiate the lift-off at a normal airspeed in both tailwheel- and nosewheel-type airplanes.
B— right rudder pressure, aileron pressure into the wind, and higher than normal lift-off airspeed in both tricycle- and conventional-gear airplanes.
C— rudder as required to maintain directional control, aileron pressure into the wind, and higher than normal lift-off airspeed in both conventional- and nosewheel-type airplanes.

5662. When turbulence is encountered during the approach to a landing, what action is recommended and for what primary reason?

A— Increase the airspeed slightly above normal approach speed to attain more positive control.
B— Decrease the airspeed slightly below normal approach speed to avoid overstressing the airplane.
C— Increase the airspeed slightly above normal approach speed to penetrate the turbulence as quickly as possible.

5663. A pilot's most immediate and vital concern in the event of complete engine failure after becoming airborne on takeoff is

A— maintaining a safe airspeed.
B— landing directly into the wind.
C— turning back to the takeoff field.

5664. Which type of approach and landing is recommended during gusty wind conditions?

A— A power-on approach and power-on landing.
B— A power-off approach and power-on landing.
C— A power-on approach and power-off landing.

5665. A proper crosswind landing on a runway requires that, at the moment of touchdown, the

A— direction of motion of the airplane and its lateral axis be perpendicular to the runway.
B— direction of motion of the airplane and its longitudinal axis be parallel to the runway.
C— downwind wing be lowered sufficiently to eliminate the tendency for the airplane to drift.

5666. What is the general direction of movement of the other aircraft if during a night flight you observe a steady white light and a rotating red light ahead and at your altitude? The other aircraft is

A— headed away from you.
B— crossing to your left.
C— approaching you head-on.

5667. To develop maximum power and thrust, a constant-speed propeller should be set to a blade angle that will produce a

A— large angle of attack and low RPM.
B— small angle of attack and high RPM.
C— large angle of attack and high RPM.

5668. For takeoff, the blade angle of a controllable-pitch propeller should be set at a

A— small angle of attack and high RPM.
B— large angle of attack and low RPM.
C— large angle of attack and high RPM.

5669. A pilot is entering an area where significant clear air turbulence has been reported. Which action is appropriate upon encountering the first ripple?

A— Maintain altitude and airspeed.
B— Adjust airspeed to that recommended for rough air.
C— Enter a shallow climb or descent at maneuvering speed.

5670. If severe turbulence is encountered during flight, the pilot should reduce the airspeed to

A— minimum control speed.
B— design-maneuvering speed.
C— maximum structural cruising speed.

*   *   *

5682. With respect to using the weight information given in a typical aircraft owner's manual for computing gross weight, it is important to know that if items have been installed in the aircraft in addition to the original equipment, the

A— allowable useful load is decreased.
B— allowable useful load remains unchanged.
C— maximum allowable gross weight is increased.

*   *   *

5689. (Refer to figure 43.)

GIVEN:

Ambient temperature .... 60 °F
Pressure altitude .... 2,000 ft

What is the rate of climb?

A— 480 ft/min.
B— 515 ft/min.
C— 540 ft/min.

5690. (Refer to figure 43.)

GIVEN:

Ambient temperature .... 80 °F
Pressure altitude .... 2,500 ft

What is the rate of climb?

A— 350 ft/min.
B— 395 ft/min.
C— 420 ft/min.

5691. (Refer to figure 44.)

GIVEN:

Ambient temperature .... 40 °F
Pressure altitude .... 1,000 ft

What is the rate of climb?

A— 810 ft/min.
B— 830 ft/min.
C— 860 ft/min.

5692. (Refer to figure 44.)

GIVEN:

Ambient temperature .... 60 °F
Pressure altitude .... 2,000 ft

What is the rate of climb?

A— 705 ft/min.
B— 630 ft/min.
C— 755 ft/min.

* * *

5739. Frost covering the upper surface of an airplane wing usually will cause

A— the airplane to stall at an angle of attack that is higher than normal.
B— the airplane to stall at an angle of attack that is lower than normal.
C— drag factors so large that sufficient speed cannot be obtained for takeoff.

5740. To determine pressure altitude prior to takeoff, the altimeter should be set to

A— the current altimeter setting.
B— 29.92" Hg and the altimeter indication noted.
C— the field elevation and the pressure reading in the altimeter setting window noted.

5741. Which is the best technique for minimizing the wing-load factor when flying in severe turbulence?

A— Change power settings, as necessary, to maintain constant airspeed.
B— Control airspeed with power, maintain wings level, and accept variations of altitude.
C— Set power and trim to obtain an airspeed at or below maneuvering speed, maintain wings level, and accept variations of airspeed and altitude.

* * *

5748. Pilots are encouraged to turn on the aircraft rotating beacon

A— just prior to taxi.
B— anytime they are in the cockpit.
C— anytime an engine is in operation.

5749. When in the vicinity of a VOR which is being used for navigation on VFR flights, it is important to

A— make 90° left and right turns to scan for other traffic.
B— exercise sustained vigilance to avoid aircraft that may be converging on the VOR from other directions.
C— pass the VOR on the right side of the radial to allow room for aircraft flying in the opposite direction on the same radial.

5750. Choose the correct statement regarding wake turbulence.

A— Vortex generation begins with the initiation of the takeoff roll.
B— The primary hazard is loss of control because of induced roll.
C— The greatest vortex strength is produced when the generating airplane is heavy, clean, and fast.

5751. During a takeoff made behind a departing large jet airplane, the pilot can minimize the hazard of wingtip vortices by

A— being airborne prior to reaching the jet's flightpath until able to turn clear of its wake.
B— maintaining extra speed on takeoff and climbout.
C— extending the takeoff roll and not rotating until well beyond the jet's rotation point.

5752. Which procedure should you follow to avoid wake turbulence if a large jet crosses your course from left to right approximately 1 mile ahead and at your altitude?

A— Make sure you are slightly above the path of the jet.
B— Slow your airspeed to V_A and maintain altitude and course.
C— Make sure you are slightly below the path of the jet and perpendicular to the course.

5753. To avoid possible wake turbulence from a large jet aircraft that has just landed prior to your takeoff, at which point on the runway should you plan to become airborne?

A— Past the point where the jet touched down.
B— At the point where the jet touched down, or just prior to this point.
C— Approximately 500 feet prior to the point where the jet touched down.

5754. When landing behind a large aircraft, which procedure should be followed for vortex avoidance?

A— Stay above its final approach flightpath all the way to touchdown.
B— Stay below and to one side of its final approach flightpath.
C— Stay well below its final approach flightpath and land at least 2,000 feet behind.

5755. With respect to vortex circulation, which is true?

A— Helicopters generate downwash turbulence, not vortex circulation.
B— The vortex strength is greatest when the generating aircraft is flying fast.
C— Vortex circulation generated by helicopters in forward flight trail behind in a manner similar to wingtip vortices generated by airplanes.

5756. Which is true with respect to vortex circulation?

A— Helicopters generate downwash turbulence only, not vortex circulation.
B— The vortex strength is greatest when the generating aircraft is heavy, clean, and slow.
C— When vortex circulation sinks into ground effect, it tends to dissipate rapidly and offer little danger.

5757. As hyperventilation progresses a pilot can experience

A— decreased breathing rate and depth.
B— heightened awareness and feeling of well being.
C— symptoms of suffocation and drowsiness.

5758. To scan properly for traffic, a pilot should

A— continuously sweep vision field.
B— concentrate on any peripheral movement detected.
C— systematically focus on different segments of vision field for short intervals.

5759. Which is a common symptom of hyperventilation?

A— Drowsiness.
B— Decreased breathing rate.
C— Euphoria - sense of well-being.

5760. Which would most likely result in hyperventilation?

A— Insufficient oxygen.
B— Excessive carbon monoxide.
C— Insufficient carbon dioxide.

5761. Hypoxia is the result of which of these conditions?

A— Excessive oxygen in the bloodstream.
B— Insufficient oxygen reaching the brain.
C— Excessive carbon dioxide in the bloodstream.

5762. To overcome the symptoms of hyperventilation, a pilot should

A— swallow or yawn.
B— slow the breathing rate.
C— increase the breathing rate.

5763. Which is true regarding the presence of alcohol within the human body?

A— A small amount of alcohol increases vision acuity.
B— An increase in altitude decreases the adverse effect of alcohol.
C— Judgment and decision-making abilities can be adversely affected by even small amounts of alcohol.

5764. Hypoxia susceptibility due to inhalation of carbon monoxide increases as

A— humidity decreases.
B— altitude increases.
C— oxygen demand increases.

5765. To best overcome the effects of spatial disorientation, a pilot should

A— rely on body sensations.
B— increase the breathing rate.
C— rely on aircraft instrument indications.

5766. During preflight in cold weather, crankcase breather lines should receive special attention because they are susceptible to being clogged by

A— congealed oil from the crankcase.
B— moisture from the outside air which has frozen.
C— ice from crankcase vapors that have condensed and subsequently frozen.

5767. Which is true regarding preheating an aircraft during cold weather operations?

A— The cabin area as well as the engine should be preheated.
B— The cabin area should not be preheated with portable heaters.
C— Hot air should be blown directly at the engine through the air intakes.

5768. If necessary to take off from a slushy runway, the freezing of landing gear mechanisms can be minimized by

A— recycling the gear.
B— delaying gear retraction.
C— increasing the airspeed to V_{LE} before retraction.

* * *

5772. A left side slip is used to counteract a crosswind drift during the final approach for landing. An over-the-top spin would most likely occur if the controls were used in which of the following ways? Holding the stick

A— too far back and applying full right rudder.
B— in the neutral position and applying full right rudder.
C— too far to the left and applying full left rudder.

* * *

5882. A change in behavior as a result of experience can be defined as

A— learning.
B— knowledge.
C— understanding.

5883. In levels of learning, what are the steps of progression?

A— Application, understanding, rote, and correlation.
B— Rote, understanding, application, and correlation.
C— Correlation, rote, understanding, and application.

5884. In the learning process, fear or the element of threat will

A— inspire the student to improve.
B— narrow the student's perceptual field.
C— decrease the rate of associative reactions.

5885. What is the basis of all learning?

A— Insight.
B— Perception.
C— Motivation.

5886. While material is being taught, students may be learning other things as well. What is the additional learning called?

A— Residual learning.
B— Conceptual learning.
C— Incidental learning.

5887. Students learn best when they are willing to learn. This feature of LAWS OF LEARNING is referred to as the law of

A— recency.
B— readiness.
C— willingness.

5888. Perceptions result when a person

A— gives meaning to sensations.
B— groups together bits of information.
C— responds to visual cues first, then aural cues, and relates these cues to ones previously learned.

5889. Which is true? Motivations

A— should be obvious to be useful.
B— must be tangible to be effective.
C— may be very subtle and difficult to identify.

5890. To effectively motivate students, an instructor should

A— promise rewards.
B— appeal to their pride and self-esteem.
C— maintain pleasant personal relationships, even if necessary to lower standards.

5891. Motivations in the form of reproof and threats should be avoided with all but the student who is

A— bored.
B— discouraged.
C— overconfident.

5892. The level of learning at which a person can repeat something without understanding is called

A— rote learning.
B— basic learning.
C— random learning.

5893. The level of learning at which the student becomes able to associate an element which has been learned with other blocks of learning is called the level of

A— application.
B— association.
C— correlation.

5894. To ensure proper habits and correct techniques during training, an instructor should

A— never repeat subject matter already taught.
B— use the "building-block" technique of instruction.
C— introduce tasks which are difficult and challenging to the student.

5895. Before a student can concentrate on learning, which of these human needs must be satisfied first?

A— Social needs.
B— Safety needs.
C— Physical needs.

5896. Although defense mechanisms can serve a useful purpose, they can also be a hindrance because they

A— alleviate the cause of problems.
B— can result in delusional behavior.
C— involve self-deception and distortion of reality.

5897. When a student asks irrelevant questions or refuses to participate in class activities, it usually is an indication of the defense mechanism known as

A— aggression.
B— resignation.
C— substitution.

5898. Taking physical or mental flight is a defense mechanism that students use when they

A— want to escape from frustrating situations.
B— become bewildered and lost in the advanced phase of training.
C— attempt to justify actions that otherwise would be unacceptable.

5899. When a student uses excuses to justify inadequate performance, it is an indication of the defense mechanism known as

A— aggression.
B— resignation.
C— rationalization.

5900. When students become so frustrated they no longer believe it possible to work further, they usually display which defense mechanism?

A— Aggression.
B— Resignation.
C— Rationalization.

5901. A student who is daydreaming is engaging in the defense mechanism known as

A— flight.
B— substitution.
C— rationalization.

5902. Which of these instructor actions would more likely result in students becoming frustrated?

A— Presenting a topic or maneuver in great detail.
B— Covering up instructor mistakes or bluffing when the instructor is in doubt.
C— Telling the students that their work is unsatisfactory without explanation.

5903. The effectiveness of communication between the instructor and the student is measured by the degree of

A— motivation manifested by the student.
B— similarity between the idea transmitted and the idea received.
C— attention the student gives to the instructor during a lesson.

5904. To communicate effectively, instructors must

A— utilize highly organized notes.
B— display an authoritarian attitude.
C— display a positive, confident attitude.

5905. Probably the greatest single barrier to effective communication is the

A— use of inaccurate statements.
B— use of abstractions by the communicator.
C— lack of a common core of experience between communicator and receiver.

5906. What is the proper sequence in which the instructor should employ the four basic steps in the teaching process?

A— Explanation, demonstration, practice, and evaluation.
B— Explanation, trial and practice, evaluation, and review.
C— Preparation, presentation, application, and review and evaluation.

5907. Evaluation of student performance and accomplishment during a lesson should be based on the

A— student's background and past experiences.
B— objectives and goals that were established in the lesson plan.
C— student's actual performance as compared to an arbitrary standard.

5908. To enhance a student's acceptance of further instruction, the instructor should

A— keep the student informed of his/her progress.
B— continually prod the student to maintain motivational levels.
C— establish performance standards a little above the student's actual ability.

5909. The method of arranging lesson material from the simple to complex, past to present, and known to unknown, is one that

A— the instructor should avoid.
B— creates student thought pattern departures.
C— indicates the relationship of the main points of the lesson.

5910. When teaching from the KNOWN to the UNKNOWN, an instructor is using the student's

A— anxieties and insecurities.
B— previous experiences and knowledge.
C— previously held opinions, both valid and invalid.

5911. In developing a lesson, the instructor must logically organize explanations and demonstrations to help the student

A— understand the separate items of knowledge.
B— understand the relationships of the main points of the lesson.
C— learn by rote so that performance of the procedure will become automatic.

5912. Which should be the first step in preparing a lecture?

A— Organizing the material.
B— Researching the subject.
C— Establishing the objective and desired outcome.

5913. What is one advantage of a lecture?

A— It provides for student participation.
B— Many ideas can be presented in a short time.
C— Maximum attainment in all types of learning outcomes is possible.

5914. In a "guided discussion," lead-off questions should usually begin with

A— "why ..."
B— "when ..."
C— "where ..."

5915. What are the essential steps in the "demonstration/performance" method of teaching?

A— Demonstration, practice, and evaluation.
B— Demonstration, student performance, and evaluation.
C— Explanation, demonstration, student performance, instructor supervision, and evaluation.

5916. Which is true about an instructor's critique of a student's performance?

A— It must be given in written form.
B— It should be subjective rather than objective.
C— It is a step in the learning process, not in the grading process.

5917. The purpose of a critique is to

A— identify only the student's faults and weaknesses.
B— give a delayed evaluation of the student's performance.
C— provide direction and guidance to raise the level of the student's performance.

5918. When an instructor critiques a student, it should always be

A— done in private.
B— subjective rather than objective.
C— conducted immediately after the student's performance.

5919. Proper quizzing by the instructor during a lesson can have which of these results?

A— It identifies points which need emphasis.
B— It encourages rote response from students.
C— It permits the introduction of new material which was not covered previously.

5920. To be effective in oral quizzing during the conduct of a lesson, a question should

A— center on only one idea.
B— include a combination of where, how, and why.
C— be easy for the student at that particular stage of training.

5921. A written test has validity when it

A— yields consistent results.
B— samples liberally whatever is being measured.
C— actually measures what it is supposed to measure and nothing else.

5922. A written test which has reliability is one which

A— yields consistent results.
B— measures small differences in the achievement of students.
C— actually measures what it is supposed to measure and nothing else.

5923. A written test is said to be comprehensive when it

A— yields consistent results.
B— includes all levels of difficulty.
C— samples liberally whatever is being measured.

5924. Which is true concerning the use of visual aids? They

A— should be used to emphasize key points in a lesson.
B— ensure getting and holding the student's attention.
C— should not be used to cover a subject in less time.

5925. Instructional aids used in the teaching/learning process should be

A— self-supporting and should require no explanation.
B— compatible with the learning outcomes to be achieved.
C— selected prior to developing and organizing the lesson plan.

5926. The professional relationship between the instructor and the student should be based upon

A— the need to disregard the student's personal faults, interests, or problems.
B— setting the learning objectives very high so that the student is continually challenged.
C— the mutual acknowledgement that they are important to each other and both are working toward the same objective.

5927. Which is true regarding professionalism as an instructor?

A— Anything less than sincere performance destroys the effectiveness of the professional instructor.
B— To achieve professionalism, actions and decisions must be limited to standard patterns and practices.
C— A single definition of professionalism would encompass all of the qualifications and considerations which must be present before true professionalism can exist.

5928. An instructor can most effectively maintain a high level of student motivation by

A— making each lesson a pleasurable experience.
B— easing the standards for an apprehensive student.
C— continually challenging the student to meet the highest objectives of training.

5929. Faulty performance due to student overconfidence should be corrected by

A— high praise when no errors are made.
B— increasing the standard of performance for each lesson.
C— providing strong, negative evaluation at the end of each lesson.

5930. What should an instructor do with a student who assumes that correction of errors is unimportant?

A— Invent student deficiencies.
B— Try to reduce the student's overconfidence.
C— Raise the standards of performance, demanding greater effort.

5931. What should an instructor do if a student's slow progress is due to discouragement and lack of confidence?

A— Assign subgoals which can be attained more easily than the normal learning goals.
B— Emphasize the negative aspects of poor performance by pointing out the serious consequences.
C— Raise the performance standards so the student will gain satisfaction in meeting higher standards.

5932. Should an instructor be concerned about an apt student who makes very few mistakes?

A— No. Some students have an innate, natural aptitude for flight.
B— Yes. Faulty performance may soon appear due to student overconfidence.
C— Yes. The student will lose confidence in the instructor if the instructor does not invent deficiencies in the student's performance.

5933. When a student correctly understands the situation and knows the correct procedure for the task, but fails to act at the proper time, the student most probably

A— lacks self-confidence.
B— will be unable to cope with the demands of flying.
C— is handicapped by indifference or lack of interest.

5934. What should an instructor do if a student is suspected of not fully understanding the principles involved in a task, even though the student can correctly perform the task?

A— Require the student to apply the same elements to the performance of other tasks.
B— Require the student to repeat the task, as necessary, until the principles are understood.
C— Repeat demonstrating the task as necessary until the student understands the principles.

5935. When under stress, normal individuals usually react

A— with marked changes in mood on different lessons.
B— with extreme overcooperation, painstaking self-control, and laughing or singing.
C— by responding rapidly and exactly, often automatically, within the limits of their experience and training.

5936. The instructor can counteract anxiety in a student by

A— treating student fear as a normal reaction.
B— allowing the student to select tasks to be performed.
C— continually citing the unhappy consequences of faulty performance.

5937. Which would most likely indicate that a student is reacting abnormally to stress?

A— Thinks and acts rapidly.
B— Extreme overcooperation.
C— Extreme sensitivity to surroundings.

5938. What is the primary consideration in determining the length and frequency of flight instruction periods?

A— Fatigue.
B— Mental acuity.
C— Physical conditioning.

5939. Students quickly become apathetic when they

A— understand the objectives toward which they are working.
B— are assigned goals that are difficult, but possible to attain.
C— recognize that their instructor is poorly prepared to conduct the lesson.

5940. In planning any instructional activity, the instructor's first consideration should be to

A— determine the overall objectives and standards.
B— identify the blocks of learning which make up the overall objective.
C— establish common ground between the instructor and students.

DEPARTMENT OF TRANSPORTATION
FEDERAL AVIATION ADMINISTRATION

SUBJECT MATTER KNOWLEDGE CODES

To determine the knowledge area in which a particular question was incorrectly answered, compare the subject matter code(s) on AC Form 8080-2, Airmen Written Test Report, to the subject matter outline that follows. The total number of test items missed may differ from the number of subject matter codes shown on the AC Form 8080-2, since you may have missed more than one question in a certain subject matter code.

FAR 1   **Definitions and Abbreviations**

A01   General Definitions
A02   Abbreviations and Symbols

FAR 25   **Airworthiness Standards: Transport Category Airplanes**

A03   General
A04   Flight
A05   Structure
A06   Design and Construction
A07   Powerplant
A08   Equipment
A09   Operating Limitations and Information

FAR 23   **Airworthiness Standards: Normal, Utility, and Acrobatic Category Aircraft**

A10   General

FAR 21   **Certification Procedures for Products and Parts**

A11   **General**

FAR 39   **Airworthiness Directives**

A13   General
A14   Subpart B—Airworthiness Directives

FAR 43   **Maintenance, Preventive Maintenance, Rebuilding, and Alteration**

A15   General
A16   Appendixes

FAR 61   **Certification: Pilots and Flight Instructors**

A20   General
A21   Aircraft Ratings and Special Certificates
A22   Student Pilots
A23   Private Pilots
A24   Commercial Pilots
A25   Airline Transport Pilots
A26   Flight Instructors
A27   Appendix A: Practical Test Requirements for Airline Transport Pilot Certificates and Associated Class and Type Ratings
A28   Appendix B: Practical Test Requirements for Rotorcraft Airline Transport Pilot Certificates with a Helicopter Class Rating and Associated Type Ratings
A29   Recreational Pilot

FAR 63   **Certification: Flight Crewmembers Other Than Pilots**

A30   General
A31   Flight Engineers
A32   Flight Navigators

AC 65-9A   **Airframe and Powerplant Mechanics General Handbook**

S01	Mathematics
S02	Aircraft Drawings
S03	Aircraft Weight and Balance
S04	Fuels and Fuel Systems
S05	Fluid Lines and Fittings
S06	Aircraft Hardware, Materials, and Processes
S07	Physics
S08	Basic Electricity
S09	Aircraft Generators and Motors
S10	Inspection Fundamentals
S11	Ground Handling, Safety, and Support Equipment

AC 65-12A   **Airframe and Powerplant Mechanics Powerplant Handbook**

S12	Theory and Construction of Aircraft Engines
S13	Induction and Exhaust Systems
S14	Engine Fuel and Metering Systems
S15	Engine Ignition and Electrical Systems
S16	Engine Starting Systems
S17	Lubrication and Cooling Systems
S18	Propellers
S19	Engine Fire Protection Systems
S20	Engine Maintenance and Operation

AC 65-15A   **Airframe and Powerplant Mechanics Airframe Handbook**

S21	Aircraft Structures
S22	Assembly and Rigging
S23	Aircraft Structural Repairs
S24	Ice and Rain Protection
S25	Hydraulic and Pneumatic Power Systems
S26	Landing Gear Systems
S27	Fire Protection Systems
S28	Aircraft Electrical Systems
S29	Aircraft Instrument Systems
S30	Communications and Navigation Systems

S31	Cabin Atmosphere Control Systems

EA-ITP-G[2]   **A and P Technician General Textbook — International Aviation Publishers (IAP), Inc., Second Edition**

S32	Mathematics
S33	Physics
S34	Basic Electricity
S35	Electrical Generators and Motors
S36	Aircraft Drawings
S37	Weight and Balance
S38	Fluid Lines and Fittings
S39	Aircraft Hardware
S40	Corrosion and Its Control
S41	Nondestructive Inspection
S42	Ground Handling and Servicing
S43	Maintenance Forms and Records
S44	Maintenance Publications

EA-ITP-P[2]   **A and P Technician Powerplant Textbook — IAP, Inc., Second Edition**

S45	Reciprocating Engines
S46	Turbine Engines
S47	Engine Removal and Replacement
S48	Engine Maintenance and Operation
S49	Induction and Exhaust Systems
S50	Engine Fuel and Fuel Metering
S51	Engine Ignition and Electrical Systems
S52	Engine Lubrication and Cooling Systems
S53	Engine Fire Protection Systems
S54	Propellers

EA-ITP-A[2]   **A and P Technician Airframe Textbook — IAP, Inc., Second Edition**

S55	Aircraft Structures
S56	Assembly and Rigging
S57	Aircraft Fabric Covering
S58	Aircraft Painting and Finishing
S59	Aircraft Metal Structural Repair
S60	Aircraft Wood and Composite Structural Repair
S61	Aircraft Welding
S62	Ice and Rain Control Systems
S63	Hydraulic and Pneumatic Power Systems

Aircraft Basic Science — McGraw-Hill, Sixth Edition

T31	Fundamentals of Mathematics
T32	Science Fundamentals
T33	Basic Aerodynamics
T34	Airfoils and their Applications
T35	Aircraft in Flight
T36	Aircraft Drawings
T37	Weight and Balance
T38	Aircraft Materials
T39	Fabrication Techniques and Processes
T40	Aircraft Hardware
T41	Aircraft Fluid Lines and their Fittings
T42	Federal Aviation Regulations and Publications
T43	Ground Handling and Safety
T44	Aircraft Inspection and Servicing

Aircraft Maintenance and Repair — McGraw-Hill, Fifth Edition

T45	Aircraft Systems
T46	Aircraft Hydraulic and Pneumatic Systems
T47	Aircraft Landing Gear Systems
T48	Aircraft Fuel Systems
T49	Environmental Systems
T50	Aircraft Instruments and Instrument Systems
T51	Auxiliary Systems
T52	Assembly and Rigging

EA-363   Transport Category Aircraft Systems — IAP, Inc.

T53	Types, Design Features and Configurations of Transport Aircraft
T54	Auxiliary Power Units, Pneumatic, and Environmental Control Systems
T55	Anti-Icing Systems and Rain Protection
T56	Electrical Power Systems
T57	Flight Control Systems
T58	Fuel Systems
T59	Hydraulic Systems
T60	Oxygen Systems
T61	Warning and Fire Protection Systems
T62	Communications, Instruments, and Navigational Systems
T63	Miscellaneous Aircraft Systems and Maintenance Information

Aircraft Electricity and Electronics — McGraw-Hill, Fourth Edition

T64	Fundamentals of Electricity
T65	Applications of Ohm's Law
T66	Aircraft Storage Batteries
T67	Alternating Current
T68	Electrical Wire and Wiring Practices
T69	Electrical Control Devices
T70	Electric Measuring Instruments
T71	DC Generators and Related Control Circuits
T72	Alternators, Inverters, and Related Controls
T73	Electric Motors
T74	Power Distribution Systems
T75	Design and Maintenance of Aircraft Electrical Systems
T76	Radio Theory
T77	Communication and Navigation Systems
T78	Weather Warning Systems
T79	Electrical Instruments and Autopilot Systems
T80	Digital Electronics

FAA Accident Prevention Program Bulletins

V01	FAA-P-8740-2, Density Altitude
V02	FAA-P-8740-5, Weight and Balance
V03	FAA-P-8740-12, Thunderstorms
V04	FAA-P-8740-19, Flying Light Twins Safely
V05	FAA-P-8740-23, Planning your Takeoff
V06	FAA-P-8740-24, Tips on Winter Flying
V07	FAA-P-8740-25, Always Leave Yourself an Out
V08	FAA-P-8740-30, How to Obtain a Good Weather Briefing
V09	FAA-P-8740-40, Wind Shear
V10	FAA-P-8740-41, Medical Facts for Pilots
V11	FAA-P-8740-44, Impossible Turns
V12	FAA-P-8740-48, On Landings, Part I
V13	FAA-P-8740-49, On Landings, Part II
V14	FAA-P-8740-50, On Landings, Part III

| V15 | FAA-P-8740-51, How to Avoid a Midair Collision |
| V16 | FAA-P-8740-52, The Silent Emergency |

EA-338 **Flight Theory for Pilots — IAP, Inc., Third Edition**

W01	Introduction
W02	Air Flow and Airspeed Measurement
W03	Aerodynamic Forces on Airfoils
W04	Lift and Stall
W05	Drag
W06	Jet Aircraft Basic Performance
W07	Jet Aircraft Applied Performance
W08	Prop Aircraft Basic Performance
W09	Prop Aircraft Applied Performance
W10	Helicopter Aerodynamics
W11	Hazards of Low Speed Flight
W12	Takeoff Performance
W13	Landing Performance
W14	Maneuvering Performance
W15	Longitudinal Stability and Control
W16	Directional and Lateral Stability and Control
W17	High Speed Flight

Fly the Wing, — Iowa State University Press/Ames, Second Edition

X01	Basic Aerodynamics
X02	High-Speed Aerodynamics
X03	High-Altitude Machs
X04	Approach Speed Control and Target Landings
X05	Preparation for Flight Training
X06	Basic Instrument Scan
X07	Takeoffs
X08	Rejected Takeoffs
X09	Climb, Cruise, and Descent
X10	Steep Turns
X11	Stalls
X12	Unusual Attitudes
X14	Maneuvers At Minimum Speed
X15	Landings: Approach Technique and Performance
X16	ILS Approaches

X17	Missed Approaches and Rejected Landings
X18	Category II and III Approaches
X19	Nonprecision and Circling Approaches
X20	Weight and Balance
X21	Flight Planning
X22	Icing
X23	Use of Anti-ice and Deice
X24	Winter Operation
X25	Thunderstorm Flight
X26	Low-Level Wind Shear

Technical Standard Orders

| Y60 | TSO-C23b, Parachute |
| Y61 | TSO-C23c, Personnel Parachute Assemblies |

Practical Test Standards

Z01	FAA-S-8081-6, Flight Instructor Practical Test Standards for Airplane
Z02	FAA-S-8081-7, Flight Instructor Practical Test Standards for Rotorcraft
Z03	FAA-S-8081-8, Flight Instructor Practical Test Standards for Glider

NOTE: AC 00-2, Advisory Circular Checklist, transmits the status of all FAA advisory circulars (AC's), as well as FAA internal publications and miscellaneous flight information such as AIM, Airport/Facility Directory, written test question books, practical test standards, and other material directly related to a certificate or rating. To obtain a free copy of the AC 00-2, send your request to:

U.S. Department of Transportation
Utilization and Storage Section, M-443.2
Washington, DC 20590

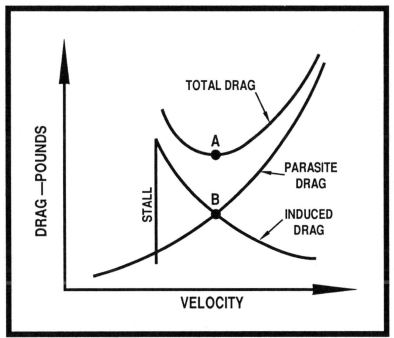

FIGURE 1.—Drag vs. Speed.

GROSS WEIGHT 2750 LBS		ANGLE OF BANK			
		LEVEL	30°	45°	60°
POWER		GEAR AND FLAPS UP			
ON	MPH	62	67	74	88
	KTS	54	58	64	76
OFF	MPH	75	81	89	106
	KTS	65	70	77	92
		GEAR AND FLAPS DOWN			
ON	MPH	54	58	64	76
	KTS	47	50	56	66
OFF	MPH	66	71	78	93
	KTS	57	62	68	81

FIGURE 2.—Stall Speeds.

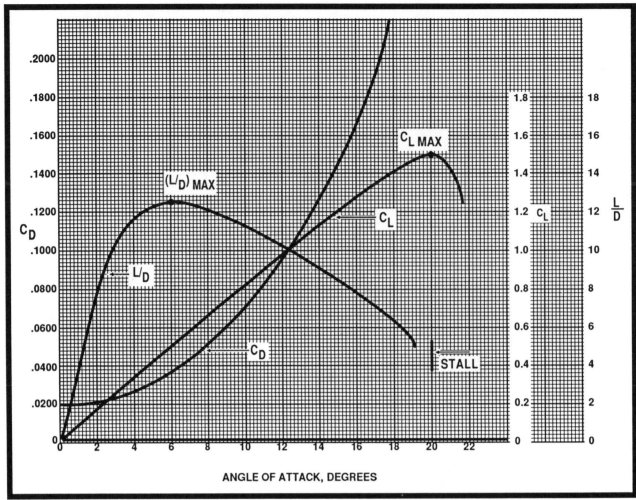

FIGURE 3.—Angle of Attack, Degrees.

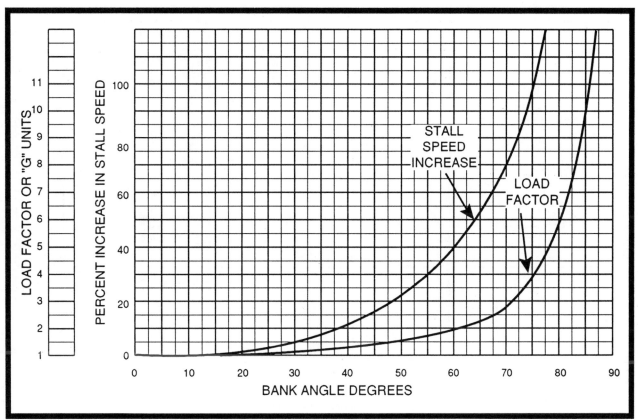

FIGURE 4.—Stall Speed/Load Factor.

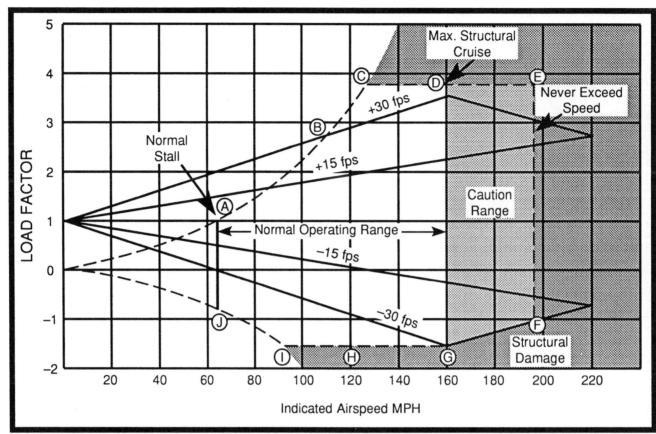

FIGURE 5.—Velocity vs. G-Loads.

* * *

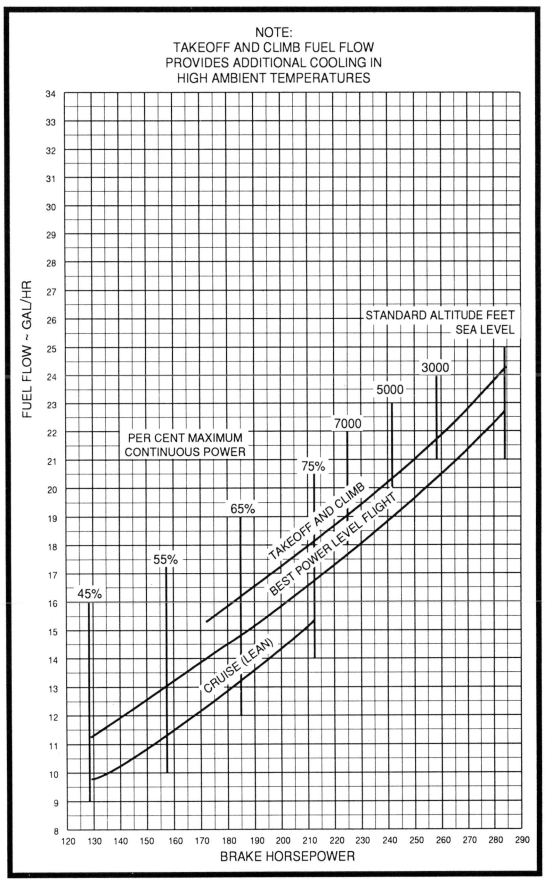

FIGURE 8.—Fuel Consumption vs. Brake Horsepower.

NORMAL CLIMB – 100 KIAS

CONDITIONS:
Flaps Up
Gear Up
2550 RPM
25 Inches MP or Full Throttle
Cowl Flaps Open
Standard Temperature

MIXTURE SETTING	
PRESS ALT	PPH
S.L. to 4000	108
8000	96
12,000	84

NOTES:
1. Add 12 pounds of fuel for engine start, taxi and takeoff allowance.
2. Increase time, fuel and distance by 10% for each 10 °C above standard temperature.
3. Distances shown are based on zero wind.

WEIGHT LBS	PRESS ALT FT	RATE OF CLIMB FPM	FROM SEA LEVEL		
			TIME MIN	FUEL USED POUNDS	DISTANCE NM
3800	S.L.	580	0	0	0
	2000	580	3	6	6
	4000	570	7	12	12
	6000	470	11	19	19
	8000	365	16	27	28
	10,000	265	22	37	40
	12,000	165	32	51	59
3500	S.L.	685	0	0	0
	2000	685	3	5	5
	4000	675	6	11	10
	6000	565	9	16	16
	8000	455	13	23	23
	10,000	350	18	31	33
	12,000	240	25	41	46
3200	S.L.	800	0	0	0
	2000	800	2	4	4
	4000	795	5	9	8
	6000	675	8	14	13
	8000	560	11	19	19
	10,000	445	15	25	27
	12,000	325	20	33	37

FIGURE 9.—Fuel, Time, and Distance to Climb.

MAXIMUM RATE OF CLIMB

CONDITIONS:
Flaps Up
Gear Up
2700 RPM
Full Throttle
Mixture Set at Placard Fuel Flow
Cowl Flaps Open
Standard Temperature

MIXTURE SETTING	
PRESS ALT	PPH
S.L.	138
4000	126
8000	114
12,000	102

NOTES:
1. Add 12 pounds of fuel for engine start, taxi and takeoff allowance.
2. Increase time, fuel and distance by 10% for each 10 °C above standard temperature.
3. Distances shown are based on zero wind.

WEIGHT LBS	PRESS ALT FT	CLIMB SPEED KIAS	RATE OF CLIMB FPM	FROM SEA LEVEL		
				TIME MIN	FUEL USED POUNDS	DISTANCE NM
3800	S.L.	97	860	0	0	0
	2000	95	760	2	6	4
	4000	94	660	5	12	9
	6000	93	565	9	18	14
	8000	91	465	13	26	21
	10,000	90	365	18	35	29
	12,000	89	265	24	47	41
3500	S.L.	95	990	0	0	0
	2000	94	885	2	5	3
	4000	93	780	5	10	7
	6000	91	675	7	16	12
	8000	90	570	11	22	17
	10,000	89	465	15	29	24
	12,000	87	360	20	38	32
3200	S.L.	94	1135	0	0	0
	2000	92	1020	2	4	3
	4000	91	910	4	9	6
	6000	90	800	6	14	10
	8000	88	685	9	19	14
	10,000	87	575	12	25	20
	12,000	86	465	16	32	26

FIGURE 10.—Fuel, Time, and Distance to Climb.

| | | | | | Gross Weight- 2300 Lbs. Standard Conditions Zero Wind   Lean Mixture | | | |

NOTE: Maximum cruise is normally limited to 75% power.

					38 GAL (NO RESERVE)		48 GAL (NO RESERVE)	
ALT.	RPM	% BHP	TAS MPH	GAL / HOUR	ENDR. HOURS	RANGE MILES	ENDR. HOURS	RANGE MILES
2500	2700	86	134	9.7	3.9	525	4.9	660
	2600	79	129	8.6	4.4	570	5.6	720
	2500	72	123	7.8	4.9	600	6.2	760
	2400	65	117	7.2	5.3	620	6.7	780
	2300	58	111	6.7	5.7	630	7.2	795
	2200	52	103	6.3	6.1	625	7.7	790
5000	2700	82	134	9.0	4.2	565	5.3	710
	2600	75	128	8.1	4.7	600	5.9	760
	2500	68	122	7.4	5.1	625	6.4	790
	2400	61	116	6.9	5.5	635	6.9	805
	2300	55	108	6.5	5.9	635	7.4	805
	2200	49	100	6.0	6.3	630	7.9	795
7500	2700	78	133	8.4	4.5	600	5.7	755
	2600	71	127	7.7	4.9	625	6.2	790
	2500	64	121	7.1	5.3	645	6.7	810
	2400	58	113	6.7	5.7	645	7.2	820
	2300	52	105	6.2	6.1	640	7.7	810
10,000	2650	70	129	7.6	5.0	640	6.3	810
	2600	67	125	7.3	5.2	650	6.5	820
	2500	61	118	6.9	5.5	655	7.0	830
	2400	55	110	6.4	5.9	650	7.5	825
	2300	49	100	6.0	6.3	635	8.0	800

FIGURE 11.—Cruise and Range Performance.

PRESSURE ALTITUDE 18,000 FEET

CONDITIONS:
4000 Pounds
Recommended Lean Mixture
Cowl Flaps Closed

NOTE
For best fuel economy at 70% power or less, operate at 6 PPH leaner than shown in this chart or at peak EGT.

		20 °C BELOW STANDARD TEMP -41 °C			STANDARD TEMPERATURE -21 °C			20 °C ABOVE STANDARD TEMP -1 °C		
RPM	MP	% BHP	KTAS	PPH	% BHP	KTAS	PPH	% BHP	KTAS	PPH
2500	30	---	---	---	81	188	106	76	185	100
	28	80	184	105	76	182	99	71	178	93
	26	75	178	99	71	176	93	67	172	88
	24	70	171	91	66	168	86	62	164	81
	22	63	162	84	60	159	79	56	155	75
2400	30	81	185	107	77	183	101	72	180	94
	28	76	179	100	72	177	94	67	173	88
	26	71	172	93	67	170	88	63	166	83
	24	66	165	87	62	163	82	58	159	77
	22	61	158	80	57	155	76	54	150	72
2300	30	79	182	103	74	180	97	70	176	91
	28	74	176	97	70	174	91	65	170	86
	26	69	170	91	65	167	86	61	163	81
	24	64	162	84	60	159	79	56	155	75
	22	58	154	77	55	150	73	51	145	65
2200	26	66	166	87	62	163	82	58	159	77
	24	61	158	80	57	154	76	54	150	72
	22	55	148	73	51	144	69	48	138	66
	20	49	136	66	46	131	63	43	124	59

FIGURE 12.—Cruise Performance.

MAXIMUM RATE OF CLIMB

CONDITIONS:
Flaps Up
Gear Up
2600 RPM
Cowl Flaps Open
Standard Temperature

PRESS ALT	MP	PPH
S.L. TO 17,000	35	162
18,000	34	156
20,000	32	144
22,000	30	132
24,000	28	120

NOTES:
1. Add 16 pounds of fuel for engine start, taxi and takeoff allowance.
2. Increase time, fuel and distance by 10% for each 10 °C above standard temperature.
3. Distances shown are based on zero wind.

WEIGHT LBS	PRESS ALT FT	CLIMB SPEED KIAS	RATE OF CLIMB FPM	FROM SEA LEVEL		
				TIME MIN	FUEL USED POUNDS	DISTANCE NM
4000	S.L.	100	930	0	0	0
	4000	100	890	4	12	7
	8000	100	845	9	24	16
	12,000	100	790	14	38	25
	16,000	100	720	19	52	36
	20,000	99	515	26	69	50
	24,000	97	270	37	92	74
3700	S.L.	99	1060	0	0	0
	4000	99	1020	4	10	6
	8000	99	975	8	21	13
	12,000	99	915	12	33	21
	16,000	99	845	17	45	30
	20,000	97	630	22	59	42
	24,000	95	370	30	77	60
3400	S.L.	97	1205	0	0	0
	4000	97	1165	3	9	5
	8000	97	1120	7	19	12
	12,000	97	1060	11	29	18
	16,000	97	985	15	39	26
	20,000	96	760	19	51	36
	24,000	94	485	26	65	50

FIGURE 13.—Fuel, Time, and Distance to Climb.

NORMAL CLIMB – 110 KIAS

CONDITIONS:
Flaps Up
Gear Up
2500 RPM
30 Inches Hg
120 PPH Fuel Flow
Cowl Flaps Open
Standard Temperature

NOTES:
1. Add 16 pounds of fuel for engine start, taxi and takeoff allowance.
2. Increase time, fuel and distance by 10% for each 7 °C above standard temperature.
3. Distances shown are based on zero wind.

WEIGHT LBS	PRESS ALT FT	RATE OF CLIMB FPM	FROM SEA LEVEL		
			TIME MIN	FUEL USED POUNDS	DISTANCE NM
4000	S.L.	605	0	0	0
	4000	570	7	14	13
	8000	530	14	28	27
	12,000	485	22	44	43
	16,000	430	31	62	63
	20,000	365	41	82	87
	S.L.	700	0	0	0
3700	4000	665	6	12	11
	8000	625	12	24	23
	12,000	580	19	37	37
	16,000	525	26	52	53
	20,000	460	34	68	72
	S.L.	810	0	0	0
	4000	775	5	10	9
3400	8000	735	10	21	20
	12,000	690	16	32	31
	16,000	635	22	44	45
	20,000	565	29	57	61

FIGURE 14.—Fuel, Time, and Distance to Climb.

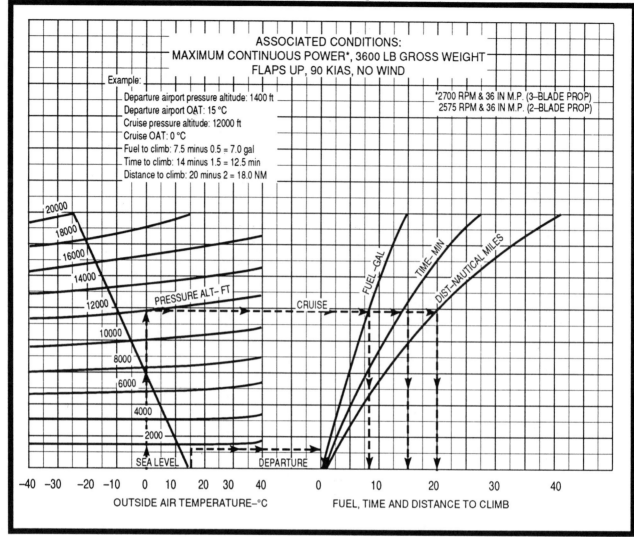

FIGURE 15.—Fuel, Time, and Distance to Climb.

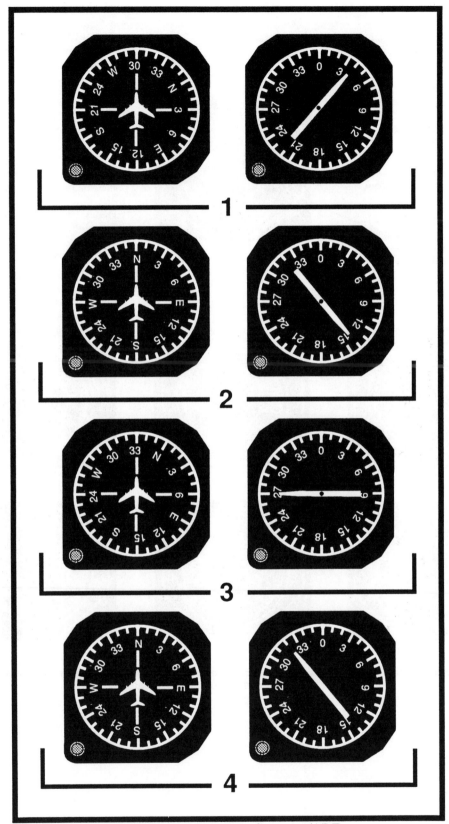

FIGURE 16.—Magnetic Compass/ADF.

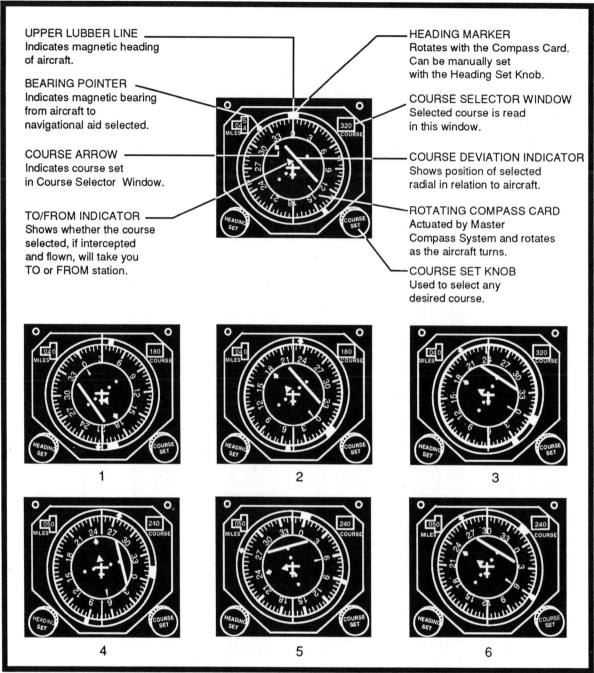

FIGURE 17.—Horizontal Situation Indicator (HSI).

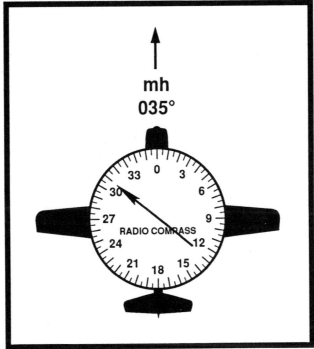

FIGURE 18.—Magnetic Heading/Radio Compass.

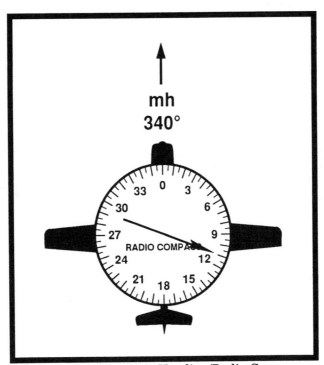

FIGURE 19.—Magnetic Heading/Radio Compass.

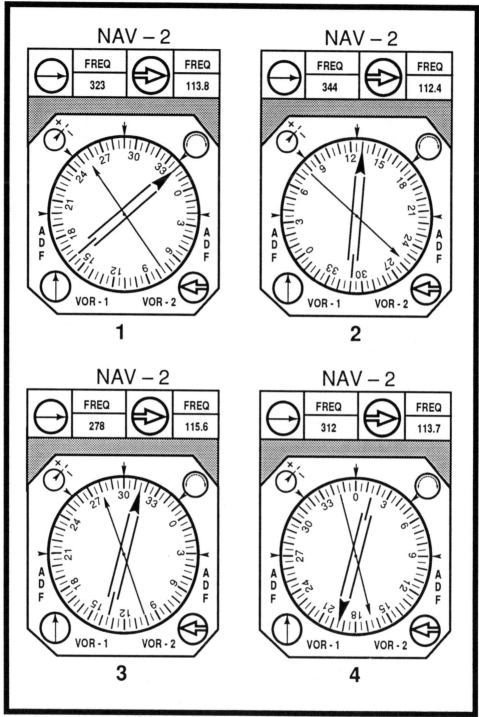

FIGURE 20.—Radio Magnetic Indicator (RMI).

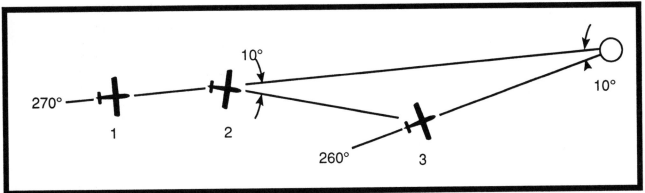

FIGURE 21.—Isosceles Triangle.

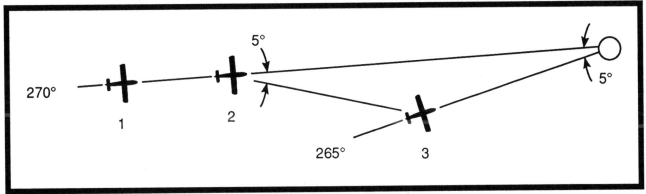

FIGURE 22.—Isosceles Triangle.

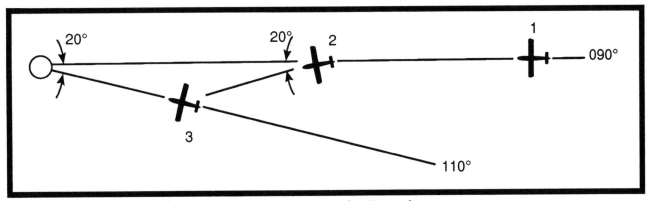

FIGURE 23.—Isosceles Triangle.

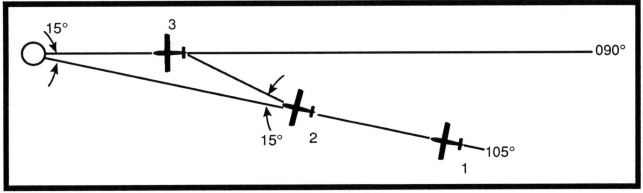

FIGURE 24.—Isosceles Triangle.

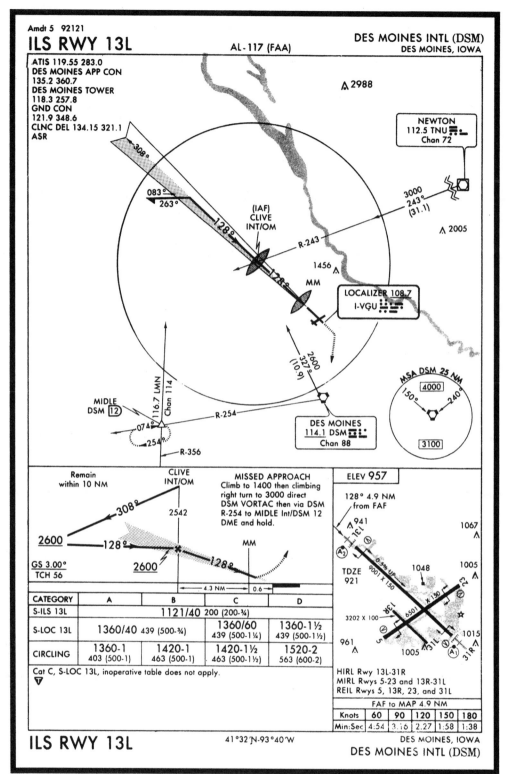

FIGURE 25.—ILS RWY 13L (DSM).

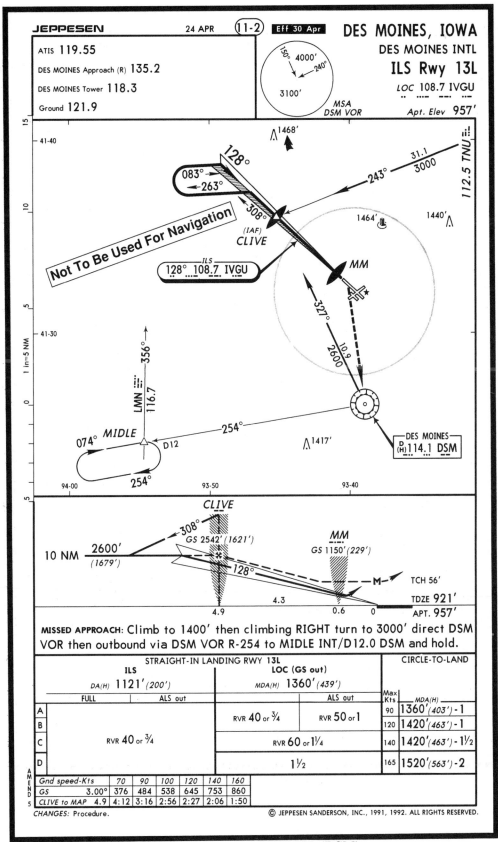

FIGURE 25A.—ILS RWY 13L (DSM).

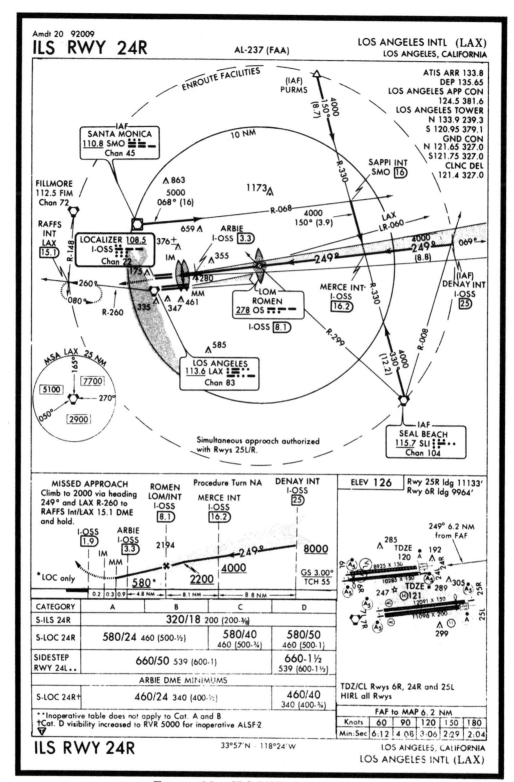

FIGURE 26.—ILS RWY 24R (LAX).

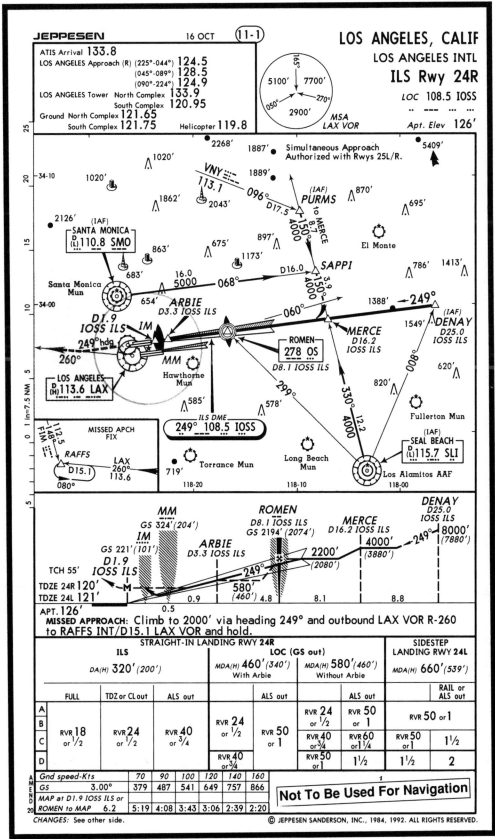

FIGURE 26A.—ILS RWY 24R (LAX).

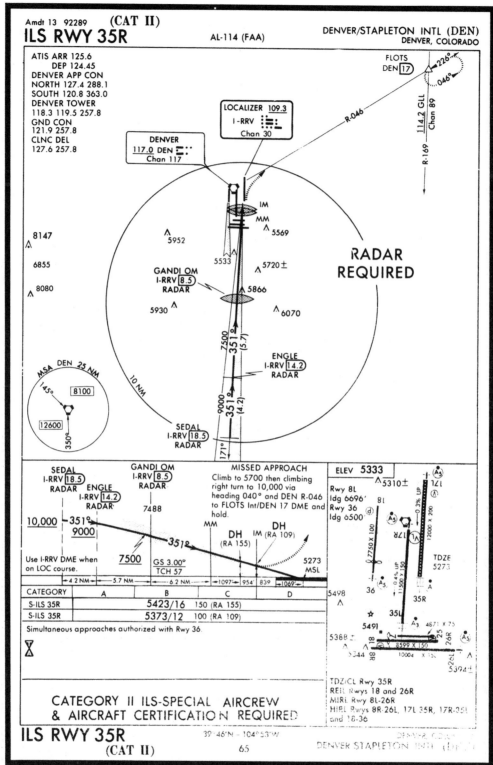

FIGURE 27.—ILS RWY 35R (CAT II) – (DEN).

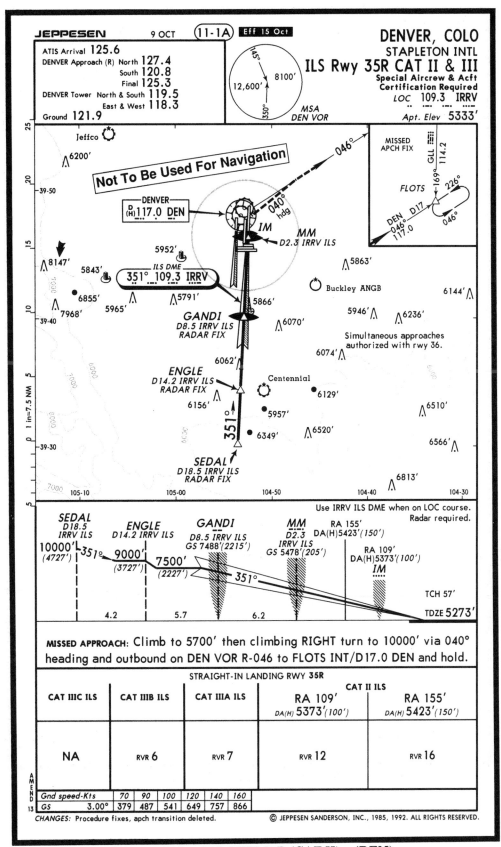

FIGURE 27A.—ILS RWY 35R (CAT II) – (DEN).

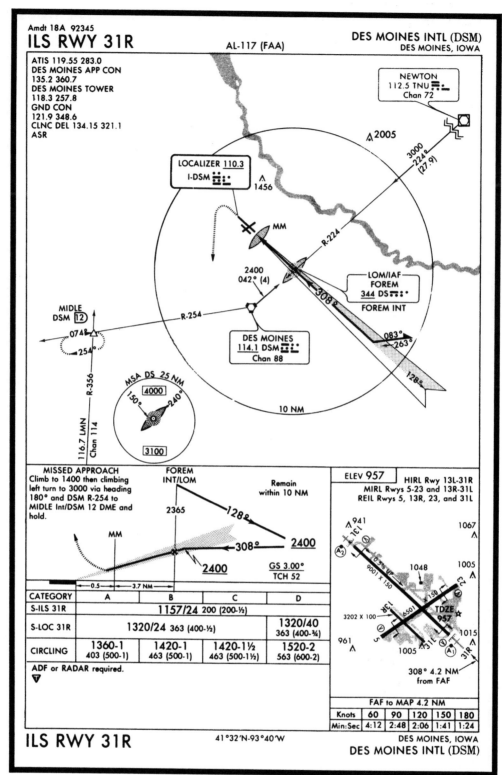

FIGURE 28.—ILS RWY 31R (DSM).

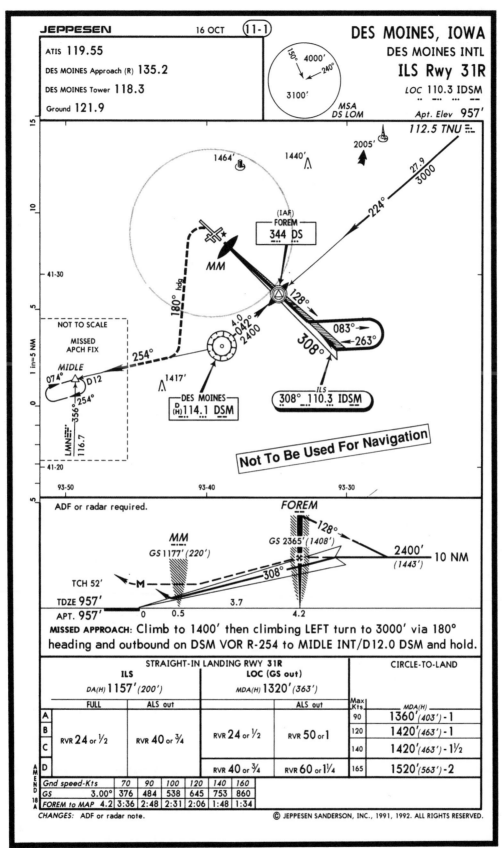

FIGURE 28A.—ILS RWY 31R (DSM).

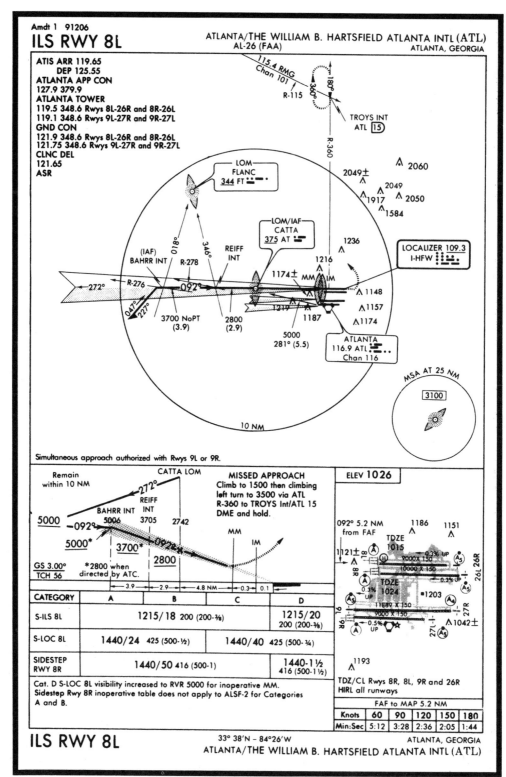

FIGURE 29.—ILS RWY 8L (ATL).

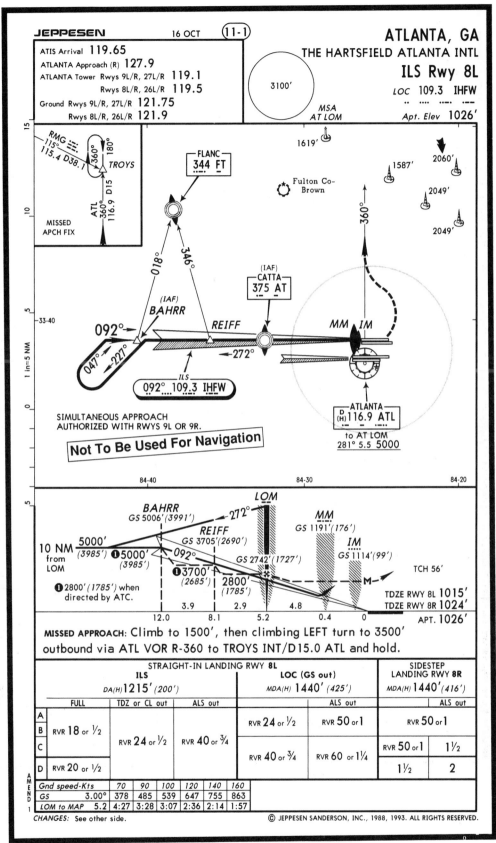

FIGURE 29A.—ILS RWY 8L (ATL).

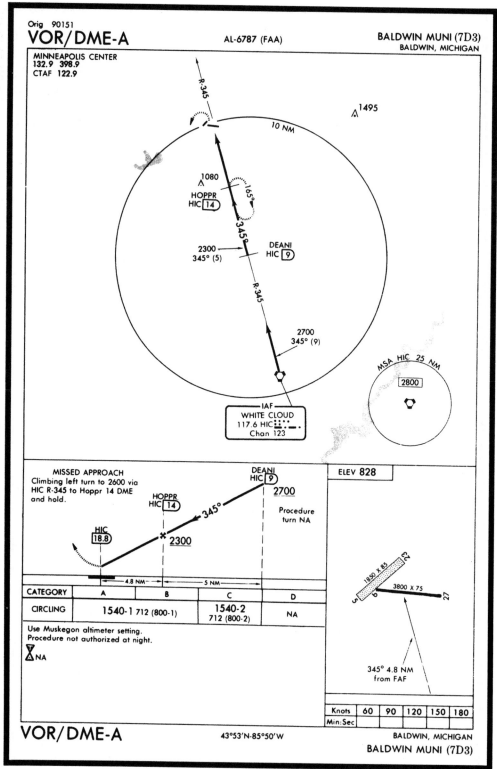

FIGURE 30.—VOR/DME-A (7D3).

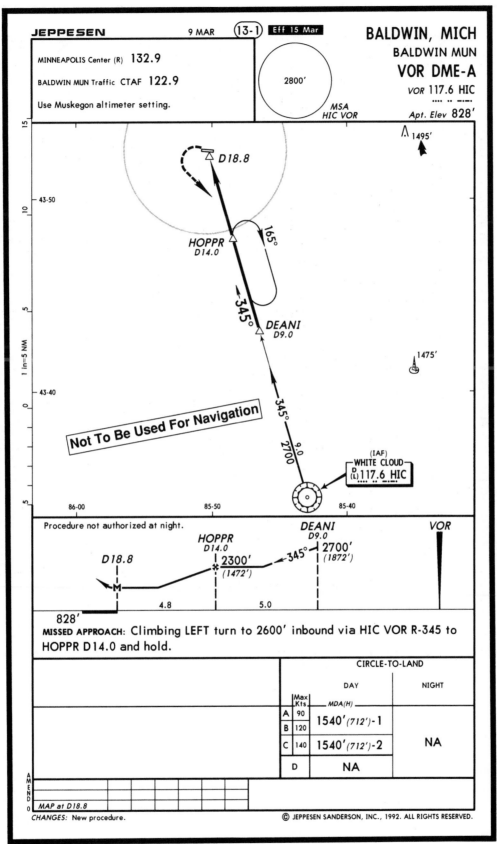

FIGURE 30A.—VOR/DME-A (7D3).

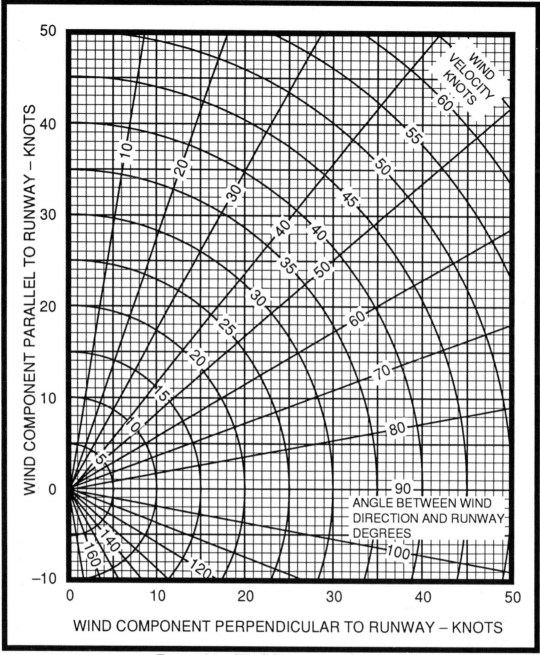

FIGURE 31.—Wind Component Chart.

ASSOCIATED CONDITIONS:

POWER	TAKEOFF POWER SET BEFORE BRAKE RELEASE
FLAPS	20°
RUNWAY	PAVED, LEVEL, DRY SURFACE
TAKEOFF SPEED	IAS AS TABULATED

NOTE: GROUND ROLL IS APPROX. 73% OF TOTAL TAKEOFF DISTANCE OVER A 50 FT OBSTACLE

EXAMPLE:

OAT	75 °F
PRESSURE ALTITUDE	4000 FT
TAKEOFF WEIGHT	3100 LB
HEADWIND	20 KNOTS

TOTAL TAKEOFF DISTANCE OVER A 50 FT OBSTACLE	1350 FT
GROUND ROLL (73% OF 1350)	986 FT
IAS TAKEOFF SPEED	
LIFT–OFF	74 MPH
AT 50 FT	74 MPH

| WEIGHT POUNDS | IAS TAKEOFF SPEED (ASSUMES ZERO INSTR. ERROR) | | | |
| | LIFT–OFF | | 50 FEET | |
	MPH	KNOTS	MPH	KNOTS
3400	77	67	77	67
3200	75	65	75	65
3000	72	63	72	63
2800	69	60	69	60
2600	66	57	66	57
2400	63	55	63	55

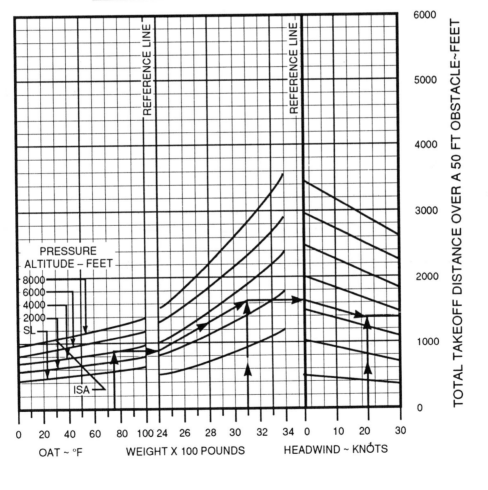

FIGURE 32.—Obstacle Take-off Chart.

CONDITIONS:
Flaps Up
Gear Up
2600 RPM
Cowl Flaps Open

PRESS ALT	MP	PPH
S.L. TO 17,000	35	162
18,000	34	156
20,000	32	144
22,000	30	132
24,000	28	120

WEIGHT LBS	PRESS ALT FT	CLIMB SPEED KIAS	RATE OF CLIMB – FPM			
			-20 °C	0 °C	20 °C	40 °C
4000	S.L.	100	1170	1035	895	755
	4000	100	1080	940	800	655
	8000	100	980	840	695	555
	12,000	100	870	730	590	---
	16,000	100	740	605	470	---
	20,000	99	485	355	---	---
	24,000	97	190	70	---	---
3700	S.L.	99	1310	1165	1020	875
	4000	99	1215	1070	925	775
	8000	99	1115	965	815	670
	12,000	99	1000	855	710	---
	16,000	99	865	730	590	---
	20,000	97	600	470	---	---
	24,000	95	295	170	---	---
3400	S.L.	97	1465	1320	1165	1015
	4000	97	1370	1220	1065	910
	8000	97	1265	1110	955	795
	12,000	97	1150	995	845	---
	16,000	97	1010	865	725	---
	20,000	96	730	595	---	---
	24,000	94	405	275	---	---

FIGURE 33.—Maximum Rate-of-Climb Chart.

PRESSURE ALTITUDE 6,000 FEET

CONDITIONS:
Recommended Lean Mixture
3800 Pounds
Cowl Flaps Closed

RPM	MP	20 °C BELOW STANDARD TEMP -17 °C			STANDARD TEMPERATURE 3 °C			20 °C ABOVE STANDARD TEMP 23 °C		
		% BHP	KTAS	PPH	% BHP	KTAS	PPH	% BHP	KTAS	PPH
2550	24	---	---	---	78	173	97	75	174	94
	23	76	167	96	74	169	92	71	171	89
	22	72	164	90	69	166	87	67	167	84
	21	68	160	85	65	162	82	63	163	80
2500	24	78	169	98	75	171	95	73	172	91
	23	74	166	93	71	167	90	69	169	87
	22	70	162	88	67	164	85	65	165	82
	21	66	158	83	63	160	80	61	160	77
2400	24	73	165	91	70	166	88	68	167	85
	23	69	161	87	67	163	84	64	164	81
	22	65	158	82	63	159	79	61	160	77
	21	61	154	77	59	155	75	57	155	73
2300	24	68	161	86	66	162	83	64	163	80
	23	65	158	82	62	159	79	60	159	76
	22	61	154	77	59	155	75	57	155	72
	21	57	150	73	55	150	71	53	150	68
2200	24	63	156	80	61	157	77	59	158	75
	23	60	152	76	58	153	73	56	154	71
	22	57	149	72	54	149	70	53	149	67
	21	53	144	68	51	144	66	49	143	64
	20	50	139	64	48	138	62	46	137	60
	19	46	133	60	44	132	58	43	131	57

FIGURE 34.—Cruise Performace Chart.

ASSOCIATED CONDITIONS:

POWER	AS REQUIRED TO MAINTAIN 800 FT/MIN DESCENT ON APPROACH
FLAPS	DOWN
RUNWAY	PAVED, LEVEL, DRY SURFACE
APPROACH SPEED	IAS A TABULATED

NOTE: GROUND ROLL IS APPROX. 53% OF TOTAL LANDING DISTANCE OVER A 50 FT OBSTACLE.

EXAMPLE:

OAT	75 °F
PRESSURE ALTITUDE	4000 FT
LANDING WEIGHT	3200 LB
HEADWIND	10 KNOTS
TOTAL LANDING DISTANCE OVER A 50 FT OBSTACLE	1475 FT
GROUND ROLL (53% OF 1475)	782 FT
IAS APPROACH SPEED	87 MPH IAS

WEIGHT POUNDS	IAS APPROACH SPEED (ASSUMES ZERO INSTR. ERROR)	
	MPH	KNOTS
3400	90	78
3200	87	76
3000	84	73
2800	81	70
2600	78	68
2400	75	65

FIGURE 35.—Normal Landing Chart.

*   *   *

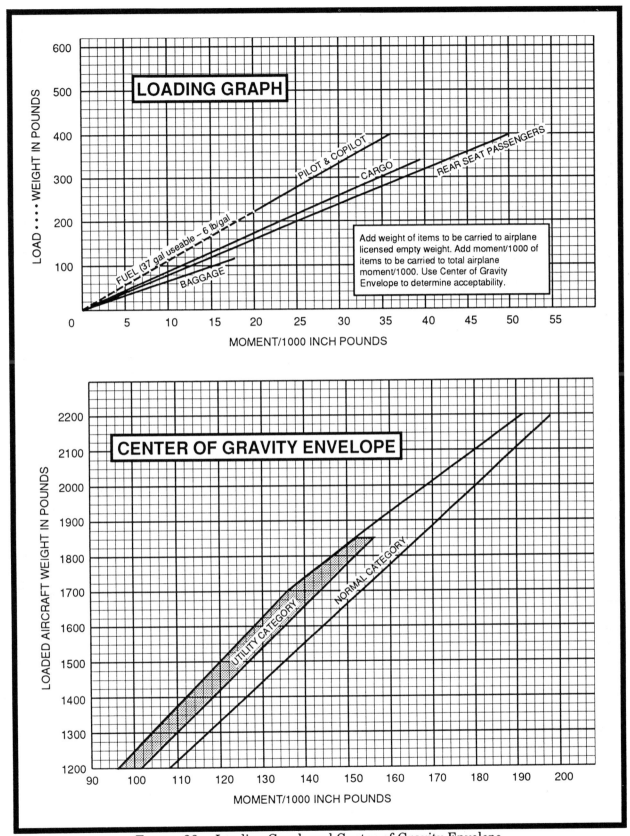

FIGURE 38.—Loading Graph and Center-of-Gravity Envelope.

*   *   *

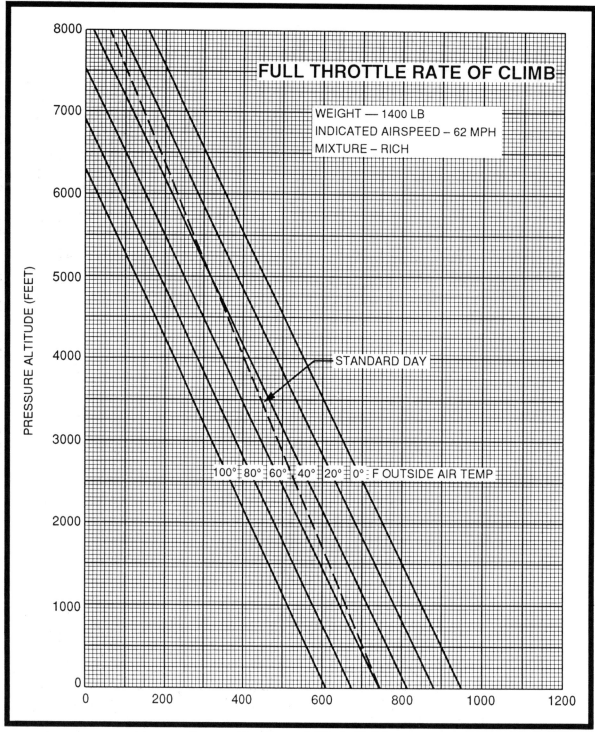

FIGURE 42.—Rate of Climb (Ft/Min).

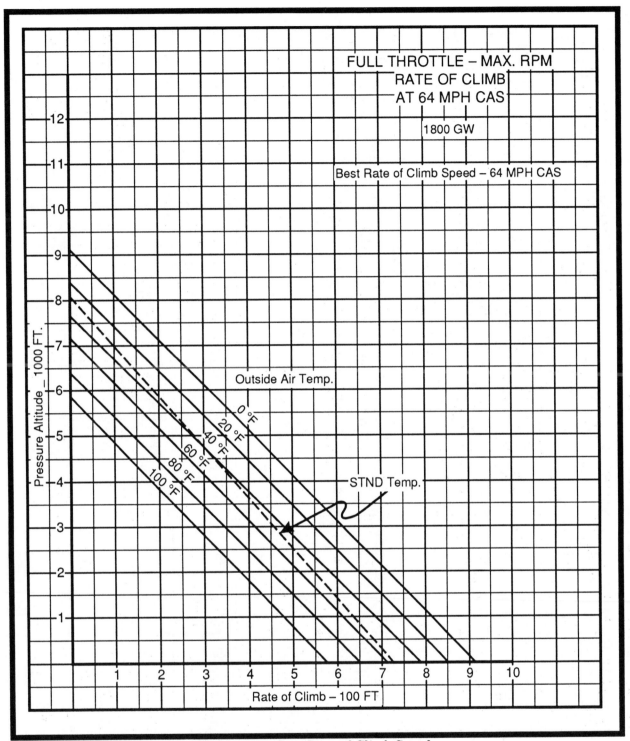

FIGURE 43.—Best Rate-of-Climb Speed.

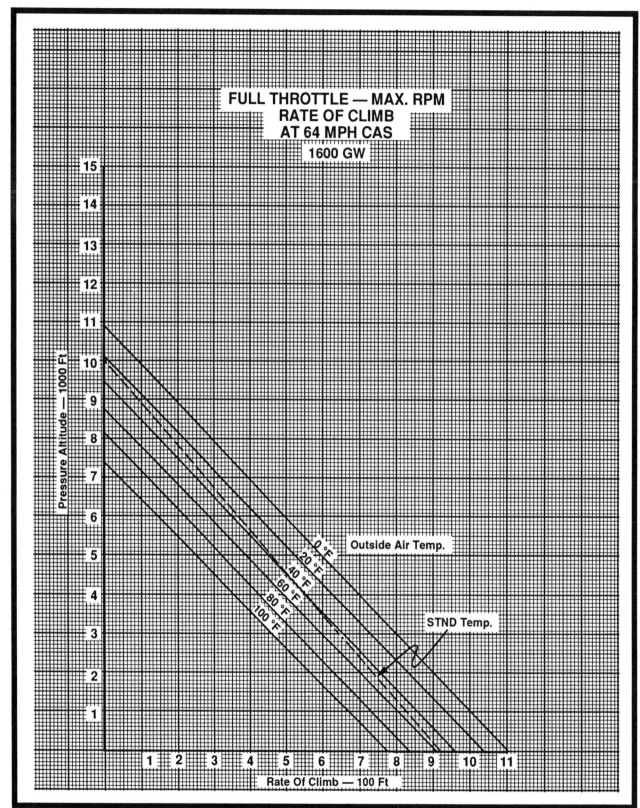

FIGURE 44.—Rate of Climb.

* * *

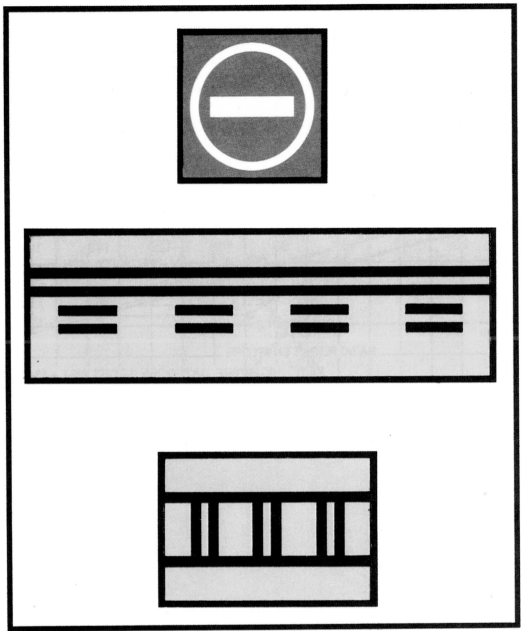

FIGURE 51.—Airport Signs.

FIGURE 52. – Sectional Chart Excerpt.

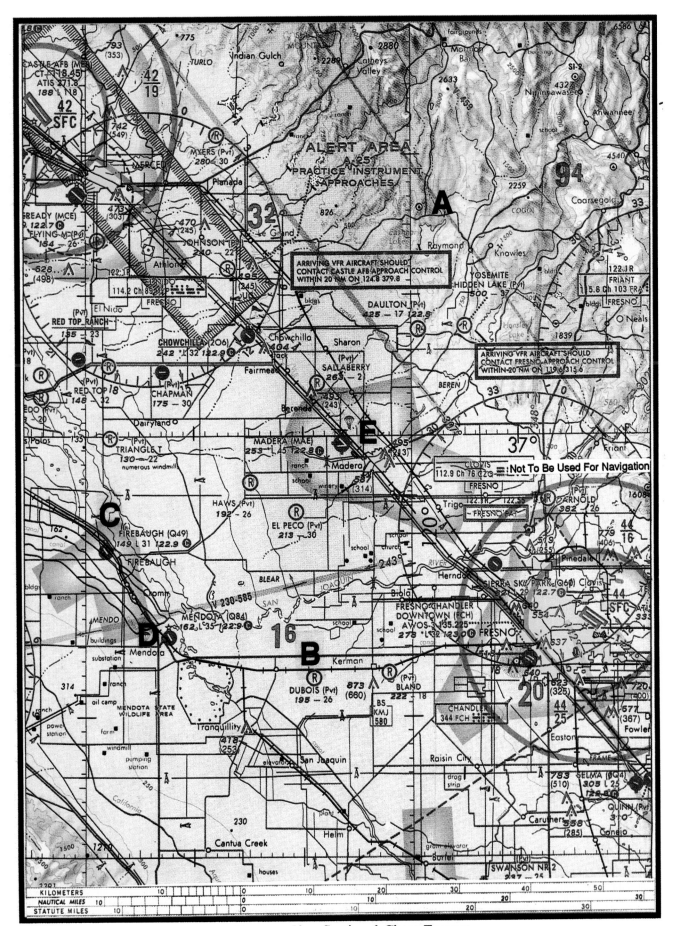

FIGURE 53.—Sectional Chart Excerpt.

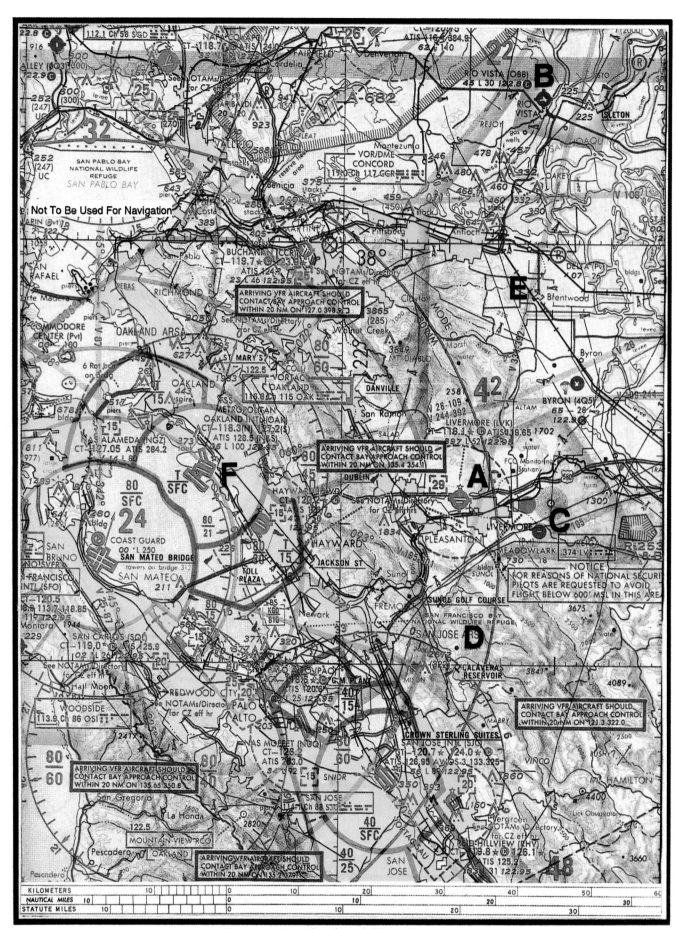

FIGURE 54.—Sectional Chart Excerpt.

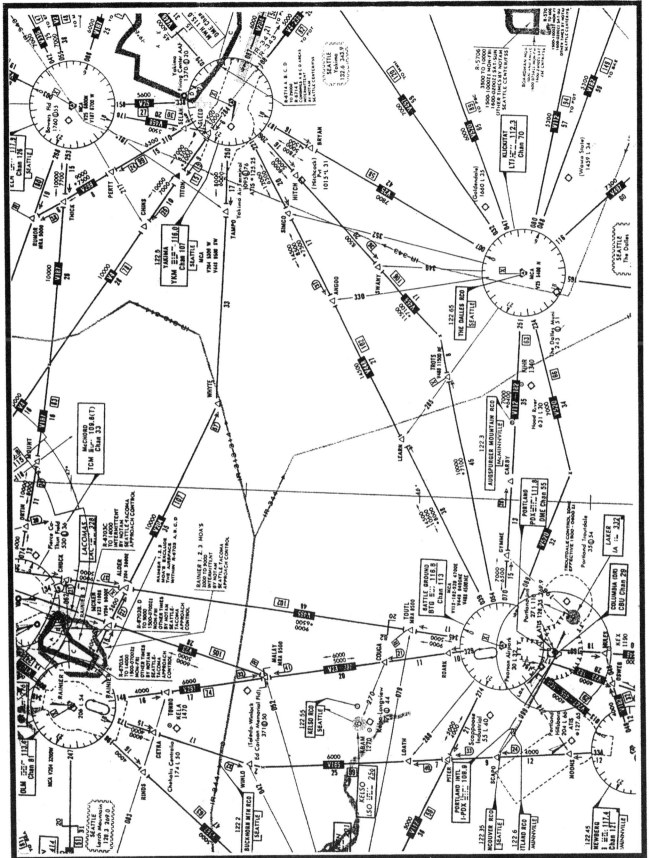

FIGURE 55.—En Route Low Altitude Chart Segment. (Chart printed in black and white for production purposes only—ISU Press)

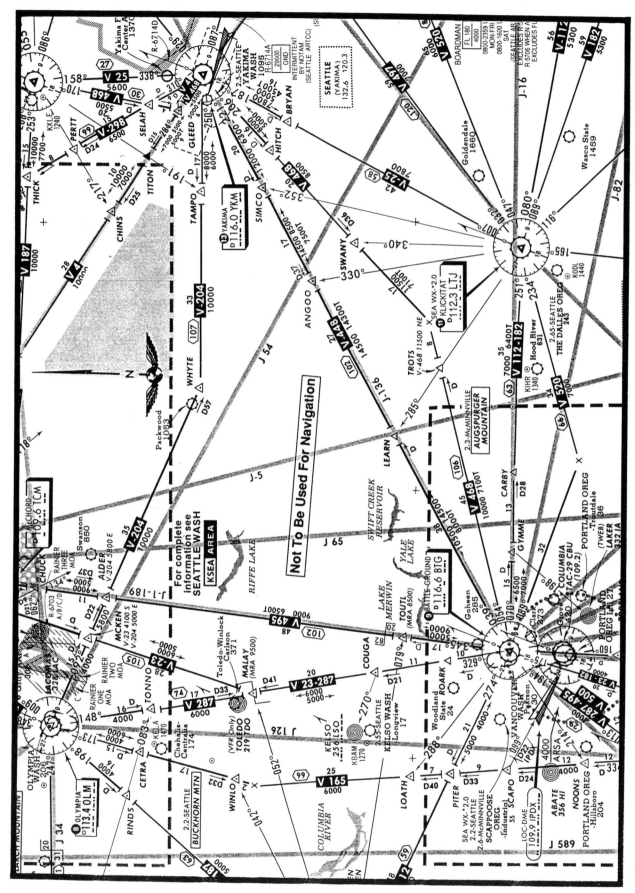

FIGURE 55A.—En Route Low Altitude Chart Segment. (Chart printed in black and white for production purposes only—ISU Press. Low altitude information, blue; J = routes, green, in actual chart)

ANSWERS AND EXPLANATIONS FOR FAA QUESTIONS

Introduction to Answers and Explanations—Read This! The following answers and explanations refer to illustrations and/or descriptions used in this book, as well as several other aviation references.

Reference abbreviations

The Advanced Pilot's Flight Manual—APFM
Aerodynamics for Naval Aviators—ANA
Airman's Information Manual—AIM
Aviation Instructor's Handbook—AIH
Aviation Weather—AW
Aviation Weather Service—AWS
Basic Aerobatic Manual—BAM
Federal Aviation Regulations—FAR 91.105 (for example)
The Flight Instructor's Manual—FIM
The Instrument Flight Manual—IFM
National Transportation Safety Board Part 830—NTSB 830

Examples:

5235. A. *APFM*, p. 24, col. 2, para. 5 (page 24, column 2, paragraph 5; count any partial paragraph at the top of a column as paragraph 1).
5491. B. *IFM*, pp. 108–14, Fig. 5-32.

If there could be confusion in the reader's mind about the wrong answers for a question, the reasons *why* they are wrong will be cited. When the steps leading to the correct answer are spelled out, in many cases it will not be necessary to explain why the other two choices were wrong.

The *Advanced Pilot's Flight Manual* was written for the pilot working on the commercial pilot certificate for *airplanes*. Only questions on airplanes from the FAA Written Test Book are answered and explained here. Questions and figures for other aircraft categories (hot air balloons, rotorcraft, blimps, and gliders) have been eliminated with a few exceptions. For instance questions 5240 through 5267 are not included here because they are not about *airplanes*. It's handled this way:

5239. When the angle of attack of a symmetrical airfoil is increased, the center of pressure will
A—have a very limited movement.
B—move aft along the airfoil surface.
C—remain unaffected.

* * *

The asterisks (*'s) following a question indicate that one or more questions not applying to *airplanes* have been deleted.

Reference figures for the Written Test have been deleted if they don't apply to airplanes (figures 6, 7, 36, 39–41, 45–50).

There are 100 questions (airplane) on the FAA Written Test and you currently have 4 hours to complete it. (Check for time limit changes with your instructor.) Those 100 questions will be taken from the questions here.

Too many people treat the Written Test as a chore that must be "gotten out of the way" so that training can proceed. You should use the review of these several hundred questions as a way to improve your knowledge of flying an airplane safely.

In earlier years, the questions used on any of the CAA/FAA Written Tests were *not* published in advance. Applicants knew only the *areas* of knowledge they would encounter when they sat down to take the test. It's believed that now, given time enough and good coaching, a person who had never even *been* to an airport could make a passing (or better) grade by studying the question books and explanations available. It is hoped that the old method of nonpublication of Written Test questions will be reinstated.

Answers and Explanations

5001. C. NTSB Part 830.2, Definitions and Part 830.5, Immediate Notification.

5002. C. NTSB 830.5, Notification.

5003. A. NTSB 830.5.

5004. A. NTSB 830.5 Discusses *in-flight* fire.

5005. C. NTSB 830.5(a)(4).

5006. A. NTSB 830.5. You have to report an accident immediately because in 830.3, one of the definitions of an accident is "substantial damage."

5007. C. NTSB 830.25(a).

5008. C. NTSB 830.25(a).

5009. B. When the control tower becomes inoperative, Class D airspace becomes Class E.

5010. C. *APFM*, FAR 1, Definitions.

5011. C. FAR 1, Operate.

5012. C. FAR 1, Operational control.

5013. B. FAR 1, V-speeds.

5014. A. FAR 1, V-speeds.

5015. A. V_F is the design flap speed.

5016. A. V_{LE} is the max gear *extended* (and locked) airspeed. Usually this is a higher airspeed than V_{LO} (max landing gear operating speed) because the landing gear and doors are more vulnerable to damage during the transition.

5017. __ No answer. Answer A says that spins are excluded, but this is not necessarily the case. Answer B says that spins are included but this is not necessarily so—utility category airplanes may meet the spin requirements (FAR 23.221) of normal category (no spins allowed) or acrobatic category, which allows the aircraft to be spun, subject to restrictions (for instance, front seat occupants only and no baggage, etc.). Answer C has the same problem because spins *may* be allowed (FAR 23.1563, Airspeed Placards and FAR 23.1583, Operating Limitations).

5018. C. FAR 61.3.

5019. C. FAR 1, Class (2).

5020. A. FAR 61.19(c).

5021. A. FAR 61.23(b).

5022. C. FAR 61.31(c).

5023. B. FAR 61.31(a)(1) and FAR 1, Definitions. "Large aircraft means aircraft of more than 12,500 pounds, maximum certificated takeoff weight."

5024. C. FAR 61.31(e).

5025. A. FAR 61.51(c)(3).

5026. A. FAR 61.51(a).

5027. C. FAR 61.57(d).

5028. B. FAR 61.57(d).

*   *   *

5031. C. FAR 61.56(c).

5032. A. FAR 61.60.

5033. B. FAR 61.69(b).

5034. C. FAR 61.69(b).

*   *   *

5039. C. FAR 61.129(a).

*   *   *

5041. C. FAR 61.195(a).

*   *   *

5043. B. FAR 71.5(c)(1).

5044. A. Class D is a cylinder (plus lateral extensions in some cases) of airspace beginning at the surface and it becomes Class E when the tower is not in operation.

5045. A. With the new airspace designations of September 16, 1993, the Continental Control Area no longer exists.

5046. C. Class C airspace extends from the surface to 2,500 feet AGL with a square depicting its top in MSL figures.

5047. B. See the answer for 5044.

*   *   *

5049. B. FAR 91.103(a).

5050. C. FAR 91.103(a)(b).

5051. B. FAR 91.105.

5052. A. FAR 91.107(a)(91)(2).

*   *   *

5055. B. FAR 91.311(a).

5056. C. FAR 91.21.

*   *   *

5059. B. FAR 91.167(a)(3).

5060. A. FAR 91.215(b)(1)(5). See answer for 5061. (*Excluding* airspace below 2,500 feet AGL.)

5061. A. FAR 91.215(b)(5).

5062. A. FAR 91.171(b)(1).

5063. C. FAR 91.211(a)(1).

5064. C. FAR 91.211(a)(3).

5065. A. FAR 91.205(c)(3).

5066. B. FAR 91.205(c)(4).

5067. B. FAR 91.205(b)(11).

*   *   *

5069. B. FAR 91.315.

5070. C. FAR 91.207(c)(1).

5071. A. FAR 91.23(c)(1).

*   *   *

5073. C. FAR 91.111(c).

5074. A. FAR 91.113(d).

5075. B. FAR 91.113(g).

5076. B. FAR 91.113(f).

5077. B. FAR 91.117(c).

5078. B. FAR 91.117(b). "Class B" was inadvertently added to this question. Check your latest FARs and note that FAR 91.117(b) does not mention "Class B," but choice B is correct.

5079. A. FAR 91.303(e)(f).

5080. A. FAR 91.209(a).

*   *   *

5082. C. FAR 91.131(b) and FAR 61.95.

5083. B. FAR 91.155.

5084. B. FAR 91.155. This one was included because it also fits powered aircraft.

5085. B. FAR 91.155.

5086. C. FAR 91.155.

5087. C. FAR 91.155(d)(1).

5088. A. FAR 91.157(b)(d)(1). That's *ground* visibility.

5089. B. FAR 91.157(d)(2).

5090. C. FAR 91.157(a)(2).

5091. B. FAR 91.159.

5092. C. FAR 91.177(a)(2).

5093. C. FAR 91.403(a).

5094. C. FAR 91.403(a).

5095. B. FAR 91.417(a)(1).

5096. C. FAR 91.417.

5097. B. FAR 91.407(b).

5098. B. FAR 91.407(a)(1)(2).

5099. C. FAR 91.409(b).

5100. B. An annual inspection may act as a 100-hour inspection but not vice versa.

5101. C. FAR 91.413(a).

5102. C. FAR 91.417(a)(2)(ii).

5103. B. FAR 91.417(a)(2)(v). Airworthiness Directives (ADs) affect the airworthiness of the aircraft and must be complied with. Some ADs may indicate that compliance must be within a certain time period, others may require compliance within a certain number of flight hours, and still others may require recurring action or inspections.

5104. C. FAR 91.421(b)(2).

5105. A. FAR 91.413(a).

5106. C. FAR 125.(1)(a).

5107. B. FAR 125.1(a)(c).

5108. C. FAR 125.3(a)(c).

5109. C. FAR 125.7(a).

5110. C. FAR 125.11(b).

5111. B. FAR 125.11(a).

5112. A. FAR 125.23(a).

5113. B. FAR 125.281(a).

5114. B. FAR 125.283(a).

5115. B. FAR 125.285(a).

5116. B. FAR 135.1(a)(1),(b)(1).

5117. C. FAR 135.1(a)(3).

*   *   *

5120. C. FAR 135.1(b).

5121. C. FAR 135.21(e).

5122. B. FAR 135.23(e).

5123. B. FAR 135.33(a).

5124. A. FAR 135.33(b).

5125. C. FAR 135.89(a)(2).

5126. C. FAR 135.85(b).

5127. B. FAR 135.87(c)(1).

5128. B. FAR 135.87(c)(1).

5129. C. FAR 135.89(a)(2).

5130. B. FAR 135.89(a)(2).

5131. A. FAR 135.93(a).

5132. C. FAR 135.105(a).

5133. C. FAR 135.107.

5134. B. FAR 135.117(c)(e).

5135. A. FAR 135.149(c).

5136. C. FAR 135.171(a).

*   *   *

5138. C. FAR 135.183(a).

5139. C. FAR 135.203(a)(2).

5140. B. FAR 135.203(a)(2).

*   *   *

5142. C. FAR 135.203(a)(1).

5143. C. FAR 135.203(a)(1).

*   *   *

5146. C. FAR 135.205(a).

*   *   *

5148. B. FAR 135.211(b)(2).

*   *   *

5150. A. FAR 135.243(c)(2).

5151. A. *APFM,* p. 145, col. 2, para. 4; also see Fig. 11-2, *APFM,* and figure 4 in Appendix 2 of this Written Test Book. The load factor equals Lift/Weight and, the stall speed is a *function of the square root* of the load factor.
B. The "aspect load" is not a known term.
C. It's the load factor alright but it *does* have a relation to stall speed (see answer A).

5152. A. See references for question 5151.
B. No, the lift is *divided* by the total weight of the airplane at the time the load is imposed.
C. No, use the *actual* weight, not the basic empty weight.

5153. A. Check Fig. 11-2 *APFM* and figure 4 in Appendix 2 of this Written Test Book.
B. If the airplane has a constant bank and is in a coordinated, *constant-altitude* turn, the rate of turn will be constant and there will be no change of load factor.
C. The load factor is constant and the stall speed will *not* decrease, but increase as in the 1-g stall.

5154. B. *APFM,* p. 142, col.1, para. 2. In a coordinated (balanced), level turn, the *angle of bank controls the stall speed* (Fig. 11-2).
   A. Well, the rate of turn goes right along with the angle of bank in a coordinated turn, but that's not the best answer.
   C. Nope, true airspeed has nothing to do with wing loading—bank controls it (balanced turn). For instance, a jet in a balanced, 30°-banked turn at 1000 knots has exactly the same load factor as a C-152 in a 30° balanced turn at 90 knots.

5155. A. The stall speed increases as a function of the square root of the load factor, whether imposed in a turn or a pull-up.

5156. B. In a 60°-banked, constant-altitude turn, the airplane would require doubling the lift to 4,000 pounds and 2 g's would be imposed (*APFM,* Fig. 11-1).

5157. B. The load factor depends on the angle of bank in a coordinated, constant-altitude turn. The airspeed for a given bank would make no difference. (See the explanation C for question 5154.) Check Turns, *APFM,* p. 8. The turn radius would be greater even though the g's imposed on the airplane and pilot are the same.

5158. A. This answer says it all, since Lift is a force. See Fig. 2-2, *APFM.*
   B. No. Is that differential pressure acting "up" or "down?"
   C. Great Scott! What does *that* mean?

5159. A. This is the closest to correct. Assuming a *balanced, constant-altitude* and constant banked turn, the radius would increase only with a change in airspeed and the load factor would not change, but the radius would:

   Turn Radius (feet) = V² knots/11.26 Tan φ

5160. B. Turbulence increases the stall speed if vertical upgusts are present. Check Fig. 11-10, *APFM,* which shows that the maneuvering speed is on the low side of the recommended gust penetration range (shaded area). The V_A is indicated as the airspeed directly below the upper left-hand corner of the maneuver envelope.

5161. C. *APFM,* p. 16, col. 1, para. 2.

5162. B. *APFM,* p. 17, Fig. 2-31. The point at which parasite drag and induced drag are equal is the minimum drag point, or the max Lift-to-Drag ratio. As the airplane is slowed from that point, the induced drag increases, thereby increasing the total drag again.

5163. C. The load factor is controlled by the bank in a balanced, constant-altitude turn. The added airspeed will increase the turn radius. See the explanation for question 5159. Since the radius is a function of V², if the airspeed is increased by a factor of 1.5 (from 90 to 135 knots) the turn radius will increase by $(1.5)^2 = 2.25$ times.

5164. B. This is a simple multiplier question: A normal category airplane has a maximum required positive load limit of 3.8 positive g's, so the baggage compartment floor could withstand up to $3.8 \times 100 = 380$ pounds without deformation (see *APFM,* p. 147 and note that the normal category plane is required to have positive g limits of 2.5 to 3.8 g's, and it's assumed that 3.8 is the number for this question). So, $90 \times 3.5 = 315$ pounds and for the assumptions stated would not be excessive.

5165. A. The low point on the drag versus velocity curve is the max Lift-to-Drag ratio or max L/D.

5166. B. The *airspeed* at point B would be the one to fly for max glide *at* a particular weight. See *APFM,* p. 7, concerning max distance glides and p. 108 also discusses this.

5167. C. *APFM,* Fig. 2-6. Induced drag and hence total drag is increased with an increase in angle of attack.

* * *

5169. B. *SPFM,* p. 51, col. 2, para. 5; *Basic Aerobatic Manual,* p. 11. This means that a mag (or both mags) is not grounded. The engine could start if someone moves the propeller, even with the key turned OFF and out of the ignition.

5170. C. The carburetor heat richens the mixture and can cause a significant loss of power on takeoff, particularly in conditions of high density-altitude.

5171. A. *Idle* the engine for this check, as indicated in this answer. Cutting the ignition off at high power settings can result in a backfire and possible engine-system damage.

5172. A. Plugs are more likely to foul if the mixture is too rich, and as the airplane climbs the mixture will become richer if no adjustment is made.

5173. C. If a ground wire is broken, that magneto is "hot," or ON. Answer A is a possibility for older airplanes that do not have a mixture control for shutting the engine down. However, answer C is the best choice here.

5174. C. This writer used to hand-prop airplanes as a line boy, and the Meyers OTW biplane with its 5-cylinder Kinner engine would often have a loose ground wire in a magneto because of vibration. The mags were always treated as if they were "hot."

5175. B. The circulation of lubricating oil has a decided effect on engine cooling. Be sure that the oil supply is at a proper level at any time, but it's particularly important during the hotter months.

5176. C. *APFM,* pp. 165–69. The mixture control is the air/fuel ratio control.

5177. C. *APFM,* pp. 7–8, 149–51. The maneuvering speed *varies* with the square root of the weight change ratio, so a fixed number would not apply.

5178. B. *APFM,* p. 59, Fig. 4-36.

5179. C. Looking at figure 2 in this Written Test Book, you see that the stall speed (the lowest available for that weight) is 47 knots with the power ON and gear and flaps down.

5180. A. The airplane stalls (power ON) with gear and flaps up at 76 knots; with gear and flaps down the stall speed is 66 knots in a 60° bank.

B. No. The stall speed with flaps up, power OFF, 60° bank is 92 knots. The wings level, power OFF, flaps down stall speed is 57 knots, a difference of 35 knots. The clean configuration stall at 60° bank is 35 knots *higher, not lower* than the flaps down, wings level condition. (Read the question carefully.)

C. No. In the clean configuration this is true (64−54 knots = 10 knots) but with the flaps down the difference is 9 knots (56−47 knots). The choice does not indicate the configuration.

5181. B. *APFM,* pp. 11−12. The raising of flaps increases the stall speed.

A. No. See above.

C. The required forward or back pressure with flaps retracting varies with the airplane type and model.

5182. B. *APFM,* p. 12, High-Lift Devices.

5183. C. *APFM,* p. 158, Prop Controls.

5184. B. *APFM,* p. 156, Using the Throttle and Propeller Controls.

5185. A. *APFM,* p. 167, col. 2.

5186. C. *APFM,* p. 167. col. 2.

5187. B. *APFM,* p. 165, Leaning.

5188. A. *APFM,* p. 165, Leaning.

5189. A. *APFM,* p. 194, col. 1, next to last paragraph.

5190. C. *APFM,* p. 167, col. 2.

5191. C. *APFM,* p. 28, col. 2, para. 9.

5192. C. *APFM,* pp. 8−9, Turns; pp. 34−37, Forces in the Turn.

5193. A. *APFM,* pp. 8−9, Turns; pp. 34−37, Forces in the Turn.

5194. A. *APFM,* pp. 34−35, Figs. 3-16 and 3-17.

5195. B. *APFM,* pp. 34−35, Figs. 3-16 and 3-17.

5196. A. The stall speed is a function of the weight or load factor and is less with power. See question 5179 and its answer again.

5197. B. *ANA,* p. 78, Fig. 1.33.

5198. A. *APFM,* chap. 3. While this is the best choice of answers, you can note that except in a constant-altitude turn, or an abrupt pull-up or pushover, lift doesn't vary much for the normal regimes of flight (straight and level, climbs and glides).

5199. C. *APFM,* p. 10, Figs. 2-5 and 2-6.

5200. C. *APFM,* p. 28. The term "in theory" is good because an airplane normally cannot double its airspeed

while maintaining a constant angle of attack. If the lift is increased four times, the airplane will be doing a 4-g pull-up or part of a loop!

5201. C. *APFM,* p. 10, Figs. 2-5 and 2-6; *ANA,* p. 19, Fig. 1.9.

5202. B. *APFM,* p. 28, col. 2.

5203. A. *APFM,* p. 28, col. 2; also see *APFM,* chap. 3; p. 145, col. 2 for more detail on forces in the turn.

5204. A. Weight, dynamic pressure (airspeed), bank angle, or pitch attitude may change, but the stall angle of attack remains the same (for a given flap configuration).

5205. B. In a spin, the airplane rotates around the CG, which moves around the spin axis, which has a position with respect to a vertical earth axis. If the CG is too far aft, a flat spin results with a difficult, if not impossible, chance of recovery. See *APFM,* p. 250, col. 1.

5206. C. *APFM,* p. 376, Instrument Indications; *FIM,* p. 228, Figs. 21-4 and 21-5. In a side-by-side airplane with the ball on the left side of the panel, the ball will be displaced to the *left in both left and right spins.*

5207. B. *APFM,* p. 122, col. 2 and Fig. 10-7. The airplane will be unstable in pitch, or around the lateral or Y axis.

5208. A. The dynamic pressure (calibrated or correct indicated airspeed) needed to produce lift at a given speed is the same at any *altitude* if weight and configuration are the same.

5209. B. *APFM,* pp. 17−18, Ground Effect.

5210. C. To maintain a constant altitude if the airspeed is increased (and it's assumed that the weight stays the same), the angle of attack must be *decreased* or the angle of bank *increased.*

5211. C. While the stall is always at the same angle of attack for a given flap configuration, the indicated or, more accurately, the calibrated stall airspeed varies as the square root of the wing loading. Also see *APFM,* p. 6, col. 2, Stall Speed for the mathematical discussion of *why.*

5212. A. *APFM,* p. 146, col. 2. The airplane can be stalled at any attitude and/or airspeed. (Don't stall it at too high an airspeed or you could overstress the airplane.)

5213. B. Looking at figure 3 in this Written Test Book at 10° angle of attack for that airplane, a L/D of 11 is found. (That's the glide ratio.) In other words the airplane will lose 1 ft for every 11 ft it moves forward:

$$5{,}280/11 = 480 \text{ ft of altitude loss.}$$

5214. C. Looking again at figure 3, for 8° you see that the L/D is 12. For 3 miles (3 × 5,280 = 15,840); 15,840/12 = 1320 ft of altitude lost.

5215. C. Using figure 3 follow the 2° angle of attack value until it intersects the L/D curve, then move to the right to re-intersect it, and then down to get an angle of attack of approximately 16.5°.

5216. A. The Lift slope (C_L vs. angle of attack) is steeper in ground effect, meaning that for a given angle of attack more Lift is attained in ground effect (*APFM,* p. 18, col. 2, para. 8). The induced Drag is decreased in ground effect as shown in *APFM,* Fig. 2-32.

5217. B. *APFM,* p. 99, col. 1, A Look at Maximum Range Conditions; and *APFM,* p. 108, para. 1, Maximum Distance Glide.

5218. C. *APFM,* p. 33, Fig. 3-13.

5219. B. Check the Lift equation (*APFM,* p. 10, col. 2). As pilots, we play angle of attack airspeed to maintain altitude as needed, from slow flight to fast cruise (slow flight = high angle of attack; fast cruise = low angle of attack).

5220. C. In the transition from straight and level to climb, the Lift is momentarily increased, but after the climb is established, Lift is less than it was in straight and level (*APFM,* Fig. 3-11).

5221. C. Looking at figure 4 in this Written Test Book, the stall speed curve shows an increase of slightly more than 40%. The new stall speed is 1.4 × 60 = 84 k. The stall speed goes up (or down) with the square root of the weight or a load factor. If you have a calculator capable of taking square roots, find the square root of the load factor and multiply that number times the 1-g stall speed (*APFM,* p. 6, Stall Speed).

5222. C. Check figure 4 and note that the load factor in a 60° bank is 2 g's, and the load factor in a 80° bank is 6 g's; the increase is 4 g's (*APFM,* p. 146, col. 1).

5223. C. *APFM,* p. 100, col. 2, para. 4. For a given condition (for instance, max range), the same indicated (calibrated) airspeed would be used, but this would mean that the TAS will be increased with altitude, making up for the lower density and therefore producing the same lift for a given angle of attack.

5224. A. *APFM,* pp. 17–18, Ground Effect; also see the answer for 5216.

5225. A. It's assumed that the bank is in a *balanced constant-altitude turn* and no added back pressure is being applied, so A is the answer.

5226. A. *APFM,* p. 137, Fig. 10-46.

5227. B. *APFM,* p. 137, Fig. 10-46. Longitudinal dynamic instability (or *negative* longitudinal dynamic stability) is shown in that figure.

5228. B. *APFM,* p. 122, col. 2, last paragraph. The elevator controls pitch (longitudinal stability motions).

5229. B. As the airplane is slowed, the decrease in dynamic pressure (airspeed) requires an increase in angle of attack (coefficient of Lift) to keep the "up" and "down" forces balanced.

5230. B. *APFM,* p. 121, Static Stability.

5231. B. *APFM,* p. 149, The Maneuver Envelope, Fig. 11-4.

5232. A. *APFM,* p. 149, Fig. 11-4. That's the upper end of the yellow arc (and also the red line).

5233. A. *APFM,* pp. 148–149. Airspeed Indicator Markings and Important Airspeeds, Fig. 11-4.

5234. A. The airplane performance depends on the pressure altitude (plus temperature), which results in density-altitude. Remember that *true altitude* is the actual height above sea level and doesn't take temperature into effect.

5235. A. *APFM,* p. 24, col. 2, para. 5.

5236. B. *APFM,* p. 21. Looking at Fig. 2-40, you see the efficiency curves of several "fixed-pitch" propellers (15°, 20°, 25° pitch) at different airspeeds. The constant-speed propeller would result in an envelope of peak efficiencies.

5237. C. *APFM,* p. 19, Propeller.

5238. B. *APFM,* p. 21, last paragraph; also see *IFM,* p. 32, Slipstream Effect. The fact that the slipstream is hitting the fin and rudder on the left side means there is a tendency to yaw left and, because the surfaces extend above the longitudinal (fuselage) axis, a roll to the right around that axis is induced.

5239. C. *ANA,* p. 49. "An increase in lift on the symmetrical airfoil produces no change in this situation and the center of pressure remains fixed at the aerodynamic center." (Also see *ANA,* p. 48, Fig. 1.21.)

* * *

5268. C. *APFM,* pp. 68–69, The Turn and Slip, and Turn Coordinator.

5269. A. *APFM,* p. 69. It's better to have different power sources for the precession (T/C and T/S) and rigidity-in-space (A/I and H/I) instruments, so a failure of either electrical or vacuum systems doesn't leave the pilot without references.

5270. B. At a standard-rate turn of 3° per second, 120 seconds, or 2 minutes, is required to complete 360° turns.

5271. A. Lycoming Service Bulletin 245 warns against abrupt throttle change (opening *or* closing) because of possible damage to the counterweights (which are there to damp out the torsion of the crankshaft as it turns). There are also other actions that can detune the counterweights. (A good book about practical aspects of engine operations is *Aircraft Engine Operating Guide* by Kas Thomas, Belvoir Publications, Greenwich, CT.)

5272. C. There is no apparent motion between the aircraft. This is the way one military pilot may "eyeball" a join-up with another aircraft. Also, if the other aircraft is level with the horizon, this means that it is on or very close to your altitude (*AIM,* 8-8).

* * *

5298. B. The best power mixture is a fuel/air ratio that allows the engine to develop the most power for a given throttle, or RPM setting, so it will vary with the horsepower being used. An excellent book on this and other engine information is *Aircraft Powerplants,* 5th Edition, by Bent and McKinley, McGraw-Hill Book Co., New York, NY.

5299. A. *APFM,* p. 167, col. 2. Detonation may be caused by a too-lean mixture, abrupt throttle opening and using a lower-grade fuel than recommended.

5300. C. *ANA,* p. 199. As the temperature increases or at high density-altitudes, the thrust decreases.

5301. A. *AW.* "Temperature variations create forces that drive the atmosphere in its endless motions."

5302. A. The standard sea level temperature is 15°C; the standard lapse rate is −2°C/1,000 feet. 15° − (10 × 2) = −5°C.

5303. C. Again, the standard sea level temperature is 15°C. 15° − (20 × 2°C) = 15 − 40 = −25°C.

5304. A. *AW.* On clear, calm, cool nights, the surface cools rapidly and the air near the surface may be cooler than the air above it (an inversion).

5305. A. Standard temperatures at sea level are 15°C, or 59°F. Pressures are 1013.2 millibars, 29.92″ Hg, 2,116 pounds per square foot, or 14.7 psi.

5306. B. One way to work the problem without getting out the computer is to review *APFM,* p. 75, col. 2, and realize that the sea level standard temperature is 59°F and the standard lapse rate is 3.5°F/1,000 feet. The standard temperature at 12,000 feet is 59° − (12 × 3.5) = 59 − 42 = 17°F, *but* the temperature given is 50°F, which is 33°F *higher than standard.* Using the procedure in *APFM,* p. 75 (add 1,000 feet of density-altitude for every 15°F *above* that altitude standard temperature), you'd add 33/15 × 1,000 = 2.2 × 1,000 = 2,200 feet. Adding 2,200 to 12,000 gives an answer of 14,200 feet, which is close to answer B.

5307. A. Okay, here Celsius is being used and for every 8.5°C above or below standard for that altitude, add or subtract 1,000 feet to get the density-altitude.

Standard at 5,000 feet = 15° − (5 × 2°C) = 5°C.
Temperature of 30°C is 25°C high.
25/8.5 = 2.94 × 1,000 = 2,940 feet.
5,000 + 2,940 = 7,940 feet density-altitude.

Using two different types of computers, the rule of thumb and a computer, the density-altitude is closest to A, or 7,800 feet. The thumb rule answer is off by 140 feet but that's reasonably close for an altitude of 7,800 feet. Use a computer if one is available.

5308. B. Pressure altitude 6,000 feet and temperature 30°F. Standard temperature at 6,000 feet (F°) = 59° − (6 × 3.5) = 59 − 21 = 38°F. By rule of thumb, the temperature is 8°F *low,* so the density-altitude will be *lower* than the pressure altitude given. Using the rule of thumb:

6000 − 8/15 × 1,000 = 6,000 − 533 = 5,467, or 5,500 feet.

Using a computer, you get 5,508 feet, so B is the answer.

5309. B. Using the thumb rule and noting that the standard temperature at 7,000 feet should be 15 − (7 × 2) = 1°C, the temperature is 14°C above standard for that pressure altitude, so the density-altitude is approximately 1,650 feet higher, or 8,650 feet. Working the problem on (1) a manual and (2) an electronic computer, you get (1) 8,600 feet and (2) 8,595 feet.

5310. C. *AW.* Pressure differences create winds as the air masses try to reach equilibrium.

5311. A. *AW.* The wind is deflected to the right in the Northern Hemisphere by the Coriolis force.

5312. A. *AW.* "When the Coriolis force deflects the wind until it is parallel to the isobars, the pressure gradient balances the Coriolis force."

5313. B. *AW.* A cyclone is a counterclockwise flow in the Northern Hemisphere.

5314. C. *AW.* ". . . closely spaced isobars mean strong winds; widely spaced isobars mean lighter wind."

5315. A. *AW.* "The pressure gradient force drives the wind and is perpendicular to the isobars . . . the instant air begins moving, Coriolis force deflects it to the right. Soon the wind is deflected a full 90° and is parallel to the isobars or contours."

5316. A. *AW.* A left crosswind in the Northern Hemisphere indicates that the aircraft is flying toward a low pressure area, or that you are flying toward an area of generally unfavorable weather conditions. Also see the answer for 5317.

5317. C. *AW.* "Highs and ridges . . . are areas of descending air. Descending air favors dissipation of cloudiness; hence the association, high pressure = good weather."

5318. B. *AW.* "Rising air is conducive to cloudiness and precipitation . . . low pressure = bad weather."

5319. B. Approaching a low pressure, the pressure gradient will be increasing, which results in stronger winds. Also see the answer for 5316.

5320. B. *AW.* "As the (temperature-dewpoint) spread becomes less, relative humidity increases and it is 100% when temperature and dewpoint are the same."

5321. A. *AW.* "Highs and ridges, therefore, are areas of descending air. . . . Winds spiral outward clockwise from high pressure. . . ."

5322. A. *AW.* "Virga—Water or ice particles falling from a cloud, usually in wisps or streaks and evaporating before reaching the ground."

5323. C. *AW.* "Evaporation is the changing of liquid water to invisible water vapor. . . . Sublimation is the changing of ice directly to water vapor."

5324. B. The surface warm front has not reached your position and the warmer rain above has frozen as it passes through the colder air below the warm front.

5325. A. *AW.* Ice pellets always indicate freezing rain at a higher altitude.

5326. C. *AW.* See answer to 5325.

5327. C. A high moisture content, unstable air, and very warm surface temperature are the ideal combination for strong updrafts with cumulonimbus clouds.

5328. C. *AW.* "Cloud base determination: Temperature and dewpoint in upward moving air converge at a rate of about 4°F or 2.2°C per 1,000 feet." Note: Other sources use 4.5°F/1,000 feet. The difference in temperature is 18°F, using 4.5°F/1,000, the added elevation is 4,000 feet for a total of 6,000 feet MSL.

5329. C. *AW.* "When stable air is forced upward, the air tends to retain horizontal flow and any cloudiness is flat and stratified." The result is little or no turbulence.

5330. B. *AW.* "Whether the air is stable or unstable within a layer largely determines cloud structure."

5331. B. Using the temperature and dewpoint spread (89 − 45 = 44°F) and dividing that by 4.4 (or 4.5 depending on your source) gives a cloud base of 10,000 feet AGL:

$$44/4.4 \times 1,000 = 10,000 \text{ feet AGL.}$$

5332. B. *AW.* "In stable air, flying is usually smooth but can sometimes be plagued by low ceiling and visibility." Stable air makes stratus-type clouds and steady precipitation.

5333. A. *AW.* "When the air near the surface is warm and moist, suspect instability."

5334. B. *AW.* "A change in ambient temperature can change this balance (between stable and unstable air)."

5335. C. *AW.* "Thunderstorms are sure signs of violently unstable air. Showers and clouds towering upward indicate strong updrafts and turbulent air."

5336. B. *AW.* "When the air near the surface is warm and moist, suspect instability." When the surface or lower air is cooler, a stable condition or inversion exists.

5337. B. *AW.* ". . . within a stable layer, clouds are stratiform." Moist air is necessary for clouds to form.

5338. C. *AW.* "A cumulous cloud . . . forms in a convective updraft and builds upward." (Cirrus and nimbostratus clouds are in a stable condition.)

5339. B. *AW.* Standing lenticular altocumulus clouds indicate very strong turbulence.

5340. B. *AW.* "Within a stable layer, clouds are stratiform . . . within an unstable layer clouds are cumuliform. . . ."

5341. B. When an unstable layer of moist air is lifted orographically, cumuliform-type clouds and showery rain (and comparatively good visibility) result.

5342. A. *AW.* ". . . clouds in stable air form in horizontal, sheet-like layers or 'strata,' . . . within a *stable* layer, clouds are *stratiform*." (The italics were added by this writer.) The other two answers are the characteristics of *unstable* air.

5343. B. A quick answer choice, because a moist unstable air mass is normally characterized by cumuliform clouds and rough air, which eliminates answers A and C.

5344. C. *AW.* Stable air normally has smooth air stratus-type clouds and poor visibility conditions, so answers A and B are eliminated.

5345. C. *AW* indicates that restricted visibility is a result of stable air.

5346. C. Stable air has continuous precipitation with stratus-type clouds.

5347. B. *AW.* In the cold front occlusion, the *coldest* air is under the warm front. The *cool* air ahead of the front is replaced by that colder air.

5348. B. *AW.* "Cool air moving over a warm surface is heated from below generating instability and increasing the possibility of showers." *Unstable air* results in cumuliform clouds, turbulent air, and good visibility, except in blowing obstructions.

5349. C. Unstable moist air with lifting action is the maker of cumulonimbus clouds and the resulting turbulent conditions.

5350. C. *AW.* "Precipitation induced fog . . . is most commonly associated with warm fronts but can occur with slow moving cold fronts and with stationary fronts."

5351. C. *AW.* Wind shear can be present at any level and can exist both horizontally (in a low-level temperature inversion or in a frontal zone) or vertically (between up and down currents in a thunderstorm).

5352. C. See the explanation for 5351.

5353. B. *AW.* If there is a low-level temperature inversion with relatively strong winds above the inversion, wind shear may exist.

5354. A. *AW.* A strong wind above a low-level inversion may create a wind shear hazard because of a possible stall.

5355. A. *AW.* Under the conditions cited, "allow a margin of airspeed above normal climb or approach speed to alleviate dangers of a stall. . . . You can be relatively certain of a shear zone in the inversion if the wind at 1,000 to 4,000 feet is 25 knots or more."

5356. A. *AW.* "Convective currents are most active on warm summer afternoons when winds are light."

5357. B. *AW.* Flying toward a mountain on the leeward side in strong winds can result in the airplane being unable to "outclimb the downdraft."

5358. C. The power and vertical velocity required to stay on the proper glide path is the answer because wind shear would not affect the trim or necessary heading changes.

5359. A. *AW.* If the aircraft encounters a sudden tailwind (or a loss of headwind) and a corresponding loss of airspeed, a stall is possible because the airplane drops, increasing its angle of attack.

5360. C. Precipitation will be in the form of rain at altitudes where the temperature is 32°F or higher. As it falls through a layer of sub-freezing air (at altitude or on the surface), freezing rain may occur on impact with the surface (or on impact with your airplane).

5361. C. Hailstones may be "thrown out" of the top of thunderstorms and be encountered several miles from the actual storms.

5362. B. Hail is formed by *very strong* vertical currents (cumulonimbus type clouds) moving drops of rain up to the freezing level. The drops then fall to gather more moisture, which builds the characteristic layers in hail. Rain at the surface does not mean that hail won't be found at higher altitudes.

5363. B. *AW.* "A squall line often contains severe steady-state thunderstorms and presents the single most intense weather hazard to aircraft."

5364. C. *AW.* "Outside the cloud, shear turbulence has been encountered several thousand feet above and 20 miles laterally from a severe (thunder) storm."

5365. A. See the answer to 5364. *AW.* "Avoid the most intense (radar) echoes by at least 20 miles; that is, echoes should be separated by at least 40 miles before you fly between them."

5366. C. *AW.* "A *squall line* is a non-frontal, narrow band of active thunderstorms. It often contains severe steady-state thunderstorms. . . ."

5367. C. *AW.* See the answer to 5363.

5368. B. *AW.* "Precipitation beginning to fall from the cloud base is your signal that a downdraft has developed and the cell has entered the mature stage."

5369. C. *AW.* "The cumulonimbus gives visual warning of violent convective turbulence. . . . The roll cloud is most prevalent with cold frontal or squall line thunderstorms and signifies an extremely turbulent zone. . . . The more frequent the lightning the more severe the thunderstorm."

5370. A. See the answer to 5368.

5371. B. *AW.* "The key feature of the cumulus stage is an updraft. . . ."

5372. C. *AW.* "Downdrafts characterize the dissipating stage of the thunderstorm cell. . . ."

5373. C. See the answer to 5365.

5374. C. *AW.* "(Precipitation-induced fog) is most commonly associated with warm fronts, but can occur with slow moving cold fronts and stationary fronts."

5375. A. *AW.* ". . . weather radar detects only precipitation drops; it does not detect minute cloud droplets. Therefore *the radar scope provides no assurance of avoiding instrument weather in clouds or fog.*"

5376. B. *AW.* "Advection fog forms when moist air moves over colder ground or water. It is most common along coastal areas but often develops deep in continental areas. At sea it is called 'sea fog.' "

5377. C. *AW.* "Advection fog deepens as the wind increases up to 15 knots. Wind much stronger than 15 knots lifts the fog into a layer of low stratus or stratocumulus."

5378. C. See the answer and explanation for 5377.

5379. A. *AW.* "Radiation fog is restricted to land because water surfaces cool little from nighttime radiation." Advection fog is most common along coastal areas. Steam fog forms over a water surface.

5380. C. *AW.* ". . . advection fog is usually more extensive and much more persistent than radiation fog. Advection fog can move in rapidly regardless of the time of day or night."

5381. B. *AW.* "An abrupt change in temperature lapse rate characterizes the tropopause."

5382. A. *AW.* "A preferred location of CAT is in an upper trough on the cold (polar) side of the jetstream."

5383. B. *AW.* ". . . when high level moisture is available, cirriform clouds form on the equatorial side of the jet(stream). . . . Such cloudiness ranges primarily from scattered to broken coverage in shallow layers or streaks."

5384. B. *AW.* "In mid-latitude, wind speed in the jetstream averages considerably stronger in winter than in summer. Also the jet shifts farther south in winter than in summer."

5385. A. See the answer to 5384.

* * *

5398. A. The facilities cited have information stored but have a request/reply service for out-of-the-ordinary weather requests.

5399. A. The FSS or WSO has the latest information. The ATIS broadcast only gives local airport information. Class II NOTAMs are normally printed and aren't up to date with the daily situation.

5400. B. *AIM*, para. 7–9.

5401. B. *AIM*, para. 7–8.

5402. C. RADAT is a contraction signifying "freezing-level data." The relative humidity was 87% and the 0°C level was at 4,500 feet MSL.

5403. B. RF2 RB12. Rain and fog are obscuring two-tenths of the sky and the rain began at 12 minutes past the hour.

5404. B. Okay, the field elevation is 3,500 feet, and the ceiling is 500 feet, so the base of the clouds is 4,000 feet MSL. The top of the overcast is reported as 7,500 feet (MSL), so the thickness of the layer is 3,500 feet.

5405. C. *AWS* indicates: "A *squall* is a sudden increase in (wind) speed of at least 15 knots to a sustained speed of 20 knots or more lasting for at least one minute."

5406. B. *AWS.* The top of the lower overcast is 2,500 feet, and the base of the second layer is 4,500 feet with its top at 9,000 feet MSL. *All PIREP heights are given as MSL.*

5407. A. Pilot reports (PIREPs) give the latest, *actual,* on-the-spot weather information. The other choices are *forecasts* of what might be.

5408. C. There is a line of echoes with eight-tenths coverage at the location from the radar cited by points 086°–40 NM, 164°–60 NM, and 199°–115 NM. MT 570 at 159/65 means that the maximum top is 57,000 feet at 159° (southwest of the station) at 65 NM.

5409. B. *AWS* MVFR conditions are: Ceiling 1,000 to 3,000 feet and/or visibility of 3 to 5 miles. Note that it says "and/or." The forecast could be for an 8,000-ft ceiling and 4 mi (or 2,000-ft ceiling and 15 mi) and it would still be forecast as MVFR.

5410. C. *AWS.* WND means that during the 6-hour categorical outlook period, winds are forecast to be 25 knots or stronger.

5411. C. *AWS.* VFR CIG ABV 100 means a forecast of ceilings above 10,000 feet and visibility more than 5 miles. ("VFR" implies visibilities greater than 5 miles and the "CIG ABV 100" may be appended to VFR at the forecaster's discretion.)

5412. B. *AWS.* "Absence of a visibility entry specifically implies visibility more than 6 *statute* miles."

5413. A. *AWS.* Terminal forecasts are issued 3 times daily for 24 hours and include a 6-hour categorical outlook.

5414. B. *AWS.* The HAZARDS section is "a 12 hour forecast that identifies and locates aviation weather hazards which meet Inflight Advisory criteria . . . ."

5415. C. *AWS.* The SGFNT CLOUD AND WX section covers the information stated in this choice. The other choices (A and B) have information that doesn't fit the criteria (such as cloud tops [A] or restricting information to weather systems that produce liquid or frozen precipitation, etc.).

5416. A. The states and areas listed are forecasting IFR conditions that meet In-flight Advisory criteria.

5417. A. *AWS.* The location of each icing phenomenon is specified by (1) the affected states or areas within the designated Area Forecast boundary and (2) the VOR points outlining the *entire* area of icing. Also given are the type, intensity, and height of the icing.

5418. A. *AWS.* The *area forecast* is the only one of the 3 choices that gives the information cited.

5419. B. *AWS.* "FA's are issued 3 times a day . . . ."

5420. C. *AWS.* "The TWEB Route Forecast is similar to the Area Forecast (FA) except information is contained in a route format."

5421. A. AWS; *AIM,* para. 7–8. "The TWEB is a continuous broadcast on low/medium frequencies (200–415 kHz) and selected VOR's (108.0–117.95 MHz)."

5422. A. AIM, Glossary. "SIGMET—A weather advisory issued concerning weather significant to the safety of all aircraft."

5423. C. AIM, Glossary. "Convective SIGMETs are issued for tornadoes, lines of thunderstorms, embedded thunderstorms of any intensity level, . . . and hail ¾ inch or greater."

5424. B. Winds Aloft are always *true* direction and in *knots.*

5425. A. *AWS.* "Isobars are solid lines depicting the sea level pressure pattern."

5426. A. *AWS.* "When the pressure gradient is weak, dashed isobars are sometimes inserted at 2 millibar levels to more clearly define the pressure pattern."

5427. A. The Surface Analysis Chart shows pressure centers and frontal positions.

5428. B. *AWS.* Since isobars are normally lined apart at 4 millibar intervals of value, closely spaced isobars mean a strong pressure change across a relatively short distance.

5429. C. *AWS,* Surface Analysis Charts.

5430. C. The Weather Depiction Chart shows IFR, MVFR, and VFR areas.

5431. B. *AWS.* "If total sky cover is few, or scattered, the cloud height entered is the base of the lowest layer."

5432. A. *AWS.* "The (Radar Summary) chart displays the type of precipitation echoes and indicates their intensity, intensity trend configuration, coverage, echo tops and bases, and movement." The chart shows lines, areas, and cells of hazardous thunderstorms.

5433. C. *AWS.* "The (Significant Weather Prognostics) charts show conditions as they are forecast to be at the valid time of the chart." The charts are based on 12- and 24-hour forecast periods.

5434. B. Check the *AWS.*

5435. C. *AWS.* "The U.S. High Level Significant Weather Prog . . . encompasses airspace from 24,000 to 63,000 feet presssure altitude."

5436. B. *AWS.* The U.S. Low Level Significant Weather Prog charts have an upper level of 24,000 feet.

* * *

5438. C. *AWS.* "The freezing level panel is an analysis of observed freezing level data from upper air observations."

5439. A. *AWS.* "The lifted index is computed as if a parcel of air near the surface were lifted to 500 millibars. The temperature the parcel would have at 500 millibars is then subtracted from the environmental 500 millibar temperature."

5440. B. *AWS,* Constant Pressure Charts. "To aid in identifying areas of strong winds, hatching denotes wind speed of 70 to 110 knots. . . ."

5441. A. *AWS.* Winds, observed temperatures, temperature-dewpoint spread, and height of the pressure surface are given on the Constant Pressure Analysis Charts.

5442. C. *AWS.* See the explanation for 5441.

5443. B. *AWS.* "Moderate Turbulence . . . where vertical wind shear values exceed 6 knots per 1000 feet."

5444. B. *AWS.* "Light turbulence . . . momentarily causes slight, erratic changes in altitude and/or attitude."

5445. C. *AWS.* "Moderate turbulence . . . changes in altitude and/or attitude occur but the aircraft remains in positive control at all times."

5446. B. *AW,* Glossary. "Clear air turbulence is turbulence encountered in air where no clouds are present; more popularly applied to high level turbulence associated with *wind shear.*"

5447. B. *AW.* "CAT is most pronounced in winter when temperature contrast is greatest between cold and warm air. Strong wind shears develop near the jet stream, especially where the curvature of the jet stream sharply increases in deepening upper troughs."

5448. C. *AW.*

5449. B. *AW.* Low Level Wind Shear is a change in wind direction and/or speed within a short distance in the atmosphere. This is a particularly dangerous phenomenon for the airplane climbing out or approaching at the relatively low airspeeds in these regimes.

5450. A. *AW.* Rotor clouds form *below* the elevation of the mountain peaks and getting *below* rotor cloud level is extremely dangerous.

For questions 5451–5489, review *APFM,* Chapter 17, "Advanced Navigation."

5451. B. Look at the problem: At 55% power-cruise (figure 8), fuel consumption is 11.3 gph. Night VFR reserve is 45 minutes, or 8.5 gallons (rounded off), which leaves 38.5 gallons at 11.3 gph for cruise, for a time of 3 hours and 24 minutes (call it 22 minutes).

5452. B. Day VFR cruise reserve equals 30 minutes at 13 gph (figure 8), or 6.5 gallons. This leaves 58.5 gallons for cruise at 13 gph, or 4.5 hours (4 hours, 30 minutes).

5453. C. Looking at figure 8, the fuel consumption is 18.2 gph. Seven minutes fuel consumption would be 7/60 × 18.2 = 2.12 gallons and C is the closest answer. Remember also that there may be a slight discrepancy in reading the chart.

5454. B. Using the same method as in the last problem: 10 minutes at 17.1 gph = 2.85 gallons (call it 2.88).

5455. A. For fuel consumption of 11.3 gph and 45 minutes reserve, take 8.5 gallons of the 38, which leaves 29.5 gallons. At 11.3 gph, this leaves 2 hours and 36 minutes, closest to answer A.

5456. C. The amount of fuel used to climb from 4,000 feet (12 pounds from sea level) to 12,000 feet (51 pounds from sea level) is 51 − 12 = 39 pounds. The temperature is 26°C, 19°C higher than the standard for 4,000 feet (15° − 4 × 2° = 7°C. The note says to add 10% for each 10°C above standard, so 19% is added, or 1.19 × 39 = 46 gallons (rounded off). Adding the 12 gallons for start and taxi, a total of 58 pounds is required.

5457. C. The amount of fuel used in a normal climb is 11 pounds from sea level to 4,000 feet. Subtract this from the total from sea level to 10,000 feet (31 pounds), for a difference of 20 pounds. The temperature is 14° above standard (+7°C) at the airport, so 14% is added to the climb fuel, or 1.14 × 20 = 22.8, plus 12 pounds for start and taxi, etc. = 34.8 pounds (call it 35).

5458. C. The amount of fuel used from sea level to 2,000 ft = 4 pounds. Fuel from sea level to 6,000 ft = 14 pounds, or 10 pounds required for the climb from 2,000 feet to 6,000 feet. The temperature is 16°C high, so add 16%, or 1.16 × 10 = 11.6 pounds. Add 12 pounds for start, etc. to get 24 pounds.

5459. C. The amount of fuel required to climb from sea level to 4,000 ft (12 pounds) and from sea level to 10,000 feet (35 pounds) at a weight of 3,800 pounds is 35 − 12 = 23 pounds. The temperature is 23°F higher than standard for 4,000 feet, so add 23% to the 23 pounds as indicated by the note, or 1.23 × 23 = 28 pounds (rounded off). Add 12 pounds (start, etc.) to get 40 pounds used.

5460. C. This could be a "gotcha." You might have used the 38-gallon column to get a range of 645 miles. (Naturally one of the answer choices.) Nope! It's 810 miles at *48* gallons.

5461. B. Looking at figure 11, check 52% power at 7,500 feet, then move across to 48 gallons, and the endurance is 7.7 gallons.

5462. C. This time in figure 11, answer C fits the parameters of 105 mph and 6.2 gph, for 52% power at 7,500 feet.

5463. B. VFR reserve is 0.5 hour at 94 pph, or 47 pounds, leaving 378 pounds for flight time. At 94 pph this is 4.02 hours, or 4 hours and 1 minute, rounded off.

5464. A. At the conditions given, the fuel consumption is 99 pph. The 45 minute reserve requirement takes 75 pounds, leaving 318 − 75 = 243 pounds at 99 pph, for a time of 2 hours and 27 minutes.

5465. C. The fuel consumption on the graph in figure 12 at −1°C is 59 pph, *but* the NOTE indicates subtracting 6 pph for the power setting given. The fuel consumption is 53 pph and subtracting 30 minutes for the VFR day reserve (27 pph) leaves a total fuel for cruise of 317 pounds. At 53 pph this gives a flight time of 5 hours 59 minutes.

5466. A. *APFM,* p. 211. This problem was worked out on an E-6B and an electronic computer. Both arrived at answer A.

5467. C. *APFM,* p. 211. Both computers agreed.

5468. C. *APFM,* p. 211. Both computers agreed.

5469. A. To travel 460 NM at 180 knots would require 460/180 = 2.56 hours (no need to convert to hours and minutes). 2.56 × 80 pounds = 205 pounds.

5470. A. This is the same type of problem as 5469. Groundspeed = 173 knots; distance of 450 NM 450/173 = 2.60 hours; 2.60 × 95 = 248 pounds. The altitude (6,500 feet) given is superfluous. It doesn't matter what the altitude is if distances, consumption, and groundspeed are given.

5471. C. The distance of 435 NM is divided by the groundspeed to get a time of 3 hours. At 12.5 gph consumption, 37.5 (call it 38) gallons are required.

5472. C. Dividing: 490/135 = 3.63 hours; 3.63 × 9.5 = 35 gallons.

5473. A. 560/167 knots = 3.35 hours; 3.35 × 14.8 = 49.58 (50 gallons).

5474. A. 612/157 = 3.9 hours; 3.9 × 14.7 = 57.33 (58 gallons).

5475. A. *APFM,* pp. 203–6. In working the earlier wind triangle problems, 3 factors of the triangle were known: (1) the wind vector, (2) the TAS, and (3) the true course. Here, the TC, groundspeed, TH, and TAS are known, so the third leg of the triangle (wind direction and velocity) must be filled in. Using both the E-6B and an electronic computer, the answer was found to be 020° and 32 knots (rounded off). You could do this on paper also, drawing the known information, then using a protractor, and "filling in" the wind line for direction and speed.

5476. B. *APFM,* pp. 203–6. This is the same type problem as 5475. Using the two types of computers (they agreed within 1° and 1 knot), an answer of 113° and 19 knots (answer B) was obtained.

5477. C. *APFM,* pp. 209–11; Fig. 17-14 and explanation on p. 210, col. 2. The tangent of the angle is 6/52 = 0.1154, or the angle is 6.6° (call it 7°). This represents the degrees of correction required to *parallel* the desired course. To converge on the destination, an *additional* change in course is required. Using *APFM,* Fig. 17-14 technique, or trigonometry, you find that an additional correction of 3° is needed, for a total of 10° (answer C). *APFM,* Fig. 1-8 may be of some help.

5478. C. *APFM,* pp. 209–11; Fig. 17-14 and explanation on p. 210, col. 2. To *parallel* the original course a change of 5.7° is required (call it 6°). To converge at the destination, a further correction of 4.3° is required, or 10° total (answer C).

5479. C. *SPFM,* p. 166, Fig. 19-6. The sectional chart is a Lambert conformal conic projection, so the meridian lines converge toward the top of the chart. Use the midpoint meridian for measuring courses.

*   *   *

5481. C. *APFM,* pp. 202–3. Working with two types of computers, a groundspeed of 81 knots and a true heading of 089° is found. To go 135 NM at 81 knots requires 1:40 (1 hour 40 minutes), or 1.67 hours, and at 105 pph, fuel required is 175 pounds.

5482. A. From sea level to 6,000 feet requires 14 pounds (interpolating) of fuel and from sea level to 16,000 feet requires 39 pounds. To climb from 6,000 to 16,000 feet requires 39 − 14 = 25 pounds. The temperature is 7° C high so add 7%, or 1.07 × 25 = 26.75 (call it 27 pounds). Adding 16 pounds for starting, etc., gives an answer of 43 pounds, closest to answer A.

5483. B. Use the same technique as shown in 5482, except this time you're dealing with time rather than pounds of fuel.

Time to climb from 2,000 to 8,000 feet is 9 − 2 = 7 minutes. Correction for the temperature (standard at 2,000 feet is 11°C; the temperature is 21°C high), so 1.21 × 7 = 8.4 minutes.

5484. C. From sea level to 4,000 feet with an aircraft weight of 3,700 pounds requires 12 pounds of fuel. Sea level to 12,000 feet requires 37 pounds, so 37 − 12 = 25 pounds required from 4,000 to 12,000 feet. The temperature (21°F) is 14° high, so 20% is added to the climb fuel or 1.2 × 25 = 30, plus 16 pounds for start, etc. giving a total of 46 pounds.

5485. C. From sea level to 4,000 feet takes 5 minutes and from sea level to 8,000 feet takes 10 minutes, so from 4,000 to 8,000 feet would take 10 − 5 = 5 minutes. The temperature is 7°C above standard, so add 10%, or 1.1 × 5 = 5.5 minutes.

5486. B. *APFM,* p. 95, Fig. 6-12. This can be a tough problem because the Fuel, Time, and Distance-to-Climb scale is "illegitimate" and hard to read in 2.5 increments.

5487. A. Again, the figure is hard to read and interpolate because of the non-standard scale.

5488. B. *APFM,* p. 211, Computing Climb and Descent Factors. Both types of computers agreed on answer B.

5489. B. Looking at the altitude to be climbed (from 1,500 to 9,500 feet, or 8,000 feet) and the rate of climb (500 fpm), the answer is 16 minutes. This eliminates answer A. Using the E-6B and electronic computers, the TAS is 153 knots and the TH is 140°. Subtracting the variation of 5°E and the deviation of −3°, the compass heading is 132°.

5490. A. *SPFM,* p. 181, Fig. 21-3.

5491. B. *IFM,* pp. 108–14, Fig. 5-32.

5492. B. Adding the heading (265°) and magnetic bearing (065°) gives an answer of 330° TO the station or 150° FROM the station.

5493. C. Adding the heading and bearing: 315° + 140° = 455° TO the station. Okay, better subtract 360° to get 095° TO the station, but the question wants a FROM answer so the reciprocal of 095° is 275° FROM. Keeping up with whether TO or FROM is required.

5494. B. There are two ways to get the magnetic bearing in this case: (1) add 350° + 240° = 590°; then subtract 590° − 360° = 230° TO or (2) the station is on a relative bearing 120° to the left, so 350° − 120° = 230° TO.

5495. C. This one's pretty simple. Heading (040°) plus relative bearing (290°) equals 330° magnetic bearing TO the station.

5496. A. Add 355° + 045° = 040° to get the magnetic bearing TO the station.

5497. C. Looking at the situation as it stands in instrument group 3 in figure 16, the heading is 330° and the relative bearing is 270°, which means that it's 240° TO or 060° FROM the station. The airplane must continue on course until it's 030° from the station, or a movement of 30° rearward for the needle (270° − 30° = 240°).

5498. C. The airplane is headed 300°, and the relative bearing is 040°. If the aircraft is turned to 090°, this means a turn to the *right* of 150°. The needle of the ADF will turn 150° to the *left* of its original bearing of 040°, or 360° − 110° = 250° (or the relative bearing is 360° + 40° = 400° − 150° = 250°).

5499. C. By turning right to a heading of 360°, the needle will indicate 330° relative bearing when that bearing to the station is intercepted at a 30° angle.

5500. A. There's no law that says you can't set a reciprocal bearing to your course, but you'll have put up with reverse sensing.

5501. C. Tracking outbound on the 180 radial, you'd set the OBS to 180° so that corrections would be made toward the needle.

5502. C. When you're tracking *inbound* on the 215 radial, the course is 035° and you'd set this on the OBS to correct toward the needle.

5503. B. There are several reasons for climbing (assuming that you're VFR, for instance) and answer B is one of them.

5504. A. For VHF/DF assistance, all you'll need is to be able to talk and listen.

5505. B. *APFM,* p. 7, Max Range Airspeed.

5506. A.

5507. C.

5508. B. At a 60° angle, the choices eliminate three of the illustrations.

5509. A. To intercept the 360 radial *inbound* at a 60° angle would require a heading of 240°. A 150° *left* turn from 030° to a heading of 240° would give an intercept angle of 60° inbound (answer A).

5510. A. The airplane is inbound on a heading of 255° with the OBS set to 240° (TO). The selected course is to the right, so the intercept will be made on the 060 radial at a 15° angle.

5511. B. Sketch what's happening and you'll see that a left turn of 125° to a 270° heading will give the required intercept angle.

5512. B.

5513. C. The airplane should be flown on the heading of 340° until the needle "head" is pointing 35° right of the tail, or 145° relative. Add 340° + 145° = 485°, then subtract 485° − 360° = 125° TO the station, or 305° FROM. Or you could use the "tail" of the needle and fly until it's 35° to the left of the 360° position; 340° − 35° = 305° FROM the station.

5514. C. Fly on a heading of 340° until the needle moves back to 30° to the right of the tail (150° relative). 340° + 150° = 490° − 360° = 130° TO or 310° FROM.

5515. C. *APFM,* pp. 211–12. Time Between Bearings. Using the rule of 60, 60/degrees change × time change = time to station. The change is from 265° to 260° = 5°, and the time change is 2 minutes. So, it would be 60°/5° × 2 = 24 minutes to station. The groundspeed is 145 knots, so the distance to the station is 24/60 × 145 = 58 NM.

5516. B. Using the formula, 60°/10° × 2 minutes = 12 minutes from the station. With a TAS of 160 knots, then 12/60 × 160 = 160/5 = 32 NM. (Here it's assumed that there's no wind when TAS is given.)

5517. C. 60°/5° × 1.5 minutes = 18 minutes to the station. At a TAS of 115 knots, 18/60 × 115 = 34.5 NM.

5518. C. 60°/5° = 12; 12 × 5 minutes = 60 minutes at 115 knots = 115 NM.

5519. A. The change is 5° in 1.5 minutes, or 18 minutes to the station.

5520. C. 60°/5° × 2.5 minutes = 30 minutes.

5521. C. 60°/5° × 2 minutes = 24 minutes.

5522. B. 10° change = 60°/10° × 2.5 = 15 minutes.

5523. B. 10° change = 60°/10° × 2.5 = 15 minutes. 15/60 × 90 = 22.5 miles.

5524. A. 10° change = 60°/10° × 4 minutes = 24 minutes. 24/60 × 11 gph = 4.4 gallons.

5525. B. Bearing change is 5° in 6 minutes. 60°/5° = 12 × 6 = 72 minutes = 1.2 hours at 12 gph, or 14.4 gallons is required.

5526. A. 60°/15° = 4; 4 × 6 = 24 minutes to the station. Fuel consumption − 8.6 gph; 24/60 × 8.6 = 3.44 gallons.

5527. A. 60°/15° = 4; 4 × 7.5 = 30 minutes to station, 42.5 miles and 4.8 gallons required.

5528. B. *FIM,* p. 342, Fig. 25-8. This is a "double the angle off the bow" problem. The two legs are equal (an isosceles triangle), so leg 2 equals leg 1 (which was 6 minutes). Sketch it on a piece of paper.

5529. A. *FIM,* p 342, Fig. 25-8. This is another isosceles triangle with equal sides (see Fig. 20-2). Leg 1 is 5 minutes long, so leg 2 is 5 minutes long, also. Read *APFM,* chapter 1 (this book) to review your trigonometry.

5530. A. This problem is like that of 5529; the airplane is flying one leg of a 45° isosceles triangle, so the 7-minute initial leg is the same as the leg to the station (7 minutes). At 135 knots, the distance is 7/60 × 135 = 16 miles.

5531. A. Another long, lean isosceles triangle; leg 1 is 5 minutes, so leg 2 must be the same. At 105 knots, the distance is 8.7 miles.

5532. B.

5533. B. The rule of 60 applies here: A one-fifth deflection of the CDI is 2°; a 2° angle at 60 miles is 2 miles. You might review *APFM,* p. 205, and Fig. 17-6.

5534. A.

5535. C.

5536. B.

5537. B.

5538. A.

5539. A. Using the rule of 60, the time required for 10° of radial change is 7 minutes (1237 to 1244); 6 × 7 = 42 minutes to the station. At a TAS of 120 knots (assume no wind), the distance to the station is 84 NM.

5540. A. Figure 21 shows an isosceles triangle, so if the leg from 2 to 3 is 13 minutes, the leg from 3 to the station must also be 13 minutes.

5541. A.

5542. B.

5543. A.

5544. B. Both legs are equal in time, since this is an isosceles triangle.

5545. A. Another isosceles triangle.

5546. B.

5547. A.

5548. B. *U.S. Terminal Procedures Charts* indicates in the legend that the altitude minimum for glide slope inoperative ILS approaches is that of the S-LOC for that runway, and 1360 feet is the minimum for 13L in figures 25 and 25A.

5549. C.

5550. C. When you can't complete an approach to the destination airport and proceed to the alternate, the minimums are as if you planned to go to the alternate in the first place. (The published landing minimums for the type of procedure now apply.)

5551. B. FAR 91.71.

5552. C. *AIM,* para. 1-4b. Remember, when using a VOT, the expression "Cessna 182" (180 TO) means that you are "north of the station" and thus on the 360 radial.

5553. B. FAR 91.171 (b)(3)(4).

*   *   *

5556. B. *AIM,* para. 5-25a(2).

5557. B. *AIM,* para. 5-40a.

5558. C. *AIM,* para. 5-46b.

5559. B. *AIM,* para. 7-9a(2).

5560. A. *AIM,* para. 7-8.

5561. B. *AIM,* Glossary, Final Approach Fix. See the lightning symbol at 2,200 feet on figure 26.

*   *   *

5564. C. Class B, C, and D airspace have airports with control towers and those airports are depicted in blue. Airports in Class E airspace (no tower) are marked in magenta.

5565. B. Class E airspace may have a base 1,200 feet AGL or may be under a transition area 700 feet AGL. Georgetown Airport is *not* under a transition area, so the floor of the Class E airspace over it is 2,588 + 1,200 = 3,788 feet MSL.

5566. C. Note that part of the town of Woodland is under "regular" Class E airspace (base 1,200 feet AGL) and the southwestern part is under a transition area (Class E base 700 feet AGL).

5567. B. University Airport is under a transition area (Class E airspace, base 700 feet AGL).

5568. C. Auburn is under "regular" Class E airspace with a base 1,200 feet AGL.

5569. B. Military training routes (MTRs) are depicted in such a manner. The type and route number are not shown on this segment.

5570. B. Check the legends of any of those sectional charts you have lying around.

*   *   *

5572. B. As shown in the dashed box in the Livermore Class D airspace, the top is at 2,900 feet MSL, so 2,901 feet MSL will clear it. A question: The altimeter may be 6 or 7 feet above the landing gear. Would you be dragging the wheels (fixed gear) through the Class D airspace at 2,901 feet indicated altitude? (Don't worry about it.)

* * *

5574. B. This is the closest answer, but it's suspected that the altitude in the question should be 3,000 feet MSL, not 300 feet MSL.

5575. A. *AIM,* Glossary, Special Use Airspace-Alert Area.

5576. B. FAR 91.215.

5577. B. "No SVFR" is an indication that such clearances are not available. Look at figure 54 on the left margin just west of the San Francisco Airport.

* * *

5581. C. The tower symbol about 4 NM south of Lincoln Airport has the "lightning strokes" depicting high-intensity lighting (299 AGL). The other choices don't have this.

* * *

5583. C. Check the legend on any of your sectional charts; this is the symbol for a non-public-use airport.

* * *

5585. B. There's a tower about 8 NM ESE. The top is 1,254 feet MSL and it's 300 feet above the ground, so the terrain elevation is 954 feet. The airport elevation is 119 feet MSL, so 954 − 199 = 835 feet (answer B).

* * *

5587. A. The Oakland Class C airspace extends up to the overlying Class B airspace, which has bases of 2,100 and 3,000 feet MSL in that area.

5588. B. With a visibility of 1 mile, you are required to stay out of Class E airspace, which, at your present position north of Madera, is from 1,200 feet AGL upward. The Class E airspace base drops to 700 feet AGL just north of the Madera Airport. To be legal you must drop down to 700 feet to Class G airspace.

* * *

5591. C. The minimum enroute altitude from BTG is 7,000 feet eastbound. You would cross GYMME at 7,000 feet. (Going *west,* the segment from GYMME to BTG is 6,500 feet.)

5592. A. One VOR receiver can pinpoint ANGOO intersection by establishing the course from YKM and then switching to LTJ and setting in 330° FROM. It's not as handy as having two VOR receivers or one VOR and a DME, but it sure can be done.

5593. C. Notice on the NOS chart that a flag (and X) denoting a Minimum Crossing Altitude of 11,500 feet MSL at TROTS when traveling NE. The Jeppesen chart also notes "V-468 11500 NE."

5594. B. *AIM,* Glossary. For approaches, the final approach fix is denoted by a "lightning arrow" on NOS charts, and in this case, it is the glide slope intercept altitude as noted (7,500) on both charts.

5595. A. Both charts (27 and 27A) note that the MSA is established on the Denver VORTAC.

5596. A. *AIM,* Glossary. ". . . when ATC directs a lower-than-published Glideslope/Path Intercept Altitude, it is the resultant actual intercept point of the glide-slope/path intercept."

5597. B. NOS, U.S. Terminal Procedures Legend, Landing Minima Format. The straight-in localizer MDA becomes the minimum if the glide slope is inoperative. Both charts (figures 28 and 28A) agree on 1,320 feet MSL; in fact, the Jeppesen chart (bottom center) shows it well.

5598. B. Both charts say that the FAF to MAP is 5.2 miles.

5599. B. *AIM,* Glossary. MSA is based on the navigation facility and both charts show that the HIC (White Cloud) VORTAC is the center of the circle.

5600. B. Well, you need azimuth and distance information, and one VOR receiver and a DME will do it. (You'll need both because there are no intersection cross-bearings required, only distance requirements.)

5601. B. FAR 91.113(d). The aircraft to the other's right has the right-of-way. The easiest way to remember, if two aircraft of the same category are converging, is that the one requiring a *right turn* to go *behind* the other one must give way.

5602. C. See the answer to 5601. (The aircraft are of the same category, that is, *airplanes.*)

5603. A. This question cites an airship but the same would apply to an airplane. If in VFR conditions on an IFR flight plan and experiencing a two-way communications loss, remain VFR and land as soon as practical.

5604. B. *APFM,* p. 151–55, The Gust Envelope.

5605. B. *APFM,* p. 148, Airspeed Indicator Markings and Important Airspeeds.

5606. C. *APFM,* p. 194, col. 1, next to last paragraph.

5607. B. *APFM,* p. 196, Loss of Oil Pressure.

5608. C. *APFM,* p. 165, Leaning.

5609. C. *APFM,* p. 165, Leaning.

5610. A. *APFM,* p. 165, Leaning.

5611. B. This is the only feasible choice. Anytime the mixture is too rich for the situation, plug fouling can be a problem.

5612. A. *APFM,* p. 57, Acceleration Errors. This is a sailplane question but it applies to airplanes as well, so it's included here.

5613. B. *APFM,* p. 57, Acceleration Errors. Okay, another mention of a sailplane, but it happens with airplanes also. Remember ANDS: *A*ccelerate—compass turns *N*orth; *D*ecelerate—compass turns *S*outh.

5614. B. *APFM,* p. 78, Runway Slope Effects.

Questions 5615–5618, assume that the runway is lined up exactly to the nearest 10°; that is, for instance, Runway 30 is exactly 300° magnetic.

5615. A. *APFM,* p. 3, Fig. 1-5. The crosswind capability is $0.2V_{so}$ so the max crosswind component is 12 knots (0.2×60 knots). The wind is 40° off the nose at 20 knots and a crosswind component of 13 knots is found. The other choices are less than this.

5616. C. *APFM,* p. 3, Fig. 1-5. The wind is 70° off the nose at 18 knots, and looking at figure 31, you see a crosswind component of 17 knots. You can use trigonometry (Fig. 1-8) with this also: wind 70° to course; sin 70° = 0.94; 0.94 × 18 knots = 17 knots.

5617. A. Okay, the wind is 50° off the runway heading at 25 knots. Using figure 31, 19 knots is the answer. Using trig. and Fig. 1-8 *APFM*: sin 50° = 0.766; 0.766 × 25 = 19.15 knots.

5618. B. *APFM,* p. 3–4, refer to Figures 1-5 and 1-8. The angle is 60° and the speed is 15 knots for an answer of 13 knots. Sin 60° = 0.866; 0.866 × 15 = 12.99 knots (go ahead and call it 13).

5619. C. Working from "both ends" of the chart, start on the right (restricted to 1,000 feet total distance) and move to the 20 knots wind value. Then working on the left for the pressure altitude and temperature, you find that the intersection of the lines is at a weight of 2,600 pounds or 300 pounds of reduction is necessary.

5620. B. This is a straightforward problem. Move up from 50°F to the sea level line, then across and up the slope of the weight lines to 2,700 pounds, and straight across to a value of 650 feet.

5621. B. The answer of 1,350 feet is the closest but the small size of the chart makes the problem difficult. Remember that the question asked for the *ground roll,* which is 0.73 of the total.

5622. C. The numbers are different but the principle is the same as for 5620 and 5621.

5623. B. A double interpolation is required here. At 4,000 feet, splitting the 20°C and 40°C (to find 30°C), the R/C is approximately 728 fpm (split 800 fpm and 655 fpm). At 8,000 feet using the same procedure, the R/C is approximately 625 fpm. So, at 5,000 feet, the rate of climb is one-fourth of the difference between what was found for 4,000 and 8,000 feet at 30°, or 728 − 625 = 103; 728 − 26 = 702 fpm.

5624. C. At 20,000 feet interpolating the rate of climb between −20°C and 0°C (to get the −10°C R/C): 600 − 470 = 130; 600 − 130/2 = 535 fpm. At 24,000 feet −10°C, R/C = 232 fpm. So, at 22,000 feet, the rate of climb is halfway between 535 and 232 = 384 fpm.

5625. B. *APFM,* pp. 104–5. At 22″ and 2,200 RPM at +3°C, the fuel consumption is 70 pph; with 465 pounds available, this gives 6 hours 39 minutes max flight time.

5626. B. Consumption is 82 pph and fuel available is 370 pounds, so 370 divided by 82 = 4.5 hours.

5627. C. Interpolation is called for here. A temperature of +13°C is exactly between the numbers for +3°C and +23°C. At 3°C and 23″ and 2,500 RPM the consumption is 90 pph. At 23°C at that power setting the consumption is 87 pph. Fuel available is 460 pounds and consumption is 88.5 pph (splitting the difference), so that 5.2 hours (5 hours 12 minutes) flight time is available.

5628. A. *APFM,* p. 120. This graph is hard to read because of its size, but 1,300 feet is the approximate distance found for the total distance. The ground roll is 0.53 of this, or 689 feet (closest).

5629. A. Remember you're looking for the ground roll, which is 742 feet.

5630. B. Because of slight differences in using the graph, plus its small size, pick the number nearest to your answer—636 feet here (answer B).

5631. B. This one calls for the *total landing distance* over a 50-foot obstacle and 1,250 feet is the closest answer.

5632. A. *APFM,* p. 132. The Basic Empty Weight (for later airplanes) contains *full oil,* unusable fuel, and hydraulics. (It's ready to fly except for usable fuel and the pilot.) Older airplanes (Licensed Empty Weight) include only undrainable oil.

5633. B. *APFM,* p. 132, Fig. 10-37. This sample airplane uses a datum just ahead of the nose, so all moments are positive. Some Cessnas use the forward face of the firewall, so any moments ahead of that station have a negative sign.

5634. C. *APFM,* p. 133, col. 1.

5635. B. *APFM,* p. 133, col. 1.

5636. B. *APFM,* p. 133, Figs. 10-38 and 10-39. Working it out:

A = 155 × 45 = 6,975 pound-inches
B = 165 × 145 = 23,925 pound-inches
C = 95 × 185 = 17,575 pound-inches
415 pounds   48,475 pound-inches

48,475/415 Total Moment = 116.8 inches aft of datum (CG)

5637. B. A = 140 × 17 = 2,380 pound-inches
B = 120 × 110 = 13,200 pound-inches
C = 85 × 210 = 17,850 pound-inches
345 pounds   33,430 pound-inches

CG = 33,430/345 = 96.9 inches (OK, 96.898551)

5638. A. 42,585 = 100.2 inches.

5639. C. 45,525/385 = 118.24 inches.

* * *

5646. A. One way of doing the problem is to find the initial total moment (4,137 × 67.8 = 280,488) and subtract the fuel moment (13.7 × 1.5 × 6 = 123.2 pounds; 123.2 ° 68 inches = 8,384 pound-inches).

4,137 − 123 = 4,014 pounds
280,488 − 8,384 = 272,104 pound-inches

272,104/4,014 = station 67.79.

5647. A. *APFM,* p. 136, col. 1.

Total Weight = 3,650 pounds
Total Moment = 3,650 × 94.0 = 343,100 pound-inches

Moving the baggage forward 140 inches (180 − 40) must result in a moment now of 3,650 × 92.0 (new CG) = 335,800 pound- inches; 343,100 − 335,800 = 7,300 pound-inches, which is the moment of the baggage to be moved.

So: 7,300 (moment)/140 (inches) = 52.14 pounds

5648. A. *APFM,* p. 136. The current moment is 4,800 × 98 = 470,400 pound-inches. By moving 90 pounds forward 100 inches you have decreased that moment by 9,000 pound-inches, or to 461,400 pound-inches.

461,400/4,800 = 96.125 inches, which is in the envelope.

5649. B. *APFM,* p. 135, Problem 1.

Fuel *weight* burned = 12.7 × 1.75 × 6 = 133.3 pounds.
Decrease in total moment = 133.3 × 68.0 = 9,068 pound-inches.

Original moment = 68.8 × 3,037 = 208,946.
208,946 − 9,068 = 199,878 pound-inches.
New weight is 3037 − 133 = 2,904 pounds.

199,878/2,904 = 68.83 inches.

5650. A. *APFM,* p. 134, col. 2. The weight is 2,133 pounds and the moment is 187,040 pound-inches after all the factors have been multiplied and added. The weight and CG are within limits.

5651. A. *APFM,* p. 134, col. 2. After working it out, a weight of 1,933 pounds and a moment of 167.24, or 167,540 pound-inches, is found. Looking at the envelope, you see that the weight and CG are well within the normal envelope category.

5652. A. You can work out the original weight and CG (2,193 and 193,940) and see that at least it started out in the envelope. Reworking the problem with 7 gallons (42 pounds) of fuel, the weight is 2,013 pounds and the moment is 177,540 pound-inches, within the envelope. Designers try to assure that fuel burn has a minimal effect on the CG.

5653. A. Carbon monoxide in the cockpit can be a real danger, and the most likely cause is a cracked or poorly fitting exhaust heating system.

5654. C. *APFM,* p. 156, Using the Throttle and Propeller Controls. Increasing the pitch by easing back on the prop controls reduces RPM.

5655. C. You're holding the ailerons so that the quartering tailwind holds down the upwind wing. With a quartering tailwind, "dive and bank *away* from the wind."

5656. C. See the explanation for 5655.

5657. C. *SPFM,* p. 48, Fig. 6-12; *AIM,* para. 2-3m(1). "The solid lines are on the side where the aircraft is to hold."

5658. B. *AIM,* Fig. 2-33(b). That's a sign prohibiting aircraft entry into an *area.* (Don't taxi onto the Interstate.)

5659. C. *AIM,* para. 1-10k(1)(2). That's the ILS Critical Area Boundary Sign.

5660. A. The top red sign prohibits aircraft entry into an area as noted in 5658.

5661. C. *SPFM,* p. 113, col. 1. You don't want a premature lift-off with the possibility of a drifting touchdown.

5662. A. You need to increase the airspeed slightly to make sure that you have control in turbulence.

5663. A. *APFM,* p. 199. Your first requirement in such a situation is to maintain control of the airplane, and that means maintaining a safe airspeed.

5664. C. This is my answer, based on over 5,000 landings on a runway on the edge of the Cumberland Plateau, where turbulence and direct crosswinds up to 25 knots are not uncommon. By using power on the approach, the varying gust effects can be better controlled. Once in position for landing, get the power off, so the airplane will not be dragged down the runway, with the possibility of ballooning, followed by a *real* drop-in.

5665. B. *APFM,* p. 177, Crosswind Landings. That's a real advantage to the wing-down landing—the longitudinal axis and direction of motion must be parallel to the runway *and,* at the moment of touchdown, the airplane should be on, or very close to being on, the runway centerline.

5666. A. The rotating beacon and the white light on the tail shows that the other aircraft is headed away from you.

5667. B. *APFM,* p. 20, last paragraph; p. 157, col. 2. A low angle of attack (low pitch) and high RPM produces the most power and thrust.

5668. A. *APFM,* p. 20, last paragraph.

5669. B. Some airplanes have a turbulence penetration airspeed, others don't, but if it's available, move to it.

5670. B. If no other information is available (turbulent penetration speed) and you know the V_A for your current weight, use it for severe turbulence.

* * *

5682. A. The items installed are added to the empty weight. Since the gross weight is constant for a particular airplane, this decreases the useful load, which is the difference between gross weight and actual empty weight.

* * *

5689. B. This question, like questions 5690–92, simply relies on your ability to read climb charts.

5690. B.

5691. C.

5692. A.

* * *

5739. B. *AW.* The frost causes early separation of flow (at a lower angle of attack).

5740. B. *APFM,* p. 49.

5741. C. Set the power and trim to get the proper airspeed and *try* to keep the wings level. Accept variations of altitude and airspeed (you won't have much choice).

* * *

5748. C. *AIM,* para. 4-72.

5749. B. *AIM,* para. 8-8e(1).

5750. B. The induced roll is the major hazard. This writer has had two real encounters with wake turbulence. The first time in 1950, the airplane (a *Stinson* 108-2) was rolled inverted on final. (I was teaching aerobatics in a *Meyers* OTW, so it came as a natural, though shaking, action to roll it back upright.) The second time was at the "cut" position in an F4U-5N *Corsair* on a carrier. Being just above a stall at that point, full recovery was impossible and it cost the taxpayers a lot of money and me some ego.

5751. A. *APFM,* p. 202, item (6).

5752. A. *APFM,* p. 201, Fig. 16-7.

5753. A. Answer A is the closest choice, but if the jet has just landed, *wait* before taking off (sometimes up to 5 minutes, depending on the meteorological conditions). It looks as if your airplane could encounter wake turbulence in all 3 choices, whether you are on the ground or airborne, so wait until you can take off behind a "large jet aircraft that has landed some time ago."

5754. A. *APFM,* p. 202, item (1).

5755. C. *AIM,* para. 7-56. "In forward flight, departing or landing helicopters produce a pair of strong, high-speed trailing vortices similar to wing tip vortices of larger fixed wing aircraft."

5756. B. *APFM,* p. 201, col. 2.

5757. C. *AIM,* para. 8-3a; *APFM,* p. 217, col. 1.

5758. C. *AIM,* para. 8-6c(2).

5759. A. *AIM,* para. 8-3a.

5760. C. *AIM,* para. 8-3a.

5761. B. *APFM,* p. 218, Hypoxia; *AIM,* para. 8-2a(1).

5762. B. *APFM,* p. 217, col. 1; *AIM,* para. 8-3.

5763. C. *AIM,* para. 8-1d.

5764. B. *APFM,* p. 218, col. 1. The already scarce oxygen at altitude is being replaced by carbon monoxide.

5765. C. Rely on the aircraft instrument indications. Don't rely on body sensations, and if you are spatially disoriented, you'll probably automatically hyperventilate (try to avoid *that*).

5766. C. SPFM, p. 34, bottom of col. 2.

5767. C. The warm air (some pilots use hairdryers or heater/blowers) should be directed both above and below the cylinders. A good book for your library that covers this and other engine operations is *Aircraft Engine Operating Guide* by Kas Thomas. The cabin area heating is of less importance than the engine. After the engine has started you can heat the cabin.

5768. A. *APFM,* p. 175, col. 2.

* * *

5772. A. *APFM,* p. 244, Takeoff and Departure Stalls. These stalls are done using power, but the normal reaction of the airplane to a slip (which is the situation cited here) is to normally go over the top.

* * *

5882. A. *AIH,* p. 1. ". . . learning can be defined as a change in behavior as *a result of experience*."

5883. B. *AIH,* p. 8–9, Levels of Learning.

5884. B. *AIH,* p. 6.

5885. C. *AIH,* p. 7.

5886. C. *AIH,* p. 3.

5887. B. *AIH,* p. 3.

5888. A. *AIH,* p. 5.

5889. C. *AIH,* p. 7.

5890. B. *AIH,* p. 7.

5891. C. *AIH,* p. 8.

5892. A. *AIH,* p. 8.

5893. C. *AIH,* p. 8–9.

5894. B. *AIH,* p. 13.

5895. C. *AIH,* p. 16.

5896. B. *AIH,* p. 17.

5897. A. *AIH,* p. 17.

5898. A. *AIH,* p. 17.

5899. C. *AIH,* p. 17.

5900. B. *AIH,* p. 18.

5901. A. *AIH,* p. 17.

5902. C. *AIH,* p. 18.

5903. B. *AIH,* p. 21.

5904. C. *AIH,* p. 22.

5905. C. *AIH,* p. 23.

5906. C. *AIH,* p. 25.

5907. B. *AIH,* p. 26.

5908. A. *AIH,* p. 26.

5909. C. *AIH,* p. 30.

5910. B. *AIH,* p. 30.

5911. B. *AIH,* p. 30.

5912. C. *AIH,* p. 31.

5913. B. *AIH,* p. 33.

5914. A. *FIM.* Telling a student *why* a lesson or maneuver is being done helps both memory and motivation.

5915. C. *AIH,* p. 36.

5916. C. *FIM,* p. 25; *AIH,* p. 39.

5917. C. *AIH,* p. 39.

5918. C. *AIH,* p. 39.

5919. A. *AIH,* p. 43.

5920. A. *AIH,* p. 44.

5921. A. *AIH,* p. 45.

5922. A. *AIH,* p. 45.

5923. C. *AIH,* p. 46.

5924. A. *AIH,* p. 53.

5925. B. *AIH,* p. 54.

5926. C. *AIH,* p. 54.

5927. A. *AIH,* p. 57.

5928. A. *AIH,* p. 61.

5929. B. *AIH,* p. 64.
A. High praise when there's really nothing to praise could cause the student to lose confidence in the instructor.
C. "Negative teaching generally results in negative learning," so it isn't C or A.

5930. C. *AIH,* p. 62.

5931. A. *AIH,* p. 62.

5932. B. *AIH,* p. 62.

5933. A. *AIH,* p. 62.

5934. A. *AIH,* p. 64.

5935. C. *AIH,* p. 65.

5936. A. *AIH,* p. 65.

5937. B. *AIH,* p. 65.

5938. A. *AIH,* p. 74.

5939. C. *AIH,* p. 74.

5940. A. *AIH,* p. 77.

21 The Practical Test

BACKGROUND

This chapter is for the private pilot with an instrument rating who is taking the practical test in a single-engine airplane. Fig. 21-1 is a checklist to be used to get ready; add or delete items as they apply to your particular situation.

You should have the latest Practical Test Standards (FAA-S-8081-12B) available to you because there may have been some minor changes since *this* book was printed; for instance, certain maneuvers may have been combined or altitude or heading limits may have been increased or decreased. The information here is intended to give a general look at the requirements of the practical test so you can see what will be expected.

The descriptions have been paraphrased and additional information is included. Also included is information from older Practical Test Standards, which I feel will be of help to you. Some of the orders of presentation have been changed for easier transitions.

The practical test will have AREAS OF OPERATION, which are phases of flight arranged in logical sequences from the preparation to the conclusion of the flight. (The examiner may, however, conduct the practical test in any sequence that results in a complete and efficient test.)

TASKS are procedures and maneuvers appropriate to an AREA OF OPERATION. The TASKS are set up for each aircraft category and class (Airplane Single-Engine Land, Airplane Multiengine Land, Rotorcraft Helicopter, Lighter-than-Air airship, etc.). As noted earlier, this chapter is aimed at the ASEL applicant.

The references for this practical test (in addition to *this* book) are

FAR Part 43 Maintenance, Preventive Maintenance, Rebuilding and Alteration
FAR Part 61 Certification: Pilots and Flight Instructors
FAR Part 91 General Operating and Flight Rules
FAR Part 97 Standard Instrument Approach Procedures
NTSB Part 830 Notification and Reporting of Aircraft Accidents and Incidents
AC 00-2 Advisory Circular Checklist
AC 00-6 Aviation Weather
AC 00-45 Aviation Weather Services
AC 61-21 Flight Training Handbook
AC 61-23 Pilot's Handbook of Aeronautical Knowledge
AC 61-27 Instrument Flying Handbook
AC 61-65 Certification: Pilots and Flight Instructors
AC 61-67 Stall and Spin Awareness Training
AC 61-84 Role of Preflight Preparation
AC 61-107 Operation of Aircraft at Altitudes Above 25,000 Feet MSL
AC 67-2 Medical Handbook for Pilots
AC 90-48 Pilot's Role in Collision Avoidance
AC 91-13 Cold Weather Operation of Aircraft
AC 91-23 Pilot's Weight and Balance Handbook
AC 91-55 Reduction of Electrical System Failures Following Aircraft Engine Starting
AIM Airman's Information Manual
AFD Airport Facility Directory
NOTAMs Notices to Airmen
Pertinent *Pilot Operating Handbook*s and FAA-Approved Airplane Flight Manual
Refer to the latest available issuance of the above references

(for example, AC 00-6A, -B, -C, or -L).

Each OBJECTIVE lists in sequence the important elements that must be satisfactorily performed to demonstrate competency in a TASK. The OBJECTIVE includes

1. Specifically what you as an applicant should be able to do.
2. The conditions under which the TASK is to be performed.
3. The minimum acceptable standards of performance. (You may be required to do some of the TASKS in a complex airplane on the flight test.)

TASK: TAXIING (ASEL)
REFERENCES: AC 61-21; *Pilot's Operating Handbook* (*POH*) or FAA-Approved Airplane Flight Manual
OBJECTIVE: To determine that the applicant

1. Exhibits knowledge of the elements related to recommended taxi procedures, including the effect of wind on the airplane during taxiing and the appropriate control position for such conditions.
2. Positions flight controls properly, considering the wind.
3. Performs a brake check immediately after the airplane begins moving.
4. Controls direction and speed without excessive use of brakes.
5. Complies with airport markings, signals, and ATC clearances.
6. Avoids other aircraft and hazards.

APPLICANT'S PRACTICAL TEST CHECKLIST

APPOINTMENT WITH EXAMINER:

EXAMINER'S NAME _____

LOCATION _____

DATE/TIME _____

ACCEPTABLE AIRCRAFT

- ☐ Aircraft Documents:
  Airworthiness Certificate
  Registration Certificate
  Operating Limitations
- ☐ Aircraft Maintenance Records:
  Logbook Record of Airworthiness Inspections and AD Compliance
- ☐ Pilot's Operating Handbook, FAA-Approved Airplane Flight Manual
- ☐ FCC Station License

PERSONAL EQUIPMENT

- ☐ View-Limiting Device
- ☐ Current Aeronautical Charts
- ☐ Computer and Plotter
- ☐ Flight Plan Form
- ☐ Flight Logs
- ☐ Current AIM, Airport Facility Directory, and Appropriate Publications

PERSONAL RECORDS

- ☐ Identification - Photo/Signature ID
- ☐ Pilot Certificate
- ☐ Current and Appropriate Medical Certificate
- ☐ Completed FAA Form 8710-1, Airman Certificate and/or Rating Application with Instructor's Signature (if applicable)
- ☐ AC Form 8080-2, Airman Written Test Report, or Computer Test Report
- ☐ Pilot Logbook with appropriate Instructor Endorsements.
- ☐ FAA Form 8060-5, Notice of Disapproval (if applicable)
- ☐ Approved School Graduation Certificate (if applicable)
- ☐ Examiner's Fee (if applicable)

Fig. 21-1. A practical test checklist.

7. Completes the prescribed checklist.

When the examiner determines during the performance of a TASK that the knowledge and skill OBJECTIVE of a similar TASK has been met, it may not be necessary to require the performance of that similar TASK.

When the demonstration of a TASK is not practicable, such as operating over a congested area or unsuitable terrain or a demonstration that does not conform to the manufacturer's recommendations, competency can be evaluated by oral testing.

The examiner may not follow the precise order in which the AREAS OF OPERATION and TASKS appear in each standard. The examiner may change the order, or in some instances combine TASKS to conserve time. Examiners should develop a plan of action that includes the order and combination of TASKS to be demonstrated by the applicant in a manner that results in an efficient and valid test. It is of utmost importance that the examiner accurately evaluate the applicant's ability to perform safely as a pilot and also recognize the applicant's weaknesses as well as satisfactory performance.

Examiners place special emphasis on the areas of aircraft operation that are most critical to flight safety, such as precise aircraft control and sound judgment in decision making. Although these areas may not be listed under each TASK, they are essential to flight safety and will receive careful evaluation throughout the practical test. If they are shown in the OBJECTIVE, additional emphasis is placed on them. The examiner will also emphasize stall/spin awareness, spatial disorientation, collision avoidance, wake turbulence avoidance, low-level wind shear, and checklist usage (other areas will be determined by future revisions of the test standard).

When you get the latest copy you'll find that practical test standards will also refer to the metric equivalent of various altitudes throughout. The metric altimeter is arranged in 10-meter increments, so the numbers are rounded off to the nearest 10-meter increment for simplicity.

Stabilized Approach.

The term "stabilized approach" as used in the PTS is not intended to be construed as the term used in the operation of large aircraft. The term "as utilized" means that the aircraft is in a position where minimum input of all controls will result in a safe landing. Excessive control input at any juncture could be an indication of improper planning.

Use of Distractions during Practical Tests.

Numerous studies indicate that many accidents have occurred when the pilot was distracted during phases of flight. And many accidents have resulted from engine failure during takeoffs and landings where safe flight would have been possible had the pilot used correct control technique and proper attention. Distractions that have been found to cause problems are

1. Preoccupation with situations inside or outside the cockpit

2. Maneuvering to avoid other traffic

3. Maneuvering to clear obstacles during takeoffs, climbs, approaches, or landings

To strengthen this area of pilot training and evaluation, the examiner will provide realistic distractions throughout the flight portion of the practical test in order to evaluate the applicant's ability to divide attention while maintaining safe flight:

1. Simulating engine failure

2. Simulating radio tuning and communication

3. Identifying a field suitable for emergency landings

4. Identifying features or objects on the ground

5. Reading the outside air temperature gage

6. Removing objects from the glove compartment or map case

7. Questioning by the examiner

Practical Test Prerequisites.

As an applicant for the commercial practical test, you are required by Federal Aviation Regulations to

1. Possess a private pilot certificate with an airplane rating, if a commercial pilot certificate with an airplane rating is sought, or meet the flight experience required for a private pilot certificate (airplane rating) and pass the private airplane written and practical test;

2. Possess an instrument rating (airplane) or the following limitation will be placed on the commercial pilot certificate: "Carrying passengers in airplanes for hire is prohibited at night and on cross-country flights of more than 50 nautical miles";

3. Pass the appropriate pilot knowledge test since the beginning of the 24th month before the month in which the practical test is taken;

4. Obtain the applicable instruction and aeronautical experience prescribed for the pilot certificate or rating sought;

5. Possess a current medical certificate appropriate to the certificate or rating sought;

6. Meet the age requirement for the issuance of the certificate or rating sought; and

7. Obtain a written statement from an appropriately certificated flight instructor certifying that you have been given flight instruction in preparation for the practical test within 60 days preceding the date of application. The statement shall also state that the instructor finds you competent to pass the practical test and that you have satisfactory knowledge of the subject area(s) in which a deficiency was indicated by the airman written test report.

Aircraft and Equipment Requirements for the Practical Test.

You are required to provide an appropriate and airworthy aircraft for the practical test. This aircraft must be capable of, and its operating limitations must not prohibit, the pilot operations required on the test. It must have fully functioning controls except as provided in FAR 61.

Flight Instructor Responsibility.

An appropriately rated flight instructor is responsible for training you as a commercial pilot applicant to acceptable standards in *all* subject matter areas, procedures, and maneuvers included in the TASKS within the appropriate commercial pilot practical test standard. Because of the impact of their teaching activities in developing safe, proficient pilots, flight instructors should exhibit a high level of knowledge, skill, and the ability to impart that knowledge and skill to students. Additionally, your flight instructor must certify that you are able to perform safely as a commercial pilot and are competent to pass the required practical test.

Throughout your training, the flight instructor is responsible for emphasizing the performance of effective visual scanning, collision avoidance, and runway incursion avoidance procedures. These areas are covered, in part, in AC 90-48, Pilot's Role in Collision Avoidance; AC 61-21, Flight Training Handbook; AC 61-23, Pilot's Handbook of Aeronautical Knowledge; and the Airman's Information Manual.

Satisfactory Performance.

Satisfactory performance to meet the requirements for certification is based on your ability to safely

1. Perform the approved areas of operation for the certificate or rating sought within the approved standards;

2. Demonstrate mastery of the aircraft with the successful outcome of each task performed never seriously in doubt;

3. Demonstrate sound judgment; and

4. Demonstrate single-pilot competence if the aircraft is type certificated for single-pilot operations.

Unsatisfactory Performance. If, in the judgment of the examiner, you don't meet the standards of performance of any TASK performed, the associated AREA OF OPERATION is failed and therefore the practical test is failed. The examiner or you may discontinue the test any time after the failure of an AREA OF OPERATION makes you ineligible for the certificate or rating sought. The test will be continued ONLY with your consent. If the test is either continued or discontinued, you are entitled credit for only those TASKS satisfactorily performed. However, during the retest and at the discretion of the examiner, any TASK may be re-evaluated, including those previously passed.

Typical areas of unsatisfactory performance and grounds for disqualification are

1. Any action or lack of action by you that requires corrective intervention by the examiner to maintain safe flight.

2. Failure to use proper and effective visual scanning techniques to clear the area before and while performing maneuvers.

3. Consistently exceeding tolerances stated in the objectives.

4. Failure to take prompt corrective action when tolerances are exceeded.

When a disapproval notice is issued, the examiner will record your unsatisfactory performance in terms of AREA OF OPERATION appropriate to the practical test conducted.

PREFLIGHT PREPARATION

Certificates and Documents.
You should understand and be able to explain pilot certificate privileges and limitations applicable to flights for compensation or hire, medical certificates, personal logbooks or flight records, and FCC station licensee and operator's permits.

DOCUMENTS THAT STAY IN THE AIRPLANE

Airplane Registration. The certificate of registration contains the name and address of the owner, the aircraft manufacturer, the model, the registration number, and the manufacturer's serial number. The registration number is painted on the airplane. You can change the registration number of your airplane by applying to the FAA and paying a small fee, assuming that the number and letter combination you have chosen is not already in use. Many corporation planes use this system; for instance, the Jones Machinery Corporation may decide that the registration "N1234P" is too ordinary so they apply for, and get, "N100JM" or some other "more suitable" number-letter combination.

The manufacturer's serial number, however, is permanent and a means of identifying the airplane even when the registration number has been changed several times. The serial number 6-1050 means that the airplane is a Zephyr model 6, the 1050th airplane of that model manufactured. The manufacturer's serial number is used for establishing the airplanes affected by new service notes or bulletins ("Zephyr Sixes, serials 6-379 through 6-614, must comply with this bulletin"); you can check the registration certificate for the manufacturer's serial number to see if your airplane is affected. If you own an airplane you'll know the serial number—or should.

When an airplane changes owners, or the registration number is changed, a new registration certificate must be obtained.

Certificate of Airworthiness. The certificate of airworthiness is a document showing that the airplane has met the safety requirements of the Federal Aviation Administration and is "airworthy." It remains in effect indefinitely, or as long as the aircraft is maintained in accordance with the requirements of the FAA. Unlike the certificate of registration, it must be dis-

played so that it can be readily seen by pilot or passenger. The airworthiness certificate itself will stay in the airplane indefinitely, but in order for it to be valid, the following must be complied with:

1. *Privately owned aircraft* (not operated for hire)—The aircraft must have had a periodic (annual) inspection within the preceding 12 calendar months in accordance with the FARs. The logbooks and inspection forms will be a voucher for this.

2. *Aircraft used for hire*—In addition to the periodic (annual) inspection, an airplane used for hire to carry passengers or for flight instruction must have had an inspection within the last 100 hr of flight time in accordance with the FARs. This interval may be exceeded by not more than 10 hr when necessary to reach a point at which the inspection may be accomplished. In any event such time must be included in the next 100-hr interval. The annual inspection is accepted as a 100-hr inspection. Both the annual and 100-hr inspections are complete inspections of the aircraft and identical in scope. In order to perform an annual inspection, however, the mechanic or facility must have inspection authorization.

3. *Progressive inspection*—The airplane you're flying may use the progressive inspection system. The owner or operator provides or makes arrangements for continuous inspection of the aircraft, so the inspection work load can be adjusted or equalized to suit the operation of the aircraft or the need of the owner. This plan permits greater utilization of the aircraft. The owner using progressive inspections must provide proper personnel, procedures, and facilities. Progressive inspections eliminate the need for periodic and 100-hr inspections during the period that this procedure is followed.

Check the logbooks and the inspection forms before taking the flight test to make sure that the airplane is airworthy. It would be plenty embarrassing for the flight examiner to find that the airplane has not been inspected as required and is not airworthy. No matter whether you begged, borrowed, hired, or stole the airplane, the final responsibility rests on you at the flight test. The owner/operator will be in trouble too, but this won't make it any easier on you.

If there is no record of the required inspections, then the airworthiness certificate is null and void.

Airplane Flight Manual or Pilot's Operating Handbook. The *POH*s for general aviation airplanes are laid out as follows for standardization purposes:

Section 1—General

This section contains a three-view of the airplane and descriptive data on engine, propeller, fuel and oil, dimensions, and weights. It contains symbols, abbreviations, and terminology used in airplane performance.

Section 2—Limitations

This section includes airspeed limitations. The primary airspeed limitations are given in knots and in both indicated and calibrated airspeeds (although some manufacturers furnish mph data as well), and the markings are in knots and indicated airspeeds.

The maneuvering speed, which is the maximum indicated airspeed at which the controls may be abruptly and fully deflected without overstressing the airplane, depends on the stall speed, which decreases as the airplane gets lighter. (Review Chap. 11.)

Included here also are power plant limitations (engine rpm limits, maximum and minimum oil pressures, and maximum oil temperature and rpm range). Weight and CG limits are included for the particular airplane.

Maneuver and flight load factor limits are listed, as well as operations limits (day and night, VFR, and IFR), fuel limitations (usable and unusable fuel), and minimum fuel grades.

An airplane may not be able to use some of the fuel in flight; this is listed as "unusable fuel." For example, one airplane has a total fuel capacity of 24 U.S. gal with 22 U.S. gal being available in flight (2 gal unusable).

Copies of composite or individual aircraft placards are included.

Section 3 – Emergency Procedures

Here are checklists for such things as engine failures at various portions of the flight; forced landings, including ditching; fires during start and in flight; icing; electrical power supply malfunctions; and airspeeds for safe operation.

Included are amplified procedures for dealing with these "problems," such as how to recover from inadvertently flying into instrument conditions, recovering after a vacuum system failure, spin recoveries, rough engine operations, and electrical problems.

Section 4 – Normal Procedures

This section has checklist procedures from preflight through climb, cruise, landing, and securing the airplane. It's followed by amplified procedures of the same material. Recommended speeds for normal operation are summarized, as well as given in the amplified procedures. Noise characteristics of the airplane may be included here.

Section 5 – Performance

Performance charts (takeoff, cruise, landing) with sample problems are included, with range and endurance information, airspeed and altimeter calibration charts for normal and alternate static sources, and stall speed charts.

Section 6 – Weight and Balance and Equipment List

Airplane weighing procedures are given here, as well as a loading graph and an equipment list with weights and arms of the various airplane components.

Section 7 – Airplane and Systems Descriptions

The airframe, with its control systems, is described and diagrammed. The landing gear, engine and engine controls, etc., and fuel, brake, electrical, hydraulic, instrument, anti-icing, ventilation, and heating systems are covered here.

Section 8 – Airplane Handling, Service, and Maintenance

Here is the information you need for preventive maintenance, ground handling, servicing and cleaning, and care for a particular airplane.

Section 9 – Supplements

This covers optional systems, with descriptions and operating procedures of the electronics, oxygen, and other nonrequired equipment.

Aircraft Radio Station License. If your airplane has any transmitting equipment, make sure the radio station license is on board and in date.

OTHER AIRCRAFT DOCUMENTS – AIRCRAFT AND ENGINE MAINTENANCE RECORDS. The FARs state that the registered owner or operator must maintain a maintenance record in a form and manner prescribed by the FAA administrator, including a current and accurate record of the total time in service on the aircraft and on each engine, propeller, and appliance of the aircraft, and a record of inspections and the record of required maintenance. Such records shall be

1. Presented for required entries each time inspection or maintenance is accomplished on the aircraft or engine.

2. Transferred to the new registered owner or operator upon disposition of the aircraft or engine involved.

3. Made available for inspection by authorized represent-

Fig. 21-2.

atives of the FAA administrator or NTSB.

Number 3 is the reason you should have the logbooks and inspection reports with you for the flight test.

Logbooks. The logbook entry must include the type and extent of maintenance, alterations, repair, overhaul, or inspection and reflect the time in service and date when completed. The logbook should have entries when mandatory notes, service bulletins, and airworthiness directives are complied with. The regulations call for a separate, current, and permanent record of maintenance accomplished on the aircraft and engine, and the logbook *is* the record. You could carve the information on a piece of granite, but this would be unhandy to haul around, so the usual procedure is to use a logbook.

The aircraft and each engine must have separate records.

Before taking the flight test, make sure your logbooks are the right ones and are up-to-date.

Record of Major Repairs and Alterations. This is FAA form 337, a special form for major changes done after the plane leaves the manufacturer. The owner/operator keeps a copy, and an entry is made in the logbook with a reference to the date or work order by number and approving agency. The FAA 337 notes the new empty Weight, useful load, and empty CG (as in the logbook) and is normally attached to the Weight and Balance form in the airplane. Review Chap. 13 for information on service bulletins and other maintenance requirements.

SUMMARY OF THE AIRCRAFT DOCUMENTS. You can accomplish a great deal by going over the documents with the owner/operator of the airplane you plan to use on the flight test. Examiners can ask embarrassing questions that would have been simple to answer had you just spent a few minutes checking the airplane's papers (Fig. 21-2).

Obtaining Weather Information. Be able to obtain *Aviation Weather Reports, Area* and *Terminal Forecasts,* and *Winds Aloft Forecasts* pertinent to a proposed flight. Know what *is* pertinent and be able to interpret and understand the significance.

A chapter on such information is *not* included in this book because the methods of presenting weather are constantly changing. The times of release and symbols used in the various reports will probably be changed from the time this book is printed to the time you are ready for the practical test. You'll be graded on reading actual information at the time of the practical test. If you haven't dealt with the workings of the National Weather Service lately, you'd better go to an FSS or Weather Service Office and get up-to-date on what information is currently available and the best way to interpret it.

Break out your copies of *Aviation Weather* and *Aviation Weather Services* beforehand for a good review of weather theory and how to interpret the information provided by the National Weather Service.

There will be emphasis on PIREPs, SIGMETs and AIRMETs. Know how to use wind shear reports.

Cross-Country Flight Planning. Your knowledge and ability to plan a cross-country flight may be based on the most complex airplane used for the practical test. In-flight demonstrations of cross-country procedures will be tested under the area of operation NAVIGATION. You'll be expected to promptly and systematically plan a VFR cross-country flight near the maximum range of the airplane, considering maximum payload and fuel, including one leg for night operations. (For Pete's sake, select and use current and appropriate aeronautical charts.) You'll plot a course with fuel stops, available alternates, and a suitable course of action for various situations.

You'll pick the best checkpoints and the most favorable altitude or flight level considering weather and equipment capabilities. You'll be expected to select appropriate radio aids for navigation and get pertinent information from the *Airport/Facility Directory* and other flight publications, including NOTAMs. You'll fill out a navigation log and simulate filing a VFR flight plan. When you select the route, check the airspace, obstructions, and terrain features. Planning on flying through a Prohibited Area can cost points.

Airplane Loading and Baggage Capacities. You'll be expected to refer to the approved Weight and Balance data for the airplane. You might review the section on Airplane Weight and Balance in Chap. 10. You'll probably be asked for some practical computations of permissible fuel and payload (baggage and passenger) distributions. The FAA considers the following as standard for Weight and Balance computations:

Fuel — 6 lb per gallon

Oil — 7½ lb per gallon

Actual weights of persons

Remember that the baggage compartment is placarded for two reasons: (1) structural and (2) CG considerations.

Weight and Balance. You'll be expected to be able to work a Weight and Balance for the airplane being used to determine that the Weight and CG are within limits. You'll naturally use the charts and graphs furnished by the manufacturer. Don't use the sample empty Weight, as given in the *POH*, unless the examiner just wants a general example. At least know that you'd use the actual empty Weight and empty CG of the airplane you're flying.

Review Chap. 10, particularly with respect to the effect of CG positions on stability and control. Also note the effects of Weight on performance and airplane stresses (Chap. 11).

Determining Performance and Limitations. You'll be expected to know the limits of your airplane, such as limit load factors and airspeeds (see Chap. 11) and to demonstrate proficient use of the appropriate performance charts, tables, and data — including cruise control, range, and endurance (Chap. 7).

You'll be expected to determine the airplane's performance in all phases of flight, so Chaps. 5 to 9 of this book might be reviewed. Be sharp with your weight and balance work, and a review of that section in Chap. 10 would be in order.

Know the effects of seasonal and atmospheric conditions on the airplane's performance (for instance, High, Hot, and Humid Hurts). You'll be expected to use sound judgment in making a competent decision on whether the required performance is within the airplane's capabilities and operating limitations. (If you come back after the flight test with a wrinkled airplane, don't expect to get a commercial certificate that trip.)

Operation of Aircraft Systems. You'll have to be familiar with the primary flight controls and trim, wing flaps, spoilers, and leading edge devices (Chap. 2).

Know the *pitot-static system* and the associated flight instruments (Chap. 4) as well as the *vacuum/pressure* systems and associated instruments that may have possible problems associated with the flight instruments and systems (Chaps. 4 and 19).

Be aware of the foibles of *retractable landing gear* with particular emphasis on the retraction system (normal and emergency), the indicators, the brakes and tires, and the nose-wheel steering (Chap. 14).

As far as the *power plant* is concerned, know the controls and indicators as well as the induction, carburetor/fuel injection, exhaust and turbocharging, and cooling and fire detection systems (Chaps. 4, 12, and 19).

Be very familiar with the *propeller* type and controls (Chaps. 2 and 12).

As far as the *fuel system* is concerned, you'd better have full knowledge of its capacity, pumps, control, and indicators plus fueling procedures (approved grade, color, and additives) and the low-level warning system. For Pete's sake know where the fuel drain valves are and in what order they should be used (Chap. 13).

The *oil system* information includes capacity, grade, and indicators (Chaps. 4 and 13).

The *hydraulic system* will be discussed with attention paid to the controls and indicators plus pumps and regulators (Chap. 14).

You might review Chap. 4 and the *Pilot Operating Handbook* for the *electrical system* of your airplane.

[Does your airplane have an alternator(s) or generator(s), and what are the advantages and disadvantages of each?] You might check Fig. 4-67 to see a simple electrical system. Know where the battery is located and note if your airplane has an auxiliary power plug. What circuit breakers or fuses protect what components? If you lost all electrical power, what systems and instruments would you lose? Be very familiar with the internal and external lighting and controls.

You might review Chap. 18 and your *POH* for the *environmental system* of your airplane, including heating, cooling and ventilation, oxygen and pressurization, and the controls and indicators for all this.

Check out the *ice prevention and elimination systems* for your airplane (Chap. 19).

Avionics is a most important system. Which antenna (top or bottom) is for what communications system?

Minimum Equipment List. Know which aircraft require the use of a minimum equipment list and the airworthiness limitations imposed on aircraft operations with inoperative instruments and equipment. Be able to explain the requirements for a letter of authorization from the FAA FSDO. You also need to be able to discuss intelligently supplemental type certificates, instrument and equipment exceptions, and special flight permits, and you should be aware of the procedures for deferring maintenance on aircraft without an approved minimum equipment list.

National Airspace System.
Know the basic weather minimums for all classes of airspace and be able to prove your knowledge of Class A, B, C, D, E, and G airspace. You'll probably be asked questions on special use airspace and other airspace areas.

Aeromedical Factors.
The *Airman's Information Manual* has an excellent chapter on "Medical Facts For Pilots," and there you can get information on hypoxia, hyperventilation, middle ear and sinus problems, spatial disorientation, motion sickness, the effects of alcohol and drugs, carbon monoxide poisoning, and stress and fatigue. (Review Chap. 18 of this book, also.) If you scuba dive and then fly too soon afterward, you could get the bends.

Night Flight Operations.
You will be asked questions about night operations but won't likely be required to fly at night.

You should be able to answer questions on night visual perception, including functions of rods and cones, how the eyes adapt to changing light conditions, and how to cope with illusions created by various light conditions. Know about aids for increasing vision effectiveness.

Be aware of personal and required airplane lighting and equipment and how a pilot can judge another airplane's probable path by light interpretation. Be able to explain airport and navigation lighting, including pilot-controlled lighting.

You could be asked to explain the steps of a night flight from preflight to landing, including possible emergencies. Know by feel where all the switches, circuit breakers, and spare fuses are hidden.

PREFLIGHT PROCEDURES

Preflight Check or Visual Inspection.
Be prepared to answer *why* you are checking certain things on the airplane.

Start the line check in the cockpit. Make sure the ignition switch (or switches) and battery (master) switch are OFF.

Use the manufacturer's recommended procedure or your own line check procedure. A pilot who finally makes up a line check only in order to pass a flight check doesn't deserve to get a higher certificate or rating. Of course, *you* have used a thorough line check for every flight since the student pilot days, so the only difference on the flight test will be explaining why each item is inspected.

It's amazing how little some pilots know about the internal workings of their airplanes. This is more often the case when the pilot has rented airplanes all along and has a blind faith in the operator. It may be possible that the pilot has never drained fuel strainers, always assuming that "the operator did it this morning." These pilots may not even know where to drain the fuel to check for water or dirt. It *has* happened.

When you become a commercial pilot or buy your own airplane you'll be carrying more of the preflight responsibility. As a commercial pilot you may operate away from the home base for days or weeks on a charter operation. Good ol' Joe, the mechanic, won't be around to drain the fuel strainer and check the oil for you. It'll be up to you to decide whether repair work should be done and whom to contact at the strange field. (Review Chaps. 12, 13, 14, and 15.)

Airplane Servicing.
You'd better know the proper grade and type of fuel and oil for your airplane and determine that there is an adequate supply of both on board. The examiner could ask questions about possible types of fuel contamination and how to eliminate it. If your airplane has oxygen equipment, know how to check the adequacy of the supply and how to use it (Chap. 18).

Cockpit Management.
You'll show that you know good procedures in cockpit management by making sure that passengers and cargo are secure and full-control movement is possible. Brief passengers (the examiner) on safety belt use and emergency procedures. Make sure that your material (charts, etc.) and equipment are readily available. Discuss with your instructor beforehand the factors of crew resource management.

Engine Starting.
Use the checklist! Be able to explain the correct starting procedures, including use of external power sources, hand propping, and the effects of incorrect starting procedures. Don't abuse the equipment. You'll be judged on positioning the airplane to avoid creating hazards, determining that the area is clear, setting up the engine controls properly, setting (holding) the brakes, avoiding excessive engine rpm and/or allowing the airplane to move too soon, and checking the engine instruments after the start.

Taxiing.
Be able to discuss all aspects of safe taxiing procedures, including the effect of wind on the airplane and the other elements in the flight test taxiing excerpts at the beginning of this chapter.

Before Takeoff Check.
Use the manufacturer's, or a recommended, checklist. If you start and make a run-up without a checklist the examiner will terminate the flight (and is right to do so). You are now working to become a *professional* pilot and probably have used a checklist during every flight anyway. If your chandelles or lazy eights aren't so hot but your other flying has been good, and if you've been conscientious about using a checklist, you're much more apt to pass than if you have outstanding chandelles but no checklist.

If you position the airplane improperly (blasting other airplanes), run up over sand or gravel (sandblasting *your* airplane's propeller), or make a long run-up headed downwind (maybe overheating the engine), you could fail this TASK.

Touch each control or switch or adjust it to the prescribed position after calling it out from the checklist.

Recognize any discrepancy and determine that the airplane is ready for flight. ("The left mag *always* drops 600 rpm.") Review critical takeoff performance, airspeeds, and distances and describe emergency procedures. Catch the takeoff and departure clearances and note the takeoff time.

AIRPORT OPERATIONS

Radio Communications and ATC Light Signals.
Be sure to think before transmitting (or listening for) a particular service and to transmit and report correctly using the recommended standard phraseology (no CB chatter). You'll be expected to be sharp in receiving, acknowledging, and complying with communications and to follow prescribed procedures for a simulated or actual communications failure. Be able to interpret and comply with ATC light signals.

Traffic Patterns.
You'll be judged on your professionalism in the traffic pattern operations at controlled and uncontrolled airports and will be expected to use proper collision avoidance procedures and established traffic pattern procedures and to stick to instructions and rules. *Avoid wake turbulence!* Fly a precise pattern and make good corrections for wind drift.

Maintain adequate spacing from other traffic (formation flying is *out*) and maintain the traffic pattern altitude within ±50 ft and the desired airspeed within ±5 K. Don't forget the checklist and don't land on the wrong runway.

Airport and Runway Markings and Lighting. You'll be expected to identify, interpret, and conform to airport, runway, and taxiing marking aids. To land on the *wrong* side of a displaced threshold or ignore the taxiway hold line could result in some disappointment.

Know and conform with airport lighting aids.

TAKEOFFS, LANDINGS, AND GO-AROUNDS

Normal and Crosswind Takeoff and Climb. Review Chaps. 5 and 6 for takeoff and climb factors. Be able to explain the elements of normal and crosswind takeoffs and climbs, including airspeeds, configurations, and emergency procedures. Adjust the mixture control as recommended (manufacturer or other reliable sources) for the existing conditions.

Note obstructions or other hazards and make sure the airplane is capable of performing the takeoff. Other factors to be considered are wind, alignment, necessary aileron deflection at the start and during the takeoff run, engine instrument check, smooth throttle operation, positive directional control (on centerline), rotation at proper airspeed, maintaining V_Y ±5 K, good wind drift correction on climbout, retraction of gear and flaps at the proper point and airspeed in climb (after a positive rate of climb is indicated), setting desired climb power at safe altitude, maintaining a straight track over the extended centerline until a turn is required, and completion of an after-takeoff checklist. If you pull the prop control back first (if the manufacturer insists that it should be the other way around) or forget to retract the gear and climb laboriously up to altitude, it could result in disqualification. Use proper noise abatement procedures. (Refer to your airplane's *POH* and Chaps. 5, 6, 12, and 14.)

Normal and Crosswind Approach and Landing. You'll be asked to explain the elements of normal and crosswind approaches and landings, including airspeeds, configurations, performance, and related safety factors.

For normal landings, the tailwheel-type airplane should touch down all three wheels simultaneously at or near the power-off stall speed. In strong gusty surface winds you'd better be prepared to use a wheel landing. In the nosewheel-type airplane, the touchdowns should be on the main gear with little or no weight on the nosewheel.

Your crosswind corrections should be made throughout the final approach and touchdown. (Don't think you can wander all over creation on final, make a last second "save" and

Fig. 21-3. The mark used for power-off accuracy landings is considered to be a deep ditch—don't undershoot.

be given a lot of credit for headwork.) Don't relax your guard during the landing roll while congratulating yourself after an extra-smooth touchdown. Don't exceed the crosswind limitations of the airplane and don't ground loop.

You'll be judged on takeoff and landing technique, judgment, drift correction, coordination, power technique, and smoothness. Keep the final approach speed within ±5 K with a gust correction applied and touchdown within 200 ft beyond a line or mark specified by the examiner.

For review purposes, take a look at these points on *power-off* accuracy landings. In a power-off approach to hit a spot, it is always better to be slightly high. If there's any question, you may slip or use flaps. Things may work out so that neither slipping nor flap application is necessary. Nothing is more embarrassing on a flight test than to think you're high, apply full flaps or make a steep slip, and discover that enthusiasm caused you to *under*shoot. The line or mark that you are required to land within 200 ft beyond is considered to be a ditch (Fig. 21-3). If you are going to undershoot, recognize the fact and apply power. An examiner who catches you trying to "stretch the glide" may get a bad impression of your flying ability.

About correcting for overshooting: although the rate of sink will increase considerably by slowing up the airplane in the glide, this is not the place to get cocked up and dangerously slow. Violent maneuvering, excessive slips, or dangerously low airspeeds will be disqualifying. One aid in telling whether you'll hit the spot or not is to watch its apparent movement as you glide toward it on final. If it moves toward you, an overshoot may occur; away, you may undershoot the spot.

Ground effect will tend to carry you farther down the field than you can determine by the apparent movement of the spot (Fig. 21-4).

Every approach will have some small amount of "float." The amount depends on the approach speed. If you approach at 140 K (normal approach speed 80 K), the float distance will

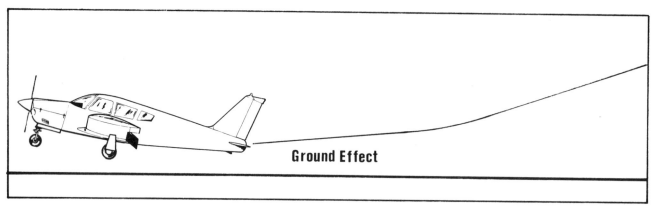

Fig. 21-4. Ground effect.

be extremely long. If you should approach at 61 K (stall speed 60 K), the float distance will be quite short (the airplane kind of "squashes" onto the ground).

Don't get so engrossed in the accuracy landing that you forget to put the wheels down, or skip other checklist items.

For points on various takeoffs and landings review Chap. 5 and 9.

A last note on the flight test landings: Improper or incomplete prelanding procedures, touching down with an excessive side load on the landing gear, and poor directional control will be disqualifying. Although it's not specifically mentioned, landing gear-up will terminate the flight test (probably this *would* be considered a result of improper or incomplete prelanding procedures).

Be aware of the possibility of wind shear or wake turbulence.

Soft-Field Takeoff and Climb.

Know *why* you are using specific techniques, configurations, and airspeeds for this TASK. You should also be able to explain the emergency procedures and hazards associated with attempting to climb at airspeeds less than V_x.

Taxi onto the takeoff surface at a speed consistent with safety, align the airplane on the takeoff path without stopping, and advance the throttle to full power smoothly. Check the engine instruments and maintain a pitch attitude that transfers the Weight from the wheels to the wings as soon as possible. Maintain directional control, lift off at the lowest possible airspeed, and stay in ground effect while accelerating. Accelerate to $V_x + 5$, -0 K, if obstructions are to be cleared, otherwise to $V_y \pm 5$ K. Retraction of flaps, gear, power use, and the flight track after takeoff will be judged. Checklist requirements are the same as for the short-field takeoff just covered (Chaps. 5, 6, 12, and 14).

Soft-Field Approach and Landing.

You'll be judged on your knowledge of what's involved in a soft-field approach and landing and *why* techniques different from the normal or short-field procedures must be used.

On the flight (practical) test you are to evaluate obstructions, landing surface, and wind conditions and select a suitable touchdown point. Establish the recommended soft-field approach and landing configuration and adjust the pitch and power to maintain a controlled approach to the touchdown point. (Maintain a controlled descent rate at the recommended airspeed (gust correction factor applied), ± 5 K or in its absence, not more than $1.3\ V_{so}$.) Be aware of the possibility of wind shear and/or wake turbulence. Make smooth and timely corrections as necessary throughout the procedure and touch down smoothly at minimum descent rate and airspeed with no drift or misalignment of the longitudinal axis. Don't ground loop. Keep the airplane moving so that you wouldn't bog down (in an actual situation).

Short-Field Takeoff and Climb.

Be able to explain *why* special techniques are required, the significance of specific airspeeds and configurations, and the expected performance for existing operating conditions. Know your emergency procedures for this phase of flight. Use the recommended flap setting and adjust the mixture control as recommended. (Start at the very beginning of the takeoff surface.) Use smooth throttle, check the engine instruments, and keep it straight on the runway. Rotate at the recommended airspeed and accelerate to $V_x + 5$, -0 K until any obstacle is cleared or until at least 50 ft above the surface, then accelerate to V_y and maintain it within ± 5 K. Retract the flaps and landing gear as recommended. (Don't retract the gear until you can no longer land on the runway.) Set desired power at a safe maneuvering altitude, maintain a straight track until a turn is required, and complete the after-takeoff checklist (Chaps. 5, 6, 12, and 14).

Short-Field Approach and Landing.

You'll be expected to touch down smoothly and within 100 ft of a specified point, with little or no float, no drift, and with the airplane longitudinal axis aligned with the runway centerline. Maintain a stabilized approach, controlled rate of descent, and recommended airspeed (or in its absence not more than $1.3\ V_{so}$) with gust correction applied, ± 5 K. (Remain aware of wind shear and/or wake turbulence.) Use that checklist! Fig. 21-4 shows ground effect. You will be expected to maintain positive directional control and apply smooth braking, as necessary to stop in the shortest distance consistent with safety. (Review the section on short-field landing and braking in Chap. 9.)

Go-Around from a Rejected (Balked) Landing.

You will likely have to explain the go-around procedure, including the recognition of the need to make a go-around, the importance of making a timely decision, the use of recommended airspeeds, the Drag effects of landing gear and flaps (retract the gear after a positive rate-of-climb indication), and properly coping with undesirable pitch and yaw tendencies. Trim the airplane to accelerate to V_y before the final flap retraction and climb at $V_y \pm 5$ K. Watch that wind drift and obstruction clearances and use that checklist. The examiner will present a situation on the flight check in which a go-around from a rejected landing is required and check that you recognize it and that your performance is acceptable. (The main requirement is to maintain good control of the airplane during the cleaning-up process and establishment of climb.)

SLOW FLIGHT AND STALLS

Slow Flight.

You will do slow flight at a safe altitude and will maneuver at an airspeed at which controllability is minimized to the point that further increasing the angle of attack or load factor would result in an immediate stall.

For good practice beforehand, do slow flight in medium-banked level, climbing, and descending turns, and straight and level flight with various flap settings in both cruising and landing configurations.

You'll be checked on your competence in establishing the minimum controllable airspeed and positive control of the airplane and in recognizing incipient stalls. Your straight and level flight should be held within limits of ± 50 ft altitude and $\pm 5°$ of the assigned heading. If you don't look around before and during the maneuver, or if you stall the airplane, the examiner will disqualify you. Primary emphasis will be placed on airspeed control.

You might review the following while getting ready for the flight test:

Remember to keep turns shallow because the stall speed increases with angle of bank. You may have to use more power to maintain altitude in the turns.

The problem that most pilots have in the straight portions is that of maintaining heading. They concentrate so hard on airspeed that the airplane is allowed to turn at will.

The following tolerances are suggested for straight and level and turning flight:

Heading — $\pm 5°$
Altitude — no change of altitude in excess of ± 50 ft
Airspeed — within ± 5 of the desired speed ($1.2\ V_{s1}$)
Bank — $\pm 10°$ in coordinated flight

A good exercise for you to practice for airplane cruise configuration is as follows:

1. Throttle back to less than the estimated power required to maintain altitude at the maximum endurance speed. Maintain altitude and heading as the airplane slows and adjust power as necessary. Fly straight and level for 2 min.

2. Increase power for climb as you raise the nose. Don't let the airspeed change. Maintain your heading—torque will now be more of a problem. Climb straight ahead for 1 min. Make shallow climbing turns in each direction (15° to 20° banks).

3. Throttle back and resume level slow flight.

4. Carburetor heat ON, throttle closed. Set up a glide, maintain the slow flight airspeed. Don't jerk the throttle closed but ease it back as the nose is lowered to the glide position (Fig. 21-5).

5. Make shallow gliding turns (20° to 30° banks) in each direction.

You can repeat the exercise with the airplane in landing configuration, except for the climb. The transition to the various attitudes will give you the most trouble. The stall warner may be sounding off throughout the exercise. Roll out on specified headings within ±5°.

Common Errors

1. Poor altitude control during the transition from cruise to slow flight.

2. Heading problems during straight and level and during climb.

3. Stalling the airplane.

4. Excessive changes of speed during transition from straight and level to climb or glide.

5. Failure to maintain a continuous surveillance of the area before and during the procedure. (Don't stare at the airspeed indicator or altimeter.)

6. Getting below 1500 ft AGL.

Straight-Ahead Stalls.
Always clear the area by making two 90° turns in opposite directions, or one 180° turn before doing stalls straight ahead. There will be a blind spot over the nose during the stall. Some pilots mechanically make these turns but don't look around. This is not only unsafe but a waste of time. If you don't look around during the turns it's as bad as no attempt to clear the area at all.

Be sure in all stalls that you have recovered at least 1500 ft above the ground.

POWER-OFF STALLS. You will maintain a heading ±10° in straight stalls.

Procedure

1. Clear the area.

2. Carburetor heat ON (if your airplane requires it), allow about 10 sec for any ice to be cleared, then set power to approach configuration. (Practice clean or in the landing configuration.)

3. Raise the nose to an angle of 10° to 15° above the horizon. Have some prominent object picked to help keep the nose lined up.

4. Pin the nose at that attitude by continued back pressure. Keep the wings level.

5. When the stall occurs, promptly lower the nose and apply full power smoothly—don't ram the throttle open.

The check pilot could ask you to make a power-off recovery, which only means that the recovery is not quite as quick as that using power but is still positive. The reason for a no-power recovery would be to simulate a dead stick glide during an emergency when you've let it get too slow and are approaching a stall (with no power available to help recover). Keep looking around during the stall process, even though you cleared the area before starting.

After the recovery, allow the airplane to accelerate to approach speed and resume the approach.

POWER-ON STALLS. The only difference between this stall and the power-off version is that cruise power is used throughout, which makes it necessary for you to raise the nose slightly higher in order to get stall indications without too much delay. Power makes a difference in nose attitude and stall speed because of the added slipstream over the wings and the airplane's vertical component of Thrust. Fig. 21-6 shows a comparison of the nose positions for the power-on and power-off approaches to a stall (pitch angles exaggerated).

The recovery for the stall consists of promptly reducing the pitch attitude and applying full throttle. Get in the habit of automatically applying full power on all stalls unless you are told otherwise by the check pilot.

In a few high-performance aircraft, the power setting may have to be reduced below the PTS guideline (no less than 55–60 percent of full power) so that you don't have excessively high-pitch attitudes (greater than 30° nose up). Such low power settings may be deemed inappropriate for this TASK for the initial commercial pilot certification. (You'll usually use the manufacturer's power setting.) Don't pull back on the wheel or stick too rapidly (easy!) or you might pitch the nose up to an uncomfortable position.

You'll be expected to recover to the point where adequate control effectiveness is regained with the minimum loss in altitude. Allow the airplane to accelerate to the best angle of climb with simulated obstacles, or the best rate of climb without simulated obstacles, and resume the climb. (See Takeoff and Departure Stalls.)

Common Errors

1. Failure to clear the area.

2. Lowering the nose before there are definite indications of the stall.

3. Not keeping the wings level throughout.

4. Letting the nose wander.

5. Not maintaining a heading within ±10°.

COMPLETE OR FULL STALL. This stall is a good exercise for keeping the wings level—and little else—but you should be

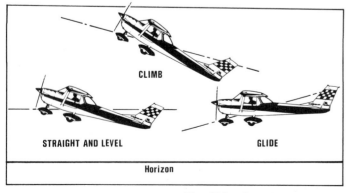

Fig. 21-5. Slow flight attitudes.

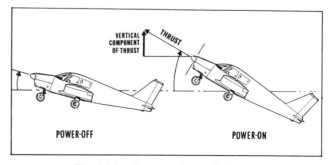

Fig. 21-6. A comparison of the attitudes of the power-off and power-on versions of a stall.

familiar with it, if only for academic interest. The maneuver may be done at cruise power or at idle, as with the first stall types mentioned.

In performing this stall pull the nose up higher than for the normal stall (up to about 30° above the horizon) and continue easing the control wheel back until the break occurs. In the complete stall do not start a recovery until the nose has fallen to the horizon (keep that wheel all the way back!) at which point you release back pressure and apply full power.

You'll find that the power-on version may give you a little trouble in keeping the wings level and that the nose tends to wander. As you can see, this is an exercise—you certainly wouldn't deliberately wait until the nose had fallen through to the horizon before starting recovery in an accidental stall at low altitudes!

SUMMARY OF SOME STRAIGHT-AHEAD STALLS

Approach to a stall—Recover before the break. (Not required on the practical test.)

Normal stall—Recover immediately after the break or when full up-elevator travel has occurred.

Complete stall—The nose is higher; recover after the break when the nose has moved down to the horizon. (Not required on the practical test.)

Always clear the area.

Note that there are six possible combinations of the above stalls—each one with and without power.

Keep the wings level with coordinated controls as the nose is lowered and don't let the nose wander.

Turning Stalls.
The heading of this section may be a little misleading because you should also practice the takeoff and departure stalls and approach to landing stalls straight ahead. However, in most cases pilots seem to get into trouble in climbing or gliding *turns* at low altitudes—hence the heading.

TAKEOFF AND DEPARTURE STALLS.
These stalls simulate a situation that happens too often—a stall occurring during the takeoff or climbout. It may be caused by the pilot's distraction at a critical time or by just showing off.

The maneuver should be done at slightly above takeoff speed, in takeoff configuration (this means flaps if you normally use them for takeoff and, of course, gear down), and at recommended takeoff power. They should be done from straight climbs *and* climbing turns of 20°, ±10° constant bank.

You may find that the "high" wing will stall first in most airplanes and the airplane will roll in that direction, the reason being that as the stall is approached the wings start losing Lift and the airplane mushes and starts to slip. The highest wing gets interference from the fuselage and quits first. You can check this by watching the ball throughout the approach and stall; if you can no longer keep the ball centered (it will indicate a slip) the high wing will stall first. Don't blindly expect this to happen because if you stall at a higher airspeed and are skidding, the bottom wing may be slowed to a point where it might stall first. There is one model trainer on the market that has a tendency in a *balanced* climbing right turn to have the inside (right wing) drop first (the left turns are as expected). Also, your particular airplane may have been rigged laterally after leaving the manufacturer so that funny things happen in the stall. Of course, that's why you practice them anyway—to see what *your* airplane does and to find the best method of recovery. But normally, you can count on an "over the top" type of stall (the airplane rolls away from the ball).

To recover, get the nose down and level the wings with coordinated controls. Unless the roll is particularly vicious you can usually recover by merely relaxing back pressure.

Procedure
1. Gently slow the airplane to about 5 K above the stall in the takeoff configuration (lift-off speed).

2. Apply climbing power and start a shallow-banked turn in either direction, pulling the nose up steeply. (Practice them from straight climbs, also.) Note the altitude at the "lift-off."

3. When the stall breaks, relax back pressure, use opposite rudder if necessary to stop rotation, and then level the wings with coordinated controls.

In practicing these stalls you'll find that if the bank is steep you'll have trouble getting a clean break. The nose may drop, causing the airplane to descend in a tight circle, shuddering and buffeting—with no stall break.

Keep your head swiveling all during the approach and stall.

Practice the stall in both directions as well as straight ahead.

Common Errors
1. Too steep a bank in the turning stalls—no definite stall break. The bank angle must be 20°.

2. Too early a recovery—recovering before a definite break.

3. Too late a recovery—the airplane is allowed to rotate too far before recovery is started.

4. Failure to make a steep climb and thereby delaying the stall as the airplane mushes.

5. Overeagerness to get the nose down; abrupt forward pressure on the wheel or stick, with the result that the nose is pushed too low and excessive altitude is lost during recovery.

APPROACH-TO-LANDING, OR GLIDING-TURN STALLS.
These stalls might be considered a power-off version of the departure stalls. The airplane will be in the landing configuration and the engine throttled back. This stall demonstrates what *could* happen if the airplane is allowed to get too slow during a landing approach. This type stall will be harder to get to break cleanly, particularly if you are practicing solo. Of course, you may have a great deal of trouble getting the airplane to stall cleanly during practice and then be complacent someday and find that the airplane *can* stall if you get sloppy and distracted. Practicing these stalls is intended to help you recognize what could happen and learn how to recover as quickly and safely as possible.

Procedure. Keep looking around throughout the approach and stall.

1. With the airplane in landing configuration, establish a normal gliding turn of 20°, ±10°, bank in either direction (after applying carburetor heat if called for). Be sure to practice the stalls in both directions—not all approaches are made from left-hand patterns. For straight-ahead versions, keep the heading within ±10° of that selected.

2. Flatten the glide through continued back pressure until the stall occurs.

3. Stop any rotation as you simultaneously release back pressure and apply *full* power.

4. Clean up the airplane and establish a climb or continue the approach as required.

Practice this stall from straight glides as well as from moderately banked (20°) turns.

It requires no will power to lower the nose when you're practicing stalls at 3000 ft. It's very easy up there—you just get the nose down and don't pay any attention to it. *But* at 200 ft or so you'd have to force yourself to release back pressure to recover from a stall. Fatal accidents have occurred because pilots have gone back to their instincts and ignored training when under stress.

Practice with your instructor recoveries without power—note the difference.

Common Errors

1. Too steep a bank in the turning stall.

2. Allowing the wings to become level through inattention during the stall approach. You wouldn't have this problem during an actual landing approach because you'd be watching the runway and would be turning as necessary to line up.

3. Too early a recovery; not allowing the stall to break.

4. Overeagerness in getting the nose down; excessive forward pressure during the recovery.

Accelerated Stalls. Here is proof positive that a stall is a matter of angle of attack, not airspeed.

You don't do any of the accelerated stalls at an airspeed of more than 1.25 times the unaccelerated stall speed because of the possibility of overstressing the airplane, particularly in gusty air. The flaps will be retracted for this same reason.

Accelerated stalls are done from a turn of 45° bank. There are two reasons for this: (1) this is the condition under which most pilots actually encounter the accelerated stall in flight—when they try to tighten the turn by pulling back on the wheel or by trying to maintain altitude without sufficient power and (2) this avoids inadvertently pulling the nose *straight up* abruptly in practice, getting a whip stall (the airplane stalls with the nose up so steeply that it tends to slide backward).

Unless you are skidding, the high wing will usually stall first, as in the departure and approach stalls, but the roll will be faster. The recovery is standard; release back pressure and return to level flight through use of coordinated controls. Plan on adding power during recovery.

In practice, recover (1) immediately upon stall recognition and (2) after a full stall develops and the nose falls below level flight attitude.

In situation 1 the recovery is simple. Relaxing the back pressure at the right time can result in the airplane's recovering in straight and level flight, if the high wing stalled first and roll occurred.

In situation 2 the nose will be low, and the airplane will probably have rolled over into a steep bank. Relax back pressure and then bring the airplane back to straight and level flight through use of coordinated controls.

Recover quickly with a minimum loss of altitude, but don't get overeager and restall it.

Don't get over cruise speed at any time during the recovery. (This stall is not required by the PTS.)

Procedure

1. Using power as needed to maintain altitude, make a 45° (or more)-banked turn. Slow the airplane to no more than 1.25 times the normal stall speed.

2. Increase the angle of attack in a moderate climb or constant altitude until a stall occurs. Power may be reduced below cruising to aid in producing the stall, but any decrease in the rate of climb or loss of altitude will relieve the load factor (and the stall is not "accelerated"). Remember the term "accelerated" means that above-normal load factors are present at the stall.

3. Release back pressure, open the throttle, and recover to straight and level flight using coordinated controls.

The 1.25 factor does not apply to an aerobatic category airplane, but keep it below the maneuvering speed or recommended speed for accelerated maneuvers.

Incidentally, some airplanes do *not* give a sharp stall break and, with these, when the wheel or stick is full back, initiate your recovery.

Common Errors

1. Jerking the wheel or stick back.

2. The opposite—timid application of back pressure.

Fig. 21-7. The pilot sees on approach that unless the rate of turn is increased he'll fly past the runway and have to turn back to it.

Fig. 21-8. This is sloppy flying and the other pilots will notice. He knows that the stall speed increases with a steeper bank so he decides to cheat by using inside rudder and skidding it around (and maybe using just a *touch* of opposite aileron).

Fig. 21-9. Inside rudder means that the outside (left) wing will speed up, steepening the right bank. He applies more opposite (left) aileron. The cycle continues until he is in a shallow banked skid with well-crossed controls at a very low speed (he is using added back pressure to keep the nose up).

Fig. 21-10. A view of the runway as seen from a near inverted position just after the stall occurs. Another statistic!

3. Too brisk forward pressure on recovery, which hangs occupants on seat belts and puts undue negative stress on the airplane.

Cross-Control (Skidding) Stalls. This stall is most likely to occur during the turn onto the final approach. A typical situation might be as follows:

You see that in the turn onto final you will go past the runway unless your turn rate is increased. Now, everybody knows that the stall speed increases with an increase in bank, so you figure that the best way to turn is by skidding around—and not increasing the bank. You start applying inside rudder, which increases the turn rate, but the outside wing is speeded up and the bank starts to increase. You take care of this by using aileron against the turn, which actually helps drag the inside wing back farther. As the airplane is in a banked attitude, application of inside rudder (and opposite aileron) tends to make the nose drop, which is counteracted by increased back pressure. The situation is perfect—for having one wing stall before the other, that is. True, the wing with the down aileron has more coefficient of Lift (the down aileron acts as a flap, increasing the coefficient of Lift), but the Drag of that wing increases even more sharply, which slows it more. So the inside wing starts dropping, which increases the angle of attack—and it stalls before the outside wing. Another term for this stall is "under-the-bottom stall"—an apt description.

Look back at Fig. 2-11 (the NASA 0006 airfoil) to see the theory behind *why* the wing with the down aileron stalls first. The coefficient of Lift (C_L) versus angle of attack curve, without flaps, stalls at about 9°. When flaps are used, the stall occurs at about 6° angle of attack. The C_L is higher at the stall but that flapped wing stalls "sooner" as both wings' angle of attack is increased from some point of reference. The down

aileron acts as a flap and the Lift of each wing is about equal, since Lift is a combination of calibrated airspeed (q) and angle of attack, or C_L, for a given airplane (the use of inside rudder speeds up the outside, unflapped wing). The stall occurs as the critical angle of attack is reached first for the wing with the down aileron.

You should be familiar with this stall and know that it *could* happen and note the best means of recovery.

Figs. 21-7 through 21-10 show the probable sequence of such an actual stall at a low altitude. The series shows a *right-hand* approach—an even more likely setup for such a stall, as you would be more apt to misjudge the turn.

Procedure

1. Practice these stalls at a safe altitude and keep an eye out for other traffic. Use carburetor heat, if required. Make a shallow gliding turn in either direction. You may have to carry some power during the practice sessions to help get a good break. Sometimes it seems it is easily accomplished only when you *don't* want to stall. In practice stalls it's probably best not to use flaps because of the possibility of exceeding the max flaps-down speed during the recovery. In an actual stall on an approach turn, you'd have the flaps down but wouldn't be worrying particularly about the max flaps-down speed during the recovery.

2. Apply more and more inside rudder to cheat on the turn. Use opposite aileron as necessary to keep the bank from increasing.

3. Keep the nose up by increasing the back pressure.

4. When the stall break occurs, the roll will be rapid. Neutralize the ailerons; stop any further rotation with opposite rudder as you relax the back pressure.

5. Then return to normal flight with coordinated controls and add power as the recovery progresses.

As the roll is fast, the bank may be vertical or past vertical. The nose will be low and speed will build up quickly. The usual error in practice is allowing the airspeed to build up too high during recovery, which wastes altitude. Recover to straight and level flight with coordinated controls as soon as possible without overstressing the airplane or getting a secondary stall.

The bad thing is that this stall is most likely to occur at lower altitudes where recovery is less sure. Practice it until you are able to recognize the conditions leading up to it—and then avoid those conditions. This stall is not required to be demonstrated on the commercial practical test but is included for information.

Common Errors

1. Not neutralizing the ailerons at the start of the recovery.

2. Using too much opposite (top) rudder to stop rotation, causing the airplane to slip badly.

3. Hesitation in recovering, with a greater than necessary altitude loss.

Spin Awareness.

While spins are not required on the commercial practical test you should have some idea of the theory behind them. *A spin is an aggravated stall resulting in autorotation.*

The airplanes that you've been flying are generally spin resistant; you have to make them spin. They should show no uncontrollable spin characteristics no matter how you use the controls. Some of the older light trainers would come out of a spin of their own accord with the pilot's hands and feet removed from the controls, but this is not the most effective spin recovery method. You remember in the departure and approach stalls and the cross-control stall that one wing stalled before the other and a rolling moment was produced. If you had held the wheel back and used rudder in the direction of roll, a spin would have likely followed. The whole theory of the spin can be understood by realizing that one wing is stalled before the other, producing an imbalance of Lift and Drag (autorotation). If you continue to hold back pressure and hold rudder into the roll, this stalled condition remains and the roll continues as the nose "falls off" downward.

BACKGROUND.

Spins and spirals are sometimes confused. The spiral is a high-speed, low-angle-of-attack, descending turn; *normal control pressures* are used to recover. The spin is at low airspeed and a high angle of attack; *mechanical control movements* are used for recovery. (More about spin recovery procedures later.)

The following factors about upright (normal) spins aren't generally known.

Rate of Descent.

In the developed spin, the average two-place trainer has a rate of descent of from 5500 to 8000 fpm, depending on the spin mode. (Usually, the flatter spin mode has the lower rate of descent, but even a "mere" 5500 fpm can be fatal.)

One question often asked is, How much altitude is lost per turn? There's not a simple answer because the greater the number of turns, the less the *loss per turn*. For instance, you'd probably do well to allow for a loss of 1000 to 1500 ft for a 1-turn spin, as altitude is also required for entry and recovery from that one turn. On the other hand, a 21-turn spin in a current trainer resulted in a total altitude loss of 4100 ft from start to level-off after recovery—an average of 195 ft per turn. In that longer spin the altitude used for entry and recovery is spread out among the 21 turns instead of being a major factor, as for the 1-turn spin.

Rate of Rotation.

One popular trainer averages 1.3 sec per turn (277° per second) in the first 5 or 6 turns, then pitches up slightly from the 6th to 9th (or 10th) turn with the rotation rate slowing to about 170° per second. You may find that the engine quits (the prop stops) in prolonged spins, but this does not affect the effectiveness of recovery. After the airplane is out of the spin, the starter can be used to get things going again. (Holler "Clear!" before using the starter, naturally.)

Instrument Indications.

The airspeed will be low and remain so if the airplane stays in the spin. If, as the rotation progresses, the airspeed continues to increase from stall or near-stall indications, the airplane is easing into a spiral and recovery should be effected immediately to avoid high-airspeed and/or high-stress problems. As mentioned, one light trainer in an extended spin changed modes, that is, moved from a comparatively steep nose-down attitude to a more pitched-up one; and the airspeed varied from 45 K in the steep mode to zero in the more pitched-up attitude.

The turn and slip needle, or the small airplane in the turn coordinator, is always leaning in the direction of the spin, but the ball is normally unreliable. For instance, the reaction of the ball depends on its relative position to the CG. (The airplane is rotating around its CG, which is moving around the spin axis, which in turn is moving in relation to a vertical, or earth-related, axis. If you think about this in a spin you may get confused enough to forget how to recover—a procedure that will be discussed shortly.) On several side-by-side airplanes, with the turn and slip or turn coordinator located on the left (pilot's) side of the panel, the ball always goes to (and stays on) the *left* side of the instrument for both *left and right developed spins*. (A slip indicator placed on the *right* side of the panel moved over to and stayed on the *right* side of the instrument in spins in both directions.) It has been noted in some sources that the ball always goes to the outside of the spin, and for recovery the pilot should "step on the ball." In some airplanes with the slip indicator in the center of the panel, a slight tendency for the ball to move outside of the spin has been noted, *but don't "predict" it for your airplane.*

In a current tandem military basic trainer, the ball in the front cockpit (near the CG) has a reaction different from the one in the rear cockpit. (In one experiment spinning in either direction, the ball in the front cockpit T/S had very small oscillations on each side of neutral and the rear cockpit ball deflected slightly *into* the spin.)

PRACTICE SPIN TO THE LEFT

1. Before doing any spins in an airplane you haven't spun before, it would be wise to have an instructor experienced in spinning it ride with you to demonstrate the entry and recovery procedures. Even if you've spun earlier models of an airplane, you'd better review the recovery procedure and either talk to some of the local instructors or get them to ride with you. In later models the manufacturer may have changed the geometry of the airplane or added other factors that affected the airplane's recovery characteristics. Such changes can surprise you on that first spin.

Of course, you should make sure that the airplane is certificated for spinning and is properly loaded. The control cables should have the proper tension because it would be "interesting," after getting into the spin, to discover that full-opposite rudder pedal deflection used for recovery only moves the rudder a few degrees.

2. Get enough altitude so that you'll be recovered by 3000 ft above the ground.

3. Clear the area and start a normal power-off stall (use carburetor heat if recommended).

4. Just as the stall break occurs, apply—and hold—full left rudder; keep the wheel or stick full back. Some airplanes

require a blast of power to get the spin started; the prop blast gives the rudder added effectiveness to yaw the airplane.

5. The nose drops as the airplane rolls, but the full up-elevator does not allow the airplane to recover from the stall. The unequal Lift of the wings gives the airplane its rotational motion.

The spin is continued as long as the rudder and wheel are held as above. The rotation of the airplane tends to continue the imbalance of Lift; the "down-moving" wing keeps its high angle of attack and remains well stalled. The "up-moving" wing maintains a lower angle of attack (and more Lift).

If you should unconsciously relax back pressure before the developed spin, a spiral will result.

The properly executed spin is no harder on the airplane than a stall. A sloppy recovery puts more stress on the airplane than the spin itself.

Don't have the flaps down when practicing spins because it might change the airplane's spin characteristics, plus the fact that you might exceed the maximum flaps-down speed during the recovery.

SPIN RECOVERY. *It would be well to take the recovery step-by-step from a theoretical standpoint first, and then bring in some practical recovery procedures.*

1. You used the rudder to induce the yaw in the spin entry, so opposite rudder should be applied to stop the yaw, equalize the Lift of the two wings, and stop autorotation. If the rudder effectively does this, it should be neutralized as soon as rotation stops or a spin in the opposite direction (a progressive spin) could be started.

2. At this instant, in a theoretical look at recovery procedures, the rudder is neutral (the rotation has stopped) but you're still holding the wheel or stick full back and the airplane is still stalled, even though the nose appears to be pointed almost straight down. If you continued to hold the wheel full back the airplane would be buffeting and could, because of rigging, tend to whip off into a new spin in either direction.

The autorotation, or imbalance of Lift and Drag, has been broken, and now the stall recovery is initiated by relaxing the back pressure *or* giving a brisk forward motion of the wheel or stick (depending on the airplane). For older and lighter trainers such as the J-3 Cub, Aeronca Champion, Taylorcrafts, or Cessna 120–140s a slight relaxing of the back pressure was enough to assure that the stall (and spin) was broken. In some later airplanes with higher wing loadings, the wheel or stick must be *briskly* moved forward, well ahead of neutral, to get the nose farther down and break the stall.

3. The third step is recovery from the dive after the autorotation and stall are broken. Sometimes the airspeed is allowed to get too high or too much back pressure is used on the pull-out (or both). Sometimes a pilot in a hurry to recover relaxes back pressure (or uses a brisk forward motion as required) and immediately pulls back on the control wheel to "get it out of the dive," which results in a quick restalling of the airplane and possibly setting off a progressive (or new) spin. You've had this experience with plain everyday stalls—a too-quick recovery can put the airplane back into a stalled condition, and the process has to be started again.

Okay, the three steps mentioned were just that, a listing of required control movements for discussion purposes. You'll find that with some airplanes the use of rudder alone won't stop the rotation, so you wouldn't wait for it to take effect before applying forward pressure, which would help not only to break the stall but also to aid the rudder in stopping the yaw and unbalanced Lift-Drag condition. In other words, you would apply full opposite rudder followed about a quarter turn later by brisk forward movement of the wheel, holding the controls this way until rotation stops. Usually in this procedure, because of the almost simultaneous application of elevator with the rudder, the nose is down and the airspeed starts picking up as soon as the rotation stops; at this point the rudder is neutralized and back pressure is again applied to ease the airplane from the dive. (Some *POH*s suggest simultaneous use of rudder and elevator in the recovery.)

For some airplanes, ailerons against the spin speed it up, but for others the rate of rotation slows if ailerons are used opposite to the roll. *A suggested all-around procedure, however, is to leave the ailerons neutral throughout the spin and recovery to avoid adding some unknown factors to the recovery.*

Usually, the steeper spin modes are more easily recoverable and have a faster rate of rotation, as was discussed earlier in this section. If in extended spins the airplane moves into a flatter mode (which usually means more time and turns required for recovery), the recovery process may move it back through the earlier, faster rotation mode as it goes back to the normal flight regime. The initial reaction by the pilot is to think that the recovery inputs are making things worse (the rotation speeded up!) when actually this is a good sign for many airplanes. Fortunately the airplane often moves through the increased rotation rate and on to recovery before the pilot has time to "start thinking" and back off from this proper recovery technique. Sometimes it seems to take longer to recover than anticipated, there's always the temptation to Try Something Else. If you are using the *POH*-recommended recovery, give it a chance, although it may seem a long time before good things start happening.

In theory, it would seem that adding power during recovery would increase the slipstream by the rudder, thereby increasing its effectiveness. The problem is that in a standard configuration, pitch-up results from added power—and *that* you don't need. A NASA study has shown that even in jets of high Thrust-to-Weight ratios, addition of power has little measurable effect in aiding recovery and in some cases may be detrimental. Also, in an extended spin, the engine may stop completely, as noted earlier, which would make academic the subject of power helping or hurting the recovery.

SUMMARY OF SPINS. The *POH* (or an instructor who has experience in spinning a particular airplane) will take precedence over the general look at spins given here, but you might keep in mind the following notes about spin recoveries.

1. Most airplanes recover more promptly if the throttle is closed before using the aerodynamic controls. Neutralize the ailerons. Then,

2. A general recovery procedure is to use full rudder opposite to the spin, followed almost immediately by a brisk forward movement, well ahead of neutral, of the wheel or stick. (Don't violently *jam* the wheel full forward—the airplane could be overstressed or an inverted spin entered.) For some airplanes the rate of rotation appears to speed up as the recovery starts, which could fool you into thinking that things are getting worse.

3. As soon as rotation has stopped, neutralize the rudder and use the elevator to help further break the stall or ease the airplane from the dive. One error made by pilots with comparatively little spin recovery experience is continuing to hold opposite rudder after the rotation has stopped and airspeed builds up; this can cause heavy side loads on the vertical tail.

4. Normally docile airplanes can bite back if the CG is near or at the aft limits of the envelope. Of course, you would not deliberately spin an airplane with people in the rear seats or with baggage back there; if you get into a stall situation with this type of loading, don't let a rotation get started. For most airplanes the first two turns are an incipient spin condition and the spin can be stopped relatively easily. After that, moments of inertia can be such in the developed spin that

recovery is impossible. If it looks like the stall is getting out of hand, get that nose down farther with a brisk forward movement of the wheel (and you may decide that opposite rudder *and* wheel action is the best move to make — you can apologize to the passengers later).

One good procedure for checking the spin characteristics (and your reaction), after getting the proper briefing and instruction and making sure the airplane is properly loaded, is setting up on that solo practice by making less than one turn, recovering, then making a turn and a half and recovering, and so on until you've gotten the feel of the airplane in this area. (Climb back up after each spin.) If things start to feel funny to you that first spin entry or two, you can break it off before any problems develop.

If one statement can be made about inadvertent spins, it is that they occur when the pilot is distracted and, particularly, in uncoordinated flight.

PERFORMANCE MANEUVERS

Steep Turns. Maximum performance maneuvers are required on the commercial flight test so that you may demonstrate your ability to fly in a precise manner. They are a measure of airmanship and are specifically planned so you fly the airplane through all speed ranges and in varying attitudes. The precision maneuvers are practice maneuvers and are seldom used in normal flying.

The maneuvers done at higher altitudes (1500 ft above the surface or higher) are considered "high work" and are normally all done at the beginning of the flight test, although there is no written law about it. High work and low-altitude maneuvers are grouped as such here to give a clearer picture of the probable sequence of the flight test. The stall series and slow flight have been covered as a separate unit.

Here's a suggestion for any climbs or glides during the flight test (or anytime). Don't climb or glide straight ahead for extended periods. Remember that there is a blind spot under the nose. Make all climbing turns *shallow* and keep a sharp lookout for other airplanes (a steeply banked climbing turn results in much turn and little climb).

You've done steep turns before but now have closer limits to stay within. To review the maneuver briefly:

The steep turn required on the commercial flight test is a steep turn with a bank of 50° ±5°. You will be allowed up to a ±100-ft altitude lapse, a ±5-K entry airspeed variation, and a rollout ±5° of the entry heading.

No slip or skid will be maintained.

You may use climb power in the turns to help maintain altitude at the steep angle of bank.

Procedure. You may have to do a steep turn in either direction, and the check pilot may require that you roll directly from one into another.

At a safe altitude and clear area pick a road or a prominent landmark on the horizon to use as a reference point. Don't just peer ahead when looking for a point — an outstanding one may be off the wing tip. Head toward the reference point and get settled on the chosen altitude.

Choose the direction of the first steep turn and, after looking to make sure that you aren't turning into another airplane, start rolling into the turn and smoothly opening the throttle to climb power. You should use a 50° bank and have climb power established before you have turned the first 45°. Your job will be to maintain a near-constant bank.

A bank of 50° is pretty steep and the usual tendency is to lose altitude. If this occurs, you know that the bank must be shallowed in order to regain altitude. If you have a tendency to climb, a slight steepening of the bank may help you — *but* you only have about 5° of bank to vary on each side of the 50°.

In several places in earlier chapters it was mentioned that the load factor was 2 in a *60°* bank and that the stall speed was increased by the factor of $\sqrt{2}$, or 1.414. The stall speed increases by 41% in a *60°*-banked, constant-altitude turn. The stall speed increases because of the bank. The airplane slows because the angle of attack is increased to maintain altitude, and you are being squeezed in the middle even at the slightly lesser bank here of 50°. The power you are using helps to lower the stall speed as well as allowing you to maintain a constant altitude at a higher airspeed.

Check the nose, wing, and altimeter as you turn. Keep a sharp eye out for the reference point and keep up with your turn. The earlier you catch deviations, the fewer problems you'll have.

If the airplane is holding the bank and altitude, don't do anything. The most common problem is that the pilot spoils the ideal setup by trying to be doing *something* at all times.

Remember "torque" effects: the airplane is slower than cruise and you are using climb power. The tendency is to skid slightly in the left turns and slip in the right turns. Slight right rudder may be needed to keep the ball centered. There's no need to go into detail about the fallacy of trying to hold up the nose with top rudder during the turn — *don't!*

The ±100-ft altitude allowance means that at *no time* during the maneuver may you exceed those limits. Some pilots figure that it doesn't matter how far they are off the original altitude during the turns as long as they are within 100 ft of it when they roll out. They find that the check pilot disagrees.

As you roll out, throttle back to cruise power, even if you plan on rolling right back into a steep turn in the opposite direction. The biggest problem most pilots have is keeping the nose from rising during the roll-out even if they have started throttling back. Imagine how tough it would be to keep from gaining altitude with excess power being used. If the check pilot wants an immediate turn in the opposite direction, you can smoothly reapply climb power as you establish the new bank.

Common Errors

1. Too much back pressure at the beginning of the roll-in; the nose rises and the airplane climbs.

2. Improper throttle handling; rough throttle operation at the beginning and end of the maneuver.

3. Attempting to use back pressure alone to bring the nose up, if it drops; forgetting that the bank must be shallowed.

4. Failure to keep up with the checkpoint.

5. Letting the nose rise on roll-out, causing the airplane to climb.

6. Slipping or skidding throughout the turns.

Summing up the check pilot's expectations for the steep power turns: you'll be asked to enter a 360° turn maintaining a bank angle of 50°, ±5° in smooth, stabilized, coordinated flight. Keep the altitude within ±100 ft and the desired airspeed within ±10 K. Keep your attention divided between orientation and airplane control. After rolling out within ±5° of the initial heading, you are to set up a turn of at least 360° in the opposite direction, with the same limits. Avoid indications of an approaching stall or a tendency to exceed the structural limits of the airplane during the turns.

Chandelles. The chandelle is a maximum performance climbing turn with a 180° change in direction (Fig. 21-11). It is a good training maneuver because of the speed changes and the requirement for careful planning. *Clear the area.*

Procedure. Use the recommended entry speed given in the *POH* or on the appropriate placard. Stay below the maneuvering speed, if you aren't sure about the entry speed. Cruise plus 10% is a quick and dirty figure for chandelle entry for many

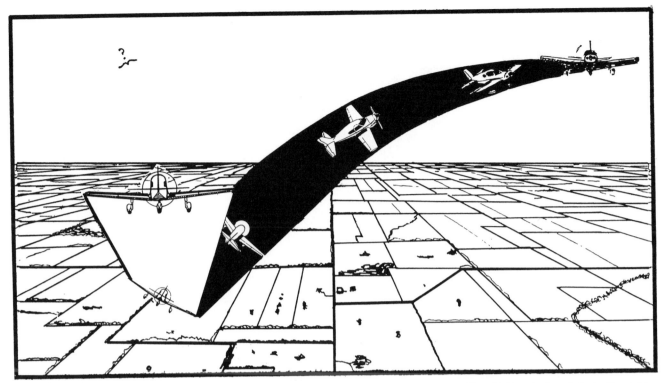

Fig. 21-11. A chandelle to the right.

airplanes. However, for some complex airplanes the maneuvering speed is lower than the usual cruise CAS, and the airplane should be slowed to V_A before starting the chandelle. As the proper speed is reached, set up a medium bank (approximately 30°). The ailerons are then neutralized. You may have to hold slight left rudder in the dive because of offset fin effect, but check it for your airplane. Apply back pressure smoothly. The airplane's bank will tend to *steepen slightly* as the nose moves up and around because of the pitch change, but the examiner will want you to maintain a constant bank. You'll be changing rudder pressure because of the torque effects as the speed changes.

The airplane will be turned slightly before you get the back pressure started—this is expected. The wrong thing to do during the initial dive and bank is to try to keep the airplane headed for the reference point by holding top rudder. Expect the slight turn and don't worry about it.

As the climb is started and the airspeed drops, smoothly increase power to full throttle but don't cause the engine to overspeed. It's better to start the dive at cruise rpm (assuming a fixed-pitch prop) and try to maintain this by opening the throttle as the airspeed decreases in the climb.

At the 90° turn position the roll-out is started; the airplane should be in a wings-level attitude with the airspeed just above the stall at the 180° position. The nose is then lowered and the airplane returned to cruise attitude. (The nose should *not* be raised or lowered further after the 90° position; the first 90° is used to bring it up to the proper pitch attitude, which is maintained during the roll-out.) The throttle is eased back to maintain cruise rpm as the speed picks up. Use whatever right rudder is necessary to take care of torque during this part of the maneuver.

Your main problem will be setting up the proper bank; too shallow and the airplane will stall before completing the turn; too steep and little climb is attained. You can visualize this by exaggeration—the effect of a 0° bank or a 90° bank in the dive portion. The exact amount of bank depends on your airplane's characteristics, but for most trainers the initial bank should fall between 25° and 30°.

It's best to do chandelles into the wind so you won't drift so far. The initial dive is done crosswind, and the turn is made into the wind. Pilots practicing chandelles have made the turns downwind and after several maneuvers have found themselves a considerable distance from the practice area. This is a very slow way to go cross-country but is fast enough to get you to a new area before you realize it. Remember that the check pilot is interested in your *planning* as well as smoothness in the maneuver.

A straight stretch of highway, railroad, or power line right-of-way is the best aid in doing a precise chandelle. You may prefer to start (and end) the maneuver parallel to the highway, but some pilots find that starting and ending perpendicularly to the reference gives them a better check at the 90°-of-turn point. As mentioned earlier, it's best to do the chandelle into the wind to avoid leaving the area.

Basically the first 90° of the chandelle is the pitch change (constant 30° bank), with the pitch at the 90° point held through the rest of the maneuver. (Don't let the nose move up *or* down after that point.) The second 90° is the constant changing (reduction) of the bank, so that with perfect timing (it says here) the roll-out is completed and the airplane on the edge of a stall just as the 180° point is reached. Incidentally, make certain that the airplane is always at least 1500 ft AGL in the chandelle or lazy eight. If you have a reliable safety pilot it's fun to do chandelles under the hood.

Common Errors

1. A too-shallow initial bank, resulting in the airplane's stalling before 180° of turn is reached.

2. A too-steep initial bank, resulting in all turn and little climb.

3. Poor coordination throughout, particularly failing to compensate for torque during the last 90° of turn.

4. Failing to roll out at 180° of turn; becoming so engrossed in the nose attitude and airspeed that the turn is neglected.

5. Excessive back pressure, stalling the airplane, or too weak back pressure, resulting in the airplane "dragging" itself

around with little evidence of a high-performance maneuver.

With underpowered airplanes you may be lucky to finish the chandelle at the same altitude you started, much less gain a great deal of altitude. This will be understood by the check pilot, who is more interested in your technique than in outstanding performance—which the underpowered airplane does not have—and who knows that if you have the skill, when you do get a chance to fly a more powerful airplane you'll get the extra performance.

You'd better perform chandelles consistently within 10° of the desired heading and recover within ±5 K of 1.2 V_{s1}.

Lazy Eights. The lazy eight is one of the best maneuvers for finding out if a pilot has the feel of the airplane. It requires constantly changing airspeed and bank, and because of this is more difficult than the chandelle.

The lazy eight gets its name from the figure the nose apparently transcribes on the horizon—a figure 8 lying on its side (a "lazy" eight) (Fig. 21-12). For the sake of clarity you can consider the lazy eight as a series of wingovers. Unlike the wingovers, however, it has no transition between maneuvers.

The turns of the lazy eights, like the chandelle, should be done into the wind to avoid drifting too far from the original area.

The airspeed should vary from cruise, or the recommended entry speed, to just above a stall at the 90° turn (max bank) point. The maximum bank at the 90° turn point should be 30°. (Divide your attention and keep an eye out for other airplanes.)

Remember that you'll want a constant change of pitch, bank, and turn rate, and the altitude and airspeed should be consistent at the 90° points, ±100 ft and ±10 K. Your heading tolerance is ±10° at each 180° point.

Procedure. Pick a well-defined reference point off the wing tip, preferably one that is into the wind. A point on the horizon is best so you won't be moving in on it and distorting your pattern. *Clear the area.*

Leaving the throttle at cruise setting, lower the nose and pick up an airspeed at cruise or V_A, whichever is lower (use the recommended entry speed, if available). Pull up smoothly and as the nose moves through the level flight pitch position start rolling into a bank toward the reference point (say, to the

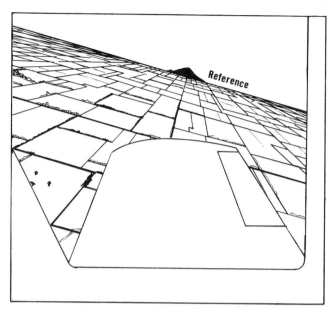

Fig. 21-13. The reference point as seen during the initial dive (lazy eight).

right). The maximum bank should be at the 90° point of turn. The airspeed should be just above a stall.

An extension of your line of sight over the nose should pass through the reference point at the 90° point of turn. The second 90° of turn consists of a shallow diving turn, rolling out until at the completion of 180° the wings are level and the reference point is off the left wing. Ease the nose up smoothly and make a climbing turn to the left, following through as before. You may continue the maneuver indefinitely.

To sum up: The maneuver is a climbing turn of ever steepening bank until the 90° point of turn is reached, after which it becomes a descending turn of ever shallowing bank until the 180° point is reached, at which the wings are level. This is followed by a 180° combination climb and descending turn in the opposite direction. Figs. 21-13, -14, and -15 show how the reference point would appear as seen from the cock-

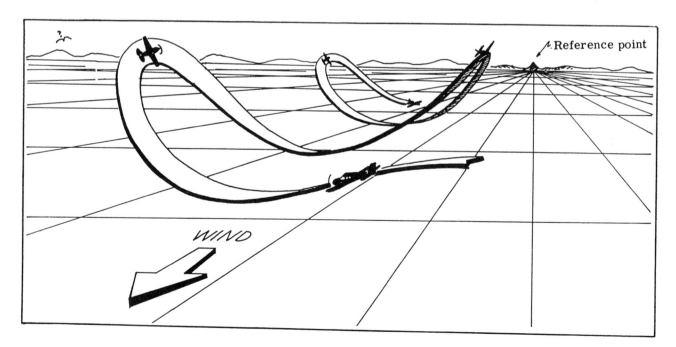

Fig. 21-12. The lazy eight.

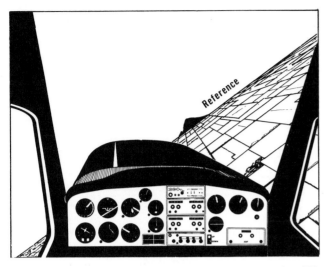

Fig. 21-14. The reference as seen at the 90° point of turn (30° bank) in the lazy eight.

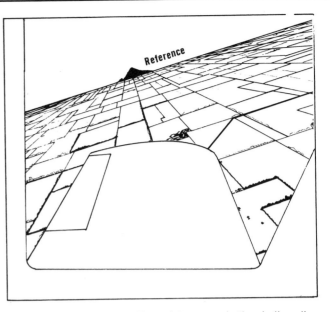

Fig. 21-15. The point as seen in the shallow dive after 180° of turn (lazy eight).

pit at different parts of the first 180° of the maneuver. The nose should have its highest pitch at 45° of turn; the lowest pitch will be at 135° of turn.

Keep the maneuver "lazy." One of the faults of most pilots is that as they get further into the series of turns, the faster and more frantic their movements. You may have to make yourself relax as the series progresses.

You should always be at the same altitude at the bottom of the dive. If you tend to climb, decrease power slightly. If you tend to lose altitude, increase power as necessary. The maneuver should be symmetrical; that is, the nose should go the same distance below the horizon as above it. By judicial use of the power, you'll attain starting altitude and airspeed at the completion of the maneuver, ±100 ft and ±10 K respectively.

You may have to consciously apply bottom rudder (and maybe opposite aileron) at the top of the "loop" to keep the ball centered at all times. Back pressure usually is needed at the peak to make sure your line of sight goes through the point without the airplane slipping.

Common Errors

1. Poor coordination; slipping and skidding.
2. Too steep a bank at the peak of the maneuver.
3. Failing to maintain the same altitude at the bottom of the descents.
4. Losing the reference point.

You will be judged on planning, orientation, coordination, smoothness, altitude control, and airspeed control.

Eights on Pylons. This maneuver (also called *on*-pylon eights) is a ground reference maneuver, but in this case, rather than flying a constant *path* with respect to the pylons, the airplane is flown so that the wing maintains a constant *reference* to them. You'll keep the wing *on* the pylon; that is, while in the turning part of the maneuver you should see the pylon remaining at a constant spot with reference to the airplane's lateral axis (or more properly, your line of sight). If you had a fixed telescopic sight at your eye level, pointing at 90° to the airplane centerline, the cross hairs should stay centered on the pylon as the airplane turns on it, although, as will be noted later, the pylon will be closer or farther away as the wind affects the pattern. The examiner could require an emergency descent (covered later) to get you down to the eights-on-pylon altitude.

At cruising airspeed (assuming no wind), you'll find that

at a certain altitude you'll be able to lay the wing on an object and keep it there indefinitely as you circle in a balanced turn. This pivotal altitude (PA) is a function of the *square* of the airspeed and can be found by the equation $PA = TAS^2$ (mph)/ 15, or $(TAS)^2$ (K)/11.3. (The number 11.3 is easier to work with than the more accurate 11.26.) A trainer flying at a TAS of 100 K would have a pivotal altitude of $100^2/11.3 = 10,000/11.3 = 885$ ft above the surface.

The pivotal altitude depends on the relative speed (squared) of the airplane to the pylon, and if wind is a factor (as it normally is) the *groundspeed* is the value to be used in the formula. An airplane flying on a pylon with a wind existing would have to change altitudes around the "circle" in order to keep the reference line (the pilot's line of sight) on the pylon. With a 10-K wind for a 100-K trainer, the pivotal altitude could vary from 717 ft when traveling directly upwind to 1071 ft when headed directly downwind. The angle of bank has nothing to do with the pivotal altitude; a 15° bank has the same pivotal altitude as a 60° bank for a given TAS (or groundspeed) (Fig. 21-16).

Fig. 21-17A shows the eights on pylons in a no-wind condition at a constant TAS. The airplane is circling each pylon at a constant bank and altitude and the circles are symmetrical. Note the "circles" in the maneuver in a wind (Fig. 21-17B) are more egg shaped than round and the line of elongation is 90° to what would be "predicted"; it would seem that the longest part of the "eggs" should be pointing downwind but this is *not* the case, as you will see when you do the maneuver.

Procedure. Pick the pylons as shown in Fig. 21-18. A medium-banked (30°–40°) pylon eight is best for getting the idea of the maneuver. A 3 to 5 second straightaway is required between circles and with a wind those legs will require a crab correction.

Enter the pattern at cruise power (or less, for the higher-performance airplanes) and make the roll-in (Fig. 21-19). Generally it's better to time it so that the roll-in is started comparatively late and is a positive one, rather than rolling in too early and then having to shallow out, resteepen, etc.

The pylon is kept at the same *relative* position around the circling part of the maneuver but the distance from the reference (and the bank required to keep it at the proper spot) changes as the airplane is affected by the wind. When the airplane is flying downwind it will be closer to the pylon than

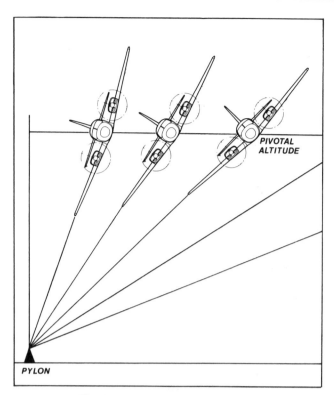

Fig. 21-16. The angle of bank does not affect the pivotal altitude if the airspeed (or more accurately, the speed relative to the pylon) is constant. The chances are very great that you would not be doing eights on pylons in a twin, particularly at such steep banks—this is only an example.

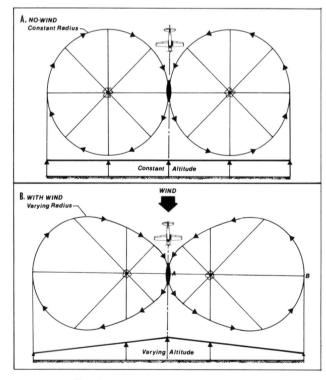

Fig. 21-17. A. A no-wind eights-on-pylons pattern. B. The same pattern in a moderate to high wind (wind effect exaggerated to make a point). The arrows indicate the path in both cases but do not represent the heading in the on-pylon eights *with wind.*

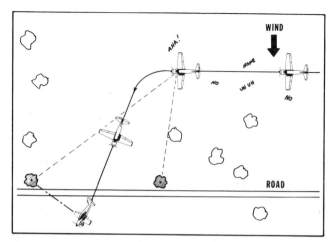

Fig. 21-18. Picking pylons precisely prevents the prolonging of practice periods.

when flying directly upwind (Fig. 21-17B). Also, the altitude must change to maintain the proper pivotal altitude for the speed relative to the pylon (groundspeed).

You might think of it as keeping the pylon centered in the cross hairs (Fig. 21-20). All flying must be coordinated and the bank varied to keep the pylon "centered." As the airplane moves into the pylon (flying downwind) the bank must be steepened (or the reference will move down out of the proper position), and as it moves away from the pylon the bank must be shallowed. You control the relative "up" and "down" motion of the pylon with *bank angle change.*

Note in Fig. 21-20 that you are looking along the imaginary dashed line along the wing; the right-seat occupant in a side-by-side trainer would use that same line (if the person in the left seat isn't in the way). However, a rear-cockpit occupant of a tandem trainer who tried to use that same point on the wingtip would be turning into the pylon (Fig. 21-21).

The correct pivotal altitude must be maintained (varied with groundspeed), or the pylon cannot be held. If the altitude is too high for the groundspeed, that is, the airplane is above that particular pivotal altitude, the airplane will fall "behind" the pylon. If the airplane is too low it will gain on the pylon, or the pylon will start dropping behind.

In the first case (the airplane falling back) the tendency is to use outside rudder to keep the wing on the point, with a slip resulting. On the other hand, if the airplane is gaining on the pylon you'll want to hold inside rudder (skid) to move the wing back to "where it belongs." The maneuver should, in theory, be perfectly coordinated throughout (it says here), but in turbulence it's more easily said than done.

So the problem of fore or aft motion of the pylon must be corrected by an altitude change. Suppose that the pylon is apparently moving ahead of the wing tip reference. The problem is either that the altitude is too high for the groundspeed or that the groundspeed is too low for the altitude. You would ease the nose over (no power change) and gain on the pylon, because (1) the increased airspeed (groundspeed) raises the pivotal altitude and (2) the loss of altitude brings you closer to the required pivotal altitude. You are bringing the airspeed and altitude requirements together with one move and would adjust altitude as the airspeed decays back to normal. As the airplane descends in the pattern, the bank must be decreased to keep the pylon at the same relative position.

If the airplane is too low and is gaining on the pylon, back pressure is used to (1) gain altitude and (2) slow the airplane up; this combination hastens the correction. The bank will have to be increased as the new, proper altitude is reached so that the correct relative position of the pylon is maintained. (Use a model and a desktop "pylon" to see the relationship.) Check Fig. 21-22.

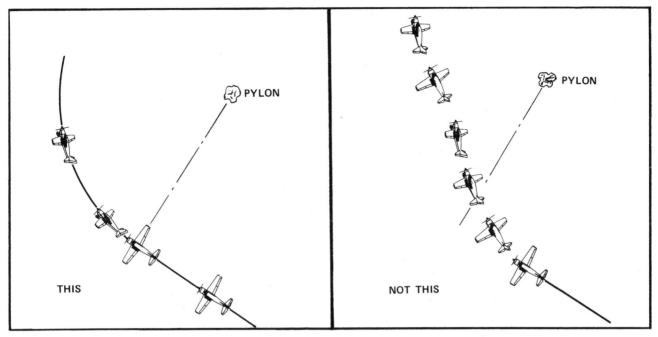

Fig. 21-19. Eights-on-pylons entry. (*Flight Instructor's Manual*)

Steep eights on pylons may be easier than medium or shallow ones because the circle portion is complete before you have a chance to get too far off the proper path. (A shallow eight can be a real challenge to some people, and as they slowly move around the larger circles, altitude and bank can vary considerably.) If you aren't organized on the roll-in of the steep eight, however, you won't catch up until that part of the maneuver is over. There's always hope for that *other* pylon, though.

Eights on pylons are excellent for learning to fly the airplane only by outside references. An airspeed or altimeter watcher will have problems with these maneuvers. By watching the pylon the pilot can maintain the proper pivotal altitude all the way around without reference to the altimeter.

Common Errors

1. Poor pylon picking; too close, too far, or easily lost.
2. Overconcentration on one pylon.
3. Poor wind drift correction in straightaways.
4. "Losing" a pylon.
5. Rolling in too soon, particularly when the pylon is on the right (in a side-by-side airplane) and is hidden.
6. Poor bank control.
7. Too slow rollout in back-to-back eights.
8. Failure to keep looking around for other traffic.
9. Skidding or slipping to hold a pylon.
10. Poor altitude control in the straightaway.

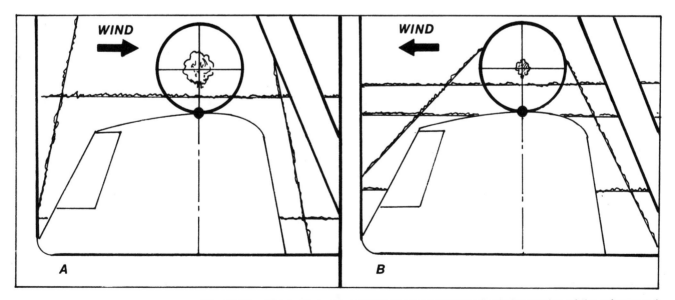

Fig. 21-20. The bank angle controls the "up" or "down" relative motion of the reference; A and B show what would be seen at positions A and B in Fig. 21-17B. The relative positions of the pylon are the same at both positions, as shown by the crosshairs, but the wind effect has changed the distances to the pylon — and the bank required to maintain the "bullseye." A is the closest point, steepest bank, and highest altitude, and B is the farthest point from the pylon, the shallowest bank, and the lowest altitude in Fig. 21-17B (slightly exaggerated).

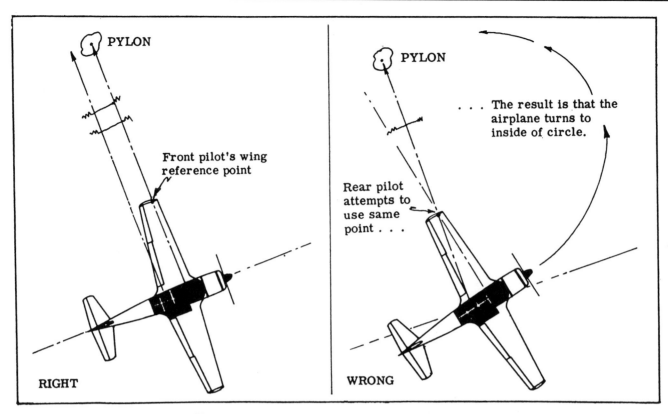

Fig. 21-21. The rear-cockpit occupant has to use a different wing tip reference or he will turn into the pylon.

NAVIGATION

Pilotage and Dead Reckoning. You'll be expected to know the elements related to pilotage and dead reckoning. You'll correctly fly at least the first planned checkpoint, to demonstrate that you were accurate in your computations. You'll consider available alternates and set suitable action for various situations, including possible route alternation by the examiner.

Follow the course solely by reference to landmarks and identify landmarks by relating the surface features with the chart symbols.

You're expected to navigate by means of precomputed headings, groundspeed, and elapsed time, and you'd better be able to verify at all times the airplane's position within 1 NM of the flight's planned route.

You'll have an ETA margin of 3 minutes for arriving at enroute checkpoints and the destination.

Correct and record the differences between the preflight fuel, groundspeed, and heading calculations and those determined enroute.

Be sure to maintain altitude (± 100 ft) and heading ($\pm 10°$) during the level portion of the flight.

Don't forget to use the checklist.

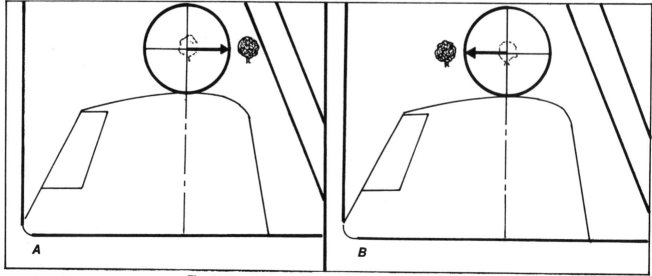

Fig. 21-22. Effects of being above or below the proper altitude for the groundspeed. A. Above the pivotal altitude the pylon moves ahead of the airplane. B. Below it the pylon appears to be falling behind.

Radio Navigation and Radar Services. You'll demonstrate a knowledge of radio navigation and ATC radar services and select and identify the appropriate facilities. You will locate the airplane's position relative to the navigation facility and intercept and track on a given radial or bearing.

You'll locate your position using cross radials or bearings and will recognize and describe the indication of a station passage.

You will be expected to recognize signal loss, take appropriate action, and use proper communications whenever utilizing ATC radar services.

Better stay on the appropriate altitude ± 100 ft.

Diversion. The examiner may ask for a diversion route to an alternate airport and you'll divert to that airport promptly. You'll give an accurate estimate of heading, groundspeed, arrival time, and fuel consumption to that point. Stay within ± 100 ft of the appropriate altitude and ± 10° of your heading.

Lost Procedure. Select the best course of action when you're given a lost situation and maintain the original or appropriate heading. If necessary, climb and attempt to identify the nearest prominent landmark(s).

Use available communications and navigation aids for help. Plan a precautionary landing if deteriorating visibility and/or fuel exhaustion is impending.

EMERGENCY OPERATIONS

Emergency Descent. You'll be required to recognize situations that require an emergency descent, such as decompression, cockpit smoke, and/or cockpit fire.

Establish the prescribed airspeed and configuration for the emergency descent as recommended by the manufacturer, without exceeding safety limitations, and be sure to know the proper engine control settings.

Use proper planning and keep your orientation (divide your attention as necessary). Keep positive load factors during the descent and, for Pete's sake, use the checklist.

Emergency Approach and Landing. You'll be expected to know and be able to explain approach and landing procedures to be used in various emergencies. When the examiner sets up the simulated emergency you are to establish and maintain the best glide airspeed (± 10 K) and the configuration required for the various parts of this problem. (One of the common errors in this exercise is to let the airspeed get too fast, above the best glide speed.) You are to pick a suitable landing area within gliding distance. Bank and look directly under the airplane; many a pilot has headed off to the far horizon, ignoring a 640-acre pasture right below. Keep the airplane in the clean configuration until the landing area (pattern) is made. Set up an emergency pattern (see Chap. 16), considering altitude, wind, terrain, obstructions, and other factors. You'll be expected to follow an appropriate checklist. (One POH emergency landing checklist requires the pilot to turn off the master switch early in the procedures and then, as a last step, notes that the *electric* flaps should be put down to decrease the impact speed.) You should work out your own procedure, perhaps moving across the cockpit from right to left (or vice versa) to set up the most logical sequence. One airplane is set up so that a right-to-left sequence works well:

1. Fuel management (on floor between seats). Depending on the altitude of the emergency and the system, it could mean switching tanks or turning the fuel off.
2. Mixture RICH (on panel)
3. Carburetor heat ON

4. Ignition switch—check mags or turn them OFF if the landing is inevitable
5. Master OFF after needed electrical components (flaps, radio, etc.) are used, but before touchdown

Review Chapter 16 for ideas on gear-up or -down landings.

After the glide is established and the landing site selected, you are to try to determine the reason for the simulated malfunction and try to remedy it. *You must remain in coordinated control of the airplane at all times.*

You'll be checked on your judgment, planning procedures, and positive control during the simulated emergencies.

Systems and Equipment Malfunctions. You'll be expected to explain indications and courses of actions for various systems and equipment malfunctions. Review the POH for your airplane and Chaps. 12, 13, 14, 16, and 19 of this book (and Chap. 15, too, if you're taking the test in a twin).

You'll analyze the situation for simulated emergencies:

1. Partial power loss (Chap. 16 and *POH*)
2. Rough-running engine or overheating (Chap. 16 and *POH*)
3. Carburetor or induction icing (Chap. 16 and *POH*)
4. Fuel starvation (Chap. 16 and *POH*)
5. Smoke or fire in flight (Chap. 16 and *POH*)
6. Electrical malfunctions (*POH*)
7. Gear or flap malfunction (including asymmetrical flap position) (Chap. 16 and *POH*)
8. Door opening in flight (Chap. 16 and *POH*)
9. Trim inoperative (*POH*)
10. Loss of pressurization (Chap. 19 and *POH*)
11. Loss of oil pressure (*POH*)
12. Icing (*POH*)
13. Pitot-static/vacuum system and associated flight instruments (*POH*)
14. Engine failure during various phases of flight (Chapter 16 and *POH*)
15. Any other emergency unique to the airplane flown
16. And, very important, make sure that there is an emergency checklist available.

Emergency Equipment and Survival Gear. You'd better know the following about the emergency equipment for your airplane by describing its

1. Location
2. Method of operation
3. Servicing requirements
4. Method of safe storage

In addition, you should be well familiar with the facts of survival gear appropriate for operation in various climatological and topographical environments.

HIGH ALTITUDE OPERATIONS

Supplemental Oxygen. Know the FARs concerning use of supplemental oxygen and distinctions between "aviators breathing oxygen" and other types. How can you determine availability of oxygen service? Know (and be able to describe) the operational characteristics of continuous flow, demand, and pressure demand systems. Are you familiar with the care and storage of high-pressure oxygen bottles?

Review Chapter 18 and your *POH*.

Pressurization. Review Chapter 19, the FARs, and your *POH,* so that you know the regulatory requirements for the use of pressurized airplane systems. Review the operational characteristics of the cabin-pressure control system. What are the hazards associated with high-altitude flight and decompression?

How about the operational and physiological reasons for completing emergency descents? Be able to describe the need for wearing safety belts and for rapid access to supplemental oxygen.

Can you operate the system properly and react promptly and accurately to pressurization malfunctions?

POSTFLIGHT PROCEDURES

After Landing. Know thoroughly the after-landing procedures, including local and ATC procedures. Pick a good parking spot and check your wind correction technique and watch for obstacles. (If you taxi into another airplane or the gas pump, you'll likely flunk the practical test.)

Parking and Securing. Review ramp safety factors such as taxi and parking signals and proper shutdown, securing, and postflight inspection. Be careful not to damage persons or property as you park and secure the airplane.

Use the checklist for sequence of shutdown, but get the engine shut down without undue delay; don't sit in the cockpit with the engine running and your head down in the cockpit, reading a complicated shutdown procedure. You should be able by now to do a good job of chocking and/or tying down the airplane and setting the control lock(s) as applicable. Perform a careful postflight inspection using a prescribed checklist.

AFTER THE FLIGHT TEST

After you've passed the flight test and are a commercial pilot you'll find a new attitude toward flying. You are a professional and will have to maintain closer standards than before. You *are* on your own and will have to make decisions on maintenance, weather, and airport operations—maybe in situations where there is no one else to discuss it with. Don't let passengers or other pilots talk you into flying when you don't feel right about it. *You* know your limitations better than anybody else, and as a professional you shouldn't let outside pressures push you. Maybe you're thinking of going with the airlines or corporate flying; don't let a poorly planned charter trip (with passenger pressure) get you into a spot that could result in a violation or an accident, which could affect your chances for later advances in your career. You'd be surprised how a firm *No* to a bad situation lets passengers know who is in command of the airplane.

Keep up your proficiency and you'll find that you're starting on the most rewarding career possible.

Happy (and safe) flying.

Bill Kershner

BIBLIOGRAPHY

Airframe & Powerplant Mechanics Handbooks. 1970. 3 vols. (AC 65-9, AC 65-12, AC 65-15). Washington, D.C.: FAA.

Berven, Lester H. 1978. *Engine-Out Characteristics of Multiengine Aircraft.* Staff Study. Washington, D.C.: FAA.

Byington, Melville R., Jr. *Optimized Engine Out Procedures for Multi Engine Airplanes.* 1988. Embry-Riddle Aeronautical University, Daytona Beach, Fla.

Commercial Pilot Question Book. 1993. FAA-T-8080-16B.

Ditching Sense. 1958. NAVAER 00-800-50.

Dommasch, Daniel O., et al. 1967. *Airplane Aerodynamics.* 4th ed. New York: Pitman.

Flyer. Williamsport, Pa.: AVCO-Lycoming.

Fung, Y. C. 1969. *An Introduction to the Theory of Elasticity.* New York: Dover.

Hurt, H. H., Jr. 1960. *Aerodynamics for Naval Aviators.* NAVWEPS 00-80T-80.

Kershner, W. K. 1993. *The Flight Instructor's Manual.* 3rd ed. Ames: Iowa State University Press.

Kershner, W. K. 1990. *The Instrument Flight Manual.* 4th ed. Ames: Iowa State University Press.

Kershner, W. K. 1993. *The Student Pilot's Flight Manual.* 7th ed. Ames: Iowa State University Press.

Liston, Joseph. 1953. *Power Plants for Aircraft.* New York: McGraw-Hill.

Lyon, Thoburn C. 1972. *Practical Air Navigation.* 11th ed. Jeppesen-Sanderson, Denver, Colo.

Medical Aspects of Flight. 1965. U.S. Steel.

Perkins, C. D., and Hage, R. E. 1949. *Airplane Performance, Stability and Control.* New York: Wiley.

Practical Test Standards—Commercial Pilot Airplane. 1994. Washington, D.C.: FAA-S-8081-12B.

Wake Turbulence. AC 90-23D.

Companies supplying *Pilot's Operating Handbooks,* products, or other information:

Barfield Instrument Corp., Miami, Fla.

Bendix Products, Aerospace Div., Bendix Aviation Corp., South Bend, Ind.

Castleberry Instruments and Avionics, Austin, Tex.

Cessna Aircraft Co., Wichita, Kans. (for models 150, 172, 180, 182, 210, 310).

Continental Development Corp., Ridgefield, Conn. (instantaneous vertical speed indicator).

Hartzell Propeller, Inc., Piqua, Ohio.

Lycoming Division, Avco, Williamsport, Pa. (detailed engine specifications and *Flyers*).

McCauley Industrial Corp., Dayton, Ohio.

Safetech, Inc., Newtown, Pa. (E-6B computer, model FDF-57-B).

Sigma-Tek, Inc., Wichita, Kans. (aircraft instruments).

INDEX